W9-AQG-885

ALSO BY THE AUTHOR

The Student Revolution: A Global Confrontation, 1969

A Presidential Nation, 1975

The Media and the Law, 1976
(WITH HOWARD SIMONS)

The Media and Business, 1979
(WITH HOWARD SIMONS)

Joseph A. Califano, Jr.

AN INSIDER'S REPORT FROM THE WHITE HOUSE AND THE CABINET

Governing America

SIMON AND SCHUSTER
NEW YORK

Published by Simon and Schuster
A Division of Gulf & Western Corporation
Simon & Schuster Building
Rockefeller Center
1230 Avenue of the Americas
New York, New York 10020
SIMON AND SCHUSTER and colophon are trademarks of Simon & Schuster
Designed by Irving Perkins
Manufactured in the United States of America
Printed and bound by Fairfield Graphics, Inc.
10 9 8 7 6 5 4 3 2 1

Library of Congress Cataloging in Publication Data

Califano, Joseph A., date
Governing America.

Bibliography: p.
Includes index.
1. United States—Social policy. 2. Social legislation—United States. 3. United States. Dept. of Health, Education, and Welfare. 4. Califano, Joseph A., date. I. Title.
HN59.C26 361.6'1'0973 81-652
AACR2

ISBN 0-671-25428-6

Acknowledgments

So many helped so much that it is difficult to express my appreciation.

A host of colleagues read all or part of the manuscript at various stages: Michael Barth, Richard Beattie, Peter Bell, Frederick Bohen, Ernest Boyer, Hale Champion, Richard Cotton, Karen Davis, Ervin Duggan, Dr. Donald Fredrickson, James Gaither, Benjamin Heineman, Jr., Michael O'Keefe, Dr. Julius Richmond, Stanford Ross, Eileen Shanahan, David Tatel, and Richard Warden. The chapter on welfare reform benefited from the case study Laurence Lynn, Jr., did for the Kennedy School of Government at Harvard.

Numerous people typed parts of the manuscript, including Joyce Bentley, Susan Brown, and Anne Spinks. Special thanks go to Gay Pirozzi, who helped assemble the original files and did all of the typing in the early months, and Dana Urban, who took on the task of typing the final versions of the manuscript and keeping everything in order at the end. They all worked with good cheer.

I am particularly indebted to Hale Champion, Ben Heineman, and Fred Bohen. Their comments, insights, and suggestions have been as invaluable to me in writing as their commitment, energy, and imagination were at HEW.

John Hughes worked with me for the entire year. He verified facts, dates, places, found documents, and then double-checked everything as I wrote and rewrote. Over the course of this work he became far more than a research assistant; he has been an important critic, always constructive, and a friend, who is headed for a significant career of his own.

I was blessed with fine editors, the overworked and dedicated Alice Mayhew, and her patient, committed colleague, John Cox. The sensitive judgment of Sterling Lord was also important.

Stanford Ross, my dear friend of more than a quarter century and my law partner, exhibited the patience of Job throughout the first year of our law firm as

I worked on this book. God has blessed him with a wise head and an understanding heart; he has never failed to share those special traits generously with me. My three children, Mark, Joe, and Claudia, all lost many weekend lunches and Sunday afternoons with me, with understanding and love. My wife, Trudy, bore a share of the burden during the months we were together while I served as HEW Secretary.

There are too many people at HEW to acknowledge all of them by name. I would like to thank Muriel Hartley and Lem Johns whose skill at scheduling and understanding me during those thirty months helped make it possible to get so much done each day. I am particularly indebted to the more than three hundred men and women who came to the Department at my request, usually at great personal sacrifice. They gave freely of themselves to their country and they gave me a very special education. Most of the ideas and proposals which our media shorthand has called mine are theirs; they brought to HEW the kind of intellect, imagination, and talent we must commit to public service if we are to solve the problems our nation faces. Finally, let me express my appreciation and admiration for the thousands of HEW employees, and their colleagues on the front lines in state and local government, who have dedicated their lives to what I have often called and truly believe to be "the noblest work of our society"—assisting the most vulnerable among us.

They all helped, but the responsibility for what's between these covers is mine alone.

JOSEPH A. CALIFANO, JR.
WASHINGTON, D.C.
JANUARY 1981

For Claudia Frances Califano

whose health, education and welfare
are very important to me

CONTENTS

PREFACE

THE SETTING of this book is my thirty months as Secretary of Health, Education, and Welfare, the most extraordinary Cabinet department ever created by an Act of Congress, the lodestone of more controversy than any other. This is not only a personal memoir. It is also a book about people trying to make government work as the 1970s gave way to the 1980s, and about the difficulties of pursuing the social agenda of America as the twentieth century is pressed aside by the twenty-first.

I have tried to portray with candor the frustration and excitement, joy and hurt, achievements and mistakes. Inevitably, the account bears my point of view. It is a view of Washington from the department of the people, a personal view from someone who had to run Great Society programs he had earlier helped create. My years with Lyndon Johnson greatly influenced my work at HEW. Where relevant, I have recounted a few of my experiences during those years to enrich the reader's understanding of the controversial events described here.

This is a story of people: Presidents Lyndon Johnson and Jimmy Carter, Vice-President Walter Mondale, Senate Finance Committee Chairman Russell Long, Senators Edward Kennedy and Daniel Patrick Moynihan, House Speaker Thomas P. (Tip) O'Neill, Ways and Means Committee Chairman Al Ullman, House leader Dan Rostenkowski, and dozens of others. They are portrayed in these pages as good, ambitious, talented, cunning, generous, petty, dedicated, self-interested, sensitive, shrewd; in short, as the human beings they are. They do have one thing in common: they have chosen public service as their way of life. Along with the rewards and accolades, they have endured the hardships, the often brutal personal bruises, the embarrassment and sometimes ignominy of public failure, the exhausting disappointments of trying to move the bureaucratic behemoths of Washington, the Congress and the executive.

For choosing that difficult life I deeply admire all of them, even though these pages reveal many of our disagreements, as well as our efforts together. The men and women whose activities are chronicled here deserve far more credit for trying to make government serve people than they will ever receive. In public life in our democracy the people give few A's for effort; they usually come, if at all, from historians long after the event.

To none is the credit for trying more due than to those who occupy the office of the presidency. I frequently saw two Presidents, Lyndon Johnson and Jimmy Carter, and occasionally a third, John Kennedy, struggle with the impossible choices that came to their desks. Within the limits of their experience, ability, political power, larger objectives, and the limited facts and even more limited time at their disposal, I believe that each sought to do what he considered in the best interest of our country.

I am too immediately and intensely involved in the controversies recounted in this book to judge them dispassionately, as a historian might do. I must leave that to others. My account is rather the raw material of history, the first of many versions that will no doubt be written.

This book necessarily plucks only some of the events from an experience as full as any person could hope to have. I left HEW greatly enriched by my experience there; a little wiser, I hope, than when I started, and considerably more realistic about the limits of government in the 1980s—but forcibly struck by the need to make government work better, confident that it can, and convinced that the time has long passed when it was enough for government to do good. Today government must do good *well*.

Why have I set forth events in such intimate detail, with plenty of who-said-what and who-did-what? Because I want people to know what governing is really like, how interest groups maneuver, how political deals are made and broken, how presidents make decisions, what it is like for a Cabinet officer to deal with the White House, the Congress and the media in Washington today. I have a free man's faith and an abiding conviction that if people know enough about these things, they will have a better chance to improve the way government works.

CHAPTER I

STARTING UP

FROM THE time I left my job at the White House as President Lyndon Johnson's staff assistant for domestic affairs in January 1969, I knew that if I ever returned to government service, I would like to be Secretary of Health, Education, and Welfare. But in light of Jimmy Carter's persistent attacks on Washington insiders during 1976, I never thought he would offer me the opportunity—until he chose Fritz Mondale, a personal and political colleague of mine since 1965, as his vice-presidential running mate. Then, shortly after the Democratic National Convention, in late July 1976, Patrick Anderson, a Washington novelist and the first Carter speechwriter, called me: "Jimmy wants to talk about the family at his first postconvention appearance in Manchester, New Hampshire. He'd like your help on the speech." The next day Mondale introduced me to "Governor Carter" over the phone.

"Too much federal policy is anti-family," Carter said. "I want to make it pro-family. The welfare system breaks up families and we've got old people living in sin because they lose Social Security benefits if they get married. . . ." After a few other comments, Carter left Mondale and me on the phone to talk about the speech.

"It's really important for you to help on this. I want Carter to get to know you," Mondale said, signaling as only a political friend can the potential ahead. Pat Anderson called two days later to say, "Jimmy wants to announce in his speech that he's asked you to do a report on how government programs affect the family." Carter also wanted to see me in New Hampshire.

I greeted Jimmy Carter beside his airplane in Manchester at mid-morning on August 3, 1976. We rode together to the shopping center where he was to speak. When we got in the car, an aide showed Carter that day's issue of the *Manchester Union Leader,* William Loeb's right-wing paper. Two vituperative front-page stories excoriated Carter. His face tightened with a hint of controlled rage as he read them. I thought to myself, this was something we would never do with Lyndon Johnson just before he was to deliver a speech; his temper would almost certainly overwhelm his discretion. As I looked at Carter to my right in the back seat, his eyes were so calculating I assumed he was more self-controlled.

When Carter stood up, he ad-libbed for fifteen angry minutes that this was likely to be one of the dirtiest campaigns in history, that the Republicans would stage an "almost unprecedented vicious personal attack" on him. I was not sure whether he was truly angry or had decided to use this as a way of positioning himself for the future, and I didn't know him well enough to ask. He then recited his prepared text on the family, with a "pledge to you that every statement I make, every decision I make will give our families a decent chance to be strong again" and the announcement that I would be his advisor on the family and make a report to him.

After the speech Carter and I lunched alone at a house adjoining the Manchester Hotel. Only one lunch was delivered: steak, some vegetables, and a big bowl of fruit. Carter pressed me to join him, cut the steak in half, and divided the single portion of vegetables. We talked for almost two hours. He first told me about himself in the cadences of a man who had done this many times. I was struck by how deeply religious he appeared and wanted to appear, how confident he was of defeating President Ford, how politically innocent about the difficulty of achieving massive reform in the national government. When I suggested the increased difficulty in moving the Congress in the wake of Vietnam and Watergate, Carter recounted an experience with the Georgia legislature. "When they didn't cooperate with me, I went across the state, speaking to their constituents. They refused to pass a consumer-protection act until I did that. If the Congress doesn't move, I'll get the American people to move them." Even though I was to underestimate the intractability of the Congress, I knew the candidate was overconfident.

As Carter questioned me, obviously briefed on my background, he struck me as superficially self-effacing but intensely shrewd. He did not disguise his intention to make honesty and competence the issues, to target on Nixon's scandals and Ford's bumbling, and he underlined his determination to run as a nonpolitician and Washington outsider. His questions about Democratic establishment figures were as penetrating as they were persevering. They reflected his early concern about the loyalty of Party Chairman Robert Strauss, and also a keen appreciation that Strauss's ambition and zest to be at the center of the action would in the end motivate him. In a colloquy about Cyrus Vance in which I said that Vance was not only brilliant but has "as much integrity as any person I've ever met," Carter asked, "I don't doubt it, but is he tough enough to be Secretary of State?"

Carter then turned to the problem of the family. He knew it was a perfect campaign issue for him, and I could sense his contentment in pursuing both good morality and good politics. He expressed his concern about the decline of the American family with the same sincere conviction he exhibited in discussing his concern about the Catholic vote. He urged me, in preparing the report on the family, to consult widely with Catholics and look for an appropriate forum for a campaign speech. Carter talked about the Great Society programs of Lyndon Johnson and my work in those years, but much of his immediate interest in me was prompted by the fact that I was a Catholic. It was the first time in my life I had been singled out (either for favor or discrimination) for that reason, but I was so interested in the outside possibility of the HEW post that I never thought twice about it at the time.

While Carter discussed the anti-family aspects of federal policy, abortion, and the politics of the Catholic vote, never once during that two-hour meeting did he mention the Democratic Party. As I thought about that on my drive back to my summer home in Wellfleet on Cape Cod, I recalled the first time I had met him, at one of Boston Mayor Kevin White's small political dinners a couple of nights after the 1974 congressional elections. We were discussing the meaning of the election.

"If anything, political party labels are a burden these days. People don't care about political parties today," Governor Jimmy Carter commented as we sat in the house on Beacon Hill.

"Yes, they do," White said, and brand-new congressman-elect from New Hampshire Norman D'Amours agreed.

Carter turned to D'Amours. "Norman, when I got off the plane to campaign for you in New Hampshire, you asked me never to mention the Democratic Party." Carter made the point quietly, but with such force that D'Amours said nothing for the rest of the evening.

After the election, Mondale told me he was urging Carter to name me to a Cabinet post, preferably HEW. In mid-November, House Speaker Tip O'Neill told me that Carter was actively considering me for a major post. "I spent the whole damn ride from Carter's house to the airport this afternoon talking about you," he said when we bumped into each other at Duke Zeibert's Washington restaurant. "He kept asking me questions about you. He mentioned two or three jobs. When he mentioned HEW, I told him you'd be a great Secretary of HEW, but I said, 'Mr. President, Joe isn't going to take a job like that. He's served his time with Lyndon Johnson. He makes a fortune as a lawyer in Washington.' "

"Tip," I exclaimed, "I'm interested in that job. I'd like to prove that HEW can be run, that those Great Society programs can work."

"You've got to be crazy," O'Neill said, then recovered quickly. "Well, I recommended you and, you poor guy, you may just get it."

The first time I saw Carter after the election was when he interviewed me on December 7 at the governor's red-brick white-collonaded mansion in Atlanta. Half of the hour-long interview was conducted with Hamilton Jordan and Charles Kirbo present; the last half was alone with the President-elect. By this time, Carter knew a great deal about me.

During my meeting with Carter, he asked me two questions that I in turn asked almost everyone I interviewed for HEW: "What is the most difficult thing you have ever done in your life?" and, "I've got a folder full of your good qualities, but what do you think your weaknesses are?"

"Most difficult?" I thought for a moment. "Working for Lyndon Johnson. But it was also the most satisfying. As for weaknesses, I suppose it's that I've never run anything larger than a law firm."

"This is my most serious doubt about you. What makes you think you can manage a large Cabinet department?" Carter asked.

I cited my experience with Secretary of Defense Robert McNamara and President Johnson, and my book *A Presidential Nation* (Carter had read it), which had a large section on government management and organization. Carter listened noncommittally, then said, "Tell me what jobs you're interested in. And don't limit me to one, because I have a lot of juggling to do." He mentioned HEW, Defense, Housing and Urban Development, and Justice. I had been one of those recommending Harold Brown for Secretary of Defense, and I said that I would not be interested in the Housing and Urban Development post.

Carter asked if I had any questions. "Only one," I responded. "Will I have the ability to pick my own people?"

"Yes. Many are presidential appointments, of course, but barring a crime, or some serious embarrassment in an FBI check, you can select your own people. I intend to keep my promise of Cabinet government to the American people."

I was pleased. Robert McNamara, when John Kennedy urged him to become Secretary of Defense, had asked only for that. He later told me it was the most important request he had made.

By Tuesday morning, December 21, Carter had named all his Cabinet except Secretary of HEW. Despite stories in the press, I had still not heard from the President. Just as I was leaving my home for the office, the phone rang.

"This is Jimmy Carter. I'd like you to be my Secretary of Health, Education, and Welfare."

"I thought you'd never ask, Mr. President," I quipped, and promptly added, "It would be an honor and a privilege."

Carter made the announcement in Plains, Georgia, two days before Christmas, as I stood by, along with Ted Sorensen, who was to be named Director of the Central Intelligence Agency, and James Schlesinger, the future Presidential Assistant on Energy. I had worked carefully on a brief acceptance statement mentioning that my mother had been a public elementary school teacher in New York and that "I consider HEW to be the department of the people." I promised a "compassionate and efficiently run" department that "would serve all the people, not any limited constituency."

I was back in Washington by midafternoon. The first person to call me was House Speaker O'Neill. "Do you have an airplane in the Public Health Service, Joe?" I didn't know. "Well, if you don't, we'll give you one so we can all get up to the Cape on weekends. You'll need it before this is over. I don't think you know what you've gotten into."

Abe Ribicoff also called. The Connecticut Senator had been HEW Secretary under President John Kennedy. "I wish you all the luck in the world and it still won't be enough for that job. In less than a year, the only way I could keep my sanity was to ask them to change the colors of the briefing books each day. You'll read more briefing books in a month than you've read in the last eight years." I laughed and thanked him for the call. "I'm serious," Ribicoff continued. "The job is truly impossible. When you walk down the corridor to your office, just see how many pictures of former HEW Secretaries hang on the wall. You're constantly caught between the President and the constituencies you represent. You can't win, because you represent the poorest people who never get their fair share, and every President has budget problems. But look, I know you. You do your best. I hope the sacrifice you're making is worth it."

House Judiciary Committee Chairman Peter Rodino called on Christmas Eve. He had recommended me and he was genuinely proud to have an Italian-American in the Cabinet. Rodino's call was particularly warm and reassuring, but any doubt I might have harbored about the controversial and public nature of the job had already ended. For eight years during the Kennedy and Johnson administrations, including four years as Johnson's assistant for domestic affairs, my phone number had been listed. But within twenty-four hours after Carter's announcement, so many calls poured into our home from dissatisfied welfare, Medicare and Social Security beneficiaries, reporters, and interest groups, that I had to obtain unlisted phone numbers on Christmas Eve so my family could get through Christmas Day in relative peace.

I knew the job would be demanding, exhausting, frustrating, and sometimes disappointing, but I was exhilarated to tackle issues that mattered, to be challenged to my limit. Robert McNamara and Lyndon Johnson had given me a first-class education in politics, people, government, and most importantly, how to handle winning and losing. At HEW there would be both for anyone who moved aggressively, and I intended to do that. From the day I was called by Jimmy Carter, I was conscious of how short four years is.

For me, after that Christmas weekend, exhilaration gave way to anxiety. My law office phones rang incessantly. Mail from job seekers, people with new program ideas, and disappointed HEW beneficiaries stacked up unopened in sacks and boxes. Interest groups wanted to press their cases with me personally. Briefings on HEW programs were scheduled in early morning and late at night. Changes had to be made in the Ford budget to reflect Carter's priorities. Courtesy calls had to be paid on senators and House members before my confirmation hearing in two weeks. How, I thought, do you run an organization that is bigger than most governments? Where do you get, in thirty to sixty days, the scores of top-level officials needed to run HEW? What are the key decisions that have to be faced in the first weeks? How will President Carter and I get along?

NEXT TO the President, the Secretary of Health, Education, and Welfare had the greatest opportunity to help the most people, particularly the weakest. And, second only to the White House, HEW was the most treacherous turf in Washington. The same laws that gave HEW the authority and responsibility to do so much good brought its Secretary up against most of the exposed nerves of American society.

The issues that HEW faced touched tradition, moral conviction, education of children, civil rights, dependency, illness, busing, welfare, family life, abortion, firmly rooted attitudes about drugs, mental health, alcohol, and teen-age sex, deep-seated resentments about government intrusion, and fear of old age. These issues came to the Secretary relentlessly, one after another, often several at once, and they were rarely put to rest. Such issues spark conflicts among the biases, economic interests, political ambitions, and personal values that divide the country—by region, religious belief, historical accident, a sense of outrage at past injustices or the means chosen to remedy them. The boundless challenge of the Secretary's job was to try to deal fairly with these issues, to promote social justice, and to persuade, educate, cajole, and plead with the people, the Congress, the public servants at HEW, and often a President and administration besieged by crises and other demands, here and abroad.

The New Deal and Great Society programs made the Department of Health, Education, and Welfare the place where human hope and human tragedy met in America. For millions of men, women, and children, HEW offered the best hope, the only chance of surviving at a minimum level of human dignity. For those seeking help, the Department could be a symbol of past personal failure or an opportunity for a personal future. My job was to make it the latter, to give new meaning to the Department's motto, *Spes Anchora Vitae,* Hope is the anchor of life.

HEW's huge budget—$200 billion in 1980 just before it was split into two separate Cabinet departments, one of Health and Human Services, the other of Education—represented the largest financial commitment to the sick, the old, the children, the poor, and the handicapped that any society had made to its most vulnerable people. In 1980, the Department's budget accounted for more than 36 percent of the total federal budget, twice the share it had taken in 1964. The combined budgets of all fifty states—not counting the federal dollars they receive—fell more than $50 billion shy of HEW's. HEW's budget was larger than that of any country's in the world, except the United States and the Soviet Union. Almost 90 percent of it—about $175 billion—transferred income through Social Security, health care, and welfare payments. Each time the consumer price index rose one point in late 1979 and early 1980, HEW's budget rose automatically by more than $2 billion.

HEW budget decisions had a special poignancy because the programs it financed were so vital to the people they served. Ironically, the Department's budget often became a battleground on which the disadvantaged fought the disadvantaged—senior citizens pressed for more Social Security benefits; blacks and Hispanics lobbied for more welfare funds for poor children; the physically handicapped, the mentally retarded, the victims of heart disease, multiple sclerosis, and crippling arthritis, those who had suffered from personal tragedies or the failures of our social policy, looked to HEW for the chance to get their fair share.

Many found relief as HEW tried to ease the pain of poverty, ill health, or old age. At the same time, others found profit. Its Medicaid program made scores of nursing home operators multimillionaires. Proprietary trade schools made millions of dollars when student aid programs paid their tuition bills. Insurance and computer companies were created and expanded to process Medicare and Medicaid bills. A $200 billion budget will inevitably attract its share of fraud, abuse, and waste: doctors who bill falsely for Medicare and Medicaid, welfare cheats, graduates refusing to repay student loans. These things may dominate newspaper headlines and consume precious seconds of television news, but they're a small part of the whole. Many times more dollars are misspent than stolen in the welfare program as a result of incomprehensible and intricate laws and regulations and the resulting administrative errors.

In 1978, we did the first thorough assessment of fraud, abuse, and waste in HEW programs. The rough estimate was that $6 billion to $7 billion—less than 4 percent of all Departmental funds—were misspent. Most of that amount was legislative and administrative waste in the health care area: Almost $5 billion would be saved if Congress were to pass a bill restraining hospital costs and would make other changes in Medicare and Medicaid, and if we eliminated unnecessary surgery, diagnostic tests, and erroneous payments. Less than 1 percent went down the drain to fraud and theft. Department stores and supermarkets would envy that record.

HEW's mistakes were well publicized, as were the abuses by a small percentage of its constituents, but life without the Department's programs would cast millions of Americans into despair and diminish the quality of life for millions more. Without Social Security, seven million elderly citizens would sink into poverty, and another five million who are under sixty-five would join them. No medical school or biomedical research center could function without support from HEW's National Institutes of Health and Public Health Service. Permanently disabled citizens would be retired to uselessness and poverty without disability payments, Medicare, and the Department's physical rehabilitation and training programs.

The Congress charged HEW with numerous compassionate assignments: To provide compensatory education in reading, writing, and arithmetic for poor children (6.5 million in the 1979–80 school year); find a cure for cancer; provide health care to Indians, Eskimos, migrant workers, and merchant seamen; reduce teen-age pregnancies and drug abuse; give 400,000 poor children a "Head Start" in learning, and all children immunization against childhood diseases; and provide income for sick coal miners through a $1 billion black-lung program.

Its programs directly served 120 million people—providing cash payments, kidney dialysis, runaway youth shelters, assistance for blind vendors, help for alcoholics, rescue for abused children, treatment for heroin addicts. They touched almost every American. When an American takes a prescription drug, its safety and effectiveness have been certified by the Food and Drug Administration, whose regulations affect products that account for 25 cents of each consumer dollar spent. Thirty-five million people are mailed Social Security checks every month from trust funds filled by payroll taxes on 115 million workers. Much of the tea Americans drink has been graded by the Department's Board of Tea Experts.

HEW provided the funds to start *Sesame Street;* financed research that led to cures for some leukemia in children; helped bright minority students become doctors, lawyers, and Ph.D.s; spearheaded the World Health Organization's successful effort to eradicate smallpox; furnished social and educational services to refugees from Southeast Asia and to Soviet Jews; and worked with the ABC, NBC, and PBS networks to caption programs for the deaf with letters visible only to those with a special attachment that Sears Roebuck manufactures and distributes at cost.

HEW did its work on a colossal scale. In 1979, its Older Americans program provided 148 million meals to 3 million senior citizens at 11,000 sites and senior centers it supported across the country, and in their homes if they were shut-ins. In 1980, Medicare paid 20 million bills each month; Medicaid 60 million, including those for drug prescriptions. That year, each day more than 22,000 Social Security claims were filed; each night the system's computers make millions of entries on wage files so workers will receive their fair benefit when they retire. Since HEW began operating student aid programs in 1965, 30 million Americans have received $26 billion in student aid to go to college and technical and professional schools.

While I was Secretary, HEW directly employed about 150,000 men and women full-time, and 4,500 persons served on advisory committees part-time. It paid the salaries of more than one million state, local, and private employees. Management, particularly the indirect management of hundreds of thousands of state and local employees paid to run such programs as Medicaid and welfare, presented unique difficulties. The fundamental complexity of the federal structure with constitutionally shared power was brought home at HEW because state and local governments—not the federal government—administered day-by-day many of its large social programs and were immediately responsible for delivering services. Of those 150,000 people on the HEW payroll, I had under the civil service system the power to replace less than 200, including secretaries.

HEW challenged those who sought to manage it not only by its magnitude but by the sheer complexity and volatility of the responsibilities the Congress placed there. It was HEW's responsibility to determine whether saccharin was carcinogenic and Laetrile efficacious, how dangerous marijuana was and if spraying it with paraquat posed a significant additional health hazard. At the Three Mile Island accident, HEW tested food and water for safety and assessed the health impact of the radiation; in Philadelphia it did the detective work to run down the cause of Legionnaire's disease; in Colorado, it assessed the health hazard in moving leaking Weteye bombs. The Congress and the President gave HEW front-line responsibility to fight discrimination on the basis of race, religion, ethnic origin, sex, handicap, and age. HEW was often charged by law to solve human problems that other institutions—the family, the schools, the economy, local governments—had failed to solve or sometimes even to address.

Such responsibilities presented obvious management and political difficulties. But they also presented bedeviling and bewildering ethical and moral conundrums, particularly in the health area. Through its National Institutes of Health, HEW funded more than 90 percent of the basic biomedical research performed in the United States, and, largely through Medicare for the elderly and disabled and Medicaid for the poor, the Department was the largest purchaser of health care in the nation. So HEW assumed center stage for such nerve-pinching issues as abortion, sterilization, the limits of exotic genetic research and cloning, and whether to fund life-saving but very expensive heart transplants under Medicare. The family planning program put relationships between parents and teen-agers into the HEW regulatory process.

Such responsibilities provoke wide-ranging and intense controversy. To fulfill his responsibility to assure an unadulterated food supply, HEW Secretary Arthur Flemming stopped the sale of all canned cranberries and cranberry products in the Northwestern United States, just before Thanksgiving in 1959. To fulfill his responsibility to eliminate race discrimination, HEW Secretary John Gardner moved to cut off federal funds to Chicago schools in 1965, at the peak of Mayor Richard Daley's national political power. To execute the law banning any food additive that caused cancer when ingested by animals, HEW Secretary Robert Finch removed cyclamates from the market in 1970, and almost destroyed the diet soft drink industry. To fulfill his public health responsibilities, HEW Secretary David Mathews pressed President Ford to mount the swine flu program in 1976, an unprecedented and ill-starred attempt to inoculate the entire American population. It should surprise no one that there were thirteen Secretaries of Health, Education, and Welfare over the tumultuous twenty-seven-year history of the Department.

There was no way for an active Secretary to avoid controversy. Even when disagreements arose, however, it was important to try to keep the confidence of the array of competing, and often conflicting, interests that confronted HEW: pharmaceutical companies and public-interest groups; business and labor; rich and poor; blacks and whites; big computer manufacturers and American Civil Liberties Union privacy lawyers; and the scores of special interest groups such as those representing women, Hispanics, the illiterate, the developmentally disabled, and the deaf, and such lobbies as those pressing for more research funds for cancer, lung disease, and blindness.

The Secretary of HEW worked in a world of molecular politics. Power has been fragmented in Washington, not just within the executive branch, but by legislative mandate within individual departments, and not just between the executive and the Congress, but within the Congress itself. We have been and always will be a nation of special interest politics. But to a degree few Americans appreciate, these interests have been institutionalized in law and regulation, in both the congressional and executive bureaucracies. More than forty committees and subcommittees claimed jurisdiction over one or another part of HEW and each month demanded hundreds of hours of testimony and thousands of documents from top departmental appointees.

Congress with more and more frequency has legislated special interests a role on the decision-maker's side of the table in the executive branch—by giving authority to narrow interest bureaus, independent of the Secretary; by creating advisory committees and requiring that specific interests be represented on them; and by legislating special relationships to the Congress, which in reality means the appropriate subcommittees and their staffs. In HEW, there were 271 health programs authorized by statute, and 298 Public Health Advisory committees, with 3,500 members (1,000 of whom changed each year) to be appointed by the Secretary.

I had been aware of the growing influence and sophistication of the special interests in Washington, if not of the extent to which they had been institutionalized in the executive and legislative bureaucracies. But I did not appreciate the extent to which the federal courts also had intruded into the management of HEW. My first sense of this came at a Washington dinner party shortly after Carter's announcement of my designation as Secretary. I sat next to Supreme Court Justice William Brennan. "I don't know if I should break bread with you, Joe. You're a party to so many cases before the Court," he said, smiling.

Indeed, HEW was a party to more cases in federal court than anyone else except that old courtroom habitué, the United States itself. All over the country, federal judges were monitoring disability determinations (and how long it took to make them), welfare systems, FDA new-drug-application procedures, civil rights programs, and HEW's administration of a host of other laws and the regulations they spawned. There were so many court orders that no one had bothered to keep track of them. (We did a survey to assure compliance and discovered that, in mid-1979, there were 225 continuing court orders against the Secretary, requiring periodic reports to judges and judicial oversight, with an average of 25 additional such orders expected each quarter.) However reluctantly judges might have been drawn into HEW affairs because the Nixon administration failed to execute certain laws, many had come to enjoy running HEW programs and they were not about to let go.

It was this Department, then, that engaged me when I took office in 1977. Indeed, it had held a special interest for me for more than ten years. At President Dwight Eisenhower's recommendation, the Congress had formed HEW in 1953 with a $5.4 billion budget and 35,000 employees. The best of the New Deal—the Social Security system (with its lesser-known Children's Bureau, and its early social service programs)—was placed in the Department. But what put HEW at the cutting edge of social policy were the Great Society programs of the Johnson years. As an assistant to President Johnson, I had helped fashion many of them. The Nixon and Ford administrations had never been committed to making them work effectively. For eight years they had accepted new programs from the Democratic Congress reluctantly, and funds often only after a presidential veto was overridden. Still, by 1977 these Great Society programs had grown dramatically from the time they started: aid to higher education from $383 million to $5.4 billion; aid to elementary schools, from $538 million to $7.3 billion; Medicaid from $770 million to $14 billion, and Medicare from $3.4 billion to $34 billion. I was convinced that most of these programs could work to the benefit of the American people, and that restoring our people's faith in government as an effective and compassionate servant depended largely on doing just that. And I began my days as Secretary with a sense that the new President, however unfamiliar with the ways of Washington, shared that conviction.

MY FIRST impressions of Jimmy Carter's presidential style came at Sea Island, Georgia, during his initial meetings with the Cabinet over the 1976 Christmas holidays. The Cabinet stayed at the Cloister, a luxury resort; the Carters at the nearby Musgrove Plantation of R. J. Reynolds Tobacco heir Smith Bagley on St. Simons Island ten minutes away. During those early days, I was struck by the ostentatiously nonpresidential ambience of both the new President and his associates. Carter brandished informalities and religion. He slouched in a sweater and jeans, spoke softly, constantly appearing to defer to comments by members of the new Cabinet, especially Cyrus Vance. He prayed before meals, exuded fundamentalist intensity, invoked the name of God frequently. In each of our rooms when we arrived at the Cloister was a small book of religious poems written by LaBelle Lance, the wife of his friend Bert, who had been named Director of the Office of Management and Budget. I attributed much of this to Carter's born-again Baptist beliefs, and suppressed my Northeastern Catholic discomfort at such public displays of fundamentalist religion.

Again and again he stressed "ethics" and the importance of avoiding conflicts of interest. He wanted us publicly to reveal information about our holdings and earnings, to set up blind trusts over which we had no control. Carter put his White House counsel Robert Lipshutz in charge. I proposed Stanford Ross, a friend and personal attorney, as my blind trustee. Lipshutz checked with Carter and told me that Ross was too close; I had to get someone independent. I, therefore, asked a casual acquaintance, Republican Peter Peterson, Chairman of Lehman Brothers Kuhn Loeb, who had been Secretary of Commerce in the Nixon administration, to be my blind trustee. When Carter ultimately selected his intimate friend and advisor Charles Kirbo to be his, I began to suspect that much of what was going on was for public consumption.

The odor of naiveté perfumed those two days off the coast of Georgia. The new President evidenced little sense of what Washington was like or of the complexities of governing. Except for Stuart Eizenstat, who had been a junior aide under Johnson and had worked on Hubert Humphrey's 1968 presidential campaign, and Jack Watson, who had conducted a wide-ranging transition study, Carter's staff seemed naive to a fault and appeared to believe the anti-Washington rhetoric that had carried Carter to the White House.

In the meetings, Carter spoke sincerely of his desire to use his presidency "for good," to restore the confidence of the people in their government, to "give them an administration as good as they are," to fulfill his campaign commitments, and to "maintain a close and intimate relationship with the voters." Hamilton Jordan worked at being the country boy from Georgia, wearing work boots, affecting boredom during much of the discussions. Jody Powell was disingenuously deferential, calling each Cabinet member Mister or Madame Secretary. Watson, the only Carter staffer with whom I had discussed organizing the government, was subdued, giving some validity to news reports that he was having his wings clipped by Jordan; Eizenstat was quiet and serious. As I sat at the meetings, I thought that Watson and Eizenstat would have to provide Carter his substantive staff advice. Bert Lance, who had been Carter's Georgia Highway Commissioner and banker, was charming, but displayed neither the personality, depth, nor motivation required to be OMB Director, and the others close to the President evidenced little interest in governing.

Mondale distributed a suggested Carter administration agenda that stressed the importance of presenting "themes," "impressions," and "images" of the administration. The "themes of the Carter administration suggested for initial emphasis" were: "(1) Carter as a President who will unify the country, healing past divisions . . . (2) Carter as an outsider who intends to shake things up in Washington, through government reorganization, conflict-of-interest rules, and other reforms . . . (3) Carter as a leader who is close to the people . . . and is determined to give them a government that is courteous, compassionate, helpful, and cares about human needs . . . (4) Carter as a President who knows how to manage the federal bureaucracy . . . (5) Carter as a President who can restore trust by openness and candor and . . . preventing abuses of the past . . . (6) Carter as a leader who is energetic and effective working to solve national . . . and international problems. . . ."

The administration agenda suggested that "effective executive leadership be demonstrated through a series of early legislative victories, projecting the image of a 'can-do' President who has taken charge in Washington. As a corollary to this, the new administration cannot afford *any* major early legislative defeats." The agenda listed initiatives in every area, but assumed that economic problems "will permit little, if any, overall increase in current policy expenditures for actions not directly tied to the recovery. Reform-oriented proposals are therefore given priority and emphasis is placed on the initiation of long-term planning for those campaign commitments that would have major budgetary impacts."

Carter intended to set a presidential calendar for his first few months in office. He spoke like an efficient planner and the agenda even included a flow chart, but his timetables were strikingly out of accord with congressional reality and the tasks specified in the materials Mondale had distributed. Carter would have an energy program to the Congress and passed within the first few months; he initially wanted welfare reform to be "acted on by the Cabinet" by the middle of March.

That phrase struck me. Did Carter view the Cabinet as a collective decision-making body? Having watched the Cabinet throughout the Johnson administration, I knew it was not. The Secretary of HEW had as little ability to inform a discussion about a major weapons system as the Secretary of Defense had to contribute to a debate on the nuances of the welfare system.

Carter wanted to "restore the Cabinet to its proper role as the President's first circle of advisors." He echoed his campaign rhetoric that there would be "no all-powerful palace guard in my White House, no anonymous aides, unelected, unknown to the public, and unconfirmed by the Senate, wielding vast power from the White House basement. . . ." Nonsense, I thought, as we sat around in a huge oval, our briefing materials in our laps or on the floor in front of us. When Nixon sat in the Pierre Hotel in New York in 1968 assembling his Cabinet and staff, he had made similar assertions. "There will be no Joe Califanos in the White House," he insisted. Then the reality of governing produced John Ehrlichman and Henry Kissinger. As Carter talked this way, I thought him either naive or disingenuous, or both.

From the moment Carter asked me to be Secretary, I began making lists of candidates for jobs. Even at the Cloister, I was jotting down names. Making those appointments was to create my first friction with the political section of the White House staff.

No post was more important to fill than that of Under Secretary. I first tried to list my own strengths and weaknesses. I knew the federal bureaucracy, the Congress, the Washington press corps. I lacked experience in state government, which ran many of HEW's programs. The McNamara Pentagon had given me priceless training in systems analysis and computers, but I had never been a line manager of a large organization. My personality was strong, so the Under Secretary had to be someone who could stand up to that. The hardest task for a top executive is to find subordinates who will tell him the truth. I particularly wanted an Under Secretary who would give me candid advice—"with the bark off," as LBJ used to say. High intelligence was essential. Also, because we would have a working lunch each day, I wanted someone with the rough sense of humor and proportion that helps the best top government officials and politicians maintain perspective in the often cruel and hyperbolic world of public service.

I then checked my assessment with two individuals who knew me well: Larry Levinson, a Gulf & Western executive, and Jim Gaither, a distinguished and thoughtful San Francisco attorney, both of whom had worked on my staff at the Johnson White House. They suggested additional attributes. "Toughness," Levinson said. "You need someone as tough as you are in pressure situations. Otherwise, you'll run over him even when he's right and you're wrong." Gaither, who on two days' notice left his law practice in California to spend three months leading my initial recruiting effort, added: "You can be awfully difficult and demanding to work for. You need someone who knows when to ignore an order you issue out of anger or frustration, someone who is secure enough to tell you to go to hell when he has to." Gaither continued, "HEW is probably the worst damn bureaucracy in the government. You'd better have someone who can knock heads together day after day, who doesn't mind the sight of a little blood, if that's what it takes to get something done."

I reviewed several candidates and interviewed a couple. Then William Gorham, the president of the Urban Institute, suggested Hale Champion. Champion had been a newspaper reporter on the *Sacramento Bee*, had held the top post in California state government as director of finance for Governor Pat Brown, and had been the vice-president for finance at Harvard for the past several years. More shrewdly and aggressively than any other top state official, Champion had put the Great Society programs to work in California. I had admired his work on a presidential commission to study government organization in the Johnson administration. I called Harvard President Derek Bok, who had been helping me identify candidates for Under Secretary. "What about Hale Champion?" I asked. Bok's pause was uncharacteristic enough for me to realize I was on the right track. "Well, he's still got work to do here. . . ." I sensed at that moment that Champion might be the right person. I found him that night at a neighbor's party in Cambridge. Within minutes after we began talking in Washington two days later, I knew it was the right fit of strengths and weaknesses. And with Champion, it was all up front. Before he agreed to become Under Secretary, he wanted me to know that he disagreed with the President's view, and mine, opposing federal funds for abortion. "But," he added with a twinkle in his eyes and a shrug of his shoulders that characterized his manner when he tried to put difficult situations in perspective, "my wife, Marie, agrees with you and Carter. I've lived with her for twenty-five years, so I guess I can live with you for four." He was clear, however, that he expected me to handle the issue.

That Champion had the necessary toughness and a sense of humor was also obvious from the way he performed his first assignment. Along with Fred Bohen, a White House aide under Lyndon Johnson, New Jersey congressional candidate, and McGeorge Bundy's top assistant at the Ford Foundation, whom I recruited to serve as HEW Executive Secretary, Champion went to a small suite of offices in the Department to begin to fire some one hundred Nixon/Ford political appointees. When he returned to my law office that first evening, tired and chomping on his half-lit cigar, he said, "Jesus, what a day. The first Nixon-Ford guy to come into the office is the head of the Rehabilitation Services Administration. In he rolls himself in a wheelchair; he's been crippled for life. 'Do you remember me?' he asks. I didn't. 'I was the chairman of Democrats for Pat Brown in San Luis Obispo County when you were running his 1966 campaign for governor.' " When I asked Champion what he'd done, he replied, "What could I do? I said, 'You sure made one helluva mistake since then'; and fired him."

For me, the Champion appointment was perfect from the start. But not for Hamilton Jordan. Despite his personal approval of the appointment, Jordan began leaking his displeasure to the press almost immediately. On January 24, the same day the Senate confirmed me as Secretary, columnist Charles Bartlett wrote that I had moved promptly on Carter's directive to the Cabinet to take charge of their own departments. His column continued: "But while Califano was taking the new President literally, Hamilton Jordan was roaring the traditional outrage of the White House aides who feel the President's interests had not been served. Some of Califano's choices, like Hale Champion of California, are politically indigestible in the Carter camp and the lines between Califano and the White House have already been bruised." I was concerned about the article, but decided to ignore it.

The following Saturday, on my way to work, I read an Evans and Novak column reporting that the White House staff was unhappy about energy advisor Schlesinger's independence and my selection of Champion. "Presidential aides feel the HEW appointment should have had closer attention at the White House than just a Jordan-Califano chat—particularly since the Under Secretary, Hale Champion, who is a Harvard University vice-president, bitterly opposed Carter in the Massachusetts presidential primary. Califano did mention Champion to Jordan, who did not recognize the name. Other Carterites who knew Champion all too well were mortified. 'It's outrageous to appoint somebody who vilified Jimmy in the campaign,' one insider told us."

When I arrived at HEW, I spoke to Hale. His activity in the presidential primary campaign on behalf of Morris Udall had involved a couple of introductions and a speech. He had never attacked Carter personally. During the Johnson years no story like this would have appeared without the President's direction. However annoyed Johnson might have been with a particular Cabinet officer and whatever he would have said in the privacy of the White House staff, he enforced his strict order that no staffer criticize any member of his administration to the press—unless he told them to.

I was aware that use of a staff member for criticism could give the President the protection of deniability: he could always say he hadn't made the charge. When Johnson was in public combat with the aluminum and steel industries to force a roll-back in their price increases, he repeatedly urged me to attack them for profiteering off the Vietnam War. I tenaciously resisted during the aluminum industry price roll-back in October 1965, but when Bethlehem Steel raised its prices on New Year's

Eve, Johnson was implacable. Finally, in a background briefing for economic reporters, I remarked that the steel executives could subject themselves to charges of being "war profiteers." Those two words dominated the headlines and stories the next day, and the backlash from business was stinging. When we finally got the steel industry to roll back its prices, one of the chief executives gently complained about the war profiteering charge. Johnson expressed annoyance bordering on anger that "some damn fool aide" had made such a statement to reporters.

Even though Carter had deniability in the Champion situation, I decided to face him directly and I called him that Saturday morning.

"How are you doing, Joe?" the President asked softly.

"I'm not sure, Mr. President, and that's what I called to talk about," I said.

"Go ahead."

I blurted out what I had rehearsed in my mind. "The Evans and Novak column this morning says the White House staff is unhappy with Hale Champion as Under Secretary. I don't know whether that's you talking or not. There's no need to talk to me through the newspapers. If you've got a problem with something I have done or intend to do, please let me know. I work for you."

"Joe, I will talk to you directly, not through the newspapers," Carter said. I noted that I had worked for a President who spoke to his Cabinet directly and who used the papers as well, adding, "But if his staff used the press, it was at his direction."

"If I'm pleased or displeased, you'll hear it directly from me." Carter was soothing.

"I'm glad to hear that. Do you have any concerns about the Champion appointment?" I asked.

"No, I have no concern about it and the Evans and Novak column does not reflect my view," Carter responded.

When I reported the conversation to Champion, he was relieved; but we were both experienced enough to realize that Carter might simply have been backing off. Even so, we hoped the call would lead him to deal directly with me when he had problems with what we were doing, or at least to stop his staff from making such comments to reporters. We were disappointed. Periodic press reports that Champion's campaign support of Udall irritated White House staffers continued. They puzzled me as much as they annoyed me. Coupled with White House staff objections to other Udall supporters, the Champion imbroglio suggested that Carter and his staff had no sense of the importance of healing the election wounds so that they could govern effectively. The concern with loyalty was understandable. I had witnessed it firsthand in the Kennedy and Johnson administrations, and as an observer of Nixon and Ford. But widespread loyalty is generated by able leadership. It would be hard enough to govern with the bulk of Democrats behind him; with power as fragmented as it was in Washington, he could be hamstrung without such support. Those early incidents created my first concerns that the President and his staff were unable or unwilling to switch gears from campaigning to governing.

(Although the political staff at the White House never accepted the Champion appointment, the President grew to respect his talents. On May 18, 1978, after a meeting on national health insurance, the President and I were talking alone in the Oval Office. Carter expressed serious concern about Hale's weight. "Talk to him about it, and I will the next time I see him," Carter said. "He's a valuable part of the administration." On another occasion, when Champion wanted to head the Social Security Administration, Carter urged him to stay where he was because, as he told me, "he's one of only two Cabinet under secretaries capable of doing the top job.")

I took Carter at his word as I pursued my recruiting for HEW. That led to my most serious political problem with the White House in the early days. After selecting Ernest Boyer, chancellor of the State Universities of New York, to be Commissioner of Education, I interviewed several candidates with elementary and secondary school experience for the number two job in that $9 billion operation. On February 14, 1977, at the recommendation of Boyer and others, I offered the post to John Ellis, superintendent of schools in Columbus, Ohio. Ellis had a distinguished career, beginning as a teacher, and had experience with school desegregation in Columbus. The *Saturday Review* had designated him as one of the ten Americans who had contributed most in education during 1976.

After Ellis resigned his Columbus post and accepted my offer, Jordan's political staff objected to his appointment, charging that he was an active Republican who had publicly campaigned for Gerald Ford and previously against former Democratic Governor John Gilligan. Leaks about White House staff objections to Ellis began appearing in the press. Gaither investigated and found that the staff charges were not true. Ford had come to a model Columbus school and Ellis had simply introduced him as "the President of the United States." As school superintendent, Ellis had publicly asserted that Gilligan and the state legislature were not spending enough on education. Since Ellis had already quit his post in Columbus and accepted the HEW job, and since the allegations were unsubstantiated, I decided to go forward with the non-presidential appointment. But before Gaither had a chance to report to Jordan's staff, and without their checking with me, they sent the President a memo setting forth the charges against Ellis.

On Friday night, February 18, Carter called me at home. Reading excerpts from a memorandum reporting "complaints from the National Education Association against Ellis," the President said, "I don't want you to hire Ellis." I began to outline Ellis's qualifications. "If you have hired him, fire him," Carter said. He was clearly in no mood to discuss the matter, so I decided not to continue the conversation.

That night I thought about the unfairness to Ellis and my own position within the HEW bureaucracy if I had to reverse my decision. At issue as well was my ability to attract first-rate talent—and most importantly, Carter's word. By making the issue public, Jordan had made my position untenable. Education Commissioner Ernie Boyer was on the verge of resigning if the Ellis appointment was revoked. After confirming with Gaither that the charges were false, I called the President the next morning. As I set forth my position, Carter seemed less tired and abrupt. He had not changed his mind, but the unyielding impatience had left his voice. Still, sensing my persistence was not persuading him, I ended the conversation and determined to try to enlist Jordan's help in reversing the President's decision.

That Saturday afternoon Gaither and I met with Jordan in his office. Tieless, white shirt open at the collar, feet in light brown working boots pressed against a low coffee table in front of the fireplace, Jordan listened to my arguments and accepted my version of the facts about Ellis. But he said his problem was politics: Ohio had been a key state, its Democrats had been early supporters, and the Ohio Education Association had been critical in the campaign. In response to his political concerns, I noted that Carter cherished his difference from Nixon, and a grossly political move on Ellis looked more like Nixon and his political hatchet man Fred Malek than Carter and his strong Cabinet. I asked for some time to work this out with the National Education Association and Democratic politicians in Ohio. If I did, Jordan promised to go back to Carter on the Ellis appointment.

Gaither and I spent that Saturday night, Sunday, and Monday on the phone with Ohio Lieutenant Governor Richard Celeste, State Democratic Party Chairman Paul Tibbs, Senators John Glenn and Howard Metzenbaum, NEA officials, and others. The politicians complained that Ellis was the fourth appointment from Ohio on which they had not even been notified, much less consulted. At my urging, they agreed to judge Ellis on the merits. I sent Ellis to see them all. Celeste revealed that the objection was coming from a state NEA official with a personal vendetta against Ellis. Celeste said he had a high opinion of Ellis, as did most Democrats and Republicans in Columbus. He confirmed that Ellis was not politically active, and thought the local NEA would support him for the job. I called Stan McFarland, NEA's chief Washington lobbyist. If he could confirm the split between the local and state NEA in Ohio, I asked him quietly to tell the White House the National NEA was neutral. He did. Then, after meeting with Ellis, Senators Glenn and Metzenbaum withdrew their objections.

I reported to Jordan. He called that same day with Carter's approval of the Ellis appointment, and later told reporters that he was "impressed with the way Califano stood up for his Department and for his people . . . and with the way Califano personally jumped in the thing and neutralized the political opposition to it." That was to be the nicest thing Jordan would say about me during my thirty months as Secretary.

The Ellis dispute was important beyond fairness to the man himself. Except for Dr. Donald Fredrickson and some others at the National Institutes of Health, HEW needed a total rejuvenation. Once we cleared out all the political appointees we had the authority to replace, we needed to identify and recruit top-flight and dedicated scientists, economists, lawyers, businessmen, and physicians, if we were to get control over the Department considered unmanageable by most. To attract such talent—and the leadership we needed to inspire the demoralized career staff—we had to make it clear that ability was the overriding characteristic we sought, and that the Secretary would stand behind appointees in political in-fighting. The Ellis incident sent that signal throughout not only HEW, but also the communities from which we searched for our key executives.

Recruiting such talent was hard work. Jim Gaither led the massive job hunt. He was joined by Peter Bell, who had been with the Ford Foundation for ten years and who took over the permanent executive recruiting effort when Gaither returned to his law practice; Leslie Sewell, who had worked in public television and went on to become Washington Bureau Chief of the National Public Radio Network; Ernest Osborne, a foundation executive and expert on community affairs; Dorothy Ross, a close friend and historian at the University of Virginia; Jonathan Fenton, an aide to Yale president Kingman Brewster; Larry Levinson; and others. They would identify the skills needed in a particular job, call around the country, assemble lists of names, check individual qualifications against required skills and against the access I would need to various interest groups. If an appointee in one post had excellent contacts in the labor movement, then an appointee to another might be preferred if he or she had an understanding of the civil rights community or the women's movement. This recruiting group made hundreds of calls to supervisors, friends, and enemies of candidates, reduced the list to between five and ten for each job, and then began interviews. Champion and I would see the top two or three who survived that process. When we were agreed, we would offer the job and begin the work of persuasion, which often took hours of conversation, partly because federal pay is comparatively so low in high offices but even more so because of the sacrifice of privacy and the shrillness of the public dialogue.

From Christmas until mid-March, I spent at least five and often ten hours a day discussing, interviewing, and selecting personnel. If necessary, I talked to candidates' spouses (sometimes helping them get jobs), bosses, and friends, assisted in making housing arrangements or getting free legal advice on conflict-of-interest problems, and even negotiated leaves of absence from their private jobs and bonuses to help them move. I had watched Lyndon Johnson press men and women into public service and I moved just as hard as he had to convince our selections to take the posts we offered. (I remembered vividly how Lyndon Johnson got Henry H. [Joe] Fowler back into his administration. When Fowler had left as Treasury Under Secretary in the Johnson administration to return to law practice, he told LBJ he would not return in any post; his wife Trudye had suffered enough of the pressure of public service. In less than a year, Douglas Dillon resigned as Secretary. Fowler, knowing Johnson well and anticipating a call from him, carefully prepared a list of characteristics the Treasury Secretary post needed, emphasizing those he lacked, and the names of candidates for the post. As expected, Johnson called. When Fowler arrived at Johnson's outer office, the President escorted him to the Cabinet Room, sat him in the Treasury Secretary's seat, walked around the table, and sat down in the President's chair. Fowler took out his notes and went through the characteristics Johnson should seek in a Treasury Secretary. When he was halfway through and before he had identified any of his candidates, Johnson, who had been pointedly distracted, looked right at Fowler and said, "All right, Joe. Let's cut the bullshit. What are we going to tell Trudye?")

One of the most common mistakes new Cabinet appointees make is underestimating the importance of three key posts: the Assistant Secretaries for Public Affairs, Legislation, and Administration. Their tendency to focus on what appear to be more "substantive" jobs and their willingness to accept a lesser standard of intelligence or experience in these three posts has come to reduce sharply the effectiveness of many department heads and programs.

The public affairs job, dealing with the press, was particularly important in a high pressure department like HEW. The Department was regarded as unmanageable partly because so many highly active political groups had fought their battles in its corridors and conference rooms. During the Nixon years, moreover, the Department had been considered a backwater for storage of liberal Republicans, and Caspar Weinberger had mounted a serious effort to dismantle many of its social programs. I was determined to invigorate HEW's activities across the board, to revitalize its civil rights effort, to move aggressively to reduce the rate of increase in health costs, and to fulfill the President's commitments to produce comprehensive welfare reform and national health plans. This meant controversy and enormous pressure. And it meant the media would be part of our daily lives.

The temptation for a government official to cut corners with the facts rises in direct proportion to the political and public pressure on him and the potential he perceives for embarrassment if all the facts are revealed. I had seen the capacity for self-delusion about one's ability to withhold or evade "bad" facts and exaggerate "good" ones trap men as disparate as John Kennedy and Lyndon Johnson. Kennedy had never quite revealed the extent or nature of our involvement in Vietnam; Johnson had juggled Vietnam budget figures to minimize immediate political problems about the deficit. I had spent hours in Johnson's Cabinet Room preparing for press conference questions and had watched the pressure build to slant or tilt the facts. I had no illusions that I would have a halo where such men were not so blessed. My nature was just as human and prone to error and the temptation to hide, evade, and exaggerate. I wanted a vigilante in the public affairs job to bring me up short and hard whenever I seemed to be succumbing.

I also wanted a press officer with the persistence and resilience to deal with someone as strong-willed as I was. I could be overbearing and use my lawyer's skill to marshal the facts I needed, not necessarily the ones I should face or present to the public. My press secretary had to be tough enough to stand firm and quick enough to be a devil's advocate on the spot. The reports on Eileen Shanahan, the brilliant economic reporter for the *New York Times* and a committed feminist, made her a prime candidate for the job. I knew her, but not well. She was a leading member of the Reporters' Committee for Freedom of the Press when I worked with it on First Amendment issues in my private law practice.

Shanahan came to my office at 9:00 A.M. on Friday, January 14. Shortly after we sat down, she said: "There's something you should know about me." I knew she'd had a heated row with *Times* editor Abe Rosenthal over sex discrimination and that she was suing the paper, but my intuition alerted me that there was something else coming.

"Your position on abortion. I think you're totally wrong." She got it out nervously fast.

"I don't intend to subject people I recruit to a test to see whether they agree with my opposition to funding abortion."

Shanahan kept going. She obviously had prepared this in her mind and was not about to be interrupted until she got it out. "I wouldn't think you'd do that. What you have to know about me is that abortion is the one subject I cannot front for you on. I cannot be your public affairs spokesperson on abortion."

I thought to myself, this is exactly the quality I want: blunt candor on what she thinks. "That's not a problem," I said. We went on to talk about HEW and its programs. We shared essentially the same philosophy. At the end of the interview, I stuck my hand out and said, "Let's go, Eileen, we've got a deal."

I was delighted Shanahan took the job. Her persistence and acerbic arguments occasionally took their toll, but I was just about never asked a question at a press conference that she had not anticipated. She was unyielding in her commitment to maintain my integrity and the Department's, and our reputation as sources of truth as best we knew it. Her loyalty once a decision was made was as fierce as her arguments for her views in the course of making the decision.

The Assistant Secretary for Legislation was another critical spot, especially in a department whose legislative program was normally more extensive than that of all other Cabinet departments combined, with scores of bills on the floor or before committees or subcommittees of the House and Senate, day after day. The job would require a keen intellect, as well as political savvy, especially in view of Carter's ambitious plans for comprehensive welfare reform and national health insurance. Nasty civil rights problems in a host of congressional districts each summer and fall, as schools sought HEW funds, would need a sensitive hand at the congressional relations helm, as would the thousands of congressional constituent complaints about Social Security and Medicare that flowed into the Department each month. It took more than one interview for me to settle on Richard Warden—and for him to be comfortable with me—but I never regretted the decision. I found Warden at the United Auto Workers, where he had been legislative director since 1975. We had never met before I interviewed him. We took each other's measure in a series of meetings. I checked him out with his friends and adversaries, and he checked with mine. Warden's commitment to liberal causes was as broad and deep as the big blue sky over Montana where he was born and educated. But he had a rare quality for someone of such commitment: He could face political realities, open his mind to alternatives, develop the respect of legislators whose views were completely opposed to his, and count votes better than anyone outside the Congress since Larry O'Brien served in the Kennedy and Johnson administrations.

When I took over HEW, the Assistant Secretary for Administration controlled personnel (including promotions, assignments, and bonuses for virtually all employees), space, equipment—the entire administrative machinery of a department outside the Comptroller's office. My predecessor, David Mathews, warned me about the incumbent at one of our first briefings: John Ottina was a Nixon enforcer at HEW. Originally named Commissioner of Education, he had moved to the critical administrative post, which was a career job. Several Democratic congressmen confirmed Mathews's assessment of Ottina. I told Gaither that he had to get him out. Ottina balked. He first said he would fight, go to court if necessary. Gaither had several discussions. Ottina resisted, threatening to complain to the press.

Finally, with a lawyer present, Gaither told Ottina, "The new Secretary may not be able to fire you, but he has every right to tell you what to do, to send you wherever he wants you to go." Ottina fidgeted slightly. Gaither continued, speaking slowly and looking hard into Ottina's eyes: "If the Secretary wanted to, he could send you to Alaska for months in the winter to look at HEW programs, and in the summer to Alabama for the same purpose. I doubt whether you'll be here on January twentieth." Ottina blinked. The next day he said he would leave, but only if he were given a one-year assignment to a university with full pay. Gaither agreed, and Ottina had worked out an arrangement with the School of Public Administration at American University by the time I arrived at HEW. Eventually I split off some duties of the administrative job and named Thomas McFee, a dedicated career personnel administrator, to replace Ottina as Assistant Secretary for Personnel Administration.

For a personal assistant, I wanted someone with a razor-sharp mind, an eloquent pen, a sense of jugular bureaucratic politics, and the ability to get along well with people. I found him in my law office—Ben Heineman, Jr., a young man with what *The New Republic* called "the best resumé in America."

An important element of mastering the HEW bureaucracy was a new office the Congress had created: the office of Inspector General. Spurred by North Carolina Congressman L. H. Fountain, and the discovery that HEW had only ten investigators to police the Department's programs and a ten-year backlog of uninvestigated cases, the Congress in 1976 had established this new office to provide an independent investigatory arm in HEW. Given unprecedented independence, the Inspector General had the power (and duty) to make his reports public within seven days of submitting them to the Secretary if he felt that the Secretary had not taken appropriate action, or that the report warranted special attention. The Inspector General reported to the Congress, as well as the Secretary, sending each a quarterly report simultaneously. The independence with which the Congress vested the office was such that Attorney General Griffin Bell thought the law was unconstitutional. In the hands of an irresponsible person, the office could run over civil liberties of individuals, continually distract the HEW Secretary and his staff, and seriously disrupt operations.

Many congressional sponsors of the bill had a cops-and-robbers view of the Inspector General, and Georgia Senator Herman Talmadge's candidate, Finance Committee staffer Jay Constantine, shared that view. When I arrived to testify at my confirmation hearings, Senate Finance Committee Chairman Russell Long handed me a letter signed by every Democrat on the committee, recommending Constantine for the post. When I privately discussed Constantine with all but one senator who had signed the letter, each indicated he did not care whether I made the appointment. One even volunteered that he was "too abrasive for the job."

I was also wary of putting in that independent slot anyone so self-interested he would not be loyal to me and the administration. I was reminded of the time when Lyndon Johnson had left Deputy Attorney General Nicholas Katzenbach sitting on the fence as "acting" Attorney General for months after Robert Kennedy resigned. At dinner one evening, weeks before Johnson had named him to the post in his own right, I argued that Katzenbach would be a superb Attorney General and that Johnson had left him in an "acting" capacity too long. I urged Johnson to make the appointment. "That's a Harvard recommendation, not a Brooklyn one," Johnson said, never missing an opportunity to remind me that what I had learned on the streets in Brooklyn was more important in Washington than what I had learned at Harvard Law School. "There are two jobs in this man's government that you want only your mother to fill —and even her not on every day: Commissioner of Internal Revenue and Attorney General."

There was now a third, I thought, and set about finding someone of impeccable integrity and fairness, but a sense of loyalty as well. Since this would be the first such office in HEW, it was important to emphasize systemic and institutional changes that could save taxpayers millions of dollars and demonstrate the value of their investment in social programs, rather than simply provide a few moments of titillation on the evening news. Both kinds of work were important, but more funds could be saved by expanding competitive bidding or computer-policing Medicaid than by highlighting isolated cases of larceny. Eventually I designated Thomas D. Morris, former Assistant Comptroller General and former Assistant Secretary of Defense, who most recently had been helping reorganize Florida's 30,000-employee department of health and rehabilitation services, as the first Inspector General.

As Morris's deputy I selected Chuck Ruff, the last Watergate Special

Prosecutor. Ruff provided the criminal-law experience needed to supplement Morris's forty years of management experience. His confirmation was delayed for months, however, by Senator Robert Dole, an otherwise amiable Republican with a good sense of humor, because of Ruff's investigation during the 1976 presidential campaign of allegations that Gerald Ford, as a congressman, had diverted large contributions from a maritime union to his personal use. Ruff found, and publicly announced in October 1976, that the charges were without substance. But Dole privately thought Ruff's investigation was unwarranted and might have been decisive in the close 1976 race. He never forgave Ruff, and he harbored the unfounded suspicion that Ruff had let the investigation drag on and was being rewarded by the Carter administration.

My most publicized appointment was hardly the most important policy position. Shortly after I became Secretary, I hired a cook, Wiley Barnes, to take advantage of the elaborate kitchen already built in the HEW headquarters to serve the Secretary's dining room, for working breakfasts and lunches with the staff, congressmen, and interest groups. Late one evening I signed a 402-word job description for Barnes as a "personal assistant" and the word "cook" or "chef" never appeared. On March 23, Associated Press reporter Mike Putzel broke a story that the "personal assistant" was a chef. His story never mentioned the fact that all other Cabinet officers have at least one chef, and much more elaborate kitchens and culinary staffs than those at HEW. In the wake of press reports about my $505,000 in legal fees the year before I became Secretary (on which I paid $276,000 in income taxes), the chef story was widely covered. Within forty-eight hours it was on all television networks.

Carter had made a big point of trimming the ostentatious symbols of office and cutting the "imperial presidency" down to human size. He repeatedly expressed his intention to cut down on "frills, pomp, and ceremony." At the January 24, 1977, Cabinet meeting, he had asked us to "reduce the perquisites of yourselves and your employees," and suggested we eat in the employee cafeterias on occasion. A week later, he had asked the Cabinet to "travel unostentatiously" and "to cut out automobiles for deputies," as he was eliminating White House cars for senior aides. I called him and offered to fire the chef if he was embarrassed about it. "Handle it your way. Whatever you do is fine with me," Carter said reassuringly.

I appreciated his confidence and support. I did not want to fire the cook, but I had to put an end to the story. Senator John Heinz and other congressmen were publicly needling me, asking for invitations to lunch when I testified on Capitol Hill. On Friday, March 25, after a meeting with Carter on welfare reform, Jody Powell urged me to try to put the story to rest with the White House press corps. I went out through the west lobby to a horde of reporters, cameras, and microphones. "What are you going to do about the chef?" ABC correspondent Sam Donaldson mischievously shouted. "I'm going to rewrite the job description to set forth candidly his duties. But the chef will save time and money over the long haul and I intend to keep him."

I returned to my office, hoping I had put an end to the story. I feared that the combined impact of the chef and the high legal income would make it impossible for me to lead HEW and effectively plead the case for the poor. At the depths of my frustration, House Speaker Tip O'Neill called: "Joseph, is it true you hired a chef for twelve thousand dollars?"

"Yes, Mr. Speaker."

"Well, I've got some advice for you: Any guy in this town that hires a chef for twelve grand had better hire a food taster." He laughed and so did I, for the first time that day. "Don't let it get you down," he added. "It'll pass. You'll do beautiful things. Just get on with it."

That evening on the television news I watched reporters scurry around Carter as he was boarding his helicopter on the south lawn of the White House for a weekend at Camp David. "Mr. Califano says he's going to keep his chef," cried a correspondent. "Do you approve?" Carter smiled and said, "I hesitate to discuss a problem so involved with so little thought." Then the smile left his face. "I trust him," Carter said, and boarded the aircraft.

Carter disliked the political aspects of the personnel process. At a Cabinet meeting early in the administration, he complained about the Congress, expressing his "disgust," particularly about House members. "I try to talk to them about substantive problems, like the energy program, and all they want to talk about is whether or not they can get their buddies appointed to some regional job in HUD or HEW." His attitude infuriated some key House members.

For example, John Brademas of Indiana, one of the three key Democratic leaders in the House, felt so deeply about the new Institute of Museum Services (created under legislation he sponsored) that he visited me on New Year's Day 1977 in my deserted law office. The Institute was to provide grants to help museums defray operating costs. Beginning that afternoon, Brademas worked back and forth with me for weeks, compiling a list of talented members for its first board. The names languished in the White House for months, even though Brademas raised the delay with the President at a leadership breakfast. Brademas was furious. He took what he perceived as Carter's cavalier treatment of his personnel recommendations as cavalier treatment of him.

Carter's assistants for personnel took their signals from their boss. They delayed decisions and embellished the process with so much red tape that even those individuals selected and approved by the President often sat in positions as consultants for precious months before their nominations went to the Senate. Those delays seriously retarded effective administration of departments, because acting appointees, awaiting the political process of Senate confirmation, do not make controversial decisions.

Carter's disdain of the political aspects of the appointment process sharply contrasted with the enthusiasm of Lyndon Johnson, who truly enjoyed this political give-and-take with the Congress. To him, the politics of personnel appointments were a key part of governing. He would ponder moves with the concentration of a chess master. He was interested in talent, but where he could combine that with a vote on a bill or a commitment to fund a program, he would. Indeed, Johnson would often tell a candidate he had already selected in his own mind to get some senators, congressmen, and interest groups to support his or her appointment. When the candidate did, Johnson would announce the selection, calling the supporters to say he had appointed their person. Months later, when the appointee took some action (often at Johnson's direction) that offended a group that supported him, he would say, "Hell, he's your man. You told me to appoint him."

Johnson never gave too much to one interest. When he picked John Connor, a drug-company chief executive, to be Secretary of Commerce, he turned down Connor's recommendation of his Washington lawyer Lloyd Cutler to be Under Secretary. Johnson thought Cutler, despite his talents, was too close to the drug industry, representing the Pharmaceutical Manufacturers Association, and gave no more lines to business than the President already had with Connor.

But Carter and Johnson did share one important personnel objective. They both pressed affirmative action in federal appointments. Carter never articulated to me what Johnson often said—that it was important for a black child to know he could grow up to be a Supreme Court justice, Cabinet officer, or member of the Federal Reserve Board. Carter had much more political benefit to gain from minority and female appointments than Johnson, since groups interested in these appointments were far better organized than they had been in 1965. But Carter's persistence was no less vigorous than Johnson's. He pressed me with notes to appoint more blacks, Hispanics, and women, and fewer white males.

WHILE PERSONNEL was the first order of business in unlocking HEW's potential, reorganizing operations along functional lines and streamlining the hierarchy were also essential. Student-aid programs were scattered in different operating agencies; Medicare and Medicaid were in separate organizations; Social Security and Supplemental Security Income programs were in one division, the welfare program in another; the federal social service programs and the funds for state social service programs directed at the same needy populations of elderly, poor children, and disabled people were in different agencies; thirty-seven people reported directly to the Assistant Secretary of Health, demanding an impossible span of control. I decided to move rapidly and secretly.

Secrecy was particularly important where virtually all constituencies prefer the comfort of the status quo to the unknown. The special insecurity of HEW constituencies—the poor, sick, aged, children, disabled—animates the turf instincts. Government is the key factor in their lives, and HEW is very much the government to them. And, within the Department's myriad bureaus, as Jack Watson aptly put it, the instinct among workers to defend turf "is about one hundred times what it is among gorillas." The problem was aggravated in HEW, for, as Senator Russell Long told me, "There are whole separate governments down there in that Department." I knew the interest groups and their representatives within HEW would try to block any change by pressing key congressmen to ask me to postpone action. I also knew that most, though not all, congressmen would be satisfied to be informed later, rather than sooner, to avoid having to ask. I realized that I would incur much wrath—and angry letters and calls from Capitol Hill—but I decided to move aggressively in the national interest as best I could perceive it, and shake (even if I could not break) some of the cozy relationships that had blocked HEW from reaching its full potential.

I myself headed a group that worked in a room a few doors from my office to put the reorganization together: Champion, Fred Bohen, and Tom Morris worked closely with Don Wortman, Bruce Cardwell, Jack Young, and Tom McFee, four top career executives. We quickly agreed on the reorganization. Morris, Wortman, and McFee worked on the details that could make or break any major change: personnel rights, titles, who gets what office space—all the bureaucratic necessities that can torpedo any significant reorganization if not delicately handled. Dick Beattie, an unusually accomplished attorney I recruited from his partnership in a New York law firm and who eventually became HEW's general counsel, did the legal work around the clock. When we finished, I had the charts and statements explaining the massive changes printed in the top-security print shop in the basement of the Pentagon.

I called Carter in late February to tell him I was ready to move with the first major component of his campaign commitment to reorganize the federal government. He asked for a briefing in the Cabinet Room on March 2. To avoid leaks, only the President, Mondale, Stu Eizenstat, and Jack Watson were there with Hale Champion and me. I sketched the largest reorganization in HEW's twenty-five-year history, moving around $52 billion in federal programs and more than 50,000 employees. Not before or since did I see such a wide-eyed look on Carter's face. He was truly excited. Jack Watson later called and said that the President was "ecstatic" about the reorganization.

I announced the plan on March 8, six weeks after assuming office. Out of the confused organization, we created five functional operating divisions:

—A Health Care Financing Administration, which for the first time combined the Medicare and Medicaid programs to the greatest extent legally permitted.

—A cash payments administration in the Social Security Administration, combining in one operating unit Social Security, Supplemental Security Income for the Aged, Blind, and Disabled, Aid for Dependent Children, and the Black Lung program.

—An Office of Human Development Services, which combined the $3 billion Title XX program of grants to states for social services with the $2 billion of federal social service programs, including the Administration on Aging, Head Start, and the Rehabilitation Services Administration.

—In the Education Division, a Bureau of Student Financial Assistance, consolidating the management of several student financial aid programs scattered around the Department.

—The Public Health Service was reorganized to reduce from thirty-seven to sixteen the people reporting to the Surgeon General and to create a set of coherent offices and bureaus, eventually including an Office on Smoking and Health and an Office for Disease Prevention and Health Promotion.

In my immediate office, I created an Assistant Secretary for Management and Budget, with functions paralleling the President's Office of Management and Budget; an Assistant Secretary for Personnel Administration; an Office of International Affairs to tap the enormous potential of the Department to promote national interests abroad; and most importantly, a strong Executive Secretariat.

I entrusted the Executive Secretariat with four major responsibilities. The Department had been inexcusably insular. The diverse bureaus rarely consulted, much less helped one another increase their leverage over a problem. The Runaway Youth Program, which funded crisis-call centers, for example, had never worked closely with the National Institute on Drug Abuse even though most youth who contacted the crisis centers had drug problems. The health, education, and welfare components had never combined their efforts on the teen-age pregnancy problem. The secretariat would try to get the various offices to help one another.

A bureaucracy of HEW's complexity, with such disparate constituencies in Washington and on Capitol Hill, required a central mechanism through which all significant policy would flow. An office such as the secretariat could also assure that staff and operating components would be accorded due process and be heard on critical policy decisions by the Secretary. I needed a way to check and improve the quality of the staff papers and to assure that I would not be blindsided by a recommendation from an interested component of the Department without adequate information about the disadvantages of accepting the recommendation or the political pitfalls. And I wanted an instrument to follow through and see that orders were carried out.

To fulfill these responsibilities, the Executive Secretary Fred Bohen and I wanted to bring the best career people to the Executive Secretariat, to give them exposure to the entire Department. When I sent out a memo asking bureau and division chiefs to recommend their "brightest young people" so that we could interview them for positions in the secretariat, within twenty-four hours an age discrimination complaint was filed against me. We revised the memo and recruited some top departmental talent to the secretariat.

On the day the reorganization was announced, Jody Powell said Carter considered it "a superb example" of what the President had made a commitment to do in his campaign, and that congressmen had told Carter the savings would be twice my $2 billion estimate by 1981. Carter wrote me his highest commendation of those early days: "I'm very proud of your reorganization effort."

On the whole, the Congress greeted the reorganization with approval. But there were complaints. House Majority Whip Brademas was annoyed. He had not been informed of the reorganization of the programs in the Rehabilitation Services Administration that he monitored until an hour before the announcement. We were close enough friends so that I was absolutely candid: "I knew there would be flack," I told him. "But this place is in such organizational disarray that I decided to take the heat to get it reorganized."

"If the reorganization is good enough, you should be able to convince us in advance, consult in advance," Brademas argued.

"These groups will never agree with any change. You assume people would judge it on the merits of efficiency," I countered.

"Washington has changed since the LBJ days. Congress is stronger. You're going to find that out." Brademas was heated.

"I know that. It's not that I'm unwilling to consult Congress. It's that issues of turf are impossible to debate with special interest groups. On those issues, they don't care about efficiency or saving tax dollars." With that, we agreed to disagree. Brademas later sent me a copy of a *Harper's Weekly* article in 1871 with a story about the stoning of a teacher, with this note: "If you think some of us on the Hill are tough on you, look at this a century ago. With warm regards from a sometime critic, but constant friend, John."

The move of Medicare out of the Social Security Administration and combining it with the Medicaid program in the Health Care Financing Administration created consternation among some interest groups and older bureaucrats. Senior citizen groups and old Social Security hands complained that they did not want their "clean" Medicare program contaminated by the "dirty" Medicaid program for the poor, including millions of blacks and Hispanics. The shift stirred even more controversy because, as part of the same reorganization, I moved the Aid to Families with Dependent Children welfare program into the Social Security Administration, so that we could manage all income maintenance programs in one place. The old-line bureaucrats of Social Security believed this further adulterated their program.

Once I had decided to merge Medicare and Medicaid to the maximum degree the law permitted, it became essential to move the personnel to the same complex in Baltimore. This meant that hundreds of District of Columbia and suburban Maryland and Virginia residents would have to move to Baltimore, commute long distances, or change jobs. Again, we had to move rapidly. Leonard Schaeffer, the tough, able Health Care Financing Administrator, moved the two groups to Baltimore during the 1978–79 congressional recess. It was imperative to make the move over the recess. Otherwise we would have been blocked by some investigation on Capitol Hill precipitated by employee unions and suburban Maryland and Virginia congressional members. As it turned out, both congressional and union representatives expressed relief to me privately that this move was accomplished swiftly during the recess

Trying to get administrative control of all aspects of HEW provided one of my more bizarre experiences there. In early 1977, the General Services Administration sought to take over allocation of precious parking spaces in HEW's headquarters building. After bickering for a year, GSA issued parking permits, claiming jurisdiction. I told Fred Bohen to ignore the action and continue to allocate parking spaces from HEW. On December 7, 1978, Administrator Jay Solomon called me to say that if we issued HEW permits, he would send armed GSA guards to prevent holders from entering the garage the next morning. Astonished, I told Solomon he had no authority to do so and directed Bohen to go forward. The next day, GSA guards let the cars with HEW permits enter the garage to park, and the GSA aide who prompted Solomon to make his call apologized to Bohen for the attempted parking putsch.

Picking the best people and reorganizing the basic structure of HEW permitted us to take maximum advantage of existing management techniques. There were, however, obvious management gaps in the Department. We attempted to close them by starting a major initiatives tracking system, a service delivery assessment program, and a regulations control system; and just before I left, by testing the extent to which individual grant, contract, and program decisions were consistent with policy directives.

A singular difficulty in government is to measure performance in a way that motivates personnel and promotes efficiency. We sought to establish numerical goals both to have a standard by which to judge individuals responsible for meeting them and also to inspire those individuals to greater productivity and efficiency. I called this the Major Initiatives Tracking System—MITS, an acronym designed to reflect hands-on management. We took everything of significance that we could measure in the Department and set quarterly targets. We measured scores of programs; for example, in the Office of Civil Rights, cases closed per investigator per year; in health, children immunized or teen-agers served with family planning; in Social Security, the number of days it took to decide a disability case; in the senior citizens programs, reducing the cost per meal; in health planning, the number of agencies certified; in education, the number of handicapped children served and of student loans collected; in welfare, the amount of child support collected from runaway fathers.*

The Service Delivery Assessment Program was designed to measure the effectiveness with which social services were delivered. This had not been done before, but I considered it essential if we were to present a persuasive brief for more funds. The object of the Service Delivery Assessment Program was to find out what services were being delivered, for what price, and whether the providers and recipients of services knew

* The major Initiatives Tracking System, with much pushing and shoving from above, had a measurable impact. While I was Secretary, for example, in the Supplemental Security Income Program, we reduced the average time required to process a claim for an aged recipient from thirty-four to eighteen days. In the Disability Insurance Program, we increased the overall accuracy of initial claims processing from 83.5 percent in July 1977 to 92.1 percent as of March 31, 1979, and we reduced the time for handling disability claims. In the Child Support Enforcement Program, we doubled collections, exceeding a $1 billion annual rate in late 1979.

what they were supposed to give and get. We began with Head Start; when we said we had 400,000 children in the Head Start program, what did that mean? Head Start programs range in quality from babysitting services to sophisticated programs designed to teach social development, digital skills, numerical identification, and even mathematics, reading, and writing. With the aid of the Service Delivery Assessment, we could impose upon each Head Start program the obligation to deliver specific services and then measure their performance against the number of children to whom they delivered those services and at what cost. Thereby a claim that so many children were in Head Start would have more meaning. We sought to assess home health care (discovering in Florida that often the doctor thought he had ordered something different from what the home health aide thought he was supposed to provide, and both differed from what the patient thought she was supposed to receive, but also learning that the elderly far preferred home health care to institutional living), family planning services for teen-agers, foster care, senior citizen centers, community health centers, education for the handicapped, rural health programs, physician assistants, boarding homes, health services on Indian reservations, community mental health centers.

In an attempt to get control of the thousands of pages of regulations published each year by HEW, we established Operation Common Sense. We set specific goals for eliminating unnecessary or unduly burdensome regulations among the six thousand pages in thirteen volumes of HEW regulations, and for writing regulations more clearly. By February 1979, we had eliminated more than six hundred pages of unnecessary regulations, 11 percent of the total. We also sought to avoid the situation where major policy issues are brought to the Secretary's attention for the first time in regulations ready to sign. The system identified those issues before the regulation-writing process began so the Secretary could decide them tentatively or order analytical work done early in the process, and the public could be widely consulted.

HEW was also a morass of unnecessary reports (often mandated by the Congress) and paperwork that were rarely, if ever, read, and so aggravated many citizens that they lost sight of the Department's important work. When I arrived at HEW, the paperwork burden the Department imposed on its grantees and contractors was 44.5 million hours each year. The Office of Education alone had required the completion of 67,000 reports taking 620,000 hours to prepare and 134,000 hours to read just for 25,000 grants. Led by Education Commissioner Boyer, we reduced those requirements sharply. By September 30, 1977, we had already eliminated 10.2 million hours of paperwork burden required by the Department—

exceeding Carter's government-wide goal of 7 million hours in his first year.

Another innovation we had just begun when I left office sought to determine the extent to which day-to-day decisions actually followed policy. Regulations set forth standards under which discretionary grants should be made in particular programs. But determining whether the individual making the grants can understand and is following those guidelines is difficult. In each area of the Department, we set in motion a system to sample individual decisions and measure that sample against the policy guidelines—legislative, regulatory, presidential, or secretarial—to see whether those decisions conformed to the guidelines. The answer would teach us how to formulate better guidelines.

THESE WERE the tools I used to try to run HEW: talented people, reorganization of operations, measurements of performance, assessment of delivery of services, clarifying regulations, and determining systematically whether employees were making decisions consistent with legislative and administrative policy. Through these techniques I hoped to demonstrate that the programs of the New Deal and Great Society and the enormous social commitment of the American people could be executed efficiently, as well as compassionately. I wanted to make HEW an example of the manageability, not the unmanageability, of government.

And the President gave us energetic charges to move. He urged us to get our policy initiatives on the table, take controversial positions early and harmonize later. "Run your departments," he said to the Cabinet on January 24, 1977. "Move on ideas fast. Do not wait. Be aggressive." I liked what I heard in the early Cabinet meetings of the Carter administration, and I intended to act on it.

Chapter II
ABORTION

THE ABORTION issue marked my initiation by public controversy as Secretary of Health, Education, and Welfare.

It was certainly not the issue I would have chosen to confront first. The abortion dispute was sure to make enemies at the beginning of my tenure when I particularly needed friends; guaranteed to divide supporters of social programs when it was especially important to unite them; and likely to spark latent and perhaps lasting suspicions about my ability to separate my private beliefs as a Roman Catholic from my public duties as the nation's chief health, education, and social service official.

The issue whether Medicaid should fund abortions for poor women was more searing than many I faced, but it was quintessentially characteristic of the problems confronting HEW. The abortion dispute summoned taproot convictions and religious beliefs, sincerely held and strenuously put forth by each side, about the rights of poor people, the use of tax dollars, the role of government in the most intimate personal decisions. The pro- and anti-abortion forces each claimed that the Constitution and the American people were on its side, and each truly believed that it was protecting human life. Wherever those forces struggled to prevail—in the courts, the Congress, the executive regulatory process, the state legislatures, and city councils—there were HEW and its Medicaid program. And there was no neutral ground on which HEW or its Secretary could comfortably stand, for any decision—to fund all, or none, or some abortions—would disappoint and enrage millions of Americans who were convinced that theirs was the only humane position.

The controversy exposed me to the world of difference between being a White House staffer—however powerful—and being a Cabinet officer, out front, responsible not only to the President as an advisor but also to the Congress and the American people. It was one thing to be Lyndon Johnson's top domestic policy advisor crafting Great Society programs, but not accountable to the Congress and not ultimately responsible. It was quite another to be the public point man on an issue as controversial as federal financing of abortions for poor people.

Lyndon Johnson had held his White House staff on a particularly short leash. We spoke only in his name—explaining what he thought, how he felt, what his hopes and objectives for America were. "The only reason Hugh Sidey [of *Time*] talks to you is to find out about me, what I think, what I want. He doesn't give a damn about you," Johnson so often told us, "so you make sure you know what I think before you tell him what you think I think." Indeed, during my lengthy press briefings on new legislative programs, as Johnson read early pages of the instantly typed transcript in his office, he sometimes sent messages to me to correct statements or misimpressions before the briefing ended.

Cabinet officers, of necessity, function with less detailed and immediate presidential guidance. It goes with the territory for a Cabinet officer to put a little distance between himself and the President, particularly on such controversial issues as abortion. Presidents expect, as they should, that their Cabinet officers will shield them from as much controversy as possible so that precious presidential capital can be spent only for overriding national objectives the President selects.

Jimmy Carter first talked to me about abortion when we lunched alone in Manchester, New Hampshire, in early August 1976. He expressed his unyielding opposition to abortion and his determination to stop federal funding of abortions. He asked me to work with Fritz Mondale to make his views known to the Catholic hierarchy and influential lay Catholics. Mondale was using his Minnesota friend Bishop James Rausch, who was then the general secretary of the National Conference of Catholic Bishops, to get Carter's view across, and Charlie Kirbo would be quietly communicating with Terence Cardinal Cooke in New York, but Carter said he wanted a "good Catholic" to spread the word of his strong opposition to abortion. I was impressed by the sincerity and depth of Carter's views on abortion and I found his determination to get credit for those views politically prudent in view of the inevitable opposition his position would incite. It later struck me that Carter never asked my views on the subject and I never expressed them. Our conversation simply assumed complete agreement.

The assumption was well grounded. I consider abortion morally wrong unless the life of the mother would be at stake if the fetus were carried to term. Under such tragic and wrenching circumstances, no human being could be faulted for making either choice, between the life of the mother and the life of the unborn child. Those are the only circumstances under which I considered federal financing of abortion appropriate.

During the 1976 presidential campaign, I never had to reconcile my beliefs as a Catholic about abortion with any potential duty to obey and execute the law as a public servant. In promulgating Carter's view, like any proponent of a presidential candidate, I took as a given his ability to translate that view into law or public policy. Since my conversations were with those who opposed abortion, no one asked me what Carter would do if the Congress enacted a different position into law.

In talks with Monsignors George Higgins and Francis Lally, and others at the Catholic Conference, I sought to convince them that Carter shared their view. Higgins was an old friend from the Johnson years and he helped get Carter's position better known in the Catholic community. But Higgins confided that nothing short of a firm commitment to a constitutional amendment outlawing abortion would satisfy the conservative elements of the Catholic hierarchy. When I reported this to Mondale, he expressed doubt that Carter would—or should—go that far, particularly since in January 1976 he had said he did "not favor a constitutional amendment abolishing abortion." I agreed.

Eventually, in response to the numerous questions on abortion during the campaign and after a meeting with Catholic bishops in Washington on August 31, 1976, Carter said that he had not yet seen any constitutional amendment he would support, but he "would never try to block . . . an amendment" prohibiting abortions. He added pointedly that any citizen had the right to seek an amendment to overturn the Supreme Court's 1973 *Roe* v. *Wade* decision, which established a woman's constitutional right to have an abortion, at least in the first trimester of pregnancy.

In November 1976, after the election, as Mondale, Tip O'Neill, and other friends reported conversations in which Carter or his close advisors such as Jordan and Kirbo were checking on my qualifications, it became clear that I was a leading candidate for the HEW post. Then, for the first time, I had to focus on the depth of my personal religious belief about abortion: As Secretary of Health, Education, and Welfare, would I be able, in good conscience, to carry out the law of the land, even if that law provided for federal funding of all abortions? I asked myself that question many times before others began asking it of me.

Both my parents are devoutly religious Catholics. Their influence and my education at St. Gregory's elementary school in Brooklyn, at the Jesuit high school Brooklyn Prep, and at the College of the Holy Cross had provided me not only with some intellectual sextants but with a moral compass as well. Like many Catholic students and young lawyers in the 1950s, I had read the works of John Courtney Murray, a leading Jesuit scholar and philosopher. His writings on the rights and duties of American Catholics in a pluralistic society and the need to accommodate private belief and public policy were guides for liberal Catholics of my generation. But even with this background, it was an exacting task in modern America to get clarity and peace in my private conscience while satisfying the legitimate demands of public service and leadership.

The abortion issue never came up in the Johnson administration. But family planning, even the aggressive promotion of the use of contraceptives to prevent pregnancy as a government policy, was an issue I had confronted in those years. President Johnson was an ardent proponent of birth control at home and abroad. He repeatedly rejected the unanimous pleas of his advisors from Secretary of State Dean Rusk to National Security Advisor Walt Rostow to ship wheat to the starving Indians during their 1966 famine. He demanded that the Indian government first agree to mount a massive birth control program. The Indians finally moved and Johnson released the wheat over a sufficiently extended period to make certain the birth control program was off the ground.

Johnson spoke so often and forcefully about birth control that the Catholic bishops denounced him publicly. He sent me to try to cool them off. Working discreetly with Monsignor Frank Hurley, then the chief lobbyist for the Catholic Conference in Washington, we reached an uneasy off-the-record truce: If LBJ would stop using the term "birth control" and refer instead to the "population problem," which allowed increased food production as a possible solution, the bishops would refrain from public attacks on him. Johnson agreed, and spoke thereafter of "the population problem"—but with equal if not greater vigor.

During my years with Lyndon Johnson, and the legislative fights to fund family planning services through the Public Health Service and the War on Poverty, I had to relate my private conscience to public policy on family planning. The alternatives of teen-age pregnancy, abortion, mental retardation, poverty, and the like were far worse than providing access to contraceptives; to expect all citizens to practice premarital celibacy or all married couples to use the rhythm method was unrealistic in America's increasingly sexually permissive society. I was able to reconcile my private conscience with public policy. I concluded that it made sense for government to fund family planning programs that offered and even encouraged artificial birth control. I had no moral qualms about such a policy in a pluralistic society so long as it respected individual dignity and religious belief. The Catholic bishops disagreed with Johnson. But among theologians there was a great diversity of opinion about the moral propriety of birth control in various personal situations; I inclined to the more liberal position.

Abortion was a far more difficult issue. Here I faced my own conviction that abortion was morally wrong except to save the life of the mother, that medically unnecessary abortions offended fundamental standards of respect for human life. It is one thing temporarily to prevent the creation of a human life; quite another level of moral values is involved in discarding a human life once created. With abortion, I had to face direct conflict between personal religious conviction and public responsibility.

I was to learn how difficult it would be to preserve the precious distinction between public duty and private belief. Setting forth my own and the President's view of appropriate public policy on federal funding of abortion, putting the issue in perspective, relating it to considerations of fairness, and striving to separate my own personal views from my responsibilities as a public official once the Congress decisively acted on the legislation were to be matters of enormous complexity and lonely personal strain. Whatever inner strength I mustered from my own religious faith, the public anguish would not be eased by the fact that I was the only Catholic in the Carter Cabinet.

The anti-abortion, right to life groups and the pro-abortion, freedom of choice organizations had turned the annual HEW appropriations bill into the national battleground over abortion. The issue was whether, and under what circumstances, HEW's Medicaid program to finance health care for poor people should pay for abortions. It would be debated and resolved in the language of the HEW appropriations law, and the regulations implementing the law. This made the Secretary of HEW an especially imposing and exposed figure on the abortion battlefield.

With the Supreme Court's *Roe* v. *Wade* decision in 1973, HEW's Medicaid program promptly began funding abortions for poor women as routinely as any other medical procedure. By 1976, estimates of the number of HEW-funded abortions ranged as high as 300,000 per year. The furies that the *Roe* decision and its impact on HEW's Medicaid program set loose turned abortion into a legal and political controversy that the courts and the Congress would toss at each other for years. The federal financing of an estimated 300,000 abortions set off an emotional stampede in the House of Representatives in 1976, led by Republican Representative Henry Hyde of Illinois, and reluctantly followed by the Senate, to attach a restriction to the 1977 HEW appropriations bill prohibiting the use of HEW funds "to perform abortions except where the life of the mother would be endangered if the fetus were carried to term."

Before the restriction took effect, pro-abortion groups obtained an injunction from Federal District Judge John F. Dooling in Brooklyn, blocking its enforcement until he could decide whether the Supreme Court decision in *Roe* v. *Wade* established an obligation of the federal government to fund abortions, as a corollary to the right to have them performed.

Whatever the courts ultimately ruled, the abortion issue would continue to be a volatile inhabitant of the political arena. Sincerely held as I believe it was, Carter's stand was also a critical part of his election victory. Betty Ford's strong pro-abortion views and Gerald Ford's ambivalence were thought by Carter to have hurt the Republican candidate.

But Carter's appointment of pro-abortionist Midge Costanza as a senior White House aide and his strong support of the Equal Rights Amendment and other feminist causes gave women's groups some hope that his position would be softened. The pro-lifers were suspicious because Carter's colors blurred on the litmus test of supporting a constitutional amendment outlawing abortion. With pro- and anti-abortion advocates poised to battle for the mind of the administration, I prepared for my confirmation hearings on January 13, 1977.

From my religious and moral convictions, I knew my conscience. From my training at Harvard Law School and my life as a lawyer and public servant, I knew my obligation to enforce the law. But on the eve of becoming a public spokesman for myself and the administration, I sought the reassurance of double-checking my moral and intellectual foundation. I consulted an extraordinary Jesuit priest, James English, my pastor at Holy Trinity Church in Georgetown. He came by my law office on the Saturday morning before the confirmation hearing. He sat on the couch against the wall; I sat across the coffee table from him. I told him I wanted to make one final assessment of my ability to deal with the abortion issue before going forward with the nomination. If I could not enforce whatever law the Congress passes, then I should not become Secretary of Health, Education, and Welfare.

Father English spoke softly about the pluralistic society and the democratic system, in which each of us has an opportunity to express his views. Most statutory law codifies morality, he noted, whether prohibiting stealing or assault, or promoting equal rights, and the arguments of citizens over what the law should be are founded in individual moral values. He said that my obligation to my personal conscience was satisfied if I expressed those views forcefully.

I postulated a law that any abortion could be funded by the federal government, simply upon the request of the woman. He said that so long as I tried to pursue the public policy I believed correct, then I was free —indeed obliged if I stayed in the job—to enforce that permissive law. I was relieved, comforted by his quiet assurance. As I thanked him for coming by, he mentioned an expert in this field, Father Richard McCormick, a Jesuit at the Kennedy Institute of Bioethics at Georgetown, whose advice I might find helpful.

On the following Monday evening, January 10, representatives of the National Women's Political Caucus sat on the same red couch Father English had occupied. It was the most intense of a series of meetings with various special interest groups.

As the women filed through the door to my office, I shook hands with each one. Their eyes seemed cold and skeptical, and reflected deep concern, even when they smiled. The warm welcome with which I greeted them masked my own foreboding about the imminence of the clash on abortion.

The discussion began on common ground: the failure of the Nixon and Ford administrations to enforce laws prohibiting sex discrimination. One after another, the representatives of each group in the women's political caucus attacked the enemy: discrimination in the Social Security system (in terms far more forceful than Jimmy Carter's quaint accusation that the benefit structure encouraged senior citizens to "live in sin"), in the federal income tax system, and on the nation's campuses. Most mentioned female appointments at HEW, but since they knew I was searching for qualified women, they did not linger on the personnel issue. Margot Polivy, a tough and talented attorney litigating to eliminate discrimination in women's athletics, pressed her case for HEW enforcement of Title IX, the law prohibiting sex discrimination at educational institutions that receive federal funds.

I shared most of the views the women expressed on these subjects and they knew it. When are they going to stop circling their prey, I thought, and ask about abortion?

Dorothy Ross, a committed feminist who had been helping me recruit for HEW jobs, was seated at my left. She had told me abortion would be the key topic and I wanted to get it over with. Then one of the women put the question: "What's your view on abortion?"

I had decided to make my view unmistakably clear. It was important to state my position on abortion before the Senate confirmation hearings.

No senator should be able to claim that his vote was cast for my confirmation without knowing my view on this subject. But in the tension of the moment, it was not easy or pleasant to get the words out.

"I believe abortion is morally wrong," I said softly and firmly. "That is my personal belief."

There was a brief moment of breathtaking at the depth of conviction in my voice. Then the women responded.

"Would you deny federal funds for abortion?" one woman angrily asked.

"I oppose federal funding for abortion." The circling was over. The questions were accusations called out like counts in an indictment.

"The Supreme Court gives a woman a right to an abortion. You would deny that right to poor women?"

"You'd deny a woman her constitutional right?"

"How can you be a liberal and hold such a view?"

"Suppose the woman's life is at stake?"

"What about rape or incest?"

"Suppose the child would be retarded, a vegetable?"

"Are you going to impose your religious views on HEW?"

The questions came with such furious vehemence that I had to interrupt to respond.

"Look," I said, "I have no intention of imposing my personal view on anybody. I am prepared to enforce the law, whatever it is."

"But how could you possibly," one of the women asked, "when you have such strong personal views, such religious commitment?"

"There's nothing wrong with religious commitment," I fired back, "and nothing about it prevents me from enforcing the law."

The women made no attempt to disguise their anger or their suspicion. I wanted to end the meeting before it further deteriorated. The subject was even more volatile than I had anticipated. I was shaken by the obvious depth and genuineness of their emotional and intellectual conviction, and the difficulty of some of the questions they had raised. But there was nothing to be gained by heated exchanges. If there were no other matters on their minds, I suggested we conclude the meeting. They were just as anxious as I to cut off discussion: they, out of a desire to report to their colleagues and plan strategy; I, out of relief.

The parting was superficially amicable, but the battle lines had been drawn. Washington's feminist network buzzed with reports of the meeting throughout that evening and the next day. Late that Tuesday afternoon I was told that the women's groups would attack my nomination on the basis of my stand on abortion.

By Wednesday, the day before my confirmation hearing, the National Abortion Rights Action League had asked to appear, on behalf of fourteen groups which supported federal funds for abortion, before both Senate committees scheduled to hear me testify on my nomination.

As I drove to my office early on Thursday morning, the radio news broadcasts were announcing that Senator Robert Packwood of Oregon, a staunch proponent of Medicaid-funded abortions and member of the Finance Committee which had jurisdiction over my nomination, would question me closely on abortion and might well oppose my nomination unless I changed my reported views.

I needed a much more sophisticated grasp of the political code words on abortion. I knew my own position, but the Senate hearing rooms of Washington were paneled and carpeted with good intentions and clear views ineptly expressed by well-meaning witnesses. I wanted to be sure I could maneuver through the verbal and emotional minefield of pro- and anti-abortionists. It was imperative for those in the abortion controversy, from Cardinal Cooke to National Abortion Rights Action League Executive Director Karen Mulhauser, to understand the words I spoke as I meant them, and I wanted to be confident that I knew what they would hear when I spoke. Far more careers have been shattered in Washington because of what people say than because of what they do—and far more often through words spoken by inadvertence or ignorance than by design.

As I parked my car, I recalled Father English's recommendation of Father Richard McCormick as an ethicist well versed in the abortion controversy. I called him as soon as I got to the office. I told him I had only a few minutes before leaving for the Senate hearing. I quickly reviewed the old ground with him, the obligation to enforce a law contrary to my personal view. Then I moved to some of the harder questions, about pursuing a public policy for our pluralistic country that differed from my personal beliefs.

"What about rape and incest? In terms of public policy, it seems to me that when a woman has been the victim of rape or incest, a case can be made to permit an immediate abortion."

"First of all," McCormick responded, "the woman may be able to solve the problem if she acts fast enough without even getting to an abortion. Even after fertilization but before implantation in the uterus, there are things like twinning and possible recombination of fertilized eggs. These things create doubt about how we ought to evaluate life at this stage. It may take as long as fourteen days for the implantation process to end."

"Do you mean that from an ethical point of view, you don't see any abortion problem for up to two weeks?" I asked.

"I mean there are sufficient doubts at this stage to lead me to believe it may not be wrong to do a dilation and curettage after rape. It's very doubtful that we ought to call this interruption an abortion. Absolutist right to life groups will still complain. But serious studies support this. The pro-abortionists feel very strongly about rape and incest."

"Suppose the doctor says the child will be retarded, or severely handicapped physically?"

"That is a much more difficult question. The Church would not permit an abortion, and the right to life and pro-abortion groups feel deeply here," McCormick replied.

"And what about some severe or permanent damage to the mother's health short of death?"

"That's another tough question in public policy terms. The Church would oppose abortion."

"Well, it's going to be an interesting morning," I mused aloud.

McCormick summed up rapidly. "You should always keep in mind three levels of distinction here. First, there is the personal conscience and belief thing. Second, there is what the appropriate public policy should be in a pluralistic democracy, which could be more liberal on funding abortions than one would personally approve as a matter of conscience or religious conviction. Actual abortion for rape and incest victims might be an example here. And third, there is the obligation of the public official to carry out the law the nation enacts."

"So I could pursue a policy for the country that funded abortion for rape and incest victims even though the Church—and I as a matter of personal and religious conviction—opposed abortion under those circumstances."

"Yes, you could."

I thanked him and rushed out of the office to my confirmation hearing.

I had to walk past a long line of people waiting to get into the standing-room-only Senate Finance Committee room in the Dirksen Building. Inside the door I had to weave through spectators and climb over legs to get to the witness table. The lights of all three networks were on me, sporadically augmented by clicking cameras and flashing bulbs from photographers sitting and kneeling on the floor in front of me. Seated behind their elevated and curved paneled rostrum, the committee members and staff looked down at me.

The hearing began promptly at 10:00 A.M. After fifteen minutes in which I made a brief opening statement and received some generous praise from Chairman Russell Long, Senator Packwood began:

"Mr. Califano, you know I have some strong feelings about abortion. . . . What is your personal view on abortion?"

The cameras turned on me.

I began by expressing my recognition of the difficulty of the abortion issue and the sincerity and depth of feeling on all sides. I noted that Carter and I shared identical views on the subject, although we came from quite different religious, cultural, and social backgrounds. I then set forth my views:

"First, I personally believe that abortion is wrong.

"Second, I believe that federal funds should not be used for the purpose of providing abortions.

"Third, I believe that it is imperative that the alternatives to abortion be made available as widely as possible. Those alternatives include everything from foster care to day care, family planning programs to sex education, and especially measures to reduce teen-age pregnancies.

"Finally, we live in a democratic society where every citizen is free to make his views known, to the Congress or to the courts. If the courts decide that there is a constitutional right in this country to have an abortion with federal funds, I will enforce that court order. If the Congress changes its mind and amends the statute which it has passed, or passes other laws which direct that funds be provided for abortion, I will enforce those laws. I will enforce those laws as vigorously as I intend to enforce the other laws that I am charged with enforcing if I am confirmed, including laws against discrimination against women on the basis of sex in Title IX, the Title VI laws."

Packwood pressed: "You are opposed and would be opposed to federal funds for abortions under any circumstances . . . if the life of the woman is jeopardized, if the fetus is carrying a genetic disease?" I testified I did not oppose federal funding of abortion where carrying the fetus to term endangered the life of the mother. That was not as far as Packwood wanted me to go.

Packwood continued: "What I am really interested in, Mr. Califano, what I would hope is that your feelings as a person would not interfere with the law, the enforcement of the laws." I assured him that my personal views would not interfere with my enforcement of the law.

Packwood asked what my recommendation would be for legislation in the future. The same as Carter's, I responded. "We would recommend that federal funds not be used to provide abortions" in Medicaid or any other program.

Packwood's first-round time was up. The tension in the room eased a little as other senators asked questions on Social Security, balancing the budget, eliminating paperwork, busing, race discrimination, a separate department of education, Medicare and Medicaid management, handicapped rehabilitation programs, fraud and abuse in the welfare program, older Americans, alcoholism, and other matters prompted by special interest constituencies and the concerns of Americans that HEW intruded too deeply in their lives. The ever-present staffers whispered in senators' ears and passed their slips of paper from which senators read questions.

Texas Senator Lloyd Bentsen tried to lighten the atmosphere as he began: "Mr. Chairman, I am very pleased to see Mr. Califano here. I have known him for many years and have had a great respect for his ability, intelligence, integrity, and judgment—until he took this job." The room burst into laughter.

At about noon, it was Packwood's turn again. When our eyes engaged, it was a signal for all the buzzing and rustling in the room to stop. As I expected, he went right to abortion, asking how I would change the law if I had the power to do so. I told him that President Carter and I would support the ban on the use of federal funds for abortions except where the mother's life was at stake. "That is the position . . . of the Carter administration," I concluded, quoting from one of the President-elect's campaign statements.

Packwood felt so strongly about the issue his face went florid with anger.

I thought for an instant about raising the issue of rape and incest, but immediately decided against it. This abortion controversy would be with me and the President for a long time and I didn't want to go any further than absolutely necessary without careful thought.

With his blue eyes blinking in disbelief, Packwood's voice rose: "If you had a choice . . . your recommendation would be that no federal funds will be used for those two hundred and fifty or three hundred thousand poor women, medically indigent, mostly minorities, who could not otherwise afford abortions?"

I reiterated: that would be my recommendation and the position of the administration. When I expressed the need to provide alternatives to abortion, Packwood interrupted: "How do you deal with teen-age pregnancies once the teen-ager is pregnant?" I said we needed more sensitive, decent human alternatives, treating the pregnant teen-ager as a person, letting her remain in school or continue her education in a home. I also recognized the need for better sex education and more effective family planning programs.

Packwood expressed support for all such programs. Then, his voice again rising, he said, "What we are saying, as far as the Carter program goes, with all the planned parenthood facilities, all the homes for unwed mothers, all the decent facilities to take care of them, if that woman wants to have an abortion and is poor and cannot afford it, tough luck." The last two words came out in angry disgust.

I could hear the whir of the television cameras.

"Senator, what I am saying is that we should reduce these cases to the greatest extent possible."

Packwood repeated for the television evening news: "Still, tough luck, as far as federal help is concerned."

I noted that "The federal government is not the only source of all funds," and private organizations were free to finance abortions. I then reminded Packwood that the administration position "is what the Congress has said in the Hyde amendment. The Senate and the House . . . voted for that amendment last year."

He asked whether the administration would oppose funding abortions in a national health insurance program. I said it would.

Packwood shook his head in apparent despair. We come to this issue from such different premises, I thought. To him, it is unfair for the government not to fund abortions for poor women when the Supreme Court has established a constitutional right to an abortion in the first trimester. To me, there is no question of equity. I thought abortion was wrong for women who could afford it unless the life of the mother was at stake, so I had no misgivings on grounds of equity in opposing the use of public funds to pay for abortions for poor women, as a matter of statutory law. Where the life of the mother was endangered, I favored public funding of abortions for the poor. The constitutional right to an abortion in the first trimester did not, in my mind, carry with it the right to public funding. The Constitution guarantees many precious rights—to speak and publish, to travel, to worship—but it does not require that the exercise of those rights be publicly funded.

Packwood cited Carter's hedging during the campaign and asked about a constitutional amendment to reverse the Supreme Court decision striking down state abortion laws. I responded that I opposed any constitutional amendment on abortion. "We run to the Constitution to stop busing, we run there on prayers in schools. We have to stop running to the Constitution to solve all of our problems." Packwood, still unsatisfied, had no further questions.

As the television crews disassembled their cameras, Senator Harry Byrd launched an attack on HEW's interference in local schools with excessively detailed civil rights questionnaires, and asked me about my support for voluntary charitable organizations.

The hearing before the Senate Finance Committee lasted so long that I had less than an hour before the Senate Committee on Labor and Public Welfare session began early the same afternoon. Within fifteen minutes of its start, Senator Jacob Javits of New York asked about my ability to carry out the law, in view of my personal beliefs. I told Javits I had no qualms of conscience about my ability to enforce the law, "whatever the law is."

After a two-and-one-half-hour interlude of questions on civil rights enforcement, the isolation of HEW from the rest of the nation, welfare reform, busing, museums, education funding, biomedical research, national health insurance, conflicts of interest, animal testing of drugs, lack of coordination among Cabinet departments, and HEW's unresponsiveness to state and local government, Maine Democratic Senator William Hathaway returned to abortion. He characterized my position as being "morally and unalterably opposed to abortion," and then asked: "Does this mean that your convictions are so strong that if Congress should enact a law, whether it is national health insurance or whatever, that did provide federal funds for abortion, that you would recommend to President Carter that he veto such legislation?"

I hedged to get time to answer this unexpected question. I had never discussed this situation with Carter and I did not want to box the President in by simply saying I would or would not recommend a veto. "I do not think President Carter, in terms of his own views, needs my advice on whether to veto that legislation."

As Hathaway pressed, asking what I would recommend if Carter sought my advice and how active a role I would take, I decided to finesse the question. "I cannot answer that question. Laws come over with lots . . . of provisions in them, and whether one provision is of such overriding importance in terms of the national administration's policy that the bill ought to be vetoed . . . is something very difficult to judge in the abstract." There was no way I would judge this issue now.

Hathaway sensed what I was thinking and helped out by noting the difference between a national health insurance program that the administration wanted with abortion funding being the only unwelcome provision and a bill that simply provided federal funds for abortion.

He then asked whether I would lobby the Congress against legislation which permitted federal funds to be spent for abortion. I told him that the administration would lobby against such legislation.

Hathaway expressed concern about anyone forcing his religious or other beliefs on the public, citing as examples a Christian Scientist HEW Secretary who did not believe in modern medicine, or a vegetarian Secretary of Agriculture who did not believe food stamps should be spent for meat. I responded firmly that if I had the slightest hesitation about enforcing whatever law the Congress passed, I would not be sitting in front of him.

Hathaway didn't question that. His concern was that no individual "should enforce his particular religious or moral beliefs into the policy-making area.'' I responded that ''the Congress had made a judgment last year that restricting federal funds for abortions was a matter appropriate for legislation.'' As to my personal views, I was expressing them so every senator who had to vote on my confirmation would know them.

Unlike the exchange with Packwood, the exchange with Hathaway ended on a conciliatory note. He appreciated my candor and hoped that I would maintain an open mind during the course of the debate on abortion.

But neither the press nor the American public was prepared for any conciliation on this issue. Before I had departed the hearing room the first of some 6,473 letters and telegrams and hundreds of phone calls, unyielding on one side or the other, began arriving at my office. That evening, the *Washington Star*'s front page headlined: ANGRY SENATOR BLASTS CALIFANO ON ABORTION. The story featured Packwood's questioning and his ''tough luck'' comment. It did report my commitment to enforce the law vigorously, and it questioned an assumption that Packwood and Hathaway had made—that the woman's right to an abortion established in *Roe* v. *Wade* implied a right to federal funds to pay for the procedure. Earlier in the week, during oral arguments before the Supreme Court on pending abortion cases, several Justices had questioned any such right to funds. There were indications that the Court would throw the scalding issue back into the legislative-executive political process. That possibility only enhanced the significance of my views—and President Carter's.

That evening Carter telephoned me: ''How did the testimony go today?''

''All right, I think, Mr. President,'' I responded hesitantly. ''I hope I didn't create any problems for you.''

''What did they ask you about?''

''Most of the questions were on your campaign promises, like welfare reform and national health insurance, and then typical special interest questions about HEW's constituencies and busing. I testified for seven hours. But the fireworks came in the thirty minutes of questioning about abortion.''

''I saw what you said in the paper and on television. You hang tough. You're saying the right things.''

''Thank you, Mr. President.''

In public comments outside the hearing, Packwood expressed deep concern and anger. Javits predicted a long and contentious struggle over the issue. And Karen Mulhauser of the National Abortion Rights Action League said it was ''unthinkable'' that a leading civil rights attorney ''would openly discriminate'' against indigent women. ''We really didn't know until this week how extreme Califano's views were,'' she added.

The lead editorial in the *Washington Post,* my former law client, was headed "Mr. Califano on Abortion," and took after me and my new boss: "The fact that each man reached this conclusion as a matter of personal conviction makes the conclusion itself no less troubling. For, personal or not, the effect of their common position would be to deny the poor what is available to the rich and not-so-rich. To argue as they do, that the emphasis should be on other medical services and/or pregnancy services does not address this inequity."

On Inauguration Day, January 20, 1977, the new President sent the nominations of the nine Cabinet members-designate whose hearings were completed to the Senate for confirmation. Eight were swiftly confirmed. Senator Packwood denied the Senate the necessary unanimous consent to consider my nomination that day.

Majority Leader Bob Byrd called my nomination to the Senate floor on January 24. Packwood was vehement. He said I held my views so passionately, so vigorously, that "I think it is impossible that Mr. Califano will be able to fairly administer the laws involving abortion, assuming that the Supreme Court says women . . . continue to have a right to an abortion, and that they continue to have a right to federal funds to help them."

Javits shared Packwood's view favoring federal funds for abortion, but he felt my qualifications in other areas merited my being confirmed. Other Republicans, from Senate Minority Leader Howard Baker to arch-conservative Carl Curtis, the ranking minority member of the Finance Committee, supported the nomination. The debate was brief, the vote 95 to Packwood's 1. Strom Thurmond was the first to phone to tell me of the Senate confirmation and congratulate me.

I called to thank each senator who had spoken on my behalf. Then I thought about Packwood. I felt that he had been petty in holding my nomination up four days, and that there had been an element of grandstanding in it. However, I had to accept the fact that his beliefs on abortion were as sincerely held as mine. From his point of view, putting that extra spotlight on me may have provided a little insurance that I would be careful to enforce a law that funded abortions more widely than I considered appropriate. I had been confirmed overwhelmingly, and I had to deal with him as a member of the Senate Finance Committee that had jurisdiction over such key HEW programs as Social Security, Medicare, Medicaid, and welfare. I swallowed a little hard and called him: "Bob, I understand your view on abortion. But I'm now Secretary and you and I agree on virtually every other social issue. I hope our differences on abortion won't prevent us from working together." Packwood, clearly surprised, thanked me for the call.

In a *New York Times* editorial on January 31 condemning my position on abortion, one element struck me as amusing: "Mr. Califano's statement in one sense represents his personal opposition to abortion. In another sense, it is a free political ride, earning credit for the administration from abortion foes without his having any real decision to make. It was Congress, though sharply split, which last fall decreed the ban on Medicaid funds for abortions. It is the courts, now scrutinizing that ban, which will decide. And Mr. Califano has pledged, as he must, to carry out the orders of the courts." I could understand the point of the editorial, but I hardly considered my experience before the Senate committees a free ride.

THE ABORTION issue would track me for most of my term as HEW Secretary. I shortly discovered that, like Champion and Shanahan, few, if any, of my colleagues at HEW shared my view or the President's on abortion. Everyone in the top HEW management who expressed his opinion disagreed with mine. Only at the Christmas open house, when they streamed through my office to shake hands and have a picture taken, would HEW employees—mostly the blacks or Catholics—whisper, "Don't let them kill those black babies," or "God bless you for your stand against abortion."

The same was true at the White House. A few staff members, such as Midge Costanza, were publicly outspoken in favor of federal funding for abortion. Shanahan called me on July 15, 1977, and said she was going to a meeting at the White House, set up by Midge Costanza to organize the women in the administration to urge Carter to change his position on abortion. Shanahan said they might draft a petition asking to see Carter and setting forth their views. I was incredulous that a White House staffer would organize such a meeting. I had no question about Shanahan's loyalty, but was appalled at Costanza's judgment and seriously questioned her loyalty to Carter. Two of the other top appointees at HEW, Assistant Secretary for Human Development Services Arabella Martinez and Assistant Secretary for Education Mary Berry, also went to the meeting.

A story was in the *Washington Post* on the morning following the Friday afternoon meeting. Jody Powell called Shanahan at about 11:00 A.M. "I just wanted to find out what right you all think you had to have a meeting like that in the White House?" Before Shanahan could respond, he answered, "No right, none at all."

"We have a right to express our views," Shanahan began.

Powell snapped, "At least General Singlaub [who disagreed with the President's policy in Korea] resigned. I can respect him."

"I did not give up my First Amendment rights when I joined the administration," Shanahan shot back.

Powell was incensed. "Most of these turkeys wouldn't have a job if it weren't for the President."

Shanahan spoke firmly, in the tense, modulated tone her voice often assumed when all her energy was devoted to maintaining her composure: "These women left damn good jobs to join the administration. Most are better qualified than men who got jobs of the same rank."

"Not you, Eileen, I don't include you," Powell responded defensively to the former economic correspondent for the *New York Times,* "but these turkeys would not have jobs if the President hadn't given them one."

When Shanahan told me about this conversation later that afternoon, she was still trembling with indignation and rage. Fortunately, she found great satisfaction in her work and she and I had developed a relationship of sufficient respect that she decided not to resign.

I assumed Carter would be enraged when he heard about the women's meeting—and he was, privately, and at the Cabinet meeting on Monday, July 18. "I don't mind vigorous debate in the administration. As a matter of fact, I welcome it," Carter said, "but I do not want leaks to the press or attacks on positions we've already established. If the forty women had listened to my campaign statements, they should know my position." Carter then contrasted Commerce Secretary Juanita Kreps and HUD Secretary Pat Harris with the group of women who met with Midge Costanza. Kreps raised her hand to speak. The President recognized her. In her soft-spoken, polite, and respectful manner, she said: "Mr. President, I appreciate the intent of your comment about me and I, of course, am loyal to you as we all are." What well-chosen words, I thought. "But"—Kreps paused to make certain we were all appropriately postured on the edge of our Cabinet chairs—"you should not take my absence from the meeting of the women as an indication of support for the administration's position on abortion."

Carter seemed somewhat surprised, not at Kreps's position, but at the quiet firmness with which she expressed her view in front of the Cabinet and the "barber shop" patrons (as I sometimes thought of the crew of aides and note-takers that sat against the wall in the Cabinet Room). From across the Cabinet table, Pat Harris promptly agreed with Kreps, but promised to keep her views within the official family. The President, so uncomfortable that he almost sounded defensive, indicated he was of course not talking about "Juanita and Pat," and reiterated his desire for "full debate," but he insisted on "complete loyalty" once an administration decision was made.

When the President walked in to begin the Cabinet meeting two weeks later, on August 1, the first Costanza had attended after her women's meeting, he put his arm around her, kissed her, and said, "Nice to see ya, darlin."

Whatever distance the President wanted from me on other policies, like school integration, the anti-smoking campaign, or Social Security cuts, he held me at his side whenever he spoke of abortion: during a March 1977 Clinton, Massachusetts, town meeting and on a Los Angeles television show in May 1977 ("Joe Califano, who is Secretary of HEW, feels the same way I do against abortions"); in Yazoo City, Mississippi, in July 1977 (". . . the Secretary of HEW agrees with me completely on this issue . . ."); at a Bangor, Maine, town meeting in February 1978 ("Joe Califano, who is head of HEW, is a very devout Catholic. . . . I happen to be a Baptist, and his views on abortion are the same as mine"); with college and regional editors and at general press conferences.

There were demonstrations, first in front of the building where my law office was located, then at the corner of Independence Avenue and Third Street, S.W., where the HEW headquarters and my offices were. The demonstrations, always peaceful but with increasingly sensational placards during 1977, were, as I looked out my window, a constant reminder of the potential of this issue to consume my energies to the detriment of other programs. A week after my confirmation, on January 31, 1977, Karen Mulhauser led a contingent of marchers from the National Abortion Rights Action League, carrying signs ("Califano Will Enslave Poor Women") that, however overdrawn they seemed to me, conveyed how many Americans felt. Coupled with the personal turmoil the issue stirred in several key managers I had recruited, both men and women, I decided it was imperative to set an overall tone and strategy from the beginning.

I was a bureaucratic child of the 1960s, acutely sensitive to the potential of an issue that touches on human life to kindle a consuming movement—as the military draft fueled the anti–Vietnam War movement. On abortion, the issue was life itself: If we all believed that life began at the same time, there would be no debate on abortion. If all citizens believed life begins at the moment of conception, then they would consider it intolerable for their national government to permit, much less fund, abortion because it involves the elimination of life. If, however, the body politic unanimously believed that life does not begin until the second or third trimester, or that there is no life until the fetus can be viable separate from the mother's body, then it would offend social justice for the government of such a single-minded people not to fund abortions for the poor when rich and middle-class women could easily obtain them to avoid serious illness or the later creation of retarded or physically handicapped life. However, the American people are far from unanimous in their view of when life begins; indeed, disagreement on that issue has been so strong it spawned as bitter a social and political dispute as the 1970s produced.

I concluded that it was not sufficient simply to express my view clearly and consistently, but that it was also essential to communicate the certainty with which I held it. Any hedging would only encourage those who disagreed to hope for a change that would not be forthcoming, and those who agreed to take steps to stiffen my resolve. By repeatedly and clearly setting forth my position, I could perhaps deflect the resources of some of the pro- and anti-abortion partisans to other targets they felt they had the opportunity to influence or the need to bolster.

My second conclusion was that I must do all I could to avoid unnecessary provocation. My obligation was to keep some measure of political decorum in this emotional debate. I did not have the luxury of an outside antagonist to be flip or hyperbolic. I refused to see or speak before pro-life groups who wanted to give me awards or roses, and I tried (not always with success) to avoid crossing picket lines or confronting demonstrators directly. In 1977, this involved going to a lot of places through the back door.

I had to display a calm and reasoned approach because of my obligation to enforce whatever law the Congress ultimately passed or the courts eventually declared constitutional. On this issue, above all, it was not enough for me to be fair; it was critical for the interested people to perceive they were being fairly treated.

Maintaining a sense of integity was important not only to the public, but to the professionals in the department. HEW's Center for Disease Control was charged with the surveillance of communicable diseases. Most commonly identified with monitoring and reporting on influenza or other communicable diseases, the center was also responsible for surveillance of abortions and abortion-related deaths in the United States. In October 1977, at the peak of the legislative debate over Medicaid funding for abortion, there were reports that an Hispanic-American woman had checked into a McAllen, Texas, hospital with complications from an abortion improperly performed in Mexico. There were allegations that the woman was covered by Medicaid and had been told by a Texas doctor that if she had only come a few weeks earlier, she would have been eligible for Medicaid funding for an abortion, but now the law prohibited it. The woman died within a few days of being admitted to the hospital.

I called Bill Foege, whom I had recently appointed director of the center, and asked him to check out the reports. He came to Washington and nervously told me that while it was difficult to establish the facts because the woman might have gone to Mexico to keep the abortion secret, she had received two Medicaid-funded abortions before the Hyde amendment took effect. "So we may have a confirmed death from an abortion improperly performed on an otherwise Medicaid-eligible woman," Foege said, resting his paper on his lap as though trying to produce relief from a tension that still persisted.

I studied him silently for a moment and then realized that he was concerned about my view of the center's role in keeping abortion statistics.

"Look," I said, "you must understand this: I want you to keep statistics as accurately as you can, to investigate as meticulously as you can. Our obligation—whatever my views—is to set the facts before the Congress and the people. Particularly on an issue like this, we must maintain the integrity of HEW's data. The only way to deal with an issue this hot is to be accurate."

His face brightened in relief. "That's just the way I feel," he said.

While I could not predict the route or timetable, I sensed that the abortion issue was inexorably headed for my desk. On June 20, 1977, the Supreme Court decided in *Beal* v. *Doe* and *Maher* v. *Roe* that the federal government had no constitutional obligation to fund discretionary abortions that were not medically necessary. Like so many ardently awaited Supreme Court decisions, this one created as much controversy as it resolved. The Court had cleared the way to having the Hyde amendment go into effect, thus restricting Medicaid funding to abortions where the life of the mother would be endangered if the fetus were carried to term. The Court had also moved the debate back into the political arena, to the floors of the House and Senate and the HEW regulatory process.

I asked my staff to prepare a guideline to implement the Hyde amendment. Judge Dooling in Brooklyn would now have to withdraw his order blocking enforcement of that amendment and I wanted to be ready to issue the necessary instructions the same day the judge acted. Any delay would only give the pro- and anti-abortionists more time to demonstrate. If I could act immediately, there would be only one day of newspaper and television coverage.

As we planned to move as quickly and quietly as possible, the President was hit with a question about the Supreme Court decision at his July 12 press conference. I was signing routine mail, casually watching the televised conference, when Judy Woodruff of NBC News caught my attention with a question asking how "comfortable" the President was with the recent Supreme Court decision "which said the federal government was not obligated to provide money for abortions for women who cannot afford to pay for them.'' The President reiterated his view that ''I would like to prevent the federal government financing abortion.''

Woodruff followed up: ''Mr. President, how fair do you believe it is then that women who can afford to get an abortion can go ahead and have one and women who cannot afford to are precluded?''

In an echo of a statement by John Kennedy, the President answered, ''Well, as you know, there are many things in life that are not fair, that wealthy people can afford and poor people can't. But I don't believe that the federal government should act to try to make these opportunities exactly equal, particularly when there is a moral factor involved.''

I had been leaning back in my chair and almost went over backward. I was stunned at the President's response. It was clear to me that he had no idea of the bitter reaction his comment would incite. It couldn't have been deliberate. At worst, it was an on-the-spot, clumsy attempt to appeal to fiscal conservatives and right-to-lifers; at best it was an inept, off-the-top-of-his-head answer to a question for which he was not prepared. Within an hour Eileen Shanahan was in my office, tears of anger welling in her eyes, to tell me that the press wanted my comment on the President's ''life is unfair'' remark. ''None, none, none,'' I said.

The only person who told me she agreed with the comment of the President was Eunice Kennedy Shriver, who wrote me on July 15: ''In terms of the equity argument, I think the President's answer is satisfactory.'' It was one of the few times I can recall disagreeing with the political judgment of this extraordinary woman. She had become and remained a dedicated and politically persistent participant in the abortion controversy, an energetic opponent of federal funding.

In July, unknown to the public, to most of the antagonists prowling the halls of Congress with roses and hangers and, indeed, to most congressmen and senators, a secret compromise remarkably close to the agreement the House and Senate would reach in December was beginning to take shape in the mind of Eunice Kennedy Shriver. She called me, as she was undoubtedly calling others, in the middle of the month, three weeks after the Supreme Court tossed the issue back to the Congress. She had ''some language that might be acceptable to both the House and Senate'' and end the widespread access to abortion. ''We've got to face the rape and incest argument, don't you think?'' And, spraying words in her staccato Massachusetts accent, she added: ''We also have to deal with serious damage to the mother—physical damage, not this fuzzy psychological stuff.''

Eunice read me some language and concluded, ''I'm sending this over to you, personally and confidentially, and you can use it as your own.''

Just as I was about to hang up, she added, "And Joseph, when we get over this, we need a teen-age pregnancy bill. I'm getting Teddy to introduce it and I want the two of you to work together on it." Eunice was working on a bill to fund centers to help teen-agers who were pregnant (she was so well connected within HEW that I got her revision of my draft testimony in support of the bill before I even received the draft from the departmental staff). Impressed by a Johns Hopkins program that helped teen-agers deal with their babies and avoid having more, she wanted to duplicate it around the nation. But even there she stood firmly on abortion. When the teen-age pregnancy bill was being considered in 1978 and HEW Deputy Assistant Secretary Peter Schuck was quoted as saying states might give funds to clinics providing abortions if they were providing services to pregnant teen-agers, Eunice sent me a strong letter: "I certainly have not worked on this bill for three years under the assumption that abortion services would be provided under the bill. . . . I will not continue, quite frankly, if abortion services are permitted under this legislation." Due in large measure to her lobbying on the Hill, when the bill was eventually enacted, no abortion services were funded under it.

The confidential proposal Eunice Shriver sent me suggested modifying the Hyde amendment to prohibit the use of funds to perform an abortion, except in cases of rape or incest, where necessary to save the life of the mother, or where the mother has an organic disease that would cause grave damage to her body if the pregnancy were continued to term. Under her proposal, she estimated that only a thousand to fifteen hundred abortions per year would be performed under Medicaid, mainly involving mothers with severe heart or kidney disease or severe diabetic conditions. "I am told," her letter concluded, "that 80 percent of the abortions performed under Medicaid would be eliminated by this language."

There were few takers for the Shriver compromise in July, but before the abortion legislation saga ended in December 1977, the House and Senate would agree on language reflecting her influence and access to key members.

On August 4, 1977, Judge Dooling reluctantly lifted his injunction against enforcing the Hyde amendment. Within hours, I announced that HEW would no longer fund abortions as a matter of course, but would provide funds "only where the attending physician, on the basis of his or her professional judgment, had certified that the abortion was necessary because the life of the mother would be endangered if the fetus were carried to term."

The House and Senate Conferees' report on the Hyde amendment approved funding for termination of an ectopic (fallopian tube) pregnancy, for drugs or devices to prevent implantation of the fertilized ovum on the uterus wall, and for "medical procedures for the treatment of rape or incest victims." I had asked Attorney General Griffin Bell to interpret that language. His opinion concluded that the Hyde amendment and the quoted language prohibited funding abortion for rape or incest (unless the life of the mother was threatened), but permitted funding for prompt treatment before the fact of pregnancy was established.

On the same day Judge Dooling lifted his injunction and I issued my guidelines under the Hyde amendment to the 1977 HEW Appropriations Act, the Senate voted by a lopsided 60 to 33 to permit payment for abortions under a broad "medically necessary" standard in 1978. Earlier that week the House had voted 238 to 182 to retain the strict Hyde amendment language.

And on that same August 4th day, the Defense Department revealed that it had funded 12,687 abortions at military hospitals between September 1, 1975, and August 31, 1976. The Pengaton policy was to fund abortions for members and dependents for reasons of physical and mental health. The *Washington Post* story reporting military abortion statistics also noted that federal employees were entitled to abortions under the general health plans, but no records were kept of the number of abortions performed for them and their dependents.

In this state of chaos and division, the House and Senate left Washington for their August recess. When the Congress reconvened in September, high on its agenda was the House and Senate Conference on the Labor-HEW appropriations bill.

There are two ways to block federal funding of a particular activity otherwise authorized. One is to pass a statute that prohibits the federal government from acting. Such legislation must be referred to the authorizing committees of the Senate and the House; normally those committees would be required to hold hearings and report the legislation before it was eligible for consideration on the floor. That can be a long and tedious process—with no certainty that the legislation will ever get to the floor of both Houses for a vote. The authorizing committee can block consideration by simply holding the bill.

The other way to block federal funding for a specific purpose is through the appropriations process, either by not providing funds, or by attaching a rider to an appropriations bill, stating that none of the appropriated funds can be spent for the proscribed activity. The appropriations rider has the same practical force as authorizing legislation, and it offers a significant advantage to legislators: Each year the appropriations bills for the executive departments must be reported by the appropriations committees and acted on by the Congress if government is to continue functioning. The disadvantage is that, unlike substantive, authorizing legislation, the appropriations rider comes up for review each year.

Until the mid-1960s, there were few such riders. By and large, House and Senate parliamentarians ruled them out of order because "substantive legislation" was not permitted on appropriations bills. But as the government funded more activities, the lines between substantive legislation and limits on the uses of federal funds became increasingly hard to draw. The more controversial the activities funded by the appropriations bill, the more frequent the attempt to restrict spending by riders.

No bill attracted more politically aggressive, true-believing interest groups than the annual HEW appropriations bill. It had become honey for a host of political bees: riders prohibiting loans or grants to students who crossed state lines to incite to riot (a hangover from the Vietnam War), forbidding the use of funds for busing, limiting the use of funds to obtain civil rights enforcement information from schools. Senator Warren Magnuson, Chairman of the Senate Appropriations Committee, told me during my first month in office, "Joe, you won't recognize the appropriations hearing for HEW. It has attracted the Goddamnedest collection of kooks you ever saw. We've got to stop all these riders. Make them go to the authorizing committees." But Magnuson's outburst was to prove nothing more than exasperated hope. For during the fall of 1977, he would be involved in the bare-knuckled, prolonged fight over the abortion rider on the HEW appropriations bill.

Some facts about abortions also helped inflame the issue. In 1975, the nation's capital had become the first city in America where abortions outnumbered births. As the congressional recess ended in September 1977, the District of Columbia government revealed that in 1976, legal abortions obtained by District residents totaled 12,945—an unprecedented one-third more than the city's 9,635 births. And 57 percent of the abortions—7,400—were paid for by the Medicaid program before the Hyde amendment went into effect on August 4. The high abortion rate in Washington, D.C., reflected the nationwide abortion rate among blacks, which was double that among whites.

With the Congress returning to Washington, the pro-abortionists moved to counter the right to life roses. On September 7, pro-abortion leader Karen Mulhauser announced a campaign to mail coat hangers to Representative Daniel Flood, the Pennsylvania Democrat who chaired the HEW appropriations subcommittee, and other anti-abortion members.

The first meeting of the House and Senate all-male cast of conferees on September 12 broke up almost as soon as it started. Magnuson and Massachusetts Republican Senator Edward Brooke (who, like Packwood, strenuously fought to fund abortions under Medicaid) vowed that they would not return to the conference table until the House voted on the Senate version of the abortion rider. House Committee Chairman Flood initially refused. But, under pressure from his colleagues who feared that funds for important HEW programs and paychecks for federal employees would be interrupted if no appropriations agreement were reached, Flood took the Senate proposal to fund abortions where "medically necessary," to the House floor. On September 27, the House overwhelmingly rejected the Senate language, 252 to 164.

Then Flood took Magnuson up on his earlier commitment to compromise if the House would first vote on the Senate language. But Magnuson was not prepared to give much and House conferees ridiculed his attempt to cover genetic disease, with statements that his suggestion would permit abortions where the child had a blue and brown eye. At one point Magnuson proposed limiting funding to situations where the life of the mother was at stake, cases of rape or incest, and situations involving "serious permanent health damage." When I heard about his proposal, I suspected the fine hand of Eunice Shriver. But Flood's initial reaction was scathing. "You could get an abortion with an ingrown toenail with that Senate language," and it went nowhere.

After House Speaker Tip O'Neill complained that only pro-abortionists Magnuson and Brooke attended the conference for the Senate, thus making compromise near-impossible with the dozen House members usually present, more Senate conferees went to the meetings. The conversation became more civil, but the conferees were no closer to agreement as September 30, the end of the fiscal year and the end of HEW's authority to spend money, arrived.

Up to that point I had decided to stay out of the congressional fight over abortion. The administration view was well known. The President did not want to be part of any compromise that was more permissive than his anti-abortion campaign statements. It was one thing to carry out whatever law the Congress passed, quite another to take an active role in easing the restriction. Carter was committed to the former; he wanted no part of the latter.

Popular sentiment, reflected in the polls, was with the strict House view, and many pro-abortionists realized that. On October 6, for example, Norman Dorsen, head of the American Civil Liberties Union, in opposing a constitutional convention, cited his concern that a nationwide convention might be used to outlaw abortion completely. With that kind of popular support, the House was likely to hold to the strict limits on federal funding for abortions that Carter favored.

Moreover, my conversations with members of Congress had led me to the conclusion that I could be of little, if any, help in drafting the substance of an eventual compromise. Abortion was such a profoundly personal issue that neither I nor a President who, during his first nine months of office, had already lost a good deal of respect on the Hill, would have much influence with individual members.

Only once had I come close publicly to entering the debate during this time. I understood the depth of conviction and humane values that motivated most abortion advocates, but I was deeply offended by the cost-control, money-saving argument pushed by the staunchly pro-abortion Alan Guttmacher Institute, the research arm of the Planned Parenthood Federation of America. In late September, the Institute published a report claiming that the Hyde amendment would cost the public at least $200 million, for the first year of their life, to take care of children who could have been aborted under Medicaid. I wanted to denounce this kind of argument in severe terms: it was appallingly materialistic and represented a selfish failure to confront moral issues as such. But in the interests of being firm yet not provocative, I waited until I was asked about it at a press conference to express my views, and then did so in muted tones.

Now, however, I had to get into the congressional fight. On October 1, I was compelled to eliminate all hiring and overtime and virtually all out-of-town travel by HEW's 150,000 employees. I also warned that they might receive only half their pay in mid-October unless the House and Senate resolved the appropriations fight over abortion. It was, so far as we could tell, unprecedented at the time for a department to have no authority to operate or spend money after the first of the new fiscal year.

Despite the situation, the conferees again failed to reach agreement on October 3, and postponed any further action until October 12, after the Columbus Day recess. That postponement jeopardized beneficiaries of HEW programs and the pay of Department employees. Across the nation, state rehabilitation agencies for the handicapped were running out of money to process claims for Social Security disability benefits; New York State would be unable to meet its payroll for employees to process disability determinations; Texas intended to furlough 612 employees on October 12; Idaho would have no money for its nutrition and community services programs for the aged.

I called Tip O'Neill and Bob Byrd on October 10th, and asked them to try to break the abortion deadlock in order to avoid severe human suffering. The next day I sent them a letter and made it public. It was, the letter charged, "grossly unfair to hold the vulnerable people of our nation and thousands of federal and state employees hostage" in the congressional dispute over the use of federal funds for abortions. If the Congress could not agree on abortion language, I urged them to pass a Continuing Resolution to give me authority to spend in early 1978 at the end-of-1977 level in order to continue HEW programs that people depend on each day. The Senate opposed a Continuing Resolution because it would also keep the Hyde amendment in effect.

I sent telegrams to the state governors alerting them to imminent funding terminations so they would press their congressmen and senators to act. I asked Labor Secretary Ray Marshall to tell the Congress and the public of the dangers of continuing to hold up 1978 funding, since his department's appropriations were tied to the HEW bill. Marshall announced that further delay could force many states to stop processing unemployment insurance claims and halt federally funded job and health safety programs. At my suggestion, President Carter told the congressional leadership on the morning of October 12 that, while we all recognized what an emotional issue abortion was, the paychecks of federal employees should not be held up while Congress tried to resolve it. House Appropriations Committee Chairman George Mahon warned of "chaos in some parts of our government." By October 13, after wrangling with each other and some spirited debate on the House floor, both legislative bodies passed a Continuing Resolution to provide funds for fifteen days until the end of the month.

On Sunday, October 16, I was scheduled to appear on the ABC-TV program *Issues and Answers*. On the Saturday morning preceding the program, I called the President to review the administration's position on abortion. The President said that his position had not changed since the campaign.

"One issue in sharp dispute is how to handle victims of rape or incest," I said, asking whether he objected to funding abortions for rape or incest victims and referring to his July 12, 1977, press conference. There Carter had said that the federal government "should not finance abortions except when the woman's life is threatened or when the pregnancy was the result of rape or incest. I think it ought to be interpreted very strictly."

I asked the President whether his "very strictly" interpretation was related to the dispute between House and Senate conferees over medical procedures short of abortion for rape or incest performed shortly after the act, as distinguished from outright abortions. Carter said he was unaware of the dispute, but wanted to stay out of it. I said that it might not be possible for me to do that. Then leave the administration position ambiguous on this issue, he suggested. "Above all I want people to understand I oppose federal funding for abortion in keeping with my campaign promise."

The words had the texture of the three dimensions that came into play when Carter discussed abortion with me: his deep personal belief, his sense (particularly in the first year) that he would violate some sacred trust if he did not adhere to his campaign statements, and his insistence on getting the political plusses out of issues that had such significant political minuses as well.

ABC White House correspondent Sam Donaldson asked the first question on the program the next day: What was the administration's position on abortion? I recited the administration position opposing federal funds for abortions "except where the life of the mother is endangered if the fetus were carried to term, or for treatment as a result of rape or incest."

After Bettina Gregory asked about teen-age pregnancy, Donaldson pressed for precision on the issue of rape or incest. "The House position . . . would not even allow abortions to be financed in the case of rape or incest, unless someone comes forward and it can be established that there is not yet a pregnancy that has been medically found. Is that reasonable?"

Trying to satisfy the President's desires, I responded: "In the case of rape or incest, you would assume that the individual would come promptly for treatment and that is a matter of several days. Doctors and experts disagree on it. It can be days or a couple of weeks."

Donaldson noted that the House would allow a dilation and curettage only where an abortion was not involved, and asked if I agreed. I hesitated, then in pursuit of the President's overriding objective to be anti-abortion, responded: "Yes, that is the way I feel; that is the way the President feels. He made that clear during the campaign repeatedly, as you are well aware, covering him during the campaign."

I then recalled my own desire to cool the debate, and added: "This is a very difficult issue; it is a very complex issue; it is a very emotional issue. There are strong feelings on all sides. I think in terms of the nation as a whole what is important is that this issue is being debated in every state in the union . . . in city after city. The way to reach a consensus in a democracy is to have people talk about it, where they live; and that is happening now in this country . . . the issue should be debated in more places than in the House and Senate."

When the Continuing Resolution ran out on October 31, House and Senate conferees agreed to language which would permit federal funding for abortion in cases of rape, including statutory rape of minors, or incest, where a prompt report was made to appropriate authorities. They were still split over Senate language which would permit abortions "where grave physical health damage to the mother would result if the pregnancy were carried to term." By the next day, however, the House conferees wanted only forced rape covered. The Senate conferees were furious, and the conference broke up in acrid charges of bad faith. This skirmish marked the first time the House conferees had agreed on abortion, as distinguished from treatment before the fact of pregnancy was established, in any rape situation. Nevertheless, with their conferees unable to agree, the House and Senate voted another Continuing Resolution, giving members a three-week respite from the issue until December 1.

But there was no respite from the demonstrations. Without fail, during the week pickets marched outside HEW. The signs got more vivid; the crude printing crueler. There were the color pictures from *Life* magazine and the roses and hangers, which had become calling cards for the protagonists. The rhetoric was increasingly sprinkled with harsh accusations of "murder" by each side—of killing unborn children by Medicaid abortion, or poor mothers by back-alley abortion. Some placards accused me of being a "murderer of poor women."

Wherever I went, pickets greeted me. When I spoke in Oregon at a Democratic political fundraiser, several hundred demonstrators from both sides paraded outside the Hilton Hotel. The Oregon Legislative Emergency Board was scheduled to decide in ten days whether to replace lost federal abortion funds with state money. The pro-abortionists angrily accused me of trying to inject my own views into the Oregon fight, which I had not heard of until arriving in Portland.

The sincerity of the Oregon demonstrators and others like them took its toll on me: earnest pleas of both sides were moving. None of the lighthearted sidebars that accompanied most demonstrations—even some during the Vietnam War—were present during pro- and anti-abortion rallies. When I avoided demonstrators by going out a side entrance, as I did that evening in Oregon, I felt like a thief in the night, denying these committed marchers even the chance to know they had been at least heard, if not heeded.

The most vehement demonstration took place in New York City's Greenwich Village on Saturday afternoon, November 12. It was my most draining emotional experience over the abortion issue.

New York University President John Sawhill invited me to receive NYU's University Medal. The award ceremony was to consist of a brief talk and an extended question and answer period. As the day approached I was told that pro-abortionists planned a major demonstration. When I arrived at the NYU Law School in Washington Square, there were several thousand demonstrators. They were overwhelmingly pro-abortion; the handful of right-to-lifers there said they had heard of the demonstration only the evening before and had no chance to mobilize their supporters. Bella Abzug reviled the "white-male dominated White House." Speaker after speaker attacked me for "imposing my Roman Catholic beliefs on poor women." "Our bodies, ourselves," protesters chanted to the beat of a big drum. "Not Califano's."

The crowd was so large and noisy, I could hear it clearly when I entered the law school around the block from the demonstrators. As I reached the back entrance, ACLU Chairman Norman Dorsen, a friend of twenty-five years, greeted me with a broad smile on his face. "It took Califano to bring the sixties back to NYU," he cracked. We all chuckled at that welcome, which broke the tension for the next few minutes.

When Dorsen, who was to moderate the question and answer period, Sawhill, and I entered the auditorium, my right arm and hand were in a cast, held by a sling, due to an operation on my thumb the week before. The auditorium was crushingly overcrowded. Every seat was taken; every inch of wall space lined with standees. The antagonism of the audience was so penetrating I could physically feel it as I sat on the elevated stage. Even the cast on my arm will evoke no sympathy here, I thought.

Sawhill spoke first about me. He then turned to give me the medal. As I rose to receive it, the last row of the audience unfurled a huge pro-abortion banner across the back of the auditorium. Fully half the audience stood and held up hangers, many with ends that had been dipped in red nail polish. When the medal was presented, at least a hundred people in the audience turned their backs to me. Many of them remained in that position throughout the entire ninety minutes of my speech and the question and answer session that followed.

The question period was largely devoted to abortion, with many emotional statements and speeches. None, however, struck me more forcefully than that of an intense woman who picked up on a comment I had made earlier that year. On the Sunday, March 20, NBC program *Meet the Press,* Carol Simpson had queried me at length on abortion and the adequacy of the administration program for alternatives to abortion. In the course of one extended response, I observed: "I have never known a woman who wanted an abortion or who was happy about having an abortion. I think it is our role to provide for those women the best we can in terms of family planning services, of day care centers for their children, of health, and prenatal services to make sure children are born healthy, and all the decent things in life that every child in this country deserves, whether it is health care or a clean home or a decent schooling, and we will do our best to do that."

To my left, about halfway down the aisle in the NYU auditorium, a woman rose to the microphone. Her head was tilted sideways, her eyes spilled over with anger, even hatred. "Look at me, Mr. Califano," she shouted with defiant emotion. "I want you to see a woman who wanted an abortion. I want you to see a woman who was happy at having an abortion. I want you to see a woman who had an abortion two weeks ago and who intends to have another abortion."

The room fell into total silence as the tone of her voice became that kind of gripping whisper everyone can hear even when they don't want to: "I want you to go back to Washington knowing that there are women who are happy who have had abortions, knowing that there are women who want abortions. I don't ever want you to make a statement like the one you made saying that you have never known a woman that wanted to have an abortion or never known a woman who was happy about having an abortion. You have now met one."

So draining was the emotional experience at NYU, that afterward, when I got into the car to Kennedy Airport to depart for England, Germany, and Italy to look at national health programs—my first trip abroad as Secretary of HEW—I instantly fell asleep and did not wake up until the driver shook me to say we had arrived at Kennedy.

The abortion issue followed me to Europe. There were questions in England and the Italians were in the midst of their own volatile parliamentary debate on the issue. The latent suspicion of my Catholicism again surfaced in Rome. Immediately after my audience with Pope Paul VI, several reporters called at the Hassler Hotel to see if the Pope talked to me about abortion. He had not mentioned the issue. His focus was on the failure of the food-rich nations such as the United States to feed the world.

I returned to Washington on Thanksgiving eve. I knew the abortion issue would erupt again when the latest Continuing Resolution expired. But I was not prepared for the news the *Washington Post* brought me on the Sunday after Thanksgiving. Connie Downey, chairperson of an HEW group on alternatives to abortion, had written a memo expressing her views to her boss, Assistant Secretary of Planning and Evaluation Henry Aaron. The *Post* headlined the most sensational portion of an otherwise typical HEW memo: TASK FORCE HEAD LISTS SUICIDE, MOTHERHOOD, AND MADNESS: ABORTION ALTERNATIVES CITED IN HEW MEMO.

The memo, written more than four months earlier on July 18, contained this paragraph: "Abortion is but one alternative solution to many of the problems . . . which may make a pregnancy unwise or unwanted. . . . It is an option, uniquely, which is exercised between conception and live birth. As such, the literal alternatives to it are suicide, motherhood, and, some would add, madness. . . ."

The memo had never reached me, but its leak provided a dramatic reminder of the potential for turmoil within HEW and raised the curtain on the final act between the House and the Senate on the fiscal 1978 HEW appropriations bill.

Returning from Thanksgiving recess, the House leadership was determined to press for a compromise. They did not want the Christmas checks of federal employees to be short. Appropriations Committee Chairman Mahon called me on November 29 to say he had decided to take the leadership completely away from Flood, who ardently opposed federal funds for abortion. "He's just implacable on the subject," Mahon said, distraught. "I'm retiring, but this kind of conduct is a disgrace to the House. We all look asinine."

In secret negotiations with Senator Brooke, Mahon eventually produced the compromise on December 7. The House voted twice within less than four hours. The first time members rejected a Mahon proposal and voted 178 to 171 to stand by their strict position against all funding for abortions except those needed to save the mother's life. Minutes later, Mahon, dejected but determined, won speedy approval of new language from the Rules Committee and rushed back to the House floor. The House reversed direction and adopted the new and relaxed standard, 181 to 167. Within two hours, with only three of its hundred members on the floor, the Senate acceded to the House language and sent the measure to President Carter for his signature.

Under the measure, no HEW funds could be used to perform abortions, "except when the life of the mother would be endangered if the fetus were carried to term, or except for such medical procedures necessary for the victims of rape or incest, when such rape or incest has been reported promptly to a law enforcement agency or public health service; or except in those instances where severe and long-lasting physical health damage to the mother would result if the pregnancy were carried to term when so determined by two physicians."

Senator Brooke described the outcome as "not really acceptable to either side, but it makes some progress." Representative Hyde said that the measure "provides for the extermination of thousands of unborn lives." Senator Javits called the action "a major victory for women's rights." ACLU Chairman Dorsen characterized it as "a brutal treatment of women with medical needs for abortion." Any relief I felt at seeing at least some resolution was lost in the knowledge that the protagonists would rearm to battle over the regulations I had to issue.

AS SOON as President Carter signed the $60 billion appropriations bill on December 9, it landed on my desk, for the final provision of the compromise language stated: "The Secretary shall promptly issue regulations and establish procedures to ensure that the provisions of this section are rigorously enforced."

The antagonists turned their attention to me. Magnuson and Brooke wrote and called with their permissive interpretation. Robert Michel, ranking Republican on the Appropriations Committee, wrote with his strict view. Dan Flood called and other members—and their even more aggressive staffs—pressed for their interpretation of words such as "medical procedures," "promptly reported," "severe and long-lasting physical health damage," and "two physicians."

There was no way in which I could avoid becoming intimately involved in making key decisions on the regulations. I decided personally to read the entire 237 pages of self-serving and often confused congressional debate and to study the ten different versions of this legislation that were passed by either the House or the Senate.

To assure objectivity, to balance any unconscious bias I might harbor, and to reduce my vulnerability to charges of personal prejudice, I assigned the actual regulation writing to individuals who did not share my strong views about abortion and, more importantly, who stood up for their own views and did not hesitate to tell me when they thought I was wrong. The bulk of the work was done by Richard Beattie, the Deputy General Counsel of HEW, and HEW attorneys June Zeitlin and David Becker, all of whom opposed any restrictions on federal funding of abortions. I also asked the Attorney General to review independently the regulations we drafted at HEW. Once they were in effect, I would establish a detailed auditing system to assure compliance and fulfill the congressional mandate "to ensure that the provisions of this section are rigorously enforced."

Finally, I decided not to consult the President about the regulations. Carter had enough controversial problems on his desk without adding this one. My responsibility under the Constitution and under our system of government was to reflect accurately the law passed by the Congress. Neither Carter's personal views nor mine were of any relevance to my legal duty to ascertain what Congress intended and write regulations that embodied that intent.

In pursuit of my overall goal of cooling the temperature of the debate, I wanted to issue the regulations more "promptly" than anyone might expect. Not relying solely on my own reading of the congressional debates, I asked the lawyers for a thorough analysis of the legislative history. We then spent hours discussing and debating what the Congress intended on several issues, frustrated by the conflicting statements in the congressional record. We determined that for rape and incest victims, the term "medical procedures" as used in this new law now clearly included abortions; that a "public health service" had to be a governmental, politically accountable institution; that short of fraud we should accept physicians' judgments as to what constituted "severe and long-lasting physical health damage"; that the two physicians whose certification was required must be financially independent of each other; and that the rape or incest victim need not personally make the required report to public authorities. We resolved a host of other issues as best we could against the backdrop of the heated and confusing congressional debate. They were wearing days, because I felt the law was too permissive, and its provisions were in conflict with my own position. I revisited many decisions several times, concerned, on overnight reflection, that I had bent too far to compensate for my personal views and approved inappropriately loose regulations, or that I was letting my personal views override congressional intent.

By far my most controversial determination was to define "reported promptly" in the context of rape and incest to cover a sixty-day period from the date of the incident. Even though the Attorney General found the judgment "within the permissible meaning of the words within the Secretary's discretion," there was a storm of controversy over this decision.

There were widely varying interpretations on the floor of the House and the Senate. Most of the legislative history on the Senate floor was made by pro-abortion Senators Magnuson and Brooke. They spoke of "months" and "ninety days" to make the period as long as possible. On the House side, Mahon and other proponents of the compromise spoke of "weeks" and "thirty days" as they cautiously maneuvered this difficult piece of legislation to passage. On the floor of Congress, pro- and anti-abortionists could express their views and protect their constituencies. But I had to select a number of days and be as certain as possible that it would stick.

After extensive internal discussion and spirited argument within the department, I concluded that a sixty-day reporting period was within the middle range of the various time limits mentioned in the debates. The dominant issues during debate were access to abortions and prevention of fraud. The sixty-day period was long enough for a frightened young girl or an embarrassed woman who might not want to report a rape or incest, or one in shock who psychologically could not, to learn whether she might be pregnant and to make the report to public authorities. Sixty days was also prompt enough to permit effective enforcement of the law.

I was ready to issue the regulations during the third week of January 1978. On Monday, January 23, the annual March for Life to protest the 1973 Supreme Court abortion decision was scheduled to file past HEW en route from the White House to the Capitol. I decided to delay issuing the regulations until later in the week. The participants were outraged at the House-Senate compromise. As march leader Nellie Gray saw it, "The life issue is not one for compromise and negotiation. Either you're for killing babies or you're against killing babies."

I issued the regulations on January 26. Attorney General Bell concluded that they were "reasonable and consistent with the language and intent of the law." The *New York Times* editorialized that I had "done [my] duty. . . . He has interpreted the nation's unfair abortion law fairly. . . . On several controversial issues Mr. Califano and his lawyers have performed admirably, hacking their way through a thicket of ambiguities in the law that passed a bitter and divided Congress in December after months of heated debate."

The right to life lobby disagreed. Thea Rossi Barron, legislative counsel for the National Right to Life Committee, called the regulations an example of "a rather blatant carrying out of a loophole to allow abortion on demand." The pro-life groups were particularly disturbed about the sixty-day reporting period for victims of rape or incest. But the most severe critic of that provision was Jimmy Carter.

In testifying before the House Appropriations Committee on the morning of February 21, 1978, less than a month after issuing the regulations, Chairman Flood and Republican Robert Michel pressed me to provide an administration position on tightening the restrictions on abortion.

I called the President during the luncheon break. The President wanted the reporting period for rape or incest shortened. He was "not happy" with the sixty-day time period in the regulations. "I believe such instances are reported promptly," he said coolly.

I told him that the sixty-day period was my best judgment of what Congress intended in the law. Carter "personally" believed sixty days permitted "too much opportunity for fraud and would encourage women to lie."

"But what counts is what the congressional intent is," I argued.

The President then said he thought the regulations did not require enough information. He particularly wanted the doctor to report to Medicaid the names and addresses of rape and incest victims. The President was also inclined to require reporting of any available information on the identity of the individual who committed the rape or incest. Carter said, "Maybe some women wake up in the morning and find their maidenhead lost, but they are damn few. That actually happened in the Bible, you know."

"Perhaps we can tighten the reporting requirements," I responded, somewhat surprised at his Biblical reference. "Do you have any strong feelings on the legislation itself?"

Carter expressed some strong feelings: "I am against permitting abortions where long-lasting and severe physical health damage might result. I think that might permit too much of a chance for abuse and fraud. I want to end the Medicaid mills and stop these doctors who do nothing but perform abortions on demand all day.''

When I testified that afternoon, I gave the House Appropriations Subcommittee some indication of the administration's views and agreed to submit a letter with the administration's position the next day.

After preparing a draft, I called the President and reviewed my proposed letter for the committee word by word. The letter set the administration position as stricter than the December compromise of the Congress. The administration opposed funding abortions in situations involving ''severe and long-lasting physical health damage to the mother.'' The President and I compromised on the rape and incest paragraph: ''In the case of rape or incest, we believe that present law requires the sixty days specified in the regulation as the period Congress intended for prompt reporting. In order to reduce the potential for fraud and abuse, it may be advisable to reduce that period to a shorter period of time.''

Just as he was hanging up the phone, Carter again directed me to tighten the reporting provisions on rape and incest. ''I want rules that will prevent abortion mills from simply filling out forms and encouraging women to lie.''

I changed the regulations to require that the names and addresses of both the victim and the person reporting the rape or incest, and the dates of both the report and the incident, be included in the documentation for Medicaid funding. This change drew immediate fire from the National Organization for Women's National Rape Task Force, but it was well within my discretion under the law and consistent with the congressional intent.

Yet the President was still not satisfied. He wanted the sixty-day reporting period shortened, regardless of congressional intent. He raised the issue again two months later at the Camp David Cabinet summit of April 17, 1978, sharply criticizing ''the regulations HEW issued on abortion'' among a series of actions by Cabinet officers with which he disagreed.

The concern of the President and others that the regulations were too loosely drawn in the rape and incest area has not turned out to be justified. During the first sixteen months under the law and regulations, until shortly before I left HEW, only 92 Medicaid abortions were funded for victims of rape or incest. The overwhelming majority of Medicaid-funded abortions—84 percent of 3,158 performed—were to save the life of the mother; 522 were to avoid severe and long-lasting health damage to the mother. Eunice Shriver's estimate of 1,000 to 1,500 Medicaid-funded abortions each year was not too far off, particularly when compared with the 250,000 to 300,000 abortions estimated to have been performed annually under Medicaid in the absence of any funding restrictions.

I came away from the abortion controversy with profound concern about the capacity of national government, in the first instance, to resolve issues so personal and so laced with individual, moral, and ethical values. The most secure way to develop a consensus in our federal system is from the bottom up. But once the Supreme Court established a woman's constitutional right to an abortion against the backdrop of federally funded health care programs, the issue was instantly nationalized. As each branch acted—the Congress with the Hyde amendment, the executive with its regulations, and the Supreme Court in its opinions—the mandates from the top down generated as much resentment as agreement. This is true even though, by 1978, many states had more restrictive provisions on abortion funding than the national government.

In 1978, the Congress extended abortion funding restrictions to the Defense Department budget. In 1979, it applied an even stricter standard to both HEW and Defense appropriations, by eliminating funding in cases of long-lasting physical health damage to the mother, thus funding abortions only when the life of the mother is at stake or in cases of rape or incest, as Carter and I proposed for HEW in February 1978. The Supreme Court in the *McRae* case upheld the constitutionality of the Hyde amendment in June of 1980, concluding that the right to an abortion did not require the government to provide the resources to exercise it and that the Congress could restrict the circumstances under which it would pay for abortions. Months later, the Senate and House agreed to place tighter restrictions on Medicaid funding of abortions. Under the 1981 appropriations legislation, such funding is permitted only where the mother's life is at stake, in cases of rape reported within 72 hours and in cases of incest. That legislation permits the states to be even more restrictive; they are "free not to fund abortions to the extent that they in their sole discretion deem appropriate." Similar language was attached to the Defense appropriations bill.

Conforming the Defense and HEW appropriations bills provides the same standards for most of the federal funding arena. So long as the Congress acts through the appropriations for each department, however, rather than by way of across-the-board authorizing legislation, there will be inconsistencies. Even within HEW, the abortion funding policy has been a quilted one. The restrictions do not apply to disabled citizens whose health bills are paid by Medicare, because that program is financed out of Social Security trust funds, not through the HEW appropriations bill. Nor do the funding limits apply to the Indian Health Service; though administered by HEW, funds for the Indian Health Service are provided in the Interior Department appropriations bill. The Congress has begun to move to prohibit the use of federal funds to pay for abortion through federal employee health insurance. The inevitable challenges in court to new restrictions and the recurrent debate in the Congress assure continuing turmoil and controversy over the abortion issue.

In personal terms, I was struck by how infinitely more complex it was to confront the abortion issue in the broader sphere of politics and public policy in our pluralistic society than it had been to face it only as a matter of private conscience. I found no automatic answers in Christian theology and the teachings of my church to the vexing questions of public policy it raised, even though I felt secure in my personal philosophical grounding.

I was offended by the constant references to me as "Secretary Califano, a Roman Catholic" in the secular press when it wrote about the abortion issue. No such reference appeared next to my name in the stories reporting my opposition to tuition tax credits favored by the Catholic Church or my disputes with the Catholic hierarchy on that issue.

I was dismayed by the number of Catholics and diocesan papers that attacked me for the regulations I issued on abortion. Their attack so concerned Notre Dame president Father Theodore Hesburgh that he urged me to speak about the conscience and duty of a Catholic as a public official at the commencement in South Bend in 1979. The assumption of many bishops that I could impose my views on the law passed by the Congress reflected a misunderstanding of my constitutional role at that stage of the democratic process. As it turned out, like the President's, their assumption that the sixty-day reporting period for rape or incest constituted a legal loophole was as ill-founded in fact as it was in law.

Throughout the abortion debate, I did—as I believe I should have—espouse a position I deeply held. I tried to recognize that to have and be guided by convictions of conscience is not a license to impose them indiscriminately on others by one-dimensionally translating them into public policy. Public policy, if it is to serve the common good of a fundamentally just and free pluralistic society, must balance competing values, such as freedom, order, equity, and justice. If I failed to weigh those competing values—or to fulfill my public obligations to be firm without being provocative, or to recognize my public duty once the Congress acted—I would have served neither my private conscience nor the public morality. I tried to do credit to both. Whether I succeeded is a judgment others must make.

CHAPTER III

HEALTH: NATIONAL HEALTH PLAN

FROM THE moment Edward M. Kennedy began questioning me about health policy during my confirmation hearing before the Senate Labor and Public Welfare Committee, I knew that national health insurance was going to be a major issue for him, for Carter, and for me. His detailed questioning about health policy stretched late into the January afternoon. Kennedy made clear his unhappiness at my previous indications that Carter was going to submit welfare reform to the Congress before a national health plan. I reassured him that national health insurance would be "a centerpiece of the Carter administration," that we would study it as soon as possible. Kennedy responded tersely, "the issue . . . has really been studied to death." Kennedy considered himself the spokesman for the Democratic Party on national health insurance. Establishing a comprehensive health insurance program was one of the major goals of his public life. This was one torch he had taken from Lyndon Johnson in January 1969 and had carried through eight years of Nixon and Ford.

In question after question about health planning, health maintenance organizations, the Food and Drug Administration, the Public Health Service, the Indian health program, Kennedy was delivering a message: I am

Mr. Health in the Democratic Party. I welcomed his interest, but I was well aware that however much we might accomplish together, our strong personalities and the public ambitions of Carter and Kennedy made some friction inevitable.

When candidate Carter took the liberal Democratic oath on national health insurance in an address to the Student National Medical Association in April 1976, Kennedy was looking over his shoulder. Carter had committed himself to federal takeover of the health care system and to a payroll tax and general revenues to finance it, and he had recited the national health insurance gospel according to the United Auto Workers and the AFL-CIO. Stu Eizenstat had negotiated the speech word by word with Lane Kirkland for the AFL-CIO and Leonard Woodcock for the UAW. Eizenstat's attempts to keep some flexibility for the President had given way to the need for UAW support in Michigan and elsewhere, and Kennedy had pushed the unions to get as much from Carter as they had already gotten from him. The candidate's speech stopped barely short of Kennedy's federal cradle-to-grave blanket, the Kennedy-Corman Health Security Act. By 1977, however, Carter had not only taken the oath on national health insurance, he had also taken the oath as President. However reluctantly he used his voice, he was now the chief Democratic spokesman on national health insurance, as on other issues.

Within days after I was sworn in, Kennedy called to urge me to get started on a national health insurance program "to fulfill the President's commitment in his speech. . . ." His tone was friendly and cooperative, "We're ready to help in any way we can," but insistent and demanding: "We want to get moving on this early in the administration." I thought about Lyndon Johnson and Robert Kennedy, and about the inevitable problem any Democratic President would have with the last Kennedy brother in the Senate.

Carter's personality is very different from Johnson's. Carter is inner-directed, more like Nixon in his shyness and desire to be alone. Johnson was consumingly extroverted. He wanted company from the moment he rose in the morning until he fell asleep reading memos and talking to an aide with a masseur kneading his back. But Carter nurtured the same resentment of the liberal, Eastern establishment as Johnson, and no person could suffer the exhausting indignities of running for President without a monumental ego and enormous self-confidence, however disguised by the image-makers who told him to carry his own suitcase.

I knew how Johnson had felt about Robert Kennedy and how some of his feelings had spilled over on Ted Kennedy near the end of his presidency in late 1968. Carter was not immune to the same feelings. I thought it was only a matter of time before Carter and Edward Kennedy became a redux of Johnson and Robert Kennedy. Only this time, I thought, national health insurance will be a crucial issue, and Califano will be the rope for the tug of war. I knew well how intense it could get. I remembered Johnson one night in June 1968, after Robert Kennedy had been shot, when he was dying on the operating table. We had known all day that Kennedy was going to die. It had been an eerie time; Johnson had asked me to draft a presidential proclamation commemorating Robert Kennedy, to be issued after he died. Late that night, as we went over it at dinner in the family dining room, Johnson kept picking up the phone attached under the table at his place, calling to get the latest reports. He was never able to disguise his hurt at the accusations of dark intentions that Kennedy had made during the heat of the 1968 presidential campaign. Nor could he hide the personal pain as another assassinated Kennedy was about to become a national hero, while his own greatness and monumental achievements were destined not to be recognized during his lifetime. Johnson was strong and publicly gracious during the next few days of mourning, and greatly admiring of Rose Kennedy, but I knew how much this tragic turn of fate hurt, and how deeply it affected him.

Johnson respected, and at times seemed to revere, John Kennedy, but even so, there had been occasional outbursts of his frustration. I was standing next to him in his office when he bent over the wire service tickers early one afternoon to read that Jacqueline Kennedy was going to marry the Greek playboy-tycoon Aristotle Onassis. "That'll sure take its toll on the Kennedy myth," he remarked half in sorrow, half in the tones of a haunted man.

Johnson liked Edward Kennedy. He used to say that Ted Kennedy had the potential to be "the best politician of the whole family," and when LBJ used the word "politician" he meant it in its finest sense. Unlike his brothers, Ted Kennedy seemed to share Johnson's love and respect for the Senate. Even here, however, his envy and the unfairness of the Kennedy myth sometimes pricked Johnson. When Ted Kennedy was pushing his family's friend Francis X. Morrissey to be a federal judge, Johnson urged us to help get votes on the Senate floor, as Kennedy had asked him to do. "Work hard on this one," Johnson told us, and with a cat-who-ate-the-canary smile on his lips, he added, "Teddy's gonna get his ass beat on this one and I don't want him to accuse me of not helping him, 'cause he ain't going to blame himself when he loses."

I knew how it felt to get squeezed between a President and a Kennedy. Johnson had used me to negotiate domestic issues with Robert Kennedy, and teased me about going to his parties at Hickory Hill. During the 1968 campaign, Johnson told me to call Kennedy, and all the other candidates, Democrat and Republican, to alert them that the Urban Institute he was creating was apolitical and would help not Johnson but whoever won. I reached Robert Kennedy at an airport in Indiana. He was too suspicious to give Johnson the benefit of political altruism, but he agreed not to criticize the announcement. Then he said, "What are you doing there? You should be here with me."

"Someone's got to prepare the orderly transition," I said, trying to deflect the Kennedy hook.

Ted Kennedy could be as stubborn and prickly as Robert. There was only one Democratic congressional leadership breakfast after Ted was elected Majority Whip in January 1969 before Johnson left office. Johnson had put a single question on the table: Should he ask the Congress to renew the 10 percent surtax on income, or should he cut the budget and leave the issue to Nixon? I had argued strenuously that he recommend the surtax. To cut the budget would be to leave office on a phony budget, or to set the stage for Nixon to savage some of the Great Society programs. I had written Johnson such a tough memorandum that he was not speaking to me, and for the past few days had prohibited me from attending budget meetings for the first time since I joined his staff in 1965.

At breakfast, Johnson described the alternatives in such a way that I expected every member of the leadership to come out against renewing the surtax. And so they did, as Johnson went from Speaker John McCormack to Senate Majority Leader Mike Mansfield and down the line until he reached Ted Kennedy. "I'd like to think about it, Mr. President," he said, "and get back to you this afternoon." I couldn't tell whether Kennedy was insecurely cautious or intuitively shrewd.

Later that morning, Kennedy called me. "I think the President should urge renewal of the surtax. He can't reduce the budget enough without fake cuts. Tell him I'm preparing a memo I'll send over this afternoon." Kennedy did not know my views or anything about my memo to the President. But against that background, I was not about to deliver his message to Johnson. "Why don't you call Jim Jones [Johnson's appointments secretary] and tell him," I suggested.

Kennedy was shrewd enough to sense he had a sympathetic ear and mischievous enough to say he didn't know Jones. "You just tell him, Joe, if you would," he responded, and hung up.

I gave Jim Jones a two-sentence note to slip to Johnson, who was in a meeting. The presidential hot line rang within three minutes. "You tell Kennedy I don't need his Goddamn memorandum. Tell him I already have it from you." Two days later, without any further discussion, Johnson called me to his office. He handed me a draft of the budget message. "This needs a lot of work. I want to go out with the best budget message I've ever submitted. You'd better rewrite it." He gave me the message, and walked to his desk, dismissing me. As I walked down the hall, I noticed that, in the dry language of the budget office, Johnson was recommending renewal of the 10 percent surtax and a solid budget.

The political chances for Carter and Kennedy to agree on a national health plan were never good, given Kennedy's ambition, his tenacious staff, and the media's great interest in reading presidential aspirations into the slightest movement of a potential challenger. Moreover, Carter was going to be as combative as Kennedy. He suspected that Kennedy might be his opponent for the 1980 nomination. Annoyed once by a Kennedy comment that he was "indefinite and imprecise on the critical issues" during the 1976 campaign, Carter remarked privately, "I'm glad I don't have to depend on Kennedy or people like that to put me in office. I don't have to kiss his ass."

Whatever the conflicting ambitions and jealousies of these two men and their staffs, I decided that it was imperative to try to forge an agreement on national health insurance. In Carter's first year, and perhaps for much of the second, both he and the Senator from Massachusetts shared that goal. But some time in 1978, and throughout 1979, the politics of the situation changed. As inflation and energy became overarching issues, Carter's advisors split on the desirability of a national health plan, congressional attitudes hardened, the President slipped in the polls, and the personal ambitions of the two men moved from covert tension to open conflict.

Once Kennedy had signaled his intention to press the Carter administration on national health insurance, the signs of presidential political conflict hung over my office. For Kennedy, commitment to national health insurance had come early, and he was devoted to achieving this goal. For Carter, that commitment came late in life and only reluctantly. He had resisted it until he needed UAW and labor help in the pivotal Pennsylvania, Michigan, and Ohio primaries in 1976. He carried to the President's office an intention to try to keep his campaign promise, but he had no idea how difficult it was going to be. For Carter, as for most elected Democrats, national health insurance was more political rhetoric than potential reality, a part of the national Democratic catechism more to be recited than honored.

I did not anticipate how unprepared HEW was to develop a national health insurance proposal. The subject might have been talked to death for a decade, but it had certainly not been studied to death as Kennedy had suggested. Despite the years of debate in the Congress and HEW, a great deal of sophisticated analysis needed to be done. The introduction of each Kennedy national health bill had been a media event but little more. The Congress had never seriously analyzed any national health plan. House Ways and Means Committee Chairman Wilbur Mills had held some hearings on the Kennedy-Mills national health insurance plan during his hundred-yard dash for the presidency in 1972. But a national health insurance bill had never been reported out of any committee in either house. Only Russell Long's proposal to provide coverage for catastrophic illnesses had come out of his Senate Finance Committee in 1970, and it had not passed the Senate.

At HEW and among its contractor-consultants, the computer programming and detailed policy development were inadequate to measure the costs of various proposals. To help correct that, I recruited Karen Davis, an intense and highly intelligent Brookings Institution Fellow who had taught economics at Rice University and worked on access to health care in rural areas with Labor Secretary Ray Marshall while he was teaching at the University of Texas.

Quite aside from the rivalry between Carter and Kennedy, the politics of health insurance were complicated on Capitol Hill. Russell Long told me early on, "Kennedy gets all the press, but the Finance Committee gets all the jurisdiction." It was Long's Finance Committee, and its health subcommittee chaired by conservative Georgian Herman Talmadge, that had jurisdiction over Medicare and Medicaid. At best, Kennedy's subcommittee would have jurisdiction over only a piece of the legislation or (as in the case of hospital-cost containment) share it with the more powerful Finance Committee. That did not give Kennedy much effective power in the Senate. And, as former Senate Majority Leader Mike Mansfield told me in 1979, "Russell is the ablest and shrewdest legislator in the Senate, if not the smartest. And he may be the smartest."

On the House side, jurisdiction was also shared. The Health Subcommittee of the House Interstate and Foreign Commerce Committee handled Medicaid, while the Ways and Means Health Subcommittee had jurisdiction over Medicare. Any national health bill would go to both. The Senate Finance and House Ways and Means committees would also decide in the first instance how to raise any funds for national health insurance. That power and the general breadth of their jurisdiction—over welfare reform, Social Security, the anti-inflation tax program, and much of the energy legislation—gave them leverage to increase their influence over health insurance legislation.

National health insurance also has a Byzantine history of special interest politics: the labor unions, the American Medical Association, the hospital associations, nurses, insurance companies, laboratories, radiologists, chiropractors, physical therapists, mental health organizations, medical equipment and device manufacturers, and scores of others had been working through the political mazes of national health insurance proposals for years. To help me through these labyrinths, I recruited Dr. James Mongan, the number-two person on the Senate Finance Committee health staff. That I had chosen well was clear not only from his work, but from Russell Long's reaction. During one of our discussions on national health insurance in 1979, Long offered to trade his top committee health staffer "one-for-one" for Mongan.

There were other key staff actors I drafted: Bill Fullerton, a savvy former House staffer who had been through most prior incarnations of national health proposals and who had the confidence of Ways and Means Committee Chairman Al Ullman, and Ruth Hanft, a senior research associate at the Institute of Medicine who had worked at HEW on national health insurance in the late 1960s and early 1970s. With these staffers, Karen Davis, and Dick Warden, I had under the HEW roof many of the key players of the 1970s in the national health insurance sweepstakes.

I would need them all. The difficulties of shaping, much less enacting, a national health proposal were formidable. The cost of any such proposal, the need to reform the health care system and restrain its inflation, the complexities of delivering health services and the stubborn commitments of twenty- and thirty-year partisans were ominous portents for the success of the endeavor. Yet, I hoped there was a chance to find common ground. I felt that most prior plans had not built on the existing structures, particularly the health insurance coverage most Americans received as part of their employment. Perhaps we could mandate some minimum level of health insurance as we had legislated the minimum wage. As for poor people and those with catastrophic illnesses, there seemed to be a sense among many legislators of the need to act. Well, I thought as I reviewed the roster of talent we had recruited for the task, we may not succeed, but there aren't any better people to try.

I APPOINTED Hale Champion chairman of the Advisory Committee on National Health Insurance Issues that I set up in April 1977, with thirty-three representatives of various interests: consumers, physicians, labor unions, other health professionals, state and local governments, business, and the hospital and health insurance industries. The committee conducted hearings across the nation on problems of delivering and financing health care services. I had two objectives in forming the committee: to show some movement to Kennedy, who was pressing for action at a time when Carter's domestic attention was focused on energy and mine on welfare reform, hospital-cost containment, and getting a handle on HEW; and to get a better sense of the points of conflict among the various interests by floating specific plans.

We decided to develop four prototype plans, one of which would be a private sector, competition-oriented plan. Despite years of lobbying efforts by the private sector, no such plan existed, and there was neither the capacity nor the will to develop one by those who had been so consistently effective in killing off national health insurance proposals. I called Alain Enthoven, a thoughtful and careful analyst I had met in the early 1960s when we both worked for Robert McNamara at the Pentagon. Enthoven was in California, teaching about health systems at Stanford's business school. I asked him to prepare a private sector health plan and funded his effort. "Whether I agree with it is not the point," I told him. "The Congress and the people should have a first-class private sector plan to look at."

I held a day-long public hearing on October 4, 1977, to listen to the interested parties. I traveled abroad to look at other national health programs: at Kennedy's suggestion, to Canada in September 1977; to England and Germany in November of that year. Every major industrialized nation except the United States has a national health program. The Canadians have established programs, funded by the central government but operated by the provinces, which reimburse physicians on a fee-for-service basis, but negotiate prospective budgets for privately run hospitals. In the British national health service, the government owns the hospitals and pays the salaries. The West Germans require employers to insure employees, leave hospitals and physicians in the private sector, and reimburse physicians on a fee-for-service basis.

Some surprising and troubling themes emerged. Each nation had bought its existing health care system just as it existed at the time the plan went into effect. Not one was able to achieve reform as part of the plan. In Britain at the end of World War II, the government already had taken over most hospitals and employed virtually all doctors to care for the casualties of war, so nationalization was in many respects the status quo. Canada in the 1940s and Germany in the 1880s had been required to accede to the demands of private physicians, hospitals, and (particularly in Germany) insurance companies to get their national health plans in place. The United States, rich as it was, could not afford to do that; our health care system was far too profligate.

Wherever the reimbursements went, the health care system followed and stayed. Canada, which had provided hospital care for years before it covered outpatient physician services, had as a result so many excess hospital beds that it had to declare a complete moratorium on hospital construction in some sections of the country for years. Even with complete control of hospitals by the government—as in Sweden, which I visited in 1979—it was at least as difficult to close an unnecessary hospital as it was in the United States. By and large these nations provided more equitable access to health care than we, but their national health systems were plagued by the same persistent inflation, waste, and utilization problems as existed in the United States. Britain was trying to put a lid on its health budget, even though many people in need of discretionary health services, such as artificial hip joint operations, had been queued up for so many years that they died before receiving them. David Ennals, Britain's Secretary of State for Social Services, told me at dinner in London one evening, "Whatever you do, decentralize. Get the decisions and the bureaucracy out in the cities and villages, and let them pick up a good share of the cost. Otherwise, the local people don't care about cost, and the system becomes more expensive and inefficient, because we can't close anything, even the most underutilized health clinic, from London." In Israel, I was told that drug prescriptions and use skyrocketed when the government paid the entire bill. When the patient was charged a small amount for each prescription, there was an immediate decline of 10 percent in drug use. Physicians abroad were not happy with any national health plan.

I received a reminder of the attitude of American physicians about national health insurance when I returned from England on Thanksgiving eve in 1977. At about 6:00 P.M., I went directly from Dulles airport to the office of one of Washington's most distinguished orthopedic surgeons, Dr. Robert Neviaser. A few days earlier, *The Wall Street Journal* had quoted me praising portions of the British national health care system. Neviaser had performed the operation on my thumb two weeks earlier and my hand and arm were in a cast. He had agreed to wash the arm and put on a new cast so that I could avoid discomfort over the Thanksgiving weekend. As he finished, he smiled and remarked, "You know, Mr. Secretary, under socialized medicine, a patient wouldn't have a doctor waiting on Thanksgiving eve to change a cast so his arm didn't itch over the weekend."

THE RHETORIC of national health insurance has little patience for the need to gather data, program computers, devise alternative plans, measure their costs, assess their administrative feasibility, and analyze the achievements and mistakes of the Great Society health programs, most notably Medicare and Medicaid. As I viewed the months of work necessary to put forth an intelligent and workable plan, I felt trapped by the nostalgic and ideological politics of those who could not accept the economic and the special interest group realities of the late 1970s and the 1980s, and the incipient presidential politics of Kennedy and Carter.

The press seemed mesmerized by the glamorous vision of the last Kennedy seeking that Holy Grail of liberal Democratic politics, national health insurance. Its coverage had been astonishingly superficial over the past fifteen years. During the introduction of Kennedy-Griffiths, Kennedy-Mills, Kennedy-Corman, Long, Long-Talmadge, Long-Talmadge-Ribicoff, Ullman, Dellums, and other bills, the media provided no serious analysis of the fatal flaws and never exposed the abysmal lack of data to support the relatively low cost claims of the sponsors.

I was appalled at the inadequacy of cost and other data in the health care field, and HEW's almost total dependence on segments of the industry, like hospitals, for financial information on which to base its projections. Little was known about what a national health plan might cost, what changes would occur in the use of health facilities, what needs would arise for health personnel under any of the Democratic proposals over the previous ten years. Financial data and facts about how people use the health care system were a decade behind the information and computer programming in income maintenance areas such as welfare and Social Security.

At my first press conference on January 26, 1977, I said, "I don't see how we can submit a well-thought-through national health insurance proposal to the Congress until next year." When Carter visited HEW employees on February 16, he said he would propose a national health program to be implemented in phases in a "year by year progression toward a comprehensive health care system."

Kennedy didn't like what he was hearing and saw no need for the Advisory Committee or other work I had put in motion. He expressed this view in amicable but certain terms at a meeting Champion and I had with him, Leonard Woodcock, Congressman Jim Corman, and some of Kennedy's staff on May 2, 1977, in the living room of his McLean, Virginia, home. To Kennedy and Woodcock, Carter's campaign speech to the medical students was an endorsement of the Kennedy-Corman bill. "The issue isn't working up a new program. We already have a program we've been working on for years," Kennedy replied in exasperation to my assertion that we needed time to produce an intelligent plan. "What we need is a political negotiation. We're ready to negotiate with the administration now. Is the administration ready to negotiate with us?" he asked.

I argued that there was no point in pressing forward urgently. The Senate Finance and House Ways and Means committees were already backed up with energy legislation; they would soon have welfare reform before them, and we had to do something quickly on Social Security financing. Kennedy did not like this reminder of where the real jurisdiction lay for national health insurance. "I'll hold hearings," he said, "to get things moving and to mobilize the groups and build pressure on the Congress to move." The meeting ended with Kennedy expressing his impatience, and me committing to move as fast as we could, but I was determined to keep the President's options open. All I knew with any certainty about Carter's view at that time was that he did not consider his campaign speech an endorsement of the Kennedy-Corman bill, and that he would be instinctively opposed to substantial expenditures.

Two weeks later, Kennedy and Carter spoke on successive days before the UAW annual convention in Los Angeles. Senator George McGovern had already criticized Carter for his conservative economic and fiscal policies. Such charges from the left of the Democratic Party were to be expected. But Kennedy's attack was sharper than we anticipated. To cheering auto workers, Kennedy charged that "health reform is in danger of becoming the missing promise" of the Carter administration. He urged the President to set a target date in 1977 for submitting national health insurance legislation to the Congress. Kennedy recalled Carter's promise to develop a "universal and mandatory" national health insurance plan that would provide uniform benefits to every citizen. While commending Carter for his energy program and work to balance the budget, Kennedy charged that, "health has been left behind." Alluding to our exchange at his home, Kennedy bellowed, "The American people should not tolerate delay on national health by Congress simply because other reforms are already lined up bumper to bumper."

Carter and I discussed Kennedy's speech. The President would commit on a target date, but he would not accept Kennedy's. I told him we would have difficulty producing a plan on either his or Kennedy's timetable. Nevertheless, the following day, as he was telling the auto workers that "We can't afford to do everything," Carter promised national health insurance "legislative proposals early next year." He repeated his preference for gradually "phasing-in" a health insurance program "during my time in office," but noted that the "achievement of all our goals depends on . . . a strong and growing economy."

This rhetorical skirmish had little impact on the schedule for producing a national health insurance plan. The energy legislation took far more time than Carter had anticipated; welfare reform was a consuming interest for HEW planners and required decisions by him and me; legislation had to be passed to bolster the Social Security system. Like all recent Presidents, Carter began to spend more time on foreign affairs, and the first full budgetary process moved into high gear throughout the fall.

As a result, the President did not give his attention to the substance of national health policy until November 9, 1977, and I was not ready for that discussion much before then. At that first presidential briefing, I described the health care system and the depth of federal involvement in it: When the tax deductions for health benefits, the massive Veterans Administration hospital system, the Defense Department and federal civilian health care programs, and the state and municipal hospital and outpatient systems were added to Medicare, Medicaid, biomedical research, and billions of dollars of other HEW health activities, the gap between rhetoric and reality in the debate on a national health insurance plan became apparent. We have the beginnings of a national health plan in this country. The issue was what steps to take next to improve it.

To this already heavy federal engagement, add the extraordinary amount of money Americans pay to the health industry. Despite this staggering investment, the United States ranks fifteenth among nations in life expectancy for men and seventh for women; our infant mortality rate is higher than in twelve other nations; 40 million Americans have little or no health insurance; almost 150 counties have no medical practitioner—doctor, nurse, or dentist. And millions of children under seventeen have never seen a doctor since they were born.

With these failures in delivery of services to some, with unnecessary services for others, and with the inflation in health care costs, there is a clear need for a national plan; we could not afford the health care system as it stood. This was the gist of my opening comments at the first briefing I gave the President. I had pressed for the meeting because I was concerned that Kennedy's private impatience would again erupt into public charges, but even more importantly, because Office of Management and Budget Director James McIntyre, Council of Economic Advisors Chairman Charles Schultze, and Treasury Secretary Mike Blumenthal were moving to influence Carter to postpone, or perhaps even drop, any national health program because of budgetary problems. They were searching for something less than the comprehensive proposal necessary to fulfill Carter's commitments and statements.

Carter first asked about the possibility of a no-cost national health insurance program financed out of current expenditures by decreasing inflation and waste. "We just can't afford to keep adding more and more to the already inefficient system."

I responded, to Carter's obvious dismay, that costs might be substantially offset by reforms, but they were still likely to exceed the savings that we would realize by reducing fraud, abuse, and waste.

"We must change the system," Carter said, "or national health insurance will not be worth pursuing." I agreed. My basic point was that we could not afford to purchase the existing system.

Carter said he wanted to have a role for the private insurance companies in any national health plan. White House domestic policy advisor Stu Eizenstat pointed out that labor interpreted Carter's April 1976 campaign speech to be an indirect endorsement of the Kennedy-Corman-labor bill, which had no role for private insurers. "Any compromise with the private insurance companies will anger labor and create a major political problem," he added.

Carter responded curtly, "Labor is wrong. I was the only Democratic candidate who did not endorse the Kennedy bill during the campaign."

Carter then spoke more generally. "Our polls consistently show public support for an improved health program, and that people would be willing to pay more taxes for health services and better health care." He said that many families seemed concerned about costs for a catastrophic illness. Then, displaying his frustration at dealing with Washington, the President sighed. "This may all change as you begin to directly engage the special interests, such as the doctors, hospitals, and insurers." He cited his losing fight to pass an energy bill in 1977. He added that doctors and hospitals, though perhaps good individually, were "bad when organized"; under the present system no one is held accountable for expenditures and the insured individuals do not care, since they "don't directly feel the fast-rising costs."

The President paused, and then continued, with real concern in his voice. He had been getting a great deal of advice about the dangers of involving himself in too many issues at once. He had to decide when to move here. Perhaps he could begin to deal with health insurance in a fireside chat, where he could simply describe the problems to the people without making specific proposals, or raising expectations, so that Americans would understand the issues better.

Hamilton Jordan and Stu Eizenstat reminded him that a number of other subjects were already lined up for the fireside chats: Panama, the economy, and welfare. The spring of 1978 would be the earliest he could get back to health insurance and get more involved. I argued that there would be pressure to do something sooner. Jordan suggested that the education and consultation process could buy Carter a year's time and give the appearance of doing something. The President pointed out that major figures on the Hill with long-standing commitments to their own approaches needed to be consulted. Carter agreed implicitly with Jordan, saying "If the UAW knows the administration is working on welfare, knows there is a fireside chat on health insurance scheduled in the spring, and knows that there will be a bill in 1979, they will be satisfied."

I welcomed time to prepare a thoughtful plan, but I doubted the UAW or Kennedy, with each prodding the other, would sit still for a year. As we left the meeting, I suggested to Eizenstat that we give some thought to announcing a set of broad principles soon, to have something in line with the early 1978 target in Carter's UAW speech, and to promising a detailed plan several months later. In my own mind, I realized we would have to devise a plan that achieved many of our objectives in the private sector, adding to federal budget expenditures only where we could not effectively mandate private coverage.

ON DECEMBER 2, I met for almost two hours with Senator Kennedy to discuss a variety of health issues that would be coming up in the Congress during the next year. Kennedy was enthusiastic about a major overhaul of the drug law that we were proposing, and the meeting went well as we reviewed a list of health laws that had to be reauthorized. Kennedy then turned to national health insurance. He was unhappy about the delays in the administration's proposals for national health insurance. "We need a legislative proposal and some hard negotiations with labor and the other groups, early in 1978."

"One possibility is for the President to send up general principles in 1978 to be followed by legislation in 1979," I suggested.

"No," Kennedy said, "that's unnecessary and unacceptable. The President put out the principles in his campaign speech."

I told Kennedy I would pass his view on to the President and Kennedy said he would also talk directly to Carter. The meeting ended amicably. We were both professional about our disagreements, we were friends, and we had some sense of humor. But there was trouble and political conflict ahead. Sentiment was increasing for a less than comprehensive plan among Carter's economic advisors and some of Eizenstat's staff. I became increasingly concerned about a collision between Carter and Kennedy, with Kennedy taking the labor groups with him. They thought Carter was foot-dragging. That was the political prize, I thought, labor support.

I remembered that in 1966, when Congress was considering legislation to end the machinists' strike against the airlines, neither Robert nor Edward Kennedy, both on the Senate Labor Committee, voted for the bill. "No Kennedy will ever vote against labor," Lyndon Johnson had said. "Any liberal Democrat with national ambitions has got to have a perfect record on hard-core labor issues. Jack Kennedy won his first congressional race in 1946. He knows how many men got to Congress that year just because their opponents voted against the draft right before World War II. The Kennedys know how important one vote can be. They won't vote against labor."

Carter had his eye on the same prize Kennedy did. During a November press conference, he gingerly modified the commitment in his UAW speech to submit national health insurance legislation "early next year." He said we were "working on this now with increasing commitment, and I think by early next year the principles of the national health program will be outlined to the American people." Kennedy, however, wanted legislation, not simply principles that would rehash Carter's campaign speech. On December 6, 1977, in response to insistent questioning by Cassie Mackin of ABC-TV, I said, "Whether the legislation . . . will go to Congress next year, which will be late in the year, or early in 1979, I don't know and I don't think anyone can know until we see what the reaction is to the principles." I sensed Carter's reluctance to move, and I knew that events would only make him more reluctant as other problems consumed his attention. Kennedy immediately asked the White House for a public clarification. He demanded to know whether a decision had been made to delay the legislation. Eizenstat publicly replied, "Califano is not speaking for us."

It was a one-day flap, lost in the HEW budget issues which were of overriding concern to me in December, but I pressed the President for another meeting to get clear guidance on what he wanted to do. My sense of Carter's reluctance to move was reinforced by his failure to schedule such a meeting for more than two months and his statement in February 1978 that "next year would be the time for the Congress to take action on [national health] legislation." The meeting finally took place on March 2, 1978. In addition to the President and me, Blumenthal, Eizenstat, and Jordan were there. The issue was whether to send a national health insurance bill forward in 1978 or 1979. Jordan and I disagreed sharply.

Carter sat behind his elaborately carved dark oak desk, the one John Kennedy had used. We were in a semicircle opposite, about ten feet distant. Carter turned to me.

"There is little stomach on the Hill for any national health legislation this year, except for Kennedy," I began. "The congressmen I talk to are worried about the Social Security tax increase they voted last December. They won't get involved in more taxes to finance national health insurance, that's too much of a political liability for them in an election year. And that could kill your chances of passing any national health bill." I urged him to stay publicly and clearly committed to a universal, mandatory, comprehensive plan, but not to send the actual legislation forward until 1979.

Blumenthal agreed. "Sending NHI forward this year will affect the tax bill most adversely."

The President snapped, "The only bill Mike Blumenthal wants to have before the Congress is *his* bill.'' It was my first indication that Carter shared the dislike of Blumenthal that some of his staff expressed anonymously to the press.

The Treasury Secretary replied crisply, ''That is not so, Mr. President. I have believed in national health insurance for twenty years.''

Eizenstat said that he shared my concerns.

Jordan disagreed. ''The President has a political commitment to the UAW, and the UAW is the best political organization in the country and the most powerful. At a time when our public opinion polls are down, we've got to stay close to powerful organizations like this.'' As I looked at Carter, I saw that Jordan was reaching him. Jordan continued, ''The President's commitment was renewed just a few weeks ago in a meeting between the President and UAW president Doug Fraser.'' Then Jordan turned to me. ''The UAW wants to go to every congressman in the country and offer to help them in their campaigns if they will support NHI. That's the way to get the bill passed.''

Before I could respond, Carter said, ''My word is at stake. I have made a commitment. It would be a lie not to send the legislation forward this year.''

I argued, with Blumenthal's support, that economic and political circumstances had changed. But the President would not change his position. As a fallback position, I suggested that we announce principles in late April 1978, to be followed by a tentative program, then by legislation. ''That's consistent with my commitments,'' Carter said.

''Mr. President, you should know this is not consistent with what Kennedy thinks your commitments are. He expects a piece of legislation, not principles,'' I said, trying to alert him to Kennedy's likely reaction. Eizenstat nodded agreement with my assessment.

''Kennedy is wrong,'' Carter said, his eyes icy blue. He instructed Eizenstat to tell Kennedy of the schedule he had outlined.

Outside the President's office, Eizenstat turned to me: ''Kennedy may be right about what Carter committed to.'' He asked me to join him later that day to meet with Kennedy, Steve Schlossberg of the UAW, and Tom Donohue of the AFL-CIO. When we met, Eizenstat and I listened as Kennedy set forth a broad outline of their plan and asked for a meeting with the President. Eizenstat never made quite clear the schedule the President had just approved. We ended by scheduling a meeting with the President for April 6.

On April 3, 1978, I circulated a memorandum to other members of the Cabinet to solicit their views on this subject. In line with my discussions with the President, the memo made one central point: ''We need a national health program, not just national health insurance.'' After describing the health care system and the government's involvement in that system, I set forth four prototype plans for comment: a private sector plan based on market forces and competition, developed by Enthoven; a targeted plan providing federal coverage for all catastrophic illnesses and comprehensive care for poor people; a mandatory employer coverage plan requiring employers to furnish private insurance for their employees and creating a public corporation to provide insurance protection for all who could not get private insurance (this was similar to the plan the administration would eventually propose); and a publicly guaranteed plan with strong federal regulatory controls, particularly over financing policy. With some important exceptions, the last plan was modeled on Kennedy's then current proposal. Additional federal expenditures under it would be much the same as under the mandatory employer coverage plan —about $25 billion—with the same benefit package and patient cost sharing. But if, as was the case with Kennedy's plan, "cost sharing were eliminated, benefits expanded to a more comprehensive . . . package, and subsidies provided to employees [otherwise] required to pay 100 percent of the premium, the resultant costs in federal expenditures could well exceed $80 billion."

On April 6, when Carter met with Kennedy, George Meany, Doug Fraser, and Lane Kirkland, it was clear that Kennedy was trying to take labor away from him. We sat around the Cabinet table, I immediately to Carter's left, Meany and Kirkland at Carter's right, Kennedy across from us, and the others scattered around the table. The President reaffirmed his commitment to national health insurance. "I believe it will work and I believe the American people want it."

Kennedy came on forcefully. "These leaders of the labor movement and I and the other organizations in our group have been working in recent months to develop a proposal that meets our concerns about the budget and that provides a role for private insurance, which you want." Kennedy described the work as "agonizing. It involves a great deal of compromise with the previous positions of these groups." Then, fixing his eyes firmly on the President, he said, "But, Mr. President, there can be no compromise on the principles of universality, comprehensive benefits, and tough controls." It's as though he's making a speech, I thought to myself, and of course he was, for the benefit of the labor groups.

Kennedy said that there was not much time left if hearings were to be held in 1978. He wanted the President's reaction to their proposal, a commitment on timing, and agreement to establish a working group with the unions and his staff.

Fraser echoed Kennedy. "We want these guys campaigning to have to declare on this issue." Meany supported Kennedy and Fraser.

Kennedy then turned his eyes on me, though speaking to the President. Raising his voice, he attacked the "unfairness" of the HEW memo I had distributed a few days before, for putting an $80 billion price tag on his plan. It was at least that much, I thought.

When the President responded, he ignored Kennedy's complaints about my memorandum. "The administration will continue to move on NHI as a high priority. Congress does not appear nearly as ready to move in this area as the administration. The process is underway; Secretary Califano is the lead Cabinet member and chief spokesman for the administration."

Carter said that I was to report to him in early May and that he would talk with Kennedy then. He then chided labor for "very little support" on his hospital-cost-containment bill. Kirkland said they did support the legislation. Carter turned to Kirkland in skeptical disbelief. Kirkland admitted that labor was opposed to the part of the bill limiting hospital wages.

Fraser and Kirkland both said it would be a mistake to view hospital-cost containment as either a test or prerequisite for NHI. The President replied that while hospital-cost containment was very important to him, his NHI timetable was "not conditioned" upon it.

Kennedy then spoke in a tone so insistent it was almost disdainful of the President. Certainly no one had ever talked to Lyndon Johnson that way. "How will the process proceed?" he demanded to know. "A working group—the administration, organized labor, and my staff—should be set up to negotiate a bill."

Carter considered such negotiations "premature" until his own presidential review process was completed.

Kennedy pressed. "Our efforts have not been fairly treated so far." I could feel the intensity of his anger directed at me and my memorandum. "It is a mistake to exclude us from your process. We should be a part of it if you want us to have confidence in it."

I almost wondered aloud: Who the hell is President here? I hoped Carter would come on strong. But he didn't. He spoke softly, too softly, I thought, as he reiterated his intention to complete his internal review before going outside the administration.

Stu Eizenstat and Jordan's aide, Landon Butler, also sensed the meeting was getting out of hand. Butler slipped the President a note: "At this point, perhaps Joe could work out this problem, and you could leave to resume your schedule," on which Eizenstat scribbled, "Just add 'We'll assure you [Kennedy] that you'll be fully involved.' "

Eizenstat is too conciliatory, I thought, as I saw the note. Kennedy wants to take over the presidential decision-making process.

The President had a better sense of the situation. A touch of firmness gave texture to his soft voice for the first time during the meeting: "Your views will be fully considered—favorably, if possible. I did not support the Kennedy-Corman bill during the campaign; I endorsed a set of principles instead. I understand how the process does not satisfy you. But it is the best I can do at the moment, given the mood of the Congress and the economy." Then, in response to Kennedy's implied lack of confidence in HEW's analysis, Carter stated, "I will make the final decision."

Kennedy retreated slightly. He said that any comments on my memo would be "on a distorted version of our proposal." The President asked Kennedy to submit his critique and "Califano will circulate it." I seconded the request, and stressed the need for better information from Kennedy and organized labor. I was about to continue, when the President signaled the close of the meeting. "I do not want an administration bill to be rejected out of hand by the Congress—I want to pass a bill. To do this, the administration must be able to defend its proposal as workable and affordable."

Well, at least he closed on the right note, I thought, but from here on out, it will be Kennedy and labor versus Carter.

The White House press corps was waiting in the driveway in front of the West Wing lobby. They surrounded Kennedy, who held forth while George Meany and I stood by, reminiscing about Lyndon Johnson. Kennedy spoke in terms of general agreement in principle and of final passage of national health insurance "no later than 1980." Kennedy hoped NHI would be an issue in the 1978 congressional campaign. He was friendly, almost jovial, when he said good-bye to me as I moved before the microphone and cameras. Much more cautiously, I said that the meeting demonstrated that "we share the same objectives."

Carter soon asked me to hold candid and private discussions with some key congressional leaders on his submitting a national health plan to the Hill. Except for California Democratic Congressman James Corman, they were opposed.

House Ways and Means Committee Chairman Al Ullman expressed disbelief that Carter was even sending me to see him on the subject. "If Carter sends an NHI bill up here, it will destroy his presidency," Ullman blurted out, "because it seems so counter to the fight on inflation."

"Suppose it does not start to become effective until 1983?" I asked.

"Even with a 1983 effective date," he responded. His voice rose in level and force. "You tell the President that I will have to publicly call the act of submitting a proposal to the Congress this year a major disaster." Then he leaned over to me. Gesturing with his right hand, he said in exasperation, "The President is in the world of enchantment; I must live in the real world. The President doesn't like me because I am in the real world."

Other key leaders on Capitol Hill echoed Ullman. Illinois Democratic Congressman Dan Rostenkowski, Chairman of the Ways and Means Health Subcommittee, asked, "Where are we going to get the dollars?" He said the congressional reaction to sending a bill up before the November 1978 election would be so adverse, "The act of sending it will be seen as another defeat for the President." Russell Long would "strenuously oppose any Kennedy-type program," and urged delay to put a compromise together. Even with a delayed effective date, Senator Ribicoff said, sending a bill up would "confuse the public and blur the President's image on inflation." Talmadge, who chaired the Senate Finance Health Subcommittee, told me it would be "foolhardy" to extend health insurance to more people until we managed better what we now had. Each senator or congressman, including Corman, made the point that the only person the President seemed to be talking to was Kennedy, and Kennedy was out of touch with the Congress.

But Kennedy continued to push. During a follow-up meeting, I told him of the general congressional reaction I was getting. Kennedy insisted that Carter had made a commitment to submit a program that year. He said he wanted another chance to convince the President to support his program. But he added, "If you're not sending up a broad and comprehensive health insurance program, then it might be better for the administration to do nothing. I've been working on this for ten years and I want to get a comprehensive bill." Kennedy ended the meeting with a pointed reminder of his power with the media and the political groups. "We're organizing a big NHI rally at Madison Square Garden in August and I'm going to speak out for a comprehensive bill."

I was so concerned about the doggedness of the congressional resistance and Kennedy's unbending and threatening posture that I asked for a private meeting with the President. On May 18, Eizenstat and I met alone with Carter. We sat in the Oval Office, the President in his salmon-silk upholstered high-backed chair, I on the end of the soft striped sofa closest to him and facing the fireplace. "I wanted to bring you into the world of reality in politics and in the Congress about national health insurance," I began.

The President grinned. "I think there is no place for the world of reality on this subject. We are all in the world of unreality on national health insurance."

I reported briefly about the difficulty of getting other executive departments to focus on our staff papers and the strong opposition on the

Hill to sending a bill up this year. "Kennedy is playing very hard ball on this, Mr. President." I passed on Kennedy's comment about the Madison Square Garden rally as an example of his "raising the stakes."

The President listened, thought for a moment, and with his hands clasped and resting on his lap, said, "You're much more concerned about Kennedy than I am. We will submit proposals this year." He promised to give the relevant Cabinet officers and key advisors "strict orders" to work with me to get the proposals to the Congress in 1978.

The following day, the President and I met in the Cabinet Room with Russell Long, Herman Talmadge, and Abe Ribicoff. Led by Long, the three senators presented their case for a health plan that made Medicaid a program funded and operated by the federal government, with uniform standards (rather than the fifty-three different federal-state programs it is) and insurance coverage of all Americans for catastrophic illnesses. Their plan made no serious attempt to reform the health care system. It could easily have required the patient to absorb $15,000 in health care bills before the illness qualified as catastrophic, thus triggering government payment for costs above that amount. Carter referred to the principles he set forth during the campaign. "That's the UAW plan," Long responded. "The UAW is engaged in a confidence game. They want coverage from Uncle Sam so they can take the four percent now spent by the auto companies on health care and turn it into higher wages."

While the President and I were meeting with congressional leaders, Kennedy was working to gain support for a new bill on Capitol Hill. He met on the evening of May 23 with Jim Corman, cosponsor of the Health Security Bill. Corman was appalled at how unworkable the revamped Kennedy bill was and at the complex regulatory scheme Kennedy proposed for private insurers. Corman had always opposed turning national health insurance over to the private insurers, as he thought Kennedy's new plan would do. On the following morning, Corman told HEW legislative assistant secretary Dick Warden that he hoped Carter would not buy the Kennedy bill, because it was a "stupid thing and I hope the President will not float it." Both on the merits and the politics of the issue, this was a major break for Carter. Corman was as experienced a legislator on national health insurance as the House had, and his credentials with the labor unions and other liberal groups were impeccable.

But problems were emerging within the administration. The four plans had been narrowed to two. The first was the targeted approach, essentially the Long catastrophic plan with some additional coverage for poor people. The second was the comprehensive plan that would require employers to provide a minimum level of coverage for each employee (thus taking advantage of the existing employment relationship to cover

156 million workers and dependents); give catastrophic coverage to all those not protected through the employer-employee relationship; federalize Medicaid into a single program, to improve benefits for the 15 million people already covered and extend those benefits to an additional 16 million poor Americans presently ineligible; and legislate several reimbursement reforms and cost controls essential to stemming the inflation and waste in the health care system.

McIntyre, Blumenthal, and Schultze favored the targeted approach. I strongly favored the comprehensive approach, as did Eizenstat, who had gained an excellent grasp of the substance and politics of national health insurance. But the President was under great pressure from his economic advisors and I was aware of the inhospitable mood of the Congress. I thought Carter should delay submission of any proposal until after the November election and set the effective dates of various phases far enough in the future to accommodate the economic and budgetary situation. To avoid a serious split with the Democratic left and to help get a better grip on health care costs and reform of the health care system, I preferred the comprehensive approach, especially with a major role for the private sector. In view of my ongoing conversations with Kennedy and labor, I wanted a clear decision to protect my own credibility before negotiating with them. On May 30, just before a key meeting set for June 1, I sent Carter a confidential memo. I noted that we could not "have continuing, good faith negotiations with Senator Kennedy and organized labor if there is a lingering possibility of a targeted approach." I was aware of the presidential prerogative to cut off limbs, and I was not going to be standing on this one when it fell.

The June 1 meeting lasted more than two hours. Carter opened by noting that he found "a paradox, an anomaly" in his situation. "I have already made a number of commitments—during my campaign and subsequently to the UAW and to Senator Kennedy. At the same time, there appears to be no significant additional money for health care available in the budget in the next few years and I will not do anything to undermine my current effort to control inflation."

As he spoke, it struck me forcibly how Carter's face was graying and aging. What a toll this job takes on a human being, I thought. And meetings like this told why. He had a tough decision to make. "I am inclined to do what I've done in the past, to tell the American people the truth and lay out the problem." He talked about health system problems and concluded, "I don't believe a comprehensive program can possibly be passed this year. It is unlikely even next year. But there are some important advantages to be gained by discussing the problem and the issue openly."

There was a brief moment of quiet around the Cabinet table and among the staff against the walls. Then OMB Director McIntyre and his aides argued the budget case against a broad national health plan, suggesting instead possible health initiatives "outside NHI" extending over the next three to five years, and a targeted approach.

As I was about to begin my briefing, Carter said: "I want you to go beyond just health insurance, and to develop a national health plan." He expressed skepticism about any plan that shifted the cost of health insurance from employers to the government. "I have no intention of shifting to the government payments currently made by employers and leaving employers free to increase wages of employees." Russell Long had made his point.

Carter said he would make the "hard choices" clear in announcing his principles, he would not "pussyfoot around." The thing to do was "face these options frankly and honestly and lay them out for the Congress and the people"—on whom Carter would rely to make "the right decision once fully informed." Listening to his words, I sensed this was a decision he truly preferred not to make.

I presented the two alternatives, and the advantages and disadvantages of each. Blumenthal argued for a targeted plan focused on cost control. Schultze strongly supported him. As I was about to speak, the President said, "A comprehensive plan could eliminate some of the political opposition to cost control." I was delighted I had not spoken. Those words were much better from the President than me.

I ended by suggesting we get the principles on a national health plan out as soon as possible, with a tentative plan to follow within a couple of months and legislation after that, perhaps in 1979. Everyone agreed to that timetable.

McIntyre and Schultze argued that without new taxes there would not be sufficient funds for any national health plan. Schultze suggested phasing benefits and coverage in tandem with effective cost controls. The President liked the idea. Eizenstat said that Kennedy and the unions were negative on such an approach, but perhaps they could be convinced. I suggested that while Schultze's idea was good, it would be extremely difficult to work out. The President had the last, frugal word: "Such phasing, though, might more than pay for national health insurance if it succeeded in realizing significant savings."

Carter then launched into the health care system. "It's horrible," he said, "and very soon will also be unsupportable." He asked whether increased national health insurance would result in better health.

"For poor people, migrant workers and the like, yes," Champion responded.

The President replied as though he were thinking aloud. "Does spending six billion dollars under the comprehensive plan to cover the thirty million people that the targeted plan does not reach represent the best way to spend that amount of money? I want to present the problem to the American people, since they currently do not understand the dilemma in terms of inflation versus health care.''

McIntyre took advantage of Carter's frustration: ''I question the politics of the timing of the announcement and the submission of the legislation so soon. Suppose Tip O'Neill throws down the gauntlet and says he doesn't want a plan this year. None of his Democratic House members want this issue in their campaigns.''

Robert Strauss, then Carter's inflation fighter, came into the Cabinet Room at that point. The President summed up the issues and asked his view. Strauss said, ''Mr. President, the most difficult question you face is the credibility of your inflation program. I have not been to a single meeting in which I don't get asked the question, 'How can you be talking about national health insurance and still be serious about inflation?' I usually give a very long and involved answer—one I don't understand myself—and try to leave the room quickly.''

Carter smiled and then said there was at least a partial answer: a good national health program could stem excessive U.S. spending on health care and spiraling hospital rates—''the prospects under the present system are horrendous if we do nothing''—and the current exclusion of payment for preventive services is ''simply adding expense'' to the current system. Turning to me, the President suggested I develop a program phased in as we could afford it in terms of inflation, cost control, and administrative feasibility, and emphasizing cost containment and prevention. ''It is ridiculous to think about endorsing a bill like Kennedy's. I am not going to destroy my credibility on inflation and budgetary matters. I intend to be honest and responsible with the American people.'' Carter did ''not simply view this as a matter of accommodating particular political pressure groups.'' It was more ''a question of what we get for different expenditures.'' He urged me to get on with drafting the principles and observed as he rose to leave the Cabinet Room, ''We are still in a quandary as to how to proceed.''

For the first time, I felt that Carter might abandon his commitment to a comprehensive plan, and with it the chance to achieve significant reform of the health system. The larger responsibilities of the presidency—to fight inflation particularly, but also as party leader to Democratic House members running for re-election in a conservative year—were weighing heavily on him. Unlike Kennedy, the President had to be an advocate of more than a single cause, however worthy.

We were clearly in a struggle for Carter's mind. I decided to try to enlist Jordan's support. I set up a breakfast meeting with him on June 22, 1978. On that morning the *Washington Post* reported the split within the administration on the front page. There was a "solid phalanx of economic advisors, including McIntryre, Schultze, Blumenthal, and Strauss" for a targeted plan, lined up against Califano and Eizenstat for a comprehensive one. McIntyre was quoted as warning that the administration "had to heed the lesson of Proposition 13." Reading the story as I traveled across town to meet with Jordan, I wondered how he would view the politics of national health insurance now.

Over scrambled eggs and bacon at Jordan's desk, Champion and I urged Jordan and Butler to weigh in for a comprehensive plan to avoid an open split with the UAW and big labor. I told Jordan that we would drive labor firmly into Kennedy's corner if the President proposed a targeted plan. As I started to explain the difference between the two plans, Jordan interrupted: "I'm not interested in the substance. I'm interested in the politics for the President."

"That's exactly why we're here," I responded. We discussed the Kennedy-Labor-Proposition 13 problems, but it was an uneasy exchange. Jordan seemed unsure whether I was arguing for a comprehensive plan because I thought the politics were good for Carter, or because I was close to Ted Kennedy. Nevertheless, I sensed Jordan was more interested in the UAW's political organization than in responding to Proposition 13. He kept his own counsel as Champion and I left.

On June 26, Carter invited Kennedy to the Oval Office at five in the afternoon. At a press conference earlier that day Carter had expressed his preference for "a comprehensive health proposal," but one that would take into account "the high inflation rate and the very tight budget constraints," and that would be phased in over a number of years. Carter wanted to have a candid political discussion with Kennedy about national health insurance, taxpayer unrest, and his fear of hurting the Democratic candidates, or the possibility that they might repudiate comprehensive national health insurance, unless he put off announcement of his plan until after the fall elections.

Despite the President's request that he come alone, Kennedy brought along his health aide Larry Horowitz. When Carter walked into the Oval Office and saw Horowitz, he turned to Kennedy and said he would prefer to see him alone. Eizenstat, Horowitz, and I left. After that meeting, during which the President and Kennedy walked around the White House grounds for the better part of an hour, Carter still held out some hope for agreement. He called me the next morning to say he wanted to review the principles of his national health plan with Kennedy before making them public.

In early July, as reports of our work on national health plan principles spread on Capitol Hill, Ullman and Rostenkowski told me they did not even want principles for the development of a national health plan released; they "absolutely" did not want the President to unfold tentative plans or options until after the election. Ullman was threateningly blunt: "You tell the President that I will publicly express the view that sending a national health plan to Congress at this time is completely irresponsible."

Nevertheless, at Carter's direction I worked during the last two weeks of July to reach agreement with Kennedy on the principles. On July 27, I met with Carter, Mondale, Eizenstat, Schultze, and McIntyre to report agreement on all but two issues: Kennedy wanted a specific commitment that Carter would send up a single bill. Moreover, while Kennedy accepted the principle of phasing, he wanted assurance that such phasing would go into effect regardless of economic or budgetary conditions. In response to my argument that such a massive undertaking required recognition of conditions of high unemployment or severe inflation, Kennedy replied, "Then let the Congress change the law. The presumption should be that the plan goes into effect. Put the burden on Congress to change the law."

I told Carter that I thought Kennedy's position on the single bill was based not only on his desire for a comprehensive program, but on his fear that, if the program were sent up in separate bills, Russell Long's Finance Committee would have far more jurisdiction than Kennedy's Health Subcommittee.

"Whatever his reasons," Carter said, "I can't make a commitment that explicit at this time."

"Kennedy's staffer Horowitz threatens that the Senator will split with the administration if you don't agree to these items," I said.

"I'm not afraid of a split with Kennedy on this issue, if it comes to that. But I'd rather have agreement," Carter responded slowly and thoughtfully. He told us to keep working for an agreement. Carter postponed my scheduled announcement of the principles for twenty-four hours and said he would ask Kennedy to meet him the next day. In separate phone conversations that evening, the President and Eizenstat told me that Kennedy had taken a "very tough line" during the President's call to set up the next day's meeting. Carter said Kennedy indicated he would publicly condemn an unsatisfactory plan.

The meeting at 9:30 A.M. on July 28 was tense. For the future record, Kennedy brought his aide Horowitz; Carter had Mondale, myself, Eizenstat, and his health aide, Joe Onek. After shaking hands with Kennedy, Carter sat down at the end of the Cabinet table facing the fireplace and the portrait of Harry Truman above it. The smile on his face was studied. He rested his arms on the table, hands joined, fingers intertwined. Once fully composed, he began: "We both want a comprehensive health plan of which we can be proud. We have a different view over tactics." He briefly reviewed the mood of the Congress, particularly the House's and Ullman's, and he also reminded us that the same committees that would consider any national health plan were backed up with welfare reform, tax legislation, the energy program, and hospital-cost containment. "Under these circumstances, is it advisable to put forth a proposal before or after the election?" he asked rhetorically.

Carter stressed his desire to get a bill passed and asked pointedly, "Where is primary jurisdiction on the health proposal? Does Kennedy have it? Does Long have it?" He said he would "get the basic principles out no later than tomorrow," but stressed that those principles "must enhance the image of fiscal responsibility" and "the phasing will be laboriously worked out to emphasize this." Kennedy shifted in his chair as though he were about to respond. But Carter continued, in a conciliatory tone, to deal with Kennedy's other point: "One bill is my preference. But I cannot promise it now. A split between us would doom prospects for health insurance." Then, fingers tightly clasped, cold blue eyes fixed directly on Kennedy, he added, "I don't fear criticism. I take crap every day, criticism every day. I can take your press conference. I would like to leave office," the President concluded, his hands relaxing, "with a comprehensive, universal health plan in place."

Carter paused. He was still looking directly at Kennedy, who initially picked up on the President's conciliatory remarks. "We want to work with the administration," Kennedy said. "You will be the first President to advocate principles of universality and comprehensiveness. I have a similar view of the mood of the Congress. Unless we develop the right kind of constituency, I don't think we'll get legislation passed probably even during our lifetimes."

Then Kennedy's tone became more firm, offering a carrot of cooperation but unyielding in setting conditions. "We want to be able to say: for the first time we have a President who stands for this." Then the condition. "But we must have a real sense that this is going to be achieved within a period of time. That's why we need one bill. I understand the need to phase, but we must understand no halting, no budgetary or unemployment delays—a firm decision on your part." His voice became noticeably harsher: "If it is not one bill, then your words have very little meaning—especially when phasing is based on forces we have very little control over. That is the heart of the issue. That is why the seriousness of the effort is questioned by the groups. . . ." Then, interrupting himself as though he thought he might have been a little too sharp, Kennedy said: "I'm willing to cooperate because I believe you, Joe, Fritz, and Stu are committed to it. If we can deal with a single bill, with one bill, with no midcourse stopping, we can have a working group and move forward." The sharp edge returned quickly to his tone. "But when the groups see two bills, more than one bill, then they're enormously concerned and question the seriousness of the effort."

Carter tried to placate Kennedy. "One bill gives us a chance to identify the issue. You can't mount a public relations campaign for several bills simultaneously. That is my preference. To make it clear: The presidential preference is for one bill. But factors might arise that will make one bill ill-advised. My hope and expectation is one bill, but I don't want to—"

Kennedy interrupted. "Factors in midcourse correction? We can't let the hospitals bring national insurance to a halt."

"The President would have to have the flexibility to delay—some flexibility on budget and economic conditions," Carter continued, showing just a hint of annoyance at Kennedy's interruptions.

Eizenstat suggested that "the political pressures are going to be to go forward to the next phase."

Horowitz responded, "The greatest fear of these groups is uncertainty. They want certainty and entitlement. If you want flexibility, let the President propose delay to the Congress. Let's make it tougher to change, not easier. National health can't compete with defense for budget dollars."

Carter commented, "Whenever social programs have started, they've been added on to." To my surprise, the President addressed Horowitz rather than Kennedy. "I must keep the trust of enough members of the Congress to keep the idea alive. If I commit myself no matter what else happens, this trust goes. I must have some flexibility to maintain fiscal responsibility."

Horowitz reiterated that the President should seek an amendment to the law, and shrugged.

"We just have differences of opinion. If I did it your way, it would never get off the ground," Carter said, looking at Kennedy with frustration tinged with the despair of a man who had tried hard but could not get through. "This is a serious disagreement."

Kennedy decided to cut off the meeting. "I don't think you'll get your proposal through. You're not going to be able to build the necessary constituency."

Carter concluded by saying, "We'll go with our statement of principles tomorrow. Joe can express my preference for, but not a commitment to, a single bill. If there are unforeseen circumstances, difficulties in administration, excessive costs, then secondary phases must be delayed. There must be flexibility.''

Kennedy rose with the President; they shook hands. Then Kennedy turned to me; ''See you in church,'' he said, referring to Father James English's Family Mass at Holy Trinity Church, which we both attended. Kennedy left, with Horowitz whispering in his ear as he followed him down the hall past the Oval Office toward the elevator.

I had been back in my office no more than an hour when Kennedy called. ''I'm besieged by press inquiries about what happened this morning,'' he said. ''I think I have to respond. Is there any way you can go with your press conference this afternoon? I don't want to be the one to announce your principles.''

Not much, I thought. ''The charts simply will not be ready. Can't you wait until tomorrow?'' I asked.

''I don't think so, Joe. There's just too much furor over this,'' Kennedy responded.

''Can't you wait just one day?'' I asked.

Kennedy was all wound up. ''I know you've got problems. You made a good try, but we can't go with that. It's not a strong kind of commitment. It should all be in one bill—prevention, benefits, bringing groups into the system, cost controls, regulation, a detailed proposal. We are getting a go-slow message on the whole thing. Those guys don't want a bill up here. We're going to continue to work.''

''The politics are terrible for national health right now,'' I interjected. ''A set of principles emphasizing careful phasing at least has a chance.''

''Our political judgment is that after the election the politics will be even worse,'' Kennedy countered. ''We're willing to fight for one bill. We'll develop a constituency, say 'this is what the President stands for,' but we will not go out and sell a preference. . . . There's a commitment to the American people. I think you're running out on it. This isn't going to meet it.''

I tried one more time. ''Say what you feel you have to, but can't you wait until we announce the principles?''

''It's too late,'' Kennedy said. We understood each other.

I reported the conversation to Eizenstat as soon as Kennedy hung up. ''That bastard,'' he said.

Dick Warden called a few minutes later. ''The word on the Hill is that Kennedy's going to hold a press conference this afternoon with Meany and Lane Kirkland.''

''Carter's been trumped,'' I said. I had to return to the White House to meet with the President to put the final touches on his memo to me setting forth the principles. I told Eileen Shanahan to have Kennedy's conference covered so I could respond immediately. "Well, one thing is certain," she replied. "You're going to have a helluva crowd to hear you announce those dreary principles tomorrow."

Flanked by George Meany, Lane Kirkland, other labor leaders, and representatives of senior citizen and church groups—the Committee for National Health Insurance that had been bankrolled by the UAW and AFL-CIO to push for national health insurance—Kennedy let it fly. He assailed Carter for a "failure of leadership on this issue," and for proposing an inadequate "piecemeal" start on a national health insurance plan. "I regret to say I believe the President has misread the mood of the people," Kennedy charged, and called Carter's phasing scheme "unacceptable." The administration proposal would "cripple any program from the start" and disappoint millions whose "voices are seldom heard in the government"—but by implication have Kennedy's ear, I thought as I was briefed on his press conference.

With cameras rolling and supporters applauding, Kennedy cited a "fundamental difference" in approach and announced his intention to "take the issue to the people" and introduce his own legislation. He wanted a single bill, rather than separate bills that could be defeated by the special interests with overflowing war chests. He said the President refused to assure him that the administration's proposal would not contain any "built-in self-destruct buttons," or "automatic triggers" that would stop the program because of economic budgetary problems.

We decided quickly that I had to get on television so that Kennedy would not have all the network time to himself. Only the White House press corps was available on such short notice that late in the afternoon, so Jody Powell hastily set up a 5:15 P.M. appearance at the White House. I rushed over to reaffirm the President's commitment to a national health plan and "to decent health care for every American," but I emphasized Carter's conviction that "health care must be phased in a rational and cautious manner that faces budgetary and economic realities, avoids excessive costs, and doesn't aggravate inflation."

The following morning my press conference to announce the President's principles was indeed crowded. I set forth the principles, stressed fiscal responsibility, cost containment, health system reform, the President's broader responsibilities, and the desire to put a program together that would have a chance of passing in the Congress. I stressed the need for a broad constituency of support, pointedly noting that over the past ten years Kennedy and labor had failed to move a national health bill in the Congress. But I did not foreclose the possibility of coming to eventual agreement with Kennedy and the unions.

The next day I appeared on *Face the Nation*. Almost the entire broadcast was devoted to national health insurance, and the clash between Kennedy and Carter. I defended the administration position, but held out an olive branch to Kennedy: "We are traveling with Senator Kennedy. We are walking down the same path, we are all going to the same place, and we are all going to get there about the same time."

The questions moved to the contrast between our ability in the Johnson administration to pass legislation and Carter's inability to get things done. While I admitted to Gannett's Carol Richards (who had asked if I had lost my touch) that "my touch has grayed a little," I pointed out the differences from the Great Society years: the fragmentation of the Congress into so many committees and subcommittees in the 1970s; the liberal, not simply Democratic, majority and powerful leadership levers of Johnson's 89th Congress; and the proliferation of special interest groups. The economic situation was vastly different as well: in the mid-1960s, the economic pie was growing for everyone; in the late 1970s, inflation and zero economic growth were prevalent.

CBS correspondent George Herman suggested another difference: Lyndon Johnson and Jimmy Carter.

"I think there's a much better analogy to President Carter than Lyndon Johnson," I answered, "and it's John Kennedy, coming in after eight years of no action on a whole host of problems. President Carter came in after eight years of no action . . . and he's taken on some very tough problems in a very courageous way. He took on the Panama Canal, and he was successful. . . . He's taking on the Turkish embargo issue. There's no Turkish vote in this country. There *is* a Greek vote in this country. He took on a very difficult attempt in his Middle East initiative, and successfully got it done. The welfare system needs to be junked and rebuilt. He took that issue on. . . . He set the agenda on tax reform."

When the broadcast ended, as we were eating finger sandwiches and having Bloody Marys at the CBS studio, I was called to the phone. It was the President. "You just did a superb job, Joe. I've been watching with Rosalynn and Cy [Vance], and we all think it was excellent. You should know that Rosalynn particularly thought you did a first-rate job for me."

At the August 7, 1978, Cabinet meeting, Carter referred to Kennedy's press conference. "Kennedy complained bitterly at his Friday press conference," Carter said. "We looked prudent and careful." Carter said that health care was costly, and in the face of inflationary concerns, we had to be on the prudent side of the issue. "We don't have anything for which we need to apologize."

The issue faded briefly over the summer congressional recess, and then took a back seat as inflation and energy problems consumed the

President's attention. Carter held to his decision not to unfold even a tentative plan until after the fall elections.

As Kennedy began charting his own political course on other issues, he continued to draw the public line on national health insurance between himself and the administration. In August, he spoke to the National Medical Association: "The President and his economic advisors, and the Secretary of HEW want to launch a ship of national health insurance with a hole beneath the waterline. . . . Now that we have parted ways with the administration, our coalition will develop its own proposals."

During the second week of October, Kennedy held three days of hearings on the framework for a national health plan. My testimony for the administration was on Friday, October 13, and Kennedy's expected reactions were a reprise of the differences he had dramatically aired in July. He listened in sympathetic and enthusiastic agreement as George Meany characterized the United States medical system as "a disaster waiting to happen" and the administration's principles as "restricted in scope and vague," and Doug Fraser called them "timid and uncertain." At one point, Kennedy asked Canadian citizens he had invited to testify what Canadians would do if a political leader "tried to take your medical plan away from you?" One witness replied, "Get rid of him."

WHILE KENNEDY focused on the political theater of national health insurance during the fall of 1978 in order to generate support for his plan, I was engaged in a major struggle with OMB Director Jim McIntyre over HEW's fiscal 1980 budget. McIntyre and his staff made it clear that HEW's discretionary programs were high on their hit list. The overwhelming proportion of HEW's budget—more than 90 percent—is spent through entitlement programs, such as Social Security and Medicare. Under such programs anyone who meets the eligibility requirements is entitled to benefits independent of the annual appropriations process. These programs can be reduced only by making changes in the laws authorizing them. The rest of the Department's budget funds hundreds of separate discretionary programs that can be cut by reducing the funds appropriated for them.

On November 29, 1978, McIntyre sent over his cuts of the budget I had recommended. His proposed actions slashed HEW health programs, with more than two hundred individual cuts. Funds for health maintenance organizations, immunization, other preventive health programs, medical schools, and research programs were either sharply reduced or eliminated. There was widespread turmoil within HEW.

Word of the drastic OMB cuts was leaking to interested constituencies—an annual rite of fall for OMB and Public Health Service staffers—when Dick Warden and I met on December 7 with Kennedy and Horowitz to discuss the legislative hearing schedule for the Senate Health Subcommittee, which Kennedy chaired. At the end of the meeting, Kennedy asked Warden and Horowitz to leave. When we were alone, Kennedy asked, "What are all the stories we hear about the health budget?"

Kennedy's sources within OMB and HEW were so good, I assumed he was already aware of OMB's proposed cuts. "We're headed for difficult times," I said. "The OMB marks are pretty severe. I have a fundamental difference of strategy with them. I'd prefer to recommend legislative reform of entitlement programs rather than cuts in scores of smaller programs."

"What are you going to do?" Kennedy asked.

"Well, the situation is still wide open. The cuts are just recommendations from McIntyre and the OMB staff. Any cuts are tough politically. I think it's better to take on one or two constituencies and amend programs that need to be changed—like Social Security—rather than taking on several dozen, which the OMB cuts will require us to do. It's not a situation to resign over; it's a situation for forceful discussion with McIntyre and the President."

Kennedy kept the office he then occupied in the Old Senate Office Building dimly lit, the venetian blinds behind his desk closed. We were sitting at a coffee table, he in a chair, I on the sofa to his left against the wall. He had been fencing with me, but now he struck. Thrusting his body very slightly forward, he said, "I think you have to resign over the health cuts."

I said nothing.

"If the cuts are anywhere near what OMB is proposing, you'll have to resign."

I started to disagree, but Kennedy was not about to be interrupted. "It'll be impossible for you to run the Department. The groups will be constantly after you, you'll be repeatedly testifying, trying to rationalize an indefensible position that you'll inevitably lose."

"Ted, no decisions have been made," I pointed out. My mind was so occupied with the larger political implications of Kennedy's suggestion that I hardly heard my own words.

"If the health funds are not restored," Kennedy pressed on, "then you have an obligation to resign." He continued talking about the improper priorities of the administration, singling out the cuts in the teenage pregnancy program, and contrasting them with defense and civil defense increases. But my mind was elsewhere and I paid scant attention.

As soon as I got back to my office, I turned my attention to the

Democratic Party midterm convention that was scheduled to begin the next day in Memphis. The highlight was a discussion of national health insurance featuring Kennedy versus Califano. The White House political staff was so concerned that they added Eizenstat to the program to bolster our position.

The President spoke to the convention on Friday night, December 8, following a film depicting his presidency and its accomplishments, and at workshops the following morning. He pledged that the sacrifices required by his budget-cutting would be fairly distributed and that the needs of the poor would be given priority. But Carter made clear his support for an increase in defense spending. "I do not have any apology to make . . . for maintaining a strong defense," he said, and "as long as I am in the White House, I will keep a strong defense."

Carter said, "My own assessment of history, my own political fortunes will be determined by Americans' judgment. When I make decisions, for instance, on the 1980 budget—has Jimmy Carter been fair? Has he been conversant with and sensitive to the social needs of our people?"

For most of the audience, the President's remarks were merely a prologue for Kennedy. If Carter provided the point, he raised expectations about Kennedy's counterpoint. That would come at the discussion on national health insurance that Saturday afternoon. The Carter people had scheduled that discussion late in hopes of dampening delegate and media interest. In fact, interest was so great that the discussion had to be moved to the largest theater available. The room was packed with liberal Kennedy partisans and press. The newly elected thirty-one-year-old governor of Arkansas, Bill Clinton, was moderator. He sat in the center of a long table. I was on his right, Kennedy on his left. To my right was Doug Fraser. Everyone at the table favored Kennedy's plan, except for me, Stu Eizenstat, and the spokesman for the American Medical Association.

I had insisted on speaking first. Before this liberal crowd, I stressed Carter's commitment to a national health plan, characterized our differences with Kennedy as largely tactical, and urged the audience to be sensitive to the President's broader responsibilities. Kennedy followed. It was the most electric speech I had ever heard him give prior to his appearance at the 1980 Democratic convention. Half-rim glasses perched on the end of his nose, fist pounding the podium, fingers alternately jabbing at the colorful charts he held and the audience he faced, Kennedy attacked "the hypocrisy" of the Congress, which had completely free health care but denied it to others. Emotionally he discussed the care "I can afford for Teddy," his son who had lost a leg to cancer, for his father after his stroke, and for himself when he broke his back in a plane crash, and asked, What about others who cannot afford such care?

Kennedy told the cheering and stomping delegates, "Sometimes a party must sail against the wind. We cannot afford to drift or lie at anchor. We cannot heed the call of those who say that it is time to furl the sail." He presented himself as keeper of the Democratic Party platform: ". . . as long as I have a vote in the United States Senate, it will be for the Democratic Party platform plan that will provide decent health care across this country, north and south, east and west, for all Americans as a matter of right and not of privilege."

Kennedy deplored "drastic slashes in the federal budget at the expense of the elderly, the poor, the sick, the cities, and the unemployed," and thundered that "the party that tore itself apart over Vietnam in the 1960s cannot afford to tear itself apart over budget cuts in basic social programs."

The stage literally trembled as the delegates clapped, whistled, and jumped to their feet on several occasions. When he closed by shouting, "The Democratic Party must choose," the crowd rose as one to cheer and shout its approval. Kennedy was so wound up that Hale Champion later said to me, "The guy is manic. I've never seen anything like it."

Before he went to the next speaker, Governor Clinton asked if I had a comment. "I'm glad I spoke before Senator Kennedy," I quipped, and the audience broke into laughter.

The rest of the panelists recited predictable lines, and Eizenstat took the podium as the final speaker. He talked about Carter's actions in the health area, mentioning his support for various programs. When Eizenstat mentioned health maintenance organizations (HMOs) and financially distressed medical institutions, I saw Kennedy open a big spread sheet. I strained to see it. My God, I thought, he's got a copy of the actual OMB budget sheets.

Eizenstat closed by reminding the audience about the importance of health care and government health programs, and Governor Clinton recognized Kennedy. "When the President reviews the budget, I hope Stu gives him the same lecture he gave us," Kennedy said.

"The President doesn't need a lecture and I don't lecture him," Eizenstat snapped back, his face taut with anger.

Then Kennedy ostentatiously held the OMB budget sheet in his left hand and, peering down periodically through his half-glasses, he gestured with his right hand and emotionally replied to Eizenstat's statements about Carter's support for health programs.

"Mr. Eizenstat talked of President Carter's support for HMOs. How much does the OMB budget mark provide for new starts for HMOs?" Kennedy shouted. "Zero," he answered, and the audience cheered him on.

Hard ball, I thought. But I was about to find out how hard.

"Joe Califano supports HMOs. I'm with Joe Califano, who's fighting for these programs," Kennedy roared, and my heart sank. What mischief, I thought. He's going to try and make his suggestion that I resign happen.

Kennedy belted out his lines. "For area health education centers, zero funds. For exceptionally needy medical students, zero. For financially distressed medical institutions, zero." He chorused each item: "Joe Califano's fighting for these funds, and I'm with him."

I have to do something, I thought. It was bad enough that someone had leaked the papers to Kennedy; but his use of them to embarrass Carter publicly before the President had made any decision could hurt the chances of getting funds restored. Carter was unaware of most of these detailed OMB cuts. Eizenstat, normally pale and nervous in public appearances, was sheet-white with barely concealed rage. Kennedy was enjoying every moment.

"These are not President Carter's decisions," I said. "OMB makes its recommendations and I make mine. But only the President decides. We should all hold our judgment until the President decides."

Kennedy and I then got into a dispute over phasing in a national health plan. Doug Fraser agreed with me that the issues were more tactical than substantive and that we all wanted a national health insurance plan.

The AMA representative then attacked the concept of any national health plan. I took advantage of that to make an impassioned plea for the poor and the old. In the background, I could hear Kennedy's stage whisper, "Atta boy, Joe. You tell 'em. Go, Joe, go!"

Mercifully, the session ended. The next morning, I decided to call the President from Memphis rather than have him get his information from press reports and from Hamilton Jordan and his aides.

Carter took the call immediately. "I think Kennedy wants very much to put me in a position adverse to the administration," I said. "Mr. President, I think he may be seeking to unravel your administration."

"I am glad you are concerned about this," the President said. "I expect many arguments like this about the budget, but none from so formidable and powerful a person as Kennedy." Pausing for effect, he added, "And none from someone with such presidential ambitions."

Carter believed he was correct on the budget. "The overwhelming majority of the American people want to cut back some programs and beef up defense. Kennedy can try to get votes in the Senate against me, but I'll win."

"It's going to be one helluva fight," I said.

"I expect complaints from Scoop Jackson that there's not enough for defense, and from other senators, but I intend to wage the budget fight because I'm convinced that I'm right and I'm convinced that the American people agree with me,'' Carter said.

At the closing Sunday session in Memphis, Fritz Mondale provided the administration's rebuttal to Kennedy. He asserted that the administration's ''most important social program'' was its anti-inflation program. If that program fails, Mondale warned, the nation could become ''a nasty, uncaring society that will destroy every social program in which we believe. It has happened to other societies and it can happen to us.''

At the Cabinet meeting on the following Monday morning, Carter underscored his conviction that the miniconvention delegates were ''far more liberal'' than most Democrats and that the American people would support a tight budget. He thought Kennedy was politically on the wrong side of the issue. ''We could have been embarrassed, but we came out very well. The people there were more activist and issue-oriented than the rest of the party.''

Mondale disagreed. ''Some of our best people have doubts about us. We must work better with responsible liberals,'' he said, looking tired, almost grim.

Carter then criticized the national health insurance demands of Kennedy. ''The Democratic conventioneers are not typical of America,'' he said. Carter had ''no concern about Kennedy's popularity,'' adding that ''the news media represent a minority of the nation.'' Carter thought a moment, then said softly and seriously, ''One failure could cause the downfall of this administration—inflation. Almost everything is subservient to it in political terms. We will hold the 1980 deficit to thirty billion dollars.''

Carter concluded, ''The issue is not whether we should have a national health plan, but on what schedule we can afford to implement such a plan. My commitment is undiminished. The critical questions relate primarily to the costs and timing of such a plan.''

Concerned about HEW's budget and social programs, I pointed out that national health was part of a larger debate within the Democratic Party and across the country over the budget and fiscal priorities. ''The debate will intensify in the months ahead, especially after Congress gets back and the interest groups focus their attention on the subcommittees and bureaus with budgets at stake.''

The HEW budget fight with OMB consumed many of the health analysts who had been working on the national health plan, and slowed our efforts to produce a program. On the Monday after the Democratic miniconvention in Memphis, Kennedy met with McIntyre and Eizenstat to urge restoration of funds OMB wanted to cut. I pressed McIntyre hard with a 300-page book we prepared appealing 129 OMB cuts involving $2.9 billion. I sent McIntyre a personal memo on December 5, saying, "These deep reductions in discretionary programs cannot be characterized as merely painful, or defended as 'a pause.' Many cut the heart out of new initiatives this administration has embraced, new directions it has sought; some are directly contrary to the President's anti-inflation program; some cut back or even eliminate programs that are working well and are cost effective—for example, health maintenance organizations and preventive medicine." I charged that "OMB's cuts sell out the future." McIntyre backed off from most of his proposed cuts, and eventually $2.5 billion was restored to the HEW budget. But his budget marks fell short of our HEW requests and shorter of what Kennedy wanted.

In the end, I personally appealed to the President on two issues—funds for the National Institutes of Health, which McIntyre wanted to cut by $340 million below the amount Congress had appropriated for the prior year, and $37 million to construct a clinical research facility for the Institute of Child Health and Human Development. The President accepted my argument on behalf of NIH research funds.

I had recommended construction of a new research center for child health and human development to Carter in 1978, both during the regular budget process and in private conversations, as a major contribution he could leave to the future of the world, not just the United States. He had come close to approving it, but had backed off just before that HEW budget was made final, deferring to OMB Director McIntyre, who opposed it with an insistence approaching obsession because Sargent and Eunice Shriver—"the Kennedys"—were such strong proponents. The Congress nevertheless appropriated funds for the building. McIntyre wanted Carter to recommend rescinding the appropriation. I disagreed and urged the President to let construction go forward. When Carter made the final decision not to fund the center, he kidded me about not constructing the "Califano Building," but it was clear that the project was too dear to the Kennedys for his support.

I thought to myself how much more limited Carter's strategic sense and vision were than Johnson's. LBJ would not only have recommended the building; he would have taken advantage of the Kennedys' support to drive it through the Congress in a tight budget year, and to ease Catholic objections to fetal research and genetic engineering. I remembered how Johnson pressed to get the Kennedy Center for the Performing Arts through the Congress in the wake of John Kennedy's assassination, using the tragedy to achieve something he and many others had wanted for the nation's capital for years. And of how, over congressional objections, he had not hesitated to name the Hirshhorn Museum after the owner and collector of the spectacular art he wanted contributed, if doing so would make possible a museum for contemporary sculpture in the nation's capital.

Kennedy made the most he could of the health budget cuts. To the chagrin of the appropriations committees, he held the first hearings on the budget on January 26, four days after the President had released it. Kennedy had tried to get McIntyre to testify. Horowitz had told Dick Warden, "The Senator doesn't want to kick Joe around." But McIntyre refused. So I appeared alone. Horowitz told me with pride the evening before, "I think it may be a nine-camera hearing." He meant television coverage and he was right.

Kennedy opened the hearing with a blistering statement that was, in my mind, not justified by the health cuts that remained in Carter's budget, many of which in the end had been made in programs that were duplicated elsewhere, or were being replaced by more efficiently targeted ones.

I tried to deflect it: "I'm delighted to be here, Mr. Chairman. I haven't looked forward to anything so much since we were together in Memphis." The tension eased a little in the small hearing room, normally full, but this morning wall-to-wall with Kennedy partisans and representatives of interest groups opposed to the budget reductions.

The hearing was a made-to-order media event. A Senate subcommittee chairman, angry about budget cuts, calls in the Secretary and follows his testimony with witnesses representing interests whose funds were cut—in this case representatives of medical schools and nurses. Kennedy's rhetoric—"I don't believe that the vision of America [these cuts reflect] is a vision that the American people share or want"—took on an Alice-in-Wonderland ambience when measured against the facts. He was arguing for an addition of only between $300 and $400 million to HEW's 1980 budget, which was up by almost $20 billion above the prior year. In the health area alone, HEW's spending was up more than $10 billion from fiscal 1978 to 1980 and the increase from 1980 over 1979 was larger than the increase in 1979 over 1978; and it was up more than 3,500 percent from the beginning of the Great Society. Indeed, in historical context, the Great Society had so dramatically reversed the defense–social program pattern of federal expenditures that Kennedy seemed to be bickering about nickels and dimes. In 1963, the HEW budget was $21 billion, some 18 percent of the federal budget. In 1980, HEW's $200 billion would take more than 36 percent of Carter's proposed budget, while Defense's $125 billion would get less than 24 percent, a sharp drop from the 43 percent share Defense commanded in 1963.

In my testimony, I also pressed the distinction between Kennedy and me—both of us interested in health spending—and the President's broader responsibility "to look across the government as a whole and to balance all the needs—foreign and domestic, urban and rural, economic and social—in proposing a total federal budget for fiscal 1980." I had prepared carefully and after the hearing, Kennedy told me privately he thought I had more than held my own for the administration. Perhaps, I thought, but I recognized that this was yet another straw in the wind reflecting both the frustration of the liberal Democrats with Carter, and that Kennedy was keeping his option to challenge Carter.

AS THE budget fights melted into the congressional appropriation process, I turned back to the national health plan. After the midterm elections, Kennedy and the unions had pressed Carter to move. On January 3, Carter had sent me a memorandum expressing his "need to decide on the national health plan before the State of the Union." There was a formal tone to the memo ("I appreciate all you are doing on this difficult and critical issue"), almost as though it were written for the record. In any event, he wanted to review options on the scope of the health plan, and the timing of submission to the Congress when he returned from the Guadeloupe summit with foreign leaders.

On January 8, I sent the President a draft national health plan. I suggested we unfold it as a tentative HEW plan after his State of the Union message, and seek comment from key members of Congress and interest groups. Carter would announce a final plan later in the year. The proposed plan, which permitted phasing in any number of ways, provided a basic benefit package for all Americans of both hospital and outpatient care (including coverage for catastrophic illnesses, but emphasizing preventive and less expensive outpatient care). For the employed Americans and their dependents—some 156 million of the 220 million American population—the employer would be required to provide this coverage, paying at least half the premium cost. Medicare would still cover senior citizens and Medicaid would be expanded and federalized into a single program with Medicare, to cover the poor and the aged. The plan contained several ideas to reform the health care system.

The President met with me on Thursday, January 18, 1979. He decided not to have me unfold a tentative plan in order to keep sufficient distance from it and preserve his options, but he did direct me to brief the interested groups and congressional leaders and report back to him. The congressional briefings were well attended, but there was not much enthusiasm for any national health plan. As House Speaker Tip O'Neill, puffing on his cigar, said, "This is the kind of program Democrats should propose, especially in an election year. But I don't know how many of these guys are really Democrats!'' He chuckled with rueful heartiness.

Senator Edmund Muskie thought that inflation would cancel out any savings from cost containment and he was worried about overloading the capacity of the payroll tax. Al Ullman remained adamantly opposed: ''There will be plenty of opposition and there is no need to focus on something that isn't going to happen for ten years or more.''

But Russell Long was up for re-election in 1980 and said he was going to hold hearings in his Senate Finance Committee on his catastrophic plan early in the year. We tried to postpone them until we were ready to begin with the administration plan. Long's refusal and his insistence on moving his own plan accelerated our schedule. Carter was politically comfortable being to the right of Kennedy, but he could not take a back seat to Russell Long on a national health plan and hope to keep peace with Democratic liberals.

I had accepted Dean Ivan Bennett's invitation to dedicate the Arnold and Marie Schwartz Pavilion at the New York University Medical Center in Manhattan on March 22, 1979. The occasion provided an opportunity to keep some momentum by announcing that Carter had approved $10 to $15 billion for the first phase cost of his health plan, which would begin in 1983, and to report that, if a national health proposal were to be sent to Capitol Hill, my congressional consultations revealed overwhelming sentiment for Carter's phased plan rather than Kennedy's one-bite proposal. The decision to use the dedication for a report on Carter's national health plan was made shortly before the event. The evening before the speech found me on one end of the phone in a Regency Hotel suite in New York, conferring with Eizenstat at the White House while he checked my language with the President. We finally agreed on the key portion of the text shortly after midnight; I went to sleep to the rhythm of the typewriter clicking and telecopier machine rolling in the next room.

Five days later, on March 27, when I testified before the Finance Committee, Long opened with a relatively conciliatory statement. But sharp differences between Long and the administration remained. Long's statement supported a plan to cover only costs of catastrophic illnesses, and he wanted to put it in operation ''at the latest'' in 1981, two years ahead of Carter's proposal. Long's plan made no attempt to change the health care system. Two Republican committee members, Senators Dole and Danforth, expressed agreement with their chairman.

I stated the administration's opposition to a plan that contained no reform of the system and would cover only catastrophic illnesses. ''Millions of low income families might be driven to financial despair'' before qualifying under a $15,000 deductible, for under Long's plan a patient might easily run up a $13,000 hospital bill, as well as $2,000 in doctors' bills, before receiving financial help. Moreover, a catastrophic illness plan would encourage "profligate" spending by hospitals. The fear of the labor movement that providing relief to the middle class for catastrophic illness costs would take the political pressure off providing health care for the poor was unarticulated, but very much on my mind as well. I outlined the first phase of the administration bill. But far more significant than Long's or my statements on the public record were my private meetings with him and Kennedy.

Late Tuesday afternoon, April 10, I met with Long in his hideaway office on the Senate side of the Capitol. As he sat down on a sofa in the sparsely furnished office, he pointed to a chair at his left. "Joe," he said, "I want a national health insurance bill this year. The President may not know how to get elected, but I'm gonna help him. We're gonna go to the American people with a law."

"But you want your bill—just catastrophic coverage," I responded. "The labor unions and Kennedy will block that."

"I'll go a ways with you. I like your idea about mandating employers to cover employees and I'll put in some expanded Medicaid coverage for poor people." Long spoke with that occasional stutter that punctuates his speech when he is excited or enthusiastic.

Negotiating with Long is a marvelous poker game and I was having difficulty restraining my own inner excitement. If only he is serious, I thought, and hoped.

"We'll take that to the floor and let Kennedy vote against it." Long laughed.

"We really have to get down to specifics," I said, remembering Lyndon Johnson's cautions about negotiating with Long.

As though reading my thoughts, Long said: "Let's do it the way Lyndon Johnson used to do it when you worked for him. I'm willing to compromise."

We talked for almost an hour about specifics. For the first time I began to think there was a glimmer of hope, that we could reach agreement with Long on a good initial phase for a national health plan.

Long said he wanted a bill to go into effect on January 1, 1980. "I want the people of this country—"

"And the people of Louisiana—" I interrupted lightly.

"Well, they're citizens of this country, the best," Long rejoined. "I want everyone to have some health benefits before the 1980 election."

"The President doesn't want any expenditures until 1983," I responded. "He wants to balance the budget in 1981."

"You don't get elected in 1980 by telling the people you'll give them something in 1983. Hell, Carter may not be here to give it to them in 1983 if he doesn't give them something in 1980.'' Long chuckled.

''I don't know whether we can get ready to administer the benefits that fast,'' I warned. ''I don't think it's possible.''

Long sat straight on the sofa he had been leaning back on and began tapping my knee with his hand. ''You're the best damn administrator HEW ever had,'' he said, flattering me to get his point across. ''You administer. You let me legislate.''

We laughed, and then we talked about whether at least parts of a plan could be made operative in six to nine months.

''Russell,'' I said as I was leaving, ''you should be up for re-election more often. We could do some great things for this country.''

I told the President about our conversation and urged him to see Long. He was reluctant. ''Do you understand him when he talks?'' Carter asked, adding, ''I never can understand him. And then I never know what he's going to do—except screw me most of the time.''

My private meetings on the House side were mixed. Ullman was unyieldingly opposed to catastrophic coverage. ''There's a moral issue,'' he said, ''in paying for all this expensive equipment to extend lives. Government shouldn't encourage that, shouldn't be making those decisions. And that's what catastrophic coverage will do.'' But my discussions with Jim Corman, cosponsor with Kennedy of the Health Security Bill, and Charlie Rangel, the new Chairman of the Ways and Means Health Subcommittee, were heartening. There was a possibility that we could put together an administration bill they would endorse.

Three days after the Long meeting, I met Kennedy over lunch at his home in McLean. It was Good Friday. I wanted to make one final attempt to come to agreement with him and the labor movement. We needed a much broader coalition than the traditional union and union-supported groups he was working with, if we were to have a chance to pass even a first phase of a national health plan. But those groups were a critical nucleus. I felt that Carter, as head of a Democratic administration, should not split with the labor unions, senior citizens, and church groups over what had been a centerpiece of Democratic Party platforms since 1948. Indeed, with an initial phase as extensive as the one Carter had me outline before Long, there was no reason—in terms of health policy—for such a split.

Kennedy welcomed me as he said good-bye to a reporter for a newspaper in Ireland. We went into his library, a room of weathered gray wood and high ceilings with exposed beams. Sitting on opposite sides of the fireplace with a warm fire, we had a drink and talked about familiar and personal things.

Over lunch in the dining room, we began to discuss the national health plan issues. Kennedy talked about a single bill and phasing. He too had been consulting members of Congress. He realized the mood on the Hill was not propitious for a one-shot national health plan. "But," he still insisted, "there can be phasing over several years for a total plan in a single bill."

Kennedy was concerned about my conversations with Russell Long. An alliance between Carter and Long would kill his hopes for a total national health program in one shot. Each time I mentioned Long, Kennedy asserted with total confidence that "a catastrophic-only bill"—even if backed by Carter as well as Long—would be killed either by filibuster in the Senate or a vote in the House.

"I'm not as certain of that as I was a year ago," I said. "And if Long will accept federalization or expansion of Medicaid for the poor—"

"If the President wants to work something out with Long," Kennedy interrupted, "what's the point in talking to me?" He shrugged; it was the only time during the lunch that his voice displayed impatience or irritability.

"I'm here to see if we can come to some agreement," I said, "not to argue."

We agreed that he would speak to Doug Fraser and Lane Kirkland, and I would talk to the White House. We would quietly get together at his home in ten days, on the evening of April 24, to make one last attempt to compromise on the same national health plan.

After lunch we returned to his library for coffee in front of the fireplace and talked about whether I should run for the Senate seat in New York in 1980. Kennedy was eloquent as he discussed the satisfactions he had found in a Senate career, although he mentioned the frustrations as the legislative process had become more complex. "A lot of guys can't stand it." Nevertheless, he was enthusiastic about my running, concerned about my ability to defeat Jack Javits ("You should take some discreet polls, cost you about $25,000, to see if he has any political vulnerabilities"). "The Democratic Party could use a strong candidate in New York," Kennedy said, with enough of a distant expression for me to conclude that he had not ruled out the possibility of running for the presidency.

On April 24th, the morning of the scheduled evening meeting, Kennedy called me. "The meeting is off. The groups just will not compromise further. Whatever is introduced will be chipped away at, so they see no point in compromising now."

"I'm truly sorry. But before this is over, we'll have to come together if anything's going to pass," I said.

Like lawyers with clients who had decided to sue, we were now in a race to the courthouse. On May 14, Kennedy announced his plan, the Health Care for All Americans Act. It was another media event in the old Senate Caucus Room, crowded with supporters and television lights and cameras. Kennedy's announcement was a political speech, calling on Carter to join in an effort to "make quality health care a right for all our people," and lashing out at any catastrophic health plan with a commitment to do "everything I can" to defeat it. Kennedy's proposal covered all Americans and resident aliens immediately, but it was less a government takeover than his previous bills. Nevertheless, his bill heavily regulated the health insurance industry, provided wide coverage, and paid the cost through "premium payments" (like taxes related to income), payroll taxes, and general federal and state revenues.

To us, Kennedy's plan looked like an administratively unworkable and politically unachievable proposal, too much too fast in terms of cost and suffocating government regulation and bureaucracy. It notably failed to take advantage of existing employer-employee relationships and private insurance systems. Nevertheless, with Carter's approval, I issued a conciliatory statement: "We are addressing the same problems, and we have many of the same goals." But I emphasized the different approach Carter would take: "To enact national health legislation in the 96th Congress—after decades of failure—we should propose only a first-phase bill. And we are convinced that this is necessary not only to secure congressional passage, but also to ensure that we carry out this great new national commitment in a prudent, cost-conscious, and noninflationary manner." I signaled that we were still prepared to work together. "It is our hope that, as national health plan legislation moves through the congressional process, the administration proposal will attract a broad base of support. . . ."

While my statements were conciliatory, there were troubling signs from Iowa and New Hampshire that same day. In Iowa, an exploratory committee for a Democratic alternative, favoring a Kennedy candidacy, was formed. From New Hampshire, the *Chicago Tribune* reported a poll showing Kennedy over Carter, 58 to 36 percent.

On May 17, 1979, I went over our proposed plan and the remaining issues within the administration with the President, Mondale, Eizenstat, Schultze, McIntyre, inflation fighter Alfred Kahn, Kreps, Blumenthal, and Hale Champion. I urged the President to expand the program somewhat to counter the appeal of Kennedy's proposal to liberals.

Getting a sense that Carter would do so, I felt it was time to persuade Congressmen Jim Corman and Charlie Rangel to support us. Corman did not like Kennedy's bill and had sent several signals that he might be willing to support Carter's. My negotiations with Corman began over a long breakfast on May 31 and continued during the next several days.

On June 6, in his office, Corman and I reached an agreement: Corman would support our proposal if our first phase provided prenatal, delivery, and first-year health care services to all mothers and infants, rather than just to the poor. In our description of phases to come, he wanted me simply to sketch out a broad commitment eventually to extend this coverage through age six. As Dick Warden and I made the brief drive back from Corman's office to HEW, I thought about LBJ's "kiddie care" program. On March 3, 1968, at Ramey Air Force Base in Puerto Rico, I had briefed the press on Johnson's last health message to the Congress. When I got back to my office, I checked that 1968 Johnson legislative message on Health in America. There LBJ had proposed the Child Health Improvement and Protection Act of 1968, to assure "adequate prenatal and postnatal care for the mother . . . a safe delivery by trained health professionals . . . competent examination of the child at birth, and expert treatment when needed . . . the best of modern medical care for the infant during his first year to prevent disease, cure illness, and correct handicaps." In his final budget message in 1969, he had reiterated that proposal. How LBJ would have loved this one, I thought—right down to Corman pulling the commitment out of the administration as a *quid pro quo* for his active support.

I urged Carter to incorporate Corman's proposal. To have Kennedy's former cosponsor introducing our national health plan would be a political coup. Moreover, Harlem Congressman Charlie Rangel, the Ways and Means Health Subcommittee chairman, would go with his old friend Corman. I wrote Carter on June 6, "I cannot overestimate the importance of . . . Corman as an up-front and vocal supporter of the administration bill."

The cost was an additional $300 million on the federal budget and $700 million to the health care system, but the savings over the lives of these children would be enormous. OMB Director McIntyre accused me of a "typical last-minute ploy" to increase the health plan. But Corman's suggestions made such good sense as public policy and politics that the President readily agreed. When Kennedy learned that Corman was about to go with us, he called him in one last-ditch effort to pull him off our bill. It was too late. The President made the changes for Corman, and he and Rangel supported Carter's plan.

I then went through my final round of calls and meetings before unveiling Carter's plan on June 12 at a White House press briefing. Long was still friendly; Ullman still opposed. The meeting with Kennedy was amicable, but clearly at arms' length. Kennedy "might not attack us," I told Carter after that meeting, "but he is going his own way, at least for now."

My meetings with Senator Abe Ribicoff added to the hopeful signs from Long and Corman. Ribicoff had decided to retire at the end of his third term in 1980. He was respected by Long and Kennedy and might be able to broker a Senate compromise on national health insurance. He was the advocate for child health on the Finance Committee and would find the Corman addition to the Carter bill appealing. "I'll do it, Joe," Ribicoff said when I finished my presentation. "I think there's something there, a chance. Both Russell and Ted have already talked to me. We may be able to do something." On the day of our announcement, Ribicoff publicly expressed his desire for a bill and his intention to work for a compromise among Long, Kennedy, and Carter.

On June 12, 1979, President Carter unveiled the administration's phase one bill in a White House briefing with Stu Eizenstat and me. He emphasized the political difficulties of Kennedy's approach: "The idea of all or nothing has been pursued now for nearly three decades . . . but [no one] has benefited from that." As finally approved by Carter, our first phase bill proposed a major overhaul of the health care system. No individual American would have to pay more than $1,250 in a given year; the government would pay costs above that. Sixty-six million aged, disabled, and poor Americans would be covered with no co-payment, thus protecting an additional sixteen million Americans and improving coverage for all in this group. Employers would be required to provide adequate health care coverage for their 156 million full-time employees and dependents, and to pay at least 75 percent of the premium cost. The remaining nine million Americans, either self-employed or working part-time, would be able to buy coverage from a government health care corporation, as would small employers who could not purchase it from private insurers. The plan's initial phase reached every American with a basic benefit package of hospital, physician, laboratory, X-ray, preventive, and mental health services. Prenatal, delivery, and first-year infant care would be provided for all with no cost sharing. The bill featured major health system reforms to reduce costs and reorient services toward preventive care. Its additional costs, based on 1980 population and dollars, were estimated at $18.2 billion in public funds and $6.1 billion for employers to cover their employees where they were not already providing the required benefits. By using the existing employer-employee relationship and the private insurers, we intended to avoid creating a massive bureaucracy to administer the plan. This phase one would go into effect in 1983.

During the detailed briefing, I stressed our desire to propose a plan that could pass. I noted that the only progress toward a national health plan had been made by Lyndon Johnson with the partial steps of Medicaid and Medicare. Since Harry Truman, the Democratic Party had tried to pass a national health plan and never succeeded. The reporters kept pressing me on Kennedy's plan. I finally responded, "There's no more chance of passing Kennedy's plan than there is of putting an elephant through a keyhole."

Kennedy's public response was cool, but not final. "If I had to vote today, I'd vote 'no' " on Carter's health plan, he said. Two days later, a huge posterboard arrived at my office. In the center, a big keyhole had been cut. In the keyhole, suspended on a spring, a small stuffed pink elephant was swinging easily back and forth. The elephant was labeled "Health Care for All Americans Act," the title of Kennedy's bill. There was a handwritten note scrawled on the left side of the poster. "Joe—It looks to me like it fits. Ted."

It was a classy, good-natured touch. I called Kennedy to thank him. "Well," he said, "I watched you say that on the six-thirty NBC News. Then I watched it on the seven P.M. CBS News and ABC News. But when I turned on the ten o'clock news and saw you saying it again, I had to do something."

"You've got a great sense of humor," I said, laughing.

"If you don't have a sense of humor in this business, you'll go crazy," Kennedy responded.

CHAPTER IV

HEALTH: COST AND ACCESS

I HAD long abandoned the image of a doctor with a little black bag dispensing homespun wisdom with castor oil, but I was not prepared for two facts about health in America: Health had become one of the three largest industries in the nation, and government had become pervasively involved in the health industry.

Health is our second largest employer (behind education) and our third largest industry in consumer spending (after food and housing), and it is growing faster than any other. Federal, state, and local governments are by far the largest purchasers of health care. Unchecked, the health industry is more likely to consume Americans' private and public dollars than the oil sheiks. In 1980, Americans spent $2 on health care for each dollar they spent on oil.

In 1965, Americans spent $39 billion, 5.9 percent of their gross national product, on health care. By 1980, Americans were spending about $230 billion, more than 9 percent. That amounts to a levy of $1,000 on each man, woman, and child in America, and the average employed American worked more than a month in 1980 to pay it. By the year 2000, under the present system, Americans will turn over at least

$1 trillion—12 percent of the gross national product—to the health care industry.

Almost seven million people are employed in the health industry, about 7 percent of the national work force, one American worker out of every fourteen. And the trend is up: from 1970 to 1978, employment in the industry increased by 60 percent, accounting for one out of every seven new jobs created. Almost 450,000 physicians practice, and about 1.5 million nurses assist them. There are more than 7,000 hospitals, with a capacity of 1.4 million beds, and more than 18,000 skilled nursing homes with another 1.4 million beds. Thousands of laboratories, hundreds of suppliers of drugs, expensive medical equipment, and all sorts of medical products and devices, and a growing army of insurance salesmen, claims processors, home health aides, and nonprofessionals in hospitals and nursing homes make their living in the health care industry.

In 1965, HEW's health budget was $1.9 billion. Fifteen years later, with Medicare and Medicaid, it was $55 billion. Payments under Medicare have risen geometrically to fund increasingly expensive equipment and procedures, and the health problems that accompany the aging American population. In 1980, about 15 cents of every tax dollar spent was paid to the health industry.

The investment of tax dollars has brought significant advances in access to quality health care. In 1980, Medicare paid $34 billion in health care bills for 28 million elderly and disabled Americans. Since Medicare began, life expectancy for the elderly has increased by almost two years; days lost from work by the elderly have decreased by 50 percent, and millions of senior citizens have access to health care only because of the program. In 1980, Medicaid paid $24.5 billion ($14.2 billion, federal; $10.3 billion, state) for the health care of 23 million poor people. During the first ten years of Medicaid, death rates from diseases that are historically prevalent among the poor declined sharply: Infant mortality rates were down by 33 percent and maternal mortality rates by 66 percent; death rates from influenza and pneumonia dropped by 28 percent, and from strokes by 30 percent. The use of preventive services by the poor has increased since Medicaid: The proportion of poor women who receive early pregnancy care from a physician rose from 17 percent in 1963 to 65 percent in 1976; the number of physician visits per year by poor children climbed by 26 percent from 1964 to 1979.

While Medicare and Medicaid have helped improve access to care and the health status of millions of elderly and poor Americans, they have also contributed to the inflation, inefficiency, and waste that have persistently characterized the health care industry. When Republican Senator Carl Curtis of Nebraska pressed me about "stampeding health costs" at my confirmation hearings, I expressed my intention to "focus our efforts on controlling costs and . . . utilization" because I considered such action essential not only for the more effective use of Medicare and Medicaid, but also to persuade Congress to improve and expand these programs. Despite the explosion of the health care industry over the 1970s, 50 million people live in areas with severe shortages of health personnel and services, and whatever the future of a national health plan, it is imperative to provide health care to the 20 million poor Americans presently not covered by Medicaid and to close gaps in coverage for the elderly, disabled, and poor already receiving benefits.

In 1965, the Ford Motor Company paid a health care bill of $68 million for its employees. By 1979, that bill exceeded $600 million—almost $3,000 for each employee. The invisible standard auto part of employee health benefits on every Ford rose from $22 in 1965 to $200 in 1979. General Motors' $1.5 billion 1980 health care bill for its employees is more than the corporation paid U.S. Steel for the steel it uses in GM cars.

The average family spends more than 12 percent of its income for health care. Private health insurance premiums went up between 16 and 18 percent a year during the two-and-a-half years I was Secretary. Hospital charges—the fastest-rising costs in the health industry—have climbed more rapidly than the consumer price index, from 1975 to 1978 rising at more than twice the general rate of inflation.

As I began work as Secretary, I quickly realized that the health industry had become bloated because of its third-party reimbursement system and the absence of the competitive forces that have been present in producing and selling goods and services from automobiles and television sets to beauty care and tennis balls.

The health business is not inflationary, inefficient, and wasteful because doctors and hospital administrators wear black hats while patients wear white ones. By and large, doctors and hospital administrators respond to the economic incentives and penalties they face, just as almost anyone in any business would. Most patients do not give sufficient attention to their hospital and doctor bills because they are not paying them directly. Under the third-party reimbursement system, 90 percent of all hospital bills and 66 percent of doctor bills are paid by Medicare, Medicaid, other government programs, or insurance companies. By contrast, fifty years ago 90 percent of all health care bills were paid by individuals. Not paying the bill directly, few patients relate it to their health insurance premiums or taxes. Those who do, conclude that asking doctors about costs and bills or questioning the need for particular medical services will have no impact on their own insurance premiums or tax payments. And millions of Americans do not pay anything for health insurance—their employer or the government picks up the bill.

In business transactions, there is normally a direct relationship between buyers and sellers and competition. When an American buys a television set or a car, he chooses the dealer and pays for his purchase directly. He discusses the price with the salesman, picks the model he wants, selects the optional features he wants.

But there is no such direct relationship between buyer and seller, and virtually no competition among sellers in the health care industry. The patient may select his family doctor, but rarely the specialist, the hospital to which he is admitted, the surgery he is told he needs, the often expensive medical tests to which he is subjected. Nobody walks into a hospital and asks for an appendectomy, hysterectomy, or a coronary bypass. The doctor determines what medical procedures are required, and he does not pay the bill.

The third-party reimbursement system and the lack of competition have helped to perpetuate expensive methods of charging for health care. Almost all health care bills are paid on a fee-for-service or cost-plus basis. The more services that are rendered, the more fees we pay. When an American goes to a doctor or hospital, the financial incentive is for the provider to supply more services. The fee-for-service system offers little financial incentive for health promotion and prevention or to cure a sick patient at the lowest cost, with the fewest services.

Moreover, the incentives and penalties encourage providing the most expensive services. Insurance covers hospital and acute care far more extensively than preventive care, such as periodic physical exams or immunization. The possibility of malpractice litigation prompts physicians to perform unnecessary tests that cost millions of dollars to protect themselves against accusations of negligence.

The absence of competition, the lack of buyer-seller tension, and the third-party and fee-for-service reimbursement systems turn the traditional concept of free enterprise on its head. The more doctors, nursing homes, and hospitals we have, the more expensive the system gets. The more specialists there are, the more referrals to specialists there are; the more equipment a hospital has, the more tests it runs on its patients. These greater expenses turn into higher health insurance premiums, higher bills from doctors, hospitals, and laboratories, and higher prices of products to recoup the more expensive employee health benefits. These higher costs in turn require higher taxes to support the biggest buyer of goods and services from America's health care colossus—the federal, state, and local governments that now pay 54 percent of all hospital bills.

State and municipal health departments have traditionally committed significant resources to health care, including the operation of hospitals and public health services. Since World War II, substantial federal money has been directed to the health care system through the Veterans Administration (particularly in recent years, with the aging of the World War II veterans), the Defense Department, and the federal employee health plans. But the greatest single infusion of federal funds came during the Great Society years of the mid-1960s when, at the insistent urging of President Lyndon Johnson, the Congress passed forty health bills. There was a need to increase the access of our people to health care. We responded with funds to pay the bills where need was most severe. To increase our ability to provide such care, we provided resources to expand enrollments in medical and nursing schools, and to build more hospitals. We had hoped that a more plentiful supply of doctors, nurses, and hospitals would curtail sharp cost increases due to the demand our programs would create.

For senior citizens over age sixty-five and for the disabled, the Great Society put together Medicare, a completely federal program financed largely out of Social Security payroll taxes. For the poor—"the medically needy," as the federal regulations call them—we established Medicaid, a program funded jointly by the federal government and the states, with wide flexibility for each state to define "medically needy," and to determine what health care services it would fund, in what proportion, and at what rate.

In the often bitter struggles to get Medicare and Medicaid enacted, the focus was almost entirely on access, rarely on cost. Sitting in Johnson's small green hideaway adjoining the Oval Office one day, White House congressional lobbyist Larry O'Brien and Wilbur Cohen (later to become HEW Secretary) responded to Johnson's demand that they move the Medicare bill out of committee. "It'll cost a half-billion dollars to make the changes in reimbursement standards to get the bill out of the Senate Finance Committee," Cohen said.

"Five hundred million. Is that all?" Johnson exclaimed with a wave of his big hand. "Do it. Move that damn bill out now, before we lose it."

The opposition to Medicare by the health industry—insurance companies, hospitals, and particularly doctors—was so unyielding that we were concerned about whether the doctors would participate in sufficient numbers. LBJ decided to invite the American Medical Association leadership to the White House as the Medicare regulations were about to be issued and the program launched. Sitting on twin sofas under a portrait of Franklin D. Roosevelt in the Oval Office, the AMA officials waited politely for Johnson to say something as he settled into his rocking chair.

The President took his time, assessing their cold stares. Then he talked not about Medicare, but of his need for physicians in Vietnam to help serve the civilian population. Would the AMA help? Could it get doctors to rotate in and out of Vietnam for a few months? "Your country needs your help. Your President needs your help," he said. He got the reply he expected. Of course, the AMA would start a program immediately, the doctors responded, almost in unison.

"Get the press in here," Johnson told Bill Moyers, his press secretary, who was sitting with me off to the side of the office.

The press tramped in, forming an uneven semicircle to Johnson's left. The President described the AMA Vietnam medical program, heaping praise on the doctors present. But the reporters' first question was about Medicare. Would the doctors support the Medicare program?

Johnson acted annoyed at the question. "These men are going to get doctors to go to Vietnam where they might be killed," he said with quite apparent indignation. "Medicare is the law of the land. Of course, they'll support the law of the land."

LBJ turned abruptly to the head of the AMA delegation. "Tell him," he said. "You tell him."

"Of course, we will," the AMA official responded.

Johnson shook hands warmly with the delegation as the cameras clicked. We all breathed a little more easily.

By the time I became Secretary, the doctors' reluctance, like that of other providers, had given way to their heavy involvement, with complaints only about filling out forms and publishing the fees participating physicians received from Medicare and Medicaid. Doctors and others were being paid billions of dollars by the two programs for whatever procedures doctors considered "medically necessary," in Medicare on the basis of their "reasonable cost and customary charges." Health insurance agencies and computer companies processed millions of claims each month for federal and state governments. The sapling nursing home business of the early 1960s had grown to a $22 billion forest, as 40 cents of each Medicaid dollar went into its coffers. Medicare guaranteed income to hospitals and profits to the high-technology medical equipment industry, often funding exotic and expensive means to extend life under extraordinary circumstances. Twenty-five percent of Medicare's $34 billion budget in 1980 was spent on care during the last year of life. With too few exceptions, Medicare reimbursed hospitals for whatever costs they incurred, whatever expensive equipment they purchased, no matter how infrequently it was used.

By 1977, the once diehard opponents of Medicare and Medicaid—the health insurers, hospital administrators, and doctors—were enjoying supping at the public table. In our rush to provide access, the Great Society had let the health industry set the prices, and had acquiesced in its reimbursement systems. Over the intervening decade, the industry had used America's quest for broad access to quality health care to protect and enhance its financial interest and solidify its legislative and regulatory position. The health industry was seated comfortably at a groaning table set by the taxpayers.

IT BECAME my task as Secretary to lead the administration's effort to try to reform the economics of the health care system. Hospitals were the first target.

The problem was not entirely new to me. I had helped draft Lyndon Johnson's 1968 message to the Congress on "Health in America." Predicting that unless we acted to restrain hospital costs the nation's health bill could reach $100 billion by 1975 (it actually hit $124 billion), Johnson cited three "major deficiencies" to be corrected: the tilt of insurance plans that "encourage doctors and patients to choose hospitalization," the fee-for-service system with "no strong economic incentives to encourage them to avoid providing care that is unnecessary," and the fact that "hospitals charge on a cost basis, which places no penalty on inefficient operations." Johnson asked for a legislative authority "to employ new methods of payment as they prove effective in providing high quality medical care more efficiently and at lower cost." The Congress failed to act despite his warning that the cost of medical care for a family would double in seven years.

I had no illusions about the difficulty of succeeding in 1977. But two factors made me believe we had a significantly better chance. We were at the beginning of a new presidential term, and the rise in hospital costs because of waste and inflation had become persistently steeper since 1968. More than 130,000 excess hospital beds cost Americans $4 billion per year. The pressure on hospital administrators to recoup the cost of excess beds leads to $1.6 billion in charges for unnecessary weekend admissions. Some hospitals have even offered chances on cruises and other prizes to patients who enter on weekends. The average length of time an individual stays in a hospital varies from coast to coast, and state to state. Some states have stays as low as 6.4 days; others, such as New York, have average hospital stays approaching 10 days for comparable patient care. If the nation could reduce its length of stay to the 6.4-day average, Americans would pay at least $3 billion less on hospital care each year.

The staff-patient ratio jumped by 44 percent from 1965 to 1978. In the

United States, that ratio was 3.2 to 1; in Germany, with a health care system as sophisticated, it was 1 to 1. In 1965, the cost of an average hospital stay here was less than $350; in 1978, it was $1,470; by 1982 it will be $2,400.

The method of paying certain hospital-based physicians has encouraged unnecessary medical procedures. Radiologists, pathologists, and anesthesiologists have often been paid, like entertainers, on the basis of a percentage of the gross receipts, although this practice appears to be changing.

Hospital administrators purchase expensive equipment such as CAT scanners—body X-ray machines—more for the convenience of doctors and the status of their institutions than out of need. There are enough CAT scanners in Southern California to serve the entire United States west of the Mississippi. At least seventeen CAT scanners have been spotted around Atlanta with a population of 1.5 million, while six have proven sufficient to serve the entire state of Connecticut, with twice that population.

As hospitals purchased too many X-ray machines, the cost-plus fee-for-service reimbursement system provided every incentive to use the machines in order to pay for them. Radiation is dangerous, and exposure to it should be limited to situations in which the benefit outweighs the risk. About half the radiation a person receives comes from the air and soil. Ninety percent of the other half comes from medical and dental X-rays. Eliminating unnecessary X-rays would save $400 to $500 million per year.

President Carter was sensitive to this. On May 3, 1977, he sent me a clipping from the *Washington Post,* reporting on an Institute of Medicine recommendation to curb the use of CAT scanners, with a handwritten note: "Let's take similar action—stronger if possible—and include other devices as advisable." At a 1979 White House briefing, Carter confessed that as a member of the Sumter County, Georgia, hospital board, he was "ripping off the people" by subjecting every patient to blood tests "to rapidly defray the cost of" a new machine the hospital had bought.

The decision of a hospital to establish its own open-heart surgery unit, obstetrical department, or artificial transplant unit is too often based on prestige. This proliferation of the medical-unit arms race has not only wasted millions of dollars, it has failed to provide the highest quality of health care.

By late 1979, a study conducted by Alain Enthoven and others at Stanford University demonstrated that death rates at hospitals performing more than 200 open-heart and coronary bypass operations a year are 23 percent lower than those at hospitals performing fewer operations. If hip replacement operations were all performed in hospitals doing fifty or more each year, 32 percent of deaths resulting from those operations could be avoided. On average, teams in hospitals performing significant amounts of heart, blood vessel, hip, and prostate surgery report 25 to 41 percent fewer deaths than those at less active hospitals.

When we put it all together—the excess beds, the profligate purchasing, and the unnecessary medical procedures and days spent in hospitals—the potential savings from containing hospital costs were enormous: $53 billion from 1980 through 1984. Twenty-two billion dollars would be saved in federal government costs, including $19 billion in hard-pressed Social Security trust funds; $6 billion in state and local government costs; $15 billion for employers and $5 billion for employees in health premium payments; $6 billion in out-of-pocket payments by individuals. Over that period, hospital-cost containment would be worth .5 to 1.2 precious percentage points on the consumer price index.

With this kind of a case to make—the potential savings in Social Security taxes alone would reach $7 billion a year by 1984—in April 1977 we recommended a bill to hold hospital charges to a rate of increase one-and-a-half times that of the consumer price index, in contrast with the two-and-a-half rate then prevalent. The lid was to be temporary while we sought more fundamental changes in the reimbursement system. In March 1979, we modified our proposal, in response to hospital and industry concerns. On both occasions, we were unable to persuade the Congress to act to restrain hospital cost increases.

Why?

We ran into effective and well-bankrolled lobbying by profit-making hospitals, the American Hospital Association, the American Medical Association, and other segments of the health care industry, a powerful anti-regulatory sentiment in the Congress, and the problem of getting the American people to appreciate the financial significance of hospital-cost containment to them personally.

The very nature of the reimbursement system—with third parties like Medicare, Medicaid, and the insurance companies paying more than 90 percent of the bills—makes it extremely difficult to stir interest among individual citizens. Most Americans do not think they are paying their hospital bills since less than 10 percent of the money that goes to hospitals is paid directly by individual patients.

To counter this impression, I tried to think up an image of hospitals that everybody would understand, and that might be popular with American cartoonists. I settled on the image of obesity. I repeatedly characterized hospitals as "obese," "overweight," as unsatisfied with one helping of dessert and gorging on a whole chocolate cream pie. The media's reaction was good. Cartoonists began to pick up on the hospital cost issue, and editorial pages of major newspapers demanded action. To no avail. When I once proudly showed Lyndon Johnson a *Washington Post* editorial supporting the administration in a dispute with Mendel Rivers, the powerful House Armed Services Committee chairman, he said, "Mendel Rivers takes those editorials to South Carolina, holds them up, and runs against them. Don't waste time talking to the *Post*. Get some South Carolina constituents to attack him and support me." That was a key part of the hospital-cost containment problem. Congressmen responded to my pleas for support by saying they had not heard from any constituents to support the legislation. Nor had the small town press joined the major dailies; they took too much pride in their local hospitals. They and many influential people in the local communities simply could not accept my characterization of their hospitals as obese.

We did get through to the hospital administrators, however. Angry mail came to me and to many congressmen complaining about the legislation and Califano's characterizations of obesity. More importantly, to counter our proposal for mandatory controls, the hospitals announced a "voluntary program" to cut costs. Administrators of hospitals around the country, state health officials, and the head of one of the major hospital associations told me that for the first time hospital administrators feared legislation because of the public attention.

I had personal experience of the impact on hospital administrators. In November 1977, for the operation on my thumb, I entered a hospital in Washington, D.C., on a Thursday evening. The operation was performed on Friday and I was discharged on Saturday. Just before discharge, a young woman from the administrative office came to my room and gave me my bill. "Just mail it to my office," I said.

"Oh, no," she replied, "my boss wanted you to review it before you left."

"Why?" I asked, smiling.

She was quite serious. "I don't know why. But when my boss found out you were coming here, he said, 'My God! Of all the hospitals in Washington, why does he have to pick this one.' "

Later, my friend and former law partner Edward Bennett Williams had an operation at Georgetown University Hospital. So many doctors and administrators talked to him about me that when I visited him, he joked, "For Joe to walk into a hospital to visit me was the greatest act of courage one man ever performed for another."

The clearer the message that we were serious about cost-containment legislation, the more energy and financial resources the hospital and medical associations devoted to killing the bill. One of their most effective tactics was to tell small communities they would lose their hospital if the Congress approved the legislation. Closing a hospital, or denying a community the opportunity to build one, is politically more difficult than closing a post office or a military installation. Catholics want hospitals with obstetrical units to protect patients from abortions or sterilizations performed in nonsectarian hospitals. Rural communities want hospitals for childbirths, emergencies, and jobs; center-city minorities want hospitals for the poor. Every community wants a hospital for prestige. Members of boards of trustees of hospitals, who would never tolerate waste and inefficiency in their own businesses and who otherwise clamored for reduction in government spending, were shrewdly mobilized to urge their representatives in Congress to defeat the cost-containment bill. These board members were usually leaders in their communities with effective access to their representatives and senators.

I had an early lesson in how emotional the hospital issue was. In 1977, evangelist Oral Roberts asked to see me about a hospital and medical school he wanted to build at Oral Roberts University in Oklahoma. Because Roberts had been a law client of mine (although not on this matter), I disqualified myself. The next evening, Oklahoma Congressman Jim Jones, a colleague from the Johnson White House staff, asked urgently that I just say hello to Roberts, which I agreed to do.

Jones and Roberts arrived around 7:30 in the evening. I met them and two of Roberts's aides in my office at HEW. We sat in a circle around the coffee table. Roberts was on the sofa to my right, powerful, imposing, eloquent, and handsomely dressed. Jim Jones was next to Roberts. In other chairs around the coffee table sat Roberts's assistants and Dick Warden, whose eyes have the twinkle of Santa Claus and whose face is framed by a bushy red beard.

Roberts loosed his booming voice, steady with the single-minded purpose with which he had built the extraordinary university in Oklahoma and inspired the flock of fundamentalists who believe in him so fervently. He wanted to build his hospital and medical school, and the local planning agencies that were funded but not controlled by HEW were opposed on the grounds that there were already too many beds in the area.

When Roberts finished, I repeated my disqualification. He understood. He rose from the couch, a towering figure looking down at me. "Well, you're not disqualified from praying for us, are you?"

He asked all of us to rise and join hands. His left hand firmly clasping my right hand, the electricity of a powerful preacher gripping us all, we stood holding hands around the coffee table, our heads bowed. Oral Roberts prayed for the construction of the hospital and medical school at his university.

BY THE late 1970s, 12 percent of hospitals—almost 800—were run as profit businesses, and with cost-plus reimbursement systems, they were distinctly lucrative and rapidly growing enterprises. In addition to efforts to stir local communities to fear loss of their hospitals, the industry's lobbyists deployed their enormous economic resources.

Hospital corporations were reporting enormous increases in profits at the end of the decade: for example, Hospital Corporation of America was up 23.4 percent for 1978 over 1977; Medicore was up 25.3 percent; American Medical International was up 52.3 percent; the following year, the profits of these companies were up over 30 percent. (Indeed, shortly after I left HEW, an investment advisor urged me to put some money into for-profit hospitals. "What safer deal could you have?" he exclaimed. "No competition; payment on a cost-plus basis; the more services you render, the more money you make.")

These profits provided resources for financial contributions to key committee members in the House. When the American Medical Association's funds were added, because it feared that cost controls on physicians could not be far behind such controls on hospitals, the combined economic interests of the industry were too powerful for the Carter administration. Of the 234 House members who voted to kill the hospital-cost-containment legislation on November 15, 1979, 202 had received contributions from the American Medical Association, totaling more than $1.6 million—an average of more than $8,000 per member. Of the 50 House members who received more than twice that amount, 48 voted against the administration's bill.

The complex congressional structure provides ample opportunity for health industry forces to spend their money and defeat or shape legislation. To become law, the hospital-cost-containment bill had to clear eleven legislative hurdles: four health subcomittees (two in each house), five full committees (Senate Finance and Human Resources; House Ways and Means, Interstate and Foreign Commerce, and Rules), and the floor of the House and Senate. A victory by the hospital industry at any of these eleven points would severely hurt the bill's chances and possibly kill it. Even prior to submission to the Congress, the industry had at least three opportunities to influence the bill: at HEW, the Office of Management and Budget, and the Domestic Policy Council of the White House staff, to say nothing of the various departments and agencies who, under OMB procedures, had a right to review the bill; for example: the Justice Department for anti-trust implications; the Council of Economic Advisors for economic considerations; the Veterans Administration and Defense

Department for its relationship to their hospital systems; the Labor Department for its impact on hospital employees and unions; the Commerce Department for its impact on business.

Our effectiveness with the hospital-cost-containment bill on the House side was complicated by Carter's perceived political weakness by key House members, and a disagreement between Illinois Congressman Dan Rostenkowski and me over the best candidate to be director of the HEW regional office headquartered in Chicago. In 1977 and 1978, Rostenkowski chaired the key Health Subcommittee of the House Ways and Means Committee and was Deputy Whip of the House. He had been raised as a politician by the Daley machine in Chicago, and he was an effective legislator. He had the utmost contempt for most of Carter's staff, particularly congressional liaison Frank Moore. "Every time he comes up here he costs us votes," Rostenkowski said. He felt Chicago Democrats were not getting their fair share of patronage from Carter's staff and he disliked presidential assistant Hamilton Jordan. "He never returns a phone call, Joe," Rostenkowski would complain.

"Don't feel slighted," I would say to the Deputy Whip. "He treats you exactly as he treats most of the Cabinet." (On one occasion, when Dick Warden had difficulty getting me a five-minute meeting on a legislative matter with Senate Human Resources Chairman Harrison Williams, the Senator's head committee staffer Steve Paradise snapped, "Can you get the Chairman five minutes with Hamilton Jordan?")

The dispute over the top job in HEW's Chicago region is a classic example of the kind of incident that can have fearsome consequences on a larger stage. Like many domestic Cabinet departments, HEW is divided into ten regions. Chicago is one of the most important. There are 13,000 HEW employees in the six-state Chicago region, an area in which the Department spent $28 billion in 1977.

Rostenkowski's candidate for the regional director's job in Chicago was Deputy Mayor Kenneth Sain, a machine Democrat who performed protocol functions for Chicago Mayor Richard Daley and his immediate successor Michael Bilandic. At Rostenkowski's request, I had interviewed Sain and was unimpressed. Our check on Sain in Chicago indicated that he did not have the ability to oversee the multibillion-dollar HEW programs in the Chicago regional office. Nor did he have the talent for leadership needed to reinvigorate HEW field operations.

Because of enormous pressure from Rostenkowski, with his strategic post as chairman of the Health Subcommittee, I proposed putting Sain in the job for a year. If he performed satisfactorily, I would leave him there. If not, Sain would resign and I would be free to appoint somebody else. I was to be the sole judge of his performance. Reluctantly, Rostenkowski agreed that I might suggest this to Sain.

Sain came to my office on August 4, 1977. He listened politely, as he sat nervously still in the chair to the right of my desk. But he turned down the proposal.

I called Rostenkowski and told him I intended to appoint Chris Cohen, son of former HEW Secretary Wilbur Cohen and an ambitious, independent Chicago alderman. The Carter administration paid substantially for this decision: in Washington and in Chicago. In Washington, Rostenkowski told the American Hospital Association that he preferred to try the voluntary effort to restrain hospital costs proposed by the industry, before "falling back" to a mandatory control system such as the one Carter proposed. That meant our bill was dead in the House Ways and Means Committee. In Chicago, Kenneth Sain became a director of the Chicago Regional Transportation Authority and got the 1977–78 city snow-removal contract from Mayor Bilandic. His inept attempts to fulfill that contract resulted in the worst transportation conditions in Chicago's history. Jane Byrne rode the Sain contract to the mayoralty as she made it the central symbol of incompetence and cronyism in Bilandic's administration. Bilandic had given Sain a job over his head and had lost his own. The once effective Democratic organization in Chicago was broken.

Unable to move the hospital-cost-containment bill out of Rostenkowski's Ways and Means Health Subcommittee, we turned our efforts to the Interstate and Foreign Commerce Health Subcommittee, where we had the enthusiastic support of Chairman Paul Rogers. Rogers moved the bill through his subcommittee in October 1977. But the key House vote on hospital-cost containment in the 95th Congress came in the full House Committee on Interstate and Foreign Commerce, on Tuesday, July 18, 1978. It was on a proposal to substitute the hospital-industry-supported voluntary program for the administration's mandatory one.

For several tense days, we survived attempts by the hospital industry to gut the bill, winning most votes by ties or a margin of one. Marty Russo, a young Democratic congressman from Chicago, had been with us on every vote. But when he cast his vote for the hospital industry's substitute proposal, Dick Warden called me frantically from the committee room. "Russo has voted against us. You've got to call him right away and try to turn him around. At least ask him to make a motion to reconsider."

With Warden on one line telling me we still had time for such a motion, I called Russo on another. "The committee has already adjourned. It's too late," Russo claimed.

This guy must be covered politically in Chicago, I thought to myself as I put down the receiver. Then Paul Rogers called, tired and uncharacteristically annoyed. He had devoted enormous energy and his considerable legislative skill to moving this bill. We shared our anger and frustration. "Russo's a young Democrat from Chicago," Rogers said. "I don't think he would have done that without telling Rostenkowski. Remember, Danny was the one who was talking to him, who was supposed to deliver his vote."

Over the previous weekend, hospital association lobbyists had talked to Russo in Chicago. Russo had returned to Washington committed to vote for the industry substitute on Tuesday and thus kill the administration's bill. Others, including Warden and I, shared Rogers's suspicion that Russo had told Rostenkowski. What made it so aggravating was that if Rostenkowski did know, he had kept the Russo defection secret from Committee Chairman Paul Rogers, the President, and me.

"We're dead in the House," I told Warden. For a few moments, I wanted to call the vote to kill our bill "the Rostenkowski hospital tax of $50 billion" (a mistake I later made with Senator Talmadge in a hasty characterization of his cost-containment proposal), because that was about how much we estimated the mandatory program would have saved over five years. But Russo was a second-term Democrat and if, as we assumed, he had confided in Rostenkowski, as dean of his Chicago delegation Rostenkowski doubtless felt some obligation to honor that confidence. Moreover, I had to work with Rostenkowski on many other matters and he was already alienated from the White House. I remembered what Lyndon Johnson had told me years before: "It feels damn good to tell someone to go to hell, especially when they've beat you or screwed you. But in politics, you don't ever tell someone to go to hell unless you're sure you can send him there."

I did issue a statement calling the industry substitute "a defeat for the public interest and a victory for the special hospital interests . . . the bill is a sham." By the time I wrote my weekly report to the President three days later, I had become convinced of larger implications. "The lack of party discipline which makes legislating today so difficult was dramatically demonstrated by Representative Russo's defection from our ranks. . . . After weeks of supporting Chairman Rogers, he quietly switched his vote, without informing Rogers . . . or the administration. . . ."

We tried to pick up the pieces in the Senate, where one of our strongest supporters was Ted Kennedy. His Human Resources Committee had already reported out a bill very similar to ours. Now we needed an ally on the Senate Finance Committee.

Senator Gaylord Nelson of Wisconsin agreed to lead the fight. Although he was willing to take on Finance Committee Chairman Russell Long, Nelson did not want to be buried under Kennedy's publicity machine. The Finance Committee favored a weak bill, backed by Herman

Talmadge of Georgia and the hospital industry. With our help, Nelson developed a substitute compromise, stronger than the Talmadge bill but not as tough as the administration bill that Kennedy's committee had reported. The Nelson bill would save $34 billion over five years, at least $19 billion less than the original administration bill, but the Talmadge legislation saved little or nothing. The Nelson substitute was not adopted by the Finance Committee, but we still hoped to win approval on the floor of the Senate.

Kennedy initially balked at our support of the Nelson substitute, arguing that we should first move with his tougher bill even though it had no chance of passage. Eventually Kennedy agreed to support the Nelson compromise, but only if his bill was voted on first and if Nelson and I would work for it. While Kennedy, Nelson, and I thought any such vote was doomed to failure, we believed that offering the Kennedy bill first would give wavering senators a vote against Kennedy and Carter, and for the hospital industry. With one such vote, some senators might find it easier to vote for the Nelson compromise.

The next step was to get the bill considered on the Senate floor. Majority Leader Robert Byrd thought hospital cost containment was "a good Democratic issue," but when I met with him, he refused to schedule the bill until I could assure him there would be no Republican filibuster. I contacted Minority Leader Howard Baker. He readily agreed to oppose a filibuster and Byrd called the bill for a vote. After the Kennedy bill was defeated 69 to 18, the Nelson compromise survived a motion to table by a 42 to 47 vote, and was passed, 64 to 22. But the 95th Congress ended three days later, before we could get the compromise bill to the House floor.

In January 1979, we tried to build on the lessons of our 1978 defeat. First, we revised the hospital-cost-containment legislation. Instead of an absolute cap related to the general consumer price index, we proposed a formula determined by the cost of the market basket of goods and services a hospital bought, changes in population served, and cost of new technology adjusted for increased productivity. Nonprofessional wage increases were excepted in deference to our need for union support. Hospitals whose voluntary programs were within the mandatory ceiling and small hospitals were exempted. Less than half the hospitals in the United States would be subject to the new proposal, which accommodated every reasonable objection we thought the hospitals had expressed in opposing our original bill. (Accommodating those concerns necessarily made the legislation more complicated and played into the hands of opponents who marshaled the growing anti-regulatory sentiment against us.)

Second, the President himself became more involved. He had not given much time to the 1978 effort, but now the bill had become one of the administration's key anti-inflation measures. On March 6, 1979, the legislation went to the Congress as a top presidential priority. In a series of East and Cabinet Room meetings organized by Anne Wexler, the President met with hundreds of representatives of groups to gain their active support.

The Senate would not take on the hospital industry again until the House acted. In the House, the committee situation was reversed. Harlem Democrat Charles Rangel of New York, the new Chairman of the Health Subcommittee of the House Ways and Means Committee, brilliantly moved a strong bill—his maiden effort—through the committee. By April 25, 1979, Rangel had the bill out of his subcommittee; on July 17, 1979, the day before Carter told me he wanted my resignation, he and Al Ullman had moved legislation through the full Ways and Means Committee, and I called the action a major step toward "a $30 billion victory for the American people."

In the House Committee on Interstate and Foreign Commerce, California Congressman Henry Waxman had replaced the retired Paul Rogers as Health Subcommittee Chairman. His support for hospital-cost containment was as strong as Rogers's, but his health subcommittee was now dominated by hospital industry allies. Republican Congressman David Stockman of Michigan, an articulate opponent, used a computer terminal in his office to help him lead the fight against the Carter bill. We had no hope of success in that committee, but we thought we might have a chance on the floor. Rangel and Speaker Tip O'Neill still had some hope, however slim, until I was fired in July 1979. In postmortems, each told me that one sure effect of my firing was, as O'Neill put it, "If it ever had a chance—and that's doubtful—cost containment is dead now."

Nevertheless, Carter and the White House staff pressed for a vote in the House on November 15, 1979, over the objection of the Speaker and the Democratic leadership. In what one lawmaker called "a kamikaze mission," the administration hospital-cost-containment bill was defeated 234 to 166.

Despite the defeat, I remain convinced that some mandatory lid is essential to restrain hospital charges. In September 1980, the *New England Journal of Medicine* reported on a study of six states (Connecticut, Maryland, Massachusetts, New Jersey, New York, and Washington) that had imposed mandatory limits on hospital rate increases. Conducted from 1975 to 1978, the study found that the average annual rate of hospital-cost increases in the six states was 3 percent lower than that of the other forty-four. The three-year savings from the mandatory constraints exceeded $3 billion, with more than two-thirds of that amount coming from New York.

If all fifty states had such programs, Americans would have saved more than $6.5 billion in hospital bills during the three-year period.

THE ATTEMPT to legislate cost controls on hospitals failed. But the effort had some impact on the behavior of hospitals, and on the insurance companies that paid their bills. We pointed out that the temperature at which hospitals boiled laundry could be safely lowered and still disinfect (I presented a $1,500 award to a San Francisco HEW employee who discovered the idea), with a potential savings of millions per year in heating costs. Eliminating energy waste in hospitals would save more than $1 billion annually. As insurance companies looked harder at hospitals, they began to question and ultimately change some of their reimbursement practices. Blue Cross and several private insurers refused to reimburse for routine hospital admission tests without specific authorization by the attending physician, in an attempt to capture some of the $300 million wasted on such tests. Hospital boards began to question expenditures by administrators, and many administrators sought ways to make physicians more conscious of the costs of the tests they ordered. But until the domination of the boards of Blue Cross and Blue Shield by physicians and hospital administrators is ended, they are not likely to realize their potential to press for cost and waste reduction.

As I tried to use my administrative authority as Secretary to reduce waste and costs, each move brought a countermove from another special interest. I used the leverage of Medicare and Medicaid to encourage the prescription of lower priced generic drugs unless physicians offered a specific reason why a more expensive brand-name drug had to be used. Despite the fact that more than 90 percent of the generic drugs are manufactured by the big brand-name drug companies, the Pharmaceutical Manufacturers Association denounced the effort. The President enthusiastically supported it, however, sending me a handwritten note: "To Joe Califano. I like the Medicaid shift to generic drugs. Please expand this effort as much as possible. J. Carter."

The financial stakes in the drug industry are so high that each attempt to loosen the hammerlock of brand-name drugs is bitterly contested. When I released a list of 2,400 generic drugs that the Food and Drug Administration found medically equivalent to more costly brand-name counterparts—and limited Medicare and Medicaid reimbursement to the lower priced generic drugs—the pharmaceutical industry sued to block widespread publication of the list.

But the warriors on the other side were just as vigorous. In August 1978, I refused to turn over to a House subcommittee information on processes used by certain major drug companies to manufacture generic drugs which were on file with the FDA. Chairman John Moss, a California Democrat, and other subcommittee members suspected that manufacturing processes used by major companies for brand-name drugs and their generic counterparts were identical, and they wanted the evidence to prove it. Attorney General Griffin Bell had advised me that I would break a federal law protecting such information if I turned the material over to the subcommittee. Moss subpoenaed me to appear and the subcommittee voted to hold me in contempt of Congress for my refusal to turn over the documents disclosing the manufacturing processes, the first such citation against a Cabinet member since 1975. Eventually, I provided some information and the subcommittee dropped the citation. But being held in contempt was an uncomfortable situation, especially since two years earlier, as a private attorney, I had represented Moss and that same subcommittee in a lawsuit that successfully obtained release from the Federal Trade Commission of information about oil companies the Commission claimed was protected under a similar federal statute.

The ability to use Medicare and Medicaid to hold down costs is severely restricted without the ability to impose payment limits on the entire system. We issued regulations limiting the amounts of payments under either or both of these programs for laboratory tests, hospitals, and nursing homes. While such limits hold down federal expenditures, in a noncompetitive system like health care the providers of goods and services can increase charges to private sector patients and/or refuse to serve Medicare and Medicaid patients. In Colorado, for example, when the state held hospital-charge increases to 5 percent under Medicaid, such increases for non-Medicaid patients rose by 40 percent.

I tried to help hospitals by easing HEW's proposed fire safety code. At the prodding of Select House Committee on Aging Chairman Claude Pepper of Florida, HEW's staff had proposed several hundred pages of detailed, plank-by-plank, nail-by-nail specifications for construction and remodeling of hospitals and nursing homes. Hale Champion and I rejected the code because of the monumental additional cost it would impose on the industries affected. Instead, at an estimated savings of $1 billion from the cost of complying with the HEW staff proposal, we ordered a simple code drafted that would require hospitals and nursing homes to provide equivalent fire safety protection, but left them the flexibility to determine how. Many senior citizens groups rebelled; the issue was unresolved when I left office, but a test of our suggestion indicated that hospitals and nursing homes could exceed the prescribed safety levels at half the cost of complying with the detailed regulations, and achieve even greater savings than we estimated.

There was limited success in other areas. Under the Medicare and Medicaid laws, health care providers such as hospitals have the sole power to select the institutions to process their claims. Since millions of claims are filed under these programs each year, processing them is a multimillion-dollar business. In May 1977, Clint Murchison, the owner of the Dallas Cowboys, came by to see me. We were friendly enemies at the resplendent NFL battles between the Washington Redskins I rooted for and his Cowboys. Murchison also owned a data-processing operation, and he wanted me to open up Medicare and Medicaid claims processing to competitive bidding. We both knew the law, but I promised to try.

I used the Secretary's authority to "demonstrate" new techniques, and announced Western New York State and Illinois claims processing for competitive bidding. The results were eye-opening: in Western New York, HEW paid $3.06 to process a single Medicare claim in 1979; in 1980, after competitive bidding, it paid $1.78. In Illinois, the cost of processing a claim went from $3.26 to $1.53. Blue Cross and Blue Shield, which controlled the overwhelming percentage of Medicare claims processing, sued to block any further competitive bidding, charging that I could not use my demonstration authority to do this. In the spring of 1980, a federal court of appeals upheld my actions. Armed with evidence of such enormous overpayments, I urged that the law be amended to permit competitive bidding in all situations. The Blues effectively opposed any change in the law.

We were able to persuade the Congress to make some legislative changes, however, although always over a lot of resistance. Once a reimbursement pattern is set in the law, it creates, protects, or enriches some economic interest, and provides it with funds to lobby for the status quo or some legislative improvement. This is particularly expensive for the taxpayer where Medicare and Medicaid reimbursement is biased toward more expensive, institutional settings, such as hospitals and nursing homes. The move toward less expensive outpatient care has met resistance.

One example involves kidney dialysis. The federal government spends well over $1 billion each year to provide kidney dialysis for about 50,000 Americans. When I became Secretary, reimbursement for kidney dialysis under Medicare encouraged treatment in hospitals or freestanding clinics. At savings of about 50 percent—hundreds of millions of dollars for taxpayers—thousands of individuals could have their kidney dialysis treatment at home.

Fearing a loss of millions of dollars, the hospital and clinic-based kidney dialysis business opposed any recommendation that the law be amended to fully and conveniently reimburse for home dialysis. Their key congressional ally, Senator Herman Talmadge, chaired the Senate Finance Committee's Health Subcommittee through which any change in reimbursement would have to pass. On May 16, 1977, I invited Talmadge to breakfast in the Secretary's private dining room at HEW.

Like most Southern politicians of his generation, Talmadge is ostentatiously gracious. But like most, he is also a shrewd and canny negotiator. Politically conservative, he knows how to protect his own interests as he protects the interests of a constituent. As we talked amiably about what little ground we shared—as a private attorney I had represented Coca-Cola, one of his key corporate constituents, and we both favored vigorous efforts to end fraud and abuse in the Medicare and Medicaid programs—I remembered my negotiations with Senator John McClellan of Arkansas in 1966. Lyndon Johnson was trying to get him to report out of his committee an administration bill to create the Department of Transportation. McClellan wanted to ease the standards by which major highway construction investments would be made. Johnson sent me up to reach a compromise with him.

When I returned to the Oval Office, I reported to Johnson that I had an agreement with McClellan and described it to him. Johnson was sitting behind his desk and I was standing to his left, leaning on the cabinet that encased the API and UPI wire service ticker machines that constantly clicked away in his office. "Open your fly," Johnson ordered. I smiled, knowing he was not serious but feeling surprised nonetheless.

"Unzip your fly," he said rising from his green chair, "because there's nothing there. John McClellan just cut it off with a razor so sharp you didn't even notice it."

Johnson hit a button on his phone. "Get Senator McClellan for me."

As he was telling me what a bad bargain I had struck, McClellan got on the phone. "John," he said, "I'm calling about Joe Califano. You cut his pecker off and put it in your desk drawer. Now I'm sending him back up there to get it from you. I can't agree to any deal like that. You got to realize that the transportation system of the country needs something besides more highways in Arkansas."

Johnson spoke a while longer with McClellan and hung up. "You go back up there right now and strike a deal like the one I just described to him."

Talmadge had the same crafty way as McClellan, I thought as we breakfasted, all wrapped up in the same Southern political charm. I was wary about how to raise the kidney dialysis issue with him. Then he inadvertently gave me an opening. Puffing on his cigar, Talmadge described a painful test recently performed on him in excruciating detail.

The test was expensive and, "When the doctor finished, he told me that if the test had been done in a hospital, Medicare would have picked up the bill. Since it was done in his office, Medicare wouldn't pay the bill. That's not sensible," the Senator concluded.

"It's a lot less expensive in his office," I said.

"That's the point, Joe," Talmadge agreed.

"Mr. Chairman, that's just like the problem we have with kidney dialysis. If it's performed in a hospital or clinic, the federal government picks up the bill. It could be performed a lot less expensively at home in many, many cases. But we can't pay the full cost for home kidney dialysis unless the law is changed."

"Let me see about that," Talmadge said, his eyes squinting with caution. He was far too experienced to take on an economic interest without some checking, and he was chary about agreeing with someone whose fundamental views on health care he questioned. When I called Talmadge a few days later, he thought the change would make some sense and, with his objection withdrawn, the law was eventually amended on June 13, 1978.

We also sought to mine the potential savings in more extensive use of nurse practitioners, who can perform many of the functions of doctors at lower cost. Their profession has not grown as it should because of restrictions placed on their activities by state laws and medical associations, which define the "practice of medicine" broadly and limit it to physicians. Many health care services—from immunizations and physical examinations to simple diagnosis and treatment—can be provided by nurse practitioners. Taxpayers were denied potential economies because Medicare and Medicaid could reimburse nurse practitioners only through physicians, as part of the doctor's bill. In areas served only by nurse practitioners, there was no effective Medicare coverage. In early 1977, we proposed legislation to permit direct reimbursement of nurse practitioners in rural areas and center cities where there were severe shortages of doctors, and where often the only primary and emergency care available was provided by paramedicals. Though the American Medical Association opposed it, the Congress gave us such authority in rural areas. The AMA successfully restricted the authority to an experimental basis in inner city areas. Minorities have less political clout than farmers and rural congressmen.

A key to persuading Congress to provide additional health care benefits to the poor, particularly children and the elderly, was to demonstrate that the existing Medicare and Medicaid programs could be operated efficiently. My reorganization of Medicare and Medicaid into a single Health Care Financing Agency and the creation of the new Inspector

General office gave us an opportunity to mount major efforts to eliminate fraud, abuse, and waste in the government health programs. The effort was critical for an administration that was asking for a major expansion of Medicaid to cover child health and prenatal care and a national health plan. Since Medicare and Medicaid involved millions of transactions each month, we used computers as policemen. We followed up with selective criminal prosecutions in each state so that the publicity would help deter future offenders.

Medicare is a single program, operated by the federal government through insurance and computer companies which process claims for payment. Individual eligibility is easy to determine: all those over sixty-five years of age and all receiving Social Security disability payments. The kinds of treatment covered are uniform nationally. Less than 1 percent of Medicare funds for the elderly are erroneously spent for ineligible individuals or to pay for health care services not covered by the program.

By contrast, in 1980, Medicaid was fifty-three different health plans —one for each state (except Arizona, which had not adopted it), the District of Columbia, and the territories. Each jurisdiction set its own income level for determining eligible individuals or families. Each has wide discretion to establish which health care services will be covered, and the portion of the charge that will be reimbursed. The millions of Medicaid transactions that occur in this complex administrative environment are prone to error and abuse. Much of the waste in Medicaid is a result of its inherent complexity. Determinations of eligibility turn on such fine points that it is not possible to train thousands of individuals to administer the program with accuracy. But the potential of computers to improve payment efficiency and accuracy was enormous, and we pressed states and cities to establish sophisticated computer systems.

In 1976 and 1977, the proportion of funds paid for individuals or medical procedures not entitled to reimbursement ranged as high as 49 percent in the District of Columbia, with several states hovering around 25 percent. With the use of computers and other quality control techniques, by 1979 we were able to cut the District of Columbia's error rate to 24 percent and reduce the states' error rates to an average just below 10 percent (significant improvements, but still unacceptably high).

When a sophisticated computer system was installed in New York City late in 1978, we immediately began saving millions of dollars each month, largely by eliminating duplicate payments. Some duplicate bills were fraudulent, most were customary thirty- or sixty-day notices for unpaid bills that older billing systems had never rejected after the original bill was paid. By paying most bills within two weeks, these computer systems provided another benefit: They encouraged doctors to accept

Medicaid patients. Because payments for services for Medicaid patients are lower than for other patients and because of the increased paperwork required to recoup late payments, it had become increasingly difficult to enlist doctors to serve Medicaid patients. When we introduced the computer system with its prompt payments in New York City, we doubled in a year the number of physicians there willing to take Medicaid patients.

Our problems with Medicaid fraud were serious and led to the development in April 1977 of one of our most ingenious computer detective systems, Project Integrity. Initially we deployed Project Integrity against Medicaid doctors and pharmacists. For physicians, we identified twenty-two common medical procedures, from office visits to hysterectomies, and established an outside number of times each procedure might be performed on an individual in a year. For example, we set forty visits for a patient to a doctor's office as the outside limit. Obviously, more than one appendectomy on an individual patient was impossible. For pharmacists, we established outside limits for twenty-six commonly prescribed drugs. More than twenty-five prescriptions for Valium in a single year for one patient appeared unreasonable.

We then ran computer tapes of the Medicaid procedures for each doctor and patient and the Medicaid prescriptions for each pharmacist and customer against our outside limits. For 1976—the first year against which we deployed these computer screens—we identified more than 47,000 physicians and pharmacists who had exceeded the outside limits.

Stunned by their number, we narrowed the list down to about five hundred cases in each state. With the state usually taking the lead, we conducted an investigation to determine the circumstances surrounding the raw computer hit, and then selected the most serious cases involving twenty-five physicians and twenty-five druggists in each jurisdiction. At first it was difficult to interest U.S. attorneys and state prosecutors in pursuing doctors and pharmacists for what they regarded as very small crimes. Even when Attorney General Griffin Bell urged them to prosecute, there was little response. I decided to publicize the Project Integrity numbers in order to interest ambitious prosecutors in taking the cases, and invite some public pressure on those less interested. It had impact. By the summer of 1979, we had hundreds of cases under criminal investigation, fifty criminal indictments, and the first convictions. Eventually, we expanded the project to dentists and hospitals, and to Medicare.

One major element of our move on fraud and abuse came fortuitously. On July 31, 1978, I was interviewed on the *Good Morning, America* show by Steve Bell in Washington. David Hartman phoned me during the commercial break immediately after the interview. "We have a reporter from the *Philadelphia Daily News* coming on later to talk about an astonishing drug rip-off of the Medicaid program. Try to listen to it. You may want to do something.''

As soon as I got to my office, I watched the program. The reporter, Hoag Levins, described an incredible racket in Philadelphia: An individual with a legitimate Medicaid card goes to a physician, called a ''croaker.'' The patient signs blank forms so that the physician can fill in bogus services. The physician gives the Medicaid patient prescriptions for drugs with a high street-sale value, such as Valium and amphetamines. The Medicaid patient goes to a pharmacist, who fills the prescriptions. The patient then sells the drugs on the street. Through Medicaid, the taxpayers pay the physician for the bogus services and the pharmacist for the prescribed drugs, which the patient sells on the street. The reporter found six croakers in Philadelphia, with unexpectedly little effort, in less than eight weeks.

I called Hartman and thanked him. My preliminary investigation indicated that the situation in Philadelphia was by no means unique and I established Operation Crackdown to eliminate this fraud in several large cities, including New York and San Francisco.

While, with effective computer policing and management, the Medicare program can be run at a high level of efficiency, Medicaid is more complicated. The most sophisticated electronic and management techniques will significantly reduce the payments to ineligible patients or for ineligible procedures, but they are not likely to achieve a program with error rates as low as Medicare. Only with major legislative surgery, such as federalization or at least uniform eligibility standards for individuals and medical procedures, will Medicaid operate efficiently. A federal takeover of the financing and operation of Medicaid may find increasing political support, as in more and more states it consumes a larger share of tax dollars than welfare. By 1978, Georgia Governor George Busbee was complaining to me that ''Medicaid is driving Georgia's budget,'' and Illinois Governor James Thompson said that ''Illinois taxpayers put almost one billion dollars in Medicaid.'' In 1980, New York Senator Pat Moynihan introduced legislation to have the federal government pay a greater share of the Medicaid bill.

The use of computerization and modern management will have an impact on the health care system. But ultimate success in reorienting that system is in the hands of the doctors. Their training, motivation, attitude, and medical practices will be decisive in dealing with cost and access. Only 20 percent, roughly $45 billion, of health care payments are made to doctors. But they order 70 percent of the health care expenditures, accounting for $160 of the $230 billion Americans spent in 1980. Moreover, the intimacy and security of the doctor-patient relationship is an essential element of our health care system. It is important to preserve the confidence of patients in their doctors and changes in the health care system must command physician support if they are to be effected.

As we looked over the physician situation in 1977, I saw a dramatic change from the mid-1960s. In the Great Society years of the 1960s, we were concerned with a doctor shortage in the United States. As Medicare and Medicaid went into effect, that concern deepened. Johnson proposed legislation to provide funds to train more health professionals, particularly encouraging medical schools to produce more doctors. The American Medical Association opposed the legislation, fearing what we hoped: that more doctors would mean more competition. We viewed more doctors as essential to provide access to health care to millions of Americans, and competition as a significant by-product of training more doctors. The Congress agreed with Johnson and swiftly enacted the legislation.

The medical schools enthusiastically accepted the federal funds and enlarged the size of their classes. By early 1977, virtually no medical school in the United States could exist without federal funds. The total revenues of medical schools in 1978–79 were $4.3 billion. Of that amount, $1 billion came from the federal government in the form of research grants, funds to train doctors, and tuition, Medicare, and Medicaid payments.

When I returned to government in 1977, the physician situation was completely different from the early Johnson years. Sparked by the Great Society legislation, the number of medical school students graduated each year had almost doubled: from 8,000 in 1963, to about 15,000. As a result, and with the influx of foreign medical-school graduates, the number of physicians had increased almost 50 percent; the ratio of physicians to population had increased from 143 to 177 per 100,000. Contrary to the AMA's fears and our hopes in 1965, the more physicians, the more medical procedures were ordered, and the higher the health care costs. By 1980, the number of medical-school graduates had jumped to 19,000.

As I came to appreciate the millions of dollars that each doctor adds to the health care system, I realized the ramifications of having too many doctors. In September 1980, the Graduate Medical Education National Advisory Committee, headed by Dr. Alvin R. Tarlov of the University of Chicago's School of Medicine, concluded that unchecked, the supply of active physicians will increase to 536,000 by 1990, providing 220 doctors for each 100,000 people in this country. The result will be a substantial oversupply of physicians: an excess of 70,000. The expected entry into practice over the next ten years of 40,000 to 50,000 graduates of foreign medical schools accounts for much of the surplus. By the year 2000, there will be an estimated 630,000 physicians, 130,000 more than we will need to serve our population.

The potential oversupply of doctors is aggravated by two other characteristics of the medical profession: lopsided geographical distribution and overspecialization. One of my initial proposals to President Carter was designed to deal with the geographic maldistribution of doctors, and it revealed the sharp edges of those smiling Carter teeth to me for the first time.

In February 1977, we frenetically patched together legislative proposals to deal with the most urgent health issues. In addition to hospital-cost containment, I suggested a program to encourage doctors to practice in underserved rural areas. In early 1977, the ratio of physicians to population in rural areas was 1 to 2,000, as compared to 1 to 300 in urban areas. The discrepancy had been widening for the past fifteen years. In many rural areas no doctors were available, and the situation was continuing to deteriorate.

One factor was the wide disparity in compensation for doctors in cities and in rural areas. Metropolitan-area doctors were paid far better, sometimes twice as much or more, than were rural doctors. We hoped that by equalizing pay we could attract more doctors to serve the 25 million Americans in rural areas.

Sitting in the Oval Office on February 15, 1977, I proposed raising the Medicare and Medicaid payments of rural doctors to close the gap.

"Let me make sure I understand," Carter said. "You will pay rural doctors more money than they are now making."

"Yes, Mr. President," I responded. "Gradually, over a period of years, we'll raise fees of rural doctors to the same level as urban doctors. It's politically impossible to set fee schedules that reduce the amounts urban doctors are now charging." Carter was skeptical, so I appealed to his desire to keep his campaign commitments. "By doing this we can help fulfill your campaign promise to get more health care to rural areas."

"I don't see why we should give doctors any more money," Carter commented.

I was prepared with an example from Georgia. "In Americus, doctors at the hospital get fifteen dollars for an examination that costs at least fifty dollars in Atlanta. That big gap discourages young doctors from going to rural areas."

"No, I don't like the program." Carter shook his head. "I am opposed to any program that would pay any doctor any more money." His eyes were icy blue and steady. He was almost staring at me. "Find another way to solve the problem."

Later that year, I got an even better sense of his moral outrage about physicians. At the June 13, 1977, Cabinet meeting, I reported that I would be delivering a strong keynote address at the American Medical Association Annual Convention the following Sunday. Carter commented sharply: "AMA doctors have never done anything for the health of their patients, just for their own health. If you receive accolades at the AMA, then you'll be the first Cabinet member to change." In the speech in San Francisco, I set forth our conviction that the health care industry was too costly, virtually noncompetitive, and in need of profound reform. AMA executive director James Sammons responded heatedly after I left, and when I read the lead story in the next morning's *Washington Post* on my way to a Cabinet meeting, I thought I had gone too far. *Post* reporter Victor Cohn's article sharpened my comments about the doctors, with the headline: Califano, AMA Trade Accusations: HEW Secretary Says System Needs Profound Reforms. As the President entered the room for the Cabinet meeting, he approached me and said, "I liked what you told the AMA. Keep it up. . . . Just keep giving 'em hell. No one deserves it more than they do."

That same month, when I first reported to Carter about our Project Integrity program to root out Medicaid fraud and abuse and noted that we had identified the first physician and pharmacist targets, he wrote in the margin, "Let's prosecute some of them. J.C." Two weeks later, in response to my further report on Medicaid fraud involving pharmacists and physicians, he wrote next to "physicians," "Try to put them in jail." I subsequently learned the Georgia Medical Association had bitterly opposed Carter in Georgia and fought many of his program initiatives.

As I looked for solutions to the geographic maldistribution of doctors, I came to conclude that uniform fees would not solve the problem. More money was not likely to lure more physicians to rural areas. I studied the same problems in England, Germany, Italy, Israel, Canada, and Poland. None of those countries had been able to attract doctors to rural areas, even with bonuses, extra vacations, and special housing privileges. Only some kind of conscription worked. In the United States, only the National Health Service Corps—a program which pays medical school tuition in return for a service commitment—was getting doctors to rural areas. By late 1978, I had decided to let medical school tuitions rise (by not increasing federal capitation grants). Ultimately, most medical students would then have to apply for National Health Service Corps scholarships, thus providing a substantial pool of physicians for underserved areas.

To ease the geographic maldistribution problem, we almost tripled the size of the National Health Service Corps, from 725 to 2,100, and the number of HEW-funded community health centers, from 302 to 876. Through Medicaid demonstrations and Public Health Service programs, we worked with states and local communities to construct clinics in rural areas and mount special efforts in inner cities, such as Harlem in New York. But for the poor and particularly for minorities, there remain serious problems of lack of access as well as poverty, and they pay a frightful price. The life expectancy of a black man in the United States is only age sixty-four, below the Social Security retirement age and eight years below life expectancy for a white man. And a black woman is two times more likely than a white woman to lose her infant or her own life in childbirth.

The second factor that aggravates the maldistribution of doctors is concentration of physicians in expensive, lucrative specialties. As the specialties and subspecialties have proliferated, there has been a decline in the number of primary-care physicians who practice in pediatrics and internal and family medicine. These doctors should be the first point of contact between the patient and the health care system. They should provide as much of the health care as they can, referring the patient to more expensive specialists only when necessary.

In 1931, 94 percent of American physicians were involved in primary care. By 1975, that figure had plummeted to 38 percent, compared to 72 percent in West Germany and 60 percent in Canada—and compared to the 50 percent minimum set by the American Association of Medical Colleges. If we continue as we have, only 35 to 40 percent of new physicians will enter the primary-care fields, and the already severe distortions in our physician profile will be exacerbated. There are some indications that the trend may be turning, but not yet sufficiently to fill our needs for primary-care physicians.

Unless the trend is sharply reversed, large numbers of patients will continue to go to expensive hospital emergency rooms for primary care because they don't have access to a family physician; the health care marketplace will be even more confused as patients act as their own medical managers, referring themselves to expensive and highly sophisticated specialists for relatively routine treatment; and the entire health care delivery system will become further tilted toward the more expensive specialty end of the spectrum.

More specialists means more specialty care. The United States has twice as many surgeons per population as England and Wales, and twice the rate of elective surgery. A 1978 survey revealed that in those parts of Maine where the ratio of surgeons to population was highest, gall bladder operations were more than double the number performed in other parts of the state. Moreover, the greater the number of surgeons in the area, the higher the surgeons' fees.

In the short run, to deal with the excess surgery resulting from overspecialization, we began a campaign to encourage patients facing discretionary surgery to get a "second opinion"—to see whether a second doctor agreed with the one who recommended the operation. The program was based on the sharp reductions in surgery—up to 31 percent—experienced by private insurance companies that had tested the concept. We changed the Medicare reimbursement to pay for a second opinion, and encouraged state Medicaid programs to do the same. We even commissioned the development of a radio and television advertising campaign with Cliff Robertson to encourage patients to seek a second opinion before submitting to surgery, and to provide them with a toll-free number to call for the names of doctors in their community who would give second opinions.

The AMA strenuously opposed the campaign. AMA doctors contended that by encouraging second opinions we were undermining the confidence of people in their doctors. The results of the campaign have been mixed. Most studies have shown a decrease in surgery, but a Blue Shield survey in New York indicated an increase over the first 1,500 second-opinion cases studied.

The issue even reached into the offices of my personal physician, John Hughes. At the end of my annual physical in 1978, Dr. Hughes was about to give me the painful proctoscope examination to check for rectal cancer. As I waited, Hughes went over to pick up the proctoscope. He began to laugh, then started shaking. "What the hell's going on?" I asked. He held the proctoscope in his left hand; the fingers of his right hand held a narrow slip of paper signed by one of his partners and taped to the proctoscope. Fighting to control himself, Hughes read it: "Tell the Secretary if he wants a second opinion, I'll give it to him free." I joined in the laughter.

To increase the number of family physicians and trim the production of specialists, we proposed to change the method by which we financed medical schools. Our HEW legislative proposal was to phase out, over a period of years, the general funds we provided on a per capita student basis regardless of the medical or specialty career pursued. At the same time, we recommended increased financial support of medical schools keyed to the numbers of primary-care physicians being trained.

The explosion of specialists had been in response to federal financial incentives, as well as the lure of higher fees. If Congress changes those incentives, it will significantly influence the types of physicians produced. There are some indications of increased interest among medical students in family medicine. But until the disparity in fees between specialists and family doctors is narrowed, the financial rewards of specialization are likely to lure young physicians. As Dr. John Zawacki put it during my 1978 tour of the University of Massachusetts hospital in Worcester where the federal government is supporting innovative primary-care residencies, "If I put my hand on a woman's stomach as an internist, it is a fifteen-dollar fee; but if I do it as a gastroenterologist, it's fifty dollars."

With hospitals, we had placed our hopes to control costs and reshape wasteful practices on a legislative lid, because we saw no way for competitive or private forces to work. In dealing with physicians, however, we turned to the private sector for key components for our strategy and sought to ignite some competitive forces.

The training of medical students was critical. The medical schools hold to the university tradition of academic freedom, but they had demonstrated a special sense of responsiveness to national goals when we asked them to expand enrollments in the late 1960s. So we asked the medical schools to review their curricula and make some changes. In private meetings with key deans, and publicly at their association meeting in New Orleans in October 1978, I urged them to focus more curriculum time on alcoholism, diet, geriatric problems, drug prescription practices, mental health, and preventive care. To the extent they could prepare the family physician to recognize and treat routine mental health problems, the need for expensive psychiatric care could be avoided. The objective of the physicians should be to treat illness at the lowest possible level of specialization. Communicating that attitude to medical students is a key to eliminating unnecessary specialization. The final element I asked the medical schools to include in their teaching was to make the students conscious in every way possible of the cost of the services they ordered or performed for patients.

The major effort to inject competition into the physician sector of the health care system was through health maintenance organizations—HMOs. By June of 1977, when I spoke to the American Medical Association, Hale Champion and I were ready to launch a major program to develop health maintenance organizations.

Most doctors operate on a fee-for-service reimbursement system: They charge for services performed. The more services performed, the more fees collected. HMOs are groups of doctors who charge a fixed amount, in advance, and guarantee to provide all, or a wide range of medical services needed over a specified period, usually a year. As a result, the financial incentive is more toward preventive and outpatient care, which is less expensive. Patients of HMOs have substantially less surgery than those of fee-for-service doctors; they spend 30 percent less time in hospitals, and pay 10 to 40 percent less for health care than under standard insurance policies. Most of that difference is attributable to a greater focus on preventive care and the incentive to employ the least radical methods available. Some, of course, may be due to the healthier patient mix of many HMOs, which often have a high proportion of younger, working people as their members.

The national government had passed legislation in 1973 to encourage the development of HMOs by setting up a system of federal qualification. Under that law, if HEW "federally qualifies" an HMO for a certain area, most employers in that area are required to offer that HMO to their employees as an option (usually less expensive) to other health care coverage.

We confronted four problems facing HMOs: the coloration of "socialized medicine" that attended their early development; the need for working capital until a sufficient patient base is developed; the cumbersome, almost obstructionist regulatory burden that HEW had placed in the way of becoming a federally qualified HMO (an average application had grown to one thousand pages); and the opposition of the AMA, which had cooled the Nixon administration's original ardor for the program.

To deal with the "socialized medicine" coloration and need for capital funds, I held a conference in March 1978, attended by representatives of more than six hundred corporations and several labor unions, to explain the benefits of HMOs. The high attendance was a response to the increasing pressure on corporations to reduce health care costs. We reorganized HEW's bureaucracy to encourage HMO development. To work with the major corporations, we recruited Leo Beebe, a former corporate executive who had helped start the National Alliance of Businessmen in 1968, and Howard Veit from the Massachusetts Public Health Department. At our and others' urging, the AMA's commission on cost containment gave a limited blessing to HMOs.

Our efforts were rewarded. In 1978, the number of people in HMOs rose by 1.4 million, an 18 percent increase over 1977, by far the largest one-year increase in the seven-year history of the program. From 1977 to 1979, the number of federally qualified HMOs more than tripled. HMOs had expanded to cover 4 percent of the population. Though still a small provider compared to fee-for-service doctors, we regarded HMOs as healthy competition, far preferable to regulation. Indeed, there was some evidence, in Minneapolis–St. Paul, for example, where HMOs served about 10 percent of the population, that the fee-for-service doctors held other charges down by as much as 15 to 20 percent below comparable national averages.

IN THE coming years and decades, the elderly will provide the greatest challenge to our ability to provide health care at reasonable cost and with human dignity. Between 1980 and 2025, under our present system, the cost of Medicare and Medicaid for treating the elderly will increase tenfold—twice as fast as the rapid increases in Social Security payments.

The enormous resources directed to the health industry for the very old gives a lie to the human indignity with which they are frequently treated. Much of those billions of dollars pays for the extraordinary array of tubes and equipment that keep people alive for days, weeks, or months, often in a comatose state. Medicare for the aged has provided a multibillion-dollar market for exotic equipment to perpetuate life and for enormously expensive, long-shot, excruciatingly painful, and often dehumanizing therapies for terminal victims of cancer and other diseases. Billions of federal, state, local, and private dollars go to warehouse elderly patients in nursing homes. Many of our elderly have no other place to go, and many homes are excellent and humane, but too often we use the drug technology of Librium and Valium and the federal funds that pay for institutional care to put our elderly and our sick out of sight, mind, and conscience. At the same time our home health care system is woefully inadequate. In Sweden, for example, there is one home health aide for every 120 people; in the United States, there is one for every 5,000.

On September 19, 1978, between campaign stops with Connecticut Governor Ella Grasso during her run for re-election, we discussed the way our society treats its elderly. She was surprised at the proportion of Medicare funds spent during the last year of life. She talked of the "hospice movement" and a hospice that was being constructed in New Haven, with $1 million of HEW funds in addition to state and private contributions. "You've got to see this," she said. "It allows the dying to stay with their families and die with some dignity."

The hospice movement began in England, Grasso explained, as a movement to make as pleasant and as dignified as possible the last days or months of terminally ill patients, usually cancer victims. Rather than tie people to machines and tubes, or subject them to the more violent chemotherapies, the hospice movement provides a "hospice cocktail" of drugs to ease the pain sufficiently to permit the patient to live at home or in an institutional hospice where no home is available. In either case, the patient is able to live in dignity, conscious of his or her surroundings, capable of human communication. Most importantly, the hospice movement provides the human support necessary in such an environment—paraprofessionals trained to work with the dying, or a priest or minister. These people work with the doctor treating the patient, although most local hospices are either run by or affiliated with a physician familiar with the psychological, religious, and pharmaceutical techniques.

Grasso took me to visit the hospice team in New Haven. We then went to visit a man who was terminally ill with cancer in his home. Only Governor Grasso and I went in. We climbed up the two tiers of steps to the porch of the house. It was a typical attached row house along one of New Haven's lower-middle-class streets.

The door opened into the living room and there, directly ahead, next to the stairs, was the man. He was sixty-eight years old, a former salesman. A hospice worker was with him, helping him sit up in his hospital-style bed. His wife was in a chair in the small living room.

Ella and I sat on the couch and talked with the couple. His wife said that it was wonderful having him at home, that they could be together, talk, and watch television. It was so much better than being in a depressing hospital. Her husband had his good moments and his bad moments, she said. But together, with the help of the hospice aide, they had come to accept his approaching death and to try, with the inevitable strain, to live these last days or weeks together. His humor was good as he spoke of what this meant to him. It was so touching that tears welled up in Governor Grasso's eyes and I was physically shaken with emotion.

I realized that this simple, unsophisticated man was more comfortable in our conversation than I was. He had come to terms with the idea of dying; I had not. I was forty-seven years old, my parents were alive, and I had never come really close to someone who was dying. I had been shielded from contact with the idea of dying. I had an almost 1984 sense of our modern, enlightened society—a society that has sought to banish the idea of death as rigidly as the Victorians sought to banish the idea of sex; a society that has hidden death away, wrapped it in nervous euphemisms, tried "not to think about such things."

We stayed about fifteen minutes. Back in the car, I asked, "How can these hospice workers endure this? These nurses have the saintliness and stamina of Mother Theresa."

"It is difficult, but enormously satisfying for them," Dr. Sylvia Lack, the woman running the New Haven hospice, responded. "We give them a great deal of time off after each patient they serve dies, and we counsel them. Most are deeply religious people."

They'd have to be, I thought. I asked what HEW could do to help the hospice movement. "Reimbursement under Medicare," Dr. Lack said. "Medicare reimburses for all the expensive therapy, but does not consider hospice care as health care." I promised to look into it. Then she added, smiling gently, "And encouragement from someone in a high place."

On the plane back to Washington, I could not get the need to do something about the hospice movement out of my mind. I tried to read memos and sign letters, but finally I let my mind dwell on the events of the morning. What a society, I thought. By banishing the idea of dying, we have banished the dying to physical and emotional isolation; to denial of reality; to unnecessary psychic and physical pain. Uncomfortable with death, our ability to comfort the dying and their families is diminished.

I vowed to do what I could to help. I began to look for ways. The first annual meeting of the hospice organizations from across the United States was scheduled for October 5, 1978, at the Shoreham Hotel in Washington. I agreed to speak at the main dinner. Setting that occasion as a deadline, we looked for ways in which we could help the hospice movement. I finally decided to use the Secretary's authority to mount demonstration projects under the Medicare program. But I wanted to move gingerly. One of the strengths of the hospice movement was its genuine grass-roots inspiration. It was growing with little or no government help. Another was its need for flexibility. I did not want to smother the movement with HEW support. There were too few islands of human dignity left at the end of life to bureaucratize this one. I announced that HEW would accept applications for a limited number of hospice demonstrations. Hundreds were received from across the nation and the first twenty-six were selected in December 1979.

The experience with Ella Grasso and the New Haven hospice was still much in my mind and heart when I left on a trip to Poland, Rome, Jerusalem, and Egypt in November 1978. The trip was memorable for several reasons, but the unforgettable moment was the private meeting in the early evening of November 10, 1978, with Stefan Cardinal Wyszynski. Health Minister Marian Sliwinski had tried to prevent the meeting from taking place. But when we finally set an actual date and time for visiting the great Cardinal, the Polish government acquiesced.

It was dark as I walked past the open gates on the street up the long driveway to his residence. There were two reporters waiting outside. Inside, I was led to a room where I sat with a Polish interpreter from the American Embassy, whom I had invited to accompany me. The Cardinal's gait was halting, but his powerful human presence filled the room. His quiet voice gripped and held my attention for the hour we spent together.

What touched me most was the central point he made about health care. "There are too many machines and tubes and wires," he said. "Even with the best machines, people often die or remain sick because they have no human contact, because they do not touch other people. Man needs contact with man to be cured." I told the Cardinal that there were increasingly difficult questions in the United States about the use of machines to extend life.

"These are fundamentally moral questions," the Cardinal said, his voice echoing inner strength. "A machine saved my life some time ago, but I am still concerned about the use of machines without adequate human contact. Even when one goes to the dentist, there are too many machines. When I was in Rome some time ago, there were so many cables and wires and electric machines that I asked the dentist if he needed all of this just to fix a tooth. The dentist replied that today, everyone had such machinery. But the machinery he was using could have killed us both."

The Cardinal asked me whether the Polish doctors I had met on my trip were sensitive to individual need, "the need for one man to touch another in order to heal." I told him that the doctors who worked at the Weiss rehabilitation center I had visited realized the importance of this. Wyszynski was concerned that "too few Polish doctors understand how important human contact is."

When I gave the Cardinal the regards of President and Mrs. Carter and Mr. Brzezinski, he said he was fond of Mrs. Carter and had seen her in Poland when the President was there. He appreciated the sensitivity of the United States government in having Brzezinski and Mrs. Carter rather than the President meet with him. "It could have created a serious problem for the Polish people if the President had come."

When I stood to leave, Cardinal Wyszynski rose and graciously walked me to the door. He made clear what sermon he was preaching to me with his final words, as we stood facing each other in the dimly lit foyer: "You are the Minister of Health. When you go back home, I hope you will urge doctors in the United States to recognize how important human contact is."

Chapter V

HEALTH PROMOTION, DISEASE PREVENTION, AND ETHICS

In health, as in no other area of responsibility at HEW, I was acutely conscious that my decisions could result in life or death for individual Americans. That sobering, indeed frightening, realization was brought home within a week after I became Secretary.

On January 29, 1977, an outbreak of A-Victoria flu in a Miami nursing home forced me to decide whether to resume the swine flu immunization program. The only vaccine that offered immunization against A-Victoria flu was mixed with the swine flu vaccine. The effort to immunize the entire population against swine flu had been a debacle for the Ford administration. Before that program was suspended in December 1976, it had paralyzed and even killed Americans who simply took their government's advice to get a swine flu shot. And it left indelible scars on those most deeply involved in developing and administering the program.

In January 1976, a soldier at Fort Dix, New Jersey, died. When lab tests revealed he had contracted swine flu, Dr. David Sencer, director of HEW's Center for Disease Control in Atlanta, reported to his bosses, Assistant Secretary for Health Dr. Theodore Cooper and HEW Secretary David Mathews. Sencer also held a press conference on February 19 to announce his findings to the public. The *New York Times* reported the next day that "the possibility was raised today that the virus that caused the greatest world epidemic of influenza in modern history—the pandemic of 1918–19—may have returned."

After consulting with other scientists in an emergency meeting on March 15, 1976, Sencer handed Mathews a memo that became a gun at the head of the Secretary and his top health assistant, Cooper. The memo reminded them that half a million Americans had died during the swine flu epidemic in 1918. Immediately after the meeting, Mathews sent a memo to the White House warning of "a major flu epidemic . . . the predictions are that this virus will kill one million Americans in 1976."

Faced with that intimidating prediction, and swept away by the sense that what could not be disproven must be acted on, President Ford and the Congress set out to inoculate the entire population against swine flu. A special law was passed, funds appropriated, vaccine manufactured. The program began on October 1, 1976. More than one million people received swine flu shots in the first ten days. On October 11, three people over the age of seventy, all with cardiac ailments, died in Pittsburgh, shortly after receiving shots at the same clinic. Cooper and Sencer, believing there was no relationship between the deaths and the inoculations, pressed to continue the program but something had to be done to reassure the public. On October 14, President Ford and his family got flu shots on television and the administration blasted the press for its "body count mentality." (Jimmy Carter refused to get a swine flu shot.)

The program continued and then, in the third week of November, a physician in Minnesota reported that a patient had contracted an ascending paralysis called Guillain-Barré syndrome after receiving the swine flu shot. Subsequently HEW's Center for Disease Control found other cases of paralysis, three in Alabama, one in New Jersey, and three more in Minnesota, including one fatality. On December 16, with forty million Americans already inoculated, President Ford suspended the swine flu program pending a detailed medical assessment.

My first sense of the personal toll the decision whether or not to resume the swine flu program could take came during my meeting with Dr. Cooper on January 4, 1977. Cooper was an able official, several congressmen had asked me to keep him in his job, and he even had mild support within the Carter campaign camp. Nevertheless, I had already decided to let him leave, but on a leisurely schedule in deference to his supporters and because I didn't yet have a suitable replacement. Fifteen minutes into the meeting, I concluded that moving Cooper quickly was critical to restoring confidence in the Public Health Service. He was badly shaken by the swine flu episode, bitter over his treatment in the press, and defensive about every judgment and recommendation he had made with respect to the swine flu program. He refused to recognize the extent to which the episode had set back all immunization efforts, even those to protect against childhood diseases such as polio and rubella. I told him I intended to replace him as soon as possible. He said he would leave by January 20.

As part of the task of restoring confidence in public health immunization programs, I also decided to replace Dr. Sencer, who had directed the Center for Disease Control for more than ten years and worked there for sixteen. Hale Champion told Sencer of the decision. Sencer promptly enlisted Georgia friends of the President to bolster his position. Carter called and asked what I intended to do with David Sencer. "I plan to replace him," I responded.

Carter said that several people in Atlanta thought Sencer was first-rate. "I'm very proud of that Center in Atlanta, and I want to keep it where it is and as it is."

I told the President, "Sencer isn't running the Center well. He's largely responsible for the swine flu program, and in the last few years the immunization of children has dropped sharply. We need new leadership just to revive our immunization program, to say nothing of all the other potential of the Center."

"I would like for you to keep him there, Joe," Carter replied.

I told the President that I thought it would be a serious mistake.

"Well, it is your decision," he said finally, with obvious reluctance. "I wanted you to know there are a lot of people in Atlanta who think Sencer is a good man. But you do what you think best."

I told Jim Gaither to accelerate the job search, but it was three months before I replaced Sencer with Dr. William Foege, who was Assistant Director of the Center for Disease Control and who had been an architect of the successful program to eradicate smallpox throughout the world.

At the time I decided to replace Cooper and Sencer, I did not expect to have to make a decision soon, or at all, on the swine flu program. Sencer had recommended resumption for high-risk individuals, such as the elderly and those with chronic respiratory ailments. Cooper concurred, but had made no decision since he was leaving in a few days. There were then no reported cases of swine flu in the world.

But the outbreak of A-Victoria flu in Miami on January 29 put the decision whether to release swine flu vaccine on my desk, red-tagged for immediate action. So certain of the swine flu scenario had Cooper and Sencer been that only two formulations of vaccine had been manufactured: monovalent, the swine flu vaccine alone; and bivalent, the swine flu vaccine with A-Victorian vaccine. These vaccines had been formulated in anticipation of the arrival of these strains in the United States in the winter of 1976–77. Killer swine flu had never arrived. A-Victoria flu was not as dangerous, but the health authorities told me that it could kill and seriously injure older persons and other high-risk individuals.

On Thursday afternoon, February 3, the Center for Disease Control in Atlanta confirmed that A-Victoria flu had struck the Florida nursing home. So far no one had died, but two patients were in serious condition. Cooper was gone. Sencer had been told he would be replaced, and in any case he could not independently review his own recommendation. Dr. David Hamburg, the president of the National Academy of Sciences' Institute of Medicine, was scheduled to see me at 6:00 P.M., just after I received word of the flu outbreak. I decided to commandeer him to advise me, along with National Institutes of Health Director Donald Fredrickson (who brought along Dr. Richard M. Krause, an immunology expert and Director of the National Institute of Allergy and Infectious Diseases) and Dr. James Dickson, Cooper's deputy and Acting Assistant Secretary of Health, who was to become one of my key personal and health policy advisors. I asked Hale Champion, Eileen Shanahan, Jim Gaither, Dick Warden, Ben Heineman, and Fred Bohen to join the meeting.

We sat around the coffee table in a corner of my office for more than three hours. Fredrickson, with his crisp, almost clipped manner, put the problem: "If the A-Victoria flu spread, the risks of influenza would far exceed the risk of Guillain-Barré. On the other hand, if the A-Victoria did not spread, release of the combined vaccine could result in more paralysis and perhaps even death as a result of Guillain-Barré syndrome."

"Is there any way to separate the vaccines?" I asked.

"No."

"Manufacture A-Victoria alone in time?"

"No," Fredrickson responded. "So you see the decision you have to make."

"I see the decision I have to make," I said ruefully. Just two weeks earlier, I had been a Washington lawyer. Now I had to make a life or death decision about swine flu vaccine. I was struck by my utter lack of knowledge, an absence so profound I was concerned about my ability to ask the right questions, much less make a wise and prudent judgment.

The first step was to understand the recent past. Dickson gave a blow-by-blow description of the swine flu program. As he recounted how President Ford has been overtaken by the scientists and sat in the Cabinet Room listening to such immunization experts as Drs. Jonas Salk and Albert Sabin, I thought to myself that the new administration would not make the same mistakes: I would keep Carter out of this controversy. At the same time, I wanted the best and broadest spectrum of advice I could get, from a circle well beyond the Center for Disease Control and the experts on the Advisory Committee on Immunization Practices, who had a strong interest in promoting immunization programs and in vindicating their earlier judgments on this one. At about 10:00 P.M., I asked Hamburg and Fredrickson to put together a broad-based group that I could call in to advise me on Monday morning on the Cooper-Sencer recommendation to resume the program. Public confidence was so shaken in the decision-making process and the swine flu program that I decided the deliberations on Monday should take place in public view.

I called the President that night to tell him how I intended to handle the problem. He agreed and asked me to inform Jody Powell so he could respond to the press if any questions were asked.

Fredrickson and Hamburg worked through most of the night putting the list of names together. The next day, I called each person on their list and asked them to come to Washington early Monday morning. Everyone I spoke to agreed to serve, including the late John Knowles, the president of the Rockefeller Foundation, and Ivan Bennett, provost of the New York University Medical Center. Several doctors remarked that it was the first time their advice had been solicited since the Johnson administration.

On Monday, the group met on the eighth floor of HEW's new building. There were many reporters, and some television cameras there. Briefly I thought about having the television cameras removed, but then decided to leave them, hoping the lights and bustle would not be too much of a distraction to the conferees. I asked the advisory group to discuss whether we should release the combined swine flu and A-Victoria vaccine, the swine flu alone, or both, or neither. If we released any vaccine, I asked them to consider the circumstances under which we should encourage its use. I listened to as much of the debate as I could over the course of the day, probed the medical experts to try to get mathematical probabilities on death and disease under various alternatives, and met with the group late in the afternoon to get their recommendations.

The next day, I adopted the advisory group's recommendations: to release only the A-Victoria vaccine combined with the swine flu vaccine and to encourage only high-risk individuals to get the shots. A reporter asked what I had considered in reaching the decision. It was a pleasure to respond: "Everything I heard, you heard if you sat through the meeting."

The reaction was good. In the *New York Times,* Harry Schwartz wrote: "The government stands now where it should have stood all along: focused on high-risk individuals and poised to do more, but only if necessary.'' The *Washington Post* editorialized, ''What struck us almost as forcefully [as the decision] was the wide open way that it was made—the 'sunshine' approach, if you will.'' I hoped that we were restoring confidence in the immunization programs. From then on, we would open wide the doors to participation and encourage decision-making in public in the health area.

If the swine flu experience had lessons to teach, it was important that we learn them. I knew I would soon be facing other difficult public health questions: setting guidelines for recombinant DNA research, issuing regulations about psychosurgery and sterilization, determining whether a particular drug constituted an ''imminent hazard to the public health'' and assessing the dangers of marijuana. I asked Richard Neustadt, a professor at Harvard's Kennedy School of Government, to dissect the swine flu decision-making process in search of lessons for the future. With Dr. Harvey Fineberg of Harvard's School of Public Health, Neustadt completed a superb study in mid-1978, which provided among other things a list of questions to be asked by any decision-maker on knotty public health issues, and stressed the need for high-level policy-makers to be skeptical about experts.

Both as a matter of fairness and to help restore confidence in immunization programs, I moved to assist families of those who were paralyzed or had died as a result of the swine flu shots President Ford had encouraged ''every man, woman and child'' to get. By mid-1978, more than fourteen hundred swine flu claims alleging $775 million in damages had been filed against the government. (By September 1980, almost three thousand claims totaling $1.7 billion had been filed; ninety suits had been settled and $7 million in damages awarded.) The government-approved warning on the consent form signed prior to receiving a shot had not even mentioned Guillain-Barré syndrome. On June 20, 1978, after protracted negotiations with the Justice Department, we announced that Guillain-Barré claimants would be entitled to relief if they showed that their condition resulted from a swine flu vaccination. There would be no need to prove negligence. The only issue would be the amount of damage suffered. When I reported my decision to Carter, he wrote to the side of my memo: ''I think this is excessively lenient. Protect U. S. government within bounds of your public statement.'' I did not agree. But Justice Department attorneys seemed to share Carter's view. They began dragging their feet on the claims, displaying even more reluctance than they had exhibited during our pre-announcement discussions.

The swine flu episode left two misimpressions: that Guillain-Barré syndrome comes only from swine flu vaccination, and that flu immunization programs are not worthwhile. Actually, the Guillain-Barré syndrome can come from a variety of infections. And, for millions of Americans, immunization for flu is one of the health areas in which benefits can clearly be shown to outweigh risks. If half of the forty million high-risk persons were to be vaccinated each year for twenty years, two hundred might die as a result of vaccine-associated Guillain-Barré syndrome. During that same period, 56,000 deaths due to influenza would be averted, even if the vaccine were only 70 percent effective. This is a benefit factor of nearly 300 to 1 in terms of lives. The net financial savings as a result of this significant decrease in illness are also substantial.

In spite of this, flu immunization programs ran into opposition at the White House and from Senator Richard Schweiker, the ranking Republican on the Senate Health Subcommittee who became President Reagan's Secretary of Health and Human Services, and others in the Congress. OMB Director McIntyre, seeking to reduce spending to meet Carter's goal of balancing the budget, saw the proposed $20 million flu immunization programs as a cut that might stick. McIntyre enlisted Gilbert Omenn, an assistant to Frank Press, the President's Science and Technology Advisor, to oppose such programs for senior citizens. Omenn argued that they were not simply by reason of age a high-risk group, and, in any case, such a characterization ran counter to the administration stand against age discrimination. The argument fell before the facts that those over age sixty-five accounted for 60 percent of all excess mortality during flu epidemics, and that of the 27,000 deaths due to flu in 1976, 22,000 were persons over sixty-five. The attempts to eliminate funding also overlooked the long-term benefit of building a solid, noncrisis-oriented program to replace the annual frantic rush to get high-risk Americans flu immunizations. I wrote McIntyre that with programs like this, "We are proposing fundamental investments in a changed health system that is more rational and cost-effective."

Schweiker spearheaded an effort to hold the immunization program hostage on Capitol Hill until HEW proposed a satisfactory method of handling all immunization liability questions, for childhood disease as well as flu. But, despite Schweiker's opposition and the legacy of distrust from the swine flu program, and with the energetic help of Arkansas Senator Dale Bumpers and Tennessee Congressman Albert Gore, we did persuade the Congress to provide modest funding. We used those funds to encourage state health departments to establish regular, annual flu immunization programs in lieu of the ad hoc scramble each fall to locate and immunize the high-risk population. A sophisticated study of liability was also begun, for unless that problem was fairly solved, it would be increasingly difficult to persuade pharmaceutical companies to manufacture vaccines.

IN CONTRAST to the swine flu imbroglio, there was widespread agreement at the White House, on Capitol Hill, and within HEW on childhood immunization. When I became Secretary, only 60 percent of America's children were immunized against the basic childhood diseases: rubella, measles, polio, diphtheria, whooping cough, tetanus, and mumps. In many communities and schools, the percentage was even lower.

The childhood immunization program began the way many things began in Carter's Washington, with a phone call from the President's wife. Early in the administration, Mrs. Carter called me. She and the President had dined with Senator Dale Bumpers and his wife the night before. "Betty has some ideas about immunizing children and I would like for you to see her."

I called Mrs. Bumpers that day and she came to my office on February 18, 1977. She explained how "When Dale was governor of Arkansas, we organized everything from the National Guard to the churches and schools to get children immunized. If you get everyone going, it'll work," she said. She was delighted that I had removed David Sencer as head of CDC, because she felt he had not been effective in the childhood immunization area.

On April 6, I announced an initiative to raise the level of childhood immunizations from 60 to 90 percent by October 1979, through a campaign involving the media, federal, state, and local officials, and private organizations, and to create, as well, a permanent system for childhood immunization. The program brought out the best in HEW. We deployed every branch of the Department. All children in the Head Start Program were required to be immunized. We placed a slip in each welfare check reminding the three million mothers on welfare to make sure their eight million children were immunized. The Office of Education took advantage of the captive audience of school children by asking school officials across the country to talk to their students about immunizations. I asked each governor to enforce state laws requiring school children to be immunized. Where such laws were inadequate, we worked with governors and state legislators to change them. The commissioners of the three big television sports—Larry O'Brien of the National Basketball Association, Pete Rozelle of the National Football League, and Baseball Commissioner Bowie Kuhn—agreed to run public service ads we had produced with the *Star Wars* movie characters to encourage childhood immunization. At my request, two of the nation's most widely read newspaper writers, Dear Abby and Ann Landers, each devoted a column to the importance of childhood immunization.

Wherever I traveled, I talked about immunization statistics to put public pressure on local officials and bring these childhood diseases to the attention of young parents. Many such parents were unaware of the crippling effects of polio, or the dangers of retardation and threats to sight or hearing from measles, because, immunized themselves, they had never known them.

By the end of 1977, the number of children immunized in publicly funded programs had increased substantially for all diseases, particularly measles (by 52.8 percent) and mumps (34.8 percent). That year, 4.5 million children were vaccinated against measles in public programs, topping the previous year by more than 1.6 million. During the last three months of 1977 and the first three of 1978, the incidence of measles dropped by 65 percent compared with the same period the year before. Because our results were so heartening, on October 4, 1978, I set new goals: the elimination of indigenous measles by October 1, 1982, and the establishment of a system to provide comprehensive immunization for all newborn children.

On December 12, 1978, Mrs. Carter came to HEW to kick off the final push toward our 1979 goal. It was a festive event, and we released some new figures reflecting our accomplishments of the past nineteen months. The press coverage the next day was light, the television coverage virtually nonexistent. Rosalynn Carter remarked to me the next day, "It makes me just furious that the press never covers good news. I'm going to get some coverage on this." She expressed angry resentment about the failure of the press in general to report "Jimmy's accomplishments," but she was particularly annoyed about this success story. A couple of weeks later, Barbara Walters asked me at a party, "Did you see Mrs. Carter in my interview? She praised the childhood immunization program. She's annoyed that the press didn't cover it."

On September 28, 1979, shortly after I left HEW, Surgeon General Julius Richmond announced that HEW had reached the goal we set in April 1977 of immunizing 90 percent of the nation's children from the major preventable childhood diseases (he excepted rubella immunization which reached 89 percent in September 1980). In the first two years of our campaign, measles cases had declined 78 percent; rubella more than 43 percent, and mumps almost 30 percent. In 1979, there were no reported cases of diphtheria and tetanus among children under age fifteen. Moreover, if these efforts continue here and abroad these childhood diseases can join smallpox as diseases eradicated throughout the world by effective immunization programs.

Childhood immunization is the flagship of preventive health programs. In addition to the human illness it prevents, dollar for dollar, childhood immunization is a superb health care investment: For every dollar spent on polio vaccine, our society saves $90 in costs, the highest cost-benefit ratio of any public health program. From 1963 to 1978, this nation's investment of $189 million in polio immunization has saved almost $2 billion in health care and rehabilitation costs. There isn't much controversy about even the most aggressive attempts to immunize children against the childhood diseases. That distinguishes this program from virtually every other preventive health care measure.

FROM MY earliest analysis of the HEW health budget, I understood what Hubert Humphrey meant when he said, "We have a system of sick care in this country, not health care." Of the almost $50 billion the federal government was spending on health care in 1977, almost 96 percent was aimed at treatment; less than 4 percent—under $2 billion—was for programs to prevent disease or promote health.

In October 1976, presidential candidate Jimmy Carter made the same point. Before the American Public Health Association in Miami, he sang the praises of disease prevention: ". . . the basic need of any health care system is to care about people and to prevent disease and injury before they happen. I intend to provide the aggressive leadership that is needed to give our people a nationwide, comprehensive, effective preventive health care program, and you can depend on that."

I agreed wholeheartedly and tried to move forcefully in the preventive care field. We issued the first Surgeon General's report on Health Promotion and Disease Prevention in history, a document I hope will signal the start of a second public health revolution in America. Our nation's first public health revolution was the struggle against infectious diseases from the late nineteenth to the mid-twentieth century. We won that battle not with cures, but with sanitation programs, pasteurization of milk, a safer food supply, the development of vaccines, and mass immunization. As a result, today only 1 percent of deaths before age seventy-five are from infectious diseases. In 1900, those diseases—influenza, pneumonia, diphtheria, tuberculosis, dysentery and the like—were the leading cause of death.

Today, heart disease, stroke, and cancer account for 70 percent of all deaths, and accidents exact a fearsome toll of disability as well as death from young Americans. Victory in the struggle against these killers lies more securely in prevention than in cure. That is also the less costly way to mount a second revolution in public health. Our scientists and physicians are developing the knowledge to win. But this battle is fraught with sharp controversy and demands a commitment of political and individual will we have yet to demonstrate. Carter took rhetorical steps in the direction of mounting a health promotion and disease prevention effort. But he had so many roads to travel in domestic and foreign affairs that he had little presidential energy to spend on this one, once he came to appreciate its steep and slippery incline.

Any major health-promotion effort involves scientific and economic ingredients, financial incentives, and individual self-discipline. A cleaner environment, better drinking water, safe and nutritious food, elimination of carcinogens in food additives, and occupational health and safety standards (20 percent of cancer incidence is associated with chemicals in the work place), for example, are all worthy objectives; but achievement of each in concrete situations is likely to provoke scientific disputes and enhance or endanger specific economic interests. Changing financial incentives—such as convincing insurance companies to cover periodical physical exams, expanding reimbursement under government programs for physical rehabilitation, and paying doctors on other than a fee-for-service basis—is no task for the timid. There is a role for schools, yet introducing anti-smoking and sex-education programs in local school systems can often not be done without sharp conflict. But nowhere does controversy reach more intense levels, and nowhere is action more important, than in the area that is the key to health and the centerpiece of any health promotion and disease prevention program—personal lifestyle. Americans can do more for their own health than any doctors, any machine or hospital, by adopting healthy lifestyles, but doing so relates to a host of personal habits, such as smoking, alcohol consumption, diet, exercise, sleep, and reducing stress. In a free society, the role of government in this area is largely limited to informing and persuading people.

Moreover, even informing and persuading can become controversial when you run up against powerful financial interests, and few are more powerful than the cigarette lobby. The cigarette industry sells a product that has killed more Americans more painfully—through heart disease, lung cancer and choking to death from emphysema—than have all our wars and all our traffic accidents combined. The industry has often successfully blocked government attempts to educate our people to the life-threatening aspect of smoking.

Even though cigarettes had almost killed him, Lyndon Johnson never took on the tobacco industry. Johnson had been terribly addicted to cigarettes, but he had quit smoking after his heart attack in 1955. Still, he often told me that a day never passed when he did not want a cigarette. I remember one Sunday evening at dinner in the family quarters, when Johnson, at one end of the table, picked up a cigarette in his hand and actually put it between his lips. "Lyndon," Lady Bird said. He ignored her. "Lyndon," she repeated as she rose and walked to his end of the table, "I wish you wouldn't do that," and she took the cigarette away from him.

When I worked for Johnson and was smoking two packs of cigarettes a day myself, I once recommended that he propose legislation to ban cigarette advertising on television. He delayed acting on the recommendation while he decided the other legislative-program issues. The next day, as we were driving around his ranch together, he stopped the car when I lit a cigarette and turned toward me. "The day you quit smoking, I'll send your bill to the Congress," he said, chuckling confidently as he resumed driving.

Perhaps Johnson, who was conscious that even he could fight only a limited number of battles with special interests, did not want to add the controversy of tobacco to his overriding quest for racial justice, which was then focused in the South. For no venture into preventive health care created more controversy than my anti-smoking campaign.

When I was designated Secretary, I had never thought about smoking as a serious health issue within my responsibility (although I had quit smoking on October 21, 1975). When President-elect Carter told me at St. Simons Island in December 1976 that he wanted to move forcefully in the area of preventive care, I began to read and question experts about such programs. Invariably, they suggested a major anti-smoking campaign as a critical element of any such effort. Moreover, my interviews of candidates for the key health jobs drove home the same point. Just about every one of the two dozen top health professionals I considered for posts in the Office of the Assistant Secretary for Health urged me to mount an anti-cigarette-smoking campaign. Each insisted that such a campaign was essential to any serious preventive health care program.

By the time Dr. Julius Richmond became the Surgeon General and the Assistant Secretary for Health in July 1977, he and I had decided to issue a new Surgeon General's report on smoking in January 1979, to celebrate the fifteenth anniversary of the original report on smoking issued by Dr. Luther Terry in 1964.

Shortly after that, I asked my staff to gather the facts on smoking and health. What most disturbed me about cigarette smoking was learning that 75 percent of the adults who smoke cigarettes were addicted before they were age twenty-one. Virtually all cigarette smokers were addicted before they were twenty-five. The number of teen-age smokers had increased from 3 million to 4.5 million between 1968 and 1974 and over that period the percentage of teen-age girls who smoked had doubled. At least 100,000 children under thirteen were regular smokers. The tobacco companies were spending about $1 billion of tax deductible money annually to advertise the pleasures of smoking cigarettes and get these youngsters hooked.

How were we to mount a truly successful anti-smoking campaign against that monumental effort? Ninety percent of adult smokers want to quit. Virtually all of them at some time or other have tried. The two thrusts of any such campaign were clear—wide publicity to spur that latent desire in adults to action and a special effort aimed at encouraging the young not to smoke in the first place. There were two ways to go about the former: by a massive public education drive and by encouraging laws to prohibit or restrict smoking in public places. At the Center for Disease Control in Atlanta such a restriction had been in effect since 1973, and the Center had the lowest per capita smoking level in HEW. (In 1977, there was little proof of danger to nonsmokers being in enclosed spaces with smokers. This proof did not come until March 1980, when the *New England Journal of Medicine* published test results documenting such health risks.)

The start was bumpy. Laura Miller and Dr. Michael McGinnis, special assistants of mine, headed the smoking and health task force we established. They had recommended that we work with the Agriculture Department to phase out market supports for tobacco. Providing that we could develop a proposal to move the small tobacco farmer into other crops or work, I thought the idea had merit. The large manufacturing corporations had already diversified, in anticipation of problems with cigarettes, and I had come to suspect that small tobacco farmers existed at their sufferance—to maintain a political base in tobacco-growing states such as North Carolina. We decided to float the idea of phasing out price supports. I did so in response to a question from television correspondent Barry Serafin in June 1977.

The agricultural interests and Agriculture Secretary Bob Bergland responded immediately. Bergland, a dedicated consumer advocate, was troubled by the health implications of cigarette smoking, but he had to be sensitive to his farmer constituency. It was clear within days that only the quixotic would tilt at turning off the subsidy for tobacco farmers. The subsidy did reflect an inconsistency in government policy—paying to encourage farmers to grow tobacco while at the same time spending money to discourage smoking—but I concluded there was no hope of convincing the President, much less the Congress, to eliminate it. Moreover, as I reflected on the cigarette habit, I realized that not one person would quit or not start smoking if price supports didn't exist. The subsidy had nothing to do with any individual decision to smoke; if anything, it made cigarette smoking more expensive. I decided to stick to a highly visible anti-smoking campaign to alert the public to the dangers.

As the HEW task force prepared its list of possible components of an anti-smoking program, leaks of items on the list (many of which, such as the proposal that HEW instigate lawsuits by individuals with lung cancer against cigarette companies, I had emphatically rejected) began to appear in the press. The leaks led me to impose tight security on the development of the program. As expected, that served to heighten interest in the announcement of the program, scheduled for January 11, 1978, the fourteenth anniversary of the first Surgeon General's report on smoking and health.

As the date approached, press speculation about a hard-hitting anti-smoking program increased, and the President's White House health aide, Dr. Peter Bourne, moved to distance Carter from the effort. In November, Bourne dismayed the American Cancer Society by attacking programs that make "outcasts" of people who smoke. Addressing the Society's Ad Hoc Committee on Tobacco and Smoking Research, Bourne said, "If our behavioral research shows that a high percentage of cigarette smokers began the habit in a rejection of authority, then we must be sure that the imposition of government authority will not do more to increase their dependence rather than encourage them to quit." Echoing Tobacco Institute dogma, Bourne spoke of smoking cigarettes as a "relaxing tranquil experience which gives [some people] pleasure and relief at times of stress." To the astonishment of his audience, he asserted that "It may be that certain of the chemical breakdown products of tobacco have beneficial or mixed effects."

Most of Washington closed down during the Christmas holidays, but not the Tobacco Institute. Institute lobbyists made several attempts to obtain a copy of my speech announcing the anti-smoking program. So did White House aide Bourne. Suspicious of his motives, we refused to give it to him. He called me the evening before the speech, urging me not to mount a major anti-smoking campaign. By that time, it was too late. Earlier that same day, the Tobacco Institute held an unprecedented press conference to attack a speech that had not yet been delivered and a program that had not yet been announced. Tobacco Institute spokesmen Horace Kornegay, a former North Carolina congressman, and William Dwyer denounced me for not giving the Institute an advance text.

I worked late with my speechwriter Ervin Duggan and with Laura Miller and Peter Bell, who ran the program in its first weeks. It was that evening I settled on calling smoking "slow motion suicide" (Duggan's phrase), and designating it as "Public Health Enemy Number One." I answered the attack by the Tobacco Institute casting me as a zealot (for having quit smoking), and set forth the hard facts that cigarette smoking kills more than 320,000 Americans each year: 220,000 from heart disease,

78,000 from lung cancer, 22,000 from other cancer, and the rest from respiratory ailments such as chronic bronchitis and emphysema. I also emphasized the enormous public and private costs of smoking each year: $7 billion in health care, $18 billion in absenteeism, lost wages, and lower productivity.

My speech was to be delivered before the National Interagency Council on Smoking and Health, which included such organizations as the American Cancer Society and the Heart and Lung associations, in a small room in the Shoreham Hotel in Washington at 9:30 A.M. We had anticipated that no more than a hundred members would be present. But the Tobacco Institute attack turned the speech into a major event. When I walked in, every foot of floor space was taken.

The theory of the campaign announced in the speech was that a choice is free only if it is informed, a decision genuinely voluntary only if it is based on all the relevant information. Its key was to offset the billions of dollars for seductive advertising spent each year by the tobacco companies. There was no hope that we could approach in federal funds the investment of the tobacco industry. But we could mount an effective public education campaign through the media if we marshaled our limited federal resources, made it newsworthy and interesting, and deployed such state and local resources as teachers, doctors, nurses, and relatives of victims of lung cancer, emphysema, and heart disease.

To do this we needed to put some catalytic funds into the anti-smoking effort and establish an active organization. In 1973, Richard Nixon, in what the Public Health Service considered a sordid acknowledgment of substantial tobacco industry support, had slashed the budget of HEW's anti-smoking program and downgraded its office from Washington to Atlanta. By the time I became Secretary, there was no Office of Smoking and Health; the anti-smoking program was in a small office in Atlanta and its annual budget of $750,000 barely supported a passive National Clearinghouse on Smoking and Health. We formed an Office of Smoking and Health in Washington, named John Pinney, who had headed the National Council on Alcoholism in Washington, to direct it, and increased the education funds under its control to $12.5 million in the 1980 budget. Over thirty months, at my recommendation, the Congress more than doubled the research and education budget for HEW's anti-smoking effort—from $19.1 million to $51.5 million.

The tobacco industry did not object to increases from $17.9 million to $33.1 million in heart, lung, and cancer research, or to efforts to develop a less hazardous cigarette. The lobby did attempt to block behavioral research funds, aimed at learning why children smoke and how to encourage people to stop. For all health education and promotion, we increased the budget from $1.2 million to $18.4 million. But the strenuous resistance of the tobacco lobby succeeded in denying all Office of Education funds to inform young people about the dangers of smoking. The targets of the industry's tenacious efforts added evidence to support the indictment that cigarette companies were seducing America's young into smoking.

Tobacco politics is a hardball game. At my invitation, Pennsylvania Democratic Congressman Fred Rooney's wife, Evie Rooney, who quit smoking during the same Smokenders session I attended, sat on the stage during my speech. When a Tobacco Institute lobbyist saw her, he told her husband that he would never get another dollar from the industry. Rooney, who had received campaign contributions of several thousand dollars from tobacco interests over many years, got no contribution for his losing 1978 campaign. Governor Jim Hunt of North Carolina said that I should travel to his state to meet with some farmers to learn what tobacco meant to the state; North Carolina Democratic Congressman Charlie Rose said, "We're going to have to educate Mr. Califano with a two-by-four, not a trip."

The effectiveness of the anti-smoking campaign owed more to grass-roots involvement than budget dollars. I wrote each of the nation's sixteen thousand school superintendents, urging them to initiate smoking and health programs, asked the governors to work to pass laws restricting smoking in public places, suggested that life insurance companies lower their premiums for non-smokers (several did), and mounted special information campaigns for high-risk groups such as pregnant women, those taking birth control pills, and asbestos workers. To set an example, smoking was prohibited in public areas and conference rooms at HEW. Any worker in an enclosed area who did not smoke had the right to a smoke-free environment and could ask others not to smoke in that area. (General Services Administrator Jay Solomon issued similar government-wide regulations before he was fired.)

The political fallout from the anti-smoking effort was intense. The tobacco industry financed bumper stickers announcing "Califano is Dangerous to My Health," and there were highway billboards saying, "Califano Blows Smoke." The White House staff judged the program politically too dangerous. As always when criticizing a member of the Cabinet, the White House staff spoke anonymously, charging I had mounted the campaign without getting "political clearance" or "thinking through the political details." A "high-ranking White House aide" said, "With all the problems Carter has in North Carolina [a reference to the court order to desegregate its higher education system that HEW was enforcing], he doesn't need an anti-smoking campaign."

The President's health advisor got very much into the act. Bourne raised repeated doubts about using publicity to encourage people to quit, spoke of the "pleasure and relief" factor, and said that "the issue of tobacco goes way beyond health considerations." Subsequently, a reporter for the *Chicago Tribune* asked Bourne whether he was supposed to be giving the "other side of the administration's view on tobacco." Bourne replied, "Let's just put it this way: I knew I was speaking for the President."

Except for the North Carolina, Kentucky, and southern Virginia newspapers, the editorial comment on the anti-smoking campaign was mostly favorable. The reaction on Capitol Hill was predictable. Senator Edward Kennedy and Congressman Paul Rogers were supportive. I asked Rogers to hold a hearing before his House Health Subcommittee. "If you're willing to take that issue on so strongly, I'll certainly support you. Let's give it a real shot," he responded. Rogers's Health Subcommittee held a hearing on February 15, 1978, at which I again set forth the case against smoking and outlined our program. Representative Andrew Maguire of New Jersey proposed a stronger warning on cigarette packages: "Warning: Cigarette Smoking Is Dangerous to Your Heart and May Cause Death from Cancer, Coronary Heart Disease, Chronic Bronchitis, Pulmonary Emphysema, and other Diseases" to replace the current one ("The Surgeon General Has Determined That Cigarette Smoking Is Dangerous to Your Health"). That was one good approach. There was another: Using even more stringent language, Sweden had adopted a "fortune cookie" system with sixteen different notices rotated among cigarette packages to increase the likelihood the warnings would be consciously read.

The President's first remark to me on the campaign came in a phone conversation on February 6, 1978. Talking about my efforts to desegregate North Carolina's higher education system, Carter said, "I think your decisions on smoking and on desegregation are correct. Unfortunately, those two items hit [North Carolina Governor] Jim Hunt at the same time that he's faced with the Wilmington Ten issue. This is tough stuff for a governor, particularly a Southern one." (The Wilmington Ten were nine blacks and a white convicted of crimes in connection with a racial firebombing and sentenced to prison terms totaling 282 years after a trial widely attacked by civil rights groups. The conviction was thrown out in the federal courts in 1980.)

The suggestion of serious trouble from the White House came on February 28, seven weeks after we began the anti-smoking campaign. Carter aide Jack Watson called to report on a meeting of the President with Governor Hunt and Senator Robert Morgan of North Carolina. Watson said Hunt and Morgan had urged the President to direct me to "cool the rhetoric on the anti-smoking campaign, to stop using phrases like 'slow motion suicide,' and to stop speaking about the subject of smoking." They argued that the anti-smoking campaign could kill any chance of beating Republican Senator Jesse Helms, and could even cost the Democrats one or two seats in the upcoming congressional elections. "Particularly in North Carolina and tobacco-growing eastern Kentucky," Watson continued, "Hunt and Morgan told the President the anti-smoking campaign was devastating politically. They told the President that Jesse Helms and the Republicans are running against Califano, not the Democratic candidates."

In the course of their discussions, Watson said, Hunt and Morgan had told the President that I should go after alcohol rather than tobacco, and, alluding to the issue of desegregation of the North Carolina university system, they added: "If North Carolina sues HEW, it could cost Carter the state in the 1980 presidential election." Watson reported that Carter was noncommittal during the meeting and did point out that it was "hard for Joe to cool the rhetoric when people like the governor of Kentucky were calling for his resignation." Watson said the President wanted to talk to me personally about the meeting.

The President never mentioned his meeting with Hunt and Morgan to me. But a few days later, on March 7, 1978, I had lunch with Vice-President Mondale. Before lunch, standing near the fireplace in his office, Mondale told me he had met recently with Hunt and Morgan, as had the President. "I want to talk to you about the anti-smoking campaign," he said.

I interrupted to say that as a result of White House staff leaks about my not clearing the politics of the campaign, I was asked at each press conference whether he or the President had talked to me about the anti-smoking campaign. "It is a serious public health campaign and I don't think it makes sense for the White House to get involved at this point. So far, I have been able to deny any White House attempts to stop the campaign."

Mondale smiled and said nothing more, and we went on to the White House mess for lunch and a rather pessimistic discussion of the administration.

Ten days later, on March 17, Carter went to North Carolina to speak in Winston-Salem on defense policy, and to shore up his political image in the wake of the anti-smoking campaign and the court-ordered desegregation of the state university system. Concerned that the political staff at the White House would distort our anti-smoking campaign, I rushed a memo to the President outlining our effort. I noted that we were spending only $30 million for smoking and health (two-thirds on research, one-third on education), compared with $174 million for alcohol programs and $275 million for drug abuse programs. I gave him the basic facts on smoking by children and teen-agers.

Carter called from his plane, just before landing, to talk about the desegregation of North Carolina's higher education system. Before he hung up, I asked him if he had read my memo on smoking. He said he had. Then a few minutes later, opening his speech on defense matters at Wake Forest University, he proclaimed: "As someone who comes from a great tobacco-producing state, it is an honor for me to be here in the capital of the greatest tobacco state in the world." During this visit to North Carolina, Carter said he could understand how I—"like every Secretary before him"—felt about smoking, defended my research and education efforts, committed his administration to "a balanced campaign to protect the health of the tobacco industry," and appeared with Commerce Secretary Juanita Kreps, who was in the state to dedicate the new R. J. Reynolds tobacco company world headquarters building.

On May 1, in a private meeting with me in the Oval Office, the President made it clear that the anti-smoking program was to be an HEW/Califano effort. Carter put "the smoking program" at the top of a list of items he wanted to "keep off my desk and on your own desk." But he expressed no objection to my energetic pursuit of the program, possibly because, as he said in January 1978, "My own father did smoke four or five packs a day and he died with lung cancer, perhaps because of cigarette smoking."

Carter's concern about tobacco politics tempered his enthusiasm for preventive health care programs. As governor of Georgia, he had published a pamphlet on "Killers and Cripplers" which profiled heart disease, cancer, stroke, and other ailments in Georgia. As President, he wanted to establish a committee to plot "a national strategy to attack the major Killers and Cripplers," and recommend a preventive care program. Peter Bourne wrote Carter that it would yield "P.R. mileage for years" and cost nothing. To capitalize on Carter's interest, I suggested instead that he become visibly involved in our work on the first Surgeon General's report on Health Promotion and Disease Prevention. Carter's Georgia pamphlet never cited smoking as a cause of heart disease, stroke, or cancer, even relating urban lung cancer in that tobacco-growing state to "increased concentrations of air pollution." So I warned him that, in addition to the difficulties of trying to influence personal lifestyles, "major recommendations of any prevention program will involve a significant anti-smoking thrust; cigarette smoking is regarded as the chief culprit in heart disease [and] cancer. . . ." Carter never mentioned the Killers and Cripplers idea again.

JILL KREMENTZ

In the private study behind the Secretary's office, talking on the phone to House Speaker O'Neill about welfare reform

With Eileen Shanahan and Ben Heineman in the Secretary's conference room, preparing for the announcement of the childhood immunization program

JILL KREMENTZ

President Johnson autographed this 1968 photo: "To Joe, who puts a lot in my ears and eyes. LBJ"

THE WHITE HOUSE

THE WHITE HOUSE

A 1966 meeting in my White House office on economic problems and tax legislation. Clockwise, President Johnson, Budget Bureau Director Charles Schultze, Defense Secretary Robert McNamara, Council of Economic Advisors Chairman Gardner Ackley, Larry O'Brien's deputy, Barefoot Sanders, White House congressional relations aide Larry O'Brien, and Treasury Secretary Henry H. (Joe) Fowler

THE WHITE HOUSE

In the Oval Office, with President Carter and Hale Champion, talking about Social Security

In the Cabinet Room, briefing the President. Jack Watson (next to flag), Stuart Eizenstat (foreground), Vice-President Mondale, President Carter, and HEW Inspector General Thomas Morris (back to camera)

THE WHITE HOUSE

JILL KREMENTZ

In Senator Edward Kennedy's office, discussing the national health plan

JILL KREMENTZ

Testifying on the program to collect $1 billion in defaulted student loans

WIDE WORLD

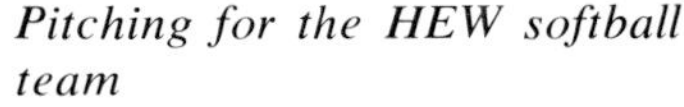

Pitching for the HEW softball team

Carter's rhetoric on preventive health care collided with tobacco politics at the Annual World Health Assembly in Geneva in May 1978. The President had sent me there, the first time any HEW Secretary had attended, to emphasize his interest in health promotion and disease prevention in the developing nations. My address focused on the President's intention to mount a global effort, particularly on childhood immunization.

After my departure from Geneva, the Saudi Arabian delegation proposed a stiff anti-smoking resolution for approval by the World Health Organization. With the exception of a prohibition against all advertising (which raised First Amendment issues and was changed at my suggestion), the Surgeon General, the remaining U.S. delegation, the State Department, and I enthusiastically supported the Saudi resolution. As cigarette consumption was being checked in industrial nations, American and Chinese cigarette companies were increasing their advertising and sales in developing nations. Several Third World health ministers had emotionally told me of their resentment and anger that the already significant rich-nation/poor-nation health gap would be aggravated by the introduction of cigarette-related diseases. I thought vigorous support of the resolution would underscore Carter's commitment to preventive health care and his desire to side with the interests of the Third World.

But the White House did not see it this way. White House political aide Anne Wexler pressed Peter Bell, HEW's Deputy Under Secretary for International Affairs, to substitute Tobacco Institute language about "*possible* harmful effects" of cigarette smoking for the Saudi proposal. Carter health aide Bourne also pressed Bell and the delegation in Geneva to soften the resolution. Wexler was concerned about the impact of supporting the resolution on U.S. tobacco interests, the re-election of Jesse Helms, and the already low standing of the administration in North Carolina. As the White House pressure mounted and the State Department told the delegation to vote against the Saudi resolution, Bell came to me. "This is incredible political intrusion into an international scientific conference," he said, distraught and angry.

"In the long run, it'll hurt, not help the President," I commented. "We won't submit the Tobacco Institute language. If necessary, I'll talk to [Secretary of State] Cy Vance or the President."

I told Bell to ignore the directive and to get Bourne to call the State Department and ease the White House pressure. "Bourne's a doctor. He can't stand public exposure of such blatant support of the tobacco interests."

Bell convinced Bourne that a vote against the Saudi resolution would do Carter more political harm than good. Bourne called the State Department. He also agreed to argue our side of the case with Hamilton Jordan's political section in the White House. But Bell and I feared he was not strong enough to counter other pressure State had received from the White House.

We had one last resort to trim the White House staff sails. We leaked to a reporter that White House staffers Wexler and Bourne were trying to put Tobacco Institute language into a Saudi resolution against smoking at the World Health Assembly, or to force the U.S. delegation to vote against it. The reporter called me later that afternoon. "There's nothing there," he said. "They strenuously deny any attempt to weaken the Saudi resolution on smoking or to get HEW to vote against it. Unless you go on the record, there's no story."

There was no need to put the charge on the record. Within half an hour, the White House pressure had subsided and we were free to support the resolution. It passed unanimously, and without any adverse domestic political implications.

Despite the White House ambivalence, there were indications that the anti-smoking program might have some impact. The response of the school superintendents was enthusiastic. Several governors, state legislatures, and county and city governments were introducing and passing clean-indoor-air acts, and some large employers were supporting anti-smoking campaigns. While I was having breakfast with Finance Committee Chairman Russell Long in the Senate dining room, Long volunteered: "I think your anti-cigarette campaign is beginning to take hold." Never without an idea, he had a theory about how to "buy out all the farmers." He said he would increase the tax on tobacco and use the receipts not for health purposes but to buy out the farmers and put them in new crops. "Not welfare," Long emphasized, "new business." He called North Carolina Senator Morgan over to our table to discuss his idea. Morgan was polite but grumpily unenthusiastic.

In early August 1978, Carter made his second of three trips to North Carolina in six months. He visited a tobacco warehouse in Wilson and spoke at a Democratic Party rally. At first the President kidded the audience about me: "I had planned today to bring Joe Califano with me, but he decided not to come. He discovered that not only is North Carolina the number-one tobacco-producing state, but that you produce more bricks than anyone in the nation as well." The crowd responded with applause mixed with laughter. "Joe Califano did encourage me to come though. He said it was time for the White House staff to start smoking something regular," an allusion to rumors of pot smoking by some members of the President's staff. The crowd loved it. The President then told the audience his family had grown tobacco in North Carolina before moving to Georgia to grow peanuts. The health program the President described, however, was hardly HEW's. As he put it, we would conduct a research plan "to make the smoking of tobacco even more safe than it is today."

When the normally mild-mannered Surgeon General Julius Richmond heard that, he immediately called me. "This is terrible. The President is either terribly ill-informed or cynically political about this." These were strong words from the most soft-spoken member of the HEW team. I told him there was nothing we could do at the moment without further embarrassing the President.

A few days later, newspaper front pages carried the results of a fourteen-year study of smoking and health financed by the tobacco companies. The headlines summarized the major conclusions: CIGARETTES ARE A MAJOR HEALTH HAZARD; SMOKING CAUSES LUNG, HEART DISEASES, MAY BE TIED TO ULCERS. So much, we all thought, for the "safer" cigarette.

Then, on August 10, the *Washington Post* carried a story headlined, SOME CIGARETTES NOW "TOLERABLE" DOCTOR SAYS. The story reported that a National Cancer Institute scientist, Dr. Gio Batta Gori, claimed that low tar and nicotine cigarettes could be called "less hazardous" and smoked in "tolerable" numbers without "appreciable" ill effects on the average smoker. Though Gori added that "The only cigarette that is safe is the cigarette that is not lit," the thrust of the story was otherwise.

Coupled with the President's comments in North Carolina, there was now a serious danger that Americans would be misinformed about the health hazards and addictive nature of cigarette smoking. The Surgeon General and the directors of the National Cancer and Heart, Lung, and Blood institutes felt they had to take public issue with the statements. "There is no known safe level of smoking any cigarette of any type," said Surgeon General Richmond. Individuals should not be misled into thinking that there was some way that "one can adjust one's smoking habits and the cigarette one smokes and thus avoid all health risks." With an eye cocked toward the White House, he concluded, "there is no data anywhere in the large body of scientific evidence on the dangers of smoking that holds out any hope that there is such a thing as a safe cigarette or safe level of smoking." In a joint statement, National Cancer Institute Director Dr. Arthur C. Upton and National Heart, Lung, and Blood Institute Director Dr. Robert I. Levy rejected "any inference that scientists now believe the use of less hazardous cigarettes may be considered 'tolerable' or safe." A report released in January 1981 indicated that users of low-tar cigarettes are somewhat less likely than other smokers to get lung cancer, but still at far greater risk than nonsmokers.

The new report of the Surgeon General on Smoking and Health was scheduled for release on Thursday, January 11, 1979. The massive, three-inch-thick book concluded that the case against cigarette smoking was "overwhelming." Indeed, the accumulation of evidence against cigarette smoking was so devastating, and the interest of government as the largest purchaser of health care so profound, that I decided to mount new and more extensive education efforts around its release. In an attempt to saturate the mass media from Thursday until Sunday, we identified anti-smoking programs in every media market for local television and radio stations and newspapers to broadcast and write about.

On Wednesday, January 10, the Tobacco Institute again attacked a report that had not been published. Again their actions raised interest in the report. This time there was a newspaper advertisement, "The Secretary of Health, Education, and Welfare invites you to a one-sided debate," before our press conference releasing the report.

On the eve of the report's release, Jody Powell called me from National Airport in Washington. "I'm headed for North Carolina to do a Democratic fundraiser tonight. Is there anything to bring me up to date on?"

"My God," I exclaimed, and told him about the release of the Surgeon General's report and the media blitz that was coming. "I don't know what you can do," I concluded.

"Smoke," Powell replied. "I'll just smoke like hell when I'm down there."

When Richmond and I walked into the press conference on the morning of January 11, the HEW auditorium was filled with more reporters and cameras than on any occasion until I was to meet the press after President Carter asked me to resign. The evening television coverage was extensive, and the next day the NBC *Today* show gave an hour to the subject and *Good Morning, America* did a forceful piece of extended coverage. Local television coverage was enormous, and so was the play in the newspapers. Only magazine coverage was moderate or light, perhaps because of the enormous amounts of cigarette advertising they carried.

The impact was stunning. A special HEW survey revealed that, in the two weeks following the release of the Surgeon General's report, more Americans tried to quit smoking than in any other two-week period since the release of the first report in 1964.

For the President, there was one unfortunate aspect of the television coverage. After reporting the case against cigarette smoking, the three networks showed footage of Carter amidst the tobacco leaves in the Wilson, North Carolina, warehouse, talking about making smoking "even more safe.'' After viewing the broadcasts, Vice-President Mondale, who never lost his wry sense of humor, called me. ''Jeez,'' he said, ''those guys in the White House really have it positioned—the President's for cancer and you're for health.''

Thereafter, we planned a year-long series of announcements and events. On April 26, I released the latest numbers on teen-age smoking: There was evidence of a decline in smoking among teen-age boys, but the increase in smoking amoung seventeen- and eighteen-year-old girls was so marked that for the first time more teen-age girls than boys smoked. I sent a letter to every seventh-grade teacher in America, asking each to start a smoking and health poster and essay contest in the classroom. We would present awards for the best.

Our survey revealed that almost four million teens and subteens were regular smokers. It also showed that children and teen-agers smoked the most heavily advertised brand—Marlboro—three times more than adults did. I wrote the chief executive officers of the major cigarette companies, asking them to devote a portion, perhaps 10 percent, of their advertising budgets to a special campaign to discourage smoking among children and teen-agers. After all, I thought, what kind of person could spend his life selling cigarettes that had been demonstrated to kill and maim millions of people? The response to my letter provided a chilling insight.

Curtis Judge, the president of Lorillard, which makes Kent and Newport, cited the fact they no longer distributed free cigarettes on college campuses as evidence the companies were not after youngsters. He never mentioned that the companies had stopped such distribution only under enormous public pressure, because their activities on college campuses had so enraged the Congress. Judge refused to do anything more.

George Weissman, board chairman of Philip Morris, which makes Marlboro, refused to use funds to urge children and teen-agers not to smoke because he did not think ''advertising is effective in altering the behavior of teen-agers in regard to the use of cigarettes.'' William Hobbs, the chief executive officer of R. J. Reynolds, which manufactures Winston and Camel, claimed that cigarette advertising played no part in encouraging teen-agers to smoke; therefore, he had no responsibility to urge them not to smoke. C. I. McCarty, of the Brown and Williamson Tobacco Corporation, which makes Kool and Raleighs, expressed no concern about addicting children and teen-agers; he was worried about whether the Department of Justice had been consulted about the antitrust aspects of mounting a public-service effort to encourage children not to smoke.

No response was more fatuous than the one from Raymond J. Mulligan, president of the Liggett Group, which sells L&M and Chesterfield cigarettes. He refused to contribute anything to a public service campaign urging children not to smoke because "the mothers and fathers of this nation, whether smokers or nonsmokers, should continue to have freedom of choice in the education and training of their children." Mulligan himself is a nonsmoker.

The anti-smoking campaign generated more political opposition than any other effort I undertook at HEW. House Speaker Tip O'Neill told me in late 1978, "You're driving the tobacco people crazy. These guys are vicious. They're out to destroy you." In April 1979, Ted Kennedy told me, "You've got to get out of the Cabinet before the election. The President can't run in North Carolina with you at HEW. He's going to have to get rid of you."

The strongest opposition came from the tobacco-state senators and representatives. Walter D. Huddleston of Kentucky and Robert Morgan of North Carolina were the most vitriolic pro-cigarette senators. On one occasion, Huddleston brought a group of senators and congressmen to meet with me in the Secretary's conference room. He wanted to smoke. As he took out a cigarette, I said, "Senator, there is no smoking in this conference room under HEW rules and regulations." Huddleston, irritated, opened his mouth to speak, but then said nothing, holding his temper as the meeting proceeded. All the senators and congressmen present argued for an end to the anti-smoking campaign. Romano (Ron) Mazzoli of Kentucky added with quiet force, "We should begin to encourage diversification of our economies and steps to protect the tobacco farmers."

Not all tobacco-state congressmen were like Huddleston and Morgan. Carl Perkins of Kentucky, the progressive chairman of the House Committee on Education and Labor, told me, "I don't agree, but I understand what you have to do about the smoking issue; you're Secretary of Health. I'll never bother you." Indeed, he often defended me to tobacco interests from his state of Kentucky, whose legislature passed a resolution in January 1978 calling for my impeachment. North Carolina Congressman Richardson Preyer, a thoughtful former judge, never attacked me personally for my actions on the smoking issue.

The anti-smoking campaign generated more mail to me than any issue I faced as Secretary, more than ten thousand letters. Fifty-four percent supported the anti-smoking campaign, 35 percent (mostly from tobacco states) opposed the campaign. The remainder were from people suggesting other anti-smoking ideas or programs. Most letters I received from North Carolina supported the anti-smoking campaign.

And the campaign had an impact. Its success was measured by a decline in per capita cigarette consumption in the United States in 1979 to its lowest level in twenty-two years and a decline in the consumption of tobacco that same year to the lowest in forty-six years. From 1977 to 1979, there was a 25 percent drop in the percentage of teen-age boys who smoked regularly, while the decline among teen-age girls was only 9 percent. There are demonstrable cultural changes in American society about smoking as well. The smoker who used to say, "Have a cigarette," now asks, "Do you mind if I smoke?" An increasing number of teen-agers—two-thirds by 1979—disapprove of smoking. No-Smoking areas abound in aircraft, trains, restaurants, and other public enclosed spaces. Children are encouraging their parents not to smoke, as my own son Joe successfully encouraged me when he asked me to quit as a present for his eleventh birthday.

THE EFFORT in health promotion also demanded initiatives in alcohol and drug abuse, exercise, diet, and other habits that are part of people's personal lifestyles.

I singled out alcoholism as Public Health Enemy Number Two, after smoking, and on May 1, 1979, we launched a program on alcohol abuse in a speech before the National Council on Alcoholism. Deaths related to problem drinking total at least 100,000 each year in the United States, without even including deaths from diseases in which alcohol is the real culprit. At least one-third of all hospital admissions are related to problem drinking, and many big-city hospitals owe 60 percent of their patient load to alcohol-related problems. The price we pay for alcohol abuse is even greater than that which we pay for cigarette smoking. Problem drinking costs American society more than $40 billion each year in lost productivity, health care, accidents, fires, social services, and the like.

Alcohol abuse is potently aggravated by the promiscuous use of drugs, particularly tranquilizers and sedatives, to ease the stress of modern life and cushion its blows to the individual spirit. Each year, Americans consume more than four billion tranquilizers and sedatives. Each day, millions of Americans take such tranquilizers as Librium and Valium. Each night, millions of Americans can't sleep without a drug; thirty-three million new or renewed prescriptions for sleeping pills were written in 1979. Getting Americans to examine the fundamental lifestyle patterns that lead to such self-abuse with drugs and alcohol is first a matter of information.

Here again, we launched an education campaign: trying to convince Americans that alcoholism is a treatable disease, to alert them to the deadly combination of tranquilizers and alcohol, and to wipe out the myth that the problem drinker is a middle-aged man headed for Skid Row like the disintegrating figure immortalized by Ray Milland in *Lost Weekend*.

The problem drinker can just as likely be a woman, often privileged, a lonely senior citizen, a clean-cut teen-ager, a famous executive or factory foreman, a community leader or clergyman, a trial lawyer who drinks for confidence, or a surgeon who refuses to admit that his drinking is getting out of control.

The attitude of the alcohol industries was in sharp contrast to that of the cigarette manufacturers as we mounted the program. The brewers and liquor and wine associations feared they would be subject to the same strong attack directed at the cigarette industry. Led by John DeLuca of the Wine Institute and Henry King of the U.S. Brewers Association, they offered to work with HEW on a major alcoholism initiative. "Men are moved by love and fear," Lyndon Johnson used to say, "and the key to persuasion is to find the right mixture of both." With the alcohol industries we seemed to have found the proper combination.

They agreed to run advertising campaigns to discourage young people from drinking (particularly beer), a critical aspect of any campaign because the number of high school students who admitted to being intoxicated at least once a month had doubled between 1966 and 1976. After I left HEW, their enthusiasm waned. But they should mount major advertising campaigns to warn the young. It is imperative for those who make such profits on liquor, wine, and beer to assume responsibility for the havoc excess consumption causes. Alcohol-related accidents are the leading cause of death in the eighteen-to-twenty-four age group, accounting for more than eight thousand; in addition more than forty thousand young people are hurt each year in drinking-and-driving accidents, many crippled for life.

From the alcohol program, I got a sense of the potential of the private sector in preventive medicine. The budget of Alcoholics Anonymous came entirely from private funds. Many alcohol-abuse programs are church-affiliated. I also noticed similarities between the work of the National Council on Alcoholism and the Cancer Society and the Heart and Lung associations in the health promotion area. By mid-1979, I realized that voluntary organizations may hold an important key to shifting Americans' emphasis to a system of health promotion and disease prevention and away from an after-the-fact, repair-oriented sick care system. In a society like ours, in which many resent the government's telling us how to lead our lives, certain preventive health programs are more acceptable coming from the private sector.

Government initiative is essential to fluoridate water systems, immunize children, keep air and water at safe levels of pollution, and take on a powerful tobacco industry. But the Scarsdale Diet and Weight Watchers are likely to accomplish more than a thousand government pronouncements about the dangers of being overweight, and privately published and promoted books on running do far more to encourage exercise than government pamphlets.

The impact of health promotion and disease prevention education efforts can be significant, at a cost far below that of treating illnesses. In 1980 as contrasted with the early 1970s, for example, Americans consumed 21 percent less milk and cheese, 28 percent less butter and 10 percent fewer eggs as they learned the importance of less fatty and cholesterol-laden diets. Over the past decade, the number of adult men and women who exercise went up 92 percent. Between 1970 and 1978, better health habits were a large part of the cause of the 20 percent decline in the death rate from heart disease and the decline in cancer mortality for those under forty-nine (except women, who are getting more lung cancer as the years of cigarette smoking take their toll).

PICKING THE occasion when government should move from informer to persuader to proscriber in preventive health care is a prickly business in a society where people prize their individual freedom to eat, drink, and live as they wish. My experience with the Food and Drug Administration bears witness. HEW's Food and Drug Administration is the government watchdog for the safety and efficacy of pharmaceutical products, medicine, and medical devices, and for the safety of food additives and much of our food supply. While I was interviewing Donald Kennedy to be FDA Commissioner in March 1977 (a job to which I subsequently appointed him), the then Acting Commissioner, Sherwin Gardner, paid an urgent call to my office. Recent Canadian tests showed that saccharin could cause cancer in mice. "Under the circumstances," Gardner said, his eyes shifting nervously, "the Delaney amendment to the basic food law requires that saccharin be taken off the market." Gardner said the FDA would announce its intention to ban saccharin the next day and that "the story was already leaking." I was disqualified from any decision about saccharin because I had worked on the issue in my private law practice, so I asked Hale Champion to take over. The FDA and Gardner moved fast, and made no attempt to neutralize the inevitable reaction. As soon as the intention to ban was announced, people responded in unprecedented numbers with unprecedented fury. The FDA announcement drew six hundred to eight hundred letters per day for weeks, 99 to 1 against, more mail to HEW than any action in the Department's history. Carter thought the decision was "senseless," and more than once he commented that he "could not understand it." On June 6, 1977, he sent me a note suggesting that instead of banning it, "Why not put 'cigarette warnings' on saccharin?'' Congress agreed. It blocked the ban and required only a warning label on products containing saccharin.

The episode prompted me to discuss the lessons of saccharin with Donald Kennedy, a distinguished biochemist, who was later to become president of Stanford. I told him that while I would defer to his scientific judgment, I must have an opportunity to review not only the FDA's major decisions, but the way they were announced and implemented.

Kennedy and Agriculture Department Assistant Secretary Carol Foreman recommended that we ban sodium nitrites—which are used as the preservatives and taste additives in about 7 percent of our food supply, including bacon, meats, fish, and virtually all cold cuts. I asked for an independent one-by-one review of the slides from the study by the scientist at the Massachusetts Institute of Technology that had found nitrites induced cancer in rats. I was not about to change the composition of or eliminate 7 percent of the nation's food supply without as much scientific care as was possible. Without nitrites as a food preservative, we ran a serious risk of deadly botulism in our food supply. The saccharin debate was still raging. The debate over cyclamates, which had been banned during Robert Finch's tour as HEW Secretary but were still used in Canada, had never ended.

If our independent study showed nitrites to be carcinogenic, Kennedy and I wanted to refine a plan for a gradual phaseout of nitrites to permit time to develop an economically viable alternative. The Attorney General, however, responding to my request for his legal opinion, found that the law provided no such flexibility. Once the determination of carcinogenicity was made, he said, the additive had to be banned immediately. This time I did not wait for the House and Senate to act. On March 30, 1979, Agriculture Secretary Bob Bergland and I asked Congress to postpone the operation of law for sufficient time to reduce the amount of nitrites in our food supply and to find an adequate substitute. In August 1980, the independent review of the MIT slides was completed. That review determined that the conclusions of the original study about the carcinogenicity of nitrites were not justified by the evidence on the slides, and found ''insufficient evidence'' to ban sodium nitrites.

Eventually, the knee-jerk operation of the Delaney amendment—which requires an immediate ban of any additive ''found to induce cancer when ingested by man or animal, or . . . found, after tests which are appropriate for the evaluation of the safety of food additives, to induce cancer in man or animal''—should be changed to permit the Secretary to weigh the health risks and benefits. Don Kennedy and I had worked on the legislative formulation of such a standard and I was preparing to make a recommendation to the Congress when I left HEW.

In the case of pharmaceuticals the legal and regulatory situation is complicated by the doctor-patient prerogatives physicians consider so precious, and by the often wrenching human tragedies involved. But the real pressure on drug administration comes from the financially interested pharmaceutical companies. In July 1977, I decided to ban phenformin, a drug then used by 350,000 diabetics that was increasingly associated with lactic acidosis, a reaction that is fatal in half the individuals it strikes. I used the Secretary's authority to ban the drug as an "imminent hazard to the public health." It was the first time the 1962 law had been invoked, yet virtually no patients or doctors complained to us. Physicians switched their patients to another insulin substitute. But the manufacturers, CIBA-GEIGY and the USV Pharmaceutical Corporation, protested the ban vigorously even though the drug was apparently responsible for up to two deaths per thousand users annually.

I did hear from patients and their relatives when terminal illness, usually from cancer, was involved. The plaintive question was: Why can't we try anything when there is no known therapy that can cure? It was an issue I faced with Laetrile. By all the science we know, Laetrile is a fool's gold for cancer victims. But for understandable reasons the frantic search by the terminally ill for a cure never ceases. As states legalized its use and judges responded to desperate cancer victims, the pressure to test Laetrile continued to build. Reluctantly, I asked Arthur Upton, the Director of the National Cancer Institute, to review the Laetrile cure cases. Doctors in Mexico and elsewhere, however, refused to give the necessary records to the Cancer Institute.

Upton himself began to feel the pressure to test Laetrile from cancer victims and even some scientists. He invited FDA head Kennedy to work with him to conduct clinical tests of Laetrile on human subjects. Among other objections, Kennedy considered such tests unethical. "To run a scientifically sound test," he explained, "you have to take the patient off every other drug. Thus, you deny the patient promising long-shot therapies that might have some chance, however slim, of working." To Kennedy, even the patient's consent did not remove the ethical objection. "It is one thing to get informed consent from a patient to test a drug we think may have some potential for cure. It's quite another when the available evidence from animal tests indicates that the drug may not be worth anything."

Upton disagreed. As long as the patient knew the risk—"and we can certainly make it clear"—Upton thought we should run the tests to put an end to the debate. "The estimate is that at least fifty thousand cancer patients in the U.S. are now taking Laetrile," he pointed out. "We have an obligation to demonstrate clearly that Laetrile is either useful or use less so the people will know." Upton argued that "There is a public health problem." He said thousands of cancer victims were spending their lifelong savings on something they know nothing about. "Shouldn't we inform them—one way or the other—and end this situation?" Upton asked. He added that the animal tests could not always be cited as 100 percent conclusory. "Mice are not men," he said.

Kennedy was concerned about setting a precedent of discarding animal tests. Such action by the FDA on Laetrile would be used by others who questioned the validity of animal tests. Kennedy expressed concern about the credibility of the FDA under such circumstances.

The Kennedy-Upton dispute broke out in the newspapers. It made no sense for two of the nation's top health officials to be involved in this kind of public dispute. It could only further confuse the public about the efficacy of Laetrile. "My decision is not to test Laetrile," I said. "So long as there is no evidence that it can effect a cure, I think Kennedy's ethical argument is right." If the situation changed, the National Cancer Institute could proceed with the tests.

But the use of Laetrile continued. By early 1980, Upton had worked out with the new FDA Commissioner, Jere Goyan, a protocol to test Laetrile. In justifying the tests, Dr. Charles Moertel of the Mayo Clinic commented that, "Laetrile has assumed proportions that no other quack medicine has assumed before."

Questions of another kind arose in connection with basic biomedical research. The government funds 90 percent of such research in the United States with more than $3 billion annually, virtually all of it at the National Institutes of Health. Only the pharmaceutical companies are in competition. And NIH has a substantial influence on them.

Dr. Donald Fredrickson had been appointed NIH Director by President Ford in the spring of 1975. He had a distinguished reputation as an administrator, and had gained international renown for his research on the role of cholesterol and other fatty substances in heart disease. During the hours of briefings on NIH and its budget, he impressed Champion and me with his articulateness, humor, and bureaucratic shrewdness. I was especially sensitive to the importance of having a scientific advisor who could speak and write English with lively clarity. His reappointment would give substance to my commitment to keep biomedical research free of any partisan politics. NIH was a research center, and I considered it my responsibility to protect it from partisan pressures, either from the Congress or the White House, particularly as we tried to open its decision-making process to wider public scrutiny.

I announced the decision to keep Fredrickson in February 1977, on my first visit to the NIH campus. The auditorium was full of doctors, scientists, and nurses in white coats, many standing in the back of the room. They cheered both the appointment and my statement that, "As far as politics is concerned, it is out of NIH." But I cautioned them that NIH was no ivory tower. "Depoliticization does not mean that scientists can be isolated from human concerns. They must still expect pressure to improve medical care and conquer diseases and do so at lower costs."

As important as freedom from partisan politics was the need to protect the institutes from control or undue influence by special interests for particular diseases, however well intentioned, and to maintain a balanced program within NIH. Nowhere was this clearer than in filling the vacancy at the top of the National Cancer Institute. The Congress enacted legislation giving the Cancer Institute special standing to send its budget directly to the President, informing the HEW Secretary at the same time. The cancer lobby had persuaded the Congress to increase the Cancer Institute's budget from $175 million in 1970 to $815 million in 1977. That 365 percent increase compared with a 98 percent increase for all the other Institutes of Health over the same period. Even in a cause as crucial as cancer research, such increases were too rapid for efficient investment in sound research, and I wanted someone with independence, who would be willing to take a hard look at the government's cancer research effort.

For director, the White House staff and Benno Schmidt, who had been appointed by Richard Nixon as Chairman of the President's Cancer Panel, pressed Dr. Arnold Brown to head the National Cancer Institute. Brown was a distinguished scientist, but immersed in the political cancer establishment. To get some flexibility, and to defuse the White House and Cancer Panel recommendations, I asked Ivan Bennett to chair a group (including Benno Schmidt) to provide me with several recommendations. Among those recommended was Arthur Upton, a soft-spoken pathologist, expert on the effects of radiation, a slight man with a mild manner but high intelligence. Besides his eminence, Upton would bring a measure of independence from the professional cancer lobby and a strong commitment to reorient the Institute's research from its obsession with therapy to a more balanced approach, with an ample commitment of resources to environmental research. I recommended him and Carter made the appointment.

With Fredrickson and Upton, and holdover scientists like Robert Levy at the Heart, Lung, and Blood Institute, and David Rall at the Environmental Health Sciences Institute, I felt we had achieved a good measure of independence. The character and intelligence of the research team would itself provide better insulation from partisan and special interest politics than I could offer.

Even so, science is too important to be left only to the scientists, so

I focused my attention on opening up the research decision-making process to the public and its informed surrogates. There was resistance, but Fredrickson agreed wholeheartedly with me, and the favorable reaction to the "sunshine" approach to the swine flu decision provided momentum.

I decided to get the word out to the interested communities that the doors were open for all sides to break long-standing logjams. The controversy over fetal and contraceptive research provided an important opportunity. McGeorge Bundy and recipients of Ford Foundation funds at the Guttmacher Institute were interested in fetal research. They carried with them the vantage of the pro-abortion and family-planning interests. Sargent and Eunice Shriver, representing the opposing Roman Catholic point of view, were also deeply engaged in this issue. Government fetal research had been held up for years because of disputes over the appropriate limits of scientific inquiry and what constitutes a human life. I invited each group to meet separately with Fredrickson and me. We reminded the Guttmacher group that there were serious moral and human rights questions, and emphasized to the Shriver group the enormous potential benefits in the area of retardation and other birth defects if such research were more vigorously pursued. We told each group we were going to call this "healthy baby research" and get away from the controversial term "fetal research." I asked both groups to put a proposed budget together. "Once you do, we will fight to get the funds." Thereafter, we got agreement on a budget and the word began to spread that the process was opening up.

Recombinant DNA research raised some of the most serious issues. The incredible work being done on the living cell and the basic life process had enormous potential for good, but entailed uncertain and monumental ethical, legal, and scientific ramifications. In 1977, the scientists approved when we set up the DNA advisory committee solely from the scientific community. But in 1978 we sparked their spirited resistance when we added a number of ethicists, clergy, lawyers, and lay persons to the committee. Fredrickson, however, saw the move as enriching the advisory group and strengthening a potential consensus on DNA research. Eventually many of the scientists who originally opposed the action appreciated some of the benefits of broad public participation.

My key effort to open up the world of NIH biomedical research to wide scrutiny was the attempt to develop, with public participation, a five-year plan to guide the allocation of research dollars. I thought that biomedical research could get some protection from the buffeting winds of partisan politics by enlisting a broader constituency. Fresh air and the sunlight of public discussion are essential to temper the forces of disease-of-the-month fashion and political influence. The explosion of the Cancer Institute budget was less a rational development of research plans, or a weighing of priorities, than a response to the access to political leaders that wealthy and politically active individuals enjoy. If we could plan research over a five-year period, providing the flexibility to shift funds in response to discoveries, unexpected breakthroughs, and serendipity, we could provide a standard against which the Congress and the executive could judge budget decisions. A measure of predictability might be assured for those involved in research. We began that process in 1978, and in early 1980 NIH published its first set of principles to guide research investment decisions over a five-year period. The harder work of putting numbers under those principles lies ahead.

A KEY element of public scrutiny for biomedical research is a full airing of the moral issues such research raises with confounding regularity. Psychosurgery, birth control, fetal research, the use of prisoners as research subjects, recombinant DNA, vital-organ transplants, and a host of other exotic research areas raise perplexing questions of ethics and human values.

My experience with family-planning programs helped focus my attention on the human and ethical questions implementing successful research can raise. The marvels of technology carry with them profound questions about the limits of government and the danger of dehumanizing health care in America, particularly as our inventiveness and technology press to dominate our delivery system. This threat struck me vividly in connection with our family-planning clinics and our treatment of the seriously ill. There is a mass-production ambience to even some of the best of our family-planning clinics and nursing homes.

Throughout the years, the pressure to deliver family-planning services to millions of young women had moved many programs, particularly large government-funded ones, in a degrading, mechanistic direction. I found visiting many family-planning clinics a depressing experience. As often as not, their clientele—many under fourteen, most of them black, often poorly educated—were treated like cattle. Even in the Grady Memorial Clinic in Atlanta, considered one of the finest, I was distressed by the way young girls were handled. Typically, a girl came to a clinic thinking she was pregnant (although most were not). She was given some forms to fill out, a brief interview, and a fifteen-minute physical examination. She awaited the results of the examination and then went to an exit interview. That interview usually lasted about fifteen minutes. If not pregnant, the girl was told about the various birth control devices—IUDs, the pill, the diaphragm, foam. The interviewer helped her choose a method and told her how to use it. The girl was asked to return in six months, sooner if she wished, and sent out with her pills or device. There was little personal counseling. There was no serious attempt to involve the parents of even the youngest clients. Many clinics were trying to interest teen-age boys in birth control, usually with little success. In cases of pregnancy, the girl was provided the customary obstetrical services.

What is needed at family-planning clinics is much more sensitive counseling, of the young girls, their boyfriends, and their parents. The federal investment in family planning is enormous—approaching $500 million in the last budget I prepared. With the leverage of that investment, we pressed to increase counseling at HEW-funded clinics. But counseling gets the government-funded programs into serious ethical issues. The programs are focused increasingly on the epidemic of teen-age pregnancy in America. One million teen-agers, one in ten, become pregnant each year; most of them keep their babies, most have more than one.

As we focused on teen-agers, our program and the regulatory process led us to seek to define the rights of the parents, the teen-ager, and the state when it comes to providing contraceptive devices to a twelve- or thirteen-year-old girl. Do the parents have a right to approve? To know? Does the thirteen-year-old have a right to privacy? Does the national government have a responsibility to enforce those rights within the family when HEW provides a half a billion dollars a year for contraceptives and family-planning clinics? Eventually, I decided to leave these questions to state law or to the local communities where clinics operated. There seemed no way any Secretary sitting in Washington could muster the wisdom to answer them in a pluralistic society.

Issues and questions such as these led me to establish an Ethics Advisory Board in the fall of 1977, chaired by Jim Gaither. A wide spectrum of opinion and experience was represented on the board, including Sissela Bok, a lecturer in medical ethics at Harvard; Father Richard McCormick; David Hamburg, from the Institute of Medicine; Jack Conway, from the United Way of America; and Maurice Lazarus, a corporate executive on the board of Massachusetts General Hospital. They joined a number of experts in obstetrics and genetics. In May 1978, I referred to the board, as a low priority, an application for funds to perform research involving human *in vitro* fertilization—the joining of sperm and ovum in a laboratory rather than within the female body, and transplantation of the embryo into the woman's womb. HEW regulations required that all such research proposals be approved personally by the Secretary.

A month later, Dr. Robert Edwards and Mr. Patrick Steptoe in England electrified the world by announcing the birth of an apparently normal child following *in vitro* fertilization. The world had its first test-tube baby, and I had one more thorny ethical problem on my desk. As Secretary, I was asked for my views almost immediately, especially since the Catholic Church had come out strongly against this kind of research. As a public official, I said my mind was open on the subject.

I began to receive moving letters from women, married and childless, who had for years yearned to have babies but could not. Some 280,000 married women who had been trying to have children might be helped by this research. It might reveal important information about normal reproductive processes, which could lead to the development of improved and ethically acceptable methods of diagnosing and preventing genetic defects. Several scientists think that an understanding of the process of cell division and growth is critical to learning what happens in abnormal cellular situations, such as cancer.

But for all the human joy successful research might hold out, there are enormous dangers. The manipulation required to develop test-tube-baby processes could create children who are severely retarded or suffer from genetic defects. The rights and responsibilities of parents, donors of eggs or sperm, research investigators, physicians, and hospitals present perplexing legal and moral issues. If a defective child resulted from such a process, legal claims and counterclaims against all involved could be imagined. The researcher might have been negligent in performing the implantation; the donor father might have withheld information about a genetic defect in his past; the mother might have smoked, drunk alcohol, or taken drugs during the pregnancy; the hospital might have mislabeled the vial containing the genetic material and the parents, therefore, received the wrong embryo. If HEW implemented a program of compensation for research-related injuries, a proposal I was actively considering, the government might have to support defective children for life.

I asked the Ethics Advisory Board to hold public hearings across the nation, to promote public discussion, and to give me its recommendations as soon as possible. The board reported in May 1979. It concluded—unanimously, to my surprise—that human *in vitro* fertilization research was ethically acceptable under certain and limited conditions, and that an embryo transfer should be attempted only with gametes obtained from married couples, in the womb of the married woman.

What haunted me more than any economic controversy during my work as Secretary of Health, was how HEW's deepening involvement in health care, delivery, and research had led to its involvement in profound moral and ethical questions, often literal questions of life and death, and how little thought we as a nation had given to this development.

It is a universal assumption among scientists, and a popular assumption among Americans generally, that all knowledge is good. But at least since the dawn of the nuclear age, we have been confronted with the uncomfortable reality that knowledge is not necessarily benign. Recent breakthroughs in biological research have stirred the kind of fears that were aroused by the revolution of physics a generation ago: that our scientists in their laboratories might be re-enacting the myth of Pandora's Box; that by their relentless exploration of the unexplored they might, however unintentionally, unleash forces of frightening potential.

At the far frontiers of biological research, scientists long ago found ways to create new molecules; now they have found ways to alter genes —to create life. Medical technology has moved into the awe-inspiring era of vital-organ transplants, some taken from dead or dying patients, and exotic technology and chemotherapy to extend life. These advances in medicine bring intellectually and morally confounding questions about when death actually occurs, whose business it is to define death, and whether such individual or society should have the right to specify when life shall no longer be sustained by extraordinary machines and chemicals. The dominating position of government in biomedical research and the billions of Medicare dollars that fund the use of life-extending equipment inevitably thrust vexing ethical questions into the arena of politics and public policy. The medical procedure of heart transplants has already prompted debate over whether it presents too expensive a bill for Medicare to pay. Other high technology procedures will face the same scrutiny. Our nation will soon face political debates on euthanasia as lacerating as those on abortion, with government once again the center of bitter controversy about what it will pay for.

When government pays the bill, it must guard against the abuse of medical procedures. To stem the widespread resort to sterilization by many doctors, particularly on poor women, I issued regulations sharply restricting funding of that procedure. All agreed that informed consent by the patient is a necessary ingredient in any decision about sterilization. But in defining informed consent, we faced such questions as whether it is possible for a minor, or a retarded or mentally incompetent adult or child, to give informed consent. Can anyone, even the spouse or parent, provide informed consent? Is there any such thing as informed consent by a young man or young woman to an irreversible procedure that goes to the essence of the life process as sterilization does? I concluded there was not, and the regulations maintained the prohibition against funding sterilization for anyone under twenty-one.

When laws fund health care that is "medically necessary" or "reasonable," in this age of need beyond resources it is unrealistic to expect the taxpayers and the government to leave those decisions solely to a doctor and patient. Not only the Congress and the executive but also the courts will get involved. While I was Secretary, a federal judge in Iowa said Medicaid did not have to fund sex change operations because they were not "medically necessary." A federal judge in Georgia ordered us to fund such operations whenever a physician found they were. Two federal courts of appeals subsequently reversed these decisions, thus funding such operations under Medicaid in Iowa, and not funding them in Georgia.

The entrance of government into the arena of moral and ethical decision-making is complicated by the blunt reality of limited resources. Limited resources sharpen the question of the extent to which it is fair to hold people responsible for their own health care before the government starts paying their bills. In an era of finite health budgets, choosing what to distribute to whom may result in life for some and death for others.

Limited resources add a moral dimension to apparently obvious judgments. All of us support the battle against cancer. But that skirts the difficult decision of what proportion of our budgets should be spent on basic research to help future generations escape the dread disease and what devoted to expensive, long-shot therapies for those now afflicted. Thanks to an effective lobby with an appealing case, the government has taken responsibility for the complete care of victims of catastrophic kidney disease with its $1 billion dialysis program. But there are other victims of other such illnesses. By what calculus of justice or mercy do we restrict their claim on limited public funds when their lives are also at stake?

Questions people once sought to have answered by prayer, issues once left for scientists to resolve in their laboratories, are now debated on the floor of Congress, by the brethren on the Supreme Court, thrown into the executive branch regulatory process, or demonstrated about under the window of the Secretary in Southwest Washington. In another age, these kinds of questions would have been fodder for Talmudic scholars, Jesuit priests, family doctors, and medical school students and professors. The peculiar and inescapable fact of the eighties is that these questions are intensely political as well.

As I reflect on my experience with the nation's health care system, I am convinced that as a matter of intellect and management, we can devise a national health care plan that the government can administer, particularly if we take advantage of the employer-employee relationship, direct the reimbursement system to reward health promotion and disease prevention, and mount massive health education efforts. Such a plan would carry the additional cost of providing proper health care to millions of Americans who do not presently have access to that care. But I believe that a well-crafted plan with the right mix of reforms in health care delivery, reimbursement incentives, and controls would cost less for each dollar of health care delivered than the present system with its rampant waste and social injustices. Indeed, I think the Carter administration proposal was a major step toward this kind of plan.

Two other nagging considerations, however, have tempered my ardor and led me to hope the private sector can do more in health care and containing costs. So long as the congressional system is as vulnerable to special-interest groups as it now is, I doubt that we have the political independence and integrity in the Congress to enact a sound national health plan. The doctors, specialists, hospitals, nurses, unions, medical equipment suppliers, pharmaceutical industry, insurance and computer companies, medical schools, and others will all demand and get significant concessions as part of any national health program. By the time they do, the resulting legislation is likely to carve in the marble of U.S. statutes many of the least effective and most costly and wasteful elements of the present system. Without substantial changes in the structure and process of the Congress, I believe that we are incapable of enacting a health plan that will serve the national interest.

The other concern that leads me to hope the private sector can do more is the ethical aspect of any national health plan. Attention is now given to the financial and administrative difficulties associated with such a law. But if our experience as a nation with federal funding of abortion provides any lessons, one surely is that federal funding of medical procedures instantly politicizes them and throws them into litigation. Ethical issues are arising in a host of other areas: psychosurgery, sterilization, the deployment of billions of taxpayer dollars for extraordinary life-extending equipment and services, the rights of terminally ill patients to try any cure—or to choose none. If the federal government funds—or mandates the funding of—most health services, it becomes the political battleground for all the ethical issues related to them. We need more experience and wisdom than we have yet displayed to learn how to cope fairly with these ethical issues in the national government of our pluralistic nation. At this stage, I believe both freedom and morality are better served by leaving these decisions to a variety of individuals, doctors, hospitals, and communities than by asking the Secretary of Health and Human Services to play Solomon.

These two considerations—the ability of the special interests to manipulate the legislative process to consolidate existing economic advantages and achieve new ones, and the difficulty of dealing with the ethical issues as national politics or in the courtroom—lead me to believe that we should move cautiously on any national health plan. This seems especially persuasive if we can maintain and increase pressure on the private sector to control health care costs.

We must, as a matter of social justice, provide health care to the millions of poor and unprotected Americans, particularly children and minorities. There are significant improvements to be made by federalizing Medicaid into a single program, opening up Medicare and Medicaid to more competition, putting a lid on hospital costs, encouraging more efficient delivery of health care services through health maintenance organizations and nurse practitioners, and moving the focus of our system from acute care to health promotion and disease prevention.

But beyond that, we may be better off as a nation giving an awakened and aroused private sector a chance to function for the next several years, perhaps under a broad mandate that employers provide a minimum level of health benefits for their employees. For every free industrial nation—Canada, England, Germany, and even socialist Sweden—has much the same problems that plague our current system. Their national health plans provide access to health care—an important objective—but their health care systems are just as expensive and profligate, and the ethical questions those systems face are no less vexing. Until we can deal with these problems, we should stop worshiping at the altar of an instant universal, mandatory, comprehensive national health plan and move instead in discrete increments to serve our most pressing health care needs, reform our reimbursement and delivery systems, and curb waste, inefficiency, and escalating costs. In the process, we can learn how better to resolve the moral and ethical issues that a government providing health care must face.

CHAPTER VI

CIVIL RIGHTS

I WAS more concerned about revitalizing HEW's civil rights role than about any other task I faced. I had witnessed the tremendous energy and commitment Lyndon Johnson brought to his assault on racism in America and his effort to provide equal opportunity for blacks and Hispanics, and I had seen what he suffered as a result. More vitriolic mail in greater quantity had arrived at the Johnson White House on civil rights issues than on the Vietnam War. The only threats to my own life came after I briefed reporters on the Fair Housing Act Johnson first sent to the Congress in 1966. City after city, North, South, East, and West, had resisted school integration. I had worked with Johnson as he called governors, and Army troops or National Guardsmen were sent to quell riots in Watts, Newark, and Detroit—and in the Nation's Capital and other cities after Martin Luther King was assassinated. And I had watched, with frustration and anger, as Nixon's Southern strategy eroded the gains of the Johnson years and interrupted the blacks' march to equality.

Like most Americans, I had been exposed to racism. I was born in Brooklyn and grew up on the border between Bedford-Stuyvesant and Crown Heights, a neighborhood that was more than 90 percent white, almost entirely Italian, Irish, and Jewish, when I was a child. We played punch ball on the street in front of my apartment and we called the one black who played with us "Snowball." But by the time I was in high school, we occasionally fought with the increasing number of black kids in the neighborhood for the right to play in the park around the Brooklyn Children's Museum. We never shared the play area in the block-square park; whoever won the fight dominated it. The day I landed on a spike of the perimeter fence in a tussle with a black my mother decided it was time to move out of the neighborhood.

Against this struggle on the street, my experience at home was quite different. In contrast to most white children in my neighborhood, I never heard my mother or father use a racial epithet. Because both my parents worked, we had a housekeeper, Mary Holly, who was black. My parents cared about her personally; she still visits them, and I see her occasionally. Although I felt antagonistic toward the blacks we engaged in the streets, my parents saved me from the infection of real hatred that has poisoned so many generations. But I was far from an activist. My concern for racial justice during my school years was limited to listening to an occasional sermon on the subject at Holy Cross College and joining the cheers for the unanimous 1954 Supreme Court decision in *Brown* v. *Board of Education* during my second year at Harvard Law School.

Later, while in the Navy Judge Advocate General's office at the Pentagon from 1955 to 1958, I was stunned to find that movie theaters in Arlington, Virginia, were still segregated. My wife and I went to some civil rights meetings and she picketed a theater on Glebe Road. I stayed home, deferring to a (probably unconstitutional) Navy regulation that prohibited military personnel from participating in demonstrations when off-duty. When I returned to New York to begin private law practice, my interest in civil rights was peripheral to my interest in the liberal Catholic movement.

It wasn't until 1962 and 1963 while I was working with Army Secretary Cyrus Vance, first as his special assistant and then as General Counsel of the Army, that I experienced the potentially glorious and sickeningly ugly sides of race relations in our nation. John Kennedy had strong commitments in the civil rights area. In response to Mississippi Governor Ross Barnett's defiance of a court order to admit James Meredith to the University of Mississippi, Kennedy dispatched federal troops to the campus. The key actors in the federal government—President Kennedy, Attorney General Robert Kennedy, Vance, Army Chief of Staff General Earle Wheeler—and all of us who worked for them knew little about handling domestic racial violence in September 1962. Partly as a result of our inexperience, death and destruction accompanied Meredith on registration day, and the Army had to station troops on the Oxford campus throughout his freshman year. (At the end of that academic year, John Doar, the top aide to Assistant Attorney General for Civil Rights Burke Marshall, and I visited the campus to see if the Army troops could then be withdrawn. White students shouted "nigger-lovers" from dormitory windows as we walked with Meredith to lunch. When we sat at a table in the dining room, students who were eating at nearby tables departed, leaving us surrounded by a ring of empty tables. That evening, the vinyl roof of Meredith's car was splattered with dozens of raw eggs.)

The drama of Meredith's enrollment and the violence on the Mississippi campus only seemed to intensify the rhetoric of the new governor of Alabama, George Wallace. At his inauguration in January 1963, Wallace noted proudly that he stood where Jefferson Davis had when he became president of the Confederate States of America. Wallace then shouted, "From this cradle of the Confederacy, this very heart of the great Anglo-Saxon Southland . . . I draw the line in the dust and toss the gauntlet before the feet of tyranny. And I say, Segregation now! Segregation tomorrow! Segregation forever!"

In June 1963, standing in front of television cameras in the doorway of the registration building at the University of Alabama, Wallace tried to bar Deputy Attorney General Nicholas Katzenbach as he accompanied Vivian Malone and James Hood, the first blacks seeking to register there. But, in the end, Wallace was not willing to risk the violence that had occurred at the University of Mississippi the year before, and also we had learned something. Instead of bringing in Army troops from outside the state, we had federalized the Alabama National Guard and they stood, Alabama citizens, obeying orders, behind Katzenbach and the two young blacks. Cy Vance, General Wheeler, and I watched and listened in the Army War Room in the Pentagon as Wallace backed down.

Two months later, in August 1963, thousands of Americans, white and black, singing hymns and civil rights songs, walked to the Lincoln Memorial in Washington, D.C., to hear Martin Luther King eloquently evoke his dream for racial justice in America. The glory of that march stirred emotions. But it did not stir the Congress until Lyndon Johnson made equal rights for blacks a non-negotiable centerpiece of his presidency, and pushed through the Civil Rights Act in 1964, the Voting Rights Act in 1965, and, in the wake of Martin Luther King's assassination, the Fair Housing Act in 1968.

Initially, the cutting edge of civil rights policy was with the Justice Department and the courts. But as cases dragged on year after year, and as its Office for Civil Rights began enforcing the new laws, HEW found itself out front, at the center of civil rights controversies. OCR had been established to make certain HEW fulfilled its responsibilities under Title VI of the Civil Rights Act of 1964, which forbids recipients of federal funds to discriminate on the basis of "race, color, or national origin." At first the efforts of the OCR were focused on education, and the original concept was to establish the Office under the Commissioner of Education, who in turn reported to the Secretary of HEW. But when I discussed that plan with President Johnson in 1965, he said the Office for Civil Rights should be free of the education bureaucracy and the school administrators, teacher unions and other lobbies the Commissioner of Education had to deal with. "It's got to be independent of them," he said. "I want the Office at the Secretary's throat, so he'll have to pay attention to civil rights."

It was still there, at the Secretary's throat, when I was sworn in more than ten years later. But it was slashing mindlessly from issue to issue, with little sense of purpose or priority, and no sense of identification with the political leadership of the administration, or loyalty to it. The years of Nixon's Southern strategy had taken a savage toll on OCR. Nixon had slowed or stopped civil rights activities across government. But he had mounted his most direct attack on civil rights where OCR was most deeply engaged, in the area of education. His particular target was school busing, the most unpopular technique to achieve elementary and secondary school desegregation. First, he ordered the Justice Department to side in court with Mississippi to delay integrating thirty-three school districts, and with other states fighting school-desegregation orders. Then, on March 16, 1972, in a nationally televised address, he proposed legislation to "call an immediate halt to all new busing orders by federal courts." Ironically precipitated by a Supreme Court opinion written by Chief Justice Warren Burger, Nixon kindled latent racism as he manipulated the concerns of white parents who, he said nodding agreement, "do not want their children bused across the city to an inferior school just to meet some social planner's concept of what is considered to be the correct racial balance or what is called 'progressive' social policy." I was appalled. If the television address went unanswered, Nixon would effectively divert attention from his dismal civil rights record by making busing appear to be the only issue. On this issue, advocates of minority rights were least likely to prevail, since Nixon was shrewdly capitalizing on the method of desegregation most feared by the white middle class, particularly in urban areas.

I had urged Johnson on prior occasions to speak out against Nixon's racial policies, to no avail. "Remember what I told you on our last night in office," he would say. "Don't criticize the President, give him a chance. There's only one pilot, and we're all on the same airplane." But that March 1972 night I remembered some other things LBJ had told me that last evening in the White House. There was a farewell buffet in the living quarters of the mansion for his immediate staff and their spouses. Johnson stood, his face inches away from mine, his right forefinger occasionally poking just below my left shoulder. He kidded me about the memos I had sent out to start new federal programs. "It's too late to get them back," he said. "Nixon is going to accuse you of being the socialist in the White House." Then he became serious. He talked about Nixon during the McCarthy years, reminiscing as he occasionally did of Helen Gahagan Douglas, the actress and congresswoman whom Nixon defeated for the Senate in 1950 by viciously (and falsely) questioning her patriotism and suggesting that she was a communist. "She was a fine woman," Johnson said sadly, "and he destroyed her."

Then Johnson looked at me, almost eyeball-to-eyeball. "Let me give you two pieces of advice. You're going to make some money now for the first time in your life. First, invest it in land. This Nixon knows nothing about the economy and it's going to go to hell. Second, when you pay your income taxes after you figure them all out, pay an additional five hundred dollars. It's not enough for Nixon to win. He's going to have to put some people in jail."

I'd never forgotten that moment, and I rolled it over in my mind as I thought about the cynical address Nixon had just delivered. Pacing in my basement room, I finally decided, though it was near midnight Eastern time, to call Johnson again. He might just be distressed enough to respond this time. I got through right away. Johnson also had watched Nixon on television. I argued that unless Nixon was brought up short on the civil rights issue, he might get the country angry enough to start repealing some of the civil rights legislation we had all worked so hard to pass. I urged Johnson to come out swinging on the civil rights issue this time. He listened, noncommittally, but there was no lecture about only one pilot for our plane, and he talked of the civil rights acts as among his greatest legacies. There were moments during our conversation when I thought Johnson was enraged. But when he ended it with a tired "thank you," I thought I had failed to persuade him. For the next several days, I despaired of his speaking out.

On April 5, while I was at the Homestead, a Virginia resort hotel, on a four-day vacation, a Johnson aide called. The former President was to speak at Tulane University on April 19 and would like to say something along the lines I had suggested to him on March 16. Would I do a draft? I was so excited that we left the Homestead the next day, but before we reached Washington, where I planned to draft the speech, a bulletin came over the radio: Johnson had suffered a heart attack while visiting his daughter Lynda and her husband, Chuck Robb, in Charlottesville, Virginia. Johnson survived, but the occasion was missed, and for months I rued the fact that fate had denied him a chance to deliver that speech.

When I looked over the situation in OCR in early 1977, I regretted even more that Johnson had not attacked Nixon for pandering to the feelings of racism that still plague the nation. For what Nixon had preached to the people, he had practiced at OCR. From the time he became President that Office began to deteriorate. What attempts HEW Secretaries Robert Finch and Elliot Richardson made in the civil rights area failed in the face of Nixon's determination to reverse Johnson's aggressive pursuit of racial justice. Demoralized because it was prevented from fulfilling its congressionally mandated mission, the Office was no place for the bright, ambitious young lawyers who had lent it prodigious energies under Johnson and HEW Secretary John Gardner. Nixon's first OCR Director, Leon Panetta, resigned in protest in 1969 (Panetta later was elected to Congress from California). Although many dedicated workers remained there, OCR became a back bench, a dumping ground for scores of unqualified bureaucrats who often hurt the cause of civil rights by their inept negotiating and by pushing frivolous issues. With an administration openly hostile to its mission, the Office for Civil Rights lost its bearings and hunkered down to survive.

David Mathews, who had taken leave as president of the University of Alabama to be HEW Secretary for Gerald Ford, concluded that the alienation of the Office for Civil Rights was beyond his recall. He told me in our first post-1976-election meeting, "That place is a law unto itself. You will find OCR takes major actions without informing you. It even attacks you in the press, attacks the Secretary." Not while I'm Secretary, I thought.

Not all the alienation of the Office for Civil Rights resulted from the Nixon-Ford policies. Some stemmed from the two faces of Congress on civil rights issues. What the Congress gave in Title VI of the 1964 Civil Rights Act, prohibiting discrimination on the basis of race, it took away in part through the annual HEW appropriations bills by forbidding the use of any funds to bus school children. The Congress energetically pursued that practice while I was Secretary. Though prohibited from using the grant or denial of HEW funds to encourage busing beyond the school nearest the home of the child, I suggested to Attorney General Griffin Bell that we might still effect some desegregation without lengthy lawsuits if HEW funds could be used to require pairing of neighboring schools. Under the proposal, two neighboring six-grade schools, one mostly white, the other mostly black, could be integrated by making one school serve grades one through three and the other grades four through six. Each would then become the nearest school. Bell concluded that the law permitted HEW to use its funds to achieve pairing. *New York Times* correspondent David Rosenbaum broke a story about our pairing idea on June 7, 1977. Nine days later, the House attached a rider to HEW's appropriations bill prohibiting the use of funds for pairing. Twelve days after that the Senate followed suit. Within three weeks, the Congress had put a new restriction on HEW's appropriations bill and on OCR's ability to enforce Title VI of the 1964 Civil Rights Act without amending that law. (In late 1980, Congress voted to further restrict federal attempts to use busing in an appropriations bill rider to prevent the Justice Department from participating in court actions to require busing to achieve desegregation, and backed down only in the face of a presidential veto at the end of the session.)

What little support the Office for Civil Rights got in the Nixon-Ford years came from the courts. To the administration's attempts to subvert enforcement efforts or ignore the mandate of the civil rights laws, OCR staffers would respond, "We've been sued," or "The court ordered us to do this." With no support from the administration, the only leverage OCR had was the courts. So its loyalty went there and to civil rights organizations that sued to compel actions OCR would have taken if it had not been for the Nixon-Ford policies. But the judicial process has its own limitations where the execution of laws is concerned, and the buffeting OCR took in litigation inhibited the Office from realizing its potential. By the time I became Secretary, more than 80 percent of OCR's work force was under the control of federal judges. The federal courts had taken over: judges reviewed HEW schedules for handling complaints of discrimination, ordered and supervised teacher and student desegregation of big-city elementary and secondary school systems, and meticulously monitored the elimination of the dual systems of higher education in Southern and border states. Given the circumstances prevailing from 1969 to 1977, there may have been no other alternative, but the court review process was hardly the most efficient way to enforce civil rights legislation.

The *Adams* case—which was to set off my controversial civil rights dispute with North Carolina—provides a good example of what happened. Through the NAACP Legal Defense and Education Fund, blacks had sued HEW in 1970 in the Federal District Court in Washington, D.C., for failure to enforce the 1964 Civil Rights law. The court found such a failure and ordered HEW to begin some desegregation activities and to step up others. The judge demanded that schedules be set to reduce the backlog of racial discrimination complaints, and began supervising OCR's operations to meet those schedules. Other minority groups who were protected by civil rights laws realized that HEW's compliance with this court order on racial discrimination would, because of limited resources, result in the neglect of their interests. Eventually Hispanics, women, and the handicapped filed suit, and the court found itself trying to manage more and more of OCR's day-to-day administration. At one point, the judge even asked HEW counsel to describe the vigor with which I was seeking additional OCR personnel slots from the Office of Management and Budget.

IT WAS imperative to breathe life into HEW's Office for Civil Rights, and the first step was to make my own commitment clear. In my confirmation hearing, I called for "full speed ahead" on desegregation: "I think the most disgraceful thing that has happened in this country is that we have shattered a generation of black children, largely in urban schools but also in rural schools. These schools have been segregated and ill-cared for." In my rounds of internal meetings with employees during my first month in office, I emphasized civil rights: "I intend to push you if you don't push me. Every time black or other minority children get inadequate education because of unequal opportunity in the classroom, we're shattering their lives, and no one gave us the right to do that. . . . We've lost too many years in the fight."

Next to my own intensity, the most effective signal of my commitment to civil rights would be the people I selected to run OCR. As Director I chose David Tatel, a committed civil rights lawyer known and respected in the black community, who was a partner in Hogan and Hartson, one of Washington's biggest law firms. Tatel is blind, but his handicap seems to have sharpened his mind and contributed to an extraordinary command of facts. Remarkably, his eyes are singularly expressive. They become intense during an argument, and twinkle once the argument is won. As Tatel's deputy, we recruited Cynthia Brown, who had worked on civil rights efforts in education for the Leadership Conference on Civil Rights and the Lawyers Committee for Civil Rights Under Law. To work with them, we selected Peter Libassi, a lawyer who had been OCR's first Director under Lyndon Johnson, to return to HEW as General Counsel.

Tatel's role as a symbol was as important as his talent. It was critical to send the word forth that HEW was once again serious about civil rights. Most Sundays that spring I pitched against civil rights superlawyer Joe Rauh, in a father/son-and-daughter softball game started thirty years earlier by *Washington Post* editorial writer Alan Barth, more to teach men how to be fathers than children how to play softball. After the games, we would stop at the Barths' for beer, lemonade, cookies, and potato chips. After the opener, Rauh commented with mischievous delight, "You picked one helluva tough guy in Tatel. He's going to burn up the road on civil rights." The word had gone out.

The next step was to get the Office operating far more efficiently. OCR investigates complaints filed by thousands of individuals seeking redress for alleged discrimination at institutions receiving HEW funds. It also conducts independent reviews of institutions, such as universities, to determine whether they are complying with the law and HEW regulations implementing the law. The Office issues policy statements to inform those who receive grants and contracts how they are expected to comply. Although responsible for enforcement across the health, education, welfare, Social Security, and social service activities of HEW, OCR's work in 1977 was focused almost entirely in education.

When I became Secretary, an OCR investigator handled only three to four complaints each year. There was a backlog of 3,500 uninvestigated complaints despite a court order directing HEW to act in a timely manner. We set productivity targets and increased the number of investigations to thirteen per staff person each year. Coupled with doubling the size of the Office, we were able to trim the backlog substantially.

It was also important, wherever possible, to bring the civil rights effort into play before it released funds. Most HEW funds, such as Social Security and Medicare, are disbursed under laws that permit no discretion. But billions of dollars go to thousands of contractors and grantees at the discretion of HEW program managers. Wherever any HEW money goes, the legal prohibitions against discrimination follow. In the past, HEW had made the grants and had subsequently reviewed compliance. At the moment of greatest leverage—when the applicant was *seeking* HEW funds—the Department did nothing beyond requiring bland assurances of compliance. Later, with the contractors and grantees in place and HEW's bargaining power at its weakest, the Department would seek to enforce the law.

We set up a program that required compliance, or a commitment that specified in detail the necessary steps to come into compliance, before contracts or grants would be awarded. To blunt any attacks for politicizing the grant or contract process, we named a career employee, Gus Cheatham from the Office of Education, to oversee it.

We also needed to reduce sharply OCR's resort to the courts. Civil rights cases take years to litigate. Particularly in the education area, those who opposed civil rights policies had learned what anti-trust lawyers have known for generations: Delay is tantamount to victory. Every four years a generation of high school or college students went through segregated schools while lawyers litigated. It was better to get most of what we wanted at the outset by negotiation. I looked for a dramatic agreement to demonstrate to the civil rights groups and the OCR bureaucracy that settling was not selling out. A possibility for such a demonstration lay in the Chicago school desegregation situation. Frank Annunzio, a Chicago congressman, and Joseph Hannon, Chicago's school superintendent, wanted a truce in the twelve-year war that had been waging between HEW and Mayor Richard Daley since HEW Secretary John Gardner had tried to cut off federal funds to Chicago's school system in 1965 on the grounds that it was segregated.

I remember the day Gardner notified the city of Chicago. President Johnson was in New York to welcome Pope Paul VI to the United States and the United Nations, and he had taken Catholics on the White House staff with him. The evening before the Pope's arrival, U.N. Ambassador Arthur Goldberg hosted a party for the President and Francis Cardinal Spellman, the powerful Catholic archbishop of New York. We had thought and debated about the protocol and politics of how Johnson should handle the Pontiff's visit. The President himself had spent hours discussing the setting for the unprecedented meeting. The chancery behind St. Patrick's Cathedral on Madison Avenue? No, an American President should not go to Catholic territory, especially when the constitutionality of some of the Great Society elementary and secondary education programs was being challenged as violating the First Amendment separation of church and state. The United Nations? No, this was an American President welcoming the Pope to the United States, and too many East European, Irish, and Italian Catholics did not like the United Nations. We finally settled for the neutral ground of the Waldorf-Astoria. There, on October 4, 1965, Lyndon Johnson became the first American President to sit down in the United States with a Roman Catholic Pope. Earlier that day, Johnson had heard that HEW Secretary Gardner had announced his intention to cut off federal funds to Chicago's school system. Mayor Richard Daley, also in New York to meet the Pope, had already called Johnson to express his angry astonishment. Johnson was extremely agitated and instructed me to have Gardner and Attorney General Katzenbach in his Oval Office on our return to Washington late that afternoon. We were going to the suite to meet the Pope, and Johnson was still talking about Chicago as we got off the elevator.

The meeting with Pope Paul VI began with great dignity and formality. First, he and Johnson shook hands and then Johnson introduced those of us who had accompanied him. Jack Valenti, the President's secretary, Marie Fehmer, and I, and other Catholic staff members filed by, knelt, and kissed the Pope's ring. Then the room cleared, with only a few of us remaining. Johnson and the Pope sat side by side. The Pope told the President how much he respected his extraordinary work in educating children, particularly poor children. The President beamed as the Pope elaborated. Then Johnson's face flushed slightly; he turned to the Pope, his enormous hands reaching out, one stopping just short of landing on the Pontiff's knee. "That's the work I want to do, your Holiness, educate poor children. But they're trying to stop me. One of my own Cabinet members wants to stop funds for poor children in one of our largest cities, run by a fine Catholic mayor. But we'll help these children."

It was vintage Johnson. The Pope was politely puzzled during the translation. I could hardly keep from laughing; I'm sure I smiled.

When we got back to the White House, Johnson made it clear to Gardner that he would not cut off funds to Chicago without giving Daley every chance to present his case and, if necessary, desegregate the schools voluntarily.

The discussions and negotiations, begun the next day, were still dragging on when I became Secretary. They had become a source of persistent friction between the city of Chicago and HEW. If I could bring any portion of the Chicago dispute to a successful conclusion, our policy of negotiating would start to take hold.

We decided to move on the opportunity Congressman Annunzio and Superintendent Hannon presented. Annunzio had been a friend of mine for fifteen years and I knew I could trust him. The most promising approaches were teacher desegregation, to eliminate the concentration of black teachers in black schools and white teachers in white schools, and the establishment of bilingual education programs for children who spoke little or no English, programs that satisfied the Supreme Court's 1974 decision in the *Lau* case. There, the Court held that children who were not proficient in English had a right to public education.

The previous negotiations had been tense and even angry. The personality clashes between OCR staffers in HEW's Chicago Regional Office and the city's education hierarchy were so marked and the bitterness so deep-seated that I took our people out of direct discussions. Conrad Harper, a partner in the New York law firm of Simpson, Thatcher, and Bartlett, agreed to be our special negotiator. I held some quiet meetings with Al Shanker, president of the American Federation of Teachers, and Robert Healy, head of its Chicago local, as well as with Annunzio and Hannon. But Harper and Tatel, with help from HEW General Counsel Peter Libassi and his deputy Richard Beattie, did most of the detailed negotiating.

The negotiators agreed on a bilingual education program in which the city undertook to provide courses in twenty languages to the disparate elements of its population (for the first time, I realized the scope of the bilingual problem in our major cities with the new wave of immigrants from Asia and elsewhere). But Tatel and Harper could not reach agreement with the Chicago School Board on one of the issues in the teacher desegregation dispute. The board wanted the open-ended right to dismiss or demote teachers on the grounds of "just cause," without publishing objective and nondiscriminatory criteria in advance and identifying which criteria a dismissed or demoted teacher failed to meet. Tatel and Harper considered this "a loophole." Shortly after 11:00 P.M., Tatel, Harper, Libassi, and Beattie recessed the negotiations and came to my office. They told me they could not reach agreement. "The School Board just won't budge," Tatel said. "They say publishing a detailed list of criteria takes away all their discretion and invites constant litigation with the teachers and the union."

"And you won't budge either," I gently chided Tatel.

"We can't, we just can't," Tatel replied. "There's too much history of recalcitrance here to trust them without this provision."

We discussed alternatives for several minutes. Harper had already tried most. Then an idea struck me. "Suppose you let them have the broad 'just cause' standard on condition that the board pays the legal fees of any teacher who challenges an adverse action. Knowing the teacher can have a lawyer at their expense will be enough of an incentive to be confident they can prove just cause. Won't that do it?"

Exhausted as they were, Tatel and Harper thought they could sell that to the board. They did, at almost the stroke of midnight. I announced the settlement of this portion of the thirteen-year-old Chicago dispute the next day. The agreement breathed life into our policy of negotiating civil rights disputes, rather than allowing them to drag on for years in administrative hearings and the courts.

It was also essential to focus OCR's efforts on the central civil rights issues. In his 1976 campaign, Carter had read correctly the voters' impatience with the federal government's intrusion in their lives, and civil rights enforcement was by its nature such an intrusion. OCR's civil rights enforcement was being undermined by its pursuit of issues that many people regarded as frivolous, matters which tended to infuriate many communities and subjected HEW to ridicule. Some of HEW's activities under the prohibition of discrimination on the basis of sex in Title IX of the Education Amendments of 1972 were examples. In 1976 and early 1977, though it had never enforced Title IX to eliminate rampant sex discrimination in intercollegiate athletics or carefully examined the Social Security system for sex discrimination, HEW was threatening to cut off federal funds to two schools for alleged violations of Title IX. One school had a boys' choir; the other had an annual father-daughter dinner. Local editorials were stinging. The boys' choir ruling had been made over the telephone by an OCR attorney in a regional office. The father-daughter judgment had also been given by a local HEW office. We reversed both rulings and directed that in the future such decisions be cleared in Washington.

OCR also had a penchant for getting involved at very detailed levels, a propensity that undermined our credibility in pursuing the central task of assuring equal opportunity. For example, some states, Iowa and Oklahoma among them, have half-court basketball for high school girls. Unlike full-court basketball, which has five players, girls' half-court basketball has six players, only three of whom are allowed to shoot baskets. The game is enormously popular where it is played, particularly in Iowa. But some girls had filed complaints with HEW alleging that limiting basketball to the half-court game discriminated against them.

The issue was so hot in Iowa that Democratic Senator Dick Clark came to my office during his 1978 campaign. "Joe, there is one thing you could do that would really help me," he said.

"What?" I asked.

Leaning over, resting his elbow on his thick leg, Clark said: "Get HEW the hell out of half-court basketball in Iowa."

"Are you serious?" I asked. He was.

I could not oblige him, because at that time there was an allegation that colleges would give basketball scholarships only to girls (and boys) who played full-court basketball. If so, the charge of discrimination might have some merit. Moreover, a federal district court in Tennessee had declared that limiting high school girls to six-player basketball was unconstitutional, citing the equal protection clause. I told Clark that, under the circumstances, the best I could do was promise not to make a decision until after the election. He was pleased, though it could not save the election for him.

Eventually, we decided that HEW should not get involved in prescribing specific sports. Its interest must simply be that high schools have athletic programs which provide equal opportunity to boys and girls. On December 26, 1978, I announced our decision: If a high school wanted half-court girls' basketball, that was up to the school so long as its overall athletic program accorded equal opportunity to girls and boys. In Iowa and Oklahoma, there was a sense that sanity had returned to HEW.

There was another chance to stop HEW from intruding where the national government had no business getting involved. A section of the Title IX regulations that President Ford had sent the Congress in 1975 (and which Congress had permitted to take effect) prohibited schools from adopting and enforcing discriminatory "rules of appearance," including hair length and dress codes for boys and girls. Some one hundred complaints had been filed with HEW under that provision. Scores of high school girls (and a few parents) had alleged that to require girls to wear brassieres without a similar dress regulation for boys constituted sex discrimination in violation of Title IX. And high school boys (and some parents) had charged sex discrimination by schools which restricted the length of their hair, since there was no such rule for girls.

I wanted to eliminate the appearance rules, which were a nuisance that cost us respect for more important sex discrimination efforts. Under the law, the President had to approve my proposed action and to submit it to the Congress, which had veto power. On my memo, President Carter checked the approved line and wrote: "Joe: Let's do more of this. J." That was May 22, 1979. By October 1979, at the recommendation of my successor at HEW, Patricia Harris, Carter had reversed himself, apparently in response to the pleas of Washington-based women's groups that had supported his successful effort to pass legislation establishing the Department of Education.

The sex discrimination issues OCR was beginning to face reflected the changing mission of the Office. Hispanics, Chicanos, Indians, and other groups had become as forceful as the blacks in asserting their rights under law. In a time of tight government budgets, enacting civil rights statutes had become a "free" means of evidencing federal concern. In short order, the Congress passed legislation prohibiting discrimination on the basis of sex, handicap, and age, adding to the prohibitions of discrimination on the basis of race, color, or national origin in Title VI of the 1964 Civil Rights Act. The legislative words were almost always identical: "No person in the United States shall . . . be excluded from participation in, be denied benefits of, or be subjected to discrimination under any program or activity receiving federal financial assistance on the basis of. . . ."

But the problems of putting regulatory oils on the legislative canvas were as varied as the different situations of the blacks, the handicapped, the old, the Hispanics, the Indians, women, and children. The Congress could relax once its broad proscription had been enacted. The OCR staff had no such luxury. Moreover, that staff was so bureaucratically exhausted by the battles over race discrimination in the schools, and its experience so confined to those battles, that it lacked the energy and imagination to tailor its efforts to the disparate needs of these new beneficiaries of congressional concern. The inadequacies of the OCR effort were further exposed as the protected groups looked beyond its education focus and sought to enforce their rights in health and social service programs. Pressed by so many claims for relief, from so many different groups, in such varied forms, the Office became almost paralyzed as its efforts to respond spawned more elaborate forms and more red tape. At times it seemed as though OCR sought in its forms and bureaucratic cant refuge from the extraordinary subtleties the second generation of civil rights issues presented.

Recipients of HEW funds reacted with understandable frustration. What was a college to do when it received a form asking about the number of blacks, Hispanics, women, handicapped, native Americans, Asians, and others in its programs? The proliferation of protected groups contributed enormously to the exasperation of middle-class white America with the civil rights movement. Vigorous civil rights enforcement would inevitably raise hackles. Even the most sensitive efforts would encounter inhospitable attitudes. But if we could eliminate irritating paperwork which was of marginal value at best and avoid the exhausting distractions of chasing frivolous issues, then OCR's energies could be centered on major areas of discrimination. With our effort so concentrated, we could move aggressively where the light of equal opportunity was clearly worth the candle—if the President would permit us to. That was the major uncertainty as I moved to rekindle the civil rights effort at HEW—the attitude of Jimmy Carter.

FROM THE first days of his presidency to his last public statement, Lyndon Johnson talked about the extra burdens the blacks and Mexican-Americans carried in a white society, how they needed some special help to cope with a history they did not make and a fate they did not choose. He spent hours persuading, threatening, cajoling, and shaming congressmen and senators to pass civil rights legislation.

The sweeping Civil Rights Act of 1964 had precipitated the longest filibuster in Senate history. President Kennedy had proposed the bill before he was assassinated, and LBJ relentlessly pushed it through the Congress. He moved the bill through the House by an overwhelming 290 to 130 vote. The Senate had never yet broken a Southern filibuster on civil rights. Led by Senator Richard Russell of Georgia, the filibuster stretched on for weeks. Johnson refused to yield. He made it clear he was prepared to suspend all other work to defeat the filibuster. When the showdown came, every senator was there. Johnson even had Clair Engle of California, who was dying of a brain tumor, wheeled in. Engle couldn't speak. Johnson had suggested he signal his aye vote by pointing to his eye. He did. The filibuster was broken and on the 83rd day of debate, the

Senate passed the bill 73 to 27. Particularly when civil rights legislation was pending, Johnson would make call after call, hold meetings into the night, review head counts of the White House staff, member by member of Congress, pressing Larry O'Brien and his congressional liaison aides to repeat the exact words on which they based their conclusion that the member would vote for or against the bill. Even when his formidable energies seemed drained, Johnson would look over the tally sheet again, make one more call, hold yet another private meeting to be sure to nail down an uncertain vote leaning his way or to persuade an opponent to change his mind.

Even when the burden of persuasion was impossibly heavy, Johnson would persist, sometimes getting exasperated, even trying to embarrass a congressman or senator into supporting his bill or at least not blocking it. When Georgia Senator Richard Russell was filibustering the voting rights legislation, Johnson invited his old friend to the White House one evening. Sitting in the small green room off the Oval Office, LBJ argued and argued with Russell. The staunch segregationist finally said, "Mr. President, I must take a stand. There comes a time when a man must take a stand."

Johnson looked at Russell for a moment and said, "You know, Dick, you remind me of the colored boy"—he delighted in using the terminology of his opponents on this issue to their faces—"who was up in bed with his master's wife. They were rolling around in the bed when her husband came home. That colored boy, he just ran to the nearest closet and that wife, she just slammed the door shut on him. Trouble is, it was the linen closet and he was pinned between the door and the shelves.

"Well, the master started shouting that someone was in the house. His wife denied it, but he didn't believe her. He looked under the bed, in all the rooms and closets, and finally came to the linen closet."

At this point Johnson rose, and gestured as though opening a door. "He opened the door and there was that colored boy, straight as a rail, arms by his side, scared to death, whites of his eyes popping out. 'What the hell are you doing here?' the master asked."

Then Johnson turned as if to face the master, standing, arms straight by his sides in the condition he had just described. "Everybody's got to stand somewhere," he said. "Everybody's got to stand somewhere." Johnson roared; Russell got the message, though he did not like it.

Johnson made enormous personal sacrifices and spent his political capital generously in the cause of civil rights and racial justice. Eventually he lost his lifelong friendship with Richard Russell over his refusal to appoint a Russell candidate he considered racist to the federal bench. Watching Johnson's heartache that night and his eloquence and sacrifice on a host of other occasions, I knew you had to have fire in your belly and inexhaustible persistence to move effectively on discrimination, and I did not know how much Jimmy Carter had.

Carter had proclaimed the liberal Democratic commandments on civil rights during his campaign, but in no area is it easier to sound like a born-again Christian and harder to be one. Across the civil rights issues, and especially in dealing with race discrimination, there is harsh resistance to overcome—state by state, city by city, institution by institution, person by person. Moreover, the issues were not drawn nearly so sharply as they had been in the mid-sixties. There were few flat-out racist Ross Barnetts in the seventies. White flight raised serious questions about the effectiveness of school desegregation as a tool of integration in Northern cities that had become overwhelmingly populated with minorities. Preferences for blacks and other minorities in jobs and education were under attack as reverse discrimination. Disproportionate economic deprivation was still visited on minorities, particularly blacks, but the lack of economic growth, higher taxes, lower take-home pay and unemployment served to reinforce white resistance to social programs for them. The Congress had passed laws to give the protection to women and handicapped and senior citizens that it had provided blacks and ethnic minorities.

These minorities looked to government—especially Washington—to help them in the area of civil rights. If Carter had the correct words on civil rights for a Democratic candidate, his speeches attacked Washington consistently as he repeated his commitment to eliminate unnecessary bureaucratic intrusions. Carter was shrewd enough to know that his attacks had subliminal appeal to those who wanted to block HEW's civil rights action. (In his gubernatorial campaign for the Democratic nomination against Carl Sanders in Georgia, Carter made Sanders's refusal to let George Wallace speak on Georgia state property a key issue, emphasizing to rural Georgians that as governor, Carter would welcome Wallace to Georgia and would form a number of interstate compacts with Alabama.) In mid-February 1977, shortly after I had announced a step-up in civil rights activity, President Carter, during a discussion of South Africa at the March 7, 1977, Cabinet meeting, said, "South Africa is like the South fifteen years ago. We knew damn well what was right, but as long as HEW was the only one putting pressure on us, we did not act. We needed other pressures—the courts."

The courts were a last resort to me, but they could provide political refuge, and Carter sought that refuge in Chicago. After reaching agreement on teacher desegregation, we sought to negotiate a settlement of the student desegregation part of the HEW-Chicago dispute. But the city was reluctant to move. HEW pressed for action, and the negotiations began to raise political temperatures. After I left the department, Carter visited Chicago. There, on October 16, 1979, he said that a court ruling "might very well be better for Chicago and the preservation of its neighborhoods and the honoring of the civil rights of the people." With that echo of his 1976 campaign commitment to the "ethnic purity" of neighborhoods, Carter dashed any hope of a negotiated settlement with HEW. Subsequently, HEW turned the case over to the Department of Justice, which settled in principle with Chicago weeks before the 1980 presidential election under an arrangement that did not require the city to produce a desegregation plan until March 1981. The NAACP cries of "foul" and legal wrangling are likely to put the matter in litigation for years.

Like Johnson, however, Carter was aware of the symbols. He put his daughter Amy in a desegregated District of Columbia public school, although that did as much for his image of being one of the common people as it did for civil rights. Also, Carter made a persistent and determined effort to place minorities, particularly women, Chicanos, and blacks, in top federal jobs. Carter's staff was conscious of his commitment to place minorities and women in visible posts in his administration and used it to attack several of my appointments.

In the autumn of 1978 the President talked to me about increasing minority appointments at HEW. On November 22, after approving Ben Heineman to be the Assistant Secretary of HEW for Planning and Evaluation, he sent me a handwritten note: "I've approved Heineman. This is the last white male I will approve for your department for a long time. Yours is the worst affirmative action record in my administration. I do not like it. J.C."

I was stunned at the note, and so annoyed at his staff-generated ignorance that I sent him a return memo within an hour: "I got your note today approving Ben Heineman. Since you talked to me about affirmative action [a few weeks before], I have made or recommended four major appointments in HEW. . . . Three of the four . . . have been minorities [one black, one Hispanic] and a woman, [she] to succeed Gene Eidenberg, a white male who was promoted to your staff. . . . As I indicated to you in our last conversation on that subject, our analysis shows this Department to be one of the best in your administration on affirmative action, particularly vis-a-vis women—e.g., there are five women presidential appointees in this Department. If you have an analysis which leads you to a different conclusion, I should like to review it with you."

The President didn't send any response, but six months later, on May 10, 1979, when he approved the appointment of Dick Beattie as General Counsel of HEW (like Heineman's a promotion from within as a reward for excellent work and a means of accelerating our momentum), Carter got off another penned note: "I've approved Beattie (white male) but this can't go on. It is embarrassing to me. What will you do about it? I do not want to handle it one (wm) appointment at a time. Thanks. J.C."

Carter sent along a selective list, prepared by his staff, of only twenty of the more than two hundred and fifty appointments we had made at HEW. The jobs were listed on the left, a column on the right showed sixteen "white males," two "white females," one "Hispanic female," and one "black female." The selection was distorted, and the house Carter lived in was made of glass. I sent back a complete list of the top twenty-three jobs on his own staff, in the same format: twenty were held by white males, two by white females, and one by a black male.

There was one appointment on which Carter and I heartily agreed, however. In mid-1979, Hale Champion decided to resign as Under Secretary and return to Harvard. After hours of interviews I persuaded Barbara Newell, the energetic and committed president of Wellesley, to replace him, not because she was a woman but because, of the scores of individuals we screened, she was the best in ability, many of her strengths complemented my weaknesses, and we would be able to function as alter egos. Carter was pleased with the appointment because he wanted "a woman, black or Hispanic" as Under Secretary of HEW, and particularly admired Newell.

Aside from his notes and conversations urging me to hire more minorities and women, and similar exhortations at Cabinet meetings, I never heard Carter speak privately with the burning conviction, much less the passion, of Lyndon Johnson about civil rights or race in America. In Carter's notes and conversations about hiring minorities and women, I sensed his desire was to appease constituencies as much as to satisfy a fundamental commitment to civil rights. When he signed his reorganization plan to strengthen the Equal Employment Opportunity Commission in February 1978, he seemed more interested in his lengthy recitation of all the organizations that were present than in using the occasion to make an eloquent plea for justice. Carter's support for the Equal Rights Amendment was unswerving, and he did nominate an unprecedented number of women and blacks for federal judgeships. Perhaps speaking out on civil rights was just not his style. It was nevertheless remarkable that a Democratic President could go through almost all of his term without delivering a fervent, ringing, major public address on civil rights (until his campaign attempt to brand Ronald Reagan as a racist). It was more extraordinary that this could happen with a President who placed such emphasis on human rights abroad.

On June 24, 1977, as the Congress blocked our attempt at pairing neighboring schools to help desegregate them, I wrote Carter urging "that you give a general but strong speech on civil rights. Such a speech would obviously complement your commitment to human rights and would help dissipate an increasingly divisive atmosphere in Congress on the subject. . . . I do think a major presidential address on equal opportunity would be an important signal to many people." He never responded to that suggestion. Carter dealt with civil rights issues when he had to, but he did not reach out with the kind of public energy and passion I thought was needed, after the setbacks of the Nixon years, to lead the nation or to break new ground.

Nevertheless, Carter had made some strong statements during his race for the presidency. I decided to take his pro–civil rights campaign rhetoric as administration policy, particularly since he was so concerned in those early months about keeping his word. Carter had gotten 90 percent of the black votes cast in 1976. Their votes exceeded his margin of victory in thirteen of the states he carried, accounting for 216 electoral votes when he won by only 56. I assumed he would want to do well by them. The first test came over an affirmative action case that made the blood of blue collar workers, urban Catholics and Jews, and a broad cross section of white America boil.

ON JUNE 4, 1965, when he addressed Howard University in one of the great speeches of his presidency, Lyndon Johnson said, "It is not enough just to open the gates of opportunity. All our citizens must have the ability to walk through those gates. That is the next . . . stage of the battle for civil rights." And in one of the final public appearances of his life, at the LBJ School in Austin, Texas, he said eloquently that "to be black in a white society is not to stand on level and equal ground. . . . [whites] stand on history's mountain and blacks stand in history's hollow." He spoke out unabashedly for special help and affirmative action to "overcome unequal history."

Once the jobs as scientists, or lawyers, or accountants were opened to blacks, it was essential to get them the training that would make them eligible. But one person's affirmative action is another's reverse discrimination. In employment and at hard-to-enter universities, affirmative action programs were coming under attack. As the job market tightened, court orders setting outright quotas for minorities in fire departments and local construction unions angered equally or better qualified whites seeking the same jobs.

In education, the issue became national in 1977 when Allan Bakke, a thirty-seven-year-old white male engineer, went all the way to the Supreme Court attacking as reverse discrimination his denial of admission to the medical school at the University of California at Davis. Bakke had been denied admission to a class of one hundred at the state-run medical school, which had reserved sixteen positions for minorities. Since his ratings by the admissions committee were higher than some of the sixteen minority students accepted, Bakke had alleged "reverse discrimination" in violation of Title VI of the Civil Rights Act of 1964 and the equal protection clause of the Constitution.

The *Bakke* case started a heated debate. For angry middle class whites, concerned about the economy and unemployment, the case provided a focus for their deeply felt but difficult-to-demonstrate sense that blacks were being favored by the government, or the schools, or their employers. For blacks, it was a litmus test. Is this nation willing to take hard steps to remedy past discrimination? Civil rights proponents came down on different sides; so did many college and university administrators.

It was on the *Bakke* case and affirmative action that I first tripped in the civil rights area. On March 17, 1977, at my initial interview with the *New York Times* after becoming Secretary, reporters David Rosenbaum and Nancy Hicks asked about the case, and about setting goals and quotas for blacks and women for jobs and for admission to schools. The next morning's page-one headline in the *Times* was accurate: CALIFANO SAYS QUOTAS ARE NECESSARY TO REDUCE BIAS IN JOBS AND SCHOOLS.

I had used the word *quota* referring to cases I had settled as a private attorney for *Newsweek* involving women and for the El Paso Natural Gas Company involving Hispanics. About the *Bakke* case, I had said: "I am not sure what the ultimate technical legal resolution of the case will be. But it is important that we not lose the ability to have affirmative action programs which could give minorities and women the opportunity to get into the major graduate schools and universities in the country." How could I or any Secretary of HEW ever "find first-class black doctors, first-class black lawyers, first-class black scientists, first-class women scientists, if these people don't have the chance to get into the best schools in the country?" Indeed, if all the black Ph.D.s that had ever lived in the United States were distributed among our colleges, there would be fewer than three at each institution.

My use of the word *quota* in the interview put me on the spot. I had meant to emphasize the need to set goals. I thought it permissible and desirable to set numerical objectives that individuals and institutions would have to make good-faith efforts to attain, the same kinds of objectives that businessmen, for example, set in other walks of life to attain sales, or growth, or increased production. But first impressions endure, especially in papers like the *New York Times,* and I was never able to shake the "quota" stamp. My use of the word *quota* had further confused the public discussion of a critical issue on which I should have been providing leadership. Many in the liberal Jewish community and many Catholics were appalled by my statement. Quotas summoned bitter memories of the twenties and thirties when major universities restricted the number of Jews and Catholics in medical and other university studies.

For older faculty members, particularly at New York's many publicly financed universities, quotas sharpened fears of being replaced by younger minority professors. They already felt they were fighting a losing battle to maintain high standards against the crush of New York City's open admissions policies, which entitled anyone who graduated from a New York City high school to go to a city college. They considered almost any kind of affirmative action a threat to their tradition of achievement; quotas were an outright insult.

On March 31, 1977, forty-four educators from leading universities across the country sent President Carter a public letter demanding that he repudiate my statement. The letter accused me of breaking trust with the constitutional principle of equality. I took advantage of the letter to take back the word. David Bird of the *New York Times* asked me to comment, and I told him that I should not have said "quota." "It's obviously a nerve-jangling word." But I reiterated that affirmative action was essential to rectify past or on-going discrimination.

The *Times,* again on page one, headlined: CALIFANO CONCEDES ERROR IN ADVOCATING JOB QUOTAS.

On seeing my comment, black leader Jesse Jackson said that my "apology" was "a direct slap in the face of the black, non-white, and women's movements." Black employees at HEW expressed their disappointment that I was "backing down." It was important for me to try to put forth a more thoughtful rationale and to set out the case for affirmative action. The commencement at City College in New York on Sunday June 5 gave me a timely opportunity. Rick Cotton, an unusually gifted attorney we had recruited from California who later became executive secretary of the Department, went to work to spell out the rationale for affirmative action and for distinguishing between goals and quotas. We labored into Saturday evening, testing each argument and measuring each word carefully. Eighty-five percent of the 1977 graduating class of CCNY came from families whose incomes were less than $14,000 a year. Fortuitously, Keith Bailey, a black admitted through one of the CCNY minority-outreach programs, was graduating summa cum laude with a perfect 4.0 average in his math major. When I stood at the podium to deliver the commencement address, I looked down across the dusty field. Directly in front of me sat several rows of liberal Jewish faculty members, most skeptical, some almost sullen. I stated that the institutions of higher education, not the government, had to open higher education to minorities and to women. They applauded gingerly. I said more strenuous efforts were required to seek out minority students—better recruitment, more imaginative programs of compensatory training, better financial aid programs. There was no applause.

Then, staring down at the faculty members in the front rows, I said loudly but slowly, to avoid running over my own words on the loudspeakers every fifteen or so rows down the long field: "If American colleges have been able to exert such efforts—special tutoring and financial aid—for star quarterbacks, surely they can do so for other Americans."

The students applauded, cheered, and whistled. Most of the faculty sat on their hands. This faculty was not going to like what was coming, I thought; I might have picked the wrong forum for the message. "It would be a bizarre society indeed—a Catch 22 society—that judged a person's potential for success by the very credentials and experience it had denied to that person by past discrimination." If we were serious about achieving minority participation in American education, I continued, then "we must have a way to measure progress. . . . Arbitrary quotas will not be part of our enforcement program; we want to rely on the good faith and special effort of all who join in the final march against discrimination."

I paused. There was impatient movement among the students, but my faculty audience was riveted. As firmly as I could, I said: "But we will also rely—because we must rely—on numerical goals as benchmarks of progress."

The mixed applause of the faculty directly below me and the cautious comments at President Robert Marshak's post-commencement cocktail party ("some interesting ideas," "I think I see your viewpoint") were like the statements of lawyers who want to read the fine print before signing up. But when I saw the *Times* headline on Monday, I knew at least that the public point had been made: CALIFANO ASKS "GOALS" NOT "QUOTAS" ON MINORITY STUDENTS IN COLLEGES.

The following Tuesday, an ad hoc group of Jewish leaders came to see me to discuss the *Bakke* case. The group gathered in the Secretary's conference room around a huge table, scarred and scratched from hundreds of meetings, that Nelson Rockefeller had given the Department when he had been an Assistant Secretary there. With twenty of us present, the table was only half used. The discussion was lively. There was distrust and skepticism about the distinction between goals and quotas. Some thought my rejection of quotas was semantic camouflage. They simply did not believe me. Their group of Jewish organizations intended to file a brief on behalf of Bakke and against quotas. When I opposed their view that Bakke should be admitted to Davis, and that the University of California's affirmative action program should be declared unconstitutional, I was accused by some of supporting quotas even for unqualified blacks. I told them I thought the administration had to support affirmative action programs and universities which were willing to provide access to minorities.

Hy Bookbinder, the Washington representative of the American Jewish Committee and a defender of equal rights with whom I had worked in the Johnson administration, called me later to say, "We've come to opposite conclusions on *Bakke*. But just as you shouldn't be automatically branded a quota lover or opponent of merit, we shouldn't be branded opponents of civil rights generally." I agreed. We were both concerned that the *Bakke* issue was exposing some of the latent tension between Jews and blacks.

The *Bakke* case presented the first real clash of the conflicting interests between constitutional concepts of equality and the need to remedy past discrimination, and tested the deep American traditions of giving everyone a fair chance and rewarding individual merit. Giving minorities preference was a temporary remedy, not a permanent fixture of America's quest for racial equality, and time would someday run out. Most black Americans knew that, but *Bakke* brought them point blank against the reality that those preferences might end long before they had a chance to catch up.

For much of white middle America, the sympathetic images of black schoolchildren in the segregated South had been tarnished by the violence of life at black-dominated urban high schools. Leading colleges accepted only a small fraction of those whites who applied, so each space given to a black under an affirmative action program was seen by white parents and students as having been taken from them. Nowhere was this feeling more explosive than in the intense competition for highly prized slots in medical schools. But this resentment extended beyond the medical schools, beyond schools in general. As unemployment spread and jobs became more precious, whites became angrier when courts ordered employers to remedy past discrimination by hiring blacks, or when the employers instituted their own affirmative action programs.

The *Bakke* case presented enormously difficult problems for the administration. Carter had never been fully trusted by either the Jewish or the black communities. The Jewish organizations had made their support of Bakke known early in the administration. And in July 1977, at his organization's annual convention, Urban League President Vernon Jordan attacked the President for his neglect of black interests, saying, "The sad fact is that the list of what this administration has not done for the blacks . . . far exceeds its list of accomplishments. . . ." Carter responded that he had "no apologies" for his record on blacks, and criticized Jordan's remarks as "demagogic and erroneous." The President's comments marshaled black leaders behind Jordan. On August 29, 1977, just a few weeks before the *Bakke* brief was due in the Supreme Court, black leaders, meeting in New York, charged that Carter had moved from "benign neglect" to "callous neglect." Jesse Jackson, spokesman for the group, cited the *Bakke* case as one of the key tests ahead for the administration.

Meanwhile, the President had stated publicly at a July 28 press conference that I would be involved: "The Secretary of HEW and the Attorney General, who are lawyers . . . will prepare our position" in the *Bakke* case. My first indication of where the Justice Department was headed came just before Labor Day. I was visiting my parents in Spring Lake, New Jersey. The *New York Times* reported that the Justice Department's draft brief argued that programs such as the one at the Davis Medical School were unconstitutional and urged that Bakke be admitted. I called Ben Heineman in Washington and discovered that the *Times* story was probably accurate. I told him to beg, borrow, or steal a copy of the brief.

The brief was worse than the report. The California supreme court had declared the Davis program unconstitutional under the equal protection clause, and had ordered Bakke admitted on factually sparse and unclear evidence. The Justice Department brief was bogged down in the inadequate and murky facts developed in the state court. The brief presented no legal or intellectual endorsement of affirmative action, and flatly argued that "racial classifications favorable to minority groups are presumptively unconstitutional." The draft rejected distinctions between the permissible use of race (to remedy past discrimination) and its impermissible use (to exclude blacks or Hispanics, for example). It rested its logic on the "overriding principle . . . that race is . . . presumptively pernicious as a basis on which to bestow or withhold benefits." It conceded the inadequacy of the record, but still concluded that the California court was correct to order Bakke's admission, "without excluding the possibility that a similar program, or indeed the [Davis] Medical School's own program, could be sustained on an adequate record." The Justice Department's brief was supported in part by a footnote: "The fact that several Jewish, Greek, Polish, Italian, and Ukrainian groups have filed *amicus* briefs in support of Bakke demonstrates that white ethnic groups are seriously concerned about the effect of the Medical School's program on them. It is difficult to dismiss these concerns without an examination of the evidence, which is not possible in this case."

I thought the brief was a chilling attack on affirmative action programs, all the more aggravating because of its admission that there was insufficient evidence in the record to judge the validity of the school's program. The record, for example, did not indicate what, if any, comparison had been made between students admitted in the regular programs and those given one of the 16 slots in the special program for minorities, why Asians were admitted through both programs, why at least one regular applicant was admitted with ratings lower than Bakke, the nature of the past discrimination, if any, the school was remedying, the relative likelihood of minority students serving minority communities woefully deficient in health care. Heineman, a former law clerk for Supreme Court Justice Potter Stewart, and Beattie and Tatel worked throughout the weekend on a memo setting out our legal arguments. If necessary, we would write a competing brief to submit to the Attorney General or the President. I spent a good part of Labor Day weekend on the phone discussing legal theories and arguing about goals and quotas.

On the morning of September 6, I called Griffin Bell to complain about the brief. He suggested that I meet with Solicitor General Wade McCree. That meeting, the next day, was deeply disturbing. McCree, who is black and had been a judge before being appointed Solicitor General, sat with two bright young white holdovers from the Nixon administration. They did not disguise their distaste for affirmative action; to them, any race-sensitive program was indeed "presumptively unconstitutional."

I was surprised at how angry I was becoming as the young lawyers spun their legalistic theories. McCree sat there, remarking simply that he had to follow the existing case law, at times seeming to acquiesce in the arguments of his aides. My God, I thought, he's bending over backward. I remembered what Lyndon Johnson said when he put the first black, Andrew Brimmer—who, like McCree, was Harvard-educated—on the Federal Reserve Board: "I want to be Goddamn sure he hasn't forgotten what it's like to be black." McCree had been an outstanding judge before becoming Solicitor General, and his temperament was to compensate for all personal biases in fulfilling the obligation to judge fairly. I was concerned that McCree was carrying so much personal freight on this issue that he could not decide it objectively.

One of McCree's lawyers thought it was impossible to write a brief that approved a special admissions policy.

"Like hell it's impossible," I said. "I don't have any problem writing it. A lot of people in this country have worked for years to try to get equality for blacks, to develop affirmative action programs, to remedy past discrimination. We're not going to have that work thrown out the window by a couple of young lawyers."

I turned to McCree. He was not yet familiar with the draft brief. I begged him to read it with special care. He could not sign a brief which said that race-sensitive programs to help minorities are presumptively unconstitutional, which in the same paragraph urged that Bakke be admitted and conceded that the record was inadequate to judge the constitutionality of the university's admission program.

As I left, I thought about the sea-change from Johnson's Justice Department. Johnson had launched federal affirmative action in 1965 by signing Executive Order 11246. He had said in his famous speech at Howard University, "You do not take a person who, for years, has been hobbled by chains and liberate him, bring him up to the starting line of a race, and then say, 'You are free to compete with all the others,' and still believe that you have been completely fair." The Justice Department's *Bakke* brief would set civil rights back a generation.

I went back to HEW and drafted a memo to Bell and McCree. This was a fight we would take to the President, but the first step was to try to turn the Justice Department around. I wrote that filing this brief would "have a serious, detrimental impact on affirmative action programs aimed at redressing the wrongs of pervasive, systemic, and long-standing racial discrimination." Efforts to make higher education accessible to disadvantaged minorities, to insure that more of tomorrow's leaders can be drawn from those minorities, must be "advanced, and not retarded by the administration's position in this highly visible case."

I had to leave for Detroit to address the National Governors' Conference on welfare reform, but I asked Heineman, Beattie and Tatel to start work on a memo to the President with our arguments on why the proposed brief was bad constitutional law. When I got back late the following afternoon, I found Bell and McCree—and the staff lawyers at the Justice Department—increasingly sensitive about my involvement. The memo that was going to the President became even more important. We worked late into the night.

I had to testify the next morning before Paul Rogers's House Health Subcommittee on our Child Health Assessment Program to expand Medicaid coverage for millions of children and pregnant mothers. As soon as I finished, I went back to the memorandum. We completed it late that evening and it began: "The draft Justice Department brief in the *Bakke* case is bad law, and pernicious social policy."

I urged Carter to become personally involved, to call a group together to discuss the administration's position, and to order a brief prepared that would argue that race-sensitive programs should be tested as to whether they had a rational, permissible goal, such as remedying past discrimination, instead of judged presumptively unconstitutional.

I reminded the President that only that week he had "promised to do something specifically directed at the shameful unemployment rate—now exceeding 40 percent in some urban areas for black teen-agers. Is your action 'presumptively unconstitutional'? . . . the virtual absence of blacks in the higher education community is at least as serious to our nation as black unemployment.'' I urged him to tell Bell and McCree to stay away from the spotty facts of the *Bakke* case, since the case had been poorly litigated in the trial court and the record was inadequate. ''The U.S. government should not fight the battle of affirmative action . . . on someone else's turf. As I have gotten more deeply into the record of the case, I have decided it is reckless—that is the most temperate word for it—for the adminstration to render a judgment on the particular facts of this case. . . .

''The most serious problem this nation continues to face is racism. Despite the herculean efforts of Earl Warren, John Kennedy, Lyndon Johnson, and others in the 1950s and 1960s, this problem still plagues our society. It pervades every aspect of social activity: unemployment, education, health, housing, urban crime, rural poverty. But the statistics are worse in the arena of higher education and professional education than in any other aspect of black-white social or economic activity.''

Our best universities, such as Harvard, were using affirmative action programs to increase participation by minorities *''where those minorities are capable of passing the courses required.''* I argued that the Justice Department's position would end those programs, and without them ''there is simply no way—for at least a decade and possibly a generation—to give minorities an opportunity at the universities of this country. . . .''

The memorandum was long because I felt I had to present a solid critique of the draft brief and thus provide sympathetic White House staffers, such as Stuart Eizenstat, with ammunition to use against the Justice Department. But I didn't know whether Carter would read a long memo, so I sent him a handwritten note for his eyes only:

Mr. President:

I believe you will make the most serious mistake of your administration in domestic policy to date if you permit the Justice Department to file the *Bakke* brief in the form I read it and under present circumstances. . . .

The brief-writing process (indeed the whole consultation process) has been so closely held—dominated through this past week by two holdover lawyers in the A.G.'s office—that even I, with a Department as deeply involved as any in the govt., with a legal background, with a presidential press statement that I would be involved, first got wind of the brief's existence in a *N.Y. Times* article over Labor Day weekend.

The brief I have read proposes new, unchartered law in your administration's name—and distinctly pernicious social policy. Race-sensitive programs are not "presumptively unconstitutional," as that brief asserts. One cannot responsibly judge the *Bakke* facts in their present state of ambiguity—and the U.S. government (your administration) need not take such a reckless and unnecessary step.

There are few, if any, more persistent, significant, or intractable problems that will touch your presidency at home than the problem of race in America. There may be no more significant signal you will send on this subject than the *Bakke* brief you eventually approve. . . .

Joe Califano

A revised Justice Department brief was produced early on September 10, somewhat improved but still dominated by its attention to the limited and incomplete facts in the record. I wrote Bell, McCree, and Drew Days, the Assistant Attorney General for Civil Rights, expressing my concern about that, and about the revised brief's failure to provide "a ringing endorsement of affirmative action" that set forth principles to guide future establishment of affirmative action programs. The new draft had dropped the "presumptively unconstitutional" language, but it still insisted that "race-sensitive admission programs have a special burden of justification, not unlike those in invidious racial classification cases." I was strenuously opposed to such a test, and asked that the brief make the distinction between goals and quotas explicit. I suggested we urge the Supreme Court to send the *Bakke* case back to the California courts, with instructions to measure the constitutionality of the Davis Medical School program under a rational relationship test.

I asked Eizenstat to convene the Justice Department lawyers and some of us from HEW to argue out the administration position in *Bakke*. He was reluctant. He said the Justice Department was "climbing the walls" about my involvement in the *Bakke* brief, and White House Counsel Bob Lipshutz thought we were meddling. "If you won't call the meeting, at least use our memoranda to argue against Justice," I pleaded. Eizenstat did jump into the dispute, and pressed Justice to change the brief.

The press kept speculating that Carter was leaning to Bakke's side. I began to receive calls from civil rights leaders and lawyers across the country, as well as from Eleanor Holmes Norton, head of the Equal Employment Opportunity Commission. "You're talking to the converted," I told Vernon Jordan. "Go see Bell and Wade McCree." I suggested the same course of action to William Coleman, the black former Secretary of Transportation. Then McGeorge Bundy called to say he had written an article for *The Atlantic Monthly* supporting affirmative action, and asked whether there was anything else he could do. Several university presidents called to express concern about the President's position. I suggested they talk to the Justice Department and the White House. I called Vice-President Mondale and he agreed to weigh in on the side of affirmative action.

The congressional Black Caucus wrote the President that the Justice brief "irretrievably undermined public and private affirmative action programs." Civil rights lawyer Joe Rauh (who Carter once told me "is the only person on my enemies list") attacked the President and commented that being pro-Bakke and pro-affirmative action was like saying "you're for peace and war."

All throughout the public and private furor, and the series of memoranda, the President gave us no indication where he stood. I became increasingly concerned. Then, on September 12, just before the Cabinet meeting that day, I saw a page-one story in the *New York Times:* Carter Said to Back Bar to Race Quotas. The story indicated that the Justice Department brief was likely to come out against the University of California program and in favor of Bakke. That did it. I decided to raise the issue at the Cabinet meeting.

Before my turn came, Carter called on Andrew Young, the Ambassador to the United Nations and a civil rights leader. Young reported on the status of relations between the British and the Rhodesians over black majority rule. His criticism of Rhodesian whites was sharp, but good-natured. He said, smiling, "Rhodesia's cabinet reminds me of a sheriff's office in Mississippi in 1950." Then he commented on the *Bakke* case stingingly. "The *Bakke* case is perceived as a betrayal of the black community by the judicial system. Blacks feel that the University of California does not want to win the case. Bakke has been denied admission by twelve other medical schools, some of which had no blacks or Chicanos, on the basis of his age."

I followed Young. I said the *Bakke* brief would be the most read brief filed by this administration. I went back over some of the points in my memoranda. I urged Carter to "take a strong stand in favor of affirmative action." Pat Harris agreed.

Bell was uncomfortable. He reported that McCree was working on the brief. Pointedly, he noted that he had been talking to the President about it, and that "the President will review it before it is submitted to the Supreme Court." After his experience with *Bakke,* Bell added, he doubted he would "circulate any more briefs in the future." The President was noncommittal.

After the meeting, I left for Canada (to find out more about its health system in preparing a national health plan for the President). I kept in touch with my staff. After some indecision, the Civil Rights Division in the Justice Department was now firmly for a brief that supported affirmative action, but Bell and McCree had cut off all contact outside the White House. The presidential tea leaves were unclear.

Later that day, the congressional Black Caucus issued a statement that Carter would "discredit his presidency in the eyes of history" if he endorsed the Justice Department brief. And the Cabinet's discussion leaked to the press. CARTER'S PLAN TO OPPOSE RACIAL QUOTAS SPLITS ADMINISTRATION, the next morning's *Washington Post* announced.

On September 15, at the end of our meeting about the national health plan, United Auto Workers President Douglas Fraser argued forcefully that the President could not come out against affirmative action in the *Bakke* case. He said Carter had to support the University of California. I passed along Fraser's comments to Eizenstat, trying to find out where the Justice brief stood. Eizenstat's reply was the first ray of hope: "Some changes are being made that you'll like."

There was a "final version" of the brief and again I pressed to see it, reminding Bell and McCree that the President had publicly stated I would be involved. Finally they consented, but on their terms. Dick Beattie had to read it at the Justice Department in the presence of one of McCree's lawyers. He could not take notes or return with a copy. He called and reported that although the brief said race-sensitive programs should be viewed "carefully," it rejected the standard of "presumptive unconstitutionality," endorsed affirmative action programs, and distinguished between goals and quotas. It urged the Supreme Court to send the case back to the California courts for reconsideration. "It's not quite how you would have written it, but it's a win for our side," Beattie said. I called Bell to congratulate him. "We ended up with everybody in the government and the nation helping us write it," he complained. Which is as it should be, I thought. The Justice Department should no more have exclusive rights to formulate positions on seminal constitutional law than the Treasury Department has to prepare tax legislation or formulate economic policy, without broad involvement of the interested government agencies.

By September 19, 1977, when the administration brief was filed with the Supreme Court, fifty-seven other *amicus* briefs had been submitted, more than the high court had received in any case in twenty years. On October 12, the Justices heard oral arguments. Archibald Cox, the former Watergate special prosecutor, representing the University of California, argued alongside McCree that racial preference was constitutionally valid. "The answer the Court gives will determine, perhaps for decades, whether members of minorities are to have meaningful access to higher education in the professions. . . .'' McCree said that ''To be blind to race today is to be blind to reality.''

The Supreme Court decided the Bakke case on June 28, 1978, endorsing affirmative action programs such as Harvard's but finding the ''quota'' system at the University of California's Davis Medical School unconstitutional and a violation of Title VI of the 1964 Civil Rights Act. Bakke was to be admitted. Those of us who administered civil rights laws were guaranteed a host of additional litigation by the Court's separate opinions, splitting 4 to 4, with Justice Lewis Powell casting the deciding vote. Justices Brennan, White, Marshall, and Blackmun blessed affirmative action programs that served important government objectives; they would not have admitted Bakke. Chief Justice Burger and Justices Stewart, Rehnquist, and Stevens essentially agreed with Powell's opinion; they voted to admit Bakke. Powell wrote that race-sensitive programs should be subjected to ''strict scrutiny'' and could survive constitutional muster where there was a compelling state interest to be served; he voted to admit Bakke. In all, there were six separate opinions, each with its own nuances. But the Court did rule that educational institutions may take race into account in the admissions process as part of an effort to obtain a diverse student body, and that when institutions have illegally discriminated against individuals from minority or disadvantaged groups, those institutions can, under the Constitution, be required by the government to adopt and carry out affirmative action programs. A meticulous legal analysis that I asked HEW lawyers to conduct in light of the decision concluded that all but one of the scores of HEW regulations, programs, and activities in this area met the Supreme Court's standards.

For me, the experience within the administration was satisfying. Our arguments and persistence had made a difference. Although I was sorry to have ruffled the feelings of Bell and McCree, both of whom I liked, they could be soothed. But the experience was also disquieting. For those who had pressed the President for a ringing endorsement of affirmative action had not been able to engage him, much less draw it out of him. He withdrew to Bell and his immediate staff. I was left with a feeling that Carter was determined to walk the tightrope between affirmative action and reverse discrimination rather than risk offending any group. He evidenced little desire to lead the nation to an understanding of the demands and subtleties of civil rights in the late 1970s and 1980s. Carter had chosen his words carefully when he visited HEW headquarters in February 1977: ''There will never be any attempt while I am President to weaken the great civil rights acts that have passed in years gone by.'' He meant what he said, and not much more.

THIS SENSE of his attitude dogged me throughout the most difficult civil rights problem of my tenure as Secretary: the effort to desegregate the Southern systems of higher education and a wrenching dispute with North Carolina. I don't think any court order created as much agony within the civil rights movement as the mandate to dismantle and desegregate the dual systems of higher education in some Southern and border states. The blacks were as much divided among themselves as were whites and blacks, and obeying the order put me in the middle of issues as complex and subtle as any I faced in this arena. I learned, as never before, what Lyndon Johnson meant when he told us it was much harder to know what was right than to do what was right.

A number of all-black colleges had grown up in the South after the Civil War. They were supposed to provide some opportunity for blacks who, both discriminated against and badly instructed, couldn't get into even the least demanding white schools. Many of the black colleges were started by the states, or else they eventually became part of the states' systems. By 1954, when, in *Brown* v. *Board of Education,* the Supreme Court held separate but equal elementary and secondary school systems to be unconstitutional, all the Southern and many of the border states had dual systems of higher education—separate, making no pretense of equality.

Brown's conclusion that separate but equal was unconstitutional was relatively easy to apply to elementary and secondary schools. But many black colleges were the only ones available to such budding black leaders as Andrew Young, Vernon Jordan, Martin Luther King, Thurgood Marshall, Kenneth Clark, Clarence Mitchell, and others. In the past, these institutions had educated the only black doctors and lawyers; they were still producing most of them. They represented some entrée for thousands of black Americans. Tuition was less than at most other colleges, and they accepted students whose poor background and education earned them lower Scholastic Aptitude Test (SAT) scores.

The Congress, at President Johnson's recommendation, recognized the special place of these black colleges in Great Society legislation. Under the euphemism "developing institutions," HEW had invested millions of dollars to keep some of these colleges going. One of my first acts as Secretary had been to push the budget up to the full $120 million authorized in the law. But by 1977, other colleges had discovered the developing institution program and for every dollar HEW had available there were requests for five. By that time, black colleges were getting only half the funds; small liberal arts colleges and community colleges, as well as predominantly Hispanic and Indian colleges, were demanding their share. In addition to these funds, black colleges received a huge proportion of their revenue from HEW grants that paid tuition, the amounts of which were determined by the income of the student's family and the school's tuition. As a result, many of these institutions got 90 percent or more of their revenues from HEW. The rest came from foundations, notably the Ford Foundation, which adopted a handful of these colleges for special attention, and from black (mostly Baptist) church collections across the South.

The years of neglect had not only taken a toll on the quality of education at these colleges, but the administrative and financial management systems were often wholly inadequate. When I examined HEW's developing institutions program, I discovered that of the 200 educational institutions in the United States with a student loan default rate in excess of 50 percent, 51 were black colleges and most of the remaining 149 were proprietary schools, run for profit, in such areas as cosmetology and low-level computer programming. We established new, objective standards for grants and, by imposing strict requirements on disbursement of the student loans, collected defaulted loans and reduced the rate of default. We acted none too soon, for, as I was to discover, financial management at some black colleges already had led to resignations, charges of misuse of funds, and convictions of federal crimes. (The General Accounting Office undertook an extensive investigation of the program and in 1979 issued a stinging indictment, filled with examples of confusion, conflict of interest, and activities lacking any coherent purpose.)

The federal court mandate to dismantle the dual system of higher education began to bite against this backdrop, but in fact it had been threatening for years. In 1969, HEW asked ten states—Arkansas, Florida, Georgia, Louisiana, Maryland, Mississippi, North Carolina, Oklahoma, Pennsylvania, and Virginia—with dual black and white systems of higher education to propose plans to eliminate them. Five states submitted inadequate plans; the other five, including North Carolina, did not submit a plan. HEW did not take action against any of them. Consequently, in October 1970 the NAACP Legal Defense and Education Fund filed a suit in the U.S. District Court for the District of Columbia to compel HEW either to obtain effective plans to desegregate higher education in the ten states, or to institute enforcement proceedings to cut off federal funds in any state that failed to submit an acceptable plan.

The case (styled *Adams* v. *Richardson* and eventually *Adams* v. *Califano*) dragged on for the next three years. On February 16, 1973, Judge John Pratt ruled in favor of the plaintiffs, and ordered the Secretary of HEW to begin enforcement proceedings within 120 days against any state that had not submitted an acceptable plan by then. HEW appealed the ruling to the Court of Appeals for the District of Columbia circuit. On June 12 that court, sitting *en banc,* unanimously affirmed Pratt's order and gave the Secretary 300 days to start proceedings against any state that did not submit an acceptable desegregation plan. The case was sent back to Judge Pratt to monitor HEW's compliance with the court's order.

Led by its shrewd and sensitive chief judge, David Bazelon, the court of appeals opinion, however, expressed concern that black colleges not be dismantled in the desegregation process until adequate opportunities for higher education existed elsewhere for the black students. Without explicitly recounting the sorry legacy of generations of third-rate schooling, the court did take judicial notice of the fact that the overwhelming majority of students in black colleges lacked the SAT scores or the funds to get into other colleges.

In 1974, HEW accepted desegregation plans from eight states: Arkansas, Florida, Georgia, Oklahoma, Maryland, North Carolina, Pennsylvania, and Virginia. Louisiana refused to submit a plan and the case was referred to the Justice Department, along with a case against Mississippi whose plan was ruled unacceptable by HEW. (These two lawsuits were still pending, tied up in pre-trial maneuvering, when I left office in August 1979, five years later).

In 1975, the NAACP plaintiffs in the original case charged that not only had HEW accepted inadequate plans; the Department had not even compelled the states to comply with them. In January 1977, four days after I became HEW Secretary, Judge Pratt agreed, and ordered HEW to negotiate with the plaintiffs to establish criteria for developing adequate plans to desegregate six states: Arkansas, Florida, Georgia, North Carolina, Oklahoma, and Virginia. Maryland had filed suit in the federal district court in Baltimore to enjoin HEW's enforcement efforts, and the Department began settlement discussions in the Pennsylvania case. (The issues with these two states remained unresolved when I left HEW.)

No criteria of the sort Judge Pratt wanted had been developed, and within weeks after I became Secretary the NAACP plaintiffs' attorney, Joe Rauh, was threatening to ask the judge to cite me for contempt for failure to develop them. During a briefing on the case it became clear that we needed time to think through our strategy before moving to dismantle the persisting separate systems of higher education. On March 22, 1977, I asked Judge Pratt for additional time to "consider carefully and fully the far-reaching social and educational ramifications of the case." On April 1, Pratt gave me three months to promulgate final criteria under which the six states still in the case should develop desegregation plans. Pratt reiterated his finding that the previous plans "did not meet important desegregation requirements and failed to achieve significant progress toward higher-education desegregation." After one more postponement, I issued the criteria on July 5.

The criteria sought to desegregate higher education by eliminating duplication of identical non-core-curriculum courses* at neighboring black and white institutions; strengthening black institutions with new courses and additional faculties to make them attractive to white students; setting immediate goals to increase the percentage of black students in the white colleges and achieve the same proportions of black and white students entering higher education as graduating from secondary school; increasing the number of black students in graduate schools; and raising the percentage of black academic and nonacademic employees and representatives on governing boards in the overall higher education system.

The proportion of white students attending traditionally black colleges was to be increased, though not in the first stages. It was thought unrealistic to set goals and timetables here because black institutions had been so neglected by the states they would not be sufficiently attractive to whites. In complying with the court's opinion, we had to take into account "the special problem of black colleges." The court recognized that more than 80 percent of all black college graduates had been trained at black colleges. In the mid-seventies, black colleges continued to graduate almost 40 percent of all blacks who received degrees. Judge Pratt's order provided that "The desegregation process should take into account the unequal status of the black colleges and the real danger that desegregation will diminish higher education opportunities for blacks." To comply, we decided that white students should not take spaces at black colleges before blacks were able to enter white ones.

Within the limits of the court orders, the means were left to the state governors, legislatures, and higher education systems. We tried to draw a line between "education decisions," properly left to the states, and decisions that perpetuated dual systems. I did not want to sink into the quicksand that had trapped so many federal judges who became the school board, the school superintendent, and the director of transportation as they tried to desegregate lower school systems. Moreover,

*The desegregation criteria recognized that certain courses—English, mathematics, literature, and the like—were part of any core curriculum essential to the educational integrity of any institution of higher education. At the same time, there are many other courses, ranging from business administration and teacher training to veterinary medicine and law, that are associated with special fields but not essential to all higher education degrees; these fell into the non-core curriculum category.

decisions such as whether to merge neighboring black and white institutions required an intimate knowledge that was beyond any HEW Secretary.

As soon as the court accepted our criteria, we began negotiating with the six states. In September 1977, each state submitted a desegregation plan to the Department for review. In February 1978, we accepted the Arkansas and Florida plans and, conditionally, the Oklahoma plan. We had anticipated little difficulty with these states, whose higher education systems already satisfied most of the criteria. Also in February, we accepted the North Carolina plan for its system of fifty-seven community colleges. But we rejected the plans for Virginia and Georgia, and for the rest of North Carolina's higher education system. I announced my intention to initiate administrative enforcement proceedings within forty-five days if the plans were not changed to meet the criteria.

Georgia then became my top priority. I was determined to settle if I had to negotiate every line of the plan myself. "We cannot have the President's state resisting desegregation of its higher education system," I told Tatel. But little progress was made until Governor George Busbee became personally involved. At breakfast in the governor's mansion I had not visited since Carter had interviewed me there, Busbee was armed with tables comparing SAT scores at the white and black colleges. He was worried that it would be impossible to integrate several of the white institutions without lowering admission standards. He emphasized that there was as much, maybe more, political pressure against desegregation from the black college presidents as from the heads of the white institutions.

Busbee suggested that we try to reach agreement with the state university system's board of trustees. But, even with the help of Busbee's top aide, Norman Underwood, negotiations between Tatel and the university representatives deadlocked, and I met Busbee again in January 1978. We lunched alone in a cavernous room in the Atlanta convention center, where a Democratic fundraiser to celebrate Carter's first year in office was to be held that night. He agreed to give the situation his personal attention. I told him that White House aides Jack Watson and Jim Parham, both Georgians, would also help muster a majority vote of the university system's board of trustees.

A few weeks later, Busbee called to urge me to meet secretly with the executive committee of the board of trustees. "It's our last hope," he said.

The meeting took place in the Secretary's conference room on February 23, 1978. I decided not to focus on the issue that divided HEW and the Georgia system—eliminating duplicate courses at neighboring black and white institutions. I rested my case on the President and Georgia. "The President of the United States has a large number of problems on his desk," I began as I looked over the executive committee around one end of the long table, and described several domestic and foreign issues facing Carter. "No one in this room should be party to a situation that puts an unnecessary burden on his shoulders." Some of the trustees seemed moved by this plea, others were stuck on the issues that remained between them and HEW. I didn't want to be drawn into any details. I simply said, "Each of you knows how the Northern liberals and the Northern press will attack the President from Georgia if his state is the only one that cannot agree on a desegregation plan that the court will approve. They'll blame him, not you."

In the end, they could not hang this burden on the President. Shortly after our meeting, the board agreed to a plan that we accepted and filed with the court.

I anticipated the greatest difficulty in Virginia. Its governor, Mills Godwin, had assailed the criteria when I had announced them. He reserved his sharpest attack for the notion of goals and timetables for desegregating the white colleges. He excoriated our proposal to set a goal of increasing black enrollment in predominately white colleges by 150 percent by 1982 as "[reducing] higher education in Virginia to a federal numbers game." Godwin had been in a running battle with HEW since 1970, during the final days of his first administration; he was still boiling over Judge Pratt's disapproval of the plan he had submitted in 1974 largely because of its failure to establish goals and timetables.

Alone among the six states' proposals, Godwin's was so out of line that we didn't think there was any point in attempting to negotiate. The plan would have had little if any impact on the fact that two-thirds of the black students in Virginia were in the two black colleges, only one-third in the twelve white colleges. Predominately white Old Dominion University and black Norfolk State College, both located in Norfolk, would remain as a classic example of the dual structure.

The only hope was incoming Republican governor John Dalton. The Virginia attorney general, J. Marshall Coleman, who had been elected along with Dalton, had secretly contacted Tatel in December 1977, before he and Dalton took office, to begin quiet exploration for a solution. I asked the court for an extension, and then I called Dalton privately on February 2, 1978, to say I wanted to settle the dispute amicably. He was surprised and wary, but he promised to take a fresh look at the situation. After some skirmishing and hard negotiation, Dalton and Coleman became convinced that we were demanding not quotas but goals. Dalton firmly corraled the presidents of the Norfolk colleges to eliminate duplication, and Virginia produced an acceptable plan, ending the ten-year battle with HEW.

Television played a role in Dalton's decision. Several times when the dual system desegregation story made network news, because of their proximity to Washington, film clips of the neighboring black and white schools in Virginia would be shown. Dalton was determined that Virginia not resuscitate its "massive resistance" national image. Just before accepting Dalton's plan, I called to congratulate him and read him a draft of my statement. "I hope the praise for your courageous leadership won't hurt you too much in Virginia," I quipped. He laughed, thanked me, and said Virginia would deliver on all its assurances in the plan.

I was privately confident we could settle with North Carolina. I had known William Friday, president of the North Carolina university system, since the Johnson administration, when he was chairman of a Great Society task force on higher education. He had struck me as a liberal, progressive spirit in the South and I had consulted him about education appointments within HEW. When he came to see me early in my tour as Secretary, he told me how delighted he was that I would be handling the higher education desegregation problem, and that he had been "rudely" treated in the past. Moreover, Governor James Hunt was a strong Carter supporter.

But an easy settlement was not to be. Indeed, North Carolina proved the most intractable state of all. Eleven of its colleges were predominantly white, five predominantly black. Ninety-four percent of the students at the white colleges were white, and 96 percent at the black colleges, black.

By its own calculation, the North Carolina university system had fifty-eight non-core-curriculum courses, in fields such as business administration and teacher training, at traditionally black schools that were duplicated at neighboring traditionally white schools in the Raleigh-Durham and Greensboro–Winston-Salem areas. We wanted these non-core courses offered in unduplicated settings in those two areas, at either the black or white college, but not both. Thus, both black and white students interested in such courses would have to go to the same school.

Since 1974, the University of North Carolina had authorized 126 new degree programs for the white schools and only 40 for the black schools, an average of 12 versus 8 per school. At the same time, North Carolina had appropriated $270 million for capital construction at the white institutions, and only $35 million for the black institutions, an average of $24 million versus $7 million per school. We sought substantial commitments for new courses and capital improvements at the black colleges, the elimination of duplication, and, at the white schools, goals and timetables to increase the number of blacks in student bodies, faculties, governing boards, and nonacademic jobs.

When the University of North Carolina board submitted its plan in August and September 1977, we had the first signal of possible difficulty. The plan was virtually identical to the 1974 plan the court had rejected, and one member of the board, Julius Chambers, a civil rights attorney from Charlotte, resigned, charging that the UNC plan "is not a sincere commitment to see that minorities are brought into the system." Negotiations dragged on through 1977 and early 1978. It took days, sometimes weeks, to reach just tentative understandings on each item on the agenda. Friday kept in close touch with Carter, largely through UNC graduate Stu Eizenstat, giving the White House his running version of negotiations with HEW. Because Eizenstat was sympathetic to Friday, and because Friday shrewdly sensed Carter's ambivalence, our bargaining hand was weakened.

As my experience with other states had demonstrated the need for political leadership to resolve these issues, I talked to Governor Hunt at a Democratic fundraiser in Atlanta on January 20, 1978, urging him to get into the problem personally. He agreed to talk to Friday, but he did not want to become involved. At this time, he was more concerned about the anti-smoking campaign I had just announced. As the pressure in North Carolina mounted on Hunt, he spoke to Commerce Secretary Juanita Kreps, who was from North Carolina, and she told Carter at a Cabinet meeting that the combined impact of desegregation and my anti-smoking campaign was hurting the administration badly in her native state. Carter teased her gently, but pointedly, saying she just wanted to keep the University of North Carolina at Chapel Hill, Duke, and Wake Forest "fancy schools." Carter later told me, "When I was kidding Juanita, I was really trying to send a message to Bill Friday. Friday's a great liberal until it begins to pinch him a little bit, just like the mayors of some of those Northern cities like Boston when desegregation was ordered." But the President's spunky attitude soon wilted under the hot lights of political pressure.

Governor Hunt and Senator Robert Morgan eventually met with Carter on February 28. They told Carter he was suffering politically in North Carolina because of my anti-smoking campaign and the move to desegregate the state's higher education system, and asked the President to blunt our efforts on both fronts.

At a Cabinet meeting on March 13, aware of the increasing political pressure on the President, I reviewed negotiations with North Carolina on school desegregation. I was seriously concerned about our ability to reach agreement before the March 22 deadline set by the court. The President asked for a brief memo on the North Carolina situation before March 16, when he was scheduled to visit North Carolina. Although my anti-smoking campaign was the king-of-the-mountain public issue when he visited North Carolina, the President privately expressed his concern to Governor Hunt about the deadlock over desegregation and urged him to negotiate with me. The next day, when I announced agreement on the Virginia desegregation plan, I made a point of the fact that only North Carolina was unsettled.

Negotiations with Bill Friday intensified over the weekend. He was reluctant to set any goals for integration of the eleven white colleges or to commit to any significant enhancement of the five black colleges. He adamantly refused to eliminate duplicative non-core-curriculum courses at the two clusters of neighboring black and white colleges. Even over the phone, I could feel Friday bridling at our insistence that these courses be eliminated. He felt he was being unfairly fingered. The black colleges had been under his jurisdiction only since 1972, and it took time to make changes. He cherished his progressive image and was annoyed and hurt by adverse *New York Times* and *Washington Post* editorials. But he was constrained by a board of governors, singularly independent, legally and emotionally, which was chaired by William A. Johnson, a conservative attorney who resented attempts to desegregate the system. My argument that the other states had agreed to eliminate duplicative courses didn't cut much ice. The other states were not North Carolina.

On the day of the deadline, I announced that HEW would begin enforcement proceedings promptly. When those proceedings began, HEW would defer consideration of future applications for funds from the affected institutions, in a carefully targeted and limited fashion, "if those new federal funds would contribute to continuing segregation in the University of North Carolina system." Coming two months after the announcement of a major anti-smoking campaign, blistering headlines, editorials, and political attacks shot back from North Carolina. Friday said the decision was "wrong." Hunt promised to seek funds from the state legislature to offset any federal cutbacks. Democratic Senator Morgan said, "Mr. Califano's demands are totally unrealistic and his inflexibility is insufferable . . . tragically unworkable, and educationally unsound." Republican Senator Jesse Helms threatened to cut off HEW funds by filibustering the HEW appropriations bill and discussing "at length Mr. Califano's harassment of the citizens and educators of North Carolina."

All this was to be expected. But civil rights groups expressed dismay that, for the first time, a deferral of less than all federal funds from HEW had been ordered. I had come to question privately and publicly the effectiveness of attempts to cut off all funds, for example, from an urban school system, when so much of HEW's money was used to help poor children. It was like opting for decapitation instead of plastic surgery to eliminate facial disfigurement. Such "atomic bomb penalties," as I called them publicly, were counterproductive. In the North Carolina case, it was particularly important to defer only those HEW funds that perpetuated the segregation. The black institutions could not possibly function without such funds. Nevertheless, NAACP Legal Defense lawyer Joe Rauh attacked my targeted deferral as inadequate and improper. Privately, Griffin Bell expressed concern about the legality of such a limited deferral. Still, I thought that targeted deferral was the only kind that made sense here.

When the public skirmishing subsided, I gave Friday, in return for his commitment to resume negotiations, an extension of the time before we would begin the fund deferral and commence the administrative proceeding. But I was now to be under an overriding deadline from the President.

In late April, Carter told me it was imperative to settle North Carolina. He wanted to call Jim Hunt himself. I urged him to hold off because I feared he would settle for too little and be embarrassed if the federal court rejected the agreement. I asked for two weeks, and sent Tatel and Beattie to negotiate with Friday.

On May 11, this handwritten note was delivered to me: "To Joe Califano: Contact me re N.C. desegregation suit. (Your two weeks are up.) Jimmy."

On that same day, Tatel reported that UNC had promised to boost black enrollment at the eleven white colleges, increase black enrollment in graduate schools, equalize black and white salaries over five years, and take other steps to meet the criteria. Tatel said Friday would not make any commitment or accept any language with respect to duplicative courses. I called Friday at home that evening and, several telephone calls later, at about one in the morning, we agreed on language committing the University of North Carolina and the state "to eliminate educationally unnecessary program duplication among traditionally white and traditionally black institutions in the same service area." North Carolina was to conduct a study to identify unnecessary duplication. With this compromise, UNC maintained its academic influence over curriculum, and we held onto the essential tool of eliminating unnecessary duplication. The President was pleased for the moment, but this was only to be a hiatus in what was to become a sad, almost bitter, struggle.

On May 25, Joe Rauh charged that I had approved an unsatisfactory plan to allay public resentment in North Carolina because of my antismoking drive. "This was clearly a political decision," he said. "Califano was burned by the tobacco leaf." He intended to ask the federal district court in Washington to cite me personally for contempt for not complying with the court order. The motion was put in abeyance when I agreed to act within ninety days of receiving the UNC study of duplicative courses. (Rauh moved so often to cite me for contempt that Griffin Bell sent me a hacksaw "in the event of incarceration.")

In December 1978, North Carolina submitted its study. It found fifty-eight duplicative programs between the two clusters of black and white schools, and concluded that none of the duplication was "educationally unnecessary." On January 10, 1979, Rauh wrote me characterizing the North Carolina study as "massive resistance to desegregation of higher education. The suggestion that the state must maintain each and every one of the . . . duplications—all the product of a century of unconstitutional segregation—is an incredible defiance of the law of the land."

Tatel was infuriated at the North Carolina response. He thought Friday was acting in bad faith. For the first time, I had real doubts about our ability to settle North Carolina and I was concerned that state politics and Friday's hurt and anger about the national press would make negotiation impossible, but I kept that feeling to myself. Particularly with Carter pressing me for settlement, I wanted to pursue every possibility. I told Tatel we had to walk the last mile. On January 18, Tatel sent Friday an OCR staff analysis rejecting the UNC conclusion that none of the fifty-eight duplicative courses could be eliminated or was educationally unnecessary. Tatel's letter deliberately did not endorse the staff analysis; he wrote that he "would welcome an opportunity to meet . . . to discuss it in detail."

On January 25, after talking to UNC Board Chairman William Johnson and Governor Hunt, Friday answered with a tough letter "intended only to respond to your specific questions as to whether the paper is acceptable as a basis for discussions. The answer is that it is not." To drive the point home, Friday returned the OCR staff analysis to Tatel, but left the door slightly open, inviting a call if Tatel wanted to discuss Friday's concerns.

In North Carolina, the presidents of the five black institutions were nervous; they were increasingly worried that their institutions might be merged out of existence, or that they might lose large numbers of students. Their opposition to any HEW desegregation plan increased. Governor Hunt phoned Tatel to ask him to meet the black chancellors and hear their views. Hunt apparently believed the meeting would work to his advantage; the chancellors would criticize us for threatening some of their black colleges. On February 6, they flew to Washington in the governor's plane. They confirmed Tatel's suspicion that Friday had been encouraging the black chancellors to think that HEW wanted to close their colleges as part of the desegregation effort. Tatel stressed, to the contrary, that we wanted to strengthen black institutions. Now, for the first time, they seemed to believe him. They invited Tatel to come to see the condition of their schools.

I told Tatel that it was a terrific opportunity, that he should go down there with a large press entourage and show everybody what those institutions were really like. "If they're as bad as you and I think they are," I said, "then I believe the people of the State of North Carolina will support an investment of substantial resources to enhance them."

Tatel was reluctant at first. He was afraid it might exacerbate the situation. I got a call from White House aide Jack Watson. Hunt and Friday wanted the trip called off. "They say it'll be a crisis," Watson argued.

"The press is the only weapon I have," I told him. "If I can get television to bring those sorry black colleges into living rooms, Hunt and Friday will have to move."

Watson did not like the idea. "What do I tell them when they call me back?"

I had half expected a call from the White House or from Hunt or Friday to stop the trip, so I was prepared: "Remind Friday what he said about black colleges. This is a direct quote. 'I believe that the State of North Carolina has done more than any other Southern state on integration and upgrading its facilities.' " If so, I told Watson, Friday has nothing to worry about. Watson wanted to think about it, but he didn't call back.

Tatel's trip had a tremendous impact. He went from campus to campus, comparing classrooms and dormitories, libraries and laboratories. Newspapers that had criticized us changed their tune. The Raleigh *News and Observer* said, "The blunt truth often hurts." It criticized Hunt and others who had committed the state to multimillion-dollar projects on white campuses while they allowed conditions "to fester for too long" on black ones, and called for a "strong commitment—this time to the advantage of black schools." Even Hunt said, "My heart just aches when I see some of the buildings those children have to go to school in," and admitted that "The state should have done a lot more a lot sooner."

Hunt and Friday increased their contacts with the White House and they had a sympathetic ear in Eizenstat. He called me with two messages: The UNC dispute was hurting the President, and HEW was hurting the university. Less forthright than Eizenstat, other White House aides anonymously told reporters that the UNC issue was damaging to the President and that the White House had its doubts about my efforts.

The greatest pressure came through an unexpected quarter. My friend Vice-President Mondale, the most committed civil rights voice in the West Wing, called me on March 8 to say, "Just before he got on the airplane to go to Cairo yesterday afternoon, the President asked me to tell you that he did not want you to bring suit in North Carolina." I said that was not the point. "The issue is whether the NAACP Legal Defense Fund, Joe Rauh, or the state of North Carolina will sue first." Mondale then said the President felt strongly about my not starting any proceedings. I told him I was seeking a settlement, but if that failed, "I must start an administrative proceeding. I have no choice."

Bill Friday came to my office on March 15, the day after the deadline for compliance. It was one of the most difficult and saddest moments of the negotiation. He looked tired, and years older than just a year before. He began by reviewing his record. I interrupted: "Bill, I've known you for years. You don't need any credentials with me." Friday then cited the political problems in North Carolina and the realities of the different student bodies: the average combined SAT scores varied from a low of about 575 at black Elizabeth City College to a high of more than 1,100 at Chapel Hill, UNC's flagship institution; the highest SAT average for a black institution was between 700 and 800. "If we don't keep places like Elizabeth City open, where will the blacks go? They will become crime problems, welfare problems." Friday shrugged.

Friday said that with the investments HEW was urging to enhance black colleges, the state legislature might adopt a standard admissions policy for all colleges, setting a minimum SAT score of 650 to 700. "That will exclude hundreds of black students each year."

Then, exhausted and in despair, Friday said he couldn't move on the duplicative course issue. It had become a matter of principle for the board. But he would put twenty-two new courses in the black institutions.

When I suggested that the alternative would be for a federal judge to take over the UNC system, Friday said, "No federal judge will take over the North Carolina system. The courts didn't take over the system in Louisiana or Mississippi."

"But they did in Tennessee, where the court merged the black and white schools. And there the judge found that the most—the only—effective tool for eliminating the dual system was to eliminate duplicate courses at the neighboring schools." The meeting ended. It was clear that Friday and I would not be able to agree on a plan that would satisfy the court. So on March 26, 1979, in order to comply with the court order, I rejected the North Carolina plan and directed HEW counsel Peter Libassi to institute administrative proceedings.

I still wanted to settle and avoid years of protracted litigation and political acrimony, and so did Carter. On April 12, as he headed for

Sapelo Island, Georgia, for Easter, he sent me a handwritten note: "To Joe Califano: Hurriedly. Do everything possible to work out an N.C. settlement by 4-30. If you wish, I can call/see Jim Hunt when I return. Jimmy."

I called Hunt, who agreed to try to bring about a settlement but warned me that the board of governors had dug in their heels. I also called North Carolina Congressmen Richardson Preyer and L. H. Fountain, both of whom had been helpful during the earlier negotiations, but they echoed Hunt's concern about the board.

Hunt called on April 14 with a proposal to spend $40 million for renovation, capital investment and program enhancement at the black colleges; to seek a legislative resolution establishing a blue-ribbon state group to assess the role of various institutions and regional needs. "To the extent that group recommends elimination of duplication, I'll go along with it," Hunt said, noting that his proposals were in addition to the twenty-two new courses Friday had previously committed to put in the black institutions.

I told Hunt his proposal was a major step forward, but that we had to find a stronger way to deal with course duplication or the court would throw out the settlement.

Hunt's voice was firm: "This is as far as we can go."

So much friction had inevitably built up between Tatel and the North Carolina education officials that I secretly sent Dick Beattie to see Hunt at his North Carolina farm on April 16, the day after Easter. Beattie made some progress, but he said that only Hunt and I could reach a final agreement.

On April 19, the Thursday after Easter, I called Hunt and we agreed to a four-point program: an investment of $40 million in the black colleges; establishment of twenty-two new programs for the black institutions; a pledge that no steps would be taken at the white institutions (such as the placement of new programs) that might impede desegregation of the overall university system; and an assurance that should the three-part plan fail to result in any significant desegregation of the black schools after four years, North Carolina would take additional steps to desegregate, including the elimination of duplicative courses at neighboring black and white institutions. Friday and Beattie worked out specific language that Friday was to present to the UNC board at its scheduled meeting the next day, April 20.

Hunt and Friday called after that meeting. They reported that Board Chairman Johnson was determined to litigate; he and his attorneys argued that if they litigated, HEW would back down or be blocked by a court injunction from going forward with the administrative proceedings. Friday did not even get a chance to present the details of our agreement with Hunt. Instead, the board of governors voted to sue HEW.

Contrary to the board request, Judge Franklin T. Dupree, in the federal district court in North Carolina, refused to enjoin HEW from proceeding against the university. He did postpone any fund cutoff until the end of the administrative proceedings. Judge Dupree closed his opinion with a reminder that, despite the emotional intensity, this litigation involved people, "Not only those to whom the University of North Carolina means so much . . . , but the dedicated public servants who work at HEW and strive to eradicate our nation's regrettable legacy of racial segregation. The protagonists in this drama do not wear black and white hats; instead they are men of conscience struggling to preserve, alter, modernize, and improve a great educational institution. In the balance rests our children's future."

A year after I left HEW, the administrative proceeding was just completing pre-hearing maneuvering and fact-finding, and the UNC board of governors had already paid more than $1 million in legal fees to block the federal government's effort to desegregate North Carolina's dual system of higher education.

BEFORE I became Secretary of HEW, my sense of civil rights, formed by my experiences in the Kennedy and Johnson years, was focused on race. I was aware of the civil rights demands from women and Hispanics, but I had never heard of "Section 504" of the Rehabilitation Act of 1973, which prohibits discrimination on the basis of handicap, mirroring the civil rights language enacted in 1964. That blanket prohibition precipitated my first civil rights confrontation and the most emotionally charged civil rights demonstration of my thirty months as Secretary.

Section 504 had been enacted into law with virtually no legislative history. There had been no hearings and the combined "debate" on the floor of both houses filled less than one page of the *Congressional Record*. Yet the sweeping language was tantamount to another major civil rights law, and it covered about thirty-five million Americans, almost one-sixth of the population. The HEW Secretary was supposed to make those words meaningful.

My predecessor, David Mathews, who was sympathetic to the rights of the handicapped, nevertheless considered this provision to be one of the most irresponsible and thoughtless acts of the Congress. His Office for Civil Rights had spent three years drafting an elaborate set of regulations. Those regulations would have required structural changes to make accessible every room in schools, colleges, libraries, hospitals, nursing homes, and other institutions that got federal funds, including mass transportation systems. The cost of compliance was estimated to run to billions of dollars. Mathews refused to sign the regulations. On his next to last day in office, he sent the 185-page text to the Congress: You passed the law with "not one day" of hearings or debate and no guidance for its implementation, he said in effect. Here is our interpretation. Is it correct?

The Committee chairmen involved—Jennings Randolph, Harrison Williams, and Claiborne Pell in the Senate, and John Brademas in the House—were irritated. They did not want the issue back in that form. It was more fun to be Moses and deliver the commandments than to be the rabbis and priests who had to make them work. Mathews's action, following the three-year delay for developing the regulations, also angered the handicapped groups. Their representatives, and the bureaucrats in OCR, pressed me just to sign the regulations, without thinking about what it would cost or even reviewing them.

The issue was not *whether* to enforce Section 504, but *how*. Those most interested, the handicapped, were, like all special interest groups, rather one-dimensional in their views. It's hard enough to deal with interest groups in black, and even gray, hats, but it's nothing like dealing with those in white hats with an unqualified ticket to equality and opportunity issued by the Congress. Relief was long overdue. Basically, we had hidden the handicapped, put them out of sight in separate schools and homes. But there were other worthy demands on the resources of the institutions that would be affected by the regulations. This was particularly true for hard-pressed universities, urban schools and libraries, and city transit systems. Preoccupied with meeting often urgent needs, these institutions and transit systems had not focused on the impact of the regulations that dealt with handicapped persons.

The law had been passed so quietly that most Americans were unaware of it, or of its ramifications. From the moment I glanced at it, I knew we were on the brink of another, though very different, civil rights revolution. I didn't want it to start from the dead-of-night posture in which the Congress had acted, so I passed the word that I intended to take ample time to review the regulations and restructure them. To signal my ultimate intention, I approved final regulations giving blind persons significantly greater priority in operating vending facilities on federal property (over the vehement objection of several federal departments and agencies). Meanwhile, handicapped groups printed signs and buttons: "Sign 504!"

Dan Marcus, a Washington attorney who had just joined us, and Libassi went to work revising the draft regulations. As the complications and cost of the regulations became apparent, I decided that we should try for program accessibility rather than structural changes. A school could move a course to a different room, rather than make every classroom accessible. Otherwise it was clear the regulations would never take effect. Once the colleges and universities grasped the cost of compliance, the Congress would postpone the effective dates, as it has done in other cases in which HEW requirements were considered excessively expensive, such as those setting standards for day care programs.

This work took time, the momentum built, more "Sign 504" buttons sprouted up. The handicapped groups announced that they would demonstrate at each of the ten HEW regional offices. I welcomed the prospect. Nothing is likelier to evoke sympathy than the poignancy of a demonstration by the handicapped—people in wheelchairs, without sight or hearing, bodies crippled by accidents or genetic defects beyond their control. I hoped the demonstrations would raise the public's awareness of the pending regulations.

I issued a statement on the day the demonstrations began. "They seek redress for discrimination they have suffered. . . . The lawful actions of handicapped men, women, and children . . . are in the great tradition of our nation. . . ." I asked HEW personnel to be "especially sensitive to these demonstrators and to respect their sincere exercise of fundamental First Amendment rights."

I was the first to be tested by my words. On Sunday, April 3, 1977, shortly before midnight, my wife was awakened by a noise outside. "I think somebody's trying to break into one of the houses," she said anxiously. I looked out our second-floor bathroom window down the long driveway to the street. A Ryder rental truck had pulled up. Some people in wheelchairs were being lowered from the back. "I think it's a demonstration," I said.

Holding lit candles, they formed a cross in the round cul-de-sac at the entrance of the driveway. As the television cameras whirred quietly, the demonstrators prayed that I would sign 504 regulations. I heard my golden retriever, Cinnamon, bark outside. "Damn," I shouted, racing down the stairs. All I needed was for Cinnamon to nip someone in a wheelchair. I didn't want to go out myself, so I called from the door, "Cinnamon, Cinnamon." There was no response.

"Cinnamon, Cinnamon," I called again.

The dog barked louder. I saw the television pictures and the newspaper headlines: CALIFANO DOG ATTACKS CRIPPLED WOMAN IN WHEELCHAIR . . . CALIFANO DOG BITES BLIND MAN. I called again as sweetly as I could, "Cinnamon, Cinnamon, come back here."

Though stopping occasionally for another bark along the way, the dog came back to the house. "Good doggie," I said. I hugged her and closed the door.

The next morning I left early through the back gate to avoid the inevitable television take of handicapped persons pleading with me to sign the regulations as I departed in my chauffeured Ford. The demonstrators later followed—first to the HEW Building, and then to the corridor outside my office—chanting "Sign 504! Sign 504!" They also demanded a meeting with me. Reluctantly, remembering Robert Finch, whose office was occupied by angry black employees in 1970, I agreed to talk to them. The television cameras moved in as I stepped nervously onto a coffee table so I could be seen above the shouting crowd.

For a moment my eyes were arrested by the sight of deaf students from Gallaudet College, signing each other in the high spirits of youth, with the manifest joy of taking action to get more control over their own lives. Then, as I felt small beads of sweat forming on my forehead and above my upper lip, I began to speak to the demonstrators. I told them I would sign 504 regulations soon and asked for time to review and revise them. I expressed sympathy for their plight and an understanding of their impatience. I told them I would act by early May and asked them to leave peacefully. They refused. (Most spent the evening at HEW, and I ordered doctors and nurses to remain on duty around the clock.) As I worked, I could hear them singing "We want 504" to the refrain of "We Shall Overcome," which I had sung so often in the 1960s. The next day they left, still denouncing me for delay. I realized that the three-year delay of the previous administration had left the demonstrators devoid of trust in HEW. They would not place any confidence in the Department or me until they saw the regulations I issued.

Cost was not the only obstacle. There was also the politically sticky issue of whether the word *handicapped* in the law included alcoholics and drug addicts. It was the only part of the regulations in which President Carter expressed any interest. At the Cabinet meeting on March 21, 1977, Carter said he did not want drug addicts or alcoholics classified as handicapped. Carter had talked to Governor Jerry Brown, who had told him that a large proportion of the disabled in California were drug addicts and alcoholics, perhaps half of them in Los Angeles. Pat Harris volunteered her agreement with Carter.

I asked Griffin Bell for his official opinion as to Congress's intent. Just before I issued the final regulations, he concluded that the law provided protection for both alcoholics and drug addicts if they could otherwise meet the qualifications for admission and matriculation, or where a job or Federal program was involved, perform the activities required. With that last issue resolved, I signed the revised 504 regulations (reflecting Bell's conclusion) on April 28, deliberately beating my publicly announced May deadline to avoid another round of demonstrations.

HEW funds already touched almost every corner of American life—from day care centers through schools to universities, the entire health care system, all state and local social service offices, and nursing homes for the elderly. Now those funds would open the door to bring handicapped citizens into the mainstream of American life. From the effective date of the regulations, all new facilities would be barrier-free; within sixty days, programs in existing facilities had to be more accessible (where possible, by moving them to accessible areas rather than making structural changes); employment barriers were knocked down. Consistent with the Education For All Handicapped Children Act, every handicapped child who could participate was entitled to a public education along with other children; and where the child was so handicapped that education in a residential setting was necessary, public authorities had to assume financial responsibility.

The regulations ordained fundamental changes in American life and in the lives of handicapped people, their relatives, and those who worked with them. Frank Bowe, Chairman of the American Coalition of Citizens with Disabilities, the umbrella group for many handicapped organizations, called the directive "an eminently fair one that will be readily enforceable and that will be viewed by disabled Americans throughout this nation as a cause for rejoicing." Others, such as columnist James J. Kilpatrick, wondered in print "What Price Califano?" He suggested that most administrators failed to object to the regulations not out of indifference, but because they were "more probably stunned."

There was one much publicized incident when overzealous enforcement and careless reporting almost turned the 504 regulations into a mockery. In October 1977, the OCR regional office in Kansas City told state agencies that every facility receiving federal funds had to be accessible to the handicapped. The Iowa State Librarian promptly told all libraries to make their facilities barrier-free. The 429 citizens of Rudd, Iowa, a small farming community with no one in a wheelchair, claimed it would cost $6,500 to build a ramp to their library. In view of the circumstances, they found it absurd to make such an investment. The press accepted the $6,500 figure (even though a wooden ramp could have been constructed for less than $500) and wrote the story as if the Iowa State Librarian's directive had been an HEW ruling. I called Tatel and we immediately told the residents of Rudd that the law was never intended to create needless hardships for institutions; they did not need to build the ramp.

There were other, more serious concerns about costs. But with intelligent enforcement, I believe the 504 regulations can play a significant role in improving the quality of life for the handicapped.

IN 1972, the Congress passed Title IX of the Education Amendments, which provided: "No person in the United States shall, on the basis of sex, be excluded from participation in, be denied the benefits of, or be subjected to discrimination under any education program or activity receiving federal financial assistance. . . ." It had grown out of an April 1970 report by President Nixon's Task Force on Women's Rights and Responsibilities. Oregon Congresswoman Edith Green, who chaired the House Special Subcommittee on Education, sponsored a forerunner of Title IX. With Green's testy persistence and Senator Birch Bayh nagging the Senate, Title IX was agreed to by a conference committee of both houses in 1972. The Senate approved it overwhelmingly; the House reluctantly went along, 218 to 180.

Soon after Title IX became law, colleges with major revenue-producing sports such as big-time football worried about the implications of treating women's sports on an equal basis with men's, in terms of recruiting, scholarships, and financial investment. Two years later, Senator John Tower of Texas introduced an amendment to exempt such revenue-producing intercollegiate sports from the law. By the time the measure cleared a Senate-House conference committee, it had been changed to a compromise proposal of Senator Jacob Javits of New York. The compromise law called for regulations implementing Title IX to have "reasonable provisions considering the nature of particular sports." The College Football Association argued that Congress intended to exempt sports like football, but President Ford rejected that argument in 1975 when he forwarded an elaborate set of Title IX regulations to Congress, and the Congress did not exercise its power to veto them. The Ford regulations covered academic programs, extracurricular activities, dress codes, and hair lengths. For athletic scholarships, they required proportionate treatment at least, but the language was unclear, and college athletic departments—like elementary and secondary schools—did not expect the regulation to be enforced. The universities howled, HEW did little enforcing, and Congress didn't press it to.

Complaints about Title IX violations were more sophisticated than those of the handicapped, blacks, or Hispanics seeking relief under 504 or Title VI. Young women moved aggressively on the admissions front, particularly at professional schools. The schools responded by opening up. But there were other issues—equal opportunity in vocational education and intercollegiate athletics, among them—on which the response was lethargic, evasive, and resistant.

Usually, when enforcing civil rights programs, HEW sent out a simple form which the federally funded institution signed, committing itself to comply with the regulations. By January 1977, that was about the only Title IX enforcement action that had been taken. Within days after becoming Secretary, I discovered that no one had ever checked to see which institutions had filed the forms and which had not; thousands of executed forms had been lost; many were in corrugated boxes, split open or scattered on floors. Some had been accidentally destroyed. It was inexcusable. We immediately sent out new forms, and by the end of 1977, sixteen thousand had been returned and properly catalogued. But that action was mostly symbolic.

Vocational education had been largely a segregated preserve and secondary school systems were reluctant to provide equal opportunities to women. It took until December 1978 to issue regulations on how to comply with Title IX in vocational education programs. The toughest Title IX problem—intercollegiate athletics—was still unresolved when I left office. In a different way, it was proving as difficult to get women a fair share of intercollegiate athletic programs at some of the big-time football colleges as it had been to get James Meredith into the University of Mississippi in 1962, but I was determined to try—not because I regarded the issue as of overriding importance (I considered the economic issues far more significant), but because it had acquired enormous symbolic value to women in education. Moreover, Title IX had a special significance for me. I wanted to move aggressively in all areas of sex discrimination to demonstrate—particularly to those who saw abortion as an overriding issue—my commitment to women's rights.

I struggled repeatedly with myself. I could not help thinking of the contrast between blacks fighting vicious racial discrimination and severe economic deprivation and women at some of our finest schools seeking equal opportunity in athletic programs. Over time, as I discussed the issue with Patricia Fleming, one of my special assistants, Eileen Shanahan, and other women I had recruited to HEW, I gained some sense of the symbolic importance of the issue to educated women. Intercollegiate athletic programs were the lunch counters in the South for these women: The point was human dignity. If athletics taught character, teamwork, and leadership, and offered the satisfactions of achievement and the discipline of defeat, should not women have the same opportunities as men to develop these traits? Aileen Hernandez, who chaired a revitalized Secretary's Advisory Committee on the Rights and Responsibilities of Women, pointed out to me what collegiate sports had done for black men in terms of personal development and post-college job opportunities, as an example of what such sports could do for women. On October 14, 1977, I wrote the President that "The question of higher education's response to women's demands for parity in athletic opportunity will become a national issue.'' The numbers dramatized the growing interest of women in athletics. From 1971 to 1976, the enrollment of women in the nation's higher education institutions rose about 40 percent. During that same period, the number of women participating in intercollegiate and intramural sports rose more than 100 percent.

I made one of my first public statements in a speech to the American Council on Education's annual dinner in Washington on December 13, 1977, discussing in general terms the era of engagement in higher education, and urging higher education to move aggressively to provide women equal athletic opportunities. I said we would issue regulations and urged the university presidents to comply immediately. I ad-libbed, ''Title IX is the law of the land. It is yours to obey and mine to enforce.'' The women in the audience cheered and the Title IX proponents on my staff glowed, but the moment of joyful rhetoric gave way to gloom as the politics of big-time football and the details of implementation began their work on my lofty words. I received letters and calls from university presidents with big-college football programs. Typical was the warning from Michigan University President Robbin Fleming about how ''controversial'' the issue of ''financing . . . athletics for men and women under Title IX was.'' He urged me to talk to ''knowledgeable people active in the field.'' House Majority Leader Jim Wright put me in a room on Capitol Hill with about thirty coaches and heads of university athletic departments. One by one each argued that football had to be exempted from Title IX because it produced revenue and entailed an especially high cost. College football would be destroyed if comparable amounts of money or a similar number of scholarships had to be given to women. The meeting lasted almost two hours. I sat and listened. There was not a woman in the room.

The argument as to whether ''revenue-producing sports''—a euphemism devised to cover big-college football, but which later spread to basketball and hockey—were within Title IX drew the most attention. HEW General Counsel Peter Libassi concluded that revenue-producing sports were clearly covered. His conclusion marked the beginning, not the end, of controversy, as the question then arose how reasonably to cover such sports.

Most women's groups wanted a dollar spent on women's athletics for each dollar spent on men's athletics, proportional to the number of men and women students enrolled in the college. Writing regulations to provide ''fair'' or ''equal'' treatment for men's and women's intercollegiate athletic programs was extraordinarily complicated by the reluctance of college administrators to give us data about their athletic finances or even about their accounting systems, and by the insistence of women's groups that every *i* be dotted and *t* crossed. At each meeting, the women cited examples of discrimination. At one Midwestern university, the men's basketball team traveled first class on aircraft and stayed in single rooms, while the women's team traveled tourist and shared rooms. The university argued that the men were taller and needed more space, and that the women should stay together as protection from being raped or molested.

Some sports require more people or more expensive equipment—for example, men's football as compared to women's field hockey. Some teams competed nationally, others regionally or locally, and expenses for travel and publicity differed.

Eventually, I issued proposed guidelines in December 1978. They required that schools have ample athletic opportunities for men and women, and that expenditures on intercollegiate athletics be proportionate to the number of men and women participating, with adjustments for nondiscriminatory factors, such as the costs of a particular sport (the football equipment required) or the scope of competition (national, regional, or local). This standard was applied to such financially measurable benefits as scholarships, recruitment, travel, and publicity. Where benefits could not easily be quantified—such as opportunities to compete and practice, or to receive coaching and academic tutoring—a rough measure of comparability was expected. The guidelines were designed to eliminate over time the effects of the traditional emphasis on men's sports, as well as to provide increased opportunities for women.

Walking the policy down the middle of the street, we were ambushed from both sides. Women's groups thought we allowed too big an exemption for football, male coaches charged that the guidelines would kill big-time football. An unexpected source of opposition came quietly, but forcefully, from many blacks, who were concerned that funds which went to women's athletic programs would reduce the number of scholarships available for black male athletics. When Tatel told me about this, urging me to "watch my black flank," I responded, "Don't worry. Those big-time basketball and football schools will always find the money to lure top-flight athletes, black and white."

When the colleges and universities became convinced that I would enforce Title IX, they moved to Capitol Hill. They hired former congressman James O'Hara and former senator William Hathaway and both proved effective lobbyists for the cause of big-time college football. For O'Hara, it was sweet revenge; he had opposed Edith Green on many issues. Hathaway had supported Title IX in the Senate. As the lobbyists went to work, I became concerned that they would get a provision attached to the HEW appropriations bill that would prohibit spending any money to enforce the Title IX intercollegiate athletic guidelines, like the prohibition against using HEW funds for school busing.

The women's groups tried to shore me up. During the spring of 1979, I received 3,646 letters about the Title IX guidelines: 3,342—98.5 percent—favored strict enforcement of my proposed guidelines. While the political groups wanted me to make the proposed guidelines final, the congressional Women's Caucus shared my concern about a legislative prohibition against the use of HEW funds to enforce Title IX for athletics. Elizabeth Holtzman and Margaret Heckler, the Caucus co-chairs, decided to take some soundings in the House.

The basic provisions of the Education Act required that final regulations, including interpretations, be submitted to the Congress. The Congress might within forty-five days void them by a resolution finding the regulations inconsistent with the law under which the Secretary issued them. As the pressure mounted from both sides, I decided to submit the Title IX guidelines to the Congress. I wanted the Congress to stand behind (at least by acquiescence) whatever interpretation I ultimatly adopted, and I wanted the women's groups to see the need to get support on Capitol Hill.

As soon as word reached the Hill that I intended to send the regulations there, both the women's groups and the congressional leadership reacted. House Majority Whip John Brademas called to say that Speaker O'Neill, Majority Leader Jim Wright, and House Education Subcommittee Chairman Bill Ford wanted a quiet, off-the-record meeting. It was held in the Speaker's private suite on March 20, 1979. When I arrived, there sat Brademas, whose district embraced Notre Dame; Jim Wright, representing big-time Texas college football; Bill Ford, speaking for Michigan and Michigan State, and the Speaker, Tip O'Neill, perhaps my closest friend in the House, a strong supporter of Boston College.

O'Neill sat me down to his right, puffed on his cigar, and asked, "Joe, how can you do this to your alma mater, Holy Cross? The Jesuits will never speak to you again." (Holy Cross had that past fall tasted the money of two regionally televised football games.) Wright spoke seriously about Texas and politics, Brademas mentioned Notre Dame, and both he and Bill Ford argued that sending the guidelines to the House for a vote posed an impossible political dilemma for Democratic congressmen: forcing them to vote to reject the position of women's groups or to take an unpopular stand against college football. "Whatever you do," Brademas said, "you can't send these guidelines to the House. All hell will break loose on the floor."

"We could end up with Title IX gutted or repealed," Bill Ford said. Brademas agreed.

"The people have had enough of HEW regulations," Wright added. "They are fed up with this kind of thing."

"Joe," the Speaker said, "this is not the time for this. The last thing we need is a major controversy—that's what it will be—on an issue like this. You'll never get cost containment for hospitals or your other bills."

But it remained for the peppery and astute Bill Ford to drive the point home: "You can lose an election on the sports pages that you'll never lose on the front pages. And that's what you'll do with this interpretation of Title IX."

I said I would talk to the congressional Women's Caucus and get back to them. I was now convinced that the House would attach a rider to the HEW appropriations bill prohibiting spending any funds to enforce Title IX for intercollegiate athletics. The threats by Republicans and conservative Democrats to do just that were mounting, and the leadership could not block such an effort. In the meantime, the members of the Women's Caucus had reached the same conclusion. They would accept an announcement that I was going to redraft the Title IX guidelines. They feared that there were enough votes in the House to cripple Title IX enforcement through the appropriations process.

I still wanted to make sure we continued to search for a workable solution, and I suggested to the women's groups, the House leadership, and some presidents of big-time football colleges that we see how the guidelines would actually apply, so we would know how to redraft viable ones. All agreed. Those who intended to attach a prohibition on the appropriations bill promised not to do so. The women's groups reluctantly accepted the alternative as the lesser of two bad deals. For the moment, the Title IX issue was defused. Once again—as with so much in the civil rights area—Congress postponed making its own sweeping rhetoric a reality.

It turned out that my insisting on testing the proposed guidelines against a variety of college situations—private colleges, state universities, those with major football teams and schools in different geographic locations—kept up enough momentum to allow HEW time to develop a new set of guidelines by the end of 1979. Though somewhat different from the ones I had proposed, the new guidelines promulgated by HEW Secretary Patricia Harris moved to fulfill the promise of Title IX.

I LEFT my civil rights responsibilities with some sense of accomplishment, but also with a lingering feeling of frustration. My experience convinced me that race remains the gut civil rights problem in America, that racism haunts our society like a malevolent ghost that refuses to leave the dark attic of the house. Without minimizing the very real civil rights problems of the handicapped, Hispanics, women, and other groups, none seems to incite the resistance of the middle class white community that actions to achieve racial justice do.

We need more candor and less cant in facing civil rights issues. The Congress has too often been hypocritical—there is no more kind or accurate word for it—in proclaiming glorious rights through authorizing statutes, and subverting the ability to enforce those rights through the appropriations process, by prohibiting the expenditure of funds to make them meaningful or providing inadequate funds. Even in more quiet ways, members of Congress slow the march to equality. I cannot remember a call from a member of Congress to step up civil rights enforcement action in the racial area; I recall scores of pleas to slow down or blunt such enforcement.

With too little consideration, Congress has passed civil rights laws that by their terms augur vast changes for our society, and then balked as the clear implications of such laws are reflected in regulations. The time to think about the political ramifications and full consequences is before taking legislative action to protect the handicapped or prohibit age discrimination, not after the executive branch issues regulations to give life to the legislation.

In HEW—and throughout most of the executive branch—there is too little sense of the different issues protection for disparate groups presents. Techniques that proved effective to eliminate discrimination on the basis of the color of a person's skin are not necessarily appropriate where the effort to root out discrimination and achieve equal opportunity faces physical or mental handicaps, biological differences between men and women, language problems of ethnic groups, or characteristics endemic to various stages of life. This inability to tailor techniques to different sorts of victims of discrimination has represented a serious obstacle to issuing sensible, creative, and clear regulations.

As is the case in so many other areas, civil rights regulations are too detailed. Much of this stems from an entrenched lack of trust by the groups seeking protection. As a result, the regulation writer casts aside the great American tradition and common law principle that every citizen is presumed to obey the law. Quite the contrary—regulations are usually written on the theory that each citizen will seek to circumvent them. We become victims of the self-defeating and self-fulfilling premise that unless we are protected by a law or regulation we are vulnerable. As civil rights regulations get into too many nooks and crannies, they create testy resistance and needlessly invite ridicule.

We must also remember the limits of law to affect human conduct, particularly in a free society. Civil laws codify moral and social standards of a nation and provide the basic framework for social justice. But by themselves they do not change the minds and hearts of citizens. Such change is an internal process. Effective leadership is critical, and no pulpit is more important here than the presidency. It is imperative for the nationally elected Chief Executive of the United States to lead the people with his eloquence, persuasion, and manifest commitment. If he fails to act with courage in the face of political resistance, few are likely to step out front on civil rights issues. The President must reach out to the private sector and encourage employers, unions, churches and others to preach and live the gospel of equal opportunity. Such conduct, far more effectively than laws and regulations, is what moves minds and hearts.

Finally, we must realize that civil rights laws are only one means to social justice, and frequently not the most efficacious. To eliminate discrimination and provide equal opportunity, there must be sound economic policies, jobs, decent housing, adequate transportation, access to health care, supportive family life—and perhaps most important of all in terms of public responsibility—education. Many individual actions are necessary, but there is no more pressing collective action—for cities, states and the national government—than to get our act together in the area of education, particularly in elementary and secondary schools. Until an individual can get the quality elementary and secondary education he or she needs to develop skills and talents, that individual cannot hope to take advantage of the higher education essential to attain positions of leadership across the varied disciplines and careers in our society. Civil rights laws are essential. But the single key that can open most all the doors of equal opportunity is education.

CHAPTER VII

EDUCATION

I CAME to HEW enthusiastic about the opportunity to improve education in America, and determined to step up federal funding sharply. I left alarmed over the deterioration of public education in America and troubled by the threat to academic freedom that the federal role, enlarged and shaped by special interests, poses.

My parents believe deeply in the importance of education. My mother taught at Public School 189 in the Crown Heights/Bedford-Stuyvesant section in Brooklyn for thirty-five years. Her students, first- and second-generation Jewish, Irish, and Italian children, had all been impressed with the need to "do well in school in order to do well in life." Both my parents paid careful attention to my grades, and sacrificed to send me to Holy Cross College and Harvard Law School. Their devotion and the value my Jesuit and Harvard Law teachers placed on academic excellence, knowledge, and the search for truth imbued me with a respect for education that bordered on religious faith.

And my schooling, especially at Harvard, had opened doors to me: Wall Street law practice at Governor Thomas E. Dewey's firm, jobs at the Pentagon with Robert McNamara and Cyrus Vance—heady stuff in the late 1950s and early 1960s for a Brooklyn boy with no contacts. Then President Johnson tapped me to be his White House assistant for domestic affairs, and I knew everything I'd been told about the value of education was true. Johnson's personal commitment to education and my work for him added a new dimension to my understanding: Education was the key to freedom, to tapping the special potential of democracy to release the talents of its citizens, providing both the common tools we all need to function in a free society and the environment to nourish our most brilliant minds.

Johnson loved to quote the president of the Republic of Texas, Mirabeau B. Lamar, with proud flourish: "Education," he would intone, "is the guardian genius of democracy . . . the only dictator that free men acknowledge, and the only security that free men desire." I sometimes wondered whether the quote was apocryphal, like Johnson's claim of direct descent from the defenders of the Alamo. But I knew he felt in every bone of his body a keen determination that "every child should have all the education he or she can take."

When Adam Clayton Powell prounounced Johnson's bill to aid elementary and secondary schools dead because of the church-state issue and a failure to provide sufficient help to black children, Johnson got him to designate Hugh Carey, then a Democratic congressman from Brooklyn, to represent the House committee in negotiations with the White House. Johnson put his top congressional aide Larry O'Brien and Carey in an office in the West Wing of the White House, telling them, "Don't come out till you have an agreement." Carey came up with a formula to provide more help to poor children and the concept of loaning textbooks to parochial schools, as library books are loaned. Johnson pushed the compromise, determined to get his bill. He invested much of his enormous energy in that task, and in 1965, proclaiming that "poverty has many roots but its taproot is ignorance," Johnson broke two decades of deadlock on federal aid to elementary and secondary education (signing the bill on April 11, 1965, Carey's birthday), and through his programs of loans and grants opened higher education to anyone with the talent to get into college.

The Great Society elementary and secondary education programs to help poor children who needed compensatory education in reading, writing, and arithmetic began at $538 million. Funds appropriated under the bill were eventually dispersed to fourteen thousand of the nation's sixteen thousand school districts under a formula related to per capita income. By 1977, despite repeated vetoes of education appropriations by Nixon and Ford, funding for the program approached $5 billion. But the Nixon-Ford vetoes took some toll, and the ravages of inflation were such that by

1977 fewer than six million of the nine million eligible children were receiving help. In higher education, the Johnson student-aid programs started with $383 million in 1966. Expanded and reshaped by the Congress over the next decade, they totaled more than $3 billion in early 1977. Yet the amounts available to help pay college costs under these programs had fallen far behind escalating room, board, and tuition fees. Middle-class families, squeezed by taxes and inflation, demanded that income restrictions on eligibility for federal help to defray college bills be eased or lifted.

I recommended steep funding increases in education programs. I also proposed legislation to concentrate at least $400 million of compensatory education funds in communities with large numbers of poor children, those 3,554 school districts where six million of the nine million eligible disadvantaged school children lived. Carter agreed wholeheartedly, and Congress made some increases of its own. Federal funding for education rose by 63 percent, up some $4.8 billion from 1977 to 1980. Funds for elementary and secondary education rose from $4.5 billion to $7 billion; for higher education, largely student aid, from $3.3 billion to $5.6 billion.

President Carter and I agreed completely on the need for these increases. But we had fundamental disputes on other education issues. The wisdom of creating a separate Department of Education was one; the federal role in elementary and secondary education was another. With respect to the separate Department of Education, the eye of Carter's camera was on the politics of renomination and re-election, and over time he seemed only to sharpen its focus. When it came to the role of the federal government, Carter's desire to improve basic skills led him to the genuine belief that HEW should run a national testing program against which elementary and secondary school children would be measured.

My concern with both these proposals stemmed from a fear that they threatened to breach the healthy limits on federal involvement in education. I also thought they gave insufficient weight to the wisdom, in a diverse democracy, of keeping primary responsibility for elementary and secondary education on states and local communities, and the danger that the increasing federal role posed to academic freedom, especially in higher education. There is no way to set educational policy in a political vacuum. But the pressures of local politics, close to the parents of the children in school, are far preferable to those of national politics where organized groups more easily lose sight of the interests of the teachers in teaching and children in learning. The proliferation of narrow programs, however well intentioned, each with its own legislative authorization or separate funding, had gone too far. Metric education, homemakers courses, ethnic studies, environmental courses, and various literacy and library programs, for example, symbolized the ability of each group to get from a pliant Congress what they were unable to get from a state legislature or local school board. Often the objectives of the national leaders of special interest groups do not reflect the fundamental interests of children and teachers in the classroom, and of society in an educated citizenry, so much as their own ambitions—for example, the emphasis of the National Education Association on teachers' salaries and the right to strike, and the perception by many Hispanic leaders of bilingual education as a political cause rather than a teaching tool.

DURING THE 1976 presidential campaign I was unaware of the extent of Carter's campaign commitment to the National Education Association to establish a separate, Cabinet-level Department of Education. Not that Carter made any attempt to hide his promise: It was printed in the June 1976 NEA *Reporter*. Carter had responded to a written question: "I'm in favor of creating a separate Cabinet-level Department of Education. Generally, I am opposed to the proliferation of federal agencies. . . . But the Department of Education would consolidate the grant programs, job training, early childhood education, literacy training, and many other functions currently scattered throughout the government. The result would be a stronger voice for education at the federal level."

Moreover, vice-presidential candidate Mondale trumpeted the promise at NEA meetings across the country. But such was the nature of special interest politics shrewdly practiced by the Carter campaign in 1976—and such was the concentration of the media on personalities and political conflicts between Carter and Ford—that few national commentators paid any attention to the commitment and even fewer discussed it in any depth. The commitment was lost in Carter's repeated assurances that he would reduce the number of government departments and agencies from 1,900 to 200 in his promised attack on Washington bureaucracy.

I first became aware of the seriousness of Carter's commitment when I met with top NEA representatives John Ryor, Stan McFarland, and Terry Herndon in my law office in early January 1977. The meeting was friendly, in sharp contrast to the emotional exchange with the women's groups over abortion.

In 1972, McFarland had retained me to do the legal work to set up the first NEA political action committee. The NEA previously had adhered to a tradition of staying out of partisan politics. When Harry Truman proposed federal grants for higher education, the NEA stated, "If we accept this gift, it will be the first step toward the degeneration of NEA into a political animal." And the NEA had not become deeply involved in Lyndon Johnson's successful effort to pass the Elementary and Secondary Education Act in 1965. It took McFarland and his colleagues the better part of a day to persuade state and local NEA representatives of the opportunities the new federal law provided, particularly if the NEA could build a political action war chest with a payroll-deduction check-off system. McFarland and I reminisced about that day as we began the meeting. "It's the best thing that happened to NEA," he said with evident satisfaction. "It's really given us some clout." How much, I would discover during the next thirty months.

Carter had promised to consult the NEA "before making education appointments," but I made clear my intention to make my own appointments. McFarland and his colleagues seemed satisfied with my assurance of an opportunity to comment on individuals under consideration for key positions. It was a common-sense political courtesy that I also afforded their rival union, the American Federation of Teachers, an AFL-CIO affiliate. McFarland, Ryor, and Herndon were confident of their ability to influence ambitious appointees, who, as a matter of self-interest, would work closely with them once in the job.

The NEA representatives were more immediately interested in money and a Cabinet-level Department of Education. I told them that I intended to seek substantial increases in federal funds for education, but that I saw little hope of achieving, in four years, the NEA goal of raising from 9 to 33 percent the federal share of the total cost of elementary and secondary education. (I did not express my own reservations about the desirability of the objective.) They nodded their understanding. "What about a Department of Education?" McFarland then asked.

"We may not agree on that," I responded. McFarland immediately reminded me of Carter's commitment to the NEA. "That's why the NEA, for the first time in its history, endorsed a candidate for President."

"I'm sure the President will try to keep all his commitments," I said cautiously, conscious of my tactical mistake. But I was far from willing at this point to agree with an idea I had rejected as Johnson's aide and in subsequent writings on government.

When I met with Albert Shanker, the president of the American Federation of Teachers, he strenuously opposed forming a separate education department. He feared that the rival and much larger NEA would control it; NEA had 1.8 million members to AFT's 500,000. Shanker was also sincerely concerned about limiting the federal role in elementary and secondary education and keeping responsibility firmly fixed on state and local government.

One other person talked to me about a separate Department of Education before I took the oath of office. During my pre-confirmation-hearing courtesy call, Abe Ribicoff told me of his determination, as chairman of the Senate committee with jurisdiction over government reorganization, to separate education from HEW. "It'll make an impossible job less impossible for you," he said. Ribicoff had never really enjoyed being Secretary of HEW in the early 1960s; he left the Kennedy administration in frustration to run for the Senate from Connecticut in 1962.

The NEA reacted to my comment by asking for a meeting with Carter. On April 25, 1977, two days before the meeting, I sent Carter a brief memo urging him to be cautious about his commitment to a separate Department of Education. "I am well aware of your campaign commitment and I am prepared to work for its implementation, if that is your final decision. However, I would like to have the opportunity to discuss the desirability of a separate education department before you firmly commit to such a proposal as President. Long before I had ever thought I would be Secretary. . . . I had written extensively about government reorganization, including arguments against creation of such a department." I stressed that the President needed fewer constituency-oriented departments, not more people reporting to him, if we were to have a bureaucracy responsive to presidential leadership. I reminded him that the health, education, and welfare combination was essential to the success of such efforts as the childhood immunization program we had undertaken, and flagged my concern about the relationship of a separate department to higher education. I suggested that Carter tell NEA officials he needed more time to examine all the reorganization options, including the possibility of a new department.

At the meeting with the NEA, Carter, Mondale, and I sat on the presidential side of the Cabinet table, our backs to the French doors leading to the Rose Garden. McFarland, Herndon, and Ryor faced us. They set forth their interests in education, stressing the importance of the separate department. To my surprise and satisfaction, Carter hedged. He mentioned some of the considerations in my memo and said he would "work on it and study it." As I sat there, I sensed that Carter, whatever he had felt during the campaign, had serious doubts whether the separate department was a good idea. McFarland's face revealed the same intuition. He sensed the danger to NEA's cherished goal; his cheeks flushed, he started to speak, but then remained silent. Carter read what I had seen in McFarland's face and said that he would have Mondale, the administration's strongest proponent for a separate department, and me review the situation.

The Vice-President and I met twice during the week of June 13. Mondale wanted Carter to state, without any further analysis and study, that he was committed to a Cabinet-level Department of Education. I argued that the President should subject the organization of education activities to a wide-ranging study by the Office of Management and Budget and HEW, with the advice of such interest groups as the NEA. At our first meeting on June 13, OMB Director Bert Lance agreed with me. During the second meeting with the Vice-President two days later, and subsequently, I realized that Mondale was far more deeply committed to the idea of a separate department than Carter, both substantively and politically. Hamilton Jordan recited his familiar lines, "I don't know anything about the merits, but I know the politics, and politically the NEA is important to us and it's important for the President to keep his word." (The 1.8 million membership of NEA was larger than Carter's margin of victory over Gerald Ford in 1976.) Mondale pressed forcefully on the merits, in addition to seconding Jordan on the politics. Nevertheless, when I urged Carter to direct a broad study before deciding whether to renew his commitment, he did so. And on July 7, 1977, after meeting with Carter, AFT President Shanker told reporters that there was "a good chance" the administration would not create a Cabinet-level post and that Carter had made "no commitment as to which way he'll go."

The OMB-HEW study was conducted against crosscurrents of persistent NEA pressure on the administration to perform on Carter's promise, and my attempt to keep the issue open. McFarland said in August 1977 that if Carter changed his mind, "We're going to have a hell of a lot of members who will feel double-crossed." Whenever I spoke at Democratic fundraisers or held out-of-town press conferences, an NEA member or a reporter often prompted by the association dutifully asked for my view on the Department of Education. I developed a stock answer, expressing my opposition, but always concluding, as I did during a press conference before meeting with Shanker and his top officials in Boston on August 18, 1977, that the President would make the decision and I would support him: "My name was not on the ballot. . . . It will be the President who will make the ultimate decision."

The issue went to Carter in November 1977. After my first year of experience at HEW, I was even more deeply troubled by the idea of a separate department and I expressed my argument strongly. From the President's point of view, such a constituency-oriented department put yet another special interest directly on his back, and no buffer of a department head with broader responsibilities to deflect some of the issues for him. Inevitably, the Secretary of such a narrowly composed department would be less responsive to the President as the daily pressure of the constituencies corroded the relationship with the White House. The narrow interest situation would be aggravated because the special interests to which an education department would be largely responsive—the NEA teachers union, school administrators, groups protecting pet programs—were not the interests it was supposed to serve; its obligations were to the students. Without any serious consolidation, the President would be adding yet another person reporting directly to him, further straining his span of control. The key commissions of the 1960s and 1970s that had studied government organization—groups chaired by Ben W. Heineman, Sr., for Lyndon Johnson and by Roy Ash and John Connally for Richard Nixon—had recommended essentially the same structure: consolidation, fewer departments and agencies, and no Department of Education.

The proposal for a separate department, I argued, would hinder effective administration of social programs. HEW's target population for welfare aid for dependent children, Medicaid, and many of its social service programs such as Head Start, was poor children and families, a target also served by its education division. The potential of school health, basic skills, adolescent pregnancy, venereal disease, anti-smoking, drug and alcohol abuse, and nutrition programs was greatly enhanced when health, education, welfare, and social service programs were together. Perhaps the most intractable management problem in government is getting people to work together; creating another special interest department exacerbated that problem. (Labor Secretary Ray Marshall and I had both energetically favored a joint Labor/HEW work-study program for high school students; yet our staffs took months to negotiate a treaty we both signed and bureaucratic jurisdiction problems still plagued the program more than a year later, when I left HEW.)

Congressional actions, particularly over the past decade, provided further clear warnings of trouble with a separate department. The Congress had lodged more than 120 programs in HEW's Education Division and was becoming increasingly intrusive in the education process. In a display worthy of Alice's looking glass, the Congress had passed a law prohibiting HEW from exercising "any direction, supervision, or control over the curriculum, program of instruction, administration, or personnel of any educational institution, school, school system, or over the selection of library resources, textbooks, or other printed or published instructional materials by any educational institution or school system. . . ." And then, over the next ten years, the same body had proceeded to write increasingly detailed directions to state and local school systems in several hundred pages of legislation, reinforced by almost two thousand pages of regulations which that legislation often explicitly ordered HEW bureaucrats to issue. With Congress more and more inclined to meddle in the curriculum, administration, and personnel of local schools *without* a separate Department of Education, I feared even more ominous intrusion in any law the Congress drafted to create one, and in its subsequent actions and those of the nearly eighteen thousand employees who would be in the department when it was created.

With federal funds go federal strings. By 1977, the federal government was paying almost 9 percent of the costs of elementary and secondary education; state government was paying about 43 percent; local government, the largest share, 48 percent. A proclaimed purpose of the NEA proposal for a separate department was to increase the federal share to one-third, and make it an "equal partner" with state and local government in financing elementary and secondary education.

The federal role has rightly been to provide access to education for all on the basis of ability and to support research efforts to advance our society. A separate department at the national level could signal a fundamental change in that role. The threat to the diversity of elementary and secondary schools, as well as the transfer of much more political responsibility for public education to the national government, was of concern to me. But the greatest danger in the creation of a separate department seemed to me to be what it might portend for higher education. There, academic freedom and excellence must be vigilantly guarded. By the end of the 1970s, the federal government was paying almost $20 billion to institutions of higher education and their research programs, more than 30 percent of all the revenues our colleges and universities received. That percentage will continue to rise in the 1980s. Today, many colleges and universities, notably including those with high enrollments of needy students such as the predominantly black colleges in the South, receive more than 90 percent of their revenues from the federal government. Others, such as the Massachusetts and California Institutes of Technology, already receive 50 percent of their revenues directly related to teaching students from the federal government, including NASA, the Agriculture, Defense, and Energy departments, and the National Institutes of Health, as well as the Education Department. If funds received by the MIT and Cal Tech laboratories are included, the federal government provides 70 percent of their revenues. Dozens of other universities get more than 30 percent of their operational budgets just from federal student aid programs, and a much higher percentage when federal research funds are included.

Under such circumstances, it is unrealistic to believe that the national government does not become involved decisively, if indirectly, in some curriculum decisions of major universities. The competition for federal research funds is intense. An integral part of winning that competition is to have on the faculty the scientific and intellectual talent to fill the government's research needs; having such talent dictates many courses offered at major universities. The federal funds bring with them

—as they should—the civil rights laws. But determining whether there has been discrimination in faculty appointments can also bring the federal bureaucrats and judges into the privacy of faculty meetings, with demands that secret ballot votes be disclosed and that Labor Department staffers be given wide access to academic files and records. The quest for equal opportunity faces one compelling social interest against another—the elimination of discrimination versus academic and intellectual freedom. But less compelling needs, such as reviews of compliance with research and other federal contracts, are already beginning to assert demands for access to records. Against this financial and bureaucratic horizon, a separate education department looms as a truly dangerous specter to our tradition of intellectual freedom of inquiry and institutional autonomy.

Moreover, a separate department would not help solve any deficiencies of our education system. The deterioration of elementary and secondary education, particularly in urban America, is far advanced. The statistics are chilling. Each year from 1962 to 1980, scores on the verbal and mathematics scholastic aptitude tests have fallen. The overall decline was 54 points on the verbal test, more than 36 points on mathematics. (Verbal scores have dropped more sharply because of television and lack of parental attention to reading. Children learn to read at home; they learn math in the classroom.) By 1975, more than twelve of every hundred seventeen-year-olds were functionally illiterate. In Washington, D.C., in 1976, a high school valedictorian was rejected by a local university because his scores on repeated tests fell far below the minimum range of acceptable applicants. In San Francisco, a high school graduate sued school officials when he discovered that his reading skills were on a fifth-grade level. In Los Angeles, 59 percent of a recent high school graduating class could not fill out applications for a driver's license.

Students' understanding of the basic structure of our government was just as depressing. In 1975, only 53 percent of seventeen-year-olds knew that each state had two senators, and that the President did not appoint members of Congress.

The HEW survey of violence in American schools was also frightening. Commissioned by the Congress in 1974 and completed during my first year as Secretary, the survey concluded that the most dangerous place for a child was in school. Although children spent only 25 percent of their waking hours in school, 40 percent of the robberies and 36 percent of the assaults on teen-agers took place there. Each *month:* 11 percent of the nation's secondary school students, about 2.4 of the 21 million, have something stolen from them; about 1.3 percent of the students, 282,000, report being attacked; some 12 percent of all secondary school teachers,

120,000 of them, have something stolen at school; approximately 5,200 teachers are physically attacked, 1,000 needing medical attention; more than 25 percent of all schools are vandalized, with an average cost of almost $100 for each act of vandalism; 10 percent of all schools are burglarized, at an average cost per burglary of $183. The statistics told me a story of an educational system in collapse.

My initial reaction to the statistical data was shock and outrage—how could the most affluent society on earth tolerate such a school system? Yet, as I came to terms with my anger, I was struck by the limited capacity of the federal government to solve the problems. School systems were already overburdened by the constitutional mandate to integrate in a society still festering with racism, and by the demands of parents that schools compensate for a decade of broken families, sexual freedom, urban violence, drugs, and a generation of urban ghettos of poverty.

Clearly, we all want better schools for our children. Perpetuation of the current situations in many rural areas and most urban centers will produce millions of functional illiterates, who will surely strain the fabric of our democracy. But a separate Cabinet-level Department of Education was at best irrelevant to these problems and at worst could further erode the responsibility of state and local school systems to deal with them.

Carter's OMB reorganization staff independently reached a similar conclusion, opposing the creation of a separate department organized narrowly around HEW education programs. We both suggested internal reorganization within HEW to cure administrative deficiencies and improve management.

On November 26, 1977, I made a final argument to Carter in a private memo: "All my experience in government—both as personal staff to a former President and as a Cabinet Secretary to you—leads me to urge, in the most forceful way I can, that you reject the narrowly based separate department on the merits as inimical to the President's policy-making, managerial, and budgetary interests." Two days later, I met with Carter and the OMB reorganization staff to discuss the options that had been developed. But Carter held his own counsel at that meeting, simply listening, asking very few questions. I learned of his decision on December 18, 1977, with the rest of America, when Rosalynn Carter responded on *Issues and Answers* to the question whether the President was going to establish a Department of Education with the statement that "I'm sure he will."

Once Carter formally committed himself to the new department in his January 19, 1978, State of the Union message, the battle opened over what it was to include. The agencies with education components predictably fought relinquishing their bureaus to the new department. While testifying before a House Appropriations subcommittee on February 21, in response to questioning about the candidates for the new department, I mentioned all of the Veterans Administration's education programs as well as those in the Defense Department, the entire National Science Foundation, the college housing loan program from the Department of Housing and Urban Development, school nutrition programs from Agriculture, and several job-training programs from Labor. Because all were logical components, turf battles instantly erupted among interest groups. OMB spokespersons said no decisions had been made; enraged White House political aides in Jordan's office scrambled to assure veterans and other groups that their pet programs would not be folded into the new department. Carter's 1976 campaign commitment for a broad-based consolidation of the education programs scattered around the government gave way to his 1980 campaign for renomination and re-election. McFarland put it bluntly: "Politically, the narrower the department is, the better off we are . . . I'd be damn happy if they took the [HEW] education division and made it a department" by itself.

At lunch on March 7, Mondale told me that the bureaucratic resistance to putting agencies outside HEW's education division in the new department was so vehement that he thought the administration should not propose any specific items for inclusion. He preferred a general endorsement of the bill Ribicoff had been introducing for several years, and then some quiet work with the Senate Government Operations Committee to put a package together. "That way we don't alienate any of the interests," Mondale said.

During the ensuing weeks, the arguments raged within the administration over what to include in Carter's proposal for the new department. Hungry for legislative victory, the administration proposal was politically forged, ignoring all but a handful of the scores of education programs scattered throughout the federal bureaucracy. For the taxpayers, the costliest missed opportunity was the failure to consolidate all the federal government's student loan and grant programs in a single Bureau of Student Financial Assistance. I had consolidated all such programs within HEW in one bureau to the full extent of my administrative authority. The OMB reorganization staff study had identified fifty-five federal student aid programs outside HEW. Fearing criticism from special interest groups, Carter recommended that only one of those programs be folded into the new department. The unnoticed failure to consolidate these programs costs the American taxpayers hundreds of millions of dollars each year.

Carter's proposal to the Congress on April 14, 1978, included HEW's Education Division, Head Start, and education responsibilities of the Office for Civil Rights, as well as Howard University, Gallaudet College, the American Printing House for the Blind, and the National Institute for the Deaf, also funded by HEW. The President recommended folding in the Agriculture Department's school breakfast, school lunch, and nutrition education programs, and its graduate school, the Department of Housing and Urban Development's college housing program, the Interior Department's Indian schools, certain science programs from the National Science Foundation, and the Defense Department's overseas schools. But the President excluded from the proposal several major education-related federal programs: The National Endowments for the Arts and for the Humanities (which the Ribicoff bill included), the Veterans Administration's education programs, the Labor Department's job-training programs, and scores of others. Bureaucratic and special interest politics had eliminated even the argument of significant consolidation.

As the date for the initial hearings before Ribicoff's Government Operations Committee neared, I faced the question of whether to testify on behalf of a proposal I considered to be bad government policy. OMB Director James McIntyre, who had succeeded Bert Lance, was demanding that I testify to "support the President." I called Eizenstat and pointed out that Republicans who opposed the concept of the new department would cite my earlier writings and testimony against such a move, and eventually draw out my honest opposition to the concept, in order to embarrass the administration. Eizenstat readily agreed that I should not testify. Under Secretary Hale Champion, armed with a letter of carefully worded, after-the-decision support from me, testified on May 17, 1978. Over the course of House and Senate hearings during 1978 and 1979, I wrote another letter of support to Ribicoff on February 7, 1979 (at the suggestion of Vice-President Mondale, "to protect yourself from accusations Jordan and [Carter legislative aide] Frank Moore are making that you're trying to derail the President's proposal"), and one to House Government Operations Committee Chairman Jack Brooks on March 27, 1979.

In addition to Champion, Education Commissioner Ernest Boyer and National Institute of Education Director Patricia Graham testified in support of Carter's proposal, even though Boyer preferred to reorganize the education division and keep it within HEW and Graham firmly opposed the idea of a separate department. Assistant Secretary of Education Mary Berry favored the new department. She helped muster black support for the proposal, partly in the futile hope that she, a black, would be the first Secretary of the new Department of Education. Carter and his staff held this possibility out to her, even inviting her to one of the President's reassessment meetings at Camp David on July 11, 1979, the day the

Education Department bill passed the House. As I watched them deal with Berry, I remembered my work for Lyndon Johnson putting together the Department of Transportation. General Bozo McKee, then head of the Federal Aviation Administration, opposed including his agency in the new department. He kept citing air safety considerations and his direct reporting line to the President. One evening, as Johnson and I reviewed the status of my efforts, we discussed the FAA and McKee. "Tell him you'll give him a higher executive level slot in the new department than he's now got," Johnson said. That just might do it, I thought. When I told McKee, he agreed to support the proposal. McKee got his higher-level job; Mary Berry did not.

As the Education Department proposal worked its way through the Congress, each special interest moved to carve out its own independent fiefdom, with legislative power and protection. This had the effect of making it virtually impossible for the Education Secretary to run the new department efficiently. The new department was also stripped of many of its components. Head Start was dropped in Ribicoff's committee, Agriculture's school-feeding programs and Interior's Bureau of Indian Education were cut out on the Senate floor. At the urging of groups of the disabled the Rehabilitation Services Administration of HEW was added (even though the median age of the population served was 32), and given even more legislative independence than it had enjoyed in HEW. By the time the amended bill passed the Senate on September 28, 1978, the power of the new department's Secretary was so circumscribed that when I offered to recommend Hale Champion for the post, he said he would never take it. "I doubt anyone in higher education will be the first Secretary. Only someone who's never been in Washington bureaucracy will take that job," he added.

Meanwhile, during the summer of 1978, after weeks of wrangling in committee and at the prodding of Vice-President Mondale, the House Government Operations Committee reported a bill similar to the Senate's. But even with the support of the disabled groups, who had gained more independence for the Rehabilitation Services Administration in the separate department, the administration was unable to muster enough votes in the House. The editorial comment across the nation was scathing, and even included the liberal *New York Times,* and *Washington Post* which said, "The bill is the inspiration of the NEA, an organization that has much the same relation to the public schools as the plumbers union has to the plumbing business." Without the votes to pass Carter's proposal, the House leadership refused to put the bill on the floor before the session ended.

Early in the next Congress, on February 8, 1979, the administration reintroduced the separate department legislation. Mondale argued at the briefing that "This is the only major industrial democracy in the world that does not have a department or a ministry of education." The administration's new proposal dropped the school lunch, school breakfast, and nutrition education programs from the Agriculture Department, and the Head Start, Indian Education and Labor Department Education and Training programs that had been included in the original proposal the year before. The bill, essentially carving the E out of HEW and not treading on anyone else's turf, easily won approval from the Senate Government Affairs Committee by a 14 to 1 vote on March 14, 1979. After four days of debate and skirmishing over various amendments, on April 30, 1979, the Senate voted 72 to 21 to create the new department.

The final battleground was the House. There, Albert Shanker, his American Federation of Teachers, the AFL-CIO, and many in the higher education community made their fight against the department. As Shanker began to collect votes—and as the editorial refrain of opposition rose from the grass roots—OMB Director McIntyre held a press conference on March 23, 1979. He made the expected arguments: The new bureaucracy would eliminate up to four hundred jobs and save $100 million annually. But then he accused me of pushing educational problems aside in favor of other interests. Education Commissioner Boyer, who had been seething for months at what he called "McIntyre trashing our accomplishments" and his work in education at HEW, was appalled. "Obviously," he told me, "to tell the story would mean we don't need a new department."

When I read the news reports of McIntyre's press conference the next morning, I called Jack Brooks and asked if the record of his House Government Operations Committee hearings included the accomplishments in education since I had been Secretary. "No," Brooks said. "I'll write you asking for them and I'll read your letter in the record." Brooks wrote on March 26, 1979, asking for "a list of achievements [of] your Department . . . in the field of education since you became Secretary. . . ." I answered him on March 27, citing the accomplishments and closing the letter with praise for Carter and carefully phrased support for his Education Department proposal: "President Carter's proposal to give Cabinet-level status to education builds on these accomplishments. . . . The President's proposal for a Cabinet-level Department of Education flows from well-established national education commitments and aspirations. By actions in his own time, the President has unmistakably signaled his conviction that education merits greater national concern and attention."

I sent McIntyre a copy of my letter. The list of accomplishments on the first pages made him so furious, he called me before reading the concluding paragraphs. I focused his attention on them, and told him that I intended publicly to answer any incorrect statement he made about Boyer's or my handling of education at HEW. McIntyre then contacted the White House staff, which led to a penned presidential note the same day: "To Sec. Califano; I want your active support in the Congress for the Department of Education legislation. J. Carter."

I responded to the President the following morning, enclosing my earlier letters of support to the House and Senate committees and noting that I had persuaded top HEW officials to testify in support of the new department although they disagreed with the concept. I offered "to do whatever else you wish" for the new department, but I expressed my disagreement with McIntyre about the attention I had given to education: "Since 1977, by far the lion's share of HEW discretionary fund increases, requested by me and enthusiastically approved by you, has gone to education. During your presidency, the HEW education budget has increased by $4.8 billion, some 63 percent. And HEW's finest legislative hours have been in this area: the new Elementary and Secondary Education Act legislation, the Middle Income Student Assistance Act, the new legislative focus on basic skills and on flexibility in using desegregation funds. Administratively, we have completely reorganized the Office of Education, and moved to clean up the student assistance programs. . . . There are arguments for a separate Department of Education. But I do not believe that a lack of accomplishment in education over the past two years—or lack of attention to it—can fairly be said to be one of those arguments."

On May 2, two days after the lopsided vote on the Senate floor, the House Government Operations Committee, by one vote, 20 to 19, reported the Education Department legislation to the House.

Shortly thereafter, while I was in China in June 1979 to sign the first Health and Education agreements to implement the protocol signed by President Carter and Vice-Premier Deng Xiaoping, the most serious incident with the White House over the Education Department erupted. Earlier, Congress had passed Carter's Ethics in Government Act, and Education Commissioner Ernie Boyer had told me that he could not wait, as planned, until the end of 1979 to leave to become President of the Carnegie Foundation. (Foundation lawyers told Boyer that the law's restrictions on post-government activities would sharply curtail his effectiveness as foundation president unless he left before it took effect on July 1, 1979.) Boyer's decision to resign before that date created the problem of whom to designate as Acting Commissioner of Education. No qualified outsider would come aboard, because the controversial proposal for a separate Department of Education was still pending.

I had settled in my own mind on either Tom Minter, who was Deputy Commissioner in Charge of Elementary and Secondary Education, or Mike Smith, the Assistant Commissioner of Education for Policy Studies. Minter was a more experienced administrator and was black. Smith had done a superb job in helping develop our elementary and secondary education legislation, and would be a key actor in the higher education legislation that would dominate congressional concern in this area for the rest of the 96th Congress. I was leaning toward Minter largely because Carter was so intent on putting more blacks and other minorities in jobs at HEW.

At a White House meeting in late March 1979 to review upcoming appointments, Peter Bell, my executive recruiter, told White House personnel aides Arnie Miller and Harley Frankel that we would fill the Acting Commissioner's position with either Minter or Smith. The White House aides told Bell that of the two, they preferred Smith. That was fine with Hale Champion and me, especially since Smith, talented as he was, would not be perceived a potential candidate for the first Secretary of Education, as Minter would. Smith would also give us someone already well versed on the details of the higher education proposals, to testify on them. So on June 15, the day I left for China, I announced to the Department that effective July 1, Mike Smith would be Acting Commissioner.

On Sunday evening, June 24, Hale Champion called me urgently in Kunming. The Smith appointment had become a major controversy. Congressional Black Caucus chairman Parren Mitchell, a Maryland Democrat, objected to it. Mitchell wanted Mary Berry in the Acting Commissioner's job, in the hope of getting a black as first Secretary of Education. Smith was one of the researchers for the book *Inequality: A Reassessment of the Effects of Family and Schooling in America,* by Christopher Jencks, founder of the Center for Educational Policy Research at the Harvard Graduate School of Education, and Mitchell alleged the book was "racist." Authored by Jencks with the aid of a team of seven assistants, including Smith, this book found, among its conclusions, that desegregation had little, if any, impact on the performance of black children in school. The book called for a major reassessment of the amount and mix of resources devoted to elementary and secondary school desegregation. The conclusions and recommendations were explicitly Jencks's. Indeed, Smith had worked and written for years, before and after, in support of desegregation and of federal funds to help educate poor children.

Mitchell threatened to lead a major assault against the Department of Education on the House floor unless the designation of Smith as Acting Commissioner was withdrawn. This concerned administration strategists, especially since many thoughtful black leaders, such as Shirley Chisholm, were already opposed to the separate department. Among other reasons, they considered it critical to keep the liberal, labor-backed programs in a single department so the lobbying efforts of individual groups would reinforce one another. They also feared, as I did, that putting the civil rights effort under the top education official, rather than independent of that official as it was in HEW, would soften enforcement. Predictably, Mitchell's threat sent shivers through White House aide Stuart Eizenstat and Vice-President Mondale.

Eizenstat called Champion and suggested that he withdraw the Smith appointment as Acting Commissioner. Champion, who had resigned effective June 30 to return to Harvard, resisted. He argued that Mitchell's effort was an "outrageous attack on intellectual inquiry" and an attempt by the Black Caucus to get a leg up on the new Cabinet post. Eizenstat pressed him for Smith's removal "to save the Education Department bill." Champion refused until he had an opportunity to discuss it with the President. "This is grossly unfair," Champion argued. "Smith is not a racist. And there'll be one helluvan academic backlash."

Mondale then called Champion. Pointedly noting that he was speaking for the President, Mondale told Champion that Smith could not be Acting Commissioner. From the Vice-President's point of view, it was a meaningless interim appointment that could block achievement of a goal he believed in. Moreover, the NEA would be critical to Carter in any primary fight and it looked more and more like Kennedy might take on the President. Mondale saw no issue of academic freedom. Hale asked for a face-to-face meeting.

Champion recited these events during his June 24 call to me in Kunming. He was so outraged, he was prepared to resign a few days early as a protest. "I will not rescind Mike's appointment. This is the grossest attack on academic freedom. It's character assassination," he shouted halfway around the world. "And it won't change a vote on the Education Department bill."

"There is an element of McCarthyism here," I noted.

"You bet there is," Champion agreed. "It's worse than that. This is book-burning." I'd never heard him so angry. I asked him whether Mondale had agreed to see him. "Not quite," he responded, "but there's a better than even chance he'll see me tomorrow. I want to make sure I know your view before I meet with Mondale."

I told Champion I agreed with him, and asked. "What about Mike Smith? How does he feel?"

"I don't know," Champion said. "They'll eventually pressure Smith to withdraw, thinking that if he did, it would solve the problem." There was a pause at the other end of the line. Then with a wry chuckle, Champion added, "But to be perfectly honest, I hope he doesn't."

As I hung up, I thought of my last brush with such an experience. In 1964, when the War on Poverty program hung in the balance in the House, word leaked that President Johnson and Sargent Shriver intended to appoint Adam Yarmolinksy, Robert McNamara's special assistant at the Pentagon, to be deputy director of the program. Yarmolinsky was unfairly and unjustly attacked for far-left views he did not harbor and held accountable politically for the views of his parents. Johnson and Shriver agreed not to make him deputy director in return for a handful of Southern votes essential to pass the War on Poverty bill. I had succeeded Yarmolinsky as McNamara's assistant, and as we discussed how outrageous Yarmolinsky's treatment had been, McNamara said, "Where the President or one of his key objectives is concerned, none of us is important." I didn't believe McNamara's assessment then; but experience has taught me that every President does. The fact that I had since learned that McNamara was correct about the harsh realities of governing has never made it easier to accept the individual injustice of such situations.

Champion did meet with Mondale the next day; he called me early in the morning in Kunming to report. Our hour-long conversation left our Chinese hosts and the American press corps waiting at a commune outside the city. "Mondale cares only about the vote on the Education Department," Champion began.

"Did he hear you out?" I asked.

"A little," Champion answered. "But what he heard, he wasn't listening to. He doesn't care about anything except the department. He virtually began the meeting by saying, 'We don't want Smith as Acting Commissioner. The appointment's got to be withdrawn.' " Hale's angry disappointment echoed through the statical connection. "I laid out our points, but he wasn't really interested. At the end, Mondale ordered me to rescind your appointment." I asked Champion how he had reacted. "I told Mondale that I would have to see what I would do, but that first I wanted to talk to Mike Smith." I asked where Smith stood. "I don't know," Champion replied, "but Mondale's staff has continued to put pressure on Smith to withdraw."

"What a mess," I said in dismay.

"This is your town," Champion said, sighing. "I don't know how you can live in it. Thank God I'm going back to Cambridge."

I asked Hale to request an appointment for me with Mondale as soon as I returned, and to let me know the outcome of his conversation with Smith.

Champion and Smith had several talks. Smith was an academic policy analyst; that was the career he cared about. He had little stomach for such brutal confrontation, but he felt as deeply as Champion about relating the appointment to his academic work. The Vice-President's staff promised him a major post in the new Education Department if he withdrew, but he had no interest in view of the events. Smith saw it as a distasteful, no-win situation; Champion eventually agreed. Acting at Smith's request, Champion reluctantly withdrew his appointment. Under White House order, Mary Berry was named Acting Commissioner. The appointment—and the signal of an inside track to be the first Secretary of Education it falsely implied—brought cheers from Parren Mitchell and those who had gone after Smith.

Others saw it quite differently. The *Washington Post* editorial called the episode ". . . a lot of shoddy dealing" and labeled the charge of racism against Smith a "breathtakingly false charge. . . ." It closed by saying that "the government could do something to repair its own integrity, which did get dirtied, by saying out loud and for the record, that it was and is a libel to accuse [Smith or Jencks] of racism in any way, shape or form." The *Post* editorial particularly hurt Mondale because it came from a friend, Meg Greenfield. The *Times* was even more critical in its editorial, "Education Disgraced": "The charge of racism is rolling too easily off too many tongues these days. . . . These smear tactics debase not only language but politics itself." The *Times* attacked the Black Caucus members for threatening to "vote against the Education Department if Mr. Smith received the interim appointment. Shamelessly, Mr. Mondale went to work, until Mr. Smith withdrew. . . . These tactics were cruel and the charges were absurd; the offending book, *Inequality* by Christopher Jencks, is a serious treatise that no responsible person would condemn as racist. Those who hurl such charges and those who appease them should never be entrusted with education or scholarship in any setting. And Mr. Smith deserves the apology of his government. Even in the politics of education, individuals are still supposed to matter."

Enroute from China, I stopped in Hawaii to meet with Governor George Ariyoshi about the refugee crisis the island state faced and to review several HEW programs. Mondale called me there on July 4 from Carter's 1979 Camp David domestic summit. Mondale never mentioned the Mike Smith incident, but he asked me to contact several congressmen to vote for the Education Department bill. The House had postponed floor consideration of the legislation several times, but the decision had been made to vote on the bill shortly after the July 4 recess. I told Mondale I would make the calls, and I mentoned that I wanted to see him as soon as I got back. He agreed to the meeting.

I returned to Washington on Saturday, July 7, and met with Mondale at 10:15 A.M. the following Monday. Mondale waved me into his office. He sat behind his desk; I sat in one of the two chairs facing it. After an exchange of pleasantries, I expressed my disappointment at how Mike Smith had been treated. My comments were restrained, between friends, but they conveyed the depth of my feeling. "When the thirty days of Mary Berry's appointment are up, we should designate Smith the Acting Commissioner," I concluded. "It's the only decent thing to do." (The law restricted the Assistant Secretary of Education from occupying the Commissioner's post for more than thirty days.)

Mondale let my comments pass. He was uncharacteristically cool and distinctly sheepish, stung not only by the bristling press comment about the Smith affair, but seemingly shaken by the experience of having to act so ruthlessly in pursuit of a presidential goal. Politics can be such a brutal profession, I thought. I knew Fritz Mondale to be one of the most decent people in it, so I too was shaken and I could feel his hurt and understand his obvious uneasiness. What I did not realize at the time was that he knew Carter was being urged to fire me and was actively considering the idea. Then the Vice-President broke the momentary silence. He said the outcome of the Education Department vote was in serious doubt and gave me a list of twenty-five House members to call. All were undecided or leaning against the bill. I promised to make the calls. As I left his office, I was sad. I sensed that something had been lost between us, that this issue had badly strained our personal friendship. Dutifully, I contacted the representatives on my list. Since my personal views were well known to most, I did not discuss the merits of the bill; I simply urged members to support the President, who was then engaged in a desperate reassessment of his presidency at Camp David. The argument may have had some effect. When the votes of the twenty-five members assigned to me were tallied, eleven had gone against the bill, two had not voted, and twelve had voted in favor of it. The legislation passed by only four votes, 210 to 206. I did not share Mondale's joy at the establishment of a new bureaucracy. The feeling in my gut was hollow as I realized that the twelve House members whom I had contacted who had voted for the bill were more than the margin of victory. Indeed, Leon Panetta, a Democrat from California, later said on the House floor that if it had not been for my call, and that of Mondale, "I do not think that I would have voted for the Department of Education."

I would never know how significant my calls had been, especially when weighed against the investment of the National Education Association and the President and Vice-President. The NEA and its local affiliates had given members of Congress who favored the bill $527,552 from 1974 through 1978, while those opposing it received only $98,880. Carter himself devoted far more time and energy to the Congress on the Department of Education bill than on any other HEW legislation. For Mondale, passing the legislation was a crusade, the only campaign pledge that unmistakably bore his name as well as Carter's, the symbol of his profound dedication to education in contrast with Edward Kennedy's commitment to health. Mondale had devoted much of his Senate career to education, was recognized as a leader by his colleagues, and had encouraged and supported every increased investment in education I recommended to Carter. If Kennedy had taken the torch of national health insurance from LBJ, Mondale had claimed the mantle of the Great Society's commitment to education.

For Carter, planting the new department in the Cabinet yielded a bumper political crop. As the United Auto Workers and Douglas Fraser edged closer to Kennedy, the troops of the National Education Association became Carter's critical forces in the early 1980 presidential primary battles in such states as Iowa and New Hampshire. NEA members delivered their enthusiastic and effective support to Carter in the Iowa caucuses and in several other states. At the 1980 Democratic convention, 464 NEA members were Carter delegates and alternates; all other unions combined produced only 200.

The political importance of the Education Department to Carter's renomination effort made support for the concept a key test of loyalty to the President. Jody Powell and Hamilton Jordan became increasingly suspicious and angry about editorials in the *Washington Post* and *New York Times* opposing the new department. Mondale warned me that Powell, Jordan, and Frank Moore were blaming the editorials on me. When the charge broke into print, it was too much for the intellectual and professional integrity of Meg Greenfield, the *Post*'s editorial page editor. She let loose in an editorial entitled, "Wherein We Confess All": "The thing about Washington is that it is even worse than Jimmy Carter and Jody Powell think it is. . . . people in this benighted town not only fall into Grievous Error, but also persist in it, sometimes for as much as a quarter of a century or more. . . . We are provoked to reveal this terrible truth by an item in yesterday's *Star*. In it, Mr. Powell disclosed to Carl Rowan the President's belief that Joseph Califano's misdemeanors included not only opposing the creation of a Department of Education, but also 'inducing *The Washington Post* to editorialize against such a department.' Our first thought on reading this was that we hoped Messrs. Powell and Carter were better at understanding the Russians, the Congress and the oil companies than they are at understanding *The Washington Post*. We will come clean: We are not one-time offenders in this business and there's no point blaming Mr. Califano for our lapse. . . . We have been fighting the creation of a separate Department of Education . . . since 1953. . . . By November of [1962] we were getting a little testy: 'We see no occasion . . . to elevate the Office of Education into a separate Cabinet department. It can function effectively as part of HEW.' So far as we can piece together from their printed biographies, Mr. Califano was at that time a sub-sub assistant at the Pentagon, Mr. Carter was in the Georgia state legislature, and Mr. Powell was at the Air Force Academy."

IF CARTER'S interest in the Department of Education was largely political in terms of his own renomination and re-election, his interest in improving the basic skills of schoolchildren was persistent and sincere. But in reaching for that goal, we encountered one of our few disagreements of fundamental principle, over the proper role of the national government in education. As I flipped through my final chart during a December 6, 1977, briefing on our Elementary and Secondary Education Act legislative proposals, standing opposite the President, who was seated in his chair, I said, "If access to education was the dominant theme of the sixties, then quality, even excellence, should be the dominant theme of the late seventies and eighties."

Carter immediately responded that he wanted the proposed legislation "to focus on achieving basic skills." He talked about his campaign trips across the country and the concern people expressed to him. "The people aren't satisfied with their schools and neither am I," he said. I found myself, as interventionist as anyone in the room, reminding him not to overestimate the ability of the federal government or misconstrue its role. But Carter saw only the overriding need to teach students reading, writing, and mathematics. I then suggested that a separate portion of the bill authorize funds to seek and encourage the best ways to teach basic skills. Carter agreed. Then he looked up at me and said with a tone of emotion he rarely exhibited: "I would consider myself a success as President if every child in third grade in America could read at a third grade level." It was one time I detected an echo of Lyndon Johnson's fierce passion about education in Carter's voice.

Though our disagreement about means was sharp, our desire to improve the teaching of basic skills was shared. My own attempt to attain our objective took a poignant turn toward the end of that same year. One Sunday evening, I watched a report on Jesse Jackson's Operation Push/Excel on CBS's *Sixty Minutes*. I had not seen Jackson since the 1960s, when he came to the Johnson White House as an angry young civil rights leader. It was an impressive program, dramatizing Jackson's campaign to get parents, students, teachers, and community leaders involved in an effort to teach and learn. Jackson went to a school, inspired the students to study, and had the parents sign cards making two pledges: They would keep the television off for several hours each evening while their children did homework, and they would go to the school periodically to pick up their children's report cards and talk to the teachers. Jackson was effective, the students were motivated, and there were early indications that attendance had improved, disciplinary problems had decreased, and marks had gone up.

The next day, Hubert Humphrey called me. In a weak voice, his strength consumed by his battle with cancer, he asked me if I had seen the *Sixty Minutes* program. When I responded, he said, "Well, then you saw what I saw. I want you to talk to Jesse Jackson and help him. He's doing something for those kids. I've talked to him this morning and told him I'd talk to you. Now you get him down to your office and help him. Will you do that for me?" I told him I would.

Humphrey's instinct was right about Jackson's Operation Push/Excel. The involvement of a parent with his or her own child turned out to be one of the few techniques that worked in improving classroom achievement. The problem with Jackson's program, it later became clear, was his inability to sustain its momentum when he was not present, its dependence on his charisma. But I discovered that the concept of involving parents with their own children was working elsewhere, most notably in Houston, Texas, which had the nation's seventh largest school district. There, led by School Superintendent Billy Reagan, the entire community had mounted Fail Safe, a campaign complete with television ads and bus advertising to get parents to follow the work of their own children in school. When Reagan took me on a tour of the Houston system in February 1979, the program had only been in effect for a year. Yet at least 70 percent of the third grade children were performing at their grade level; typically in urban schools across the nation, less than 50 percent of third grade children were performing that well.

As I was becoming aware that parental involvement was crucial, many Americans saw achievement tests as the solution to the decline of our nation's schools. These tests measure knowledge in reading, writing, and arithmetic as well as such other subjects as history, the sciences and geography. Proponents view them as a means of determining grade-level performance, and of assessing teacher capability. They had become widely popular in 1977. President Carter, aware of this, called me before the August congressional recess that year.

He had just talked to Rhode Island Senator Claiborne Pell, whose vote he had been soliciting for one of his programs. During their conversation, Pell, who chaired the Senate Education Subcommittee, asked Carter to support legislation he was preparing to direct the Secretary of

HEW to develop national achievement tests for use in elementary and secondary schools. Carter liked Pell's idea and told me to move forward with it. Up to that point, I had not focused on the national testing proposal. But I had become increasingly concerned about the need to safeguard the independence and intellectual freedom of the education system and conscious of how insensitive federal bureaucracy could be to these values, so I cautioned the President that we think carefully before having HEW establish national achievement tests. Carter brushed aside my concern and suggested I talk to Pell and Admiral Hyman Rickover, who had also discussed the need for national achievement tests with the President.

Pell repeated to me the same suggestions he had made to Carter. I met with Rickover in my office on August 23, 1977. The Admiral's demeanor had not changed from the early 1960s when I worked in the Pentagon. Accompanied by a bright young military aide whose hair was clipped unfashionably close, Rickover took a seat on the sofa to the right of my rocking chair. Cocky, secure in the knowledge that he had the President's attention, Rickover lashed out at HEW's "incompetent and counterproductive" Office of Education ("the last people you should listen to"), teachers who do not teach, and schools that "are so pleased to achieve mediocrity they mistake it for excellence." Rickover's solution was a "voluntary" national test. He was so single-minded that I felt there was no point expressing my concerns. I listened and promised to look at his idea.

To get a less committed view, I sought out Willard Wirtz, Secretary of Labor during the Johnson administration. Wirtz chaired the Advisory Panel on the Scholastic Aptitude Test Score Decline, which had just analyzed the steady declines in scores during the fourteen-year period from 1962 to 1976. Over lunch in my small dining room, Wirtz agreed with my concern about national achievement tests for elementary and secondary school children. Wirtz pointed out that whoever wrote the questions would have enormous power over what was taught. "That's a power I don't want and no HEW Secretary should have," I said.

When I expresssed these same concerns to the President, he dismissed them. His enthusiasm for a national achievement test was undiminished. Failing to move him on education policy grounds, I sought to enlist his political instincts by noting that the National Education Association strongly opposed any national test, even a voluntary one, to measure elementary and secondary school children. Carter's response was clipped: "Teachers just don't want people judging their performance. That's why the teacher unions oppose this." With the increased funding for education he was seeking and his support for the separate education department, Carter knew he could ignore the NEA on this. He then urged me to at least make a speech on testing just to demonstrate some interest in the subject. "The people want to know we're interested," he said.

The national test concept picked up surprising momentum from conservatives. Ohio Democratic Congressman Ronald Mottl held hearings on his bill authorizing HEW to work with the states to develop and fund mandatory minimum-competency testing programs. Several House members expressed support. It was clearly time to speak out and put the testing issues in perspective. But first I had to let the President know what I intended to say.

On October 14, 1977, I wrote Carter that I would speak later that month to the College Entrance Examination Board. Noting that twenty-six states had basic-skills competency tests and most others were considering adopting them, I advised: "I will encourage development of state and local accountability programs, and announce HEW initiatives—research, evaluation, teacher training, and demonstration projects—to assist states and localities in shaping and interpreting testing programs. At the same time, I will caution against a preoccupation with tests that I fear may be developing, and stress that many qualities we hope school children will acquire—initiative, self-esteem, self-discipline, honesty, morality—cannot be measured on standardized tests."

Then I reiterated the problem with a national test: "I also intend to indicate that creation of a national test would be a mistake at this time. . . . I have talked to Admiral Rickover, and . . . given careful thought to his proposal that a voluntary national test be written. Such a proposal raises the specter of questionable power in the federal government: to set basic tests for *all* children. Moreover, there is an enormous number of unanswered questions about testing—including what it can and cannot measure, what subjects should be included, what kinds of tests should be used, how to eliminate cultural bias, and how to interpret test scores. . . . The appropriate strategy . . . is to encourage diversity by assisting states and localities in implementing and evaluating a variety of testing and basic skills programs."

At the bottom of my memo, Carter wrote, "I'm afraid your speech might *discourage* testing. Don't. Every state should do so, and we should help. J."

Deferring to Carter in my San Francisco speech, I supported achievement tests at the state and local level, and softened my criticism of over-reliance on tests: "Achievement . . . testing is not the only way, but it is an important way, of getting information to point—and keep—us on the right course." I gave examples of valid uses of testing: to diagnose individual learning problems, to certify that students at a particular level possess certain basic abilities, and to make our schools more responsive to parents and taxpayers vitally concerned with educational quality. I committed HEW resources to assist states and localities in developing their own testing programs, and to better develop basic skills.

Then I discussed the limitations and dangers of testing, including the difficult questions about what tests truly measure which are disguised by the beguiling precision of scores. But the part of the speech I felt the deepest obligation to deliver drew the most fire: "Having said all this, am I advocating . . . a program of national tests, or national standards of scholastic achievement? Absolutely not. I believe that proposals for federal testing programs, however well-intentioned, are misguided; that even a wholly voluntary national test or set of standards would be a step in precisely the wrong direction."

I noted that no single test was right for every school, and that questions arise even in testing the three Rs: Should mathematical reasoning, or computation be stressed? Should the examples used to test competency in arithmetic or reading be different for farm children than for those whose experience is limited to urban streets? Tests whose main purpose is individual diagnosis may be inadequate for evaluating curriculum. But my greatest concern was that "in this country, control of curriculum has always rested with states and localities, not with Washington. Any set of test questions that the federal government prescribed should surely be suspect as a first step toward a national curriculum. . . . In its most extreme form, national control of curriculum is a form of national control of ideas. We should be very wary of treading in that direction; the traditional role of federal support for education has been to encourage diversity—not rigid uniformity."

The audience of professional testers and academics reacted well. But curiously, the conservative press and the letters to HEW attacked my position. California Senator S. I. Hayakawa wrote Carter that he was "both puzzled and disappointed" about my view; and urged the establishment of "national scholastic standards and tests" on a voluntary basis "if this administration genuinely wants to improve the quality of education in America. . . ." Carter responded by noting that he had instituted a testing program when he was governor of Georgia. He wrote Hayakawa that he had already taken the initiative to "explore the pros and cons of national standard education achievement tests to be used at the option of state and/or local school systems." Carter penned a P.S. aimed at me: "We will *act* within sixty days. J.C. cc: Califano."

On November 28, Carter sent me a handwritten note: "To Joe Califano: I believe we need some national standard education achievement tests—to be used only optionally when states and/or local school systems want them. How do you suggest we do this—through HEW, or National Science Foundation? J.C.''

I understood Carter's threat to turn national testing over to the National Science Foundation, but I was more concerned about the fact that I had failed to convince him of its dangers. On December 2, I sent him a copy of my speech on testing and wrote that there was ''no shortage of standardized achievement tests,'' thanks to commercial test publishers and nonprofit organizations that had produced high quality tests in reading, writing, mathematics, science, and history. Where there was a gap, as in testing noncollege-bound high school students, we were moving to fill it. I listed other steps we were taking, most notably drafting the Educational Quality Act Carter wanted to help focus state and local school systems on basic skills.

But I re-emphasized my opposition to establishing a national achievement test in basic skills: ''Such a step raises the specter of questionable power in the federal government. There would be great political opposition in the educational community and in the Congress to the perceived infringement of local control.'' Moreover, it made ''little practical sense'' to have the same standard for Westchester County and the South Bronx: a standard too low to encourage Westchester County students to achieve their full potential might be so high for South Bronx students they would become discouraged by their failure to meet it.

Carter penned a sharp response three days later. ''To Joe Califano. Your memo on testing does not answer the question. What can we do (without deliberate evasion or delay) to provide local and state government with funds & satisfactory tests, and to encourage—not require—their use? Just a brief (one page) answer. J.C.''

I answered within a couple of hours, but I was just repeating myself now. I told Carter that we would create a bank of achievement tests on which states and localities could draw, fill gaps where no tests existed, organize regional or local workshops, publicize successful testing programs. I promised to convene an HEW conference of state education officials on testing. ''Thanks,'' Carter wrote on my memo, returning it to me by messenger. At the beginning of my briefing on elementary and secondary education the next day, the President opened the meeting by saying, ''I didn't mean to be so harsh in my note on testing.''

At the HEW conference on testing in early March 1978, the National Academy of Education, a distinguished group of scholars, released its report on testing. The report unequivocally opposed a national achievement test, mandatory or voluntary. But its most startling finding revealed a great deal about what was wrong with education in America: even at our ''relatively good'' schools, only 18 percent of the time in school was actually spent on scholastic work. The report warned that "any setting of statewide minimum competency standards for awarding the high school diploma—however understandable the high public clamor which has produced the current movement and expectation—is basically unworkable, exceeds the current measurement arts of the testing profession, and will create more social problems than it can conceivably solve."

Senator Pell, who had triggered Carter's pressure on me, asked the conference audience of several hundred chief state school officers, representatives of parents and civil rights groups, teachers, and congressional staffers, "How many of you agree with the idea of a national achievement test?" Two hands went up. Pell never introduced a bill on national testing.

That conference helped cool the President's ardor. He spoke to me about testing only once again. At a Cabinet meeting on September 25, 1978, he asked me to look at North Carolina's new statewide testing program set up by Governor Jim Hunt. National Institute of Education Director Patricia Graham looked at the program and I reported to the President on December 22 that it was too early to judge its effectiveness. Moreover, a class action challenging its constitutionality had been filed by eleventh- and twelfth-grade blacks, lower income whites, and American Indians. Carter did not comment on my report.

THE FAILURE of children to learn and teachers to teach basic skills was symptomatic of the disintegration of public education in America. In many states, up to 20 percent of the teachers themselves lacked competence in basic English; those who could teach were often terrorized, particularly in urban schools. Just as the nation had gotten in place student aid programs that permit anyone with the talent to go to any college he or she chooses, regardless of economic situation, a deteriorating system of public elementary and secondary education was unable to prepare deserving boys and girls to take advantage of the opportunities those programs offered.

With the decline of public schools, parents turned elsewhere for their children's education—in cities, to Catholic elementary and secondary schools; throughout the country, where they had the money, to private schools. The chasm between children educated in most urban public schools and those in parochial or private schools widened, as the public systems produced hundreds of thousands of functional illiterates, and the nonpublic schools developed an educated elite. The danger to democracy of this situation—and the human tragedy of so many missed personal opportunities—made it essential to rebuild our system of public education. While I recognized HEW's limitations in any such effort, I did consider it imperative not to take any steps that might further jeopardize public schools. That conviction was central to my strenuous opposition to the proposals for tuition tax credits to permit a taxpayer to subtract, dollar for dollar from taxes otherwise due, a portion of the private or parochial school tuition paid for each child.

Unlike the abortion dispute, my opposition to tuition tax credits pitted me against the Roman Catholic bishops, who wanted such credits to bolster the financial condition of parochial school systems. One opponent remained the same, however: Oregon Senator Robert Packwood, whose proselytizing for tuition tax credits allied him shoulder to shoulder with the Catholic hierarchy he opposed on federal funding for abortion.

Republican Senator William Roth of Delaware introduced legislation on January 18, 1977, to establish a tax credit of up to $250 for tuition paid to a college, university, or post-secondary vocational school. In May of that year, New York Democratic Senator Pat Moynihan proposed increasing the credit to $500 and extending it to tuition paid to elementary and secondary schools. In September, he was joined by Packwood and enough other co-sponsors to signal a major fight.

The battle began without the public-parochial school issue, when, on November 4, the Senate voted 61 to 11 to attach Roth's $250 tuition tax credit for higher education to "must" Social Security financing legislation. Roth's amendment would cost $1.2 billion in lost revenues, effectively increasing federal student aid programs by more than 25 percent. It would put two more congressional committees, Senate Finance and House Ways and Means, and the Treasury Department into the education policy area. Since the credit went in equal amount to each student, financially pressed colleges would likely increase their tuitions by that amount. I thought Senate Finance Committee Chairman Russell Long would drop the proposal in conference without much argument, since it was not attached to the House-passed version of the Social Security financing bill. But when Long designated Roth one of the Senate conferees on the Social Security bill, it was clear that we would have to pay a price to get rid of the tuition tax credit, because Long would use it to hold Roth's vote on other issues.

After three fruitless House/Senate Conference Committee sessions, Long and Ways and Means Committee Chairman Al Ullman secretly agreed on December 7 to a Social Security package that would have put the Roth tuition tax credit for higher education into effect for one year. Informed of this, I told Ullman the administration could not accept any tuition tax credit. We knew that most House conferees would not accept it. When committee member Dan Rostenkowski found out about Ullman's agreement on the tuition tax credit, he was furious. "The House will never take it," he told me in a phone conversation on December 9. "There've never been any hearings. We've got to get rid of it or we'll blow the Social Security bill." At the committee meeting that Friday evening, the House and Senate conferees tentatively agreed on a $227 billion Social Security financing package, but the Senate would not retreat on Roth's tuition tax credit. Long taunted Ullman and the House conferees by insisting they take the tuition tax credit to the House floor for a vote, where he knew it would pass overwhelmingly. Angry at Long's teasing demand, the House conferees walked out.

I called House Speaker Tip O'Neill early Saturday morning. He agreed with Rostenkowski's judgment that the House conferees would let the Social Security financing bill die before accepting the tuition tax credit. O'Neill also confirmed my concern that we could not pass these new Social Security taxes the following year because of the 1978 congressional elections. I called the President, brought him up to date, and suggested that I hold a tough press conference, at the White House, indicating that "I would recommend a veto if the Social Security bill is sent to you with the tuition tax credit in it." Carter agreed, but wanted me to soften my statement about a veto to preserve his flexibility.

I then called Nelson Cruikshank, the White House Counselor on Aging, who was deeply interested in the Social Security bill. He said he would let the aging groups in Delaware know that Senator Roth was holding up legislation needed to preserve the financial viability of the Social Security system.

At the White House that afternoon, I denounced the Roth proposal. I pointed out that his tuition tax credit was irrelevant to the Social Security bill, and "an incoherent way to make education policy." I accused Roth of "holding the viability of the Social Security program" and America's elderly "hostage" to a tax credit that would help the wealthy send their children to private schools. I talked to Long that afternoon; he was still noncommittal, waiting to assess the impact of the press conference and pressure on Roth before deciding what to do.

On the following Tuesday morning, Louisiana Congressman Joe Waggoner, a Russell Long intimate who opposed the tuition tax credit, told me, "That was some press conference. All we heard in Louisiana Saturday night and Sunday morning after church was about this tuition tax credit jeopardizing the Social Security system. I think we can kill it now." By Wednesday, Roth agreed to drop the tuition tax credit from the Social Security bill in return for Long's commitment to take it up early in the next Congress.

We won the first round on the tuition tax credit largely on the basis of its irrelevance to the Social Security legislation, the opposition of the House conferees because no hearings had been held on the House side, and the threat of a presidential veto. But the broader Packwood-Moynihan proposal was gaining momentum as more and more senators and representatives expressed support. Senate Finance Committee hearings were scheduled for January 1978. In his State of the Union message the evening before the hearings began, Carter announced a 14 percent increase in education funding and promised financial aid to middle class college students. Still, the hearings left no doubt that the tuition tax credit proposal would sail through the Senate. Russell Long warned me, "If you want to beat it, you'd better get something more to beat it with than a vague promise."

On January 27, I had breakfast with House education leaders John Brademas, Bill Ford, who chaired the House Education Subcommittee, and Frank Thompson. "If Carter doesn't propose something, we will," Ford warned.

"If the President thinks Long is difficult to deal with now, remind him that Russell will have jurisdiction over education if the tax credit passes," Brademas added.

"And so will the House Ways and Means Committee," I said, smiling as I kidded my friends on the House Education and Labor Committee.

Clearly some relief was needed for middle income Americans. By the 1977–78 school year, the cost for tuition, room, and board at a private college was averaging $5,000 per year; at some of the nation's best colleges, it was more than $7,000. Many public universities charged more than $2,500 per year. These costs had risen far more rapidly than inflation generally, and they did not include the related expenses of laboratory fees, books, athletic equipment, clothing, and travel that added at least another $1,000 to the annual bill. For a family earning $25,000 in 1977—then the 80th percentile of income in this country—a $5,000-to-$7,000-a-year education expense was an unwieldy burden; it was a financially unbearable one for a family with the median income of $15,000.

Working with House Education and Labor Committee Chairman Carl Perkins, Bill Ford, Claiborne Pell, and others, we prepared a program and sent it to Carter on February 4. We proposed to raise the amounts a family could earn and still remain eligible for student grants and loans, in order to provide grants for the neediest and loans to ease the cash flow problems of those with more family income. My memorandum noted that the $500 Packwood-Moynihan tax credit was estimated to cost $4.4 billion just for higher education. Even at that cost, the credit was too little to help needy families and not enough to have any effect on the educational decision of wealthy families. Unlike a low-interest loan, it failed to meet the need of a middle income family to spread a much larger share of educational costs over a longer time.

I set forth the arguments against a credit for elementary and secondary schools, pointing out that the Packwood-Moynihan proposal would provide $500 per student at a private or parochial school, while at the same time federal funds for public schools averaged less than $140 per student in 1978. The proposal stood traditional concepts of government support for public education on their head. Such a lopsided shift in the federal investment in elementary and secondary education could have a ruinous impact on public schools. I recommended prompt action: "We must move quickly if we are to seize the initiative on this very hot issue. . . . The congressional education committees are so fearful of losing jurisdiction over education finances that they will go without us—at a very high price." Concern about separation of church and state also drove many on those committees to oppose the tuition tax credit proposals for lower schools.

Two days later, Carter agreed to our proposal. Within ninety minutes after the President spoke to me, OMB Director McIntyre called, annoyed that Carter had approved the $1.2 billion package. "I had only an hour to comment on a $1.2 billion proposal. I'm losing my credibility as OMB Director. I testified only last week about a $700 million proposal," McIntyre shouted into the phone. I suggested he talk to his own staff, which had been involved in developing the proposal. "When your top staff is informed, I assume you are informed." McIntyre was exasperated, frustrated by his bureaucracy: "Don't you worry. I've been kicking a lot of asses on my own staff, but I'm still going to appeal to the President."

Despite McIntyre's last-minute objections, the President, flanked by key congressional leaders, announced the Middle Income Student Assistance plan on February 8, 1978. He warned that the Congress must choose between the tuition tax credit and his plan: "This nation cannot afford, and I will not accept, both." Bill Ford was delighted with a program that increased student aid for higher education by almost 40 percent in one year, and the number of students receiving aid from three million to five million. "This is the single biggest infusion of funding for middle income students since the adoption of the GI Bill at the end of World War II," Ford exulted, as Carter winced since he had just presented his proposal as frugal compared to the tuition tax credits before the Congress.

The same day that the President unfolded the administration's Middle Income Student Assistance bill, I asked Attorney General Griffin Bell for his formal opinion on the constitutionality of tax credits for parochial elementary and secondary schools. On March 17, Bell responded to my request and a similar one from Missouri Democratic Senator Thomas Eagleton. The Attorney General concluded that "tax programs of the sort contemplated here would be held unconstitutional insofar as they would provide aid at the elementary and secondary school levels. However . . . similar aid at the college level would be constitutional. . . ." Bell concluded that the tax credit, dollar for dollar up to a certain amount, was in effect a federal payment to a parochial school for whatever purpose the school decided to use it, and so was unconstitutional. He cited 1973 Supreme Court decisions in *Committee For Public Education* v. *Nyquist* and *Sloan* v. *Lemon* holding similar New York and Pennsylvania tuition tax credit schemes for elementary and secondary schools unconstitutional.

The Catholic bishops attacked the President's and my failure to support the Packwood-Moynihan tax credit. Virgil Blum, the president of the Independent Catholic League for Religious and Civil Rights, an organization allied with the U. S. Catholic Conference, condemned the administration's proposal as a "renunciation of the President's campaign promises to aid pupils who attend parochial schools." Actually, Carter had limited his commitment to "finding a constitutionally acceptable method of providing aid to parents of children attending parochial schools." Among Catholic organizations, only the Association of Jesuit Colleges and Universities supported our proposal. Some sophisticated Catholic lobbyists were wary of the tuition tax credit for parochial schools because they feared it would lead to a general reassessment of tax policies affecting religious institutions. But the Catholic bishops, hard-pressed to finance huge parochial school systems in big cities, pressed their case aggressively. When I argued that Catholic schools would never see any money from a tax credit at elementary and secondary schools because litigation would tie up the funds for years, the bill was changed to mandate an immediate constitutional test in the courts.

While Carter and I refused to hold out false hopes of unconstitutional relief for parochial schools as Nixon had cynically done, we did work to help such schools in every constitutional way. For the first time, I used HEW's authority to bypass state and local school districts that did not provide a fair share of federal funds to parochial elementary and secondary schools for compensatory education, books, equipment, and other materials and services. We invoked the law to provide funds to parochial schools in Missouri, Virginia, and Wisconsin and proposed legislative expansion of this authority. I urged Catholic schools to monitor the performance of the states carefully. I established HEW's first Office of Nonpublic Schools, appointing as director Edward D'Alessio, president of Our Lady of the Elm College in Chicopee, Massachusetts, and former head of the elementary and secondary education division for the U. S. Catholic Conference.

The President's press conference on February 8 set off a race to complete congressional action. Within ten days, I testified before the House Ways and Means Committee and an extraordinary joint hearing of the House Committee on Education and Labor and the Senate Committee on Human Resources. On February 23, the Senate Finance Committee approved, 14 to 1, a bill providing tuition tax credits for elementary, secondary, and post-secondary students. I called the Finance Committee's action "a devastating blow to public school education in this country that would skew federal benefits toward parochial schools."

The next day the Senate Human Resources Committee approved unanimously the administration's proposal to expand existing student aid programs. This put the administration's plan neck-and-neck with the tuition tax credit plan in the race for the Senate floor. The Human Resources Committee bill lifted completely the income ceiling on eligibility for student loans because our proposed $45,000 lid made 94 percent of the population eligible. At Senator Jacob Javits's suggestion, the lid was lifted to ease paperwork. An enormous increase in student loan demand has resulted with this money available to all college students at low interest rates; outstanding loans jumped from $5 billion to $8 billion at the beginning of the 1980–81 school year.

Four days later, on February 28, Ford's House Education Subcommittee unanimously voted for an expanded version of our Middle Income Student Assistance proposal. That same day, in his message to the Congress on Elementary and Secondary Education Act amendments, Carter attacked the college tuition tax credit concept, but he reserved his sharpest criticism for the private elementary and secondary school tax credit proposals: "First, there is grave doubt that such a tax credit program can meet constitutional requirements concerning separation of church and state. Second, the federal government provides funding primarily to help meet the needs of public school children who are disadvantaged, or handicapped, or bilingual, or who have some other form of special need. We do not provide general support for public schools and it would be unfair to extend such support, through a general tax credit, to private schools." On March 8, the full House Education and Labor Committee approved our Middle Income Student Assistance bill by a vote of 32 to 3.

We tried to pass our student aid bill on the suspension calendar on March 20, a procedure that blocked any amendments, including those to add or substitute a tuition tax credit. Although we mustered a 218 to 156 majority, we failed to get the two-thirds vote necessary for passage under suspended rules. That forced our bill to the Rules Committee, chaired by

Brooklyn Democrat James Delaney, who strongly supported tuition tax credits, so Speaker O'Neill postponed House floor action until after the Easter recess.

During the Easter recess, the Catholic bishops mounted a massive lobbying campaign. When the Congress returned on April 3, House Ways and Means Committee Chairman Al Ullman said his committee would act on a tuition tax credit proposal by Cleveland Democrat Charles Vanik. Vanik suggested a tax credit of up to $100 for each student in elementary and secondary school and $250 for each in college. On April 9, the day before the committee vote, Treasury Secretary Mike Blumenthal and I wrote each member of the committee. Our letter opposed the Vanik proposal: "An elementary and secondary tax credit . . . will be . . . held unconstitutional in the end . . . tax credits impose a high, continuing, and uncontrollable drain on the Treasury—one that is not carefully targeted on real need . . . when both the administration and the Congress should be deeply concerned about inflation and budgetary pressures. . . ." After a series of sharply contested and close votes, the Ways and Means Committee approved Vanik's proposal for a tuition tax credit up to $250 per student for post-secondary education. But an unusual combination of Southern congressmen opposed to aid for parochial schools and civil rights advocates concerned that tax credits would provide financial assistance for segregated schools, defeated the credit for elementary and secondary schools by a 20 to 16 vote.

The formation of this coalition, and particularly the opposition of the civil rights groups, angered Catholic lobbyists. On April 15, the Catholic Conference accused me of inciting civil rights opposition and distorting the amount of money the federal government spent to aid pupils in nonpublic elementary and secondary schools.

On May 10, the House Rules Committee voted to send the Ways and Means Committee tax credit plan for higher education to the House floor ahead of the administration's student aid plan, and to permit a floor amendment to reinsert the credit for elementary and secondary education. On June 1, the amendment to add elementary and secondary schools passed a closely divided House, 209 to 194. The House then passed, 237 to 158, a tuition tax credit bill that applied to private elementary and secondary school students, as well as all college students. I called the House vote to provide a credit for parochial schools "a hollow gesture" that would "only delay the search for constitutional means of assistance to parochial education . . . the parochial schools of this country will never see a dollar of the unconstitutional aid the House voted today because the courts will invalidate it."

On August 3, the Senate Finance Committee scaled down its tuition tax credit for elementary and secondary schools to half the cost of its original bill. Senator Roth said, "We feel as though we have marched halfway up Pennsylvania Avenue." The key battleground became the floor of the Senate. If a tax credit for elementary and secondary schools passed the Senate, then the only way to stop it from becoming law would be presidential veto, an action Carter preferred not to face. We mounted a major effort to defeat the tax credit on the Senate floor, with South Carolina Senator Fritz Hollings leading the way, and Edward Kennedy spearheading the liberals concerned about civil rights as well as separation of church and state. On August 15, after three days of sometimes nasty debate, the Senate voted 56 to 41 in favor of the Hollings motion to strike the tuition tax credit for elementary and secondary schools from the bill. The tax credit for higher education then passed by an overwhelming 65 to 27 vote. The very next day, the Senate passed by a similarly lopsided 68 to 28 vote the administration's Middle Income Student Assistance program of loans and grants.

The Congress recessed for two weeks with the different tax credit bills passed by each House poised for conference, but with the administration bill passed only by the Senate. The administration student aid program was still held up in the House Rules Committee. Over the recess, I got a sense of how deeply this issue cut with many Americans. While we were fishing together on Cape Cod, Leo Diehl, Speaker O'Neill's closest aide, told me that the mail and pressure on House members to support a tuition tax credit for elementary and secondary schools was greater than on any issue since Watergate. On the third Sunday in August, I sat in our Lady of Lourdes Church on Main Street in Wellfleet, Massachusetts, where my summer home is located. During his sermon, the pastor spoke with hearty approval of the tuition tax credit and asked "all parishioners"—then he noticed me and amended his request to "all parishioners who wish to do so"—to sign petitions to President Carter, available at the back of the church, for a tuition tax credit bill for elementary and secondary schools. As virtually every parishioner signed the petitions, they talked about how the government discriminated against parochial schools.

After the recess, the conference between House Ways and Means Committee and Senate Finance Committee members was a difficult one. Not until Russell Long refused to sign the conference report unless the tax credit for elementary and secondary school tuition was eliminated did the House retreat. On September 28, the conferees agreed on a bill that provided tax credits up to $250 per student for post-secondary education. Carter was pleased; this meant he would not have to veto a bill with widespread Catholic support. Now the veto, if necessary, could be directed only at the higher education tax credit. Since most colleges preferred the administration student aid program of loans and grants, that veto would be a politically palatable one.

Then, on Thursday night, October 12, Dick Warden called me. "The House just rejected the conference report and sent it back to include a tax credit for elementary and secondary schools." The next day, rushing toward adjournment, the House and Senate conferees agreed to extend a tax credit to secondary school students, still leaving out elementary schools.

The following Saturday night, the House passed by voice vote the administration's proposal for Middle Income Student Assistance, identical to the one approved by the Senate in August. This sent the President the bill he wanted.

On Sunday morning the handful of senators still on the floor at breakfast time sent back to conference the measure that would have extended tuition tax credits to high school as well as college students, a move at that late hour tantamount to killing the legislation. A last-ditch effort of the tuition tax credit proponents to attach their proposal to the general tax bill failed.

Carter had his legislative victory without the need to veto the tuition tax credit, even for higher education. He signed the Middle Income Student Assistance Act into law on November 1, 1978. But the scars were not easily healed.

On November 11, the President met with leaders of the National Conference of Catholic Bishops, who told him of their "growing dissatisfaction" with the administration's failure to support tuition tax credits for parents of parochial school children. On December 6, at my invitation, representatives of the Catholic bishops, colleges, and elementary and secondary schools came to HEW to discuss the issue. The group was made up predominantly of clergy with a few laymen. The atmosphere was icy as I began the meeting in the Secretary's conference room. I asked what we could do to help them in the area of education. Some scoffed at the question. Then the meeting broke into sharp denunciations of Carter, punctuated with words like "broken promises" and "betrayal." When I mentioned that Senator Edward Kennedy and Carter were on the same side of this issue, there was a chorus of adverse comment, with one priest noting sarcastically, "I'd hardly call Kennedy a Catholic legislator with his stand on abortion and his opposition to tuition tax credits." Eventually we agreed to try to seek areas of common interest. But they were so worried about the financial plight of big-city parochial schools, they could not see the threat to public education and to the constitutional separation of church and state posed by the tuition tax credit. I was disappointed that they so vigorously disagreed with me, but I could understand their concern.

ONE OF the arguments of proponents of the tuition tax credit was that it was less cumbersome to manage and less prone to fraud and leakage of federal funds than the student loan and grant programs with their elaborate forms and administrative requirements. This argument was based on reports of widespread failure of students to repay loans after completing their studies. When I examined those reports, I found them to be understated—but the students were not the chief culprits.

The reorganization of the student aid programs into a single bureau gave me a precious new position to fill. As with so much of the work at HEW, the skills we needed in the Bureau of Student Financial Assistance were managerial; they had little to do with education policy. So I recruited Leo Kornfeld, a computer-systems expert and consultant on education administration from New York. Kornfeld joined HEW in August 1977. It was none too soon, when we discovered what a monumental mess we had on our hands.

There are two major student loan programs, and when we examined them, we found defaults totaling $1 billion. The Guaranteed Student Loan Program is largely operated by banks, with the government responsible for collection of defaulted loans. We found at least 300,000 of these loans in default, involving well over $300 million. If we did not act, the defaults would top $450 million in less than a year. The other, the National Direct Student Loan Program, is administered by colleges and other educational institutions, which in the first instance are responsible for collection of defaulted loans. Here we found almost 700,000 loans in default, involving more than $600 million in unpaid principal alone.

Over the years these two programs had grown rapidly. Not only did millions of college students use them, but proprietary schools (those run for a profit) that taught everything from meat cutting to television repair and secretarial skills expanded rapidly with students eligible for these loans. By January 1977, there were nine million clients in these programs and a net increase of about one million each year.

What we learned put the fault squarely on HEW and the schools. Virtually no student had ever been sent a bill for repayment when a loan went into default. Fewer than one in eight of the educational institutions was independently audited each year, and HEW certified schools as eligible to participate in the programs without imposing any fiscal or administrative standards on them.

At least 200 of the 3,400 participating institutions had student loan default rates in excess of 50 percent; some exceeded 80 percent. Since records were so poorly kept and since many institutions had not made any reports, I assumed these numbers were low. But it was clear that a better job could be done: 1,071 of the 3,400 participating institutions had default rates of less than 10 percent.

Fraud was rampant, particularly among the for-profit schools. Many fly-by-night proprietary schools took money borrowed by students and then did not provide the promised training. Others created "phantom students," fraudulently pocketing money they claimed was lent to students who did not exist. Recruiting of ineligible students and false representation of the eligibility were common. At some colleges and universities, student grant and loan funds had been improperly converted to the personal use of school officials.

The HEW record in the Guaranteed Student Loan Program was also dismal. In several of HEW's ten regions, records were kept on index cards in shoeboxes; in others, what little computer programming existed was woefully inadequate to the task of collection. The backlog of alleged fraud cases in this program alone equaled three years of work for the available HEW investigative staff.

The first step in an aggressive collection effort was to computerize these student loan programs. Developing the computer programs gave us all a lesson in civil service bureaucracy. Kornfeld discovered that, short of himself, no one in the entire one-thousand-person Bureau of Student Financial Assistance knew how to program computers to handle a problem of this magnitude. It would take us a year to eighteen months to get people qualified to do the job through the civil service process. I told Kornfeld to recruit the four or five people we needed to do the computer programming and hire them as consultants until we could get them into the federal civil service.

We had to clean our own house, so the collection effort was initially directed at federal employees. We dubbed that effort Operation Cross-Check, a computer match of the federal civilian payroll against the Guaranteed Student Loan Program default file. Of 150,000 HEW employees, we discovered 317 matches, 222 of them still on the HEW payroll. Of the approximately 2.7 million federal civilian employees, there were 6,900 matches. We moved to collect from the HEW employees and pressed other agency heads to encourage their own defaulters to pay up.

To increase collections throughout the program, we ran a competition among the ten HEW regions. The number of defaulted loans had grown to slightly more than 400,000 by May of 1978. But as our collection efforts took hold, the default backlog dropped to 374,000 in June. When I left HEW in August 1979, it was down to 237,000.

In the first nine months of our new program, we referred 1,500 civil cases to U. S. attorneys, three times the total that had been referred over the prior five years. Where U. S. attorneys moved aggressively, as in New Jersey, the impact was significant: As soon as their court actions were publicized, student defaulters jammed HEW phone lines volunteering to repay their loans. But these cases were small potatoes for overloaded U. S. attorneys, and even with a push from Attorney General Bell, it was difficult to get them interested in prosecuting them.

Our campus-based loan-program-collection effort was much less effective. We mounted an attack on fraud in the proprietary schools and in some colleges. We provided funds and technical assistance to improve administration of the program. We stepped up audits from one thousand to four thousand per year and issued strict regulations to disqualify institutions with unsatisfactory default rates from participating in the program. But colleges and universities are not well suited to mount collection efforts. Their administrative offices are not organized for such work and they resist becoming collection agencies. By early 1979, defaults in the campus-based program had risen to more than $700 million. Ultimately I concluded that the collection function should be turned over to the federal government, with the colleges given responsibility to put the overall assistance package together for each student.

The BEOG—Basic Educational Opportunity Grant—program, which is run by the government largely through contractors, had an equally lax administrative history. In 1977, that program provided about two million students individual grants up to $1,600, depending on family income and tuition costs. The government had never undertaken any systematic effort to validate the information on the grant applications. When we computer-screened the 3.4 million applications for the 1978–79 school year, 1.3 million were rejected for inaccuracy, incompleteness, or internal inconsistencies. Of those, 500,000 did not even reapply for grants. We conservatively estimated that $100 million to $150 million had been given to ineligible students each year since the program began in 1973.

In addition to screening the grant applications, we also began computer policing to see whether BEOG students received money from other federal programs. The first matches revealed the difficulty of policing against fraud, abuse, and waste with so many duplicative programs, and supported the arguments for consolidation. For the 1977–78 year, we discovered that approximately 159,000 BEOG applicants received Veterans Administration student benefits, with 19,000 failing to report their VA benefits, and that 600,000 BEOG applicants received Social Security student benefits, with 113,833 failing to report them. When we matched welfare rolls in twenty-two jurisdictions against BEOG applications, we found that almost 20,000 applicants did not report receiving AFDC (Aid to Families with Dependent Children) benefits. It is not necessarily illegal to receive funds from more than one program; but since eligibility for a BEOG grant and the size of the grant are determined in part by the income from other sources, it is a violation of law not to report such income on the application. After reviewing the problems throughout all the student aid programs, I concluded that at least $1 billion a year could be saved by consolidating student aid programs across the government and tightening administration, and by forceful collection efforts.

THE STUDENT aid programs were administered ineptly, but the bilingual program was flawed because its purpose had become confused and the intended beneficiaries—non-English-speaking children—had become helpless victims of weak HEW management in the face of shortsighted ethnic politics.

During the Johnson years, my interest in bilingual education was prompted by sociologist James Coleman's 1966 study of educational opportunity which showed that students of Mexican, Puerto Rican, and American-Indian background were completing high school at achievement levels far below the national norm. Language schools, meanwhile, were compiling persuasive evidence that children learn most readily in their native language. In 1968, the Congress enacted our recommendation to add a bilingual-education demonstration program to the 1965 Elementary and Secondary Education Act. The purpose of the program was to teach non-English-speaking children English as rapidly as possible, and to teach other courses in their native language until they could be taught in English. The hope was that this would help prevent bilingual students from falling behind while they learned English.

When the program was enacted, no state required bilingual teaching; indeed, almost half forbade it by law. In 1974, the Supreme Court ruled in *Lau* v. *Nichols* that a San Francisco school district had denied Chinese students equal access to education by ignoring their language problems. The political impact of that decision, the lack of focus of HEW's Office of Education and Office for Civil Rights, and the demand by numerous ethnic politicians for bicultural education programs changed the bilingual landscape. The Spanish-speaking community—Chicanos in the Southwest, Puerto Ricans and others in New York—regarded the bilingual program as theirs for they had the overwhelmingly greater number of students. But other groups—American Indians, Eskimos, Poles, Italians, Germans, Southeast Asians, African blacks, Chinese, Haitians, Greeks, and other nationalities—also asked for and got bilingual programs in their own languages. By 1977, eleven states required some form of bilingual schooling and dozens of large urban school districts had established projects on their own. HEW funded bilingual programs in sixty-seven languages in forty-two states, serving some 255,000 out of an estimated 3.6 million eligible children. The cost of educating the unserved population of more than three million children—excluding undocumented aliens—was well over $1 billion. Even with Mondale and me pressing for more funds, however, because of tight spending ceilings, the federal bilingual program went from only $115 million in Ford's last budget to $166 million in 1980.

Of most serious concern to me was that HEW's bilingual program had become captive of the professional Hispanic and other ethnic groups, with their understandably emotional but often exaggerated political rhetoric of biculturalism. As a result, too little attention was paid to teaching children English, and far too many children were kept in bilingual classes long after they acquired the necessary proficiency to be taught in English. Due in part to the misguided administration of bilingual programs, 40 percent of students whose first language is Spanish dropped out of school before earning a high school diploma. Society's interest in integrating these children so they could get jobs that required English and have the potential for upward mobility is so strong that I was determined to put the program back on course. I recognized the importance of bicultural education, but that was not the purpose of this program. Champion and I made our views clear: this federal program was to teach children English, and to teach them other subjects in their native language only so long as they were not adept at learning in English. Within that guideline, local school districts could put individual programs together. We soon ran into the vocal opposition of the political leaders of Hispanic organizations. In 1980, pushed by Hispanic groups, the new Education Department attempted to put in effect detailed regulations, prescribing exactly how local school systems should meet the *Lau* standards. Congress rebelled, placing a rider on an appropriations bill blocking the regulation from being issued at least until June 1981. Weeks after assuming office, the Reagan administration revoked the regulation, noting that in *Lau,* the Supreme Court left the precise method of fulfilling the right of children not proficient in English to a public education up to local school systems.

Our attempt to focus the program on teaching English also ran into the attitude of vice-presidential staffers, who viewed biculturalism as "one of the few things these groups have" and who were inclined to "let them run their own program." Mondale's staff had pressed to leave the objectives of the program fuzzy. "That's what the Vice-President wants,'' they repeatedly asserted, although Mondale himself never made this point to me.

When I briefed President Carter on this program, I was anxious about his reaction. But he came on strongly: ''Teach these kids English.'' And in the margin of a memo I had sent him about my standards for a new director for the Office of Bilingual Education, Carter wrote, ''I want language taught—not ethnic 'culture,' etc. J.''

So I ignored the demands of many professional Hispanic politicians and others and tried to focus the program clearly on teaching English, using bicultural sidebars only as a means of helping youngsters learn English, not as an end in themselves. We sought to measure the success of the individual bilingual programs on the basis of how rapidly they moved children out of them. As the program meets this standard, I believe the American people will be more likely to increase the woefully inadequate funds now committed to it, and get on with the critical task of enrolling the millions of unserved eligible children.

BILINGUAL EDUCATION is not the only federal program that needs reshaping and in which the funds committed are not sufficient to get the job done. In 1975, the Congress passed the Education for All Handicapped Children Act. The law required that each state identify and provide ''a free appropriate public education'' for a gradually increasing percentage of handicapped children until all were served at the end of five years. The objective was to mainstream as many of the ''8 million handicapped children'' as possible in regular classrooms, and to provide whatever special classroom or institutional settings those who could not be mainstreamed in regular classrooms needed.

The law set hortatory objectives as to the rising share of the extra cost of compliance that the federal government should bear. It called for federal funds to pick up 10 percent of these costs in 1979, rising to 40 percent in 1982. It was, however, left to the appropriations committees and the annual executive-legislative budget process to set the amounts the government would actually provide. During the Ford years, the federal government fell far behind. But even with an increase from $469 million in Ford's 1977 budget to $875 million in Carter's 1980 budget, when the law had set 20 percent as its fair share, the federal government paid less than 12 percent of the extra cost imposed on states for the education of handicapped children. Once again, the Congress was having its cake and eating it too. The law forced states and cities to comply with its requirements to serve larger and larger numbers of handicapped children or lose other federal education funds. Governors and mayors bridled at the legislative special interest squeeze on them, but Congress could not change the law in the face of subcommittees responsive to handicapped groups.

No one can deny the laudable objectives of the program, or the need for more funds to treat handicapped children fairly in our educational system. But the sad reality we face here, as in so many other areas, is that need has far outpaced the resources our people are willing to commit.

MY EXPERIENCE at HEW renewed my conviction that the federal programs begun in the 1960s and expanded and shaped by the Congress in the 1970s are critical to the future of education in America. But I also came away with serious misgivings about how to execute the federal role, and about the quality of education in America generally.

The vast bulk of the money the federal government provides to education should go with as few strings as possible, providing maximum freedom to state and local school systems. Essentially, the Elementary and Secondary Education Act tracks this principle, providing funds under a formula for disadvantaged children who need compensatory education. There are also matters of overriding national concern that affect the cohesion of our society—desegregation, bilingual education, and education for handicapped children, for example—that merit federal resources. The national government should even provide funds for experimental local and state programs (including those for teachers), research, and the dissemination of materials among school systems. But a troubling tendency has developed in the education bureaucracies, in both the executive and the Congress, to set curriculum priorities from Washington. Pressed by special interest groups, the Congress provides more and more funds for relatively narrow specific subjects of education (metric education, environmental or ethnic studies) and objects of concern (the gifted or developmentally disabled child). Indulging these tendencies moves the federal government closer to involvement in what our children are taught. It is one thing to give school districts money to test new ways of teaching basic skills; providing money to teach a specific subject is an order of intrusive magnitude closer to interfering in school curriculum.

This is not a conservative-liberal issue. A Russian sputnik can cause conservatives to stampede to mandate more science education from Washington as effectively as some liberals rushed legislatively to champion black studies from the floor of Congress in the late 1960s. The issue is not whether the cause is worthy; granting that, the question persists about the appropriate role of the federal government.

The role of the national government should be strictly limited in the elementary and secondary education field. As Lyndon Johnson put it in 1965, the federal government "can contribute to providing the necessary and needed tools. But the final decision, the last responsibility, the ultimate control, must, and will, always rest with local communities." The *must* in Johnson's quote was hortatory; the *will* was hope. But he was right. We should not confuse the responsibility for elementary and secondary education or further encourage interest groups to seek at the federal level what they cannot obtain at state and local levels. Responsibility for education of our children should be fixed firmly on their parents and teachers, and the federal government should not act to weaken, but to enhance that responsibility.

There is much to do in education. There is a special need to rethink the role of the high schools in America and there is a fundamental requirement to better teach the basic skills in elementary schools. We should not underestimate the difficulty or importance of these tasks. We are releasing to society, with and without high school diplomas, millions of youngsters who are functionally illiterate, ill-prepared for work, ignorant of how the American system of government works, oblivious of their obligations as citizens. We are setting off a time bomb of young Americans who are unable to function in a democratic society. With the potential offered by modern communications for demagogic leadership, an inflation so persistent, and foreign business competition so aggressive that they may render inevitable a future less affluent than the present, and a steady television diet of international crises and bizarre violence at home, the presence of an ever-increasing population of the functionally illiterate and politically naive and ignorant poses a clear and present danger to our society. The job-training programs of the federal government and business must be integrated with the academic side of high school; the basic concept of how we view those four years must be re-examined in light of the crisis we face. But the gravity of the situation calls for state and local school systems to shape and execute the response, not for the federal government to take over responsibility for a solution. If these state and local systems fail, we may reach a point in our mobile, post-industrial society where the federal role could become dominant—but that is the least desirable approach.

While education has much to do, we must also recognize the limits of elementary and secondary schools and teachers. When we ask schools to shoulder the burden of desegregation after generations of discrimination and racism, we should not be surprised when racial problems erupt in the classroom. When society becomes more permissive sexually or more materialistic, we cannot expect in an age of modern communication that the schools will be cloisters. In areas of poverty—where every child in an urban elementary school is on welfare, where high school students are frisked for weapons before entering each day, or teachers are locked in their classrooms for their own safety—we must recognize the limits of the schools and the teachers on the front lines.

At the end of a two-hour visit to a South Bronx elementary school, I asked the black principal, Albert Oliver, what he would do with more money. "Twenty thousand dollars?" he queried. What would he do? I repeated, surprised at the small amount he mentioned. "I'd hire a nurse to take care of pregnant women as soon as they become pregnant." He saw the surprise on my face and explained. "So many of these kids have problems because of birth defects or inadequate diet or care during pregnancy and the preschool years. We have many fourteen-year-old mothers in this neighborhood, lots of grandmothers in their thirties. In a school like this, we know when any child's mother is pregnant. I'd send the nurse out to see them, teach them how to take care of themselves and their babies. We'd solve maybe half our problems at the school."

If the condition of elementary and secondary education menaces the civility of our society, the pressures on higher education threaten our greatness as a nation; and the relentless increase in higher education's dependence on the federal government for funds threatens our tradition of academic freedom. The dramatic demographic changes coming in the eighteen- to twenty-four-year-old population during the 1980s and 1990s will give colleges and universities an increased incentive to press for more federal funds to survive.

Over the 1960–1980 period, college enrollment tripled. However, between 1980 and 1990, the eighteen- to twenty-four-year-old population is expected to decline by 20 percent. Assuming college enrollment at the rate of the 1970s, if the total projected enrollment decline occurred in public higher education (where the average school has 5,940 students), the resulting vacant spaces would empty 229 of the 1,488 public institutions. If the total projected decline occurred in private higher education (where the average school has 1,500 students), the vacant spaces would empty 907 of the 1,685 private colleges. That represents almost 60 percent of all private institutions.

With the coming shrinkage of the eighteen- to twenty-four-year-old population, colleges and universities must either reduce the size of their faculties or seek to maintain present enrollment numbers. Faced with such alternatives (or some combination of them) and rising costs, these institutions will be tempted to maintain enrollment numbers even where that requires lowering their standards, to raise tuition as much as they can in response to increases in federal student aid programs, and to accelerate the increase in part-time, adult, and foreign students that began in the 1970s.

The present system of federal aid provides an incentive for schools to increase tuition charges or to maintain the number of students, because the amount of aid increases with the number of students or the price of tuition. Moreover, the premium our society puts on a college diploma encourages many colleges to follow this course. Schools—and more importantly parents and employers—need to recognize that a college education does not make sense for every high school graduate.

One potential source of additional qualified students is foreign countries. It will take some political courage to fund costs of foreign students during an era of limited resources, but it would make sense to do so. The thirst for education in the underdeveloped world is largely unquenched. It is far better for us to satisfy that thirst than to leave the task to our enemies. (During my 1979 trip to China, I was approached repeatedly by doctors who proudly revealed that they had studied or completed medical residencies in the 1930s and 1940s at Stanford in California, Bellevue in New York, or somewhere else in the United States.)

Even with a significant influx of foreign students, there will be some shrinkage in the size of student bodies. The accompanying reduction in faculties will present severe strains at our best universities, for the key to academic and intellectual preeminence is to attract—and find space for —the best young minds. At many universities, that means excruciating changes in the tenure system and retiring older faculty members. There is no federal role in this critical component of excellence. But there is a federal role in helping to rejuvenate the research facilities at our major universities. Many of these facilities have not been significantly modernized since they were constructed during World War II. Between 1965 and 1975, without taking account of inflation, annual federal underwriting of research and development plants at colleges and universities declined by 81 percent, from $126 million to $24 million. At the same time, cost increases for such research equipment as scientific instrumentation have been running about 4 to 5 percentage points higher than the general inflation rate. Research capacity at our major universities is central not simply in terms of national defense, but in terms of economic growth, health care, social progress, and the quality of life generally.

In a 1977 report, the presidents of fifteen major research universities estimated that $100 million would be needed for each of the next three years to reduce the current backlog of equipment needs, and $150 million annually over an extended period to renovate obsolete facilities and build new ones. A survey of nine major research universities that we did at HEW in 1979 revealed those numbers to be low. As a result, we included in our 1979 Higher Education Act proposals to Congress changes to authorize the federal government to begin to meet these needs. Immediately the issue became how to spread the funds to more universities, rather than focusing them on our key research centers. Fortunately, as passed, the law authorizes the Secretary to make grants for the renovation or construction of research facilities with only two limitations: the total payment to institutions in a single state may not exceed 12.5 percent of the appropriation for the year and no grant can exceed 50 percent of the total cost of the project involved. The law thus provides the flexibility to rebuild our capacity at the 20 to 30 "world class" public and private university research centers. It is important that the Congress avoid logrolling in the appropriations process and not dilute the funds available for this critical purpose. We must recognize that excellence at these key centers means a better life for all of us; in this situation, the investment in the few is the truly egalitarian course.

It is doubtful that any college or university in America can survive in the 1980s without federal assistance. That fact alone calls for the construction of legal safeguards to preserve academic independence and freedom of inquiry as permanent and impenetrable as we can devise. Financial need must not subvert academic freedom and unwittingly create a national university system subservient to the federal government. In my years as HEW Secretary, scores of college representatives and presidents asked me for financial assistance. Yet, rarely did one seriously discuss the need for safeguards to protect academic freedom. They complained about regulation as an economic or administrative burden, but not as a threat to our tradition of intellectual independence and freedom of inquiry. Recently, as it is becoming evident that the federal government will, by the end of the decade, provide more than half the revenues higher education receives, and as federal bureaucrats seek to examine the decision-making process, reconstruct faculty meetings, audit hours spent on research projects, and search academic files, more leaders of education are expressing concern. My experience with the executive and congressional bureaucracies makes clear that their concern is fully warranted.

These two dangers, not unrelated—mediocrity at the price of excellence and financial dependence to the point of relinquishing academic freedom—pose as great a threat to our democracy as the military-industrial complex that concerned President Dwight Eisenhower in 1960. Neither of these two dangers will materialize overnight. They will seep slowly into the system, unnoticed for years. But as is the case with the physical cancer they mimic, prevention is the only sure cure.

Chapter VIII

WELFARE REFORM

WELFARE REFORM was, along with "a government as decent and competent as the American people," a constant commitment of Jimmy Carter's candidacy, but it was an impossible, eventually abandoned dream of Jimmy Carter's presidency. Candidate Carter, all throughout 1976, repeated the promise—"If I'm elected President, you're going to have welfare reform next year"—and he always drew satisfying applause, whoever his audience: chic Manhattan liberals, street blacks in Detroit, Southern Baptist church-goers, white hard-hats on construction sites, conservative Midwest farmers, or the nation's governors in conference. "Cleaning up the welfare mess" was the best ear-of-the-listener issue in Carter's campaign lexicon.

And when candidate Carter promised to reform the welfare system, his air of sincerity and the conviction in his voice carried through to the electorate, each of us hearing what we wanted to hear. For liberals, welfare reform meant more money for the poor and fewer degrading procedures. Conservatives heard, "Get the bums off welfare." Northern industrial states thought welfare reform was a promise of fiscal relief—the federal government would pay more or all of the tab. In Los Angeles, county welfare offices expected deliverance from the array of forms that spread seventy feet from end to end for each applicant. Millions of American taxpayers believed that reform spelled an end to fraud and abuse, and fewer ripped-off tax dollars. When Carter punctuated his promise of welfare reform with, "You can depend on it," as he often did, there was an implied contrast with Richard Nixon, who had tried the Family Assistance Plan and failed, and with Gerald Ford, who had not attempted anything so substantial.

During two years of campaigning for the presidency, Jimmy Carter never had to say precisely what welfare reform meant to him. He could, and of course did, embellish the chameleon commitment in order to help people hear what they were listening for: in one speech, stressing simplification; in another, a "uniform national payment, varying according to cost-of-living differences between communities"; in yet another and another, eliminating "waste," ending the "present anti-work, anti-family" system, stopping "fraud," or relieving local communities and the states of suffocating financial burdens. It was enough that candidate Carter promised to overhaul welfare from top to bottom and replace it with a system that "encourages work and encourages family life and reflects both the competence and compassion of the American people."

President Carter did not have such political luxury. He had, at last, to say what candidate Carter intended, to make the unpleasant choices forced by limited resources, by interest groups, by congressional politics. And, eventually, he had to send a 136-page bill to the six committees of the Congress that claimed jurisdiction over some part of the legislation, and to constituencies poised to receive what they thought they had heard during the campaign.

The story of how those decisions were made in the new administration, and of what became of them, and of the new President's coming to the realization that welfare reform was easier to articulate than deliver on, is a parable of modern American politics. It was a tragi-comedy of naiveté, of guarding institutional interests, and of clashing personalities. Events both within and beyond the administration's control brought me, on May 2, 1977, to call welfare reform "the Middle East of domestic politics" at a press briefing. The analogy fit not just the intractable Arab-Israeli situation, but referred to the tale of the scorpion who asked the camel to carry him across the Nile. The camel said, "But if you get on my back, you will sting me and kill me." The scorpion replied, "Then we would both drown." The camel thought a moment, decided the scorpion made sense, and told him to get on his back. Halfway across the river, in the deepest and most treacherous currents, the scorpion stung the camel.

"Why?" asked the astonished camel. "Now we will both drown." "This is the Middle East, my friend," responded the scorpion.

The President wanted a complete overhaul of our nation's welfare system to be one of the first proposals he sent to Congress. He made that clear to me during our meetings at the Smith Bagley plantation on St. Simons Island, Georgia, in December 1976. I assumed, though I did not state it to Carter explicitly, that welfare reform would cost more money, so I told reporters there that I thought reform might have to await economic recovery. The following day at a press conference, Carter rode over my statement: He would complete a design for basic welfare reform and send it to the Congress in 1977. What he did not say to the press—and what he did not say to me until a briefing in March 1977—was that he hoped to have comprehensive welfare reform at no additional cost to the federal budget.

There was a good deal of interest in reforming the system in the early months of 1977. Russell Long addressed me directly at my confirmation hearing: "We have worked long enough in this vineyard in trying to help disadvantaged people so that by now we should know that we do someone a far greater favor to give him an opportunity to do something useful for society in return for adequate compensation . . . rather than the demoralizing alternative of simply paying a person to sit idly doing nothing. . . . People deteriorate when they have nothing to do. I would hope that the experience that you have observed and participated in through the years now would have convinced you that just paying people money for doing nothing is a very inadequate answer to a problem. . . ."

Newly elected Senator Daniel Patrick Moynihan, Democrat of New York, the midwife and brilliant biographer of Nixon's ill-starred Family Assistance Plan, had just become Chairman of the brand-new Senate Finance Subcommittee on Public Assistance. From the moment he set foot in the Senate, Moynihan began insisting that Carter fulfill "his campaign commitment and the solemn Democratic platform pledge," for which Moynihan had battled at the 1976 Democratic National Convention, to provide New York City financial relief from its welfare burden. On the House side, liberal California Congressman James Corman, who chaired the Ways and Means Subcommittee on Unemployment Compensation and Public Assistance, was excited at the possibility of comprehensive welfare reform, one of his lifetime commitments. His close friend and working associate Democrat Charles Rangel from Harlem shared his hope. Both were more interested in increasing benefits to poor people than they were in fiscal relief or in Long's anti-fraud and abuse measures. The first time Rangel talked to me on Long's concern about welfare reform and fraud, he said, "The object is to give welfare mothers enough to live on and feed their kids. The poor will never be smart enough to rip off as much as the rich."

Unfortunately, House Ways and Means Committee Chairman Al Ullman of Oregon, who had been burned and exhausted in the Family Assistance Plan fight during the Nixon administration, had no stomach for another welfare reform push. In 1970, the House had passed Nixon's reform plan for a guaranteed minimum income by 243 to 155, under the leadership of Wilbur Mills, Ullman's predecessor. Ullman remembered the demonstrations, the attacks from left and right, the final bitterness in pushing House members to vote on this thorny and unpopular program that he himself opposed. At that point, Delaware Republican Senator John J. Williams had HEW prepare worst-case data. They showed that a family which increased its earnings from work from $720 to $5,560 under Nixon's plan would drop from $6,128 to $6,109 in spendable income, "$19 less than if they sit in a rocking chair earning only $720." That was it. Russell Long wrote the epitaph for the Family Assistance Plan with his question: "What is the point of requiring the man to go to work if he's going to end up with less money?" House members who had voted for the plan were asked that question repeatedly when they next campaigned. George Bush's vote for Nixon's plan was part of the reason he lost his Senate race in Texas. Ullman remembered all of this, and then some, and he recounted it to me on more than one occasion. It wasn't good enough that Moynihan now chaired the Senate's Subcommittee. "The liberals want too much and the conservatives want to cut back," Ullman told me, "and you can't get through the ambush. It's so complicated, whatever you do, you're going to have situations like the ones Williams found in FAP. All you need is one and your bill's dead." Even so, with all the different concerns and the contradictory solutions and passions, both on and off Capitol Hill, almost everyone agreed: Leaving politics aside, it was clear that welfare needed to be overhauled.

The five basic parts of the system paid out almost $30 billion a year when Carter took office. The Aid to Families with Dependent Children (AFDC) program was paying $6.2 billion in federal and $5.3 billion in state funds to 11.4 million recipients—one American in twenty. More than 90 percent of those recipients were mothers (3 million) and children under the age of eighteen (8 million). The rest were fathers, principally in such states as New York, California, and Wisconsin, which paid benefits to intact families. The Supplemental Security Income Program (SSI) paid $5.3 billion in federal funds and almost $2 billion in state funds to 4.4 million aged, blind, and disabled people. Some were on Social Security, but most were ineligible for it. The Food Stamp Program paid $5.6 billion in federal funds and about $300 million in state funds to 17.2 million people for stamps that could be used to purchase food. (Unlike the AFDC program, food stamps are indexed to inflation; as a result, it is the fastest-growing welfare program, likely to exceed $10 billion in 1981.) The Earned Income Tax Credit provided $1.3 billion to 20 million families with an employed member who did not earn enough to pay income tax, and received funds through the income tax system. State and local General Assistance provided $1.2 billion to almost 1 million people who did not fit into any of the other categories. Most of this money went to poor single persons and to childless couples in the big industrial states.

Since many individuals received benefits from more than one program—AFDC and SSI beneficiaries commonly received food stamps; more than 40 percent of the recipients got benefits from at least three programs; almost 20 percent from at least five—the number of Americans who received assistance was difficult to determine, but it was estimated at about 30 million when Carter took office. In spite of all this, more than 25 million people lived below the official poverty line in the richest nation in the history of civilization.

There were other cash assistance programs that helped keep millions of Americans out of poverty, and many of those who were eligible for the basic welfare programs also received some of those benefits. In 1977, Social Security paid about $90 billion to 33 million recipients; Medicare and Medicaid paid almost $40 billion for health care bills of almost 50 million old, disabled, or poor people; and additional billions were paid through disability insurance, workmen's compensation, veterans compensation, veterans pensions (which, unlike veterans compensation, are means-tested with benefits related to an individual's income and assets like other welfare programs); railroad retirement and black lung payments; rent supplements (cash payments based on family income and rent); and basic educational opportunity grants (means-tested payments to students for post-secondary school tuition). None of these programs, however, bore the stigma of welfare.

When people talk about welfare, they are, on the whole, talking about the AFDC program—the mothers and children, and the two-parent families with children, who receive cash assistance. It is not HEW or the federal government, but the states that administer the AFDC program. When I became Secretary, HEW financed from 50 to 83 percent of the program's cost, varying from state to state, depending on the level of payment and average income in the state as compared to the nation. Mississippi had the lowest monthly payment ($60 for a family of four); New York, the most publicized ($430); Hawaii, the highest ($533); the average was about $320. HEW provided some of the regulatory framework and paid a good portion of the salaries of the state and local employees who administered the programs. Within that framework, those employees set the standards for eligibility, determined whether individuals met the standards, and made the cash payments. But as Secretary, I carried political responsibility for this program that was administered by state or local governments once or twice removed from my direct management control.

Where states or cities have high payments and a relatively lower percentage of federal cost-sharing, the cry for fiscal relief is loudest, as in New York and California, where 25 percent of the nation's welfare recipients live among 18 percent of the nation's population. But whether benefits are high or low and whether state, city, or county runs the program, it has become incredibly complex. In 1977, there were 1,400 separate welfare forms in Illinois and a typical AFDC case required the completion of from twenty to thirty of them before a payment could be made. The federal courts have further complicated the program by imposing requirements for hearings where applicants may question the denial or amount of benefits on an increasing number of grounds at earlier stages of the administrative process. It is no wonder that mistakes were made in 44 percent of the AFDC cases in 1974. Contrary to the popular wisdom, most of the errors were made by the administrators, and not because of fraud by the recipients but because the whole process is so intricate. Welfare is a maze; it is easy to lose one's way. There are different eligibility standards and different forms for SSI, AFDC, food stamps, the earned income credit, and whatever general or other assistance programs may be available.

Welfare needed reform, and I had a mandate from the President to put a plan together. But what was best and what was possible were substantively difficult and politically treacherous questions to answer. My only guidance from the President was to develop "a comprehensive plan that was pro-work and pro-family." To keep faith with his speeches and the Democratic platform, the plan had to provide some fiscal relief for states and localities. And Carter wanted a plan fast. In November 1976, before I was a serious candidate for HEW Secretary, Carter had asked me on the phone how fast a welfare reform plan could be developed. I had answered him off-the-cuff, "By next May." Then, at the meetings on St. Simons Island, the President-elect referred to May as the month for welfare reform. Shortly after he assumed office, Carter gave the May deadline a demanding life of its own, announcing it from Washington, D.C., and at a town meeting in Clinton, Massachusetts: "On May first, Joe Califano, a tough, knowledgeable administrator . . . will come forward, after working with [Massachusetts Governor] Mike Dukakis and many other governors and local officials, and propose to the Congress a comprehensive revision of the entire welfare system.'' He told me that he would attend several hours of deliberation ''when you think it's beginning to firm up and you need me,'' but he did not want to become prematurely engaged. The ball was in my court.

My last look at income maintenance programs, in the mid-sixties for Lyndon Johnson, had been cursory. Economists like James Tobin at Yale had suggested a variety of negative income tax schemes to pay money to poor people through the tax system, and other consolidations of cash assistance programs into an integrated system of income maintenance. Johnson sent me to talk to them and review the government's welfare, unemployment compensation, and other cash payment programs. He made his objective clear: ''I want to get more money into the hands of poor people who can't get jobs.'' We quickly concluded that though the concept of an integrated income maintenance program made sense, it was politically unacceptable to the Congress and the majority of the American people. Once Johnson saw that, he told me to prepare legislative recommendations to increase the minimum payments of existing cash assistance programs as much as possible. So he proposed and the Congress enacted increases in the minimum payment for Social Security (asking for 59 percent in 1966) and significant hikes in certain veterans benefits, and payments for poor single-parent families, and the aged, blind, and disabled. At the same time, Johnson set up an income maintenance commission, chaired by Chicago businessman Ben Heineman, Sr., and composed of moderate Americans, to get the idea of income maintenance into the mainstream of political debate and to give us a framework for such a proposal in a second term, which never materialized.

This time, Carter wanted a comprehensive plan, and although the timetable was short, the chance to succeed where so many others had failed was exhilarating, and the hope of restructuring a system that degraded and left out so many poor in our rich country, provided ample adrenaline for the demanding effort. More than 40 percent of America's poor—primarily single persons, and couples with and without children—did not qualify under AFDC or SSI, the key cash assistance programs for the needy, and most of those who did qualify received benefits well below the poverty line.

Where was I to begin? Welfare was so encrusted with myth, demagoguery, regional politics, and racial prejudice that I thought I must start with a major consultation and education effort. The day after I was sworn in, I announced that we would try to develop a reform program working with other federal agencies, key Senate and House committee staffers, governors, mayors, and county and state legislators. The Welfare Reform

Consulting Group was to be chaired by Henry Aaron, the HEW Assistant Secretary for Planning and Evaluation and an expert on income maintenance. I had recruited him from the Brookings Institution with welfare reform very much in mind. Charlie Schultze (whom Carter named as Chairman of the Council of Economic Advisers) and Joe Pechman at the Brookings Institution had both told me Aaron was brilliant, and though Aaron had an air of impatience and annoyance that often attends high intelligence, I wanted imagination and thoughtful analysis from him, and he delivered.

Educating the public on welfare was critical. In 1967, when I had been Johnson's aide for domestic affairs, I had given a speech to the Washington chapter of Sigma Delta Chi at the National Press Club on the planning, programming, and budgeting systems we had been developing in the domestic departments. I emphasized the importance of facts. The key illustration was a study William Gorham, the first person to hold Aaron's job at HEW, made to find out how many of the 7.3 million Americans who were then on welfare were capable of working. After excepting mothers, children, those over sixty-five, and the disabled, he counted fewer than fifty thousand able-bodied males—less than 1 percent of the welfare population—who could be expected to work. The facts got a lot of attention, but the myths about laziness and cheating persisted (and still persist), and I knew I had to keep hammering away.

Myth Number One, the most pernicious, is that people are poor because they do not want to work. The facts contradict this. Seventeen percent of the poor work full time, throughout the year; another 31 percent work at some time during the year. Nearly 71 percent of the twenty-five million poor are individuals who would not normally be asked to work—children under sixteen, the aged, the severely disabled, students, or mothers with children under six. Almost 90 percent of impoverished Americans either work full time, or are persons no civilized society would require to work. Of the remaining 10 percent, 8 percent are women, many of whom have children between six and seventeen. Only 2 percent of the twenty-five million poor people even resemble the mythical stereotype—healthy males who do not work. The overwhelming proportion of poor people who can and should work do so. They stay poor because they do not earn enough money.

Myth Number Two is that most of the poor are poor for life. To the contrary, the poverty population is fluid. Each year about 7.5 million to 10 million people move above the poverty line (which in 1980 was $7,500 for a family of four), and a like number sink below it. Only 3 percent of the American population were poor in every one of the six years from 1967 to 1972. While the percentage of poor hovered around 11 percent, actually about twice that number of Americans—21 percent—were poor during at least one year of that period.

Myth Number Three is that the poor are primarily black. Actually, 67 percent of the American poor are white (though that is proportionately less than the 87 percent of the American population that is white). Thirty-one percent of the poor are black (though they constitute only 12 percent of the population).

Myth Number Four is that the poor squander their money. What evidence we have (developed before LBJ's Great Society programs provided so many benefits, such as those to provide food stamps and health care, and subsidized housing and transportation) shows that low-income people spend a somewhat greater proportion, about 88 percent, of their income on food, clothing, housing, medical care, and transportation, than those with higher incomes.

Why should there be twenty-five million poor people in a country that has a minimum wage required by law and so many cash assistance programs? The federal minimum wage is set at a level that puts a family of four with one wage earner below the poverty line. In almost half the states, including most of the South, the combined level of AFDC and food stamp benefits is less than three-fourths of the poverty income level.

In 1977, in addition to blasting away at these myths, I began to move toward another objective that I thought necessary to persuade the Congress that we should have welfare reform—wringing out all the waste and fraud we could administratively, without changing the law. Only if that action were taken could we argue that legislation was needed to improve efficiency; we would already be doing all we could, and additional funds would not be lost to waste and fraud. We drove the payment error rate down, holding frequent meetings, demanding periodic reports, calling governors, visiting field offices, sending teams to work side by side with state and city welfare departments. By mid-1979, just before I left HEW, the percentage of AFDC funds spent on excessive or ineligible payments had dropped from 8.6 percent in early 1977 to 7.1 percent, for a savings of some $100 million annually; and the SSI error rate was down to 4.6 percent. We had also introduced Project Match—a computer check of the welfare rolls against employment and Social Security rolls, to identify overpayments and cheaters. (Even this effort to eliminate fraud and waste was not without controversy. Welfare recipients and their advocates accused us of perpetuating the myth that most of those on welfare were cheaters or lazy.)

As we were busy chipping away at some of the misconceptions that distract from understanding welfare and poverty, and trying to administer the programs more efficiently, I expressed hope for our reform effort: "There will be a great national debate on welfare. . . . We welcome that debate because only with the broadest understanding of each other's views can we devise an income security system that reflects the compassion and decency of the American people and their willingness to help provide for those who cannot provide for themselves the means to live in human dignity and with peace of mind." That hope was never realized.

THE FIRST sense of the frustration and trouble that might lie ahead came as I attempted to educate myself and prepare to brief the President. I asked Henry Aaron and his experts to give me a crash lecture series on income maintenance programs, their history, the problems of equity, and the economic and political shoals on which prior programs had foundered. Once or twice a week for several weeks, I sat for hours in the early evening, as Aaron and his able deputies Mike Barth and John Todd lectured.

My education faltered as other business interrupted our sessions, but also because abstract theories and intellectual disputes did not deal with the regional, local, partisan, legislative, and special interest politics. The contrast came home deeply on March 10, 1977, as I sat alone from 8:30 in the morning until 6:00 in the evening and heard witnesses in a public hearing on welfare reform. As I listened to a parade of contentious welfare mothers, labor leaders, Hispanics and blacks, handicapped citizens, program administrators, and congressmen, I wondered to myself about the computers that worked around the clock to help Aaron and his team analyze the consequences of various changes in the welfare laws. They were throwing out numbers just as Jackson Pollock splattered paint on a canvas: how many would remain poor or near-poor, who would be better off or worse off, what were the break-even points and marginal tax rates. Eventually they would provide a design. But would it be a design that attracted sufficient acclaim and consensus from the disparate, frustrated, sometimes angry critics?

By late March, we were ready for our first presidential briefing and Carter called it for Friday, March 25, in the Cabinet Room. I wanted to give him a picture of the existing system and of the problems involved in shaping a reform proposal. I hoped to move back the May 1 target date, and to get a sense of the President's tilt on which government programs to include, how and at what level to set a minimum national standard for payment, whether we should cover intact as well as one-parent families, and whether he was prepared to guarantee employable recipients special public service jobs, if no jobs were available in the private or regular public sector. Really, I was hoping to discover what Jimmy Carter meant by welfare reform.

Vice-President Mondale was there; so were Labor Secretary Ray Marshall, Charles Schultze, White House aides Eizenstat and Watson, and top staffers from other interested government departments such as Agriculture and Treasury, and the Office of Management and Budget. The usual supporting cast of junior White House staffers ranged themselves along the wall, framing the room, and Aaron and Barth accompanied me. Hamilton Jordan and Jody Powell came in and out during the two hours.

The President sat in his usual place at the middle of the long Cabinet table. I stood opposite him with my charts, pointer in hand. The reaction at the meeting, and thereafter, to any mention of programs that were not already administered by HEW provided ample evidence to support the old proposition: in Washington, where one stands depends on where one sits. Marshall saw no reason to include any part of the Labor Department's unemployment compensation program, and for interminable hours during the spring and summer of 1977 the difficulty of integrating jobs and cash assistance was compounded in turf-dominated discussions between Marshall's assistant Arnold Packer and Aaron and his staff. Agriculture Secretary Bob Bergland maneuvered to keep the food stamp program in his department, despite the fact that, at the recommendation of the administration, the stamps were soon to be issued free with no co-payment required, and would thus be virtually the same as money.

The mere mention of veterans pensions and rent supplements sent their bureaucratic constitutencies to war. At one point, Carter stopped me to make sure he understood that the veterans pension payments were, like welfare, related to income. When I said yes, he shook his head. Powell, seated behind him to his left, remarked, "Let's remember what happened when we took on the veterans in Georgia." Someone else brought up the reaction of the veterans groups to Carter's amnesty for Vietnam draft-evaders. I knew then, and so did everyone else in the room, that we would not include this program in the reform package. Indeed, off a leak from that briefing, Senate Majority Whip Alan Cranston of California and House Veterans Committee Chairman Ray Roberts locked the fence securely around all veterans programs with a tough letter to the President demanding that the administration keep my hands off and not tarnish veterans with the welfare stigma. Carter agreed. He cautioned me that there was no point in angering veterans by calling attention to the fact that their pensions, like the welfare payments, were tested according to need.

The most public explosion came from Housing and Urban Development Secretary Patricia Harris when she heard about my suggestion during the briefing that any program, such as HUD's rent supplements, which in essence provides cash to limit a poor family's rental payment to 25 percent of its income, was a means-tested program, and ought to be examined during the reform study. Harris complained to Eizenstat and he called me. "She's so furious. Your point is right, but it isn't worth making." The matter was dropped until Carter sent Harris, Charles Schultze, and me a memo on July 7, 1977. "During our discussions on the 1979 budget, OMB raised the issue of welfare reform and its implications for federally subsidized housing programs," the President's memo said, continuing: "I have asked Bert Lance to take the lead in developing a more detailed analysis of the issue, including alternative ways in which housing subsidies and the welfare system might relate to each other." Lance's OMB staff paper suggested how inefficiently HUD's $5 billion in such subsidies were distributed: "Of those eligible, only 8 percent now receive housing subsidies. At the current program level, coverage would increase by about 1.25 percentage points annually." OMB acknowledged that distributing housing subsidies to all who qualified under welfare reform would reduce the average subsidy for each recipient. But it argued that, "The resulting distribution of benefits would be far more equitable and would leave the great majority of poverty households better off. . . . Most families can obtain decent housing for less than it costs the government to obtain it on their behalf [and] most families would not choose to devote the full amount spent on their behalf under the subsidy programs to housing if they were given cash instead."

Harris was enraged. She accused me of trying to take over her housing programs. She protested to Hamilton Jordan and when she received no satisfaction, a story based on a leaked copy of the OMB paper appeared on the front page of the *Washington Post* on July 14. "A major battle has erupted within the Carter administration over a proposal that virtually all federal housing subsidy programs be scrapped to provide money for welfare reform." The White House phone lines were busy with calls from congressional backers of housing, builders, and bankers, but not from any public interest organizations representing the poor. When Hale Champion heard that not one of the furious calls, letters, or telegrams came from a poor people's organization but rather from mortgage bankers and building contractors, he said, "At least we know who really benefits from that program." I urged OMB to drop the issue, and told Carter that "my best political judgment is that the misery is not worth the fight." Carter suggested once more to Eizenstat that we integrate housing subsidies with welfare reform, but when he learned that Lance and Eizenstat held the same view as mine, he backed off reluctantly.

At the March 25 briefing, after the reactions to my description of the $183 billion constellation of all cash payments, including Social Security, through federal, state, and local programs, I concluded in my own mind that we would be able at best to consolidate AFDC, SSI, and the food stamp program into a single cash payment to poor people. I then focused on some of the inequities in the present welfare system. It was in reality 54 widely disparate systems, one for each state, the District of Columbia, Puerto Rico, Guam, and the Virgin Islands. Mississippi benefits for a family of four amounted to 13 percent of the poverty threshold. In Wisconsin, benefits went to 80 percent.

As I gave Carter examples of work disincentives, he seemed genuinely distressed. In Michigan, a family of four, with the father working at the minimum wage, had a total income of $5,678 and the family had to pay its own medical bills. In contrast, a single-parent family of four, with a nonworking mother on welfare, had a total income of $7,161 (including the insurance value of Medicaid). I explained to the President that, should that Michigan mother decide to work full time at the minimum wage, her income would rise to only $9,350—even though that was far above the income of the working two-parent family. Carter literally blinked. When I said that the quickest way for the working father to increase his family's income, under the Michigan welfare system which paid benefits only to single-parent families, would be to leave his family, he considered it disgraceful.

I offered another example from Wisconsin, which paid welfare to intact families. A man with a wife and two children who worked half-time at the minimum wage and received welfare would get $8,628; if he worked full-time, his income would drop by about $3,000. Losing most of his welfare benefits, he would end up with only $5,691.

The President shook his head from side to side, partly in dismay, partly in disbelief. When I said—and I had a graphic chart that illustrated the point—that a family head with two children would make a net of only $5 for the next $100 earned above the minimum wage because of the loss of $95 in AFDC, food stamps, housing allowance, and the earned income tax credit, Carter said, "When the American people understand this mess, I'm sure they'll do something about it!" My short discussion of the administrative complexities got more presidential nods of dismay.

Then I described the technically rigid and politically explosive relationship between the amount of welfare benefits a family with no earnings receives and the amount of earnings at which that family loses all benefits. The relation between those two amounts determines the rate at which earnings reduce benefits. If that rate is too high, it has a motivating impact on poor people similar to the impact confiscatory tax rates would have on wealthy people: Why work? To maintain a steady rate of loss of earnings that still provides a financial incentive to work, each time the benefits for a family with no earnings are increased, the point at which all benefits are cut off must be proportionately increased. If, for example, the benefit for a family with no earnings were $4,200 and the point of benefit elimination $8,400, the family would keep 50 cents of each dollar it earned up to $8,400. If the $4,200 is raised to $4,700, then the $8,400 must be raised to $9,400 to avoid the family's loss of more than 50 cents for each dollar of earnings. If the $4,200 is increased without increasing the $8,400, then the family will lose more than 50 cents of benefits for each dollar earned and the incentive to work will decrease. On the other hand, the higher the earnings permitted before all benefits are cut off, the more people there are on welfare. Political attacks wait in both wings: for creating a benefit structure that discourages work or for paying welfare benefits to people with earnings too high and increasing the number of people on welfare.

I had a sense that the intrinsic complexity was distasteful to Carter. He wanted a "simplified program," and I could feel his frustration as the realization came over him that no such reform was possible. Then I told him about what the income maintenance experts call "notches." A notch is any point at which a dollar of earnings results in loss of more than a dollar of benefits. The big bad wolf of notches is Medicaid. Since eligibility for Medicaid is based largely on eligibility for AFDC or SSI benefits, the point at which families or individuals earn the dollar that renders them ineligible for AFDC or SSI cash assistance is also the point at which they lose Medicaid benefits, worth hundreds, often thousands of dollars each year.

Now Carter was visibly impatient. As I described the job program Ray Marshall had put together, the President relaxed. During the briefing, there were remarkably few questions. When it ended, Carter reiterated his desire for comprehensive reform, and said that he would not decide any of the consolidation issues with their prickly turf problems at this time. He was interested in simplifying the system, and he wanted to put people on welfare in jobs, and to eliminate fraud. He did recognize, however, that the most we could accomplish by early May was to announce a set of principles that would guide the development of a detailed program.

Although Carter had administered the Georgia AFDC program, I don't think anyone had ever exposed him to the intricacy and inequity of the welfare system in this depth on a national scale, and he seemed to recoil from it. "If you could start over, what would you do?" he asked me. I wasn't sure. "Well," he said, "you take the amount of money now being spent on welfare programs and redesign the whole system from scratch."

"It will cost money to get a better system," I said. "I'll design a new system, but there'll be some cost."

Carter gazed at me as though I had missed his point. "I want a welfare reform program that doesn't cost anything more," he said.

"Mr. President, I don't think it's possible to put together any program like that which makes sense or has a chance of passing," I responded.

The President's eyes were cold, his voice was soft but stern. "I want you to give me a comprehensive program at no additional cost."

I protested.

After some discussion, though, he was still insisting on a no-additional-cost comprehensive reform. At the very end of the meeting, Carter acceded to my request to submit additional cost items in order of their priority—"one billion dollars at a time."

Henry Aaron was despondent. We had been working on the assumption that there would be funds for reform. "It's impossible; what he wants is impossible," Aaron kept repeating as we drove back to HEW. When candidate Carter had said "welfare reform," Aaron and his planners had heard "decent standard of living for poor people."

I tried to buoy Aaron up by telling him that the President was simply using a time-honored management tool: See what you can get for the same amount you are now spending before increasing it. "I've done it myself," I told him. "Whenever someone proposes a new program, I ask what program they're going to eliminate to pay for it." But I was less certain in my own mind. I was disappointed. I was afraid I hadn't gotten through to the President on the political and human prices a zero-cost plan would exact, particularly from the poor who would receive no help, from those people who would be worse off, and from the states and cities who needed fiscal relief. I believed that Carter thought the only way to make reform politically palatable was to encapsulate it in a plan that cost nothing more, or saved money, and I had failed to demonstrate to him that his objective was incompatible with his campaign commitment to comprehensive reform. In any case, he wanted us to reassemble in two weeks to review zero-cost options, and we had to get them ready. At first Ray Marshall and his aide, Arnold Packer, did not want to give the President any zero-cost major reform options because they considered all such options unsound. Even the tight-fisted OMB staff believed that, "At zero cost, [no plan] is worth pursuing," because so many recipients would receive lower benefits.

I searched for ways to ease the zero-cost restriction. To the extent that Carter might be concerned about his commitment to balance the budget in 1981, we could make any costly aspects of the plan effective in 1982. I sought to include every possible program in the existing cost base to make "zero cost" as large as possible. We tried to include savings that would accrue to other programs, such as unemployment compensation or rent supplement payments, and from more equitably distributed welfare benefits, and to take credit for Social Security taxes that would be paid by those in the special public service jobs program and for projected decreases in the Labor Department's Comprehensive Employment Training Act (CETA) job program. Then we prepared a menu of desirable reforms above zero cost for Carter to consider.

The briefing on the zero-cost options was again in the Cabinet Room, at 1:00 P.M., April 11. I had charts outlining three plans: one concentrated on consolidating cash assistance programs; the other two were variations that emphasized jobs. For each of the plans, I tried to focus the President's attention on the inequities and political pitfalls of pursuing reform at zero cost. The consolidated cash plan left millions of recipients with lower benefits and (because of the sharp decline in benefits for each dollar earned) decidedly inadequate work incentives; to the extent that fiscal relief was provided to states and cities to ease their burden of welfare payments, it came from the pockets of poor families. The job-oriented programs reduced all public service jobs to the minimum wage (anathema to organized labor because prevailing wages for many of those jobs were higher); these programs did not change unjustified welfare benefit disparities among the states, were administratively complex, and provided little or no fiscal relief.

Carter didn't enjoy the briefing. He questioned me impatiently, probing to see whether I had truly tried to honor his request for zero-cost alternatives. He reacted almost petulantly to my pointing out the problems of such an approach. When I had reviewed desirable reforms that required additional expenditures, I concluded, "At zero cost, it may be that no one would recommend any more than tinkering to improve program administration and creating a hundred thousand public service jobs for the poor." The President was almost scowling, but I felt I had to finish even though he clearly did not want to hear it. "If you want a politically viable welfare reform plan that helps poor people, then we need to abandon zero cost, and we need to face some of the difficulties of creating so many jobs for this population." Carter was getting angry, so I rushed through the last sentence. "Mr. President, I don't think any of these plans is adequate unless we increase spending, and I am asking you to approve that."

Carter sat there, and asked querulously: "At zero cost, is the present system the best one?"

Aaron said something about not being able to ignore prior history. Eizenstat started to remind Carter of his "promise to [New York City Mayor Abe] Beame to reduce the local share of costs."

Carter ignored them. His eyes were indignantly locked on mine. "As you've explained it, we should just leave the system as it is. We don't have $5 billion to $10 billion to put in a new system. Why don't we just say, the hell with it!"

I tried to duck the assault. "If we don't have money now, we can always use Russell Long's approach of demonstration programs, holding costly changes for later years."

The President was in no mood to be mollified. "I was pleased with your first presentation two weeks ago because you showed the inequities and abuse in the welfare system. But now, if you're going to keep inviolate the privilege of making $8,000 or $10,000 a year on welfare, then I agree with you. Nothing can be done. Let people rip off the system. It's a travesty on the American taxpayer. We're just wasting our time."

I had never seen Carter like this. He resolutely did not want to hear what I had said; he refused to accept it. Maybe I could talk him through it piece by piece, I thought. "There's no more than $1.7 billion savings in stopping cheating in all the welfare programs, at the most," I said. I gave him the highest estimate we had, and that included the food stamp program.

"What about administrative graft?" he shot back at me. "Are there zero savings from that?" Then, turning to the room, Carter added sarcastically, "The American people will be delighted to know that we have the best system possible at the present cost."

Marshall said he thought we could make some improvements in the program even at zero cost. I disagreed. "At zero cost, we retain so many inequities we'd be shot out of the water."

Carter ignored my exchange with Marshall and kept talking to me. "I don't buy the assumption that once you set a benefit level you have to bring everybody up to it, that you have to take the highest benefit level and pay everybody the same." He rambled, agreeing with my desire to change the state welfare payment structure, emphasizing that a family with a working member should always get more than a comparable one without a working member, indicating his ambivalence on the amount and timing of fiscal relief, and expressing willingness to limit the Labor Department's special public employment program to minimum wage levels. Then, glaring at me, he said, "Stop protecting those receiving welfare benefits."

When Carter got around to talking about jobs, he was not facing up to the realities of the welfare population—mostly illiterate, unskilled teenage mothers and thirty- to-forty-year-old grandmothers. I recognized the importance of providing jobs, but expressed doubts about creating such a large number of jobs for this population in any short time frame. "It will take several years." Charlie Schultze revealed even stronger misgivings about creating over one million jobs. "I just don't think you can do it," he said.

Carter glowered. "Why? Sixty percent of the people who work in Plains [Georgia] are high school drop-outs. They work."

Henry Aaron repeated the point: "It will be very difficult to create jobs for such an illiterate and unskilled population."

The President would have none of it. "People on my farm work machinery, drive fork lifts, put herbicide on peanut plants, which has to be done just right to kill the bugs and not the plants. And when it comes time to cash their paychecks, they sign with an X."

Schultze began to speak, but Carter continued. "If we created one million or so jobs, Plains would have to provide three jobs, that's all. There are three jobs that need to be done in Plains."

"My town in Minnesota would have to find only eight or nine," said Mondale.

Schultze's face crinkled with incredulity at the comments. "But what about [New York City Mayor] Abe Beame? He needs at least 150,000!"

There were some comments on other issues from those in the room, but Carter returned constantly to reducing benefit levels. "People move from Chicago to New York to get higher welfare benefits. New York benefits are too high due to politics and poor administration. Government should be holding families together instead of encouraging vast movements of population." I knew the movements were shifting out of New York and to the Sun Belt, but this was not my day to challenge Carter on relatively marginal misunderstandings.

Then, to my surprise, the President implied that he recognized the need for more money. He volunteered that he would consider increasing the amount of the zero-cost base. "I might be able to give you some money by reducing LEAA [Law Enforcement Assistance Administration] grants to states and revenue sharing, especially if we do relieve states of some welfare cost." When he saw the hint of satisfaction on my face, he warned me again about costs. As we talked about the next steps, Carter asked me to provide a draft of guiding principles that he could announce on May 1, and under which work would proceed. There was to be another meeting in two weeks.

Back at HEW, I wondered why Carter had been so irritable and angry at the briefing. Perhaps he was sensing, as I was, the dilemma we faced: with zero cost, there could be no welfare reform without making some draconian proposals; however, each dollar of additional cost subjected the reform plan to attack as giving more money to people on welfare. If that's what's bothering him, then it's imperative, I thought, to focus on the anti-fraud and -waste aspects of the plan that improved efficiency, and on work incentives.

I promptly drew up and sent a memorandum to the President with proposed principles, which included ones to: integrate in one related cash assistance program AFDC, SSI, food stamps, housing supplements related to income, extended unemployment benefits, and the earned income tax credit (but merge only AFDC, SSI, and food stamps); redirect the special jobs program to the poorest people able to work with ancillary health, training, and social services; freeze state welfare supplements so the cost to states would not rise in the future; provide a universal minimum federal benefit with some variation based on the cost of living in different communities; and make certain that working families always made more money than comparable nonworking families. I asked him again for additional funds, "to increase equity and make the package more politically attractive."

At HEW and Labor, we turned to preparing more detailed proposals for reform, reflecting those principles and what little guidance Carter had provided at the second briefing. At zero cost, the departmental staffs were in constant tension over funds for jobs versus funds for cash assistance, and the computers ground away to provide some sense of the human and economic ramifications of varying cash payments, earned income tax credits, and priorities for jobs, and how many and who were worse or better off under each variation. Despite successive and uninterrupted fifteen-to-eighteen-hour days, too much economic theory, social philosophy, and protection of institutional prerogative separated the Labor and HEW staffs to reach agreement in two weeks. I arrived at the White House on April 26 with two plans, one job-oriented, the other centered on cash assistance reform, with charts depicting the pros and cons of each alternative.

Carter seemed more relaxed as I began once again with my pointer in hand. Henry Aaron and Arnold Packer, the chief staff protagonists, frequently clashed at a level of detail that was unnecessary for a President, but Carter listened as they argued, and he made clear that his focus was jobs. I shared his desire to provide jobs; indeed, I saw it as a critical moral and political component of a decent program. But I was worried about overpromising. When Charlie Schultze again asserted that the Labor Department might be overestimating its ability to create jobs,

Carter's response was, "So what? What difference does it make?" I responded, "Perhaps none, so long as we have an adequate cash assistance net to catch those we don't produce jobs for. But there is always the specter of lost hope and failure if we promise 1.4 million jobs and deliver only a few hundred thousand."

Carter agreed. "If we produced only 600,000 jobs, it would be a tremendous achievement. But it would look like we had failed. Let's not promise a particular number; let's just try to create jobs."

I had now talked to enough senators and representatives to describe the bleak outlook for any welfare reform proposal in Congress. "We'll be sending our plan to reluctant members, except Moynihan, and he wants fiscal relief."

I doubted that Moynihan would support any zero-cost plan. He had already begun to criticize the administration for delay. Just the day before, he had warned that welfare reform might be lost in the excitement surrounding the energy crisis. "This is HEW at it again. HEW cannot produce a welfare reform proposal. The Assistant Secretary in charge [Aaron] has written one of those books saying it can't be done, and he seems bent on proving it." Moynihan characterized HEW as "a murky and often inaccessible environ into which many proposals have gone but few have emerged." He was disappointed that all the administration would announce on May 2 were principles. "You can draft that bill in a morning," he said.

In view of my concern about the Congress, Marshall suggested to Carter that the jobs program could move to the Congress separately and first. Without the jobs program, welfare reform lost whatever chance it might have, so I disagreed. So did the President. "At present, we have the people's attention," Carter said. "Damn if they don't want something done on this issue. I'm willing to have a session with the governors, Long, Corman, and others, and go to blows if necessary." It was one of the few truly enthusiastic statements I heard him make about welfare reform in private.

The group then got into a discussion of the difficulty of passing a negative income tax and guaranteed minimum income. The President was confident that he could "sell the income assistance as part of a comprehensive reform. Pat Caddell's polls show that."

"In any case," I said, "let's get rid of these red-flag catchwords and labels. Let's just call it the Carter plan."

"Joe," Carter said, smiling, "when you want to call it the Califano plan, then I'll know we have a good one." We all laughed.

Carter told us to combine the cash assistance and jobs programs. This attempt to integrate a major jobs effort with cash assistance would be a major step in welfare reform. Carter would announce principles in May, a program in August, and legislation in September. "I am determined to meet my commitment of making an announcement on May second," he said. Blumenthal asked how such a schedule would affect "the timing of tax reform." Carter replied that "My preference is to move ahead on everything at once."

Carter than left the meeting without giving ground on the zero-cost issue. We all sent Carter memos over the weekend before the May 2 announcement.

As I worked on mine, I thought about what an impossible problem we faced: Comprehensive reform would cost money, however we tried to disguise it. More modest proposals with decidedly lower price tags would alienate the liberals, like Corman, who chaired the key subcommittees in the house, and critical governors like Hugh Carey of New York and Mike Dukakis of Massachusetts, as well as Moynihan, because they provided too little help to the poor and insufficient fiscal relief for the states. And those were the people emotionally committed to reform. Moreover, Carter was already being accused privately of temporizing on his campaign commitment. We had to start with a substantial plan to have a chance to get anything worthwhile, I concluded, believing we would begin in the House and ultimately face a tough negotiation with Russell Long in the Senate. We'd need everything we could get out of the House to barter with him. If we started big and the President stayed with it, we'd have a chance, probably our only chance, of ending up with something worthwhile. So in my memo, I urged Carter to "announce your intention to scrap the entire welfare system," consolidate AFDC, SSI, and food stamps into a single cash assistance program to help reduce waste and abuse, set up a special new employment program targeted on the welfare population, and recite the pro-family, pro-work principles that were being drafted. I was concerned that the President not commit publicly to a zero-cost principle and that Ray Marshall be at least amenable to finessing our disagreements.

I invited Marshall and Charlie Schultze to breakfast on Saturday morning, April 30. Marshall was willing to paint over our differences temporarily, but no agreement was in sight on the dispute for resources between jobs and cash assistance for the poor. Carter's speechwriter James Fallows tried his hand at the presidential announcement of principles, and sent them around on Sunday morning. That night, Carter called Eizenstat, Marshall, and me to the White House. He had dictated his own version of principles, and the first one hit me between the eyes: "We have established the following goals: 1. No higher cost than the original system." True, it was only stated as a goal, but I was troubled that after all that had gone on in our meetings, Carter still clung to this concept. I made my arguments again, and Marshall and Eizenstat concurred, but to little avail. Then Eizenstat, with the quiet effectiveness and persistence that I saw persuade Carter on other occasions, recounted the dangers of zero cost once more and suggested that one word be added, "No higher *initial* cost than the present system." Carter agreed, reluctant to the end.

The rest of the principles were essentially those Eizenstat, Marshall, and I had suggested. The head of a family with children would have access to a job; a person would always make more money in the private sector than in a special public service employment job, and anyone would make more money working than on welfare. There would be incentives for families to stay together and to eliminate fraud; and there would be simple administration. As for fiscal relief, Carter would state that, "The unpredictable and growing financial burden on state and local governments should be reduced as rapidly as federal resources permit. . . ." I urged him to make clear that it would take years to put such a massive change in the infrastructure in place, noting that it made political sense to set the start after 1981, the year Carter had promised to balance the budget. He agreed. "If the new legislation can be adopted early in 1978, an additional three years will be required to implement the program."

The news stories about the announcement highlighted the President's statement that, "The present welfare programs should be scrapped and a totally new system implemented," and his honestly felt conviction that "It's much worse than we had anticipated." But at his press conference, Carter noted that energy legislation was his "first priority for Congress" and other proposals, including Social Security and tax reform, would have to be considered by the same panels that had jurisdiction over welfare reform and energy. I flinched when he added, "I'll have to depend on congressional leaders to decide in which order they will address these major efforts."

My concern about the sensitivities of the supporters of comprehensive welfare reform on the Hill was unhappily vindicated when I testified before the House Ways and Means Public Assistance and Unemployment Compensation Subcommittee on May 4. "It now seems clear that the needs of the poor are not a clear priority of this administration," Rangel commented, referring to Carter's no-initial-cost goal, and to his desultory approach to the congressional calendar. Corman added, "Some of us thought that the administration would pass us the ball on the fifty-yard line. We are now on our own two, and we had best go down the field together."

The next morning, I testified before the Senate Welfare Subcommittee chaired by Moynihan. He was expansive: "This effort that has eluded three Presidents is yours to triumphantly resolve.'' But he also pressed for fiscal relief for states and cities and attacked the ''no-higher-initial-cost'' goal. . . . ''Take a message back to the Director of the Office of Management and Budget. . . . He has sent you up here to make bricks without straw, and it is not so easy to do.''

I was already deeply worried that the President would hold to the no-cost goal, even if it meant proposing welfare reform that had no chance of congressional passage, because he was convinced that the best politics for him was to balance the budget and project a tight-fisted frugality. The increasingly conservative vibrations from Lance, McIntyre, and their staff at OMB were buttressing his sense of where the country was. Moynihan's jab at OMB gave me an opportunity to press my case. ''Mr. Chairman, if you would like to directly deliver the message to the Director of the Office of Management and Budget, I would be delighted.'' At another point, I noted that, ''No initial cost [was] set as a goal, not an unwavering objective'' and that, ''I would like to have all the money I could get my hands on to put together a welfare reform proposal. . . .''

The high point of the hearing came when Russell Long volunteered to me, ''I personally am pleased about the way you are going about it. . . . I would hope . . . that this time [as contrasted with Nixon's Family Assistance Plan] we can arrive at a product that we are all very proud of.'' Moynihan added, ''We could not possibly end these hearings on a more hopeful note,'' and gaveled adjournment with his usual flourish.

When Ray Marshall testified the following week, the atmosphere was still friendly, but Moynihan raised a series of pointed, occasionally ridiculing, questions about some of the jobs Marshall proposed for welfare mothers—as carpenters, in National Parks, weatherizing homes. Marshall said he would go back to work on the jobs program before the specific plan was proposed, and he emphasized the importance of trying to integrate jobs with cash assistance and provide work for those we were trying to get off welfare. (In September 1980, Marshall reported that demonstrations of the jobs program were proving more successful than anticipated: 60 percent of welfare recipients put to work under the pilot program had obtained jobs in private industry; in Lowell, Massachusetts, the savings in welfare payments not made to those working exceeded the cost of the jobs program.)

THE TWO weeks after the President's announcement were frantic at Labor and HEW. A draft plan had to be produced and approved by Carter in order to provide us an opportunity for meaningful consultation with the governors and mayors, and representatives and senators on Capitol Hill.

The staffs were coming closer. Broad outlines for consolidated cash assistance and jobs programs started to take shape. But Marshall was consumed with other pressing matters and he did not have time to get into the necessary detail to reach agreement. I had no power alone to resolve disagreements between Labor and HEW staffs, since Marshall and I were Cabinet peers. I called Eizenstat and asked him to get Packer from Labor and Aaron, Mike Barth, and John Todd from HEW together and to close an agreement among them. He agreed to do it, and on May 19 I was able to send Carter a memo that began, "Secretary Marshall and I—working with Charlie Schultze, Stu Eizenstat, and [others]—have reached agreement on the broad outlines of a welfare reform proposal." It was a no-higher-initial-cost approach and it had some severe problems, I pointed out, most notably the fact that through technical changes in defining a family filing unit, thousands of aged and disabled SSI beneficiaries living with AFDC families would lose all or some benefits. "The aged and disabled are likely to oppose this change most strongly. To hold them harmless (which I personally prefer) would cost about an additional one billion dollars."

Aside from the cost constraint, which limited fiscal relief, payments to the poor, and work incentives, the basic contour of the plan made sense of the system. The three major cash assistance programs, AFDC, SSI, and food stamps, would be consolidated into one, with all the advantages of simplification and more efficient and less error- and fraud-prone administration. Poor two-parent families, childless couples, and singles would receive benefits. The needy would be put on two tiers: those expected to work (two-parent families with children, singles, childless couples, and single-parent families with older children, who would receive lower benefits to encourage them to take advantage of the 1.4 million special public service jobs we would try to create); and those not expected to work (the aged, blind, and disabled, and single-parent families with younger children, who would receive higher benefits since there was no need to provide a strong incentive to get a job). Those expected to work would always make more money in a specially created public service employment job than on welfare, and always even more in a regular public or private job than in one specially created. If we were unable to provide a job after a certain time, individual or family members expected to work would move to the higher benefit tier. The minimum benefit in 1980 dollars for a family of four on the higher, not-expected-to-work tier with no earnings would be $4,700; the benefits would stop when the family earned $9,400. There was no guarantee of fiscal relief for states and localities in this proposal; that depended on the extent to which each state decided to supplement the basic federal payment.

While we had a basic structure, we still believed that a no-cost welfare plan would fail. I tried to make this point forcefully to the President, and to keep the door open. "The politics of welfare reform are treacherous under any circumstances, and they can be impossible at no higher initial cost, because it is likely that so many people who are now receiving benefits will be hurt. The states are our natural allies in welfare reform—most members of Congress would still prefer not to deal with the subject at all—and there is virtually no relief in the proposal for governors and mayors. In addition, there will be problems in cutting benefits for the aged, the disabled, and the blind, and there will be disputes over our ability to put a significant number of the 3.4 million mothers on welfare to work.

"I suggest that we stress to the states and to the Congress that we are only presenting a working plan and that we are engaging in this process before submitting legislation in order to assess impact and to determine what improvements are necessary to make the plan work fairly and effectively for all—beneficiaries, states, cities, and taxpayers."

Carter was concerned about reduced benefits for the aged, blind, and disabled. He also agreed that I should hold a press briefing on May 25 to outline the entire plan, in the hope of avoiding distortions that could come from partial and self-interested leaks. But he gave me no sense that he would relax his tight cost constraint.

Forty minutes before my briefing, the President called. Jack Watson and Jim Parham (a White House staffer who had run the Georgia welfare program) had sent him a memo expressing apprehension that millions of previously ineligible families would receive a federal check each month and that the benefit levels were too high. "The $9,400 break-even point constitutes approximately 70 percent of the median family income in Georgia," the memo stated. Carter was worried about "the political and social implications of this." I told him that it was essential to include more families—"otherwise we won't cover intact families"—and that benefits were still significantly below the poverty line.

Carter acquiesced on covering more families, but he insisted that $9,400 was too high. "The American people will not stand for payments like that. In the South, people just won't understand payments that high."

I reminded him that all our calculations were based on those numbers, and that I was supposed to brief the press in thirty minutes.

"I don't want you to use those numbers," he said. "The benefits are too high."

Desperate, I had an idea. "All the numbers are in 1978 dollars. I can probably reduce them at least 10 percent if I bring them back to 1976 dollars."

Carter responded, "That's good. It's probably all you can do under the circumstances." We hung up and I scurried to change my statement to emphasize the 1976 dollar numbers, relegating the 1978 dollar numbers to parenthetical amounts.

At the briefing, I stressed that I was revealing a "working plan," that it was "tentative," that we would embark on a state-by-state consultation process to go over our numbers and the hosts of technical changes with individual states and localities that administered welfare programs. I emphasized "that no final decisions have been made on welfare reform," and that the figures might well change. I outlined the anti-fraud aspect of consolidating the cash programs: a state or local welfare administrator would have on his or her desk a television screen and a typewriter plugged into a computer terminal. On typing the name and Social Security number of the welfare applicant, the administrator could retrieve any and all cash payments that applicant was receiving from the federal government, and the Social Security taxes, if any, the individual was paying.

Meeting the President's no-higher-initial-cost mandate required numerous technical changes that would place millions of welfare recipients in a worse position than existing law, so I avoided those details. There was still hope that, given sufficient time, Carter would change his mind, especially since Eizenstat and Mondale held the same view I did. I stressed that we would "do everything we can to attempt to produce" 1.4 million jobs, explicitly telling the reporters around the conference room table that we were not guaranteeing that number because of the enormous difficulty of creating such special jobs, and the fact that government had never attempted to create even half as many before. I stayed away from any commitments on fiscal relief. I once again expressed disappointment that the President was "standing firmly" behind his no-higher-initial-cost constraint. Carter had never objected to my public statements along this line. I had the distinct impression that he enjoyed, and found politically advantageous, his tight-fisted posture as opposed to the position of his liberal HEW Secretary.

Those who were sophisticated about the welfare system immediately saw the potential impact of the President's restriction. Congressmen Corman and Rangel, among the most knowledgeable in the House, called me to complain, but they agreed to ease their criticism for the moment, and help try to turn Carter around. Senator Moynihan took his complaints to the public. In a May 26 speech to the Weschester County Association, Moynihan asked rhetorically: "What animates the administration? An indomitable innocence or profound cynicism? Are they sending us a welfare program that will do such injury to welfare recipients that we will not enact it? Are they sending us a program that provides no relief to state and local governments—relief that has been solemnly pledged by the President—such that state and local governments will urge us not to enact it?"

Carter held fast. At a press conference on May 26, he repeated that, "One of the requirements I have laid down . . . is no additional cost above what we have now." Carter was in a nasty dispute with the Congress over his effort to block several Western water projects, and during the same press conference he threatened to veto the bills containing those projects, and impact school aid legislation and farm price supports if lawmakers refused to curb what he attacked as "excessive" spending.

More informed second-day stories in the *New York Times* and *Washington Post* revealed how many worse-off beneficiaries there would be under the Carter limitation. HEW and Labor analysts, exhausted by the series of demanding deadlines, continued to haggle over each element of the program and I thought we might lose sight of the political forest in the technical trees. Now I would have to make scores of decisions. There were lengthy negotiations ahead within HEW as well as with Labor, the White House staff, OMB, and the Council of Economic Advisors. Any policy decisions would need a good serving of political yeast, as governors, mayors, public interest groups, and respresentatives of the beneficiaries would press their views.

I asked my executive assistant, Ben Heineman, to filter these discussions for me, arbitrating as much as he could along the way. I also enlisted Deputy General Counsel Dan Marcus, a meticulously careful attorney, to draft the legislation and lawyer the issues as they were raised, and Bruce Cardwell, then Social Security Commissioner with responsibility for administering the AFDC and SSI programs, to take responsibility for the administrative issues. Marcus, Cardwell, Aaron, and his top staffers, Mike Barth and John Todd, would meet to decide issues tentatively. Marcus and Barth would review them with Heineman in the early evenings. Heineman would go over them with me later that night. When I was working on more immediate problems, I instructed Heineman to make any decisions necessary to maintain the extraordinary momentum Carter's schedule demanded.

The most fruitful meetings were between the HEW and Labor staffs and the state and local officials. For hundreds of hours all through June and July, Barth, sometimes joined by Jodie Allen, an economist and welfare expert Marshall had recruited as his special assistant, met with welfare experts from each state and several cities to put together a reform package that made sense. In terms of fiscal relief, administration, inflation adjustments, regional cost-of-living differentials, the relationship of welfare reform to Medicaid, such services as day care and job training, and other issues, they sought to craft a plan acceptable to a sufficient number of states to have a chance of congressional enactment. Out of these meetings came numerous adjustments and the governors were grateful to have a real participation in the process. But serious issues remained unresolved. While Barry Van Lare, the chief staffer and lobbyist on welfare reform for the New Coalition of States, Cities, and Counties was questioning our ability to produce the number of jobs even remotely adequate for those expected to work and was, therefore, opposed to lowering the benefit levels for that group, Carter continued to stew about the benefit levels being too high and adding people to the welfare rolls.

New York City officials were increasingly concerned about the lack of clarity on fiscal relief. On July 26, Mayor Abe Beame charged that Carter had reneged on his campaign promise to relieve the city of its crushing welfare costs. Beame read aloud a letter candidate Carter had sent him on May 25, 1976, when the mayor had delivered a timely political endorsement: "This national program of welfare benefits would be funded in substantial part by the federal government. . . . My concept of substantial funding by the federal government would include as soon as possible the federal assumption of the local government's share and the phased reduction of the state's share."

The day after he made the charges, Beame, along with four other big-city mayors, came to see me. They were more interested in fiscal relief than any other part of the program. There was nothing I could commit, except my energy to fight for it and Carter's often repeated desire to keep his campaign promises. It was an uneasy meeting. The mayors were well aware that there would be little or no fiscal relief if Carter persisted in his no-higher-initial-cost limit, and they vowed to "keep up the pressure."

Moynihan decided not to wait. At his urging, the Senate Finance Committee voted on July 28 to give the states and cities $1 billion, over two years, in special fiscal relief to ease their welfare burden. Moynihan cited the Democratic Party platform statement that "as a means of providing immediate federal fiscal relief to state and local governments, local governments should no longer be required to bear the burden of welfare costs." Since the Carter plan would not take effect until after 1980, Moynihan asserted that fiscal relief should be provided immediately. Wavering under the building pressure, Carter at a mid-morning press conference that same day said that even if he achieved his goal of limiting first year costs to current levels, the reform package might cost more in future years. Senator Ribicoff, weary of the President's insistence on no higher cost and comprehensive reform, and sensing the President's floundering, said: "With all due respect for the administration, they don't know what the hell they are doing with welfare reform. They're changing their minds every day."

On July 25, I sent a sixty-two-page memo (with another seventy-five pages of appendices, containing details for the staffs around the government) to Carter setting forth a no-higher-initial-cost program, and recommended additions above the limit. Carter set a meeting for 2:00 P.M. on July 28 to discuss the proposals. Mondale, Marshall, Blumenthal, Eizenstat, Schultze, top OMB aides, and all our staffs were there. Carter had apparently read all 137 pages. He promptly went after the minimum benefit. I had lowered it from $4,700 to $4,200 in 1978 dollars, which reduced the earnings point at which no benefits were received from $9,400 to $8,400, but Carter wanted to lower it even more. He remained concerned that it would be more than many Southern states would politically accept. I argued that any further reduction would make so many recipients worse off, or require such increases in state supplementary payments, that we could not hope to pass welfare reform. As to local fiscal relief, Carter maintained that he had always couched his campaign commitment in terms of "as soon as possible" or "as soon as federal resources permit," phrases, he said, "Mayor Beame and Senator Moynihan prefer to ignore."

We talked about labor's opposition to the proposal. Carter understood that the AFL-CIO wanted to keep welfare benefits for striking workers, set a prevailing wage for the special public service jobs (which would almost always be higher than the minimum wage), and make clear that the new special jobs program would be in addition to existing ones. Marshall said the unions were worried that the cash supplements given those who were found jobs might carry the stigma of welfare.

"This is a voluntary program, isn't it?" the President asked, annoyed both at the union reaction and at what might be one last attempt by the Labor Department to administer this part of the cash payment program.

"Yes," said Marshall.

"Well, then, no one is going to be forced to accept these benefits."

However, Marshall ended the discussion of union attitudes on an optimistic note. "The labor leaders are more inclined to accept the program now that they understand the jobs part is in addition to existing programs."

I raised another dimension of the stigma issue: The aged, blind, and disabled SSI beneficiaries would resist becoming part of the same cash payments system as the AFDC welfare recipients. Carter said we should think of "attractive semantical phrases" to overcome these problems.

There followed a spirited and detailed discussion of what was to be included in the zero-cost base. Mike Blumenthal and I argued whether some $3 billion of the earned income tax credit should be counted as a cost of tax reform or welfare reform. Carter decided not to include it as a cost of welfare reform, but to charge it to tax reform. Carter also approved crediting to the no-cost base of welfare reform: some $1 billion of extended unemployment insurance compensation, $1.3 billion as the portion of the $50 rebate from the well-head tax (we hoped to pass) allocable to the poor, $400 million in Social Security taxes that would be paid by those working in the special jobs program, and $5.3 billion from the Labor Department CETA jobs program. Smiling as he reviewed the credits, Carter said, "There no longer seems to to be a no-cost proposal." Carter then urged me to see Russell Long and Al Ullman as soon as possible, and ended by telling Eizenstat to block out Sunday afternoon and evening for him to make the final decisions on welfare reform.

The President agreed to our recommendation not to reduce the federal cash benefit further because of the thousands of AFDC, SSI, and food stamp recipients who would get lower benefits. White House aides Jim Parham and Jack Watson had told the President that "adjusted for eight years of inflation, the guarantee discussed by President Nixon [eight years before] may turn out to be relatively more generous than [your] plan. . . ." Carter indicated his inclination to approve complex formulas for state shares of welfare payments estimated to provide about $2 billion in fiscal relief when the plan was fully effective. While we needed fiscal relief for political viability, I urged Carter to reduce the number of recipients who would be worse off, "especially . . . those below the poverty line, even at the cost of initial year fiscal relief."

On Sunday, July 31, we sent Carter the final decision memo, and he acted the following morning. He was still worried about cost, and over Pat Harris's intense objections, he added to the no-cost base $500 million in HUD rent supplements, saved as a result of more and higher welfare payments and wages from the special jobs program. Carter approved other items of reform that added $2 billion above his no-higher-initial-cost limit and rejected $1 billion in additions. Considering where he'd started from, we were relatively pleased. Even the no-initial-cost amount was higher than we had expected because Carter had included so many credits. Eizenstat and I welcomed the higher base, but we felt we had to alert Carter that many in Congress would attack the credit offsets, particularly the $5.3 billion for Labor Department jobs programs that were projected to decline as unemployment decreased. But we were all caught by Carter's rhetoric. Rather than drop the no-higher-initial-cost promise, Carter resorted to budgetary gimmickry. Eizenstat and I were so anxious to get more funds for welfare reform that we readily played the same game. I made sure the critical elements of our cost calculations—the offsets and the use of 1978 dollars—were set forth prominently in our presentations. I then turned my concern to the prospect of three committees in each House reviewing the plan, with all the personalities and arguments about areas of responsibility that would entail. Russell Long and Al Ullman were the key chairmen.

Carter had talked briefly with Long on the phone and I sat with him on July 29, a week before we intended to reveal the plan to Congress. Long understood the technical nuances of the welfare program as few legislators did and he had strong views. He favored consolidating such programs as SSI, AFDC, and food stamps, and, as always, making working more rewarding than not, and working in the private or regular public sector better-paying than in the special public service jobs.

Long opposed a national minimum payment and he wanted lower benefits for everyone. He also was committed to requiring mothers with young children to seek work. Under the law, the existing work-incentive program exempted only women with children aged six and below, but Long knew that the law's mandate to cut off benefits for refusal of other mothers to work had not been enforced by states. I told Long that we were proposing to make the work requirement real for mothers with children fourteen years or older by providing them jobs and cutting off benefits if they refused to accept them. "That only takes 10 percent of the people off AFDC," Long said. "Lower the age to six, and you take more than half the people off AFDC. That's what the President ought to be trying to do—get people off welfare. That's what the people want. That will be a popular proposal that will get him re-elected."

I argued that it was bad social policy to take a mother away from such a young child. He said other welfare mothers could be paid to take care of the children. Lots of women work with children under six. Why should welfare mothers be any different?"

I thought back ten years to sitting in Johnson's Oval Office. House Ways and Means Committee Chairman Wilbur Mills was there, arguing about a congressional resolution to put a lid on government spending as a part of the price of passing the 10 percent income tax surcharge Johnson had proposed. Mills wanted a ceiling on the federal money that went to the states for AFDC. Johnson was against it; no one could predict how many people would be on welfare; they were poor and Mills's proposal could hurt them badly.

"Mr. President," Mills argued, "across town from my mother in Arkansas a Negro woman has a baby every year. Every time I go home, my mother complains. She's now got eleven children. My proposal will stop this. Let the states pay for more than a small number of children." Mills never did convince Johnson. And Long was not convincing me.

Long suggested a pilot program that would encourage mothers with children under six to work. "There are women in Louisiana," Long told me, "who work right up to a week before they have a child, and start again a few weeks after they deliver. If women who are not on welfare can do that, women on welfare can do it, too." He liked the concept of having an "expected-to-work" group and one that was not expected to work, such as the blind, aged, and disabled. He was set against letting anyone on the "expected-to-work" tier get on the more generous "not-expected-to-work" tier of higher benefits. "You'll be bogged down in all kinds of legal and administrative hearings, like the Social Security disability program. The Supreme Court will give them rights to hearings and nobody will ever move back down to the lower tier."

But what he returned to again and again was requiring mothers to work. "Even mothers with children under six should be required to work part-time in sheltered workshops, while other welfare mothers take care of their kids."

"Why not let women who prefer to take care of their young children do so? Won't that be better for the family in the long run?" I asked.

"Joe, I'll make a deal with you right now," Long said, with a twinkle in his eye. "You get these women with children under six working in a sheltered workshop, you get all women with children six and older working, and I'll give you five billion dollars more than the current welfare system costs for *your* ideas."

"Propose that to the President, if you're really serious," I said. "He might accept it."

Al Ullman and I had breakfast in my office on Monday, August 1. He made it clear at the outset that he was talking only on the assumption that nothing could dissuade Carter from sending Congress a welfare reform proposal. He agreed with Long that mothers should work if the youngest child were six years of age, but he was opposed to creating jobs. "I don't like make-work jobs where people just sit in sheltered workshops or at courthouse desks." He was also opposed to paying cash to individuals who worked. He seemed unable to accept the fact that many people on welfare already worked, but his main objection went to the core of the welfare system: "I do not like any payments geared to the size of the family. These payments encourage people to have children. This is one of the fundamental flaws of the entire system." He also questioned the wisdom of cashing out the food stamp program, frankly doubted the administration's ability to create enough new jobs, and thought the House would overwhelmingly agree with Long's requirement that women with children six or older work.

A meeting between the President and Ullman the next day did not go well. Ullman repeated his objections to any proposal that continued to relate payments to family size, and as soon as the meeting ended, he told the press his view directly.

Carter's meeting with Long on the following day was also difficult. The Senator tried to persuade the President to require mothers to work "as soon after their child is born as possible, but no later than six." Before the meeting, Carter had settled tentatively on age fourteen. Now, as Long made his pitch, the President listened; he promised to reconsider, but he was noncommittal. Like Ullman, Long urged delay in sending the reform package to Congress. Carter refused. "We have always had August in mind as the date. There has been wide consultation. Now is the time to send the legislation up and to start the long, tough negotiations and the public hearings I hope you will hold." Long was more conciliatory to the waiting White House press corps than Ullman had been, but he emphasized that "I don't like the concept that some people, like mothers, are not expected to work."

I met again with Ullman to try to ease his objections, but with no effect. Then I called Speaker O'Neill for help. "I'll try," he said, "but you've got real problems on your bill with Al Ullman." I then made a suggestion to him. "We can at least move in the early stages if you'll set up a special committee along the lines of the energy committee." O'Neill said he'd think about it and he set a meeting for that evening with Ullman, Education and Labor Committee Chairman Carl Perkins, Agriculture Committee Chairman Tom Foley, Dick Warden, and me.

He talked to me alone before the meeting. He would not set up a special committee which, like the energy committee, would have the power to report legislation to the House. He was willing to try a special subcommittee that would report legislation back to parent committees who could then decide whether to report to the House on the portions they had jurisdiction over. The jobs program would go back to the Education and Labor Committee; the cash-out of food stamps to the Agriculture Committee; welfare benefit changes to the Ways and Means Committee.

When the three full-committee chairmen arrived, each expressed reservations. O'Neill defused most of their objections and planted the idea of having Jim Corman as the special subcommittee chairman. Perkins was satisfied; Foley was uneasy but willing; Ullman objected. There was no decision. Later, O'Neill sought unsuccessfully to bring Ullman around, but he told me he would keep working at it.

On Wednesday, after meeting with Eizenstat and me, Carter made the final decision to go forward. In order to broaden his political support and to guarantee fiscal relief, Carter agreed to additional costs that brought the total to $2.8 billion above his original no-higher-cost goal. He also set a work requirement obliging welfare mothers to seek employment when their youngest child reached age seven. Carter delayed his announcement until Saturday. O'Neill was afraid that the controversial welfare reform proposal could jeopardize the vote on energy legislation that was set for House floor action late Friday.

I spent most of Friday preparing for the press briefing, but I did take time to go by and visit Hubert Humphrey in his Senate office. His body was ravaged by cancer and chemotherapy; we hardly shook hands, instead gently hugging each other. Yet he saw that I was concerned about something. "I'm so pessimistic about welfare reform," I said. "The politics are just impossible."

"You've just got to keep pushing. You not only have my support on the welfare reform plan, you have my support any time you need it up here in the Senate, so long as I'm here." I was deeply touched. Humphrey was dying, but he had lost none of his enthusiasm. "And remember, Joe, you're fighting the good fight. No one will ever get a complete overhaul of the welfare system in one bite. But you'll make some progress and you'll win a few more allies each time you try. Stick with it." What an extraordinary human being, I thought as I left his office. We had been through many battles together. And his judgment was reassuring.

That evening, Ray Marshall and his staff, Henry Aaron, Ben Heineman, and I flew to Americus, Georgia, for the presidential announcement the next day. Late in the evening, Senator Javits of New York called: "The *New York Times* just called me. They said that the *Daily News* is going to have a break on the President's welfare program in the morning and asked me if I would help them. You know, Joe, the *Times* will write a much more favorable story than the conservative *News* if the President's got a good progressive program. From everything that I hear, he does."

"Jack, we've heard nothing from the *News*. I can't believe there's any leak," I said.

"Well, if there is anything you can give me, I think it would be a big help for the *Times*."

"We'll just have to take our chances. We have a big press conference tomorrow and the President is the one who should release the details of his plan." Javits hung up. (I have always been puzzled about whether the *New York Times* was trying to trick Javits, or Javits was trying to trick me. There is such pressure among politicians for coverage and such competition among major media for big stories that either could be true. The *News* had no break on the story.)

The following morning we drove to Plains and sat in the President's living room going over the final points of the briefing. Then Carter went out and announced his comprehensive reform of the "anti-work and anti-family" welfare program that "would not be incompatible with the dream to balance the budget by 1981." He called his plan the Program for Better Jobs and Income, a name he selected himself. Thanks to Tip O'Neill's continuing work on Al Ullman, Carter was also able to announce that the three House committees with jurisdiction over pieces of welfare reform had agreed to establish a special joint subcommittee.

I flew back to Washington that afternoon and stopped in at a party the exhausted HEW staff was having to celebrate the announcement. Throughout the months of work, Heineman and I had come to refer to them as the "wizards." I gave the leaders, Henry Aaron, Mike Barth, and John Todd, "Wizard" T-shirts, and Aaron a magic wand.

THE REACTION was good. Mayor Beame of New York and many governors praised the plan. Even Vernon Jordan, who had accused Carter of reneging on support to the urban poor, called the package "an encouraging one." Russell Long made conciliatory sounds, saying the plan had "laudable objectives" and that some changes had been made to accommodate him. Pat Moynihan called the plan "magnificent and superbly crafted." A Lou Harris poll showed 70 percent of the public in favor of welfare reform, 13 percent opposed. On *Face the Nation,* trying to build momentum, I said optimistically that I thought welfare reform would pass in a year. And while I was on CBS, John Anderson, then third-ranking Republican in the House, expressed his support of the general concept of Carter's plan on NBC's *Meet the Press.*

After the television interview, I flew to my house in Wellfleet, where my family was vacationing. I was looking for them on the beach at Newcomb's Hollow, when Jerry Wurf, the head of the American Federation of State, County, and Municipal Employees Union, roared at me across twenty yards of beach blankets, "That is the worst Goddamn welfare proposal I have ever heard of. Creating all those jobs for welfare people at lower pay than my employees are getting is an outrage. You've got to change that if you want any help from me!" My early-morning optimism gave way to the reality I already knew and had expressed: Welfare reform is indeed the Middle East of domestic politics.

By the time I returned to Washington on August 15, Pat Moynihan had sent me a copy of his book *The Politics of a Guaranteed Income: The Nixon Administration and the Family Assistance Plan,* inscribed, "Joe —Better luck this time. Pat." But the ideological conflict relating to welfare reform was never far beneath the surface. Later that day, Henry

Aaron noticed Moynihan's book on my desk. I mentioned with delight the inscription and spoke highly of the book. About a half hour later arrived Aaron's article from the *Yale Law Journal* of July 1973, inscribed, "To Joe Califano, An antidote to that big yellow-covered book. Hank." It was a blistering review of Moynihan's work.

The additional funds that had swung traditional Democratic liberals and the cities behind our welfare reform proposal had also invited the kind of criticism that concerned Carter. Republican Representative Wil-lian Goodling of Pennsylvania voiced the reaction of conservatives and most Republicans: "To finance it the country will have to find a money tree somewhere." Speaking back home for his Louisiana constituents, Russell Long abandoned his early conciliatory attitude, saying passage would be "foolhardy" except on an experimental basis. My response for the press remained optimistic—"There's always some preparation before people go dancing together; the music is just beginning to play on this" —but I was deeply concerned that we were caught in the deadly fire of charges and countercharges between liberals and conservatives that had thwarted previous efforts.

On September 19, the day the Justice Department filed the *Bakke* brief, I testified before the Special Welfare Reform Subcommittee in the House. Al Ullman came by just long enough to characterize the Carter plan as "unworkable," and accuse us of trying to add sixteen million people to the welfare rolls. This referred mostly to the millions already receiving food stamps who would get the same amount in cash under the administration plan. Ullman declared his unyielding opposition to payments related to family size. Republicans and conservatives seized on the Ullman charge. Together with allegations that by eliminating the credits set forth in my presentation the true added cost of the program became $18 billion, rather than the $2.8 billion we claimed, it formed the basis for their labeling the reform as a big-spending, high-cost giveaway.

The Special Welfare Reform Subcommittee, which Corman chaired, was far more liberal than the three parent committees, the full House or the country. Dominated by forceful champions from such big states as New York, California, and Michigan, there were indications that the subcommittee might add as much as $3 billion to the administration bill. These moves sparked interest in incremental rather than total reform and in reduction of the size of the jobs program, which some maintained was unrealistic. At the same time, it was rumored that Ullman was preparing his own bill.

Corman and I were sufficiently worried to urge Carter to meet with the full Welfare Reform Subcommittee, which had been at work for weeks. The President talked to the members of the subcommittee on

December 1, in the Cabinet Room, urging prompt action and restraint in increasing costs, and stressing that the jobs for welfare recipients were in addition to existing job programs. But it was a lackluster performance and some subcommittee members left wondering how serious the President was about welfare reform.

The subcommittee nevertheless redoubled its efforts. On December 8, it voted 16 to 12 to consolidate AFDC, SSI, and food stamps into the single cash-payments program we had recommended. Ullman, who had fought the decision, predicted it would doom the Carter proposal. Agriculture Committee Chairman Tom Foley also opposed consolidation, and since his committee had jurisdiction over the matter, I expected trouble. But Education and Labor Committee Chairman Carl Perkins argued that "we ought to give the President of the United States the opportunity to bring order out of chaos."

In other votes favorable to us, the subcommittee extended coverage to singles and to childless couples, kept a lower benefit tier for families expected to work, and refused to raise the federal portion of the benefits to the poverty line. The subcommittee did, however, reject some Carter proposals, by voting to index benefits to cost of living increases and to provide higher federal subsidies for states. I kept the President informed in weekly reports, and I told him that the subcommittee's liberalizations were likely to be overturned by the full House. But Carter was beginning to edge away from welfare reform, and he was unwilling to devote much of his time and dwindling political capital to it. In an interview published in the *New York Times* in December, he omitted welfare reform from a rundown of administration initiatives that he thought would succeed in 1978, and said only that "we will have good progress made on welfare reform." In his January 1978 State of the Union address, he listed his primary legislative objectives for the year, including ratification of the Panama Canal Treaties, energy legislation, a separate Department of Education, and tax reform. "Welfare reform," the words that candidate Carter had invoked at campaign stop after campaign stop in 1975 and 1976, did not make his list.

After a brief Christmas recess, the subcommittee returned in January to complete work on the bill in hopes that welfare reform could pass the House before July 1. Just as its meeting started on January 25, and the day after I had breakfast with Corman to plan strategy, the *Washington Post* carried a front-page headline: CARTER AIDES SEE DELAY IN PASSING WELFARE REVISION. Anonymously and in separate interviews, two senior White House aides had told the *Post* they did not believe welfare reform could pass in the current session of Congress. When Corman was called by a reporter, he responded: "Obviously, tomorrow, members are going to be saying to me, 'What the hell are we doing batting our brains out?' I can't believe the administration would be putting us through what they are putting us through if they're not serious about getting welfare reform.''

I read the story as I was eating breakfast alone in the dining room behind my office at HEW. I was angry and called Carter. As soon as I mentioned the story, the President expressed his own anger. ''When I saw that story, I began to look for somebody's ass to chew,'' he said. He asked if I knew who would say ''such a stupid thing.'' Suspecting Carter held the view expressed in the story and knew as well as I who probably leaked it, I said I thought it had to be Hamilton Jordan and Stu Eizenstat from the way the story was written. I urged him to call Corman and tell him that the story was incorrect and that he wanted a welfare reform bill ''this year.'' The President thought it would be a better idea to send a note, and promised to write one immediately. When I hung up, Corman was waiting on another line. He was livid. I told him about my conversation with the President. Corman said he needed that note in an hour to read to his subcommittee when it reconvened.

A few minutes later, Eizenstat called and asked me to dictate a short note the President could handwrite to Corman. ''The President's so concerned that he's told me to deliver the letter personally to Corman.'' Eizenstat told me that the *Post* had misquoted him, but he was clearly annoyed with himself. He had worked hard to get the reform proposal this far and didn't want to do anything to hurt its chances. He had not realized a reporter had also talked to Jordan. In any case, by the time I called Eizenstat's secretary with a brief note, the President had already written Corman, with copies to all the committee members, expressing ''every hope and every expectation that the welfare reform proposals will be passed by the Congress this year if the superb work of you and your committee continues. Although it will not be easy, there is growing interest in the Senate. We will do our best in cooperation with you, Senator Moynihan, and others to be successful this year. Call on me directly when I can be of help, and of course Secretary Califano. . . .''

I called Long and told him that the President had written Corman telling him that the story in the *Post* did not reflect his views and that he expected a welfare reform bill this year. Long laughed. ''Joe, as soon as I picked up the *Post* this morning, I knew you'd be on your soap box. I said to Carolyn [his delightful wife], 'Joe Califano will be on his soap box this morning.' ''

''Russell, none of us can be responsible for all the things our aides say. You've told me that many times when I thought I had agreements with your aides,'' I teased.

We were both chuckling. Long asked, "Did the President sign the letter himself, or did you forge his signature?"

"I just called because I knew you'd be anxious to hear that we intended to hold you to your promise to have hearings on welfare reform later this year."

Jody Powell, backpedaling for the White House, said the presidential aides "were trying to indicate the difficulties" facing the proposal "and maybe they overdid it a little." But Powell kept Carter's distance by adding that the President "hopes to see it passed, but he is not laying odds on it."

Moynihan was also distressed. His major concern was the same as my own, although I could not let him know I shared it: the suspicion that Carter, confronted with the perilous and unpopular politics of welfare reform at the same time as he faced the fallout over the Bert Lance affair and widespread criticism for ineptitude from Congress and the press, had decided to cut his losses and back off from a plan he now saw as too liberal. There were actions more concrete than the statements coming from the White House that seemed to provide evidence of this kind of change of mood—in the President's decision to send his anti-three-martini-lunch tax reform program to the Ways and Means Committee ahead of welfare reform, and his personal aloofness from our efforts to move the bill in the House or the Senate.

The evening of the *Post* story, Moynihan, Corman, Dick Warden, and I met in Corman's office to breathe some legislative life into welfare reform. Moynihan said that a bill could be acted on by the Senate that year if the House passed it by April 1. Corman claimed he could meet that deadline. Cheered, Corman pushed his subcommittee. On January 26, he won approval of the new public service employment program of 1.1 million jobs, at salaries ranging from $7,000 to about $9,200 for the heads of welfare families who were unable to find work in the private sector.

On February 1 (the same day Congressman Rostenkowski asked the hospital industry to fashion a voluntary cost containment plan in lieu of Carter's mandatory bill), Al Ullman countered with his own welfare reform proposal, saying, "I'm not doing this as any power play; I'm doing it regretfully." He did not think there was "the time or the climate in the Congress to push through a massive, all-or-nothing welfare program this year." Ullman had fashioned a complex system of incremental adjustments that he claimed would be easier to pass, and would cost $12 billion a year less than the administration's plan. "My job is to look beyond the subcommittee to the mood of the Congress and get something achievable," Ullman said. Corman replied simply, "We have never been in agreement on welfare."

Despite Ullman's move and the gloom of some subcommittee members who said that there would not be time for the Senate to act on the legislation in 1978, Corman pushed ahead, even when Ullman stated that his full Ways and Means Committee would be occupied with Carter's tax-reform proposals throughout March and could not begin to look at welfare before April 1.

Meanwhile, Moynihan opened hearings before his Senate subcommittee on February 7. I testified that the administration would not abandon its bill, and strongly opposed Ullman's proposal as "less efficient, and less equitable." Much of my testimony was a criticism of Ullman's plan, on which the special House subcommittee was scheduled to vote the following day. But it was Moynihan's show and he gave a flamboyant, if mercurial performance. In the course of the same day of hearings, Moynihan both called the welfare reform legislation "one of the most important pieces of social legislation in history," and attacked the Department of HEW for "lying" and "dumb insolence," and allowing me to testify "naked of fact," when I said that our bill was pro-family.

During the Nixon administration, when Moynihan had done battle over the Family Assistance Plan, he had been unable to respond concretely to questions concerning the extent to which the welfare program contributed to breaking up families. Although the information had passed through my office, I wasn't personally aware that preliminary data from HEW-funded experiments, conducted by the Stanford Research Institute in Denver and Seattle, provided some indications that higher payments to intact and working families do not necessarily hold them together or reduce divorce or family breakup; the preliminary data raised at least as many questions as they answered. Moynihan, who knew of the data, was angry. "You haven't five cents of honest inquiry as to whether this [present] system really does break up families. . . . The tradition of your Department has been obfuscation, frequently lying, but in any case avoidance of this issue." So hyperbolic was his attack on me that Missouri Republican John Danforth quipped, "But other than that, you're doing fine."

Then the Moynihan-Aaron clash broke out into the open. Aaron responded coldly to Moynihan's outburst: "The burden of proof should rest on those who deny" that Carter's massive welfare overhaul "would encourage couples to stay together."

Moynihan rejoined sarcastically, "Dr. Aaron, that is not a burden that will weigh heavily on the shoulders of this committee."

In spite of all this, Moynihan turned to me and said, "I support this program completely."

The next day, the Special Welfare Reform Subcommittee of the House voted 16 to 13 to reject Ullman's proposal and, by a vote of 23 to

6, reported to the three full committees a bill similar to, but more costly than, the President's proposal.

Despite Corman's push, it looked as though it would be increasingly difficult to pass welfare reform that year—through the three full House committees, the Rules Committee, the full House, the three Senate committees, and the Senate. I urged Carter to make a major personal effort. He was unwilling to meet separately with Long, Moynihan, Ullman, and Corman. But he finally agreed to sit down with all four of them on March 10.

The evening before the meeting, I sent Carter a one-page memo expressing my hope to get legislation "that will be a significant improvement over the present system." I urged him to seek a commitment from Ullman to report a bill out by a certain date, to press Ullman, Corman, and me to work together (to get some momentum, we needed a compromise that Ullman and Corman could agree to), and to get Moynihan to reopen and complete his hearings so we would be poised to move in the Senate if we got a bill out of the House.

The meeting was in the Cabinet Room. The President made no opening pitch for welfare reform. Instead, looking tired and gray, he turned to Ullman and asked him about his schedule. Ullman said that energy was the first priority, then tax reform. That would take the committee through mid-May. After that, welfare reform and, finally, hospital-cost containment. I sat watching with disbelief as Carter accepted this. Then Ullman said, "Mr. President, I am totally dedicated to getting a welfare bill out of committee in the middle of May."

Carter asked Moynihan what his schedule was. Moynihan smiled, "I'll do it any way, Mr. President, so long as it's Russell Long's way."

At Carter's nod, Long had the floor. He believed that an expanded earned income tax credit could be passed, but "the other parts of the program can't be done unless there are jobs for mothers who have preschool-age children."

Corman, barely masking his disdain for Carter's passivity, and making no attempt to disguise his irritation with Ullman, pleaded that all the hard work of his subcommittee not be wasted.

After another ten minutes of repetitive conversation, the President gave an almost resigned pep talk: "Let's do whatever we can agree on. It would be tragic not to move further politically. The differences we have this year we will have next year, so let's move this year."

Concerned that Long would read Carter's resignation as a license to pass just those pieces of welfare reform the Senator favored, Corman interjected: "If all we can get are little pieces of legislation and if the Senate isn't going to pass major legislation this year, then we should abandon welfare reform until next year."

That brought on a general discussion of whether we should hold out for the whole package or try to "get as much as we can." Carter commented, "I will take as much as I can get," paused, and then added, almost as an afterthought but to protect his urban flank, "But I'll be in there fighting like hell to get the rest of the package."

Long said at the end that there was no way he would agree to legislation unless women with children under six were required to work, at least as a pilot program. Corman expressed his "unalterable opposition."

As House members began to appreciate the generous contours of the Corman subcommittee bill, it became clear that enormous difficulties lay in the way of ever getting it to the floor. Even the cash consolidation portion of the plan was in serious trouble. The Agriculture Committee opposed cashing out the food stamp program, even for the aged, blind, and disabled whose physical disability often made it impossible for them to obtain stamps. (For committee members and staffers, it was a matter of turf: Agriculture had jurisdiction over stamps; Ways and Means over cash.) Aged, blind, and disabled SSI beneficiaries were, as I had feared, asking members not to lump them with AFDC mothers and children, the "dirty" part of the welfare program.

Russell Long's attack on the national minimum benefit was echoed by House conservatives. The jobs program was running into trouble from labor unions, who were concerned that it would become a substitute for other jobs programs and that the higher wages voted in Corman's subcommittee would not survive the more conservative House floor.

In April and early May, Dick Warden and I talked to Corman, who was not inclined to work with Ullman, since he did not believe Ullman was serious about a comprehensive bill and thought any such bill would be interpreted as a victory for Ullman rather than Carter. Corman also had policy differences with Ullman that he believed could not be reconciled. Privately, Corman thought the real enemies of welfare reform were Treasury Secretary Blumenthal, who had insisted the tax bill be taken up before welfare, and the White House staff. "They're trying to torpedo welfare through the scheduling decisions," Corman said. "I'm being flimflammed by those guys." When I mentioned that the President at least had held a meeting with the key congressional players, Corman shot back, "The President's meeting with Moynihan, Ullman, Long, and me was a waste of time. Hell, Ullman now says the Ways and Means full committee cannot begin work on welfare until June third."

"Our only hope is to develop some kind of compromise that helps poor people, which is your ultimate objective," I said, but Corman said he didn't think it was possible.

Over the next weeks, Warden and I talked separately to Corman and Ullman to find a compromise that we could move through Ways and

Means, and then through the House. I had lunch with Senators Abe Ribicoff, Henry Bellmon, John Danforth, and Howard Baker on April 26. They had suggested a compromise bill, with some of our features, that they thought might move through the Senate. I was concerned about the congressional politics, and wanted an outside source to suggest a compromise proposal. I called Massachusetts Governor Michael Dukakis, who headed the New Coalition, an organization of states, cities, and counties deeply interested in welfare reform, and asked if he would take the lead, assuring him of our staff support. He agreed. I then called Ullman and Corman and suggested the New Coalition work on a compromise, and they both publicly challenged the group to put a proposal together.

I also asked House Speaker Tip O'Neill if he would try to get Corman and Ullman together to work toward a bill. He set up a luncheon for them, Charles Rangel, and me on May 24. In a memo to Carter the day before the lunch, I reported on these activities and asked his approval to seek a compromise bill with a net cost (using 1982 dollars and none of the controversial offsets) of $10 billion to $11.5 billion, as compared to estimates of $18 billion net cost for our original bill and $20.2 billion for Corman's. Carter endorsed the undertaking, subject to his approval of the details. Ullman, Corman, Dukakis, and I seemed to be getting close, and Eizenstat was showing renewed interest. A meeting was set for June 7 in the Speaker's office with Corman, Ullman, Eizenstat, Dukakis, and me.

Then, on June 6, the citizens of California, in revolt against government spending, voted overwhelmingly for Proposition 13, a proposal to slash state property taxes. The next day, as I was heading to the Speaker's office, Tom Foley, Chairman of the Agriculture Committee, stopped me in the hall outside the House floor. "Joe, you've got to bury that damn welfare bill. With this vote in California, these guys will destroy it on the floor and the President will suffer a humiliating defeat." As I continued walking, through the Rayburn Room where members meet constituents off the floor, I knew Foley was right. A few minutes later, the Speaker confirmed it for all of us. Proposition 13 had put the final nail in the coffin of welfare reform for 1978.

We did draft a $10 billion reform plan in the hope of getting a head start in the next Congress. For by now, after ten years of debate on welfare reform, we had an emerging consensus. The Baker-Ribicoff-Bellmon-Danforth bill, Corman's bill, Ullman's bill, and the administration bill had several common themes: all had some national minimum benefit; coverage of two-parent families; expansion of the earned-income tax credit; special jobs programs; some fiscal relief and cash consolidation; and changes to simplify administration. These emerging areas of agreement, coupled with the fact that Moynihan and Corman were chairing key subcommittees, gave me some heart until I reflected on the demands Russell Long would make to report a welfare reform bill out of the Senate Finance Committee.

And there was a more serious obstacle. The President no longer cared, and it was showing. Ullman doubted that Carter was serious about welfare reform; he thought he just wanted to have his "big program announced and then forget about it," so he did not think Carter would compromise. In the wake of Proposition 13, Carter was determined to regain his frugal, budget-balancing image. More than vindicating Ullman's judgment, a White House source supplied Charles Peters, who was writing an Op Ed piece for the *New York Times,* with false information that Carter had not understood the original additional cost figure of $2.8 billion for welfare reform because he had been "misled" by a White House aide, an assistant director of OMB, and me. Once the President discovered the deception, the anonymous aide told Peters, "He did not feel he could admit the true dimensions of the error without seeming incompetent." Aaron was so angry when he read the Op Ed story, he insisted on sending a letter to the *Times* characterizing it as "false. The estimates," he explained, "were discussed in detail among all the Cabinet officers involved, with all appropriate members of the President's staff and, finally, at some length with the President himself." Indeed, Carter had heard repeated debate and disagreement over the credits in the no-higher-initial-cost package, personally discussed them with me, and approved them, down to the final $500 million from lower rent supplement payments which he personally okayed on the eve of announcing the plan. At one point, Carter had even asked why we did not take credit for additional HUD rent supplement payments.

Without the President's support, with pressure in the House not to put any welfare reform proposal on the floor, and with Senate Majority Leader Robert Byrd saying it would not be taken up in the Senate during 1978, there was nothing to do except let the staffs on the Hill and in the executive work out a compromise plan for the next Congress. Moynihan, California Democratic Senator Alan Cranston, and Long announced a $5 billion "no frills" bill that provided about $2 billion in fiscal relief, an expanded earned income tax credit, and a private-sector jobs credit, but that was hardly welfare reform. Senator Kennedy introduced a proposal similar to the New Coalition compromise and the Baker-Bellmon-Ribicoff-Danforth bill. But there was no hope left for 1978. On June 22, I acknowledged the realities of the calendar and politics in a public statement that also called attention to wide areas of agreement, and to the enormous effort involved in the "search for a more sensible, more just welfare system; I am hopeful that we can take advantage of that effort next year."

There was an attempt to revive a modest reform program in 1979. Working closely with Ullman and Corman, who were by now far more important than Carter to the reform effort, we developed a plan and submitted it to the President in late 1978. The proposal elicited from Carter a request that we consult with "interested parties." After much delay, consultation, and minor massaging by departmental staffs and executive office aides, Carter, months later, on May 15, 1979, approved going forward with a $5.7 billion reform package that set a national minimum payment, covered intact families, cashed out food stamps for the aged, blind, and disabled, increased the earned income tax credit, and funded a modest special jobs program. But the President had lost his appetite for welfare reform. He was increasingly engaged with his own re-election, and he was concerned about his posture vis-a-vis Senator Kennedy on national health insurance. The welfare program was there now to help defend his left flank, not to mount an offensive.

None of the hoopla that energized the Plains, Georgia, unveiling of Carter's comprehensive welfare reform plan in 1977 attended the announcement on May 23, 1979. Ray Marshall, Stu Eizenstat, and I unfolded the more modest proposal in the Executive Office Building across from the West Wing of the White House to a scattering of reporters and weary staff. Carter didn't make an appearance. In his written message to the Congress, the President said, with no apparent irony, "No legislative struggle has provided so much hopeful rhetoric and so much disappointment and frustration."

The cash assistance reform bill, costing $2.7 billion of the $5.7 billion package, sailed through the Public Assistance Subcommittee just before I left HEW. It passed the full House by a 222 to 184 vote on November 7, 1979. But in election year 1980, with budget balancing, recession, inflation, and foreign affairs dominating the national and political agenda, the Senate had no interest in welfare reform and Carter had no desire to stir up any. Welfare reform was once again dead.

WHY IS it so difficult to reform the welfare system, when everyone agrees it is a mess?

Each attempt brings us closer to consensus on broad concepts, but agreement on specifics that require hard choices is hard to come by. Nothing may seem clearer, for example, than the concept that a person should always make more money working than he or she would on welfare. But then the questions emerge: Should the jobs pay prevailing wages to protect existing workers, even when minimum wage jobs cost less and pay more than welfare? What about Medicaid? Its payment of the health care bills of a sizable welfare family may be worth thousands of dollars that can't be matched in any private job. What value should be placed on homemaking and mothering? Is that worthy of less pay than mopping floors? In a mobile society, with high welfare payments in some states and low wages in others, is it possible to implement a concept of always making more money working than on welfare without disrupting local, state, and regional economies?

There is no strong constituency for welfare recipients. They are the poor of our nation, and we do not like to be reminded that there are so many of them among us. Workers do not readily approve of tax dollars "going to people who don't work." Welfare recipients tend to get the worst publicity for themselves, making angry demands, often appearing vulgar to the vast middle class. The poor are most visible, perhaps, as blacks in the big cities, and that infects reform attempts with the vicious resistance of racism. Welfare reform is a victim of many myths.

It is also the victim of our monumental bureaucracies, of both fragmentation and concentration of power. Twelve of the thirteen Cabinet departments and at least seven agencies administer income security programs, and 119 of the more than 300 congressional committees and subcommittees oversee their operations. In addition, these programs are shaped in part by 50 state legislatures, 54 state and territorial welfare agencies and more than 1,500 county and city welfare departments, and by the Supreme Court and scores of lower courts. Carter's original reform proposal, which affected only four of the income maintenance programs, would have had to clear six congressional committees and the House Rules Committee just to reach the floor of the House and Senate. The jurisdictional concentration of power in the Senate Finance and House Ways and Means committees also poses a serious obstacle for welfare reform. The reach of those committees extends not only to welfare, but as well to tax legislation, Social Security, unemployment compensation, Medicare, any national health plan, tariffs, and a lion's share of energy and foreign trade legislation. The concentration not only puts enormous power in those committees, it also poses scheduling problems, with welfare reform inevitably at the end of the day.

Almost any federal change in the welfare system will affect some states, counties, and cities adversely while it affects others favorably, and not simply in terms of the number of individuals covered but also in terms of the level of state reimbursement. Any plan that will attract the support of a persuasive coalition of state governments is going to cost money. There is no free reform of the welfare system. In a time of limited resources, the need for funds to reform welfare vies with severe demands for funds from other deserving interests—senior citizens who seek to bolster Social Security, for example, a far more effective lobby than welfare recipients. And it collides with the sad reality that Americans are simply not willing to invest the significant sums necessary for comprehensive welfare reform.

Any possible reform effort has to have constant, persistent, almost stubborn support from the President and the Congress. Jimmy Carter, as it turns out, was no more willing than Richard Nixon to commit the necessary political capital. Perhaps he never had it to commit. He recoiled from being *President* Carter on this issue, and seemed always to long to retreat to the more comfortable ground of *candidate* Carter. And events—such as the tax revolt in California and the conservative swing across the nation—certainly overtook him. The congressional leadership, particularly the Speaker of the House, was more than willing to move with welfare reform. But the power of the leadership has been sapped over the past several years, as special interest politics have eroded party loyalty of members, and as a result of committee fragmentation and well-intentioned internal reforms. Even if that leadership were able to muster the political staying energy for the task of welfare reform, it is not clear how many followers it would have.

Without broad economic expansion and a reorganization that would deny so many bureaucracies and interests a veto over comprehensive reform, the only elements of welfare reform likely to pass in the next few years will be those with modest cost that command wide agreement across region, party, and interest group. A program similar to the 1979 Carter Administration proposal—or one even more modest—may have a chance.

As for the more extensive or controversial elements of reform, if they can clear the House, they must then face the Senate Finance Committee, which has members deeply interested and holding strong views on the welfare system. During the many hours we discussed the subject, Russell Long gave some indication of the fate of such proposals, should they ever reach that committee. We were sitting in his office under the Capitol Dome at about eight o'clock one evening, getting ready to break. "I have a proposition for you," Long said.

"Russell, Lyndon Johnson told me that whenever Russell Long said he had a proposition for me, I should put one hand over my wallet and the other over my testicles and hang on for dear life."

Long shook with laughter. "This is the kind of compromise Lyndon would understand. I don't know if Jimmy Carter will understand it, but Lyndon would understand it."

"What is it?"

"You try a demonstration of my welfare program and I will try a demonstration of any welfare program you want."

I thought for a minute. "There is no way the House will go along with that. You know how strongly Corman and the liberals feel about comprehensive reform."

"I'll make you an even better deal. You test my welfare program and I'll get legislation to finance not only that, but a demonstration of your welfare program and a demonstration of any welfare program that Corman wants."

I brushed his proposal gently by Jim Corman, Charlie Rangel, and some other liberals in the House. They all rejected it out of hand because they distrusted Long on this issue. When I mentioned it to the HEW staff, they argued that most elements of our proposed changes had already been proven in demonstrations. But not to the satisfaction of Russell Long, and most members of the Finance Committee.

The future of welfare reform may rest in moving modestly in areas of broad agreement, and taking up an offer to test various solutions to the more controversial elements of comprehensive reform.

CHAPTER IX

SOCIAL SECURITY

WHEN FRANKLIN DELANO ROOSEVELT proposed a Social Security system providing income for Americans over sixty-five, the life expectancy for males was less than sixty, and for females less than sixty-four. By the time of my confirmation hearings, some forty years later, when I was assuring Texas Senator Lloyd Bentsen and the Finance Committee that "We will absolutely guarantee the financial integrity of the Social Security system," life expectancy was over seventy for a man, and over seventy-seven for a woman. And the millions more men who lived to sixty-five had life expectancies of at least another fourteen years; the women, at least another eighteen.

I knew there would be financial problems with the Social Security system when the post–World War II babies retired, but I thought New Mexico Republican Senator Harrison Schmitt was puffing for the cameras when he called it a "time bomb ticking." From 1940, when the first monthly checks went out, to 1977, the system had grown from a $35 million program serving 220,000 beneficiaries, to an almost $100 billion program serving 33 million people, one out of every seven Americans.

Even so, Social Security was widely regarded as one of the best-managed programs in the government.

There had been ominous warnings. For each of the three years before I took office, the trustees of the system—the Secretaries of Treasury, Labor, and Health, Education, and Welfare—had alerted the Congress to the growing deficit in the system. Russell Long and Al Ullman had each told me to assess its financial integrity and make legislative proposals in 1977. But compared to the need to reorganize and manage the rest of HEW's programs, to devise workable welfare reform and national health plans, to attend to federal funding of abortion and student loan defaults, and to revitalize the Department's civil rights effort, I thought the Social Security problems could be placed, at least for a time, on the back burner. When I first talked in January 1977 to Social Security Commissioner Bruce Cardwell, a career man appointed by Nixon, I assured him that he could complete the year of federal service he needed for retirement. He was pleased that I brushed aside his suggestion that I might want my own man in the job immediately to deal with the Social Security financing problems. "In the unlikely event we have to move that quickly, you'll be my man," I told him.

But when Cardwell and his associates briefed Champion and me in late January and February on the program, it was clear that Senator Schmitt had understated the problem. Funds were needed urgently to keep the system from going broke by the early 1980s. The dry tones in which Cardwell and his staff talked about the problems didn't match the reality of the potential political explosion and economic troubles.

The Social Security system is divided into three trust funds: old age (retirement) and survivors, disability, and hospital insurance (Medicare). The old age and survivors, disability, and the hospital services portion of health insurance trusts are funded by earmarked payroll taxes, most of which are paid to beneficiaries about as fast as they are collected. The physician services part of health insurance is funded by individual premiums and through general tax revenues. Without additional money, the disability trust fund (in 1977 paying $12 billion to more than four million people) would go broke in 1978; and the old age and survivors (paying $75 billion to twenty-nine million retirees, surviving spouses and dependents) and Medicare trust funds (paying $25 billion in health bills of the aged and disabled) would go broke within five years. The demography of the nation posed serious long-term trouble for the system, as the post–World War II baby boom would be transformed into a senior boom by the end of the first quarter of the twenty-first century, and the decline in births would reduce the working contributors from 3.3 for each beneficiary in 1979 to fewer than 2 in the year 2030.

It was clear that a major part of the immediate solution was more tax revenue, and I knew we would have to move fast because it was critical to get the Congress to act in 1977. No election-year Congress was going to pass a multibillion-dollar tax increase, even for senior citizens, one of the most potent lobbies in Washington. Three government agencies touch virtually every American: the Internal Revenue Service, the Postal Service, and HEW's Social Security Administration, and only one, Social Security, has the favorable approval of most Americans. I wanted to keep Social Security that way.

Income security programs are the single largest function of the United States government. One out of every four Americans—about fifty-five million people—look to them for all, or at least a significant part, of their income. Through these programs, the federal government transfers roughly 20 percent of the gross national product from one group of Americans to another. Many—among them the welfare program for dependent children and the food stamp and black lung programs—are politically controversial and administrative nightmares. Social Security, by far the largest, had so far avoided those problems.

Social Security's coverage had greatly expanded from the simple retirement and widows' pension program it originated as. During the 1950s and 1960s, taxes and benefits were extended to the self-employed, such as farmers and lawyers, and by 1980 more than 90 percent of the work force was covered. In 1956, disability benefits were added; in 1965, Medicare was established to provide first the aged and then the disabled hospital insurance and the option to purchase heavily subsidized insurance for physician expenses. As the system matured, by 1980 more than 95 percent of the over-sixty-five population received benefits, along with three million survivors of deceased workers who were under sixty-five, and five million beneficiaries of the disability program. Social Security has become the largest single program in the federal budget; by 1980, its payments exceeded military expenditures by more than $20 billion.

The Congress had periodically increased benefits during the 1950s and 1960s. Some of the biggest increases since the program began and a whopping hike in the minimum benefit came during the Great Society years, when President Johnson sought to increase the minimum payment to help old poor people. To the protests that we were turning Social Security into a "welfare program" unworthy of our senior citizens, Johnson pointed out that in 1965 more than five million of the seventeen million Americans over sixty-five were struggling to survive below the poverty line, even though they had spent most of their lives working. We won most of what we asked for on Capitol Hill, and lifted two million Americans above the poverty line. That increase, and the ripple effect up the scale of retirement benefits, is a large part of the reason why Social Security payments presently keep seven million older Americans out of poverty. Nevertheless, more than three million citizens over sixty-five, 80 percent of whom receive Social Security benefits, have incomes below the poverty line.

During the Johnson years there were periodic proposals to index the Social Security system—to increase payments automatically as the consumer price index rose. We resisted them strenuously, in part because we believed such an automatic increase would fan inflation. But we were also concerned that so insulating millions of senior citizens would neutralize the most effective group that pressed Congress to fight inflation. We persuaded the Congress not to index the program. In 1972, with inflation higher, and the President, the House, and a third of the Senate up for reelection, Nixon recommended that Social Security payments be increased automatically in relation to the cost of living. Moving fast, Congress enacted a faulty law that double-indexed Social Security benefits—providing for increases geared to both prices and wages. When I became HEW Secretary five years later, it was clear that a significant number of workers, as a result of the double-indexing, would eventually receive more money in retirement benefits than they had earned working.

Economic forces joined demographic and political ones to threaten the system. The Social Security trust funds are supplied by payroll taxes, shared equally by employees and employers. When the recession of the mid-seventies increased unemployment, it reduced Social Security tax revenues. For each of the two years prior to the time I took office, the system had operated at a deficit, and a third straight deficit was expected in 1977. The reserves were perilously low, far under recommended minimums of at least 50 percent of the next year's anticipated payments (60 percent for health insurance) before taking into account tax revenues for that year.

A final storm was blowing up, and would hit with magnum force as we entered the eighties—runaway inflation, arm-in-arm with recession. For the Social Security year—July 1, 1980, to June 30, 1981—the legally mandated 14.3 percent inflation adjustment would alone increase Social Security payments and the taxpayers' bill by more than $17 billion.

A system as intimately related to people as Social Security is caught up inevitably in cultural change. The steep rise in divorce, the sharp increase in numbers of working women, and the legal and social demands for equal rights for women have had a significant impact. In the 1977 *Goldfarb* decision, the Supreme Court held that the system violated the equal protection clause by denying husbands and widowers survivor benefits unless they could prove that their working wives had provided one-half their support, when no such requirement was placed on wives and widows of working husbands. Compliance with the decision added $500 million to $1 billion in benefits each year. Combined with other pending lawsuits and the demand to recognize the economic value of homemakers, the case signaled the need for a thorough analysis of how the system treated women.

THE IMMINENT exhaustion of the disability insurance trust fund, with the depletion of the old age and survivors trust fund close behind, required action within weeks of my becoming Secretary. The longer-term problem was no less disturbing. If we did not get rid of the faulty mechanism to adjust for inflation, payroll taxes would have to double, starting immediately, in order to finance benefits provided by existing law. In late March 1977, I alerted President Carter that we would have to propose substantial additional taxes in 1977 to bolster the Social Security system, and I asked him to set a meeting to make some decisions by the end of April. We needed a proposal that could pass Congress in 1977 and would keep the system solvent for as long as possible.

Payroll tax revenues can be raised by increasing the rate of tax applied to the payroll, or the portion of the payroll taxed. During the 1976 campaign Carter, and many Democrats in Congress, had promised not to raise, and hopefully to reduce the tax rate increases scheduled to go into effect in 1978 and 1981. During the campaign, Carter had also committed himself to restoring the financial integrity of the system, but he never had to face what it would cost in taxes to keep that commitment. Less than three months after he became President, I brought Carter the news that, even were those rate increases to take effect and to raise an estimated $33 billion, the trust funds would still run a hefty deficit. We needed billions in additional revenues just to get over the next few years, through 1982. And we needed to deal with the long-term viability of the system through the turn of the century.

At HEW, I soon discovered there was no easy way, in terms of taxes or politics, to restore the integrity of the system. Dissatisfied with traditional approaches, Champion and I set up competing teams in the Social Security Administration (led by Commissioner Bruce Cardwell) and in the Office of the Assistant Secretary for Planning and Evaluation (led by Henry Aaron) to make recommendations. For hours, sitting in the green chairs or pacing around the table in the Secretary's conference room, we listened to Cardwell and Aaron and their staffs debate different approaches. At first the disagreements were sharp; the memos and tables put forth by one side were criticized severely by the other.

But as the staffs talked, and as Champion and I questioned and listened, elements of common ground began to emerge. Champion and I soon decided in our own minds that the payroll tax on employees was very near the limits of its economic validity and political acceptability. The first areas of agreement among all of us came in what we decided not to recommend. The disability fund was in danger of immediate exhaustion and there was some sentiment, briefly expressed, for just a quick fix to replenish that fund, either by modest tax increases or by borrowing from the relatively solvent hospital trust fund to get the disability fund over the next few years. Despite its appeal, we rejected this suggestion. We feared it would create anxiety among older and disabled Americans. Moreover, to postpone facing the harder short-term problems would make them even more painful to resolve in a couple of years. This Band-Aid was not large enough to cover the wound in the Social Security system.

We looked at a series of conventional tax increases, raising to various levels the wage base and/or the tax rate equally for employers and employees. To do the job required quite substantial increases that would place a heavy added burden on workers and employers, particularly if we were to increase the trust fund reserves to 50 percent of the amount of anticipated payments in a given year. That percentage was needed to weather a recession comparable to the one that had buffeted the trust funds in the mid-1970s. We eventually rejected this approach. Payroll tax-rate increases on employee wages were regressive, and raising the amount of wages subject to tax created additional long-term costs for the system because the amount a retired worker or survivor received from Social Security rose with each increase in the amount of wages subjected to Social Security taxes.

What then? How could we avoid these problems and deal with the short-run need for $83 billion over the next five years? Prodded by the concerns Champion and I raised, Cardwell, Aaron, and Larry Thompson, a thoughtful and imaginative career economist, came up with an ingenious approach to get the needed funds. Whenever the unemployment rate exceeded 6 percent, the amount of money lost because of wages not subjected to payroll taxes would be transferred from general revenues to the Social Security trust funds. This transfer not only protected against losing income at times of high unemployment; it also avoided the need to raise taxes during a recession, an action that could hinder economic recovery. Of major importance in terms of taxes, this idea also made it possible safely to maintain a lower reserve level in the trust funds—35 percent, instead of 50 percent—because funds would flow automatically into the trust funds in time of recession; this alone reduced the need for new taxes by $24 billion. We offered two arguments to allay concerns that financing Social Security out of general revenues created too great a temptation to raise benefits to excessive levels because there was no need to raise taxes to pay for benefit increases. First, general revenues would be available only in years when unemployment exceeded 6 percent; second, we devised a narrow formula to fix the amount of general revenues transferred to the trust funds.

The next proposal was to remove, in three stages, the ceiling on the amount of an individual's wages on which the employer paid a tax, while holding the employee ceiling at lower levels. This would produce some $30 billion in revenues for the trust funds by 1982, and at the same time impose a tax burden $4 billion lower than employers would have paid under a conventional financing plan, adequate to bolster the reserves, that taxed employers and employees equally. Already, 87.8 percent of payroll in the United States was subject to employer taxes. Almost all small businessmen were paying taxes on 100 percent of their payroll because the highest salaries they paid were at or below the reach of the payroll tax under existing law; thus, the tax would have no impact on them. We felt these points would overcome inevitable objections to "violating the principle" of the original system which taxed employers and employees equally on the same wage base.

The other elements of the short-term financing plan were traditional: increasing the tax rate for the self-employed, raising the employee wage base, accelerating the timing of scheduled tax-rate increases.

The meeting with the President took place on May 4, the eve of Carter's first European trip. Treasury Secretary Mike Blumenthal, Commerce Secretary Juanita Kreps, Labor Secretary Ray Marshall, Vice-President Fritz Mondale, OMB Director Bert Lance, top economic advisor Charles Schultze, and Hale Champion were there. As I reviewed the recommendations we had developed, Carter made clear his impatience and his annoyance that this problem distracted him from preparations for his European summits. There were no comments when I noted that we had to keep the scheduled 1978 and 1981 tax increases. I discussed the countercyclical use of general revenues, raised by the more progressive income tax, to supplement the more regressive payroll taxes to the extent unemployment exceeded 6 percent. Our recommendation seemed to be generally accepted.

Then I described our proposal to tax the employer on his entire payroll, and keep a lid, though somewhat raised, on the amount of the employee's pay that was taxed; for the first time the employer would be taxed on more of the payroll than the employees. Juanita Kreps opposed this as anti-business. I argued that the employer, unlike the employee, could deduct this tax from corporate income taxes, and thus could more easily bear this burden. Kreps then charged the proposal was inflationary, with some support from Charles Schultze. I pointed out that any tax on employers could be inflationary, but that this was $4 billion lower than any conventional alternative that would be sufficient to rebuild the trust funds. The President was in no mood to hear their arguments, and he shortly overruled Kreps. He was more interested in the contrast between his no-tax-rate-increase position during the 1976 campaign and Gerald Ford's proposals to raise the tax rate.

To meet the deficit crunch in the disability fund over the next few years, I proposed that we seek authority to borrow from the hospital trust fund and repay it later. For the long term I also suggested eliminating the double adjustment for inflation by eliminating adjustments for wages, and raising benefits only in response to prices, noting that there seemed to be general agreement in the key committees on this point. If the estimates of Social Security actuaries held up, the package would get us to the turn of the century without undue resort to the increasingly unpopular and economically regressive payroll tax.

Other long-run problems—the explosion in the number of disability beneficiaries, the sex discrimination issues, and adjustments for demographic changes—needed study before we could even make intelligent proposals. The American pension system, public and private, was confusing and ominously overextended—the possibility of collapse of key segments of it was real—so I suggested that the President establish a major commission, with representatives of the government and private sectors, employers and employees, the insurance companies, and others, to take a hard look at the situation and to arouse public interest. (Congress provided for such a commission in the 1977 Social Security legislation.)

The only serious alternative to our proposals was put forward by Energy Secretary James Schlesinger. He suggested that we dedicate $32 billion to the trust funds from the wellhead tax on oil and gas that Carter had recommended as part of his first energy program. Schlesinger thought this proposal would help pass the tax. I opposed his idea because I thought it would add controversy to a financing proposal that already contained two major innovations—the countercyclical dip into general revenues, and the increase in the employer's payroll base that broke the tradition of equal employer-employee shares. Moreover, since the wellhead tax was not likely to pass in time to ease the immediately threatened Social Security deficit, I feared that, with the Schlesinger proposal, the President would be accused of playing fast and loose with the trust funds.

After remarkably little discussion, Carter agreed with my recommendations, rejecting Schlesinger's idea and overriding Kreps and Schultze. He made it clear that his political commitments were to restore the financial integrity of the system, and to disassociate himself from increasing the payroll tax rate. He also expressed his conviction that "disability determinations were often abused." In less than an hour, the President had approved a proposal that, modified by the Congress, would be the largest single peacetime tax bill in our history. As he left, he asked Vice-President Mondale and me to unveil the proposals while he was in Europe.

Mondale and I made the announcement five days later, and Ullman immediately condemned the use of general revenues to bolster the trust funds during times of high unemployment, stating that it "violates the general principle of having a contributory system and makes it easy to move into a broad welfare concept." Bill Archer of Texas, the ranking Republican member of the Ways and Means Subcommittee on Social Security, attacked Carter for telling a May 4 meeting of energy legislators "that he had considered the use of general revenue financing for Social Security, but that he had rejected it. Now he is pushing it—a remarkable feat of mental agility . . . the blind leading the blind . . . [a] most brazen demonstration of fiscal legerdemain. . . ." On May 24, 1977, former President Gerald Ford attacked our proposal to use general revenues as "one of the most dangerous and shortsighted policies I can imagine." Observing that Social Security payments in the last decade had increased from $28 billion to $104 billion, Ford said that using general revenues to help shore up the system would add to the country's long-term debt and aggravate inflation.

On June 13, I testified before the Senate Finance Subcommittee on Social Security. Russell Long railed against using general revenues. With a $60 billion deficit in fiscal 1978, he argued, there were no general revenues to use. Congress should have "enough courage to vote for the taxes to fund" Social Security instead of accepting Carter's offer of "the easy way out." In private, Long made his feelings clear. "Joe, if we don't impose some discipline on the floor of the Senate, we'll bankrupt this country with the Social Security program."

The alternative to tapping general revenues or increasing payroll taxes was some reduction in benefits, and there was little stomach for that, aside from fixing the double-indexing for inflation. Hospital-cost containment could reduce substantially the drain on the hospital trust fund, but resistance developing to that proposal presaged a long fight.

Kreps suggested in an interview on July 30, 1977, that, "if you were to extend work life until sixty-eight, and not start Social Security benefits until sixty-eight, you would reduce enormously the Social Security burden." Her remarks set off a furor. The traditional supporters of Social Security, such as the AFL-CIO and the senior citizens groups it bankrolls, hold inviolate entitlement to partial benefits at sixty-two, and full benefits at sixty-five. Since a diversion on the retirement-age issue was the last thing we needed to get a bill passed, I had to publicly renounce Kreps's proposal, even though I personally considered it an important option for the future. But my comments weren't enough for the Social Security lions. They demanded that Kreps and the White House repent. On September 1, she issued a statement that "no change in the present system is imminent and . . . the administration is not actively considering any proposal to alter the present arrangement for retirement with full benefits at sixty-five." She added that she had offered no formal proposal. So her idea was effectively killed, but as Congress began to sniff the financial trouble ahead, it eventually agreed to put in the 1977 law a provision to encourage later retirement by increasing benefits for each year of work after sixty-five up to sixty-eight.

The need for more revenue and the impulse to avoid more taxes led the House to consider the concept of universal coverage, mandating the inclusion of all federal, state, and local employees and certain nonprofit workers in the Social Security system. The program already included more than 90 percent of American workers. Universal coverage would have added seven million persons and $11 billion a year to the trust funds by 1980, a big help in the short run although over the long run such coverage would have its costs as large numbers of federal and other employees became eligible for benefits. The House Ways and Means Committee reported a bill in October 1977 that folded in those employees. The government employee unions—particularly the federal employee unions, who feared losing some of their rich federal retirement benefits—complained, and the House recanted. Instead, it directed the Secretary of HEW to study and report on integrating the two retirement systems. By a vote of 386 to 38, the House imposed additional taxes to compensate for the revenues lost by not mandating coverage for federal, state, local, and certain nonprofit employees. After days of debate, on October 27, the House approved, 275 to 146, a multibillion-dollar payroll tax increase, with the maximum taxes rising from $965 in 1977 to $2,854 in 1986. It was an astonishing action to have passed a tax increase that large by such a decisive vote.

The President was immediately sensitive to the high taxes. The day after the House vote, Carter said that higher Social Security taxes were likely to be inflationary and "might be a dampening effect on the economy. . . . If the Social Security tax increase is substantial after the Congress gets through with it, we'll try to compensate for this in the tax reform package."

The Social Security tax bill had a more Byzantine passage through the Senate, with Finance Committee senators seeking to amend the bill to serve their own interests. Senator Herman Talmadge fought our proposal to borrow from the coffer-filled Hospital Insurance Trust Fund to help the Disability Trust Fund over its critical 1979–80 shortfall. Talmadge chaired the Finance Committee's Health Subcommittee, and he feared any shift of hospital trust funds might be a step toward general revenue financing of Medicare. Such financing would jeopardize his subcommittee's exclusive jurisdiction over Medicare and give Kennedy's Human Resources Committee's Health Subcommittee an arguable claim over it.

Senator Moynihan saw a chance to get some fiscal relief for New York City. As he balanced the "must" nature of the Social Security bill against the precarious life of the welfare reform proposal pending before the same Senate Finance Committee, he let Long and me know that the price of his support was to add the fiscal relief for states and localities promised in Carter's welfare reform package to the Social Security bill. I refused to agree. It would have taken away much of the motivation of the states and cities to push for welfare reform. Moynihan and Long then tried to attach fiscal relief and some of Long's welfare proposals to the Social Security financing bill. We strenuously opposed the Moynihan and Long motion and it lost on a tie vote. Meeting over lunch with Mondale, Eizenstat, and me, Moynihan charged the President and the administration with bad faith on fiscal relief. He claimed that Carter had reneged on his commitment to provide New York the fiscal relief he had promised during the campaign.

After the meeting, Moynihan wrote the President a note saying, "I am sorry to have to say that I found the welfare reform *bill* to be grievously disappointing, as compared with the promise of your message in August." At first, Eizenstat was annoyed. He felt Moynihan's position on welfare reform, as on the administration's foster care proposals (where, Eizenstat noted, Moynihan had initially supported, and then questioned our bill to continue welfare payments for children after adoption and to fund state adoption law reform), revealed "a disturbing pattern of first endorsing administration proposals and then backing off in order to obtain further concessions." Eventually, Eizenstat agreed that we should try to compromise, because of Moynihan's potential as an ally in welfare reform.

Just as we reached that conclusion, Russell Long told me I would have to find some accommodation with Moynihan to move the Social Security bill, and the President suggested I work out a compromise. After protracted negotiations, Moynihan and I agreed on authorizing, in the Social Security bill, $374 million in 1978 for fiscal relief for states and localities. An additional $453 million in 1979 and almost $1 billion in 1980 were to be part of our welfare reform legislation, and subject to state-by-state reduction in the percentage of welfare funds erroneously paid through mistake or fraud. In return, Moynihan agreed to support actively the President's Social Security and welfare reform bills. Although I had sent Carter a memo proposing the compromise on October 28, apparently he never received it. As soon thereafter as Moynihan and I reached agreement, I called Carter and told him. The President said nothing at the time, but at the April 1978 Camp David Cabinet meeting, he cited it as an example of his not being informed until after the fact.

The most fascinating dealings, as always with the Finance Committee, were with its chairman, Russell Long. For years, Long had been developing proposals, many considered too harsh by liberals in the Senate and House, to tighten up the welfare system. Many of his proposals were in a bill, H.R. 7200, that he wanted to include in the Social Security legislation.

Beginning on September 19, 1977, we met perhaps half a dozen times in Long's hideaway office on the Senate side of the Capitol in the early evening, and discussed at length changes in the welfare program as the foreplay to a Social Security bill. They were remarkable sessions, candid, funny, tough-minded, each of us with his own biases, but each fundamentally wanting to make both programs work better.

Long began by talking about his pet Child Support Enforcement Program, through which HEW provides funds to states to establish programs to locate absent fathers and get them to make child-support payments. The HEW staff nicknamed the program "Nab-a-Dad." Where the children were on welfare, the amount of child support from the father would reduce the welfare payment. But Long reminded me that the program was not limited to fathers of welfare children. "When I was dictating this bill to a secretary," he said, "she asked me why it should be limited just to people on welfare. Her own husband had run out on her and her kids and she thought she should be eligible. So I said, 'Why not? Put it in!' And that's why the bill applies to everyone whose daddy has run away from making support payments."

I thought to myself how often personal interests affect legislation. While I was working for President Johnson, my three-year-old son Joseph got into an aspirin bottle and had to be rushed to Sibley Hospital in Washington to have his stomach pumped. I was there when President Johnson called me about something else. After he got over his irritation at my absence from the White House, he found out why I was at the hospital. "There ought to be safety caps on those bottles so kids can't open them. When you get back here, I want to send a bill up to the Hill so we can require safety caps on drugs like this. Then kids like little Joe won't be able to open them and hurt themselves.'' We did send such legislation forward in 1966, it was finally passed in 1970, and that is how safety caps came to be on so many drug bottles.

Long brought me out of my reverie with a loud question. ''Joe, you've got to really do something about the fellas who don't pay their child support.'' I told him I was. The program made sense from a moral as well as a taxpayer's view. ''I know you are,'' Long said, changing pace. ''That's why I want to help you with a few amendments to the Social Security bill.''

Long's proposals were inventive. He wanted to withhold federal welfare funds from states that did not have long-arm statutes for absent fathers in paternity and child-support cases; to pay the salaries of state and local judges and law clerks to hear child-support cases; and to give the HEW Secretary authority to designate and help fund twenty-four-hour-a-day laboratories to run blood tests in paternity cases.

''Russell,'' I said, ''give me a chance to work with what I have.''

''You're too damn liberal,'' he kidded pointedly. ''We've got to do some of these things to get the program under control.'' I agreed, but after several hours of meetings he said he would let me step up the Child Support Enforcement Program under existing authority before pressing his proposals. I did, and by the time I left as Secretary, the program moved from child-support collections of $600 million in 1976 to $1.3 billion in 1979, including almost $596 million that reduced welfare payments.

Initially, Long was in no mood to compromise. Then, in the last week of September, when he lost his motion with Moynihan to attach all of his H.R. 7200 welfare proposals to the Social Security bill in the tie vote, we began to work out a compromise. He would agree to limit Moynihan's fiscal relief to one year and no more outside of welfare reform. I would support his amendment to authorize legislatively the match of welfare rolls against Social Security and unemployment compensation lists, which I had already begun in the absence of any explicit prohibition. We agreed on financial incentives for states that reduced welfare-payment error rates below 4 percent. We disagreed about reinstituting his workfare program that would have required some mothers to work or lose welfare payments, but settled on my promise to try a few demonstration projects.

With those understandings, the skirmishes within the Finance Committee were all directed at Social Security provisions. With Long on our side for the most part, the committee reported a Social Security financing bill on November 1, although without providing any authority to borrow from the general revenues to bolster the disability insurance trust fund as the House bill had provided. Long strongly supported the higher wage base for employers, and the Senate bill would, by 1985, have taxed the employer on payroll up to $75,000 per employee, while holding to $30,300 individual employee pay subject to tax.

The next day's action on the Senate floor was dicey. The level of new taxes was beginning to sink into the electorate and the Senators approached the bill far more gingerly than their colleagues in the House had. Republican Senator Henry Bellmon's motion to kill the bill got thirty-six enthusiastic votes. And on November 4, we had to make sure that Vice-President Mondale was in the chair as President of the Senate in order to break a 41–41 tie to win final passage.

After that, I held separate private meetings with Long and Ullman in an attempt to get the House conferees to accept the Senate's higher wage base for employers, and to get Long to accept the authority in the House bill to borrow from the general revenues to carry the disability trust fund over its difficult years. Those meetings, and others with House and Senate conferees, made it clear that the conference would impose higher taxes on workers before adopting each other's proposals.

On the evening of December 7, Ullman and Long met secretly and agreed to a compromise eliminating most provisions that increased benefits, the borrowing authority in the House bill, and the higher wage base for employer taxes in the Senate bill, but accepting, for a year, the tuition tax credit the administration opposed and the few welfare proposals Long and I had agreed to.

When Ullman informed me of the compromise later that evening, I expressed concern that his committee members would revolt, and said I would have to see whether the President would agree. I told him Carter would not accept any form of tuition tax credit. Ullman exploded: "You tell the President to stay out, not to get involved in any heavy-handed way, because it is too late for him or the administration to do anything about the legislation."

"We have to be involved," I said. "We have a responsibility just as you do."

"We've all worked our butts off to get a Social Security bill this year, and you should tell the President to be grateful that there will be a good bill. Nobody wants to listen to him up here."

When a majority of Ullman's committee renounced his compromise with Long, we all got involved in a desperate attempt to salvage a bill. Finally, the House and Senate conferees stripped the bill of the tuition tax credit and other frills, and Jim Corman, chairman of the Special Welfare Reform Subcommittee, accepted the welfare proposals Long and I had agreed to because he did "not want to be the guy who stopped the Social Security bill." On December 15, 1977, the conferees agreed on the largest payroll tax increase in the history of the United States—$227 billion in new taxes within ten years. The Senate passed the bill overwhelmingly, 56 to 21; the House by a far more cautious 189 to 163. Both tax-rate and wage-base increases were included, but the sharpest hikes were set to begin in January 1981, after the 1980 presidential elections. By the mid-1980s, the employee and employer would each be paying taxes of more than 7 percent on wages up to $42,000—combined taxes of more than $6,000 per year, a far cry from the initial tax of 1 percent on wages up to $3,000 that American workers and employers each paid in 1936.

Carter was concerned enough about the heavy tax burden to sign the bill in a small ceremony in the Indian Treaty Room of the Executive Office Building, rather than in the White House. He did praise the Congress for its "political courage in restoring the Social Security system to a sound basis," but in a politically calculated low key. Former HEW Secretary Wilbur Cohen, standing near me, did not like Carter's reserved ceremony. But driving back to HEW after the signing, Eileen Shanahan said to me, "Don't get too far out in front on the Social Security bill. Those taxes are too heavy. Every time you mention the bill, remind people that if they'd adopted your version, there wouldn't be those heavy taxes on the workers."

As soon as the Congress reconvened, the cries to roll back the taxes could be heard throughout Washington. Frank Church, the Democratic Chairman of the Select Senate Committee on Aging, charged that the taxes fell most heavily on those least able to pay. Ullman said a new tax would have to be devised, urging, at one point, use of funds from the crude-oil equalization tax; at another, suggesting a value-added tax. Wisconsin Democratic Senator Gaylord Nelson wanted to tap the general revenues to support the hospital and disability insurance trust funds.

On February 24, 1978, Mondale met briefly with Hale Champion, Treasury Secretary Mike Blumenthal, OMB Director Jim McIntyre, CEA Chairman Charles Schultze, Stu Eizenstat, and me to devise contingency planning, should "congressional pressure to change Social Security financing become irresistible." Blumenthal and Schultze wanted to soften the inflationary impact of the 1979 and 1981 tax increases. I had no objection, but I strongly opposed changing the Social Security tax itself because of the political difficulty of getting any more money into the system. "Someone's got to pay for the benefits," I said.

"You're beginning to sound like Russell Long," Mondale, a former member of the Senate Finance Committee, chided.

Pressure on the Hill to roll back the taxes continued to mount. Long told me he wanted to provide "about five billion dollars in relief from

Social Security taxes.'' Speaker Tip O'Neill said the House would rescind part of the tax increase it had voted in 1977.

The President preferred to hold fast, but he kept his options open. In a meeting with newspaper editors on March 16, he said that he was ''trying to hold our tax package together'' and ''prevent a reopening of the entire question of Social Security again. . . .'' At the same time, however, a White House spokesperson confirmed that the administration was studying a roll-back proposal, but only ''so that we will be in a position to respond'' to the Congress. After much discussion within the administration, it became clear that, whatever its problems, the system so desperately needed funds that it was better to leave the taxes in place, at least for the moment.

Despite a 150 to 57 vote of the House Democratic Caucus to roll back the taxes, Carter stiffened his opposition to any change in the 1977 Social Security legislation. When Jody Powell made it clear on April 5 that ''the administration is opposed to the reopening of this immensely complicated issue,'' Long and Ullman moved to a firm public position against any change. On April 7, I said a roll-back would ''raise hell'' with the soundness of the system. On May 16, in our annual trustees report, Blumenthal, Marshall, and I argued that a roll-back would endanger the financial integrity of the system. The next day, as Speaker O'Neill announced that Carter would veto a roll-back, the House Ways and Means Committee reversed its earlier vote favoring it, with Dan Rostenkowski helping lead the way. Rostenkowski chaired the Ways and Means Health Subcommittee and, like Talmadge, he was reluctant to relinquish any jurisdiction. Part of the committee's roll-back proposals would have financed the hospital insurance trust fund with general revenues. That would have jeopardized Rostenkowski's exclusive jurisdiction over Medicare, subjecting it at least to concurrent, and possibly exclusive, jurisdiction of Paul Rogers's Health Subcommittee of the House Interstate and Foreign Commerce Committee.

With the reversal, serious talk of a Social Security tax roll-back faded. And as the system was squeezed by inflation and stagnation turning into recession, there was no serious discussion of relief from the tax rise.

The 1980 trustees report revealed that yet more revenues will be needed to forestall financial collapse of the Social Security trust funds. Under decidedly rosy economic assumptions, the report projected that in 1980, the combined revenues of all three trust funds would fall short of payments, but that the disability and hospital funds would improve somewhat in the next few years. However, in each of the years 1980 through 1984, the retirement and survivors program, Social Security's largest, would pay out more than it would receive in taxes, beginning with a $5.8 billion shortfall in 1980 and steadily rising to a $16.2 billion shortfall in 1984. All accumulated surpluses would be wiped out by 1983 and from that year on, the fund would be bankrupt.

Methods to soften the inflationary impact of the sharp payroll tax increases were still discussed; but all such proposals had to face the fact that the Social Security system's appetite for funds was growing voraciously. For the first five years of the 1980s, without changes in benefits or containment of hospital costs, the Congress must find at least $100 billion, and probably more, in revenues above those that the steep tax increases going into effect will raise. Even with such an infusion of funds, the Congress will have to take a second look at the point-for-point percentage increases in Social Security in response to changes in the consumer price index, as Great Britain and some other European countries are now doing.

In January 1981, Ronald Reagan became the third successive president, following Ford and Carter, to face a crisis in Social Security financing.

DURING MY review of the system in 1977, I came to appreciate the congressional concern about the Social Security disability program. Russell Long had been troubled for several years about the growth of the program, and the House Ways and Means Subcommittee on Social Security had held extensive hearings and advanced suggested changes. Repeatedly Carter had expressed to me his belief that the disability program was being "ripped off," that "drug addicts and alcoholics" were filling the disability rolls, as were many others who could work. He was reflecting what he had been told by voters during the presidential campaign. As is often the case when the voter reacts sourly to the bureaucratic maze of modern government, the intuition that something was wrong was correct, but the diagnosis was oversimplified.

I opened a dialogue on the disability program at the Economic Club of Chicago on April 20, 1978. In 1965, there were less than one million people receiving disability benefits, at a cost of about $1.5 billion. By the time I spoke in Chicago, there were more than four million, and the annual cost was $13 billion. Modest assumptions pegged the program's cost at $30 billion by 1985.

How did this happen? There were a variety of causes. The benefits were rich for many Americans: 6 percent of those receiving disability insurance, particularly younger disabled workers, got more money than they had earned on the job; another 14 percent got 80 percent or more of their pre-disability earnings plus medical benefits. The program actually contained powerful incentives not to return to work: those who did so lost their medical benefits as well as their disability payments, and it took at least two years to get them back if their disability again forced them to stop working. Since most disabled people are difficult to insure for health care and are understandably insecure, the loss of these benefits discouraged attempts to go back to work.

Not only were people staying unnecessarily on the disability rolls, but a sharply increasing number were getting on them as lawyers became more sophisticated about the opportunities to get benefits, and administrators and judges displayed generous compassion in applying the statutory standard for disability. The courts also established numerous due-process opportunities to dispute denials of benefits. All this, in turn, attracted more applicants. When I became HEW Secretary, there were so many claimants seeking benefits through HEW's internal adjudicatory process that the Department employed more administrative law judges just to hear their cases than there were judges in the entire federal court system. After that review, so many Social Security disability cases spilled over into the federal courts—about 18,000 were pending at any given time—that they were clogging the judicial system.

I moved administratively to tighten standards, to shorten the time within which disability claims were decided, to speed administrative-law judge decisions, and, until the rehabilitation program was moved to the Education Department, to try to put rehabilitation services at the same place as claims offices to provide immediate help. We were able to make some improvements: The number of applications decreased from 1.23 million in 1976 to 1.18 million in 1978; the number of awards dropped from 552,000 in 1976 to 456,000 in 1978; the recovery and return-to-work rates improved (helped somewhat by improved economic conditions); the error rate for disability determinations dropped. Under a lot of pressure from me, the administrative law judges greatly increased their decisions to thirty per month per judge; most were rightly proud of their achievement, but a few rebelled and sued me, alleging I was making them work so hard they could not decide cases fairly.

The program needed a legislative overhaul as well, and building on the work of the House Ways and Means Committee and its Social Security Subcommittee and staff, we recommended major changes in early 1979. An insurance program that provides more income for beneficiaries when they are not working than when they are, is unacceptable. We recommended a ceiling on benefits to keep them below the worker's pre-disability earnings. We still left benefits above those of private insurers, which generally set a limit of two-thirds of earnings, because our program had the important social goal of providing an adequate living for lower-income workers. No one on the disability rolls would suffer a reduction in benefits; the reductions applied only to those who came on the rolls in the future.

Our proposals also focused on work incentives and rehabilitation. We recommended several measures to encourage disabled beneficiaries to try to return to work: automatic reinstatement of benefits to one who returns to work but then finds, within a year, that he is unable to continue; Medicare and Medicaid for three years after cash benefits ended for disability beneficiaries who returned to work; Medicare coverage immediately for a worker who becomes disabled again within five years of the previous disability; more realistic deductions for disability-related work expenses; and payments during trial work periods.

Although they supported most provisions of the bill, the proposal to cap benefits sufficiently below pre-disability earnings to provide a work incentive was mightily resisted by the disabled groups. They crowded hearings, some in wheelchairs, others blind and crippled. Like any other political action group, they used all their persuasive powers. Social Security Subcommittee Chairman Jake Pickle told me that the House Rules Committee session to clear the bill for floor action was the most emotional committee meeting he ever attended. There was barely enough room for committee members amidst the wheelchairs. Eventually, a cap was approved to hold benefits significantly below pre-disability earnings. The Congress also approved most of our recommendations on work incentives and rehabilitation, and part of our proposal to give more finality to the decisions of administrative law judges and ease the jamming of the federal courts with disability cases. The bill, passed and signed by the President in June 1980, was the most far-reaching reform in the history of the disability program. It provided forceful incentives for those disabled who could return to work, and was expected to reduce Social Security and Supplemental Security Income payments for disability by $2.6 billion in the first five years.

THE 1980 disability reforms are the result of years of work. While controversial—and bitterly contested by many old Social Security hands—they will strengthen the program and maintain taxpayer support for it. As I renewed my involvement in the other Social Security programs, I came to realize that sweeping reform of the entire system is needed. During the Johnson years, we had moved to expand the program—by increasing benefit levels, adding new benefits, and covering more workers. We viewed Social Security as one of our most effective weapons in the war on poverty, both in the immediate and the long term. Benefit increases were quickly adopted on Capitol Hill; funds could always be given to the elderly, particularly those in need, without the resistance that emerged when welfare or other means-tested programs for the poor were proposed. During the Great Society years, the economy was expanding so rapidly that more could be invested through the public sector, and even with higher payroll taxes the take-home pay of workers still went up. In those years, Social Security was sacrosanct; the social value of its benefits was never tested against other public needs; it wasn't even part of the federal budget.

Everyone accepted the political rhetoric of Social Security: that benefits were an "earned right," that the worker made a "contribution" to the trust funds, and that the system operated on "actuarily sound" principles for each individual. Indeed, President Johnson and those of us pressing for his liberalizations of the program, often invoked that rhetoric in advocating our cause. A decade later, as I assumed executive responsibility for this program, I soon realized that the days of expansion were over, that Social Security program costs had to be measured against other social needs in an era of limited resources, that the program was now very much a part of the federal budget, and that over the long haul, maintaining support for the heavy taxes necessary to provide adequately for our senior citizens would require a sensitive disciplining of the system.

By 1978, in the course of preparing the budget to be submitted to the Congress in January 1979, it was evident that we would have to begin facing the prospect of reducing benefits for those who would become eligible in the future. That required a dispassionate look at the rhetoric that had cloaked the Social Security system for more than a generation.

It is a misconception to call Social Security benefits an "earned right." The Congress has repeatedly revised Social Security benefits, most often to increase them but also sometimes to reduce them, as it did when it stopped the double-indexing geared to both wage and price inflation. As a matter of law the "right" to receive benefits under the Social Security system is no stronger than any other right under a federal statute that bestows benefits. The Social Security legislation was passed by a majority of the Congress and signed by the President, and can be changed in the same way. In fairness, those already receiving benefits should not suffer any reduction; but only to this extent can the concept of "earned right" be held clearly to have validity.

The workers and employers pay taxes; they do not make contributions. As is the case with income, estate, sales, and property taxes, no one subject to Social Security taxes can refuse to pay them.

No worker pays Social Security taxes in the amount a private insurance company would require in order to run an actuarily sound program that would provide the benefits he or she is expected to receive after retirement. Nor are payments proportional to earnings and taxes. Particularly since the Great Society's increases in the minimum payment and others that came in the early 1970s, the lower-paid worker receives a much higher proportion of his previous earnings than the higher-paid worker. As former Social Security Commissioner Stanford Ross tried to point out, Social Security is very much an income transfer program, with desirable social goals that have so far justified its existence and the increasingly heavy taxes necessary to support it.

Moreover, Social Security is a pay-as-you-go system, not funded in advance. In 1979, the old age, survivor, and disability trust funds would have required reserves of more than $4 trillion to cover their obligations to contributing workers. Those funds then held only $30 billion, less than 1 percent of their projected needs.

Once those realities are squarely faced, it becomes possible to look at Social Security with a view toward eliminating unnecessary benefits, such as those provided elsewhere by the federal government, and changing the system to accommodate the needs of the 1980s and beyond. We considered such actions essential to bolster taxpayer support for adequate benefits for the elderly and taxes to fund those benefits. This is what led to my controversial recommendations to Carter in late 1978. The proposals for change were, as Hale Champion put it, "shin-kickers and knee-knockers."

On December 5, 1978, in response to his request for ways to move toward a balanced budget in 1981, I wrote Carter suggesting that we tax a portion of Social Security payments on which no tax had previously been levied. The tax would apply only to individuals who had an annual gross income over $20,000 a year, or in the case of couples, over $25,000, independent of Social Security benefits. It would affect about 1.5 million persons, less than 5 percent of the more than 34 million Social Security beneficiaries.

At that time, an individual's payroll tax payments generally averaged 8 percent, at most 18 to 20 percent, of the Social Security benefits he or she could expect to receive. Benefit payments in excess of the individual's contribution represent, in effect, employers' contributions that had been deducted from income tax and interest that had never been taxed. In any other retirement plan, these items would be counted as income, and properly subject to tax. My proposal would tax no more than 75 percent of Social Security benefits. All revenues from the tax would be dedicated to the Social Security trust funds.

In 1977, the administration had proposed and the Congress had readily adopted, a plan to tax unemployment compensation on the same principles. But now, Carter rejected the proposal to tax Social Security payments without any serious discussion, as politically explosive. He never even commented about it directly to me. (His political instincts were vindicated in 1980 when the House overwhelmingly voted a resolution that Social Security benefits "are and should remain exempt from federal taxation.")

In addition to the disability program reform and the limited taxation of Social Security benefits, I recommended a number of other changes, including three key ones: raising gradually, over several years, the age for eligibility for any retirement benefits from sixty-two to sixty-five; phasing out benefits for post–secondary school students over four years since there were other student-aid programs; and eliminating the $255 lump-sum death benefit for burial that was enacted in 1954 and worth only $90 in 1978. These reforms would apply only to those who became entitled to benefits in the future. Those receiving benefits prior to the law's enactment would be grandfathered under the existing benefits. We regarded these as modest reforms that would effect a 1 percent reduction in the cost of the program, estimated to exceed $100 billion in 1980 and, as presently constituted, certain to more than double, perhaps even approaching $400 billion, before the end of the 1980s.

My proposals infuriated and alienated three colleagues who were among the architects and high priests of the Social Security program: Robert Ball, Social Security Commissioner during most of the 1960s and early 1970s, who had helped draft Carter's Social Security position during the 1976 campaign; Wilbur Cohen, a treasured friend and a social activist, the HEW Secretary for the last several months of the Johnson administration; and Nelson Cruikshank, who was Carter's White House Counselor and Chairman of the Federal Council on Aging. (Cruikshank was appointed at my recommendation, in response to "the only must appointment we will lay on you," as Lane Kirkland put it to me for the AFL-CIO in February 1977.)

My proposals were discussed at length with Eizenstat and McIntyre during the budget and legislative process in the fall of 1978 and I reviewed them in detail with the President in early December. I reminded him often that the proposals would be controversial, and that senior citizens vote in far greater numbers than younger Americans. Still, Carter seemed willing to bite the bullet because of the obvious need to recognize the realities of the 1980s, his desire to eventually balance the budget, and his hope to avoid the less palatable alternatives of cutting scores of programs that would anger even more constituencies.

When Cruikshank, Ball, and Cohen sensed that I was beginning to convince the President, they delivered a strong memorandum and met with him privately on December 20, 1978. They argued that the Social Security program should be considered independent of the budget, and that Social Security policy should be self-contained and not weighed against other priorities or fiscal needs as were general revenue programs. They warned Carter that the "budget game" of asking for Social Security reductions "grows out of the fact that since fiscal year 1969, the separately financed benefits of Social Security have been lumped with the general revenue expenditures of the rest of HEW in the budget ceiling given the Department. Thus, the Department makes proposals to cut Social Security benefits as a way of protecting other Department programs. Then, when the Social Security proposals are not accepted by Congress, the total HEW budget is greater than would otherwise have been the case."

Carter sent their memo over to me with a handwritten note, "These arguments are very persuasive. Please answer by Friday [December 22]." As I read their paper, I recalled that the Johnson administration had moved to create a unified budget that included Social Security. A bipartisan report approved the economic sense of such a budget, and the inclusion of the revenues from payroll taxes then helped reduce the federal deficit.

I was convinced that it was essential to begin to target Social Security where the elderly and disabled needed most help, if we were to avoid dangerous erosion of support for the program from young workers irritated with higher taxes and lower take-home pay. On Friday, December 22, I wrote Carter a note, with which OMB Director McIntyre agreed, taking sharp issue with Ball, Cohen, and Cruikshank. "These individuals, more than any others, have been responsible for the development and expansion of these programs over the last forty years. They deserve both respect and appreciation for their many contributions. Their criticisms, however, miss the mark; they are wrong with respect to the concepts, motives, and decision-making processes involved in these proposals. Their criticisms do serve one purpose well, i.e., the sharpening of the principle issue: What approach to Social Security programs best serves both the programs and the commitment of our nation to social justice for our elderly at this point in time?"

I reminded the President that "Social Security in FY [fiscal year] 1980 is presently expected to pay out more than $100 billion in benefits to about thirty-five million beneficiaries. There are obligations in future years to more than a hundred million American workers who are presently paying payroll taxes." Aside from defending my specific proposals, I set out three reasons for reforming the system: it was still not financially sound; the budget deficit had to be reduced to fight inflation; and congressional pressure to reduce payroll taxes scheduled for 1979 and 1981 could precipitate irresponsible action. "In short, the Social Security program *must* be disciplined and refined in this environment by those who believe in these programs, or the programs will not survive as we know them."

Ball, Cohen, and Cruikshank came to see me at 6:00 P.M. on Friday, December 22, 1978. Hale Champion and Social Security Commissioner Stanford Ross joined us. The two-and-one-half-hour meeting was so emotional, angry, and loud that outside the thick closed door, there were moments when my secretary wondered whether we were exchanging blows. I sat in a rocking chair in the corner of my office. Hale Champion was in an upholstered chair to my left; Bob Ball and Ross were on my immediate right on one couch; Cruikshank and Cohen to Champion's left on another. I began by telling them we disagreed with their memo, and that I was recommending the changes not just for budgetary purposes but as "administrative reforms to improve the program."

"That's nonsense, Joe," Wilbur Cohen shot back. "They're just budget-savers."

"These changes save less than $1.5 billion out of a program of well over $100 billion," I said. "The disability program changes save a little. But they are basically designed to encourage people to become self-sufficient, to get off the disability rolls. Some of these changes, like extending medical benefits, cost money."

"But you are cutting benefits," Cruikshank argued. "These benefits are earned rights that people have paid for and are entitled to."

"They're disastrous changes," Cohen said. "There've never been reductions like these in benefits."

"That's not true. In 1977, we recommended substantial reductions in benefits and the Congress went further. It cut $1.8 billion as reforms, not as budget slashes," I said. "You didn't oppose those changes."

"If we had thought you were serious in 1977 when you recommended them, we would have fought them," Cohen said. He stood up and began pacing behind the couch.

"Did you think we were going through a charade? When we propose legislative changes, we try to get them enacted," Champion commented.

"What Wilbur means is that for years—since Social Security was folded into the budget—HEW Secretaries have proposed benefit reductions to save other less popular programs. Presidents recommend them, but the Congress never accepts them," Ball explained.

"Especially with McIntyre, who is no match for you guys. We thought you were just trying to get over the budget crunch," Cohen said.

"Well, we were, and are, serious," I said.

''Then we're going to fight,'' Wilbur said, his face reddening.

Cruikshank said no changes of any significance had ever been made without wide consultation, especially with the Social Security Advisory Council. When I told Cruikshank he was wrong, and cited examples, it only made him madder. Ball, his face now splotching with anger, said no cuts in the basic program should ever be made.

''There are reductions of over one billion dollars in benefits that people have earned,'' Cohen was almost shouting.

I responded firmly, trying to measure my words. ''These are not 'earned' in any true sense. People get a lot more out of Social Security than they put in. Any program has to be changed as the times change. Benefits were added when the system had surplus funds. Today, it's under a severe financial strain that's going to get worse. In these times, if people don't need it, government doesn't do it,'' I said.

''The worst mistake,'' Cohen said, ''was when Social Security became part of the federal budget. We should go back to separating it out. Then you wouldn't cut it to meet a budget target.''

''The worst mistake would be to treat it separately.'' I was now getting annoyed. ''The claims of senior citizens for tight dollars have to be weighed against other claims. The unified budget faces up to those kinds of considerations.''

Cohen exploded. ''What you just said proves you don't believe in the Social Security program. It is a separate program. People have rights. You don't believe that.''

''Social Security needs to be reviewed periodically like every other program. We can ease the impact of cuts by not letting them apply to anyone now receiving those benefits. But changes have to be made,'' I responded.

When we got into a discussion on the disability program, the only concession was made by Bob Ball. He agreed that a person should not receive more on disability than while working, but he wanted even that change made somewhat differently.

When we talked about moving the age for eligibility for any retirement benefits from sixty-two to sixty-five, Cruikshank's hands began to tremble with rage. ''That is a fundamental change in the program. You have no right to make it.''

''The life span of Americans has grown dramatically,'' I argued. ''What was age sixty forty years ago when the program started is more like seventy today. Today, millions more people get benefits and proportionately fewer pay for them.''

Cruikshank shouted, ''That is wrong, wrong, wrong. You cannot take away some fundamental right that many people need.''

"We're taking care of poor people through the Supplemental Security Income program by reducing the eligibility age there to sixty-two," I responded.

"That's awful." Cruikshank was now joined by Cohen and Ball, in angry refrain. "The Social Security Program should not be mixed up with a welfare program like SSI."

Wilbur Cohen shouted at me, "You'll destroy the Social Security program by what you're doing."

"I'm trying to save it," I said, and Champion added, "With so many demands on public resources, we can still justify a means-tested early retirement at age sixty-two. But we can no longer justify to taxpayers a sixty-two-year-old retirement for those who do not need the funds and who can work. We're trying to bolster weakening public support among workers. This kind of a change will do that."

Ross then emphasized the need to focus benefits carefully where need was greatest in times of limited resources. "That's the way to support the program." As Ross spoke, Cruikshank and Cohen looked at him with undisguised anger. Cruikshank had opposed his appointment for the very reasons I had made it—to get someone outside the Social Security clique to take a hard look at the program. Ross had a broad government background in tax policy at Treasury, on the Johnson White House staff, and as general counsel of the Transportation Department, but his specialty was taxes and he had begun to turn his fresh mind to the Social Security tax system.

"If you want to support the program, why don't you speak out for it?" Cohen almost spit the words at Ross.

"He has, on many occasions," I said and then tried to move the conversation back to the proposed changes. I described how we wanted to remove the payments for post–secondary school students who were dependents of survivors, over a four-year period, so that no present student would lose benefits. That benefit had been placed in the Social Security law in 1965, before we had such a comprehensive student aid program of grants and low interest loans, and now cost $2.1 billion each year. I mentioned the complications of having so many different student aid programs, and the General Accounting Office charge that as much as $500 million per year was spent in the Social Security student aid program without verifying eligibility.

Cohen was calmed for the moment. He agreed with the goal of administrating student aid programs better. But just as I thought the meeting might become more equable, his face flushed again. "When I heard about this, I thought you were just using an idea from the Ford administration to protect your other programs. But you're serious!" Cohen paused, then standing behind the couch to my left, he pointed his finger out repeatedly as he shouted, "Joe, if you go forward with this, I will organize every educational institution in this country against HEW."

The discussion of our proposal to eliminate the lump-sum death benefit of $255, while providing funds to the poor through the SSI program, also drew their ire. When I pointed out that the $255 of 1954 was worth less than $100 in 1978, Bob Ball said, "That's why I favor increasing it to $1,000."

"Then the funeral parlors and burial services would get $1,000 instead of $255 off the top," I snapped. I thought to myself, as Ball spoke, that he, Cohen, and Cruikshank were still thinking of expanding benefits, while Champion, Ross, and I were pressing to hold the existing benefits in place, trim away the fat, and run the program more tightly. "Bob, the only expansion of benefits will be the automatic increases as the cost of living goes up. That eats up billions each year. There's no money for further expansion of Social Security."

"If you need more funds," Ball said, "tax Social Security benefits and put the revenues in the trust funds." I did not feel free to say that I had already recommended that to the President, so I simply indicated I was giving it some thought.

Wilbur Cohen again stood up, lecturing me. "You do not even defend the taxes that are already passed."

"That's not true," I said. "I have defended the nineteen-seventy-seven taxes and opposed reducing them, despite all the pressure on the Hill. But you cannot consider the Social Security tax in isolation. It relates to other taxes, to inflation. There's a limit to how much tax people will pay."

"But you have prepared tax reduction proposals," he insisted.

"Only as a contingency. If there's going to be a reduction, we want an intelligent one. If the President or the Congress wants to reduce the nineteen-eighty-one tax, it should be done in a way that makes sense."

Cohen threw his arms up in exasperation. "We talked to the President. He doesn't know much about your changes."

"I have briefed him in detail," I replied. But all three made it clear that they had left the presidential meeting with the distinct impression that Carter was not familiar with my proposals in any depth—a posture I concluded he assumed because the three of them were so opposed to my suggestions. It was a posture I did not have the luxury of taking.

"Your heart is not in the Social Security program." Cohen's eyes were glassy as his voice rose.

"It's not a question just of heart." I softened my own voice now out of concern. "We differ on how to preserve the program."

"You're trying to dismantle it. You never speak up for the program," Cohen charged, moving sideways and back and forth on the balls of his feet like a fighter ready to uncork a barrage of jabs. "If you propose these changes, I'm going to organize all the senior citizens groups to picket you wherever you speak. Wherever you go, they'll be there picketing you."

"I talk repeatedly about the program. I call it a great program. But I've also got to educate the American people about its problems as well as its benefits," I said, "and to make it clear that with so many unsatisfied public needs, government should target help where it's most needed."

Cohen was still standing, his face florid, his whole being shaking with rage. "You do not believe in the Social Security program; you never try and get good press for it. Instead of talking so much about smoking, you ought to be talking about what a great thing Social Security is for this country. You ought to be defending it and building up confidence in it. These changes will destroy it."

Cruikshank agreed heatedly. I started to respond, then hesitated. It was 8:30 P.M. on the last working day before Christmas. I was tired. I decided to end the meeting before I said something I would later regret.

I dropped the proposal to increase the retirement eligibility age from sixty-two to sixty-five, and Carter eventually decided to accept all the other recommended reforms. He briefly considered reducing the coming increases in Social Security taxes, but chose instead to lower the deficit, and cling to the hope of balancing the budget in fiscal 1981.

The press briefing on the 1980 budget was set for Saturday, January 20, 1979. McIntyre, Schultze, and Blumenthal summarized in the morning. The departments gave the details of their proposals in the afternoon. The President called me an hour before I was scheduled to brief. "I'm concerned about the proposed cuts in Social Security," he said. "I want you to keep me as far away from them as you can."

"But they're in your budget message. They're a major part of your program."

"When you brief on them, say they're your proposals," Carter insisted.

"Of course," I said, disappointed, but understanding his desire for some political protection and my own responsibility to provide it.

The President then talked about his political problems with Nelson Cruikshank. "Cruikshank is very much opposed to these proposals. But if you say you're going to refer them to the Social Security Advisory Committee, I think that we can handle him."

"But they're going to the Congress," I pointed out.

"Can't you send them to the Advisory Committee at the same time? Congress won't get to them for a while," Carter said.

"All except the disability proposals," I agreed. "The committees are ready to move on those."

I followed the President's instructions. One of the last questions of the briefing, from Spencer Rich of the *Washington Post,* referred to attacks Wilbur Cohen had begun on the proposals and on me. In my response, I said, "Wilbur Cohen . . . has done a great deal for this country, and has a great deal more to do. . . . [Though we disagree on this one] Wilbur Cohen and I will be fighting more battles together [for social justice], as we have in the past. . . ."

By Monday, January 22, the HEW press office was getting calls, based on leaks from the White House, that the President had doubts about the changes I was pushing in the Social Security program, and that was why he had told me to refer them to the Social Security Advisory Committee.

Then, on January 24th, Carter called. "Cruikshank is threatening to resign as my Counselor on Aging unless he can speak out publicly against the Social Security reduction proposals."

"I don't see how you can run your government and let a presidential aide attack the President's proposals," I responded.

"Hamilton [Jordan] is concerned that if Cruikshank quits, he will organize all the senior citizens groups against us," Carter said.

"Can't he just stay on and keep quiet? Just not support the proposals actively?" I suggested, seeking to salvage the situation.

"I tried that. But Cruikshank wants to oppose them publicly," Carter said.

"Mr. President, it demonstrates a severe lack of discipline in your administration. You made those proposals after hearing Cruikshank out at length, along with Ball and Cohen." I sensed I was not making any headway, so I tried another argument. "A sharp contrast will be made between letting Cruikshank stay and attack your proposals, and your firing Bella Abzug, a woman, for criticizing your programs as inadequate in terms of women's rights."

"I think just the opposite, Joe." Carter had already considered it. "I don't want to have both an Abzug incident and a Cruikshank incident in the same week. I hope you'll be able to live with this if I decide to let him stay on and speak out."

"It won't be easy. But it's your administration," I said softly.

The President decided to let Cruikshank stay. Within a few days, Florida Congressman Claude Pepper called a special hearing before the House Select Committee on Aging he chaired. I called Eizenstat and told him Cruikshank was scheduled to be the lead-off witness in a day of hearings that would attack the proposals. The night before the hearing,

Eizenstat tried to soften Cruikshank's testimony, but Cruikshank said the President had assured him he could speak out. When Eizenstat reported this to me, I said, "We've been sandbagged." Carter wanted it both ways, I thought as I hung up. It was so important to him to hold the senior citizens groups that he would risk the knocks from the women and more charges that he was a weak President.

On February 7, 1979, Cruikshank delivered a stinging attack on the Social Security proposals before the Committee on Aging. "In my view, reducing benefits on a budgetary consideration represents a breach of faith between the government and the millions of Social Security contributors and could go a long way toward eroding the confidence people have in their government." Cohen and Ball testified along the same lines.

Cohen also organized SOS—Save Our Security—to picket me and pressure the Congress. The first picketing occurred when I addressed the Consumer Federation of America Assembly at the Capital Hilton on Sixteenth Street in downtown Washington. As I emerged, about fifty senior citizens were picketing. I went over and talked to them. Some asked for my autograph; one kissed me on the cheek after she had a friend take her picture with me. It was the only time SOS picketed me.

On January 26, in a nationally televised press conference, Carter responded to a question on the Social Security proposals: "This is not a politically popular proposal . . . but in the long run, we have got to make sure that, within the limited Social Security funding, which is derived from those who are working now, that the allocation of funds goes to those who need it most, who don't have any other way to derive benefits. And with a limited amount of money, it is imperative that the system be efficient and that benefits go where they are most needed." That was Carter's only defense of his Social Security proposals after the budget and written report on the State of the Union went to the Congress. Except for the overhaul of the disability system, the proposals for reform of the Social Security system were abandoned. Within days of their announcement, Mondale (who had opposed all reductions in benefits) told me he thought the Social Security proposals were "the worst political mistake in the 1980 budget and legislative program." The Congress apparently agreed: Except for disability reform, we couldn't get anyone in either house to introduce our proposals.

WHATEVER THE short-term politics of Social Security and aging in America, we must face the fact that the nation is at the dawn of a four-generation society. Great-grandparents are becoming a common phenomenon, and we will soon see many families with two generations on Social Security at the same time. The aging of the American population must be brought into political focus if we hope to have a timely consideration of its economic ramifications.

Phenomenal advances in medical technology, increasing life expectancies, a declining proportion of workers to retirees, the pincer combination of high inflation and persistent unemployment, the cultural revolution in the roles of the sexes, and the multigeneration family have combined to subject all our social systems for the elderly to enormous tensions. Social Security is the most visibly expensive—likely to top $200 billion by 1983—but our nursing homes, outpatient care, and hospital and medical facilities also generate staggering public costs, at least another $100 billion a year and perhaps twice that amount.

The proportion of the federal budget spent on programs for the elderly has been rising steeply. In 1980, it was 25 percent; by the turn of the century it will approach 35 percent; and when the senior boom hits in 2025, it will hit about 65 percent. In fiscal 1981, the Department of Health and Human Services will spend about $140 billion of its $225 billion budget on the elderly in Social Security, health care, welfare, and social services payments. On top of that, veterans payments, military and civil service pensions, and scores of other federal programs spend billions on the elderly. Those billions will sharply increase as the need for and cost of health care and social services rise.

Life expectancy has increased by more than ten years since 1940. By the year 2030, the proportion of our citizens over sixty-five will have almost doubled, to fifty-five million people. In 1940, only 30 percent of the elderly were over seventy-five; by the end of this century, 45 percent will be over seventy-five. While Americans are living longer, they are retiring earlier: in 1950, nearly one half of men over sixty-five were in the work force; that figure dropped to one in five for men and one in twelve for women in 1978. The ratio of Americans aged twenty to sixty-four to those over sixty-five is undergoing extraordinary change; it was 9 to 1 in 1940, 6 to 1 in 1978, and will be only 3 to 1 in 2030.

To provide a fair Social Security system for our elderly will require additional taxes, reduced benefits for some, or some combination of both. Today, American workers and employers are far better off than those in other industrialized nations; even with the 1981 tax increase, they pay less than 15 percent of payroll for retirement, survivors, and disability Social Security, compared with about 20 percent in Germany, Austria, and Sweden, 25 percent in Italy, and 30 percent in the Netherlands. A lower proportion of our gross national product goes to Social Security and disability insurance payments than that of most industrialized nations. Abroad, the population is graying more rapidly than in the United

States, with some advanced nations already down to two contributors for each beneficiary, while we are at three. Both here and in Europe, the projection and ratios get distinctly less favorable once we reach two decades into the next century. So the burden on pay-as-you-go Social Security and retirement systems is a phenomenon that will test the economies and political will of all the industrialized world.

The strain on our country's pensions is already revealing serious weaknesses. The Social Security system dominates the pension landscape, not simply in size, but in reliability. Unlike most employer pension plans, it covers nearly the entire population. It provides more effective protection against inflation than private pension plans or savings. The Supplemental Security Income program is also larger than most people realize: in 1980, it reached 2.3 million aged beneficiaries, more than 75 percent of whom also received Social Security.

There are more than 40 different retirement plans in the federal government, more than 6,600 state and local pension plans, and thousands of private plans. Jointly, these pension plans in 1980 paid out close to $70 billion in benefits to more than 51 million people. Almost 50 percent of all new Social Security retirees have other pension income. These pension plans vary widely in contributions, benefits and financing, and they are subject to a maze of sometimes inconsistent legal, regulatory and tax treatments.

Most public pension plans are indexed in some way to inflation; most private ones are not. A federal worker who retired at $25,000 per year in 1970 received a $35,000 pension in 1980; a private employee retiring at $25,000 in 1970 under a typical corporate pension plan had no change, and his pension, including Social Security, was worth only $19,000 in 1980.

The incoherent array of pensions in an era of limited resources, the pressures of inflation, and the increase in unfunded pension liabilities threaten to turn the dream of a secure retirement into a terrifying nightmare of anxiety and even poverty for millions of American senior citizens. In 1980, federal pension plans had unfunded liabilities of between $500 billion and $650 billion. For state and local pension plans, the estimated unfunded liability is between $150 billion and $350 billion. The estimate for private plans is conservatively set at $300 billion. Together, these unfunded liabilities exceed the national debt of some $1 trillion. In 1980, at least six of the largest industrial corporations in America had unfunded pension liabilities equal to a third or more of their net worth; at least seven had unfunded liabilities in excess of the aggregate market value of their common stock. The relationship among the patchwork pension systems, public and private, must be reexamined and restructured if we are to fulfill the obligation that social justice imposes on a society to take care of all its elderly, and particularly those in most need.

The Social Security system is already especially attentive to the neediest elderly. The ratio between prior earnings subject to tax and benefits received is not fixed: on average, it is close to 50 percent, but for low-income workers, the ratio is 64 percent. This is a key strategy for ensuring that we do not leave old people in abject poverty. Without this tilt toward the low-income earners, the number of older Americans in 1979 with income below the poverty line would have more than tripled. Due largely to Social Security, over the last twenty years the fraction of the elderly living below the poverty line has fallen from more than one in three to one in seven. Yet, even today about one-quarter of our senior citizens are either poor or near poor.

Social Security alone cannot do the job of providing an adequate income to the retired. Private pensions now cover about half the private work force, but they are not rationally integrated with Social Security and they are not adequately related to goals of social justice. With tax breaks accorded private pension plans approaching $18 billion in fiscal 1980, and growing rapidly, it seems fair to ask that these plans be keyed to some overall social objectives.

Public pension plans should also be integrated with Social Security. About 45 percent of civil service retirees receive Social Security in addition to their federal pensions, and many receive another pension as well. When workers move in and out of different jobs, many obtain a handsome combination of pensions and Social Security; others fail to qualify for substantial benefits either under pension plans or Social Security. Income maintenance policy for the elderly should not be a game with complex rules, winners who get windfalls, and losers who get nothing; it should be a rational system meeting definable human needs.

Furthermore, any integration of public and private pension systems with Social Security must devote careful attention to the treatment of women in the Social Security system. On February 15, 1979, I sent to Congress a report on the changing roles of men and women and how they affect the Social Security system. The report demonstrated that the Social Security system discriminates against women. For example: if women take time out from paid work to bear and raise children, they unfairly lose protection against disability and receive reduced Social Security protection when they reach retirement age. Couples in which both spouses work receive less from Social Security than those in which only the husband works, even if they have identical total earnings. There are no benefits for children of deceased homemakers. The discrimination against women was not deliberately crafted into the system. But it must be eliminated as a social, legal, moral, and political anachronism. And it will cost money to do equity here.

Finally, we should rethink our concepts of old age and retirement. At present, we operate with two distinct concepts of retirement. The more traditional concept is as support for workers who have reached old age and can no longer work. The second views retirement as a reward not necessarily related to old age, but rather for a certain period of work, typically twenty to thirty years. In the military, for example, a pension is available after only twenty years of service, regardless of age. Workers in the Federal Civil Service, and in many state and local governments, can retire on full pension at age fifty-five with thirty years of service. Social Security is now available on a reduced basis, at age sixty-two. Many pension plans provide benefits at that age or earlier, with no reduction in benefits. In 1980, the federal government paid almost $15 billion in retirement benefits to persons under sixty-five. Clearly, this concept of retirement is expensive. It was born of choices that affluence without inflation offered in past years. It is time to re-examine the existing incentives for early retirement. We should explore new kinds of work arrangements that might accommodate greater numbers of older Americans in the work force, such as phased retirement and increased part-time work. Older workers can contribute to economic growth, enhance their purchasing power, and help create a need for more jobs for younger workers, rather than replace them.

These concerns about financing retirement are critical, but they are only part of the challenge older Americans pose. Our health care, housing, transportation, and social service systems will also be under enormous tension and will call for imaginative restructuring to accommodate the graying of our nation. Solutions will not come easily—or cheaply. The long-term care problems of the elderly short of hospitalization demand such enormous expenditures that neither the Kennedy nor the Carter national health plans dared attempt to provide such coverage. But, like the retirement income issues, we must confront these problems squarely. A key test of the moral fiber of a society is how it treats its elderly.

The time to come to terms with the first four-generation society in history is now. This requires careful planning rather than rhetoric calculated to get the votes of the elderly. To confront the graying of America may demand more political courage than any other domestic issue of the 1980s.

CHAPTER X

COMING APART

THE EARLY months of the Carter administration were charged with hope and expectation, but the anticipated political honeymoon never took shape and the innocence of Carter and his closest aides about governing and Washington provided cause for misgivings. The new President did wade into some tough problems—energy, SALT II, the Panama Canal Treaties, the Middle East, the Third World, welfare and tax reform—and at first his willingness to take them on was itself enough, a refreshing change from the laid-back presidency of Gerald Ford.

Carter also seemed determined to change the ambience of the federal government: to reorganize the bureaucracy more efficiently, reduce paperwork, eliminate irritating and unnecessary regulations, make those who sign regulations read every word of them, get rid of perks such as cars and chauffeurs. He intended to honor all his campaign commitments and the White House staff compiled a book dubbed "Promises, Promises" to keep them on the front burner.

Carter was bent on mastering every detail, and as his reading load increased, he and Rosalynn took a speed reading course on Tuesday nights at the White House and invited any interested members of the

Cabinet to join them. Lyndon Johnson would have said, "Put a welfare reform program together that gives poor people some money and encourages people to work and keep their families together," and left all but the key policy and political judgments to his staff. Carter read hundreds of pages of material on welfare programs and did almost everything but draft the legislation. He displayed the same fervor for total immersion in energy, the African subcontinent, tax reform, and SALT II. In addition to being President, he was, as an HEW staffer remarked after one of my welfare reform briefings, the highest paid assistant secretary for planning that ever put a reform proposal together.

In the beginning, he never let his penchant for detail temper his attempt to fulfill his commitment to Cabinet government. There were weekly Cabinet meetings that first year, and in the early months they were preceded by a prayer breakfast in the White House mess, presided over by Bert Lance with the President's enthusiastic encouragement.

The Cabinet meetings provided an opportunity for the members to get to know each other and to size up the President and seek some physical communion with him. Each member of the Cabinet would give a brief report of departmental activities the past week and a preview of what was coming up. Carter went around the table, one week beginning with Cy Vance on his right, the next going clockwise from Harold Brown on his left. Occasionally, Carter would interject his own comments or suggestions, but usually he waited until each of us had spoken and then told us what was on his mind, large and small: one week emphasizing human rights, deregulation, balancing the budget, or getting more minorities and women in top jobs, the next asking us to keep the weekly reports we sent him each Friday presidentially relevant and short "in the style of the Kiplinger Report" or to set up hot lines for citizen complaints, see our congressional liaison assistants at the start of each day, or get out of Washington and see what the country was really like.

The President displayed occasional flashes of humor. When Robert Strauss, then serving as U.S. Trade Negotiator, noted that he was flying tourist class to Japan for the first time in his life, Carter cracked that he was buying three adjacent seats so he could make them into a bed. When Griffin Bell reported that he was surveying the attorneys throughout the government to see if there were too many, Carter quipped, "Keep the lawyers in the government. That keeps them out of the private sector." When Treasury Under Secretary Robert Carswell said that nothing of substance had transpired at the International Monetary Fund meeting during the previous week, Carter teasingly asked, "You're including my remarks?"

In late March 1977, Carter pronounced the weekly Cabinet meetings "extremely useful" to him. Though he was not shaping a team out of the individual players and it was not his style to give orders crisply, I thought the meetings had provided an important opportunity for Cabinet members to get a sense of each other's problems and personalities. The jobs are so consuming that all of us were quickly preoccupied with our own concerns and we rarely worked closely together. Indeed, while HEW Secretary I was so immersed in information and issues relating to health, education, welfare, Social Security, human services, and civil rights, that I was less informed about all other public policy matters than I had been in private law practice.

The meetings were no forum in which to make decisions, and with some notable exceptions, such as the dispute over *Bakke,* comments were tempered, and tough problems were reserved for discussion in smaller groups with the President. The reports of individual Cabinet members soon took on a "show and tell" atmosphere, and Carter began to display some boredom. As programs faltered on Capitol Hill and the Carter staff began to realize that the image of a "can-do" President was getting tarnished, the search for scapegoats began, as did the unfortunate, anonymous attacks in the press. Initially, Carter appeared genuinely concerned, although he never seemed to fully appreciate how damaging to the morale and coherence of his administration these stories were. At the August 29, 1977, Cabinet meeting, Carter expressed considerable irritation at an "inaccurate and utterly baseless" *Chicago Tribune* article, reportedly from an anonymous White House source, which was highly critical of the Cabinet's performance. "If I ever have the slightest concern about the performance of a Cabinet member, I will talk to him—or her—directly." Noting that "The Washington news scene is grossly unrepresentative of the rest of the country," he insisted that such stories were "completely fabricated," that he had "never said a single word of criticism about any Cabinet member." Moreover, if anyone on his staff did, and he could find out who it was, he would "fire them."

Despite Carter's outburst, anonymous White House criticism of the Cabinet continued. At the October 17, 1977, Cabinet meeting, the President knocked down an Evans and Novak column which "falsely attributed some comments to Hamilton Jordan about the Cabinet." Carter added that it was "completely fabricated, pitiful. Something should be done about it. How to deal with news people who have no integrity escapes me." The President found it necessary once again to affirm his "profound respect and appreciation" for each member of the Cabinet. He asked them to pay no attention to totally inaccurate press articles purporting to reflect his criticism of some of them. "I have never criticized any Cabinet member in public or in private. I will fire any member of my staff who is ever identified as a source of the kind of inaccurate rumors, back-biting, and malicious gossip that have been reported in the press concerning my relationship with the Cabinet.'' He repeated that if he ever had a problem with a Cabinet member's performance, he would communicate directly with that member. Juanita Kreps said, with apparent sincerity, that the Cabinet knew the stories caused the President more pain than they caused any member of his Cabinet. Perhaps, I thought; certainly Carter had been more than generous in talking to me about my performance, but it was possible that the stories were substantially accurate reflections of Carter's angry comments about some Cabinet members, and other White House staffers said privately that they had heard Jordan make the quoted statements.

As his first year in office ended, Carter was in trouble as both executive and leader. His administration lacked cohesion. The Office of Management and Budget and its new Director, James McIntyre, floundered along a conservative course while Eizenstat and the Domestic Policy Council steered toward a liberal one. Zbigniew Brzezinski sniped at Cyrus Vance in the press, and Jordan and Powell continued to cut up several Cabinet members anonymously, Mike Blumenthal being their favorite target. Most Cabinet officers and department heads tried to read what Carter wanted and sought to serve him and his administration, each in his own way. Excepting Stu Eizenstat and Jack Watson, they had little respect for the Carter staff and no clear sense of where the President was leading them. At the same time, there was a real decline in public confidence. You could measure it not only by polls, but every time we left Washington people were anxious to tell us about it. Political leaders around the country had begun to ridicule the ''governor from Georgia.'' ''The job is too big for him,'' was what most business and labor leaders told us.

Things were even worse on Capitol Hill. House Speaker Tip O'Neill had been insulted by the arrogance of the Georgians in the early days. Ineptness in handling appointments and making announcements, in introducing and pushing legislation had alienated many key Democrats. The administration's initiatives were failing. Congress was questioning the energy program that the President had called the ''moral equivalent of war,'' and was angry about Carter's attempt to block Western water projects.

The dollar was at an all-time low. In January 1978, at a Cabinet meeting, Mike Blumenthal told us we were ''bluffing with a pair of jacks. If anybody calls us, we are in trouble.'' With no action on energy, he was concerned about the ''risk of real financial panic.'' Commerce Secretary

Juanita Kreps agreed that "we should be very much concerned about a financial panic" because of the dollar's instability, the international money markets, and the falling stock market.

The President seemed somehow oblivious to the fears his lack of leadership was engendering. While Blumenthal warned of a financial panic, Carter told us he had "a sense of euphoria about the White House staff and the Cabinet. There is no one I want to change. I want you all around four years from now." He put down a gloomy *New York Times* poll showing the lack of confidence business had in his administration, citing instead General Motors' favorable public assessment of the administration. At the March 6, 1978, Cabinet meeting, Carter said, "We have a lot of problems, but I do not feel beleaguered. I have confidence in you all." I couldn't tell whether the President believed what he was saying or whether he was trying to raise our spirits. He has, I thought, eventually to deal more candidly with us and himself.

The administration's situation continued to sour, Cabinet officers began to question the value of the weekly meetings, and self-interested leaks and internecine back-biting increased. The President gave the first indication of a desire to do something at a Cabinet meeting on April 10, 1978. He wanted the Cabinet to come to Camp David the next weekend to "think long-range about problems among ourselves, to express criticism freely about the relationship between the White House and your own departments." At last, Carter seemed ready to acknowledge a serious problem in Cabinet–White House staff relations. The number of articles—based on anonymous White House sources—critical of the Cabinet had continued to accumulate. Carter had dismissed them on several occasions, but did so less convincingly as time passed.

The senior White House staff arrived at Camp David early on Sunday afternoon, April 16, and Carter met with them separately. The Cabinet arrived that evening for cocktails and dinner in Laurel Lodge. The next morning, Brock Adams and I played a pleasant game of tennis with Mike Blumenthal and Hamilton Jordan before the Cabinet meeting began at 9:00 A.M. The Cabinet members sat around the long table in the Laurel Lodge conference room, except for Harold Brown and Cy Vance, who were represented by their deputies, Charles Duncan and Warren Christopher. Rosalynn Carter, Charles Kirbo, and Carter's personal secretary, Susan Clough, sat in chairs against the wall. They were the only other persons present as the meeting started.

Carter, casually dressed in a cardigan sweater and sport shirt, sat at the center. He had some notes in front of him. He said he had a good administration, a superb Cabinet, and an excellent White House staff, but he had serious problems. "Pat Caddell's polls show a drop from seventy-three to fifty-eight percent from January to December; and the Gallup and

Harris polls are down to fifty percent." While half the public thinks "we are doing a pretty good job," Carter felt he was doing too many things and clouding the public's mind about his achievements. "I'm especially proud of our effort to bring down unemployment, but we get no credit for it."

Carter thought his progress on international affairs "good. We have turned world opinion around on nonproliferation, made remarkable success in human rights, and unbelievable progress on Panama." It showed, he said, that "even in the most difficult circumstances, when we work as a team we succeed." But he was unhappy with progress at home. "I was not tough enough," he said, on the legislation to create an independent agency for consumer affairs: "We lost a battle that was symbolically significant." With respect to the Western water projects he had tried to kill, the President said tersely: "If I had to do it all over again, I would have vetoed the hell out of the water bill. Roosevelt made it a practice to veto twenty-five to thirty bills a year. I have a sense of partial victory, but also a sense of disappointment because I lost a chance to veto."

He recited several pending administration efforts—SALT, energy, civil service reorganization, welfare reform, national health insurance—and said with just a hint of bitterness, "Contrary to the general public view, neither Roosevelt nor Johnson ever put together a series of proposals that will equal ours." Then, more defensively, he said, "Part of the reason why we are not getting credit is that I do not speak often enough. I intend to set out all my positions in a major presidential speech. I need to do more of that."

Carter paused before turning to internal difficulties. "The problems that we do have I attribute primarily to the White House. Some leaks from the White House are inexcusable—derogatory remarks about Mike [Blumenthal] or Pat [Harris] or Brock [Adams]. If I could find one who did it, I would kick his ass out of the White House." I was incredulous. By now I suspected he had ordered or at least condoned much of it. My God, there is some Elmer Gantry in this born-again President, I thought. Carter then turned briefly to self-criticism. "We have a lack of Washington experience. We need to learn more. Fritz has helped there." The White House was taking too long to fill personnel vacancies; he had built up excessive expectations in the public mind; and he had "overestimated how rapidly Congress would move." His eyes scanned those seated at the table as he returned to his main theme. "There are times when you do not support White House policy; I need your absolute loyalty. When you have hurt me, I think it is because you haven't had strong enough direction. I have no doubt about anybody's loyalty, but you have to demonstrate loyalty."

Carter criticized Bob Bergland first, for conducting an independent negotiation on the Hill to keep the food stamp program in the Agriculture Department, rather than cashing it into the welfare program in HEW. He was annoyed with his friend Attorney General Griffin Bell for taking an administration position on the revision of the criminal code without consulting him. His tone sharpened as he took Treasury Secretary Mike Blumenthal to task for dealing on his own in the New York City financial bailout. "I didn't know about the proposal until after Mike did it. Mike should have given me a call." Then he turned to me. He said he was not informed of the agreement for fiscal relief I made with Senator Moynihan to shake loose the Social Security bill until "after the fact." He expressed even more serious concern about the regulations on abortion funding: The sixty-day period for reporting rape or incest was "too loose. The regulations were different from what I would have done."

Carter complained that federal grants were being announced by Republicans, rather than Democrats. "We are trying to whip Strom Thurmond's ass in South Carolina and seventy-five percent of the announcements in South Carolina are made by Thurmond." He sounded just like John Kennedy and Lyndon Johnson, I thought. At least he realized that it is important to notify congressmen in advance, since they have few opportunities to get favorable coverage in their local papers.

Carter said there were long delays in answering White House mail that was sent around the government for reply. He recited the number of days it took individual departments to respond, and asked us to set up special systems to answer such mail promptly. Turning to politics, he urged everyone to bend over backward to help Democrats. Looking at Blumenthal chewing his cigar, he added, "You have to go the second mile to get more involved in politics."

Carter then turned the meeting over to the Vice-President. Mondale said that some leaks were inevitable in the development of public policy. "But leaks have turned into a tidal wave; everything is in the press, at great expense to all of us." He cited leaks about the neutron bomb, a highly classified cable from Cuba with copies distributed only to five people that the newspapers had quoted verbatim, major domestic policy leaks, and a very confidential Eizenstat memo that was leaked "either to make someone look good or to pressure the President to do something. These particularly candid remarks ought to be kept private. Leaking goes to the whole nature and quality of government. We all have to get much tougher on leaks, not a gestapo or siege mentality, but we have to get much tougher."

Carter approved Mondale's remarks and then asked for comments. Energy Secretary James Schlesinger was first to speak. (Shortly after he began, Hamilton Jordan, Stu Eizenstat, Midge Costanza, Jack Watson,

Frank Moore, and Bob Lipshutz joined the meeting.) Schlesinger agreed with the President about loyalty, and criticized the executive office for not speaking clearly. "The Executive Office of the President must speak clearly and forcefully in the voice of the President." Clearer lines delegating responsibility were needed; it took ten to twelve days for him to get a paper on substance to the President "while it rattled around your staff." Using the nuclear test ban treaty as an example, Schlesinger expressed "deep concern that you are not getting the difficult issues presented to you." He said that Carter spent more time on detail than any President in history. None of us thought it was a wise investment of the President's time and I was delighted that Schlesinger had brought it up so directly. He ended by contrasting Nixon's and Carter's administrations. "This administration's image is less than the sum of its parts; the Nixon administration's image was more than the sum of its parts."

Robert Strauss, Carter's shrewd White House political handyman, spoke next. Picking up on Schlesinger's concern with image, he said, "The overall problem is a very serious one. No one is for us—not business, not labor, not politicians, not big unions. Only the National Education Association is for us. We deserve better than that. We have positioned ourselves poorly on a lot of issues. We have to do more things to get people for us—make an attack on the federal bureaucracy. The American public wants to see that attack made."

Attorney General Griffin Bell said he had already conducted several investigations of leaks "very carefully through the Office of Professional Responsibility." He agreed with Carter and Mondale that "leaks are killing you, but it's leaks in the White House, not the departments." As to confusion in the public mind, Bell said that most lower-level White House staffers can be traced to specific interest groups, and "that is part of why there is such an indecisive appearance."

Brzezinski said that leaks were inevitable so long as "any middle level official can give interviews." The major image problem Brzezinski saw was that "the historical profile of the administration was not clear." As to the public mood, Brzezinski believed that "like Eisenhower, Carter faced a society that was tired and conservative and wanted to pull back."

As though Strauss's suggestion had just sunk in, Carter interjected some criticism of the federal bureaucracy, its "disloyalty and distrust," and complained that he could "get nothing through Congress." He then said he had been reading Robert Donovan's book on Harry Truman, and urged us to do so.

Pat Harris said the problem between the Cabinet and the White House staff was the "we all–you all mentality." She was shocked to hear White House staffers say, "I represent the President of the United

States.'' Looking right at Carter, she said, "I feel I represent only you.'' Harris thought that leaks were designed to discredit people as well as to curry favor: "An anonymous attack out of the White House makes it difficult to get things done.''

Blumenthal agreed. We had to recognize, he said, that we were "all one team.'' His gray face souring, he continued, "The most serious leaks from the White House are about Cabinet officers, and they make Cabinet officers impotent.'' He noted that leaks were used constantly against people who gave advice others did not like. "Simply because we give advice that people don't like, we can't have our loyalty questioned.''

He called attention to the simultaneous pursuit both of national health insurance *and* a tight budget to fight inflation as an example of the administration's confusion.

Carter interrupted somewhat impatiently, "I have a commitment to the United Auto Workers, and I intend to keep that commitment.''

Blumenthal let the President's interruption pass. Instead, responding to Carter's earlier admonition "to go the second mile to get more involved in politics,'' Blumenthal objected strenuously to the idea of political activities by the Secretary of the Treasury, whose position he compared to those of State and Defense.

Strauss could not restrain himself. "The Secretaries of Treasury, State, and Defense are three of the most influential members of the Cabinet. They are not free from politics. Look at Henry Morgenthau. Look at George Shultz, Bill Simon and John Connally. We sure have to give President Ford credit for one thing: He kept his Cabinet in line.'' The acid scowl on Blumenthal's face only hinted at the animosity that had developed between him and Strauss.

Bergland urged the President to be "a bit imperial. The time has come to crack some political heads. You're not breaking enough arms.''

Kreps, in her own softly sardonic tone, said, "The Cabinet meetings are fairly useless.'' If they continued, Cabinet meetings should be less frequent and the President should use them to set forth priorities and provide direction. As for image, Kreps believed we needed "a name, today's equivalent of a 'Great Society.' '' Glancing disdainfully at Blumenthal and then looking at Carter, she said firmly, "I think the domestic goals are clear: more jobs and less inflation.''

Labor Secretary Ray Marshall said that he thought the administration did have a theme—"Responsive and Responsible.'' He did, however, believe that we needed a better sense of priorities.

It was my turn. I told Carter that there was a lack of trust between the Cabinet and the White House staff and that the leaks presented a very serious problem. "Under any circumstances it is hard for you to get candid advice. It is particularly difficult, perhaps impossible, where Cabinet officers or others fear that what they tell you will be leaked to the press.'' I cited the example of Secretary of Defense McNamara and Secretary of State Dean Rusk during the Kennedy-Johnson years. Early in the Kennedy administration, McNamara and Rusk decided they would not present candid controversial advice to President Kennedy in large groups because of the leaks. After National Security Council meetings, McNamara and Rusk would go alone to the Oval Office with Kennedy or Johnson. ''As good and as fine as those men were, from the President's point of view, their advice was not tested on the spot in a larger forum.'' I echoed Strauss's theme that we were an administration without friends in business, labor, or Congress. And I said, ''We need a major legislative victory.''

Carter then turned to Hamilton Jordan, who replied, ''The mood of the country is passive and nonpartisan. Americans want better government, not more government. That is why Carter was elected. The people do not want more programs.'' He said there was ''no party loyalty, no discipline within the Congress.'' The administration was dealing with 535 members and thirty or forty interest groups within the Congress itself, as well as ''dozens and dozens'' of other pressure groups. ''We are not tough; we are not in charge; we are not managing the mechanisms of government. If this persists for three or four months, it will be irreversible. The worst thing is for [the Congress] to lose respect for us as politicians. We do not know how to use our resources politically—no rewards, no retributions. We need a system for doing better.'' He described himself ''as basically an optimist,'' but said, ''We must move in the next four or five months or we cannot govern. We need successes.'' Jordan thought civil service reform was a candidate because it was ''such good politics.''

Carter, looking suddenly tired, said he felt ''like the referee between the Cabinet and the White House staff.'' At his meeting with the White House staff the day before, many ''statements and insinuations were made that the Cabinet goes behind our back. Ninety percent of those could be resolved by thrashing issues out.'' He said we did not know Jody and Ham well enough, that we should meet with them on a Saturday morning. I wondered if he knew that Jordan never returned phone calls from most of us. Carter went on in a monotone, ''If Ham or Stu or Jack calls on my behalf, take their word as coming directly from me. You have been overly reluctant to respond when the White House staff calls you.''

As Charlie Schultze was saying that Carter was not ''tough enough on us,'' I recalled how Lyndon Johnson told the Cabinet, when I was his aide working on the legislative program, ''When Joe speaks, that's my voice you hear,'' and how he had dressed down Labor Secretary Willard Wirtz when Wirtz failed to follow a presidential order relayed by a staff member. Johnson had wanted Wirtz to get a letter to Carl Albert, Majority Leader of the House, so Albert could read it on the floor before a crucial vote. I was away that evening, so he had told my deputy Larry Levinson to pass the message to Wirtz. Wirtz had questioned the ''authority'' on which Levinson was calling. Early the next morning, in the Oval Office, Johnson asked Levinson and me if Wirtz had sent the letter. Levinson didn't know. Johnson hit a button on the green phone on his desk and told the White House operator to ''Get me Willard Wirtz.'' When Wirtz got on the phone, Johnson asked if he had sent the letter. Wirtz said he hadn't been sure the request had come from the President. Johnson blew up. Everyone knew he issued orders to the nearest person, expecting them to be passed along. He shouted into the speaker phone, ''If you get a call from anyone over here, if you get a call from the cleaning woman who mops the floors at three A.M. and she tells you the President wants you to do something, you do it! Now you write that letter and bring it to Albert yourself.'' Johnson hit the button to disconnect as Wirtz was hoarsely saying, ''Yes, Mr. President.''

Carter turned to Eizenstat, who spoke from notes on a legal-size yellow pad. Eizenstat believed we were trying to do ''too much, too fast, too comprehensively, and that we have overloaded the systems.'' I guessed he was repeating what he had said to the White House staff the day before. ''The American system is incremental. Congress can't handle too much at the same time. We are moving too fast, contrary to the mood of the people.'' As for the leaks, ''We are all guilty of that. No person around this table has leaked anything that has hurt anyone else; they all hurt the President.''

Jody Powell warmed to that. ''The Cabinet is not without power to control leaks. Leaks are management problems. We need to make an extra effort to win the loyalty of the people who work for us.'' We had to ''cut down on access and the amount of material given to lower-level people.'' He did not believe the personal sniping was coming from the top. ''What happens is that someone gets angry with someone else and throws a temper tantrum in front of lower-level staff people. We can't afford to let these things drive us apart.'' (So many reporters had told me that the personal sniping from the White House was coming from Powell and Jordan that it was difficult to take his comments seriously.)

Carter then urged us to get rid of congressional relations people who were not doing their jobs. ''[House Appropriations Committee Chairman George] Mahon says he's never seen so many attempts in the departments to circumvent administration budget decisions. Maybe it's because I haven't raised hell about it." The President paused and said slowly, "In the future I intend to come down hard on you. Congress does not think I have control over our own government or that you have control over your own departments."

Jack Watson spoke with sincerity about the need to trust in one another. "The erosion of our loyalty to each other is eroding our loyalty to the President." He said we must leave that room determined to do better and to "get a better sense of each other as people." He leaned forward. "But we must be strong. They do not respect us because we are not using power well; we must punish those who punish us."

Bergland agreed. "There's not enough fear of this administration. If the image of incompetence persists much longer, then it will be set in concrete."

Carter summed up. "The reason we are all up here is because I could see a deterioration of our position and public esteem. I don't disagree with the public's view. What bothers me is the lack of team spirit and cohesion. . . . There are Cabinet officers who do not know what to do in their own departments. The White House staff over this weekend has gotten a better sense of itself. But the growing sense of loyalty on the White House staff is not adequately shared. This is a damn good administration, a good Cabinet, and a fine staff. I want all of you to get to know each other as well as I know each of you personally." Then, with a smile, he concluded, "I'll try to be meaner in the future, so you can see the hard, steely side of me."

We all boarded helicopters to go back to Washington. By and large, the Cabinet members felt it had been a good idea, this short weekend at Camp David. But nothing changed. The Saturday morning meetings with Powell and Jordan never took place. Jordan remained inaccessible; Powell and some others continued to leak stories about Cabinet members they disliked. Legislative relations continued to deteriorate, and key senators and representatives were openly contemptuous of White House liaison Frank Moore and, on occasion, even of the President.

At the April 24, 1978, Cabinet meeting, Carter said that there would be another Camp David meeting in two months, and that the Vice-President was reassessing the administration's priorities. Carter himself was going to "make a complete review of presidential appointees. Any that can't be relied on, let's fire them and get new ones. If you have second thoughts, let's get rid of them; now is the time." He asked for candid written assessments of key departmental personnel. He didn't get unvarnished evaluations from most Cabinet members because they feared Jordan would use them to embarrass anyone he didn't like. Carter had let the sniping and leaks go on too long to get forthright advice about such matters on paper. I responded cautiously in writing, and then talked frankly about shortcomings at HEW when I was alone with the President.

INEXORABLY, THE press became a target. Early in the administration, I had been struck by the difference in attitude toward the press between Carter and Johnson. Johnson gobbled up every printed and televised morsel. Just to his left, as he sat behind his desk in the Oval Office, the Associated Press and United Press International tickers clicked all day. Next to them, three television sets were set for each network so that Johnson could watch all the newscasts simultaneously. In his small private office and his bedroom in the mansion, three television sets were similarly set, as they were in several of our offices. In order to keep up with Johnson, I had the wire copy delivered to my office periodically throughout the day. I once asked White House Counsel Lee White how he functioned in the instant news world of the Johnson White House without having the wires delivered to him. "Hell," he said, "I've got the greatest ticker reader in the world working for me. He calls immediately if there's anything I need to know."

Carter exhibited none of Johnson's insatiable appetite for the news. Though he was always concerned about unauthorized releases of classified information, in the early days he displayed little animosity toward the Washington press corps. But as leaks and editorial criticism began, his attitude changed. I believe that change in attitude had a particular impact on my relations with the White House. I had been counsel to the *Washington Post* before joining the administration. I had lived through the Watergate experience, representing reporters Bob Woodward and Carl Bernstein, and Richard Cohen when his notes were subpoenaed by Vice-President Spiro Agnew. I had also represented Daniel Schorr during the controversial congressional hearing when he refused to reveal his source of the classified Pike Committee report. Many of my friends were reporters and editors. To be sure, Robert Strauss had recommended me for the Cabinet in good part because he thought I'd give Carter a needed window to the Washington press establishment. But messages and messengers often get confused, and the sense of trust essential to avoid that confusion never developed between Jordan and Powell and me.

The *Post* editors bent over backward to demonstrate their independence of me. Executive Editor Ben Bradlee told a *Chicago Sun-Times* reporter, "We give Califano more shit than anyone else. We are tough on him. You should see some of the pictures we run of him. They're almost always the worst ones, and then they are cropped out there by *Post* staffers to make him look like an idiot." After applauding my appointment, the *Post*'s first editorial comment had attacked my position on abortion.

A month into his administration, Carter had expressed anger and surprise that Bradlee had refused to delay publishing a story that the United States had been paying King Hussein of Jordan $1 million per year for several years. When reporter Bob Woodward checked his story with the White House, the President had offered to meet with Bradlee, if that would help him decide whether to print. Carter argued to Bradlee that publication would damage U.S. interests in the Middle East. He said neither Henry Kissinger nor George Bush had told him about the payments, and he asked Bradlee at least to delay publication a day or two until Cy Vance could personally alert Hussein. Bradlee thought about it, and later told the President that he was going to print the story, but that he would delay it for twenty-four hours. At a Cabinet meeting on February 21, 1977, Carter said he could not understand how Bradlee could publish a story that would hurt the United States. (A year later, at lunch with Rosalynn and Bradlee, Carter said that publication of the story had had no impact on U.S. interests in the Middle East.)

Mondale said it was important to do something about the excessive number of people, particularly in Congress, who know about things like this. The President said he would like to see a law that makes publication of national security information a felony, adding, "Some congressman who is drunk or nuts can do this." Two weeks later, he returned to this concern: "We have to reduce the number of members of Congress who have access to intelligence data."

Much of the President's criticism was leveled at television. Carter began the January 9, 1978, Cabinet meeting by reporting his extensive foreign trip, covered, he said sarcastically, "by our foremost diplomatic reporter, Barbara Walters." He complained that the press had overemphasized the incident in which the interpreter had translated Carter's statement that "I have come to understand your desires for the future" in Polish words that meant "I desire you carnally" or "I lust after the Poles." (Brzezinski expressed the "strong suspicion that the Poles deliberately stressed the goof of the translator to embarrass the President," and effectively manipulated the American press.) When Carter returned from Panama in June, he said his trip was "beautiful, the largest crowd I've ever seen supporting us. The news reports did not do it justice. They always cover the irresponsible and the radical." Meanwhile, at the March 6, 1978, Cabinet meeting, Carter was distraught over the coal strike and the need to enforce the law. He blistered the television coverage for encouraging defiance. "It was absolutely irresponsible media coverage I watched last night. They interviewed nine or ten miners—and instead of commentators and reporters pointing out the needs of the country, they singled out miners who would defy the law, who said this contract was worse than their old one."

Still, the Washington press corps was his favorite mark. At the August 1, 1977, Cabinet meeting, when Juanita Kreps had complained that a *New York Times* story by James Wooten inaccurately reported that no money was reaching farmers under the administration's drought program when "in fact we are distributing funds according to schedule," Carter suggested issuing a press release to attack and correct the inaccurate story. He urged us to get on the Sunday television interview shows, "to talk directly to the people," not through the Washington press corps.

As Carter's distrust of the press grew, my relations with the *Washington Post* became increasingly suspect. For more than a decade, I had been close friends with *Post* editors Bradlee, Howard Simons, Phil Geyelin, and Meg Greenfield. The *Post*'s publisher, Katharine Graham, had introduced me to my former law partner Edward Bennett Williams. Powell and Jordan appeared to believe that the *Post* would write what I wanted.

One late Sunday afternoon, November 6, 1977, Jody Powell tested that theory. He called me at home. Had I read *Post* Style Section reporter Sally Quinn's story on Susan Clough? I had not. Powell said the President was "very distressed" about speculation in the story that there were intimate relations between Susan Clough and the President, or Susan Clough and himself. I promised to read the story and call him back. When I called him back, I said I thought he was overreacting. Powell cited a quote from Clough, responding to Quinn's suggestions of staff insinuations about Clough and Carter. "I don't think Jimmy has ever had an affair with anybody but Rosalynn," Clough had told Quinn. I said Clough's statement flatly denied the insinuation; maybe he or I wouldn't have printed it, but I thought he should forget about the Quinn piece, let it die. Powell wasn't satisfied. "It's an outrage that a reporter can speculate about that kind of thing between the President and his secretary." Powell thought "someone who knew Katharine Graham should talk to her about it." I tried to dissuade him, observing that a conversation with the *Post* would heighten, not lessen, any impressions that might be between the lines, and any conversation would probably be considered on the record. Powell still was not satisfied. "Surely *you* can call Katharine Graham off the record," he said. "As soon as I do, she'll have Bradlee call me and that'll all be on the record," I responded. Powell also knew that Bradlee, who later married Quinn, was then living with her. He hung up, then called back a few minutes later, apparently after talking to the President and/or Mrs. Carter. He asked me again to "talk to Mrs. Graham.'' I finally said that if the occasion arose informally, I would mention the story to her.

The President never discussed that incident with me, but his antipathy toward the Washington press continued to grow. Leaks out of Cabinet meetings—where there were usually twenty or more White House staffers and others sitting around the wall—prompted him to stop briefings by Powell's deputy, Rex Granum. ''Granum now simply engages in rumor control,'' Carter said. Jack Anderson had begun occasionally to carry excerpts from Cabinet meeting minutes in his column. After asking Jack Watson to ''review the situation,'' Carter told us to treat minutes of the Cabinet meetings ''with the care that should be given highly classified documents.'' The minutes would be distributed to Cabinet members marked ''for your eyes only,'' he said. ''We've got to stop Jack Anderson putting in his column what's going on at Cabinet meetings.'' He only whetted Anderson's appetite. I was among those from whom the aggressive columnist sought copies thereafter; I refused, but Anderson got them somewhere else.

I first fully sensed the consuming animosity the President harbored for the Washington press corps in a half-hour meeting alone with him on May 1, 1978. He was reflecting on the fact that he had acted in his early months out of ''appalling ignorance'' of Washington. He intended to change that, he said firmly, but he didn't think he could do anything about the press. ''The press has been very unfair, particularly the White House press corps.'' He cited pessimistic and highly critical *Time* and *Newsweek* stories of the previous week, even though, ''I got the second Panama Canal Treaty approved by the Senate and a compromise worked out on the energy legislation.'' Then, in a voice in which despair and bitterness vied, he said: ''There is nothing I know to do about the Washington press corps. I think it will be even more unfair to my successor.'' I had to respond. ''You can't ever stop trying, Mr. President.'' I suggested he see key editors and columnists in small groups in informal settings.

Thereafter, Carter's view of the press began to affect the policy-making process. On May 25, he told the Cabinet of his determination to hold the fiscal 1980 deficit below fiscal 1979's. His budget sessions had ''not been pleasant.'' He asked that we reduce ''confrontation with me and Jim McIntyre on one side and your department on the other. . . . Any conflict becomes a matter of great press attention and that shows weakness in the administration.''

The *Washington Post* was Carter's preeminent target. He told us at the June 5 Cabinet meeting that ''news reports, particularly in the *Post,* about the NATO meetings were abominable. There were no reports of substantial progress, the fifteen-year commitment to strengthen NATO, the agreement to increase our contributions three percent in real dollars." He attacked "a completely erroneous SALT story in the *Washington Post* that made a liar out of Jody by putting the denial in the third paragraph." Brzezinski joined in enthusiastically. "The *Post* is waging a political campaign to influence policy on its front pages." Carter said there were "responsible people on the editorial page, but not on the news pages. There's more and more editorializing on the news pages." When Griffin Bell said that the editors he talked to were having a difficult time controlling young reporters, Carter ignored him. "The *Post* does not report what is important. . . . not a single word about the three basic purposes of NATO. . . . the *Post* had no interest in what we were doing [at the NATO meetings]."

On July 26, 1979, he wrote Bradlee: "Other than a non-headlined notice in an 'On Capitol Hill' column, the *Post* did not even mention the passage of the Trade Act. It was different in 1962. [Then, the success of the Kennedy round of trade negotiations and legislation was widely publicized.] Strauss & the Congress deserve recognition & the Act is very important. A reader, Jimmy Carter."

DURING 1977, Carter rarely discussed partisan politics with the Cabinet. Even his private conversations with those of us in politically sensitive departments, such as Interior Secretary Cecil Andrus, Agriculture Secretary Bob Bergland, and me, were so focused on substantive issues that we exchanged concerns among ourselves about his failure to pay enough attention to the political ramifications of what he was doing. Carter had so compartmentalized policy and politics that the annual budget process seemed to take place in an apolitical vacuum.

The April 1978 Camp David meeting brought a reassessment. Carter intended to use the federal grant announcement process—and the awarding of grants themselves—to help the administration's friends and get votes on such key legislation as the Panama Canal Treaties. In May 1978, he asked each Cabinet member to schedule at least two Democratic campaign appearances a month to help governors, senators, and congressmen up for election.

Carter's stature as President peaked in September of that year with the Camp David accords on the Middle East. The announcement in the East Room with Anwar Sadat and Menachem Begin attending was the high point of the term. The following morning, I wrote Carter: "I have long believed that it is one thing to be elected President and quite another for a man to become President. Yesterday, you decisively became President of this great nation." But even the aura of Camp David wore off and the administration fell back into the inept and confused vacillation that Carter had deplored in April.

It wasn't until February 5, 1979, that Carter began to get serious with us about presidential politics. He adjourned the Cabinet meeting that morning at 10:30, and asked all White House staffers to leave so he could talk privately with the Cabinet. I was away, but Hale Champion reported to me when I called in from Texas that afternoon. "The President sent his staff out, announced that he was going to run, but that nothing would be made public until late this year. Fritz will meet privately with members of the Cabinet to go over campaign plans, including fundraising and speeches. Jordan and Tim Kraft will be there, and the meeting will work off Jordan's plan and agenda, but he wants each Cabinet member to bring his own agenda and suggestions."

I asked Champion whether the President had anything specific for us to do. "Each Cabinet member is supposed to look at the constituent groups of his department and suggest how to get closer to them. The President said your Social Security proposals presented the toughest political issue, but that we were right on it and that we have to stress the twelve percent budget increase for the elderly," Champion responded.

"I missed an interesting session," I said.

"You did," Hale agreed, then added, "Oh, yeah, the President does not plan any changes in the Cabinet; he intends to work with you all. He said he 'wants this group to stay together into the second term.' "

"Is that it?" I asked.

"Just about," Hale said, then chuckled. "Anyone concerned about possible improprieties in campaign activities should talk to the President directly. I think that was for Blumenthal."

Fritz Mondale held the campaign-planning meeting over dinner at his Naval Observatory home on March 6, 1979. In addition to the Cabinet, Hamilton Jordan, Jody Powell, and Tim Kraft were there. After cocktails, we ate at several round tables. I was seated at Mondale's left. After dinner, he introduced Hamilton Jordan.

Standing in a corner of the dining room, Jordan said he expected Carter's re-election attempt to be "strongly contested within the party." He thought Ford "lost the general election because he ran a poor primary campaign." Jordan said that Reagan thought Ford "vulnerable" and that Ford did a "poor job on fundraising." He then talked about Carter. "We are well aware that Carter almost lost the general election. We all have to get over the myth about the incumbent President getting re-elected. Truman withdrew in fifty-two. Johnson withdrew in sixty-eight." For as long as possible, Jordan said, Carter would assume the "public posture of noncandidate." This was essential because of the bipartisan support we needed in the Congress. An exploratory committee would be formed late in the year. "The election," he said, "will be decided in the first half dozen, or at most ten, states that hold caucuses and primaries." The key states he listed included Iowa, New Hampshire, Massachusetts, and Florida. He wanted the Cabinet to begin appearing in those states.

Tim Kraft said that each Cabinet officer would be asked to speak at least once a month for the White House, and that each should give a travel schedule to the White House so that political events could be worked in around departmental business. When a Cabinet officer was in a particular city on departmental business, he or she would stay a couple of hours and do an event to help raise money for the Carter campaign.

Blumenthal muttered, "I don't think the Secretary of Treasury should raise money for the campaign." Juanita Kreps, seated at the same table, said in a whisper that was meant to carry, "I never heard such nonsense."

Powell said we needed a "relationship of support to one another," and that "we should defend each other with the press and defend and promote the Carter administration policies. We do not have to take the crap we've been taking." Powell's comments brought a shower of replies from Pat Harris, Blumenthal, and others—saying the White House should be supporting, instead of anonymously criticizing, the Cabinet in the press. I was about to join the chorus, but Mondale placed his left hand on my arm to restrain me.

Then the Vice-President spoke to cool the atmosphere, saying it was important for us to be much more political than we had been in the past. Kraft said, "I can't recall an editorial ever knocking us for being too harsh politically." Strauss said, "Amen," and urged that we begin taking the Congress on publicly. Griffin Bell said that we should put some praise for the President in every speech we give.

Almost everyone left the dinner promptly, but Cy Vance and I stayed for a nightcap with Mondale. We talked about how difficult this campaign was going to be.

Events continued to deteriorate. In the spring of 1979, the government's index of leading economic indicators declined 3.3 percent, the steepest drop since the 1974 recession. Inflation hovered at 14 percent; housing starts were flat. The Congress refused to respond to Carter's requests for energy, hospital-cost containment, and tax reform legislation. The President continued to sink in the polls.

Within the administration, it was becoming increasingly difficult to get anything done. With the exception of his deputy, John White, OMB Director Jim McIntyre had not been able to attract much talent to his staff or to lead the career talent that was there, and OMB declined to its lowest level of competence and effectiveness in recent years. The economic situation defied our best brains, and Carter himself wavered inconsistently on economic and domestic policy. I was so frustrated myself that in mid-March I asked a friend and wise colleague from the Johnson years, Harry McPherson, to come by for lunch. I spoke to him about my concern that it was becoming impossible to get anything done and bewailed the vast chasm between Carter and the Congress. After discussing the question of whether I should leave the administration, McPherson and I agreed that to leave when Carter was so down would be like abandoning a scuttled boat. I knew that was right and put all thought of departing early out of my head after our March 14 lunch. As Eileen Shanahan, FDA Commissioner Don Kennedy, and Hale Champion told me they were leaving HEW, I called Jim Gaither back in from San Francisco. We went over all vacancies and needs for additional strength to support incumbent appointees. With Peter Bell, we set up a plan to staff the department for the rest of Carter's term.

To add to Carter's troubles, on March 28 the accident at the Three Mile Island nuclear power plant occurred, setting off vocal anti-nuclear-power forces in the country. At HEW, where we were already leading a comprehensive study of low-level radiation, we were deeply concerned about radiation effects and the lack of coordination on this subject within the government. The Nuclear Regulatory Commission was going its own way, trying to ignore our concerns at HEW and those of Doug Costle at the Environmental Protection Agency. I called Carter and urged him to designate someone on the White House staff to fill the vacuum. He chose Jack Watson.

Admidst the uncertainty of the impact of the accident, Senator Edward Kennedy pressed to hold hearings before his Health Subcommittee on Saturday afternoon, March 31. I told his aide Larry Horowitz that we were too busy watching the unpredictable situation to testify. Watson talked to Kennedy and Kennedy promised not to hold the hearing on March 31 if the administration committed to give him first crack at Environmental Protection Agency Administrator Doug Costle, Nuclear Energy Commissioner Chairman Joseph Hendrie, and me. Watson agreed.

Press coverage of the accident was saturating, and Carter did not like it. At the April 2 Cabinet meeting, he acknowledged that this was "a very emotional issue," but said news reports were "grossly inaccurate and exaggerated. . . . They'll use any scientist. It's disgusting." The President criticized scientists for making "irresponsible statements. . . . It was a serious incident, but the scare statements have been overly publicized." He noted that nuclear reactors had never caused a fatality or a serious injury. "I was in the control room at Three Mile Island, a hundred feet from the reactor, and I got one-third of the radiation a passenger gets in a flight from New York to Los Angeles." He was concerned that "the nuclear industry had been severely damaged by this incident."

Kennedy held his hearings on April 4. My testimony was uneventful. However, on Thursday, May 3, before the Senate Subcommittee on Energy, Nuclear Proliferation, and Federal Services, chaired by John Glenn, the testimony I gave turned out to be controversial and disturbing to Carter. Drawing on our knowledge immediately after the accident, I had told Kennedy's Health Subcommittee that we did not anticipate any additional deaths from cancer as a result of the Three Mile Island accident. By the time I testified before Glenn's subcommittee, we had more data, and we projected that, within a radius of fifty miles, where 325,000 people were destined to die of cancer without the accident, the accident would cause one additional death. I also indicated that some scientists thought as many as ten additional cancer deaths could result, but I emphasized that those scientists were distinctly in the minority.

The statement about one additional cancer death appeared on all television evening news networks and the front pages of virtually all Friday newspapers. I was surprised, because in order to get a statistic of even one additional death, we had had to extend to a radius of fifty miles and a population of two million people.

The President was on a weekend trip to Iowa and California when the stories about my testimony broke. Jody Powell called on Saturday morning to say the President was incensed to have been caught by surprise in this way, and when he was in California. I acknowledged that I should have notified the White House, but said I had not expected my testimony to get so much coverage. I told him I would have a chance to place it in perspective, as I was taping *Issues and Answers* before leaving with Mrs. Carter in the evening for the World Health Assembly in Geneva. Powell said Carter would be calling me.

I was preparing to leave for Andrews Air Force Base to join Mrs. Carter when the President called. He wanted to talk about two things: First, he wanted to alert me to "Rosalynn's concern about anti-nuclear-power groups, North Carolina, and other political issues. She is very partisan for me and she is going to talk to you in a way that you will think is pretty tough." Somewhat puzzled, I said I'd be delighted to talk to her. "She is more partisan for me than I am for myself," Carter said, and then added cryptically, "I think so much of you that I want the two of you to get along." He said he had suggested to Rosalynn that she have dinner with me on the plane.

The President said he did not "appreciate being caught by surprise" by my assertion that there would be at least one additional cancer death as a result of the Three Mile Island accident. "It's my mistake," I responded, "not notifying you in advance."

Driving to the airport, I was bewildered about the meeting with Mrs. Carter, but I thought it could be a productive one. The administration was in deep trouble, particularly on the domestic side. We were not working together and the meeting might be an opportunity to talk candidly about this. Rosalynn Carter was a key advisor to Jimmy Carter. She attended any critical meetings, such as the April 1978 Camp David meeting at which the President reassessed the administration with the Cabinet. She had a working lunch with the President every week and was, in Jimmy Carter's own words, "a perfect extension of myself."

I knew from personal experience that Rosalynn Carter could make things move. My initial contacts with her were related to the childhood immunization and mental health programs. She was deeply interested in mental health and had helped get additional funds from the Office of Management and Budget. I thought we had worked well together, drafting the legislation to implement the recommendations of the President's Commission on Mental Health which she chaired. We shared a desire to get mental health services into the mainstream of other health care and to eliminate the stigma such services entailed.

I was smiling, recalling Mrs. Carter's spirit and determination, as my car pulled up to the airplane for the flight to Geneva, where she was scheduled to address a special session of the Assembly. She arrived shortly and we sat in her compartment with her press secretary Mary Hoyt, her assistants Madeline McBean and Kathryn Cade, and Amy Carter.

At dinner, I sat opposite Mrs. Carter at a separate table. She first began talking about the nuclear power issue. "This is a very dangerous one for Jimmy." She said she was concerned about the anti-nuclear demonstration scheduled to take place in Washington the following day, starring Jane Fonda, Tom Hayden, and California Governor Jerry Brown. She wondered whether "Jimmy should meet with the demonstrators." I thought it depended on the size and nature of the demonstration. "I think it will be large," she said. (About 65,000 people demonstrated and Carter did meet, on Monday, May 7, the day after the demonstration, with those in charge.) "The nuclear power issue has the potential to turn on the left wing and the young like the anti–Vietnam War movement," she continued.

I doubted it had that kind of appeal. "There is no draft, and that was the biggest thing that turned the young against the war," I said.

She thought for a moment. "I think Jimmy should stop construction of nuclear power plants—especially since they won't allow any to be built anyway."

I thought, what a political animal this woman is. She then asked me about desegregation of the North Carolina higher education system. I described my negotiations and told her I believed I had a settlement with Governor Jim Hunt, but that the university board was opposed.

"Jimmy has got to have North Carolina resolved," she said. Her unblinking eyes were focused directly on mine.

I told her that we would do everything possible to settle, but unlike governors of other states, Hunt had no control over the board of governors. I mentioned the anti-smoking campaign, but she seemed more concerned about the desegregation of the university. "That's the issue that hurts Jimmy so politically."

Mrs. Carter then talked about the relationship between the White House staff and me. "I'm concerned about the lack of trust," she said, referring to Jody Powell and Hamilton Jordan.

"So am I," I replied. "One of the biggest problems is that we never talk to each other."

"There needs to be a much closer relationship."

"I agree. But Jordan particularly is inaccessible. The President told me that he would have Jordan or Powell call for lunch. They never did. In the Camp David meeting last year, he said the two of them would meet with Cabinet officers on Saturday mornings to get to know them better, but that hasn't happened."

Mrs. Carter would not be deterred: "We have to have closer working relationships if we're going to pull the administration together."

I took advantage of the opportunity to propose something I'd favored for some time, long before I became Secretary. "The President should have periodic meetings with his staff and key domestic officials, like the ones he has with Vance, Brown, and Brzezinski."

Mrs. Carter thought it was an excellent idea. "What about you, Pat Harris, and Ray Marshall?"

"Fine, but it's important to have the key White House staff there, particularly Jordan and Eizenstat."

She agreed, and suggested adding Powell and Gerry Rafshoon, Carter's television and public relations advisor. Mrs. Carter was making notes as we talked, so I sensed the idea was taking. She said, "I think this is an excellent idea. If Jimmy won't hold these meetings, I will."

When I returned from Europe in mid-May, Eizenstat told me the President thought the idea I had suggested to Mrs. Carter was very good and intended to begin holding the meetings. Carter called on May 14 and

15, talked about the meetings, and said he would hold them every other Tuesday, alternating with the congressional leadership breakfast. He thought he would keep the group to Labor Secretary Marshall, Eizenstat, Jordan, Powell, Rafshoon, and me. "We can bring in other domestic Cabinet officers as we need them on particular issues." I was delighted.

No meeting ever took place.

The morning of May 15 provided a happy respite for the White House and HEW. The President, Mrs. Carter, and I held a press conference to release the presidential message on mental health and proposed legislation based on the recommendations of the President's Commission. The legislation would establish a new relationship between the federal government and the states in providing mental health services; it sought to assure that the chronically ill no longer were stigmatized, or faced with the dismal alternatives of institutionalization or inadequate care in the community. Mrs. Carter was energetically supportive. She planned to be the first presidential wife to testify in Congress since Eleanor Roosevelt. I said that "there is no lobbyist I would rather have working for the legislation than the First Lady."

But the respite was brief. On May 22, New York Senator Moynihan expressed the opinion that unless Carter acted quickly to take charge, he would soon find "that he's governing by the sufferance of" Senator Edward Kennedy. And the next day, five House Democrats started their own "Dump Carter–Draft Kennedy" movement. Kennedy refused to unequivocally take himself out of the presidential race.

During May and the first days of June, the Congress defeated Carter's proposals for Rhodesian sanctions, gasoline rationing, and decontrol of oil prices. Despite what then seemed like a bravado claim that he would "whip Kennedy's ass" in a fight for the Democratic nomination, Carter was beginning to reveal his own discouragement publicly. Addressing the Democratic National Committee on May 25, he said the American people saw "a Congress twisted and pulled in every direction by hundreds of well-financed and powerful special interests. . . . every extreme position imaginable defended to the last breath, almost to the last vote, by one unyielding, powerful group or another." He conceded that the public saw a government "incapable of action," bogged down in "paralysis, stagnation, and drift." Answering a question about failure to pass such key legislation as the wage insurance and hospital-cost containment proposals, the President responded, "Maybe if I was a better politician, I would have gotten these bills through the Congress." But before the Democratic National Committee and elsewhere, he left no doubt about his political intentions: "I have never backed down from a fight. I have never been afraid of public opinion polls, and if and when I decide to run, it will be in every precinct of this country, no matter who else ran, and I have no doubt that it would be successful."

Although veiled in anonymity, the back-biting that invariably accompanies failure in Washington was daily evident in the press. White House aides said Energy Secretary Schlesinger's days were numbered. Transportation Secretary Brock Adams was reported to be too interested in a Senate race in his home state of Washington to run his department or bear allegiance to Carter. Eizenstat's personal and ideological feud with McIntyre was now in print. Sources close to the White House expressed concern about Blumenthal's and my independence. Former Carter speechwriter James Fallows wrote a tale of incompetence, mediocrity, and sniping on the White House staff for *Atlantic Monthly*.

By June 1, I was so concerned about the deterioration that I wrote Carter: "I think it would be a good idea to have your Cabinet (and your top aides) to Camp David again. My sense is that we are all suffering a little from the two-and-a-half-year doldrums and it would be good to have another session similar to the one that you had before. Also, there seems to be little sense of the fact that we are well into the political season, and have an election to win and a record to run on and defend. A night and a day at Camp David, with a pep talk, seems to me a much better environment to get this across than a Cabinet meeting." My words were subdued compared to the depth of my concern, but I thought the President was so down there was no point in stomping him.

The President did not respond to my suggestion. Our conversations in early June were devoted largely to the National Health Plan we announced together on June 12. On June 14, I testified on behalf of the administration's mental health legislation before the House Health Subcommittee; on Friday, the 15th, before the Ways and Means Public Assistance and Unemployment Compensation Subcommittee in support of the administration's scaled-down welfare reform plan. Late that afternoon, I left for Sweden for the Fourth World Conference on Smoking and Health; the Peoples Republic of China to sign unprecedented agreements in health and education, and Hawaii to confer with Governor Ariyoshi on his problems with the massive influx of Southeast Asian refugees that constituted at least one of every 255 residents of the state.

On Monday, June 18, Carter and Brezhnev signed SALT II with a diplomatic kiss. Carter returned from Vienna and addressed a Joint Session of the Congress to pump for his controversial treaty. Ten days later, he left for the economic summit in Japan, with the heads of state of France, Italy, Great Britain, Japan, Canada, and West Germany. But the pomp and ceremony abroad had little effect on the President's decline in the polls. By late June, Gallup had his approval rating at 29, a seventeen-point decline in less than three months; ABC/Harris, at an even lower 25, one point below Nixon's lowest rating two months before he resigned; and a poll of Democrats in the South placed him eleven points behind Kennedy. OPEC raised its prices by 15 percent as the summit opened, but perhaps most importantly, automobiles formed longer and longer lines in more and more cities as drivers baked in summer sun waiting for a few gallons of gas, and Eizenstat's political memo to Carter leaked:

"I do not need to detail for you the political damage we are suffering from all this. . . . nothing which has occurred in the administration to date—not the Soviet Agreement on the Middle East, nor the Lance matter, not the Panama Canal Treaties, not the defeat of several major domestic legislative proposals, not the sparring with Kennedy, or even double-digit inflation—have [*sic*] added so much water to our ship. . . . Nothing else has so frustrated, confused, angered the American people or so targeted their distress at you personally.

"But I honestly believe we have a better opportunity than ever before to assert leadership over an apparently insolvable problem, to shift the cause of inflation and energy problems to OPEC. . . . If we fail to do so, the late hour may foreclose a similar opportunity again. . . . With strong steps we can mobilize the nation around a real crisis and with a clear enemy—OPEC."

Eizenstat suggested a major speech on energy. On Monday, July 2, when Carter returned, he spent the day in meetings on energy and decided to address the nation seventy-two hours later, on July 5. With a Cabinet-level group rushing to put an energy plan before him, he helicoptered to Camp David on July 3. On Wednesday, July 4, he received speechwriter Rick Hertzberg's draft at about 1:00 P.M. At about 3:00, he put a conference call through to Mondale, Jordan, Rafshoon, and the White House press office and instructed his closest aides to cancel the July 5 speech and not to give any reasons.

WORD OF Carter's cancellation reached me only in the newspapers. I was as puzzled as any other citizen. When Mondale called me from Camp David on July 4 about getting House votes for the Education Department bill, I asked what was going on, but he indicated he was not in a position to talk.

Remaining at Camp David, Carter met with his staff, mostly political aides. On Friday, July 6, a parade of leaders to the mountain began with eight governors going to the presidential retreat. The meetings lasted almost two weeks. During that time, the Education Department legislation passed the House. Finally, on July 15, Carter came down from the mountain to address the nation. The speech proposed major new energy initiatives, but the emphasis was on Carter's self-proclaimed "crisis of the American spirit."

The President talked about his Camp David visitors. One had told him, "Mr. President, you're not leading this nation, you're just managing the government." He promised to change that: "I will lead the fight. . . . and above all, I will act. But there is no way to avoid sacrifice." Another visitor had told him, "Some of your Cabinet members don't seem loyal. There is not enough discipline among your disciples." He apologized for getting too absorbed with "what the isolated world of Washington thinks is important" and losing touch with America in the process. "Washington, D.C., has become an island. The gap between our citizens and our government has never been so wide." Like the American people on that July evening, Carter saw "paralysis and stagnation and drift. You don't like it, and neither do I." He said he discovered a crisis of confidence, "a crisis that strikes at the very heart, soul, and spirit of our national will . . . [and] is threatening to destroy the social and political fabric of America." Carter described a nation "at a turning point in our history. There are two paths to choose. One is the path . . . that leads to fragmentation and self-interest . . . conflict between narrow interests, ending in chaos and immobility. . . . Another path [is] the path of common purpose and the restoration of American values." And then he closed with a Nixonesque exhortation to the people: "Let your voice be heard. Wherever you have a chance, say something good about our country."

The President had invited the Cabinet to view the address on television in the Roosevelt Room. There were Cokes, diet soda, beer, and sandwiches. I watched in amazement. How could we run against Washington and government when the President was both? Was I a disciple without discipline? I could see the columns: Carter drops in the polls, so there's something wrong with us. It was a banal address, written, as Elizabeth Drew later painstakingly documented in *The New Yorker*, for Pat Caddell's polls and to manipulate the emotions of the people exposed in them. After the speech, Carter walked through the room briefly. On cue, we all rose and applauded as he entered, more out of hope than conviction. He walked around the room, clearly pleased with himself, shaking hands with each of us. I had a few seconds to think about what to say. "It's the best-delivered speech I've seen you give," I blurted out as we shook hands. Carter's face was masked in his public smile and he passed on to the next Cabinet officer.

On Monday, July 16, Carter echoed his Sunday night address in Kansas City, Missouri, and Detroit, adding more specifics of his new energy program. He promised to "fight any selfish interest that undermines our national purpose." His approval rating rose ten points, and I began to wonder whether, despite my misgivings, Carter might be onto something. But I had little time to think about it because rumors of a Carter hit list—Schlesinger, Blumenthal, and myself—were mounting.

On Tuesday morning, Carter had breakfast with the congressional leadership to push for early consideration of his energy proposals. After breakfast, he and Hamilton Jordan met with the White House senior staff. Carter told them that Jordan would be Chief of Staff and that he was not satisfied with their performance: "While some good things had been done, there were not enough of them."

At 10:30 A.M., the special Cabinet meeting for "principals only" began, with Hamilton Jordan as the only non-Cabinet member present, sitting in Mondale's chair across the table from the President. Mondale was on the road, pumping for the SALT Treaty and traveling abroad, trying to get as far away as possible from what was coming.

It was to be the most intense Cabinet meeting of the Carter administration. The Washington press corps had begun the race to discover who would go. Rumors tumbled over one another, but my name was appearing on every list. Carter entered smiling; but his smile did not soften the taut lines on his face. He took his chair with its slightly higher back. Nixon had introduced that more formal chair as a symbol of the change from Johnson, who had sat in a reclining, high-back desk chair. Ford had replaced Nixon's with a chair the same size as all the others. Carter had brought back the Nixon chair.

The President began softly. "I have deliberately excluded most of you from my life for the past couple of weeks." He said he had "wanted to get away from you and from Washington." He felt an obligation to reassess his presidency, to have "serious private talks about my role as President." His words were pessimistic, his voice somber. It was as close to quiet desperation as I had ever seen him. There has been "a lot of effort wasted on misdirections," he said. "My government is not leading the country. The people have lost confidence in me, in the Congress, in themselves, and in this nation." He talked of the "alarming deterioration in attitude of people toward their country." Then a tone of teeth-gritted determination came into his voice. He had held a host of meetings with all kinds of groups from all across the country. He had asked them about his Cabinet and his staff. The comments about his Cabinet were "serious and condemnatory. I was told, they are not working for you, but for themselves." He said that he had "repeatedly been told" that there was disloyalty "among some Cabinet members," that many had been the source of leaks that had hurt him. With a studied expression of hurt on his face, Carter allowed that he had given "great loyalty" to his Cabinet and had "great appreciation" for their sacrifice and service.

He paused. "I have decided to change my lifestyle, and my calendar. I have one and one-half years left as President, and I don't deserve to be re-elected if I can't do a better job. I intend to run for office and I intend to be re-elected." To get ready for this effort over the next eighteen months, personnel changes would be made in the Cabinet and the White House staff. "I will make the changes over the course of next week." He intended to change the administration's "way of doing business" as well as the "identity of key members of the administration." He complained that "some Cabinet officers do not have support among their constituents."

I thought of my proposals to discipline the Social Security system and the reaction of senior citizens groups; of the National Education Association, whose pressure for a separate education department I had resisted; and of my battles to restrain health care costs.

He spoke to us about Jordan. "Hamilton will be Chief of Staff. He is like a son to me. He doesn't want to be Chief of Staff, but I've told him he has to be Chief of Staff. As an Assistant, he will be superior to Stu, Jody, Frank, Jack, and the others." Carter admitted that "Ham is not a detail man," but "he will bring in a deputy who will put a management system together and carry it out."

Cy Vance said characteristically that the Cabinet would give "complete support to Ham."

The President nodded perfunctorily. He reaffirmed his satisfaction with his own retreat at Camp David, and suggested that the Cabinet members "go off for a weekend of contemplation about where you are going, and ask yourselves how can you do better in supporting the President."

Turning enough to his left to look straight at Blumenthal, he said that it was imperative he have "loyalty from my Cabinet members." Scanning the table, he added, "I want each of you to assess your subordinates, their loyalty to us, whether they are team players, whether they will speak with one voice, whether they are good staff." Then he said that he wanted us all to submit "pro forma resignations." He was evaluating each of us and he would decide whether to accept the resignations or not. He wanted "written resignations from each member of the Cabinet."

Vance immediately opposed the idea, and was supported by Brown, and then most of the Cabinet. It would be "too much like Nixon in 1972," we said like a Greek chorus.

The President thought for a moment. "You all seem averse to submitting written resignations. We will think about it and then Hamilton will call you this afternoon."

Carter wanted us also to fill out personnel evaluations of each of our key staff members. Hamilton would distribute some "tough forms" to fill out on each one. He wanted us to review the work of our subordinates, and "get rid of all of those who are incompetent, except minorities and women." No woman or minority member could be fired; their situations were to be discussed with the White House, the President said.

Then the President opened the meeting. Blumenthal spoke briefly about "the difference between arguing for a point of view and disloyalty." Carter hardly listened. Pat Harris said, "We can move government forward by putting phones in the White House staff offices and the staff using them." She complained that her calls were never returned by White House aides. She said it was important to "fight fiercely for our point of view," that it was not "disloyal to disagree with the White House staff, provided one supports the administration when the decision is made."

U.N. Ambassador Andrew Young began to speak, echoing Harris's concern. The President's face reddened. He interrupted Young: "You have repeatedly embarrassed the administration. I was told this again and again at Camp David. . . . You have caused embarrassment to me by calling Britain the most racist country in history . . . saying Cuban troops in Angola were a stabilizing influence . . . saying there are hundreds of political prisoners in the United States."

Usually, Carter was uncomfortable when Cabinet members argued back to him, but now his voice and eyes were so angry that by the time he had ended his attack on Young, he had killed any other meaningful comment. He turned to Jordan.

Jordan admitted that after two and a half years "I have no relationship with many of you." He said the Cabinet had to be "more accountable, better disciplined," that we had to "resolve the little problems and not send them to the President." The redness of anger faded from Carter's face and he looked like a proud father as Jordan continued: The medium-sized problems would come to him for decision; McIntyre and Eizenstat would be involved in domestic issues, Brzezinski in foreign policy. The White House staff would "work as an organization, not as a democracy," he said. "The personnel changes will be made quickly, and the discipline will be imposed immediately, including over leaks."

Carter added an admonition to complete the personnel evaluation forms promptly, to get them back within a few days, and he left the room. Jordan distributed the personnel evaluation forms—so patently amateurish and preposterous that the expressions on several Cabinet members' faces were open-mouthed. I could think only of what a disaster Carter was headed for. This was going to destroy any benefits he had derived from his Sunday night speech.

I left for lunch with House Speaker O'Neill and his top assistant, Leo Diehl. We ate cold cuts around a table in the Speaker's private office, behind the large Rayburn Room off the House floor. O'Neill could not believe what was happening. "The guy told me this morning at breakfast that he was going to get rid of a couple of Cabinet officers. I assume it will be Griffin Bell, who's leaving anyway, and Jim Schlesinger."

"I'm not so sure," I said.

"Well, hell, Joe, I can't believe he would ever get rid of you. You're the best damn Cabinet officer he's got," my friend the Speaker said. Then he paused for a moment and added, "Although those tobacco guys would do anything they could to get you out of that job. Boy, do they hate you!"

We agreed that Carter had picked up a little momentum from his Sunday night speech. "I hope he doesn't blow it," O'Neill said.

We talked about whether Teddy Kennedy would run, a topic in every Washington conversation in July 1979. "I hope not," O'Neill said. "It's not just his family; I think he's just too liberal for these times. And Chappaquiddick. Twenty-five percent of the voters will never vote for him. So he's got to get fifty-one percent out of seventy-five percent. I don't think even he can do it."

O'Neill said that he had made his view of me clear to the President and he offered to tell Carter again if I wanted him to. I told the Speaker that I thought the President should make up his own mind.

At 3:00 that afternoon, Jordan placed a conference call to all Cabinet members. The President had decided not to ask for written resignations, but Powell would issue a statement that Jordan now read to us: "The President had serious and lengthy discussions with his Cabinet and senior White House staff about the priorities of his administration. He reviewed with them progress of the past few years and the problems that remain. All members of the Cabinet and senior staff have offered their resignations to the President during this period of evaluation. The President will review these offers carefully and expeditiously." Jordan said that Carter would be in touch with us individually.

I was stunned when I put down the phone. From a number of third parties Jordan and Powell had talked to, I knew I was high on their list for firing. But my relationship with Carter had always been good. It was nothing like the intimacy I had shared with Johnson, but it was a professional relationship, I had thought, with mutual respect, recognition of each other's interests, strengths, and weaknesses, and a sense of trust. On balance, I did not think he would accept my resignation. Then I thought of what chaos an announcement of mass resignations could cause in the stock market and I wondered if Carter realized that. Lyndon Johnson had been so sensitive to the impact of his words and actions on the stock market that he often tried to use them to drive the market up, or a particular company's stock down if we were trying to roll back a price increase.

As soon as the announcement was made, one of my assistants reminded me that Richard Nixon had written of the similar action after his re-election in 1972, "I see this now as a mistake. I did not take into account the chilling effect this action would have on the morale of the people . . . in the government."

My son Mark, who was working at the *Washington Post* as a copy aide for the summer, called late that afternoon. He kidded me, as much to deal with his own concern as allay mine. "Do you still have a job, Dad? We're running a story tomorrow that says you and Mr. Blumenthal and Mr. Schlesinger are going to be fired."

"Whose story?" I asked.

"David Broder and Ed Walsh," he said.

"I may be in trouble, but I have no idea."

The following morning, July 18, I had a quiet breakfast with my friend and former law partner Edward Bennett Williams at the Metropolitan Club in Washington. Sitting virtually alone in the vast dining room on the fourth floor, I talked about the possibility that Carter might fire me.

"I can't believe it," Williams said. "It doesn't make any sense."

I still thought it was a possibility: "I can't believe any President would let his staff put this stuff out to the press unless he had blessed it, or at a minimum they knew that I was on the way out."

Williams then said, leaning across the table, "It would be the best damn thing that could happen to you. The guy is through and it will give you a way to get out. You ought to hope he fires you. You may not be that lucky."

At noon, I went to Woodlawn in Baltimore to celebrate the anniversary of my reorganization of Medicare and Medicaid into the Health Care Financing Administration. When I got back, Susanna McBee, who had been named to succeed Eileen Shanahan as Assistant Secretary for Public Affairs at HEW, told me that Pat Harris had been to see Carter, but that no word of what occurred had leaked. Heineman reported that OMB and Domestic Policy staff aides were suggesting me to their bosses as Secretary of Energy.

I was preparing for my testimony the next morning on the administration's Higher Education Act proposals when the President called me at 5:19 P.M. "Joe, how you doing?" he asked softly.

"Fine, Mr. President," I responded.

"Can you come over here this afternoon?"

"Any time," I said. The President asked me to come right away.

I was prepared for whichever decision Carter reached, although I did not really think he would accept my resignation, despite all the published evidence to the contrary, because we always seemed to have gotten along well.

I walked into Nell Yates's office, between the Cabinet Room and the Oval Office. She had been Jack Valenti's secretary when I first met her on the LBJ staff. We chatted aimlessly as I watched the President in the Rose Garden through the French doors. He was looking up at the trees at some birds. As he came through the French doors, he said, "I think I may have seen one of Cec's peregrine falcons." He was referring to the birds that Interior Secretary Andrus had saved and brought to Washington.

Carter ushered me through the Oval Office into his small study. He sat behind his desk, and I sat on a couch to the right against the wall. In his desk chair, the President was perched slightly higher than me, as I sank into the soft-cushioned white couch.

"I have decided to accept your resignation," he said through a nervous smile.

"Mr. President, you are entitled to have the Cabinet people you want. I will work for an orderly transition." I recited the words I had rehearsed in my mind as the rumors had increased. I was surprised at how nervous my voice was as I spoke them.

"Your performance as Secretary has been outstanding," the President said. "You have put that Department in better shape than it has ever been in before. You've been the best Secretary of HEW. The Department has never been better managed."

I thanked him for his generous comments.

"I have never said a bad word about you or your performance and I never will. If anyone does around here, I will fire him."

I just sat, now a little stunned, but my instincts told me to be careful, to stay alert.

"I intend to name Pat Harris Secretary of HEW. I talked to her this morning and she wanted time to think about it. She told me she did not think she could do as good a job as you were doing, but I told her you have the Department in such good shape, she will be able to take over easily." Carter paused, smiling again. Then, as though he could hear the "Why?" in my mind, he explained. "The problem is the friction with the White House staff. The same qualities and drive and managerial ability that make you such a superb Secretary create problems with the White House staff. No one on the staff questions your performance as Secretary. Stu [Eizenstat] and Fritz are very high on you. Stu will be particularly disappointed with my decision. But you and some members of the staff—particularly Ham, Jody, and Frank Moore—have not gotten along."

All I could say was "It's your decision, Mr. President." His last statement rang true to me.

The President continued, "We have to get the Cabinet and the administration in shape for the nineteen-eighty election." I was not surprised at this comment, either, since at the Cabinet meeting the morning before he had said he intended to run for re-election and win. He asked if I were interested in another job in the government. I told him I was not. "Perhaps a foreign position?" he suggested.

"No," I said.

"Would you like to be Ambassador to Italy?" Carter asked.

"No. There is someone else in that job. And he's a good ambassador."

The President persisted. "He's been there two and a half years and he can be moved."

I told Carter that I definitely was not interested, beginning to think that he must be concerned that I would hurt him, perhaps with Kennedy, if I were a free agent. He wanted to do this in a way that "helped" me, he continued. "I assume you have no financial problems." I nodded. "Perhaps you'll go back to law practice," he said. "Whatever you do, I'd like to help."

"I've been totally involved in this job and just haven't thought about anything else," I said.

Carter responded, "I know. You have put as much of yourself into HEW as I have put of myself into the presidency." At that moment, he seemed sincerely sympathetic.

Carter invited me to Camp David for the weekend. I told him I had planned to spend the weekend with my children. "Bring your children along." I said I appreciated the invitation and would think about it. "If you want to, you can go up there alone, and I won't go," he said. I shook my head and he pressed. "Then come with me and bring your children. We can leave in a helicopter from the White House lawn Friday afternoon. Rosalynn will not be there Saturday night; we can play some tennis and have a chance to talk to each other about the future."

I was beginning to hurt a little and I felt it was time to move to the business at hand. I asked him what schedule he wanted to move on.

"Any that's convenient to you."

I thought there should be an announcement as promptly as possible, and I suggested that we exchange letters.

"That's fine," Carter said. "I will write my letter myself and I will say in it the things I said to you this afternoon.'' I said I would bring my letter to him in the morning, between 7:00 and 7:30.

When I rose to leave, Carter stood, shook my hand and renewed his invitation to Camp David. I told him I would respond the next morning. I hesitated, looking at the two doors out of his office, one leading to the corridor, the other through the Oval Office.

''Which door do you want to go out?'' he asked. ''You probably know your way around this place better than I do,'' he said, smiling as I left through the door to the corridor.

I went back to my office at HEW shaken, though the full impact of being fired had not yet come home. I asked Hale Champion, who happened to be back in town, and Ben Heineman in, told them Carter had accepted my resignation, and then called my secretary, Gay Pirozzi, and dictated a memo for the record. When I said that the President told me he had decided to accept my resignation, she started crying, and at the first interruption, put her pad and pen on my desk and raced out of the office. She returned and I finished the memo. Later, I talked to Champion, Heineman, Fred Bohen, Rick Cotton, Peter Hamilton, Dick Warden and one or two other close aides, and then sat alone for two hours, writing my letter of resignation. At about 11:00 P.M., I went to The Palm restaurant for dinner with my immediate staff.

The following morning I delivered my letter to the President at about 7:15. There was no one in his outer office, so I walked into the Oval Office. The President was sitting to the right, in the high-backed upholstered chair, reading the *New York Times*. He pointed me to the loveseat to his right. I was facing the fireplace, conscious of sitting under the portrait of George Washington. I handed the President my letter of resignation. It was sealed. I suggested that he open it. Carter opened the letter and read it slowly.

Dear Mr. President:

In accord with our conversation yesterday afternoon, I hereby formally tender my resignation as Secretary of Health, Education, and Welfare.

For me, it has been a deeply enjoyable and satisfying experience to administer so many of the programs enacted into law under President Lyndon Johnson.

I have called HEW the Department of the people because its programs touch the lives of so many Americans each day. The Department reflects the compassion of the American people. It tends to the needs of the old and the young, of the poor, the ill, and the handicapped. It exists to protect the health of all Americans, to assure equal educational opportunity for all citizens, and to guarantee the individual rights of victims of discrimination of all kinds. It administers Social Security and the other basic income-maintenance programs of our nation.

My goal as Secretary has been to demonstrate that Government can do all these things, not only with compassion, but with competence. Achieving that goal is urgently necessary because there are still in this nation millions of people whose needs can be met only by Government—and they are the most vulnerable among us.

To do this job effectively, I needed the authority to run this Department and the freedom to decide and speak out on controversial public issues. You have given me that authority and freedom, and I appreciate it.

Whenever the laws that the Congress charges the Secretary of HEW to execute are administered with vigor, there will be controversy. I have tried to execute these laws vigorously.

I appreciate the opportunity you have given me to serve our nation and you.

I wish you well as you continue striving to fulfill the enormous responsibilities of your office, and to build upon your achievements, of which you can be justly proud.

Sincerely,
Joseph A. Califano, Jr.

Carter looked up. "It's a beautiful letter," he said. "I will try to write one just as fine." I asked him for his letter that morning because I had to meet with my staff and wanted to read it to them. Carter promised to get his letter to me "well before noon."

We discussed the public announcement. I suggested he announce it that morning. "The sooner, the better," Carter agreed. Since Carter was sending his letter before noon, I said I would meet with my staff at 12 noon and with the press at 12:30. "That's fine," he said.

The President asked me again about Camp David. "I've decided not to go. I think I should try to spend the weekend with my children. This could well be a disquieting event for them." Carter said, "Fine, if that's what you want to do. I want you to know that you are welcome there with or without me."

Carter asked me whether I might run for the Senate in New York. When I indicated that was a possibility, he said he thought I would be a good senator, that "we needed more good senators," and added, somewhat incongruously, that he had "great difficulty communicating with Russell Long, difficulty understanding him. Sometimes he's just not coherent." He then repeated some of the comments about my "outstanding performance" and said he would mention them in his letter. I rose to leave. Carter also got up. We shook hands. "I'll pray for you," he said.

I returned to the office, and began working with Erv Duggan, my speechwriter, on an opening statement for the press conference. It was a sad meeting. Champion and Heineman were also helping. The deadline neared and the letter from the President had not come. Susan Clough phoned Rick Cotton, the HEW Executive Secretary who had succeeded Fred Bohen, to say that the President's letter would be delayed. I called Clough and told her that we had already announced a press conference at 12:30 and a staff meeting at noon. Jody Powell called to say that the President simply could not get the letter over in time. I said we would have to put a postponement of the conference on the AP and UPI wires. Minutes later Powell called and said to leave everything as it was, they would get a letter over. Champion, who had sat through all the calls, said, "Those bastards have seen his letter. He wrote what he told you this morning and last night, and they told him how preposterous it is for him to fire you and say those things. They're rewriting the letter. You're not going to get a good letter from the President."

The handwritten letter arrived just before noon.

To Secretary Joe Califano:

I accept your resignation with a genuine feeling of appreciation and of recognition for your notable accomplishments as Secretary of Health, Education, and Welfare.

You have, indeed, demonstrated that major public service can exemplify both competence and compassion.

My desire is that you continue to serve with my confidence and support until your successor assumes the office. Your pledge of a smooth, harmonious and orderly transition is typical of your attitude and performance.

You have my personal best wishes and friendship.

Sincerely,
Jimmy Carter

My staff had been waiting for me to speak to them, and the press conference was backed up behind that meeting. As I entered the room across the hall from my office to talk to the staff, they applauded. I motioned them to stop, but the applause continued. As I began to speak, my eyes filled and the lump in my throat thickened. Through the tears, in a voice trembling with emotion, I mustered all my will, held the sides of the podium to steady myself, and said that in a few moments at a press conference I would talk about the rewards of being HEW Secretary. I praised them for their work and reminded them that millions of people depended on HEW. I said being Secretary had been the "greatest honor of my life." I appreciated the honor of working with them and urged them to continue the "noble work of helping the most vulnerable people among us." That was all I could get out. Tears had begun to overflow my eyes. I was on the verge of uncontrollable sobbing. I turned and left to their applause. I could still hear it as I crossed the hall and went into my office. I headed straight for the bathroom. I could not stop crying. I blotted my eyes with the end of a towel soaked in cold water. I prayed for the strength to control myself and get through the press conference. Then I went with Susie McBee to meet the press downstairs.

The auditorium was overflowing, with hundreds of employees outside in the hall of the Humphrey Building. At least twelve television cameras were squeezed where ordinarily three or four were set up. There were national reporters and columnists in addition to the usual HEW press corps. The lights seemed brighter as I stood behind the podium on the stage. I was sure they exposed my red eyes. I tried to find space to put my statement down among the microphones taped and clipped to the podium. I took a sip of water to steady myself, breathed deeply, and began reading my statement, hoping I sounded firmer than I felt, and trying with all the concentration I could summon not to break down and cry again.

"I remember reading, a few years ago, a wise admonition for those who would understand our politics: Try to tell the difference between tides, waves, and ripples," I began. "By that measure, the matter of which individual runs a government department—or for how long—is surely little more than a ripple; the matter of who wins next year's election, a wave. Certain issues, however, are truly tidal in their magnitude and meaning. Civil rights is one such issue. The issue of guaranteeing a fair share of this nation's plenty to poor, old, and helpless people is another. The issue of enhancing health and education for millions of people is yet another."

I was getting a sense of self-control. My voice was regaining its natural timbre. I began to think I might make it.

"These great tidal issues describe the mandate of this Department. And in the past thirty months, as Secretary of Health, Education, and Welfare, I have found myself immersed in all of them. That experience has brought some frustrations. But I find myself thinking now only of the satisfactions. There is the satisfaction of having attracted to this Department—from the nation's universities and law firms, from the foundations and from within government itself—the best people to serve in a government department, in my judgment, since the days of the New Frontier. There is the satisfaction of having reorganized the Department, to help it become a more vibrant, effective institution and to recover hundreds of millions of tax dollars previously lost through fraud, abuse, and waste.

There is the satisfaction of having designed major legislative proposals: the national health plan, restoring the financial integrity of the Social Security system, recasting the nation's education laws with a 40 percent increase in funding, hospital-cost containment, welfare reform, and child health. Some of these have been passed by Congress; some have not. All, I believe, will stand the test of time. . . . There is the satisfaction of enforcing the nation's laws against discrimination with renewed energy and vigor. There is the satisfaction of speaking out in defense of the public health on issues from childhood immunization to the dangers of smoking to adequate budget support for basic scientific research.

"Much of what we began in these last thirty months, of course, is not yet finished. I can understand, however, that the President could feel the need to reorient his priorities, to rely more heavily on his personal staff, and to prepare his administration for the challenges of the next eighteen months.

"I wish the President well as he continues striving to fulfill the enormous responsibilities of his office, and to build upon his achievements, of which he can be justly proud.

"Inevitably, there will be those who will say, in trying to explain this event, that I made waves. I hope I did—but I will leave that judgment to you and to the passage of time. Meanwhile, I will cherish the opportunity I have had to move with some of those great tides—and perhaps to have given them added momentum."

I looked for the first question. Did I think I was a "scapegoat"? I responded that the President had a right to pick his own people. Then, the second question: Did I expect to support President Carter for reelection? I paused for a moment and decided to answer by echoing Senator Edward Kennedy's standard response during the months before he announced his candidacy: "I expect the President to be nominated for reelection and I expect to support him." The audience burst into laughter and applause. The laughter broke the tension that had gripped my body. For the first time, I was confident I would make it through the press conference.

When asked about my relations with Carter, I responded: ". . . I feel I have fulfilled my responsibilities to the Congress, to execute the law, and my responsibilities to the President, and I think he feels that way. He told me yesterday when he met with me . . . he thought the performance over here had been superb. He said the qualities of the leadership and drive and management and independence that made me such a good Secretary of HEW, he said the best Secretary of HEW, were the same qualities that created friction with certain members of the staff." I noted that "My dealings have always been fine and first rate with the President."

I was asked the reason the President gave for firing me. I answered, "He said that he thought there were two problems . . . one related to friction with certain members of the White House staff . . . and the other . . . that he had to get the Cabinet and the administration ready for the nineteen-eighty election." Later in the press conference, I identified Hamilton Jordan, Jody Powell, and Frank Moore as the three senior White House staffers he named. I refused to criticize the White House staff. I said I had spent no more than two hours with Hamilton Jordan in two and one-half years. "The only member of the . . . staff that I have close daily contact with is Stuart Eizenstat, and I think he is doing an excellent job for the President . . . and I hope he continues to do that job."

When asked whether the controversy surrounding my time as Secretary had hurt Carter in the polls, I suggested, "You would have to ask Pat Caddell what the problems are as far as the polls are concerned . . . on many issues in this Department, you are fortunate if you have fifty-one percent of the people on your side." When asked whether I was "mad" or thought I had "been unfairly dealt with," I echoed President John Kennedy's remark about the draft, "Somebody once said that life is unfair. I am a realist . . . I have tried my best to make this Department work better. . . . to demonstrate that government can help people."

I was asked about Carter's attack on the Washington establishment and government, and I felt I had to respond because I thought the President was seriously undermining our system. "It has become as fashionable to attack Washington today as it was to attack Brooklyn when I was a kid. Government is not the enemy of the people; government is the servant of the people. The important thing is to recognize that in a free society there are certain limited numbers of things that government does. By and large, most of those things can be done by no one else, and the things that this Department does and is charged to do are things for people who cannot find help anywhere else."

As the press conference closed, the HEW employees and reporters in the audience stood and applauded. Four congressmen were to the side of the stage as I came down the stairs: Toby Moffett of Connecticut, who angrily called my firing "a victory for Marlboro country"; Andy Maguire of New Jersey; Jim Shannon of Massachusetts; and Tom Downey of New York. Their presence helped immeasurably.

The reaction on Capitol Hill was heartening. I had canceled my scheduled appearance that morning before the House Education and Labor Committee, where I had been going to present our proposals for overhauling the Higher Education Act. Before hearing from Fred Bohen, who testified in my place, several members commented on my dismissal.

Chairman Carl Perkins of Kentucky, with whom I had worked in the 1960s to get the first funds for Johnson's poverty program, said, "Joe Califano is not only one of our great scholars in America; but he happens to be one of the greatest administrators in this nation, and he is the first Secretary in my memory who has taken hold of a disorganized Department. . . ." Perkins attributed the firing to the "jealousy of Jordan and that group."

Ted Weiss of New York said that "in the course of the past two and one-half years, the most noteworthy achievements and movements made in this country and administration have come from the Secretary and the Department of HEW." Bill Ford of Michigan said, "Joe Califano has set . . . a standard about what it means to be virtually a personification of the American dream, to be a young man who believes in his government, believes in the political process, rises to a position of great power, then remembers at every stage of the operation that the purpose he had in mind was to get that power so he could use it for the good of the people."

During the day, congressmen on both sides of the aisle both called me and made public statements. David Obey of Wisconsin said pubicly that "it is inconceivable . . . that they should dismiss the only effective Secretary of HEW I have seen in my ten years in Congress while retaining second- and third-raters" like McIntyre and Jordan. Speaker Tip O'Neill said, "No other Cabinet officer has ever served his President on Capitol Hill with greater dedication and loyalty. . . . As one of the most able and talented men I have ever known in Washington, Joe Califano brought . . . competence, experience, and an independent style. . . . He has not hesitated to take controversial positions whenever these stands were in the best interests of the nation and the only right course to pursue." Jake Pickle of Texas said, "We've probably lost the most talented man in the Cabinet."

Senator Edward Kennedy got word of my resignation during the Senate floor debate on the HEW appropriations bill. He said it was "an extraordinary irony that when the nation's attention is focused on energy and inflation, the first casualty is the Cabinet member most concerned with those unable to look after themselves, the millions of ill, handicapped, and poor Americans. Califano has been truly one of the outstanding individuals to serve President Carter . . . a man of extraordinary dedication and loyalty to President Carter." Senator Thomas Eagleton, who had given us gutsy support on a number of issues of no political advantage to him, called me "far and away the best Secretary of HEW" in his experience. Senator Abe Ribicoff said that the President "had made a serious mistake. Important programs for the nation will suffer without Joe Califano's leadership."

But there were voices on the other side. Senator Walter Huddleston, speaking for those who opposed the anti-smoking campaign, said, "Mr. Califano was a good place for Carter to start restructuring the Cabinet." The day my resignation was announced, special phone calls from the White House informed the North Carolina congressional delegation, most of whom (with the exception of Richardson Preyer) applauded the action publicly. North Carolina Governor Jim Hunt, who had jogged around the grounds with Carter on the first day of his Camp David retreat, said, "You don't see me crying." Hamilton Jordan, appearing on the *MacNeil-Lehrer Report* television program that night, claimed the changes were designed to increase White House control. "It's not a question of loyalty, it's a question of competence."

But Jack Watson called, with his deputy Gene Eidenberg, who had started in the administration with Champion and me to help HEW work more effectively with the states. "This is the most incredible display of stupidity and bad judgment in a long time," Watson said. Stu Eizenstat called, his voice choked with emotion, to say he was "stunned by the President's decision." Eizenstat later told HEW General Counsel Dick Beattie that "I had never seen hatred like that on the part of Hamilton and Jody. They were vituperative. They kept telling the President that 'Joe was going his own way.' I told the President I worked with Joe and it just wasn't so."

Governors called, such as Hugh Carey of New York ("You're the only one who really cared about New York"), Ella Grasso of Connecticut ("This is terrible, Joe. You care so much"), and Carter-supporter Bill Clinton of Arkansas ("If you go into elective politics, I'll help").

There were other, sometimes more pungent, comments, many from outside government. Ralph Nader said that Carter's action was like "firing Mickey Mantle because he couldn't get along with the bat boy." Urban League President Vernon Jordan left a message with Gay Pirozzi: "Tell Joe never to trust a born-again Baptist, especially a Southern white one." Representative Charles Wilson of Texas said, "they're cutting down the biggest trees and keeping the monkeys." And Art Buchwald called from Martha's Vineyard. "Joey," he said, stressing the "ey" appellation we use to tease each other, "I was worried about the country, with an energy crisis that can destroy us, when Carter called Jesse Jackson to consult him about it. But now I feel better about the energy crisis because he's fired his Secretary of Health, Education, and Welfare." He drew out the title as he said it and then we both broke into laughter. "I just want you to remember that at least once today you laughed," he said.

Blumenthal's dismissal was announced that afternoon and there was an indication that more firings were coming. I talked to my sons and they were puzzled, but fine. That evening, still in a state of shock, I had a long-scheduled dinner in Tiberio's restaurant with Ben Bradlee, Sally Quinn, Ed Williams, and his daughter, Ellen. The next morning, Jody Powell snapped at the *Post* White House correspondent, "I hear Califano was out celebrating with your boss and the *Washington Post* gang last night."

That Friday morning, I went through the ritual of appearances on the *Today Show* and the CBS Morning News. I had taped *Good Morning, America* the afternoon before. During the day, Griffin Bell, James Schlesinger, and Brock Adams resigned. Reporters were now openly questioning Carter's stability, as well as his judgment and competence. In rambling remarks in the Rose Garden, Carter talked about "love within the family, honesty, friendship among people, a desire for peace, a respect for one another" as things that, presumably unlike Cabinet officers, "do not change." A White House aide, refusing to be identified, said, "We've burned down the house to roast the pig."

By late afternoon, Carter felt it necessary to read a brief statement to the White House press corps: "I am well pleased with all the changes that have been made. Every single change has been a positive change. There is absolutely no doubt in my mind that I and my administration will now be better able to serve this country and to resolve these problems and to meet those challenges that I described to the American people in my television address Sunday night." He refused questions, turned on his heel, and walked out.

That same afternoon, Susie McBee told me that Powell was leaking denials that Carter had ever told me I did an outstanding job or was the best HEW Secretary. Reporters wanted my comment. I told her to avoid a "who-said-what" contest, but authorized her to say that Carter and I had been alone, that he and I knew what he said, and that I had accurately reported it at my press conference. Taking that back to the White House, reporters demanded that Powell go on the record. He did so, adding that Carter never mentioned the 1980 election or friction with any White House staff members; however his denials failed to convince the press. Because what Carter had said about my performance was so consistent with his attitudes in the past, and because no one had contradicted my account for more than twenty-four hours, the press, despite continued backgrounding, simply did not believe Powell or Jordan, on or off the record. The weakness of the White House version was further magnified by statements of two congressmen quoted in Saturday morning's papers. Charlie Rangel and Jim Corman, both Carter supporters, revealed that each had called the President earlier in the week to urge him to keep me in the Cabinet. Corman said that Carter called me an "excellent HEW Secretary." Rangel added that Carter's praise was so high, "I almost thought the President was going to name him his Chief of Staff." In Rangel's judgment, the reasons Carter gave him for my dismissal were "consistent with" those reported by me.

As the criticism mounted, Carter held a background news conference on Saturday afternoon, July 21. According to reporters who were present, he questioned the accuracy of my report about his statements at our private meeting together, but he refused to go on the record or permit direct quotation. Still, the Sunday papers made it clear the President was seeking to portray me as inaccurately repeating what was said. I was shocked and angry as I went to meet with my key staff before going on ABC's *Issues and Answers.* I told them that I would set forth what happened and try to close the matter with dignity. There would be no public statements after *Issues and Answers.* The American people would have to make their own judgments.

I took my three children, Mark, Joe, and Claudia, with me. It is not pleasant to have your children see you accused of twisting the facts by the President of the United States and some of his aides, and I wanted my sons and daughter to see and hear me respond.

ABC reporter Bob Clark put the question right to me: "I don't really know how to bring this matter up delicately, so I will begin by quoting these words from the front page of yesterday's *Washington Post:* 'The President put out the word that Califano was lying about the reasons given for his being fired as Secretary of Health, Education, and Welfare.' Would you begin by telling us just what the President did say to you as he accepted your resignation?" After I repeated what I had said at my press conference, Clark said that Carter and Powell had "denied almost every element specifically of what you said. . . . Who is right about this?"

"There were two people at that meeting, the President and me, and I know what he said to me. It was one of the most attentive and searing moments of my entire life," I replied. "But I would also like to say something else that I think is important. The President is not well served by this kind of a who-said-what or this kind of a personality discussion. The country is not well served by this, and I, myself, to the extent I have the power to do anything about it, intend to put an end to it." Throughout the interview, I underscored the importance of dealing with the issues—poverty, health care, education—and not just personalities.

In a session with government employees three days later, Carter spoke quite differently from Jordan or Powell, or the reports of his own Saturday background briefing for the press. At 7:00 P.M., he met in the East Room of the White House with sub-Cabinet-level presidential appointees to stem plummeting morale in the wake of the personnel evaluation forms and Cabinet shake-up. Carter said that he and I "worked together harmoniously on the national health program.'' He emphasized that he was ''not saying any critical remark about any Cabinet member.'' He asserted ''I have had no problem at all with the campaign to control smoking. If you were to ask Secretary Califano, he would say that I have never tried to restrain his enthusiastic drive to lessen the threat of smoking to health.'' Then he noted that he had studied opinion polls, not just political polls; he felt the cohesion of the nation was deteriorating, with ''divisiveness everywhere'' because of Vietnam, assassinations, Watergate, CIA revelations, and rising inflation. He spoke of his own failings. ''I have not succeeded in letting my voice build confidence in the future and increasing trust in government. Maybe Churchill or Franklin Roosevelt could have made a difference. . . .'' Before concluding, he returned to a favorite topic. ''The Washington press corps, I think, deliberately has grossly distorted [Jordan's] role as Chief of Staff.'' Carter accused the Washington press corps of looking upon Jordan as ''some sort of ogre who is trying to take over.'' Then he warned the audience not to make off-hand remarks about their staff or others because ''Washington is the richest soil I know for the nurturing of critical comments and debilitating taunts. I have erred in that respect on a few occasions; I have made off-hand remarks which have hurt someone I did not mean to hurt.''

My remaining days in office are a blur. There was a breakfast with successor Pat Harris, my only meeting with her before she took office; numerous day-to-day discussions on the danger of paraquat; the decision of the Public Health Service that homosexuality was no longer considered ''a mental disease or defect'' in terms of the immigration laws; signing regulations to cut the cost of health programs; and final recommendations to the President on radiation hazards to health. I made no decisions that would have required continuing action by Harris and no controversial decisions other than those Harris did not want to make. I tried unsuccessfully to persuade the White House not to pull back Susie McBee's presidential nomination from the Senate, which had not yet acted on it, because she had already served ninety days without it. I felt terrible about the loss to the government of Barbara Newell, Wellesley's president, who had been set to succeed Champion as Under Secretary and had been sitting in on lengthy June budget meetings to get a running start. Carter had even included her among the first groups he had invited to Camp David in July.

We packed boxes of political cartoons and personal papers. I talked with New York congressmen John LaFalce and Charlie Rangel about running for the Senate in New York. There was a moving and jolly reception given by House members at which they sang a song to the tune of ''That's Amore'' (''When Jimmeeee hits your eye with a big fat good-bye . . . that's amore'') and a warm and funny farewell from some staffers.

But permeating everything was the realization that it was over. I was no longer Secretary; I did not have the position in the government which, next to the President, offered more opportunity to do good than any other. I left on August 3. The office was cleaned out, I took my last jog on the Mall, showered, penned a personal note to Pat Harris wishing her good luck in the best job in the Cabinet, and was leaving for lunch with a few staffers at 12:50 P.M. Pat Harris would be sworn in at the White House at 1:00 and all key HEW officials except me had been invited. The phone rang. It was Jack Watson.

''The President wants you to come to the swearing in,'' he said.

''You can't be serious,'' I replied. ''Anyway, I'm on the way to lunch with my staff.''

''He asked me to call you. He would really appreciate it,'' Jack dutifully argued.

''I can't.''

''You've got to do this last thing for him.''

''I simply can't,'' I said firmly.

''I understand,'' Watson responded gently.

My next official contact with Carter was on May 14, 1980. The seal of the new Department of Health and Human Services was being unveiled. Former HEW Secretaries David Mathews, Wilbur Cohen, John Gardner, and I were there, along with Agriculture Secretary Bob Bergland, HHS Under Secretary Nathan Stark, and Pat Harris. We assembled in a holding room. The President was coming.

All except Harris went to the stage on the ground floor of the Humphrey Building before Carter arrived. Stark introduced us. I was the last person introduced. The audience clapped and cheered louder and longer than for anyone, including the President when he was later introduced. I was emotionally overwhelmed. I realized how lasting was the bond I felt with these people, whom I had worked with for thirty months. I was touched that they thought I had cared and tried.

The band struck up ''Hail to the Chief'' and Harris and Carter entered. Along with Gardner and Stark, they were in the front row. The rest of us—Bergland, Cohen, Mathews, and I—were in the back row. Carter walked across the front row, shaking hands with Stark and Gardner. He ingored the back row. When he looked back as the new seal behind us was unveiled, he avoided my eyes, though I looked straight at him. Carter spoke. He used phrases I had put into the HEW lexicon—the budget ''bigger than any except that of the governments of the Soviet Union and the United States,'' the ''vulnerable people.'' He cited programs such as childhood immunization that I had put together. Then he finished. He jumped off the front of the elevated platform, ignoring those of us in the back, shook hands with two handicapped HEW employees, and walked out.

Pat Harris presented some awards. Two of the three top ones for loyal and effective service in putting the new department together and separating out education went to Fred Bohen and Dick Beattie, whom I had brought to HEW.

The ceremony ended. The memories of this great department, this unique commitment to compassion, of opportunities I had grasped—and missed—while Secretary were vivid as I returned to my law office.

The next day I received this handwritten note in the mail:

5-14-80

To Joe Califano

I really appreciated your being at the ceremony this morning. You did an outstanding job as Secretary. On occasion, I would like to call on you to help me again.

Best wishes,
Jimmy Carter.

P.S. The C David invitation stands.

AFTERWORD

BY AND LARGE these events speak for themselves. But I lived these experiences and came away with some lessons learned.

Governing America—making government work for all the people—is not only a matter of ideology. What the proper role of government should be, what services it should provide to whom, these are matters on which ideological sides may be chosen, and conservatives, liberals and socialists may draw different conclusions. But for those who have the responsibility for performing the tasks, those labels don't offer much help.

Those who try to govern well must be tenacious and pragmatic. The task is not for anyone who thinks that deciding an issue, signing a memorandum, or ordering that something be done is the end of the matter. It is only the first step in an arduous journey of thousands of bureaucratic miles.

The time it takes to get something done underlines the necessity for persistence. It's rare to get a bill passed in a two-year Congress, much less a one-year session. Most legislation percolates for years until interested groups believe they understand all the consequences and have extracted whatever protection or advantage they can. Three of every four dollars in the federal budget must be spent unless legislation is passed amending already existing laws. Changing the course of the federal budget, therefore, takes time.

Open-minded pragmatism is required. Central administration could improve Medicaid, but it would undermine our educational system, where the more closely we fix responsibility on people to whom parents have immediate access, the better the schooling is likely to be, and the less the danger to academic freedom.

Few government solutions are permanent. The President and the Congress set out to create more doctors in the mid-sixties and succeeded beyond their expectations. Now the growing surplus of physicians threatens to increase health care costs without sufficient gains in terms of quality or access.

Management is the key to making social programs work, and far too little attention is paid to it. Management of federal programs is a complex, delicate, three-dimensional effort. There is the administrative dimension—what the businessman ordinarily thinks of as management—computerization, quality control systems, developing and motivating personnel, cost effectiveness. Even with the special problems of civil service, administrative management is the least demanding chore. Political management—negotiating the treacherous straits among islands of special interest in and out of government—is infinitely more difficult. Third, there is the dimension of once-removed management, where state, city and county officials, and an army of private employees and consultants, run federally financed and regulated programs. All three levels of management must be mastered, whether the aim is to cut the federal budget or to provide more resources for the neediest.

Both within the executive branch and in Congress, the matter of turf is the key roadblock. Outside government, the self-interest of narrow groups mines the road to progress. The proliferation of these groups is an increasing problem, and the difficulty is not simply related to any particular group's ideological bent, whether they are good guys or bad guys as measured against some political philosophy. Nothing is more appealing than helping people who are physically crippled, but the focus on the handicapped alone, like all one-dimensional views of the world, is too narrow for the formulation of broad policies in the national interest.

Single-issue groups subvert the ability of the political system to compromise, regroup and move forward. If interest groups face off against each other on only one issue, they need not worry about their adversaries tomorrow on another. They tend to see only the horns protruding from their opponents' heads and the halos floating above their own. For leaders and followers of single-interest groups, the past embitters the future; it rarely, if ever, becomes prologue for constructive change.

I believe the severest threat to governing for all the people comes from the penetration of the executive and legislative branches by narrow interest groups. It is true that many of the Great Society programs deliberately set out to develop constituency groups—for poor people, children, and medical research. A diverse, contentious, pluralistic democratic society will work best when the voices of special interests can be heard and their claims evaluated fairly.

But what is pernicious as we enter the 1980s is that we have institutionalized, in law and in bureaucracy, single-interest organizations that can accede only in the narrow interest and are incapable of adjudicating in the national interest. Congress has more than three hundred committees, subcommittees and select committees which are sedulously attended by narrow-interest groups that have weight with individual committee members—whose political campaigns depend on private financing—far beyond their voting power in the electorate as a whole. Because of this, Congress is eager to establish for each interest its own executive bureau or independent board. This structure complicates the ability of the executive branch and of the cities and states to deliver services with the efficiency that the taxpayer deserves and this age of limited resources demands. The molecular politics of Washington, with power, and often authority and responsibility, fragmented among increasingly narrow, what's-in-it-for-me groups and their responsive counterparts in the executive and legislative branches, has the centrifugal force to tear the national interest to shreds.

The most hobbling consequence of the institutionalization of special interests is the detail in which Congress addresses small issues. Detailed legislation generates chain letters of intricate federal regulations, which in turn encourage even lengthier and more specific rules as state, local and private institutions scramble to comply with the federal guidelines. University administrators, doctors, social case workers, governors, mayors, county executives, and ordinary people trying to help each other feel suffocated, frustrated to the edge of despair, as their freedom to act on matters they face each day is increasingly circumscribed. The ability of our institutions and our nation to change, the key to so much of our human and economic progress, is dangerously inhibited, and the time it takes to change grows too long.

The millions of words of laws and regulations are an unprecedented invitation to litigation by any disappointed interest group. As a result, in addition to their black robes, federal judges have donned the hats of Congressional committee chairmen, executive bureau chiefs, regulation writers, education and health policy makers, and even personnel managers and budget analysts. The judiciary is becoming a new, powerful—and with life tenure, politically unaccountable—federal bureaucracy, spinning a web of red tape that would delight the most finicky bureaucrat.

Has political self-interest become national self-indulgence? My experience inclines me to say yes.

In a time of limited resources, when to give to Paul we must take from Peter, it will not be easy to restore our sense of trust in government. And by indulging each narrow political self-interest without regard to the commonweal, we render that goal even more elusive. The eagle that once symbolized our nation—powerful, protective, armed with both sword and olive branch, head held proudly, ready to soar—is perilously close to being pushed off its perch by the vulture—also powerful, but self-interested, armed only with vicious talons, head down, poised for its carnivorous descent. Such self-indulgence encourages our citizens to see government playing the "they" to "we the people," because there seems to be no place to go for fair treatment. Only a selection of narrow-interest bureaus are available for redress, so we each seek our own.

As HEW Secretary, I learned firsthand that the social programs discussed in this book are as important to those who need them as police and fire protection are to all of us. That is why we must make government work and restore trust in its capacity to do so. Trust depends on strong, competent leadership, thoughtful policies consistently and reliably pursued, believable rhetoric, institutional regeneration, good management, and judgments fairly rendered and perceived as fairly rendered. We must have people and institutions—and systems for identifying and nourishing them—that will render national policy more than the sum of the atomistic interests. We must design bureaucratic structures that permit and encourage top government officials to assess special interests, rather than pander to them.

Solutions to these problems will not, I think, emerge from ideology or dogma. They will require sophisticated analysis, hard work, creative imagination, sensitivity to individual rights, delicate management skills, deep knowledge . . . and then political leadership, to gain acceptance of sensible changes that inevitably will distress existing power centers and disrupt comfortable institutional relationships. The work can be exasperating. But the rewards in a democracy are far greater for those who strive persistently to build and shape government to serve the people than for those who lash out in despair and frustraiton because the task is too much for them.

I loved being Secretary of HEW, and I worked at the job with all the energy I could muster. I felt the frustration, sometimes anger, of failure:

in welfare reform, national health, and the difficulty of erasing racial discrimination. I experienced the aching exhaustion that follows the loss by a single vote of a major program like hospital cost containment, and the special pain that comes from not convincing a President how important a center for fetal and child health research is, or not persuading a Congressional committee of the desperate plight of millions of poor children without health care and the benefit to all of us if we provide it.

It hurts. It hurts when you find yourself in bitter disagreement with a colleague and ally of twenty years. It hurts to be ridiculed or attacked for positions in which you deeply believe. It hurts to lose or botch programs you think will assist people. It hurts most late in the evening or the following morning when you think of something more you might have done, or done differently, or some mistake you made that might have caused the defeat. It hurts not only because you lose, but because of *what* you lose—for those who need a special education program, day care, health care, or a head start—essentially the kinds of things most of us received from parents who had the love and made the sacrifices to give them to us.

The rewards of such a job are enormous. Some of the big ones get reported: immunizing children, alerting millions of people to the dangers of smoking, integrating higher education in several states, helping spark a handicapped rights revolution in America, reducing fraud and abuse in Medicaid, student loan and welfare programs. But the one-on-one moments are even more satisfying and moving: seeing the hospice movement at work in the home of a terminally ill man; being clumsily and lovingly touched by the stunted hand of a dwarfed woman in a wheelchair; being hugged by an old black woman in Texas for "helping my grandchildren"; sitting with Mercedes McCambridge in my office as she talked through her tears about the frightening destruction of young women by alcohol abuse; dancing with an eighty-year-old woman at a senior citizen center in Queens; seeing Asian refugees learn English in San Francisco, and retarded and physically crippled children learn digital skills in Memphis so they can communicate through special typewriters.

Being Secretary of HEW was always having too much to do. There was always another meeting to hold, a phone call from a senator that had to be returned, a group of senior citizens, or women, or voluntary organizations to see, a budget fight with an appropriations committee, a key job to fill, a crisis unfolding in the morning *Washington Post,* a goal that wasn't quite met. But there was an exhilaration that came from the ability to do so much for so many, however limited it might seem at any given moment, and an adrenaline that came from getting each step closer to passing a bill, integrating a school district, launching an alcohol abuse program, understanding the teenage pregnancy problem, moving an unsafe drug off the market or releasing a new miracle drug to the public promptly. There was never enough time to savor success or lick the wounds of failure. There was always another problem to face, another opportunity to grasp. And it was always worth trying because it could be done better the next time and the rewards of success could be so great.

I cherish every moment of my time at HEW. I left, and remain, full of hope, with an intuitive and empirical conviction that we can govern with competence and compassion. Too many of us, including some in government, don't try because the tasks seem too difficult, sometimes impossible. Of course those who govern will make mistakes, plenty of them. But we must not fear failure. What we should fear above all is the judgment of God and history if the most affluent people on earth, free to act as they wish, choose not to govern justly, distribute our riches fairly and help the most vulnerable among us—or worse, choose not even to try.

INDEX